W9-AQH-842

Selections from

Ralph Waldo Emerson

RIVERSIDE EDITIONS

RIVERSIDE EDITIONS

UNDER THE GENERAL EDITORSHIP OF

Gordon N. Ray

Selections from

Ralph Waldo Emerson

AN ORGANIC ANTHOLOGY

EDITED BY

STEPHEN E. WHICHER

CORNELL UNIVERSITY

HOUGHTON MIFFLIN COMPANY

BOSTON

1960 impression

COPYRIGHT ©, 1957, BY STEPHEN E. WHICHER

ALL RIGHTS RESERVED

PRINTED IN THE U.S.A.

ISBN: 0-395-05112-6

Foreword

He in whom the love of truth predominates will keep himself aloof from all the moorings, and afloat. He will abstain from dogmatism, and recognize all the opposite negations between which, as walls, his being is swung.

The one thing in the world, of value, is the active soul.

THE PURPOSE of this volume is to encourage a fresh approach to Emerson. Its aim is to shift attention from the familiar teacher and preacher of the essays to the "active soul" of his neglected masterwork, the journals. In so doing it responds to the modern re-evaluation of Emerson, which stresses not his doctrine but his spirit and method, his enactment of the self-created role of Man Thinking.

Thinking, for Emerson, was not the contemplation of final Truth, but the daily encounter of an active mind with its environment; it was not a special activity but life itself. His lifelong enterprise was what has been the main enterprise of the American imagination: to launch filaments of order, like Whitman's spider, over the unknown until they catch somewhere on experience. His journals, with the essays and poems that grew from them, are among the most impressive quests for order which America has yet produced. Once we come, through them, to participate in the whole life of the man's mind, we discover a strongly living Emerson and are redeemed from facile condescension.

This book therefore departs from the plan of conventional anthologies, which have printed excerpts from the journals in a separate section if at all. Instead, it is built on journal passages, amounting to about a third of the total text, which are carefully chosen to convey the organic continuity and dynamic range of Emerson's thought as we experience it in the complete journals. From the matrix of this miniature journal the twelve and a half essays here included should emerge, not as meteors from the tenth heaven, but as natural growths from the soil of his thought at the time of their writing. Thus even the Divinity School *Address*, often omitted in other anthologies, is here reinvigorated by its journal context and restored to its rightful place as marking a critical moment in the story of Emerson's thought.

The order of selections is generally chronological but not mechanically so. Passages are often juxtaposed to link with or strike sparks from each other, always with the intent to bring out not just the particular passage but the whole life of the mind from which it sprang. More broadly, the selections are grouped into ten chronological sections (an eleventh contains the poems), each with an introduction of its own. No other scheme makes possible in a single volume that integration of the public with the private Emerson which alone can give new life to the whole man.

Contents

1803–1832: *Discovery*

1833–1836: *First Fruits*

1837–1838: *Challenge*

1841–1843: *Lords of Life*

1844–1845: *Skepticism*

1846–1852: *Fate*

Poems

Introduction

BY STEPHEN E. WHICHER

EMERSON is one of America's best known authors and one of the least known. The reason is that he fought two battles at once: a public and a private one. Though neither was easy, he succeeded all too well for his present reputation in the first, becoming one of the spiritual leaders of his era. Now that the issues have altered it appears that this leader is being abandoned. The result, however, is not to discredit Emerson, as some have hastily decided, but to bring to light a second figure who, it turns out, was fighting part of our battle all along. The purpose of these selections is to throw Emerson's work into such a perspective as will permit him to speak to us. A generous reading is necessary, certainly, one that will suspend judgment and use imagination to see past the familiar public image to the man. The reward will be to re-establish communication with one of the seminal minds of our literature.

Undeniably, as Henry James said, "there were certain chords in Emerson that did not vibrate at all" — notably the chord of outgoing affection and compassion which we rightly value in other authors. He was condemned by temperament, much against his will, to a lonely life of the mind. But this limitation was his strength and his opportunity. Because he was distracted by little else he experienced and conveyed the adventure of thought, the daily plunge of the mind into the unknown, with an urgency almost unique in literature. If the function of an artist is to bring something to life for us, to make us see, then Emerson is an artist who makes us see the creative energy of thinking, the original leap and grasp of the mind in action. His achievement can be described, with little adaptation, in the words Coleridge used to describe Wordsworth's purpose in *Lyrical Ballads*: ". . . to give the charm of novelty to *a thing* of every day, and to excite a feeling analogous to the supernatural, by awakening the mind's attention to the lethargy of custom, and directing it to . . . the wonders of the *power within* us; an inexhaustible treasure, but for which, in consequence of the film of familiarity and selfish solicitude we have eyes, yet see not, ears that hear not, and *minds* that neither feel nor understand." *

This way of seeing Emerson is relatively new and must still compete with his older reputation as a religious teacher, "the friend and aider of those who would live in the spirit," as Matthew Arnold called him, a reputation which reached a high point at the time of his death in 1882 and held firm until about 1930. He was then subjected to wholesale attack as a friend and aider of juveniles (Adams) or of juvenile delinquents (Winters) and his stock took a sharp drop. At the present time it shows signs of recovery. Current research is greatly enlarging our picture of the range and creative vigor of his reading. Recent studies of his "angle of vision" or "formalistic method" or "sacred science" or use of the "organic metaphor" have also revealed an original and athletic mind at work to throw into a large, fresh perspective the central issues of the day. These and other investigations are steadily directing attention away from the conclusions of his thought to a remarkable man thinking. Their cumulative effect is to make possible a fresh reading of Emerson. That is also the aim of the present anthology.

Its guiding point of view was well stated by an early German reader of Emerson, Herman Grimm: "What he has written is like life itself — the unbroken thread ever lengthened through the addition of the small events which make up each day's experience. . . . His sentences are a series of thoughts. He begins as if continuing a discourse whose opening we had not heard, and ends as if only pausing to take breath before going on." One gradually comes to realize that all his work is like one great essay, whose subject is "Man Thinking." Or put it that he is essentially a journalist, an intellectual diarist, and that his essays and lectures take their place as an extension of his daily autobiography. Each selection in this book is accordingly intended to have a double interest: in itself, and as part of his continuing discourse. For this reason the arrangement is in general chronological but with some grouping also to permit passages to comment on each other. Similarly the essays that are included complete are set in their chronological context and also when possible in one that suggests the lines of thought which led to them. The various headnotes

* *Biographia Literaria*, Chapter XIV, second paragraph. The italicized words are altered from the original.

distributed through the text are designed to call attention to what was most alive in Emerson's thought at a given period. The central purpose is to create in miniature the same sense of the "life itself" of a mind which is created by his work as a whole.* The particular issues he faced, the ideas he used as weapons, the specific content of his thought may now belong in large part to a past age. His "natural history" of a mind at work to build its own world from the materials at hand is emerging to new life.

II

The particular issues Emerson faced are nevertheless important to understand; thought that matters is concerned with problems that matter. Emerson's service to his contemporaries was to meet a spiritual emergency. His story has its heroism, for leadership has seldom grown from more crippling beginnings. One of five sons of a minister's widow, church-poor, tubercular, provincially educated, a "prodigy of shyness" like so many of his tribe, zealously orthodox, no more seemed possible for him than the traditional round of the New England preacher, if indeed he did not die before beginning his work, as was true of two of his brothers. By the time he began his ministry, however, even this career was closing to him. The Unitarian church he had entered was the extreme liberal wing of the New England church of his day, heavily influenced by the rationalism of the eighteenth century. In the name of reason Unitarians had attacked and rejected a number of the central doctrines of the still dominant Calvinism, notably the "monstrous" doctrine of man's total depravity by nature. Although they still accepted the Christian revelation to which the Calvinists appealed, therefore, they were forced in effect to subject it to the test of reason and to abandon the unquestioning submission to God's arbitrary sovereignty which had been Calvinism's secret strength. By the time Emerson was reaching maturity, however, they had become uneasily aware that not merely Christian revelation but all the tenets of supposedly "rational religion" — immortality, the moral law, the very existence of God — had been repeatedly and plausibly challenged in the name of the same reason on which they relied. French

---

* For convenience of use, the poems are grouped together in one place. They also are arranged in rough chronological order and are tied to the prose by a number of cross-references.

materialists, German higher critics, above all the "Scotch Goliath," David Hume, haunted their councils, yearly refuted and yearly rising up to be refuted once more. The net result of these rumors of rational irreligion was to shake the authority of reason as the Unitarians had previously shaken the authority of revelation. Consequently the young minister found himself, without quite knowing how he came there, standing disarmed before the threat of unbelief, face to face, as he once put it, with "the ghastly reality of things."

In this end was his beginning. A stubborn independence lay beneath his quiet reserve; he met the threat of annihilation with the will of a born warrior. Fortunately reinforcements were at hand. His crisis of faith was a late American analogue to the crises that had faced a series of Europeans from Goethe to Carlyle, for whom the rational world of the eighteenth century, "locked and chained" in the law of physical cause and effect, had become a world of death. From such sources, by a "shock of recognition" more than by any close study, he caught the characteristic tactic by which they went about to solve the problem of freedom in a world of fate: they superimposed the first on the second. Above the mechanical system of necessity in which man was an ordered part like any other collocation of atoms was a vital world of freedom of which man's free spirit gave him immediate warrant. As Kant had put it, though the order of necessity admitted no rational exception, the rational conduct of life demanded that man live *as if* he were free. Or in the words of Coleridge's "Mystos," "The world in which I exist is another world indeed, but not to come."

The transformation this new light caused in the shy young Unitarian was no less decisive for being gradual. Abandoning with relief all allegiance to historical Christianity, he rested his faith on the "other world" of God and Freedom assured him by his own immediate intuitions. Both historical revelation and discursive reason were made superfluous by this continuing revelation within him: "The faith is the evidence." The soul of man did not merely contain, as Unitarians had believed, a spark or light of God; it *was* God. An astonishing surge of power and confidence followed the discovery of this reservoir of faith and strength within himself. Thereafter life acquired a new dimension. Unlike Melville, his tragic complement, he could counter his problems by transcending them. Readers of these selections will notice how regularly they are controlled by an outward expansion from his private self to the "Universal" and then a return to the "conduct of life." He made it his chief task as a writer "to celebrate the spiritual powers in their infinite contrast to the mechanical powers and the mechanical philosophy of this time." His success is writ large in the literature, the philosophy and the religion of America from his day to our own.

III

The road he opened to his contemporaries, however, is largely closed to us. Modern thought, as reoriented since Darwin, makes possible and necessary a union of "Mind" and "Nature" on a naturalistic basis to which such naive Idealism no longer seems relevant. Though we can and must share his vision, by a willing suspension of disbelief, if we are to read him at all, relatively few readers now find him a source of faith. Theological seminaries ignore him. Moreover, we see more clearly than his contemporaries could how much his thought was, in Santayana's words, "not a philosophy passing into a religion, but a religion expressing itself as a philosophy." Much of his teaching — Compensation is a plain case — is essentially "reminiscent Puritanism" thinly disguised as philosophy, and as these ways of thought have dropped into the past it also has lost cogency. Even his beloved Self-Reliance, whose Puritan derivation is certainly less evident, has faded badly, now seeming unacceptable with its religious basis and unimpressive without it.

The first step toward a living Emerson, as his best readers have always seen, is to move behind the teacher to the man. When we put aside the mantle of dignity in which Emerson felt it necessary to wrap himself and read him with an ear for the human overtones of his words, we begin to see a far more complex and interesting figure. Our ruling impression then becomes one of forces in collision, an action and reaction from which his doctrines and his whole literary work were ejected at high pressure. One main force is a passion for freedom, an almost desperate need for release, expansion, power; to which is matched a fixed decorum that holds him fast in a narrow mold and cannot expand or give. Nature is in undeclared rebellion against second nature. Quite unlike the Olympian Emerson of legend, the man divides through the middle into the elements of the culture-bound and the autonomous, the lawful and the anarchic, the conventional and the wild. Thus in his political opinions he became for a while a totalminded radical who contemplated the existing structure of society with the contempt of a Gulliver among Lilliputians, or a Communist among New Dealers; yet in the same years whenever confronted with a specific choice between political possibilities he instinctively preferred the conservative option.

The closer we approach him, in fact, the more we realize how entirely his thought was controlled by a shifting, complex dialectic of opposites: a painful conflict, for example, between his wish for companionship and his "doom" of solitude; a mingled revulsion at and devotion to the confined life of the "scholar"; an alternation between his active and passive impulses, the egoist and the "Buddhist"; and others besides. "The path of life," Frederick Woodbridge once wrote, "is not around a center, but generated by the push and pull of contrary directions." We move in ellipses, not circles. Emerson is a central instance of this truth. Though he dreamed of intellectual system and much regretted his lack of it, his thought survives precisely because he refused to violate its living multiplicity with an imposed unity. Instead his guiding conviction that the unfettered action of the whole mind bears truth as naturally as a tree bears fruit led him to a radically organic method of thought whose modernity is still not adequately recognized.

IV

To see Emerson's original approach to the enterprise of thought we must return to his starting point, the moment of immediate insight. This was not only, he came to believe, the source of a special kind of truth; it was the source of any truth. In fact, truth existed, lived only in a present act of vision and ceased to live as that ended. Such an act did not have merely an instrumental value as it led to a "true" statement; rather, the statement it led to was to be valued as an organic part of the process that created it. What mattered, then, was not so much truth as truth-making, not thoughts but thinking. It was not important that the statement of one moment might contradict that of another. Emerson's verdict here was simple and final: "Damn consistency!" Any statement of truth is necessarily partial anyhow and implies the potential truth of its opposite also. The essential thing is not any given insight but the vital capacity to move from one to the next according to the natural rhythm of thought. The life of the mind is a perpetual voyage of discovery, a swinging of one circle around the last with no end but "old age."

A failure to appreciate his method is responsible for a number of traditional errors about Emerson; for example, that he was not aware of evil. Preoccupied with his voyage of mind, reassured by the Over-Soul, hardened by the "cosmic optimism" he inherited from his ancestors, he certainly did not have what is conventionally considered a tragic view of life; but it is simply not true that he did not feel the reality of evil. He felt keenly — *his* evil; what that was is not hard to see. Since the active soul was for him "the one thing in the world, of value," it follows that the inactive soul was his evil — and that is what we find. "Sleep," "indigence of vital power," "routine" — a lament at *incapacity* runs in a recurrent elegiac refrain throughout his work, especially in the difficult years of the 1840's when he was freshly conscious of it. Counterpointing his regret is a savage scorn of the "dead alive" whose souls are never active at all. While his faith in the God Within affirmed "the perfect Adam" in the heart, in this original nonentity he found his own Fall of Man. His affirmative good was constantly blotted out from him by some pervasive shadowy negative, for which there was finally no remedy but the stoic patience that was so conspicuous a part of his character. "Our faith comes in moments; our vice is habitual," he wrote at the start of his most affirmative essay. In darker moods, which were not infrequent, he felt almost swallowed up in illusion, vacancy, unreality. In our time, writes Paul Tillich, "the anxiety of emptiness and meaninglessness is dominant. We are under the threat of spiritual non-being." Emerson listed "the trials of this age" as "early old age, pyrrhonism,* and apathy." Granted that he had a source of reassurance denied most of us, it would still seem possible that his condition was much closer to ours than we now credit.

An insight into his method also helps to clear up some persistent misapprehensions about what he is doing as a writer. Most of them proceed from the assumption that he is some kind of philosopher, or at least a "sage." This old mistake blocks him

---

* A comprehensive skepticism.

off from us, as every collection of "Nuggets from Emerson" demonstrates. A favorable and not unjust way to put the matter is his own: ". . . a philosopher must be much more than a philosopher. Plato is a poet." Emerson too is a poet — a poet of ideas. The concern of the poet, Eliot has said, is not thought but "the emotional equivalent of thought." The phrase exactly describes Emerson's concern also. His value to his time and ours was not in new ideas thrown into circulation but in the human urgency, the imaginative vividness he gave, not just to the particular ideas which concerned him, but to the life of thought itself. He makes apparent what philosophers who are no more than philosophers tend to ignore — that thought is not an affair of the intellect alone but of the whole man. To accept an idea, he sees, is not to *speculate*, as we say, but to invest one's life. The play of the mind is for mortal stakes; "to think is to act."

To say this may seem to contradict what was said above about the contradictions in Emerson's thought. Actually the two together permit us to take a further step, now with particular reference to his method in public work like the speeches and essays. (The poems are discussed in another place.) If a thought is an act of choice, and if he was aware of many competing possible choices, each with a claim, if not always an equal one, to consideration, the stage was set for him to "play" various choices and set off one role against another in some kind of dialogue of ideas. Poet that he was, he had considerable natural taste for this. He apprehended ideas dramatically, not intellectually; to him they were ideas *of a person*, functional parts of a personal confrontation of the world, attitudes that implied a dramatic speaker. Instinctively he threw a sharp light on them and made them "tell." His thought is unqualified, not because he was incapable of second thoughts, but because the laborious *ifs* and *buts* of ratiocination had no relevance to his purpose. The accident that the rhetorical tradition in which his prose style was formed has gone out of fashion, while it puts an added distance between him and us, permits us to observe more clearly than his hearers the conscious artistry with which he worked up his part for each platform appearance. Significantly, as his art matured and he found his proper method he became more overtly dramatic. Even *Nature*, where he is least himself, rises to the words of the "Orphic poet" at the end. In the 1840's he commonly assigned his ideas to appropriate type-characters: the Conservative, the Transcend-entalist, the Poet, the Skeptic, and so on. The later essays, too, are sprinkled with imaginary *alter egos* who speak his thoughts for him. Again and again, even when no speaker is named, we find that he has assumed a dramatic personality and is projecting this "slip-off section" of himself with something of the disengagement of an artist of fiction, though so slyly — or perhaps one should say with so little artistic self-consciousness — that we read him heavily and literally, taking every speaker to be the author.

If the preceding remarks give the impression that Emerson is even more elusive than has been supposed, that is no more than the truth. The strongest part of him escapes statement. This is as it should be, for he was a believer in unseizable possibilities and would have been glad to think that he suggested them. There is a secret spring of power in him, a fire at the core "under the Andes," that is felt in all his work without being identifiable in any. It is no moral quality nor literary skill nor any one personal trait but a charged atmosphere which we can sense but not define. The best image for him is perhaps his own Uriel, archangel of the sun, who stands outside human life and yet shakes it with his truth. Through his words we intuit, almost in spite of any intention of his own, a primal realm of being — pure energy, naked spirit, unincarnate life — which lies barely within the reach of thought. Emerson is one of those writers who have enlarged the possibilities of experience.

Note on the Text

WITH the exception of Ralph L. Rusk's *Letters of Ralph Waldo Emerson* (1939) there is no definitive text of any part of Emerson's writings, and important parts are in the process of publication or republication. Considerable effort has been exerted to make the text of these selections as accurate as is possible under the circumstances. Apart from the correction of a few errors, the text of the essays and the poems is that in *The Complete Works of Ralph Waldo Emerson* (1904), edited with notes by his son, Edward Waldo Emerson, the so-called Centenary Edition. At the present time this is generally accepted as the standard edition. Kenneth W. Cameron's collation of the texts of *Nature* (Scholars' Facsimiles and Reprints, 1940) indicates that this edition is a careful and reliable one, barring minor errors and inconsistencies.

The text of the selections from the journals follows that of the only published edition, the *Journals* of 1909–1914, edited by Edward W. Emerson and Waldo E. Forbes. All selections from the journals, however, have been newly corrected and amplified from the manuscripts, for which privilege I particularly want to thank Professor Edward Waldo Forbes and the Emerson Memorial Association. This anthology, consequently, contains the most complete and accurate text of these selections that is in print, pending the publication of the new edition of the journals now in preparation. In most cases the dating of passages is based on the printed *Journals*. The text of the letters follows Rusk, though I have regularized it for ease of reading. The letters to Carlyle come from *Correspondence of Thomas Carlyle and Ralph Waldo Emerson* (1883); those to Ward from *Letters from Ralph Waldo Emerson to a Friend* (1899), both edited by Charles Eliot Norton. It has not been possible to check the MSS. of these. A few selections come from other sources as indicated.

Any anthology based as much as this one is on the journals must encounter the problem of a large and sometimes indispensable group of journal passages that are not yet published and are not now available for publication, namely those Emerson revised and used in his essays. I have adopted the best expedient possible by extracting a minimum number of these from essays not here reprinted and including each under the date of the original journal passage. Since in these cases the text is not that of the manuscript journal, however, I have enclosed the date of all such passages in brackets. The reader should understand, therefore, that the text of a passage under a bracketed date is, in whole or in part, *not* the version in the journal for that

date. When the entire passage comes from an essay, that fact is indicated at the end of the passage (i.e., "From 'The Over-Soul,' " etc.).
When the date is bracketed and there is no source indication at the
end, then the passage is a composite one put together partly from the
printed *Journals* and partly from the *Works* to approximate as closely
as is possible a continuous passage in the manuscript journals. The
exact sources of all selections are given in the notes (p. 510).

The notes are based on those supplied the *Works* and *Journals* by
Edward Waldo Emerson; those signed "E.W.E." are his verbatim,
or nearly so. These have been supplemented from the researches of
Ralph L. Rusk, Kenneth W. Cameron, Carl F. Strauch and other
such sources. The information on the MS. relations of the essays to
the journals and the lectures is based on unpublished research by the
editor.

Further Reading

MANY good guides to the Emerson literature are easily available. The
student should start with the bibliographies in *Emerson Handbook*
(1953), by Frederic Ives Carpenter, which also contains much other
useful information. Other good annotated lists are in *Eight American
Authors* (1956), edited by Floyd Stovall, and in the bibliography edited
by Thomas Johnson in R. E. Spiller *et al.*, *Literary History of the
United States* (1948), Vol. III. The basic biography, for facts, is
Ralph L. Rusk, *The Life of Ralph Waldo Emerson* (1949). A good
introduction to the man is Bliss Perry, *Emerson Today* (1931). Useful
accounts of his thought are Henry David Gray, *Emerson* (1917) and
Stephen E. Whicher, *Freedom and Fate* (1953). The best comments
on Emerson as an artist are in F. O. Matthiessen, *American Renais-
sance* (1941). The most intelligent anti-Emerson statements are
perhaps James Truslow Adams, "Emerson Reread," in *Atlantic
Monthly* (1930), and the chapter on Emerson in Yvor Winters,
Maule's Curse (1938). The Emerson bibliography includes essays,
pro and con, by nearly every first-rate mind in American intellectual
history (on Emerson abroad, see *Emerson Handbook*). Perhaps the
most brilliant sympathetic discussion is in John Jay Chapman, *Emerson and Other Essays* (1898).

Other bibliographical references bearing on particular questions
are included in the notes.

Acknowledgments   I wish to thank Professor Edward Waldo Forbes and the Emerson Memorial Association for extending me permission to use excerpts from the *Letters*, the *Journals*, and the Centenary *Works*; also Professor Ralph L. Rusk and the Columbia University Press for their permission to use the *Letters*; Professor Frederic I. Carpenter and Hendricks House for permission to quote from *Emerson Handbook*; the President and Fellows of Harvard College and Professor Carl F. Strauch for permission to quote from his article "The Sources of Emerson's 'Song of Nature'" in the *Harvard Library Bulletin* IX (1955); Mr. John A. Woodbridge for permission to quote from an unpublished letter from his father, Dean Frederick Woodbridge; and Professors Rusk, Carpenter, Strauch, Kenneth W. Cameron, Townsend Scudder, and Lucius Shero for various help and courtesies.

Chronology

1803   (May 25) Born at Boston, Massachusetts.

1821   (August) Graduated from Harvard College.

1826   (October 10) Approbated to preach as a Unitarian minister.

1829   (March 11) Ordination at Second Church, Boston.
       (September 30) Married to Ellen Tucker.

1831   (February 8) Death of Ellen.

1832   (October 28) Resignation from Second Church accepted.

1832–33   (December–October) Travel in Europe.

1834   (November) Moved to Concord.

1835   (January–March) Lectures on *Biography*.
       (September 14) Married to Lydia Jackson ("Lidian").

1835–36   (November–January) Lectures on *English Literature*.

1836   (May 9) Death of brother Charles.
       (September 9) *Nature* published.
       (October 30) Birth of son Waldo.

1836–37   (December–March) Lectures on *The Philosophy of History*.

1837   (August 31) Oration on "The American Scholar."

1837–38   (December–February) Lectures on *Human Culture*.

1838   (July 15) Address at Divinity School, Cambridge.

1838–39   (December–February) Lectures on *Human Life*.

1839   (February 24) Birth of daughter Ellen.

1839–40   (December–February) Lectures on *The Present Age*.

1841   (January 25) Lecture on "Man the Reformer."
       (March 20) *Essays, First Series* published.
       (November 22) Birth of daughter Edith.

1841–42   (December–January) Lectures on *The Times* (published, in part, 1849).

1842   (January 27) Death of Waldo.

1844   (July 10) Birth of son Edward.
       (October 19) *Essays, Second Series* published.

1845–46   (December–January) Lectures on *Representative Men* (published 1850).

1846   (December 25) *Poems* published.

1847–48   (October–July) Travel in England and France.

1851   (March–April) Lectures on *The Conduct of Life* (published 1860).

1856   (August 6) *English Traits* published.

1862   (May 9) Address on "Thoreau."
1867   (April 28) *May-Day and Other Pieces* published.
1872   (July 24) Burning of house.
1872–73   (October–May) Travel in Europe and the Near East.
1882   (April 27) Death at Concord, Massachusetts.

Discovery

"What are my advantages?" Emerson once asked, and answered, "The total New England." Stern habits of plain living and high thinking, enhanced in his own case by early poverty; an outer reserve and an inner zeal; a humility before the Lord and an independence before men; a respect for facts and a contempt for worldliness — these were all traits bred in him by the New England of his youth. In addition, his heritage as a descendant of clergymen, "born to be educated," together with the family curse, tuberculosis, combined to cut him off from the games and sports of normal youth and subject him to "the pressure of I know not how many literary atmospheres," as one early friend put it. From the first to the last, books were his element of life, contrary doctrines notwithstanding; his own name for himself was "the scholar." When he came, for lecture purposes, to sketch an ideal portrait of "the poor but educated family," the pleasures of books were virtually all he found worth remembering.

These — and the companionship of brothers. Emerson was a clansman. No relationship, not even the beautiful dream of his first marriage, ever meant as much to him as that with his brothers, William, Edward, and Charles — above all, Charles. The early deaths first of Edward and then of Charles fixed his temperamental solitude; no new friendship could take the place of their lost comradeship. The mentor of this band of brothers was an extraordinary woman, their Aunt Mary Moody Emerson, who fired the boys with her own enthusiastic faith and scorn of smallness. Emerson's zealous ambition in later life to become the prophet of a new truth reflects to an important degree her secret wish that her boys should be the ones to rekindle the spirit of the old religion in a new age.

Unlike his brothers, the young Ralph dedicated himself to the church, for motives that seem as much literary as spiritual. Poor health delayed until 1829 his accepting a regular position, and meanwhile doubts of the "rational Christianity" he had been taught to profess increasingly sapped his zeal. Gradually he groped his way through thickets of skepticism and self-distrust toward independence and faith, until new lights from "modern philosophy," chiefly Coleridge, led him to the "amazing revelation" of a God within his own heart and released him from the "yoke of men's opinions." The tragic death by consumption in 1831 of his beautiful young wife, Ellen Tucker, whom he had married just eighteen months before, marked the end not only of his youthful happiness but also of the chief tie that bound him to his conventional profession. These inner and outer changes brought their inevitable result when he broke with his parish in 1832 over the celebration of the Lord's Supper; after his resignation was accepted in October, he sailed for a year's travel in Europe before beginning a new life of self-reliance.

⚔

May 7, 1837

. . . I cannot hear the young men whose theological instruction is exclusively owed to Cambridge and to public institution,[1] without feeling how much happier was my star, which rained on me influences of ancestral religion. The depth of the religious sentiment which I knew in my Aunt Mary, imbuing all her genius and derived to her from such hoarded family traditions, from so many godly lives and godly deaths of sainted kindred at Concord, Malden, York, was itself a culture, an education. I heard with awe her tales of the pale stranger who, at the time her grandfather lay on his death-bed, tapped at the window and asked to come in. The dying man said, "Open the door"; but the timid family did not; immediately he breathed his last, and they said one to another, "It was the Angel of Death." Another of her ancestors, when near his end, had lost the power of speech, and his minister came to him and said, "If the Lord Christ is with you, hold up your hand"; and he stretched up both hands and died. With these I heard the anecdotes of the charities of Father

[1] I.e., to the Harvard Divinity School (the Unitarian center) and to public instruction.

Moody [2] and his commanding administration of his holy office. When the offended parishioners would rise to go out of the church he cried, "Come back, you graceless sinner, come back!" And when his parishioners ventured into the ale-house on a Saturday night, the valiant pastor went in, collared them, and dragged them forth and sent them home. Charity then went hand in hand with zeal. They gave alms profusely, and the barrel of meal wasted not. Who was it among this venerable line who, whilst his house was burning, stood apart with some of his church and sang, "There is a house not made with hands"? Another was wont to go into the road whenever a traveler past on Sunday, and entreat him to tarry with him during holy time, himself furnishing food for man and beast.

In my childhood, Aunt Mary herself wrote the prayers which first my brother William, and, when he went to college, I read aloud morning and evening at the family devotions, and they still sound in my ear with their prophetic and apocalyptic ejaculations. Religion was her occupation, and when, years after, I came to write sermons for my own church, I could not find any examples or treasuries of piety so high-toned, so profound, or promising such rich influence, as my remembrances of her conversation and letters.

May 6, 1841

. . . I doubt if the interior and spiritual history of New England could be trulier told than through the exhibition of family history such as this, the picture of this group of Aunt Mary and the boys, mainly Charles. The genius of that woman, the key to her life is in the conflict of the new and the old ideas in New England. The heir of whatever was rich and profound and efficient in thought and emotion in the old religion which planted and peopled this land, she strangely united to this passionate piety the fatal gifts of penetration, a love of philosophy, an impatience of words, and was thus a religious skeptic. She held on with both hands to the faith of the past generation as to the Palladium of all that was good and hopeful in the physical and metaphysical worlds; and in all companies and on all occasions and especially with these darling nephews of her hope and pride, extolled and poetized this beloved Calvinism. Yet all the time she doubted and denied it, and could not tell whether to be more glad or sorry

2 Rev. Samuel Moody, Emerson's great-great-grandfather.

to find that these boys were irremediably born to the adoption and furtherance of the new ideas. . . . These combined traits in Aunt Mary's character gave the new direction to her hope, that these boys should be richly and holily qualified and bred to purify the old faith of what narrowness and error adhered to it, and import all its fire into the new age, — such a gift should her Prometheus bring to men. She hated the poor, low, thin, unprofitable, unpoetical Humanitarians as the devastators of the Church and robbers of the soul, and never wearies with piling on them new terms of slight and weariness. "Ah!" she said, "what a poet would Byron have been, if he had been born and bred a Calvinist."

To William Emerson

February 10, 1850

. . . This is the third application within a twelvemonth that has come to me to write a memoir of our father. . . . But I have no recollections of him that can serve me. I was eight years old when he died, and only remember a somewhat social gentleman, but severe to us children, who twice or thrice put me in mortal terror by forcing me into the salt water off some wharf or bathing house, and I still recall the fright with which, after some of this salt experience, I heard his voice one day, (as Adam that of the Lord God in the garden,) summoning us to a new bath, and I vainly endeavoring to hide myself. I have never heard any sentence or sentiment of his repeated by Mother or Aunt, and his printed or written papers, as far as I know, only show candor and taste, or I should almost say, docility, the principal merit possible to that early ignorant and transitional *Month-of-March* in our New England culture. His literary merits really are that he fostered the Anthology and the Athenaeum.[3] . . .

To Nathaniel Frothingham

December 3, 1853

My mother was born in Boston, 9 November 1768, and had therefore completed 85 years a week before her death. Her father, Captain John Haskins, whose distillery on Harrison Avenue was pulled down not many years ago, was an industrious thriving man with a family of thirteen living children. He was an Episcopalian and up to the time of the Revolution a Tory. My mother was

[3] *The Monthly Anthology and Boston Review*, a literary journal; the Boston Athenaeum, a literary association, notable for its library (see pp. 81–82).

bred in the English church, and always retained an affection for the Book of Common Prayer. She married in 1796 and all her subsequent family connections were in the Congregational Church. At the time of her marriage her husband was settled in Harvard, Mass. In [1799] they removed to Boston on his installation at First Church. He died in 1812 and left her with six children and without property. She kept her family together and at once adopted the only means open to her by receiving boarders into her house, and by the assistance of some excellent friends, she carried four of her five sons through Harvard College. The family was never broken up until 1826, when on the death of Dr. Ripley's [4] daughter (my father's half-sister) she accepted the Doctor's earnest invitation to make her home at his house. She remained there until my marriage in 1830, when she came to live with me. After my housekeeping was broken up in 1832, and on my return from Europe in 1833, she went with me to Concord,[5] and we became boarders in Doctor Ripley's family, until I bought a house and took her home with me in 1835. This was her permanent home until her death. I hardly know what to add to these few dates. I have been in the habit of esteeming her manners and character the fruit of a past age. She was born a subject of King George, had lived through the whole existence of the Republic, remembered and described with interesting details the appearance of Washington at the Assemblies in Boston after the war, when every lady wore his name on her scarf; and had derived from that period her punctilious courtesy extended to every person and continued to the last hour of her life. Her children as they grew up had abundant reason to thank her prudence which secured to them an education, which in the circumstances was the most judicious provision that could be made for them. I remember being struck with the comment of a lady who said in my family, when some debate arose about my Mother's thrift in her time, the lady said, "Ah, but she secured the essentials. She got the children educated."

[November 25, 1837]

What is that society which unites the most advantages to the culture of each? The poor but educated family. The eager blushing boys discharging as they can their household chores, and hastening into the sitting-room to the study of tomorrow's merci-

[4] See p. 12.
[5] Actually in the autumn of 1834.

less lesson, yet stealing time to read one chapter more of the novel hardly smuggled into the tolerance of father and mother, — atoning for the same by some pages of Plutarch or Goldsmith; the warm sympathy with which they kindle each other in school-yard or in barn or woodshed with scraps of poetry or song, with phrases of the last oration, or mimicry of the orator; the youthful criticism, on Sunday, of the sermons; the school declamation faithfully rehearsed at home, sometimes to the fatigue, sometimes to the admiration of sisters; the first solitary joys of literary vanity, when the translation or the theme has been completed, sitting alone near the top of the house; the cautious comparison of the attractive advertisement of the arrival of Macready, Booth, or Kemble,[6] or of the discourse of a well-known speaker, with the expense of the entertainment; the affectionate delight with which they greet the return of each one after the early separations which school or business require; the foresight with which, during such absences, they hive the honey which opportunity offers, for the ear and imagination of the others; and the unrestrained glee with which they disburden themselves of their early mental treasures when the holidays bring them again together. What is the hoop that holds them staunch? It is the iron band of poverty, of necessity, of austerity, which, excluding them from the sensual enjoyments which make other boys too early old, has directed their activity in safe and right channels, and made them, despite themselves, reverers of the grand, the beautiful and the good.[7] . . .

※ ※

April 18, 1824

Myself. — . . . I am beginning my professional studies. In a month I shall be legally a man. And I deliberately dedicate my time, my talents, and my hopes to the Church. . . .

I cannot dissemble that my abilities are below my ambition. . . . I have, or had, a strong imagination, and consequently a keen relish for the beauties of poetry. The exercise which the practice of composition gives to this faculty is the cause of my immoderate fondness for writing, which has swelled these pages to a voluminous extent. My reasoning faculty is proportionably weak, nor can I ever hope to write a Butler's Analogy or an Essay of Hume. Nor is it strange that with this confession I should choose

---

[6] Actors.
[7] Cf. "Grace," p. 412.

theology, which is from everlasting to everlasting "debateable ground." For, the highest species of reasoning upon divine subjects is rather the fruit of a sort of moral imagination, than of the "Reasoning Machines," such as Locke and Clarke and David Hume. Dr. Channing's Dudleian Lecture [8] is the model of what I mean, and the faculty which produced this is akin to the higher flights of the fancy. I may add that the preaching most in vogue at the present day depends chiefly on imagination for its success, and asks those accomplishments which I believe are most within my grasp. I have set down little which can gratify my vanity, and I must further say that every comparison of myself with my mates that six or seven, perhaps sixteen or seventeen, years have made, has convinced me that there exists a signal defect of character which neutralizes in great part the just influence my talents ought to have. Whether that defect be in the *address*, in the fault of good forms, — which, Queen Isabella said, were like perpetual letters-commendatory — or deeper seated in an absence of common *sympathies*, or even in a levity of the understanding, I cannot tell. But its bitter fruits are a sore uneasiness in the company of most men and women, a frigid fear of offending and jealousy of disrespect, an inability to lead and an unwillingness to follow the current conversation, which contrive to make me second with all those among whom chiefly I wish to be first. . . .

NB

But in Divinity I hope to thrive. I inherit from my sire a formality of manner and speech, but I derive from him, or his patriotic parent,[9] a passionate love for the strains of eloquence. I burn after the *"aliquid immensum infinitumque"* [1] which Cicero desired. What we ardently love we learn to imitate. My understanding venerates and my heart loves that cause which is dear to God and man — the laws of morals, the Revelations which sanction, and the blood of martyrs and triumphant suffering of the saints which seal them. In my better hours, I am the believer (if not the dupe) of brilliant promises, and can respect myself as the possessor of those powers which command the reason and passions of the multitude. . . . My trust is that my profession shall be my regeneration of mind, manners, inward and outward estate; or rather my starting-point, for I have hoped to put on eloquence as a robe, and by goodness and zeal and the awfulness of Virtue to

[8] "The Evidences of Revealed Religion," March 14, 1821.
[9] Rev. William Emerson, minister at Concord during the Revolution.
[1] Something unlimited and boundless.

press and prevail over the false judgments, the rebel passions and corrupt habits of men. . . .

To Mary Moody Emerson
August 1, 1826

. . . In the fall, I propose to be *approbated*, to have the privilege, though not at present the purpose, of preaching but at intervals. I do not now find in me any objections to this step. — 'Tis a queer life, and the only humor proper to it seems quiet astonishment. Others laugh, weep, sell, or proselyte. I admire.[2] There are, I take it, in each man's history insignificant passages which he feels to be to him not insignificant; little coincidences in little things, which touch all the springs of wonder, and startle the sleeper conscience in the deepest cell of his repose; the mind standing forth in alarm with all her faculties, suspicious of a Presence which it behoves her deeply to respect. . . . These are not the state reasons by which we can enforce the burdensome doctrine of a Deity on the world, but make often, I apprehend, the body of evidence on which private conviction is built. . . .

To Mary Moody Emerson
September 23, 1826

. . . Is it not true that modern philosophy by a stout reaction has got to be very conversant with feelings? Bare reason, cold as cucumber, was all that was tolerated in aforetime, till men grew disgusted at the skeleton and have now given him in ward into the hands of his sister, blushing, shining, changing Sentiment. . . . Be that as it may, it is one of the *feelings* of modern philosophy, that it is wrong to regard ourselves so much in a *historical* light as we do, putting Time between God and us; and that it were fitter to account every moment of the existence of the Universe as a new Creation, and *all* as a revelation proceeding each moment from the Divinity to the mind of the observer. . . .

September 27, 1830

Self-Reliance. — . . . Every man has his own voice, manner, eloquence, and, just as much, his own sort of love and grief and imagination and action. Let him scorn to imitate any being, let him scorn to be a secondary man, let him fully trust his own share of God's goodness, that, correctly used, it will lead him on

2 I wonder.

to perfection which has no type yet in the universe, save only in the Divine Mind.

July 29, 1831

Suicidal is this distrust of reason; this fear to think; this doctrine that 'tis pious to believe on other's words, impious to trust entirely to yourself. . . . To reflect is to receive truth immediately from God without any medium. That is living faith. To take on trust certain facts is a dead faith, inoperative. A trust in yourself is the height, not of pride, but of piety, an unwillingness to learn of any but God himself. It will come only to one who feels that he is nothing. It is by yourself without ambassador that God speaks to you. . . .

October 27, 1831

. . . Is it not all in us, how strangely! Look at this congregation of men; — the words might be spoken, — though now there be none here to speak them, — but the words might be said that would make them stagger and reel like a drunken man. Who doubts it? Were you ever instructed by a wise and eloquent man? Remember then, were not the words that made your blood run cold, that brought the blood to your cheeks, that made you tremble or delighted you, — did they not sound to you as old as yourself? Was it not truth that you knew before, or do you ever expect to be moved from the pulpit or from man by anything but plain truth? Never. It is God in you that responds to God without, or affirms his own words trembling on the lips of another.

June 2, 1832

Cold, cold. Thermometer says temperate. Yet a week of moral excitement.[3]

It is years and nations that guide my pen.

I have sometimes thought that, in order to be a good minister, it was necessary to leave the ministry. The profession is antiquated. In an altered age, we worship in the dead forms of our forefathers. Were not a Socratic paganism better than an effete, superannuated Christianity?

[3] Emerson was soon to take issue with his congregation on the mode of celebration of the Lord's Supper.

White Mountains, July 15, 1832

A few low mountains, a great many clouds always covering the great peaks, a circle of woods to the horizon, a peacock on the fence or in the yard, and two travelers no better contented than myself in the plain parlor of this house make up the whole picture of this unsabbatized Sunday. But the hours pass on, creep or fly, and bear me and my fellows to the decision of questions of duty; to the crises of our fate; and to the solution of this mortal problem. Welcome and farewell to them; fair come, fair go. God is, and we in him.

The hour of decision. It seems not worth while for them who charge others with exalting forms above the moon to fear forms themselves with extravagant dislike. . . . The Communicant celebrates on a foundation either of authority or of tradition an ordinance which has been the occasion to thousands, — I hope to thousands of thousands, — of contrition, of gratitude, of prayer, of faith, of love and of holy living. Far be it from any of my friends, — God forbid it be in my heart, — to interrupt any occasion thus blessed of God's influences upon the human mind. . . . But this ordinance is esteemed the most sacred of religious institutions, and I cannot go habitually to an institution which they esteem holiest with indifference and dislike.

October 1, 1832

Has the doctrine ever been fairly preached of man's moral nature? The whole world holds on to formal Christianity, and nobody teaches the essential truth, the heart of Christianity, for fear of shocking, etc. Every teacher, when once he finds himself insisting with all his might upon a great truth, turns up the ends of it at last with a cautious showing *how* it is agreeable to the life and teaching of Jesus, as if that was any recommendation, as if the blessedness of Jesus' life and teaching were not because they were agreeable to the truth. Well, this cripples his teaching. It bereaves the truth he inculcates of more than half its force, by representing it as something secondary that can't stand alone. The truth of truth consists in this, that it is self-evident, self-subsistent. It is light. You don't get a candle to see the sun rise.

Instead of making Christianity a vehicle of truth, you make truth only a horse for Christianity. It is a very operose way of making people good. You must be humble because Christ says, "Be humble." "But why must I obey Christ?" "Because God sent him." But how do I know God sent him? Because your own heart teaches

the same thing he taught. Why then shall I not go to my own
heart at first?

October 2, 1832

The Terrible Freedom. — It well deserves attention what is
said in *New Jerusalem Magazine* [4] concerning External Restraint.
It is awful to look into the mind of man and see how free we
are, to what frightful excesses our vices may run under the whited
wall of a respectable reputation. Outside, among your fellows,
among strangers, you must preserve appearances, a hundred
things you cannot do; but inside, the terrible freedom! [5]

October, 1832

I will not live out of me.
I will not see with others' eyes;
My good is good, my evil ill.
I would be free; I cannot be
While I take things as others please to rate them.
I dare attempt to lay out my own road.
That which myself delights in shall be Good,
That which I do not want, indifferent;
That which I hate is Bad. That's flat.

Henceforth, please God, forever I forego
The yoke of men's opinions. I will be
Light-hearted as a bird and live with God. . . .
Who says the heart's a blind guide? It is not.
My heart did never counsel me to sin. . . .
I never taught it what it teaches me,
I only follow when I act aright.
Whence then did this omniscient spirit come?
From God it came. It is the Deity.

[4] See p. 471.
[5] Cf. "Grace" (p. 412), written about this time.

1833–1836

First Fruits

Emerson's year of travel did something to build up his health and more to build his confidence, chiefly by removing his superstitious reverence for great reputations, in men or in art. He could lean without fear on his own tastes; his age and his region, like all times and all regions, were very good ones, if he but knew what to do with them. He was thinking of a "book about Nature" when he was scarcely out of sight of England, and at sea, discomfited one gathers by some priest-baiter among the passengers, he set down in his cabin the most passionate defense of the faith he was returning to teach that he was ever to write.

The years that immediately followed, however, were ones of quiet exploration, of recurrent doubts and griefs soon submerged again in an expanding sense of hope and power. In 1834 he moved to Concord, where his step-grandfather, Dr. Ezra Ripley, was minister, as had been Emersons before him, and in 1835 he married a Plymouth girl, Lydia Jackson, after a sober courtship, and bought the large house near the meadows and woods on the outskirts of town which was thereafter his home. The greatest blow of this time was the death of his brother Charles in May, 1836. A legacy from Ellen, when finally paid, half-solved his financial problems; for the rest he continued to preach, filling pulpits as far away as Maine, and more and more turned to lecturing before the multiplying adult education societies, the so-called Lyceums.

His first topics seem far removed from the message he felt committed to him, being general discussions of the uses of natural history. Lectures on the subject, to be sure, were in popular demand — but Emerson was intrigued on his own account by the puzzle of the world around him and the hints of unsuspected relation that science provided, and he wished to test nature's responses to the touchstone he was eagerly applying to every question: How does this stand in relation to myself? In the same spirit he read widely in whatever "scriptures" spoke to him: Plato and the Platonists, Swedenborg and the Swedenborgians, George Fox and the Quakers, Goethe, Shakespeare, Coleridge, Carlyle — always searching for "the glimmering of that pure, plastic Idea," the moment of original insight. His method was similar when he lectured in 1835 on "Biography" and on "English Literature." He was following in advance the advice of the "Orphic poet" who speaks in Nature: "Build therefore your own world."

The results of his rapid exploration of his world he brought together, with the enthusiasm of the pioneer, in his first book, Nature (1836). It might have exchanged titles with Poe's Eureka. Beginning with deceptive show of system as an inquiry into the "theory of creation" ("to what end is Nature?"), it increasingly bursts the strait jacket of sermon-style firstlies and secondlies to become a rapt vision of redemption. Man, now a "God in ruins," is "entitled to the world by his constitution." Let him think and act from the God within him, in truth and love, and "his victorious thought comes up with and reduces all things, until the world becomes at last only a realized will, — the double of the man," and "evil is no more seen." The style is stiff and naïf, the organization over-elaborate, the thought gowned in unbecoming borrowed terminology; yet this sober-sided rhapsody, in its odd combination of provinciality and profundity, bookishness and originality, inhibition and power, was one of the most extraordinary pieces of writing yet to come from an American. It made him unexpected friends at home and abroad; and far from rolling his universe into a ball, it started one pregnant topic after another to grow and ramify in his further thought.

⚜⚜

Liverpool, September 1, 1833

I thank the Great God who has led me through this European scene, this last schoolroom in which he has pleased to instruct me, from Malta's isle, through Sicily, through Italy, through Switzerland, through France, through England, through Scotland, in safety and pleasure, and has now brought me to the shore and the ship that steers westward. He has shown me the men I wished to see, — Landor, Coleridge, Carlyle, Wordsworth; he has thereby comforted and confirmed me in my convictions.

Many things I owe to the sight of these men. I shall judge more justly, less timidly, of wise men forevermore. To be sure not one of these is a mind of the very first class, but what the intercourse with each of these suggests is true of intercourse with better men, that they never *fill the ear* — fill the mind — no, it is an *idealized* portrait which always we draw of them. Upon an intelligent man, wholly a stranger to their names, they would make in conversation no deep impression, none of a world-filling fame; — they would be remembered as sensible, well-read, earnest men, not more. Especially are they all deficient, all these four, — in different degrees, but all deficient, — in insight into religious truth. They have no idea of that species of moral truth which I call the first philosophy. . . .

September 6, 1833

Fair; fine wind; still in the Channel, off the coast of Ireland, but not in sight of land. This morning 37 sail in sight.

I like my book about Nature, and wish I knew where and how I ought to live. God will show me. I am glad to be on my way home, yet not so glad as others, and my way to the bottom I could find perchance with less regret, for I think it would not hurt me, — that is, the ducking or drowning.

At Sea, September 17, 1833

Yesterday I was asked what I mean by morals. I reply that I cannot define, and care not to define. It is man's business to observe, and the definition of moral nature must be the slow result of years, of lives, of states, perhaps of being. Yet in the morning watch on my berth I thought that morals is the science of the laws of human action as respects right and wrong. Then I shall be asked, And what is Right? Right is a conformity to the laws of nature as far as they are known to the human mind. These for the occasion. but I propound definitions with more than the reserve of the feeling above-named, — with more, because my own conceptions are so dim and vague. But nevertheless nothing darkens, nothing shakes, nothing diminishes my constant conviction of the eternal concord of these laws which are perfect music, and of which every high sentiment and every great action is only a new statement, and therefore and insomuch speaks aloud to the whole race of man. I conceive of them by no types, but the apparent hollow sphere of the whole firmament wherein this ball of the earth swims. Not easy are they to be enumerated, but he has some idea of them who considers such propositions as St. Bernard's, — Nobody can harm me but myself, — or who develops the doctrine in his own experience that nothing can be given or taken without an equivalent.

Milton describes himself in his letter to Diodati as enamored of moral perfection. He did not love it more than I. That which I cannot yet declare has been my angel from childhood until now. It has separated me from men. It has watered my pillow, it has driven sleep from my bed. It has tortured me for my guilt. It has inspired me with hope. It cannot be defeated by my defeats. It cannot be questioned, though all the martyrs apostatize It is always the glory that shall be revealed; it is the "open secret" of the universe; and it is only the feebleness and dust of the observer that makes it future, the whole *is* now potentially in the bottom of his heart. It is the soul of religion. Keeping my eye on this, I understand all heroism, the history of loyalty and of martydom and of bigotry, the heat of the Methodist, the nonconformity of the Dissenter, the patience of the Quaker.

But what shall the hour say for distinctions such as these, this hour of southwest gales and rain-dripping cabin? As the law of light is, fits of easy transmission and reflection, such is also the soul's law. She is only superior at intervals to pain, to fear, to temptation, only in raptures unites herself to God; and Wordsworth truly said, —

> " 'Tis the most difficult of tasks to keep
> Heights which the soul is competent to gain."

What is this they say about wanting mathematical certainty for moral truths. I have always affirmed they had it. Yet they ask me whether I know the soul immortal. No. But do I not know the Now to be eternal?

Is it not a sufficient reply to the red and angry worldling, coloring as he affirms his unbelief, to say, Think on living, I have to do no more than you with that question of another life? I believe in this life. I believe it continues. As long as I am here I plainly read my duties as writ with pencil of fire; they speak not of death. They are woven of immortal thread.

Men seem to be constitutionally believers and unbelievers. There is no bridge that can cross from a mind in one state to a mind in the other. All my opinions, affections, whimsies, are tinged with belief, — incline to that side. All that is generous, elegant, rich, wise, looks that way. But I cannot give reasons to a person of a different persuasion that are at all adequate to the force of my conviction. Yet when I fail to find the reason, my faith is not less. . . .

December 14, 1833

I please myself with contemplating the felicity of my present situation. May it last. It seems to me singularly free, and it invites me to every virtue and to great improvement.

January 1 ?, 1834

This Book is my Savings Bank. I grow richer because I have somewhere to deposit my earnings; and fractions are worth more to me because corresponding fractions are waiting here that shall be made integers by their addition.

April 10, 1834

Is it possible that, in the solitude I seek, I shall have the resolution, the force, to work as I ought to work, as I project in highest, most far-sighted hours? Well, and what do you project? Nothing less than to look at every object in its relation to myself.

April 20, 1834

Awake, arm of the Lord! Awake, thou Godlike that sleepest! Dear God that sleepest in man, I have served my apprenticeship of bows and blushes, of fears and references, of excessive admiration.

The whole secret of the teacher's force lies in the conviction that men are convertible. And they are. They want awakening. Get the soul out of bed, out of her deep habitual sleep, out into God's universe, to a perception of its beauty, and hearing of its call, and your vulgar man, your prosy, selfish sensualist awakes, a god, and is conscious of force to shake the world.

April 22, 1835

"We only row, we're steered by fate."

The involuntary education is all. See how we are mastered. With the desire of dogmatizing, here we sit chatting. With desire of poetic reputation, we still prose. We would be Teachers, but in spite of us we are kept out of the pulpit, and thrust into

the pew. Who doth it? No man: only Lethe, only Time; only
negatives; indisposition; delay; nothing.

October, 1835

Far off, no doubt, is the perfectibility; so far off as to be ridiculous to all but a few. Yet wrote I once that, God keeping a private
door to each soul, nothing transcends the bounds of reasonable
expectation from a man. Now what imperfect tadpoles we are!
an arm or a leg, an eye or an antenna, is unfolded, — all the rest
is yet in the chrysalis. Who does not feel in him budding the
powers of a Persuasion that by and by will be irresistible? . . .

May 3, 1834

The Idea according to which the Universe is made is wholly
wanting to us; is it not? Yet it may or will be found to be con-
structed on as harmonious and perfect a thought, self-explaining,
as a problem in geometry. The classification of all natural science
is arbitrary, I believe; no method philosophical in any one. And
yet in all the permutations and combinations supposable, might
not a cabinet of shells or a Flora be thrown into one which should
flash on us the very thought? We take them out of composition,
and so lose their greatest beauty. The moon is an unsatisfactory
sight if the eye be exclusively directed to it, and a shell retains
but a small part of its beauty when examined separately.[1] All our
classifications are introductory and very convenient, but must be
looked on as temporary, and the eye always watching for
the glimmering of that pure, plastic Idea. . . .

This is evidently what Goethe aimed to do, in seeking the
arch-plant, which, being known, would give, not only all actual,
but all possible vegetable forms. Thus to study would be to hold
the bottle under water instead of filling it drop by drop.

June 4, 1836

Here are two or three facts respecting science. 1. The tendency to order and classification in the mind. 2. The correspondent order actually subsisting in nature. 3. Hence the humanity
of science or the naturalness of knowing; the perception that
the world was made by mind like ours; the recognition of design
like ours; the seeing in the brutes analogous intelligence to
ours. . . .

[1] Cf. "Each and All" (p. 413).

History teaches 1. The presence of spirit; 2. The antecedence of spirit; 3. The humanity of spirit.

Corollary: Science must be studied humanly.

Maine, December 14, 1834

Yesterday, I sealed and dispatched my letter to Carlyle. Today, riding to East Sudbury, I pleased myself with the beauties and terrors of the snow; the oak leaf hurrying over the banks is fit ornament. . . . I know no aisle so stately as the roads through the pine woods in Maine. Cold is the snow-drift, topping itself with sand. How intense are our affinities: acids and alkalis. The moment we indulge our affections, the earth is metamorphosed: all its tragedies and ennuis vanish, all duties even; nothing remains to fill eternity with but two or three persons. But then a person is a *cause*. What is Luther but Protestantism? or Columbus but Columbia? And were I assured of meeting Ellen tomorrow, would it be less than a world, a personal world? Death has no bitterness in the light of that thought.

January 13, 1835

The great value of Biography consists in the perfect sympathy that exists between like minds. Space and time are an absolute nullity to this principle. An action of Luther's that I heartily approve I do adopt also. . . . Socrates, St. Paul, Antoninus, Luther, Milton have lived for us as much as for their contemporaries, if by books or by tradition their life and words come to my ear. . . . It is a beautiful fact in human nature that the roar of separating oceans, no, nor the roar of rising and falling empires, cannot hinder the ear from hearing the music of the most distant voices; that the trumpet of Homer's poetry yet shrills in the closet of the retired scholar across three thousand years; that the reproof of Socrates stings us like the bite of a serpent, as it did Alcibiades. These affinities atone to us for the narrowness of our society, and the prison of our single lot, by making the human race our society, and the vast variety of human fortune the arena of actions on which we, by passing judgment, take part. . . .

December 9, 1834

. . . It is said that the people can look after their own interests; that "common sense, though no science, is fairly worth the seven"; that a plain, practical man is better to the state than a scholar, etc. He were a benefactor to his countrymen who would expose and pillory this stale sophism. We hold indeed . . . that there is imparted to every man the Divine light of reason, sufficient not only to plant corn and grind wheat by, but also to illuminate all his life, his social, political, religious actions. . . . But does it mean that because a farmer, acting on deep conviction, shall give a reason as good as Bacon could have given, that therefore the ordinary arguments of farmers are to be preferred to those of statesmen? that whatever crude remarks a circle of people talking in a bar-room throw out, are entitled to equal weight with the sifted and chosen conclusions of experienced public men? And because God has made you capable of Reason, therefore must I hear and accept all your selfish railing, your proven falsehoods, your unconsidered guesses as truth? No; I appeal from you to your Reason, which, with me, condemns you. . . . Democracy, Freedom, has its root in the sacred truth that every man hath in him the divine Reason, or that, though few men since the creation of the world live according to the dictates of Reason, yet all men are created capable of so doing. That is the equality and the only equality of all men. To this truth we look when we say, Reverence thyself; Be true to thyself. Because every man has within him somewhat really divine, therefore is slavery the unpardonable outrage it is.

To Lydia Jackson [2]

February 1, 1835

. . . Under this morning's severe but beautiful light I thought, dear friend, that hardly should I get away from Concord. I must win you to love it. I am born a poet, of a low class without doubt, yet a poet. That is my nature and vocation. My singing, be sure, is very "husky," and is for the most part in prose. Still am I a poet in the sense of a perceiver and dear lover of the harmonies that are in the soul and in matter, and specially of the correspondences between these and those. A sunset, a forest, a snow-storm, a certain river-view, are more to me than many friends and do ordinarily divide my day with my books. Wherever I go therefore I guard and study my rambling propensities with a care that is ridiculous to people, but to me is the care of my high calling. . . .[3]

April 16, 1835

This snow in summer which falls so fast today is like a wound from a friend. Dr. R[ipley] calls it "robin-snow."

[2] His fiancée. When they were married, he renamed her Lidian.
[3] Cf. "The Apology" (p. 424).

Why must always the philosopher mince his words and fatigue us with explanation? He speaks from the Reason, and being, of course, contradicted word for word by the Understanding,[4] he stops like a cog-wheel at every notch to explain. Let him say, *I idealize,* and let that be once for all; or, *I sensualize,* and then the Rationalist may stop his ears. Empedocles said bravely, "I am God; I am immortal; I contemn human affairs"; and all men hated him. Yet every one of the same men had had his religious hour when he said the same thing. Fable avoids the difficulty, is at once exoteric and esoteric, and is clapped by both sides. Plato and Jesus used it. And History is such a fable. Plato had a secret doctrine, — had he? What secret can he conceal from the eyes of Montaigne, of Bacon, of Kant?

July 30, 1835

You affirm that the moral development contains all the intellectual, and that Jesus was the perfect man. I bow in reverence unfeigned before that benign man. I know more, hope more, am more, because he has lived. But, if you tell me that in your opinion he has fulfilled all the conditions of man's existence, carried out to the utmost, at least by implication, all man's powers, I suspend my assent. I do not see in him cheerfulness: I do not see in him the love of natural science: I see in him no kindness for art; I see in him nothing of Socrates, of Laplace, of Shakespeare. The perfect man should remind us of all great men. Do you ask me if I would rather resemble Jesus than any other man? If I should say Yes, I should suspect myself of superstition.

August 5, 1835

The human mind seems a lens formed to concentrate the rays of the Divine laws to a focus, which shall be the personality of God. But that focus falls so far into the infinite that the form or person of God is not within the ken of the mind. Yet must that ever be the effort of a good mind, because the avowal of our sincere doubts leaves us in a less favorable mood for action, and the statement of our best thoughts, or those of our convictions that make most for theism, induces new courage and force.

[4] See note, p. 470.

[*December, 1835*]

God offers to every mind its choice between truth and repose. Take which you please, — you can never have both. Between these, as a pendulum, man oscillates. He in whom the love of repose predominates will accept the first creed, the first philosophy, the first political party he meets, — most likely his father's. He gets rest, commodity and reputation; but he shuts the door of truth. He in whom the love of truth predominates will keep himself aloof from all the moorings, and afloat. He will abstain from dogmatism, and recognize all the opposite negations between which, as walls, his being is swung. He submits to the inconvenience of suspense and imperfect opinion, but he is a candidate for truth, as the other is not, and respects the highest law of his being.   *From "Intellect"*

✠✠

Nature

references to the eye

"Nature is but an image or imitation of wisdom,
the last thing of the soul; nature being a thing
which doth only do, but not know." — PLOTINUS
(*Motto of 1836*)

A subtle chain of countless rings
The next unto the farthest brings;
The eye reads omens where it goes,
And speaks all languages the rose;
And, striving to be man, the worm
Mounts through all the spires of form.
(*Motto of 1849*)

INTRODUCTION

tombs

OUR age is retrospective. It builds the (sepulchres) of the fathers. It writes biographies, histories, and criticism. The foregoing generations beheld God and nature face to face; we, through their eyes. Why should not we also enjoy an original relation to the universe? Why should not we have a poetry and philosophy of insight and not of tradition, and a religion by revelation to us, and not the history of theirs? Embosomed for a season in nature, whose floods of life stream around and through us, and invite us, by the powers they supply, to action proportioned to nature, why should we grope among the dry bones of the past, or put the

The American Scholar

living generation into masquerade out of its faded wardrobe? The sun shines today also. There is more wool and flax in the fields. There are new lands, new men, new thoughts. Let us demand our own works and laws and worship.

—Undoubtedly we have no questions to ask which are unanswerable. We must trust the perfection of the creation so far as to believe that whatever curiosity the order of things has awakened in our minds, the order of things can satisfy. Every man's condition is a solution in hieroglyphic to those inquiries he would put. He acts it as life, before he apprehends it as truth. In like manner, nature is already, in its forms and tendencies, describing its own design. Let us interrogate the great apparition that shines so peacefully around us. Let us inquire, to what end is nature?

All science has one aim, namely, to find a theory of nature. We have theories of races and of functions, but scarcely yet a remote approach to an idea of creation. We are now so far from the road to truth, that religious teachers dispute and hate each other, and speculative men are esteemed unsound and frivolous. But to a sound judgment, the most abstract truth is the most practical. Whenever a true theory appears, it will be its own evidence. Its test is, that it will explain all phenomena. Now many are thought not only unexplained but inexplicable; as language, sleep, madness, dreams, beasts, sex.

Philosophically considered, the universe is composed of Nature and the Soul. Strictly speaking, therefore, all that is separate from us, all which Philosophy distinguishes as the NOT ME, that is, both nature and art, all other men and my own body, must be ranked under this name, NATURE. In enumerating the values of nature and casting up their sum, I shall use the word in both senses;— in its common and in its philosophical import. In inquiries so general as our present one, the inaccuracy is not material; no confusion of thought will occur. *Nature*, in the common sense, refers to essences unchanged by man; space, the air, the river, the leaf. *Art* is applied to the mixture of his will with the same things, as in a house, a canal, a statue, a picture. But his operations taken together are so insignificant, a little chipping, baking, patching, and washing, that in an impression so grand as that of the world on the human mind, they do not vary the result.

1. NATURE

To go into solitude, a man needs to retire as much from his chamber as from society. I am not solitary whilst I read and write, though nobody is with me. But if a man would be alone, let him look at the stars. The rays that come from those heavenly worlds will separate between him and what he touches. One might think the atmosphere was made transparent with this design, to give man, in the heavenly bodies, the perpetual presence of the sublime. Seen in the streets of cities, how great they are! If the stars should appear one night in a thousand years, how would men believe and adore; and preserve for many generations the remembrance of the city of God which had been shown! But every night come out these envoys of beauty, and light the universe with their admonishing smile.

The stars awaken a certain reverence, because though always present, they are inaccessible; but all natural objects make a kindred impression, when the mind is open to their influence. Nature never wears a mean appearance. Neither does the wisest man extort her secret, and lose his curiosity by finding out all her perfection. Nature never became a toy to a wise spirit. The flowers, the animals, the mountains, reflected the wisdom of his best hour, as much as they had delighted the simplicity of his childhood.

When we speak of nature in this manner, we have a distinct but most poetical sense in the mind. We mean the integrity of impression made by manifold natural objects. It is this which distinguishes the stick of timber of the wood-cutter from the tree of the poet. The charming landscape which I saw this morning is indubitably made up of some twenty or thirty farms. Miller owns this field, Locke that, and Manning the woodland beyond. But none of them owns the landscape. There is a property in the horizon which no man has but he whose eye can integrate all the parts, that is, the poet. This is the best part of these men's farms, yet to this their warranty-deeds give no title.

To speak truly, few adult persons can see nature. Most persons do not see the sun. At least they have a very superficial seeing. The sun illuminates only the eye of the man, but shines into the eye and the heart of the child. The lover of nature is he whose inward and outward senses are still truly adjusted to each other; who has retained the spirit of infancy even into the era of manhood. His intercourse with heaven and earth becomes part of his daily food. In the presence of nature a wild delight runs through the man, in spite of real sorrows. Nature says, — he is my creature, and maugre all his impertinent griefs, he shall be glad with me. Not the sun or the summer alone, but every hour and season yields its tribute of delight; for every hour and change corresponds to and authorizes a different state of the mind, from breathless noon to grimmest midnight. Nature is a setting that fits equally well a comic or a mourning piece. In good health, the air is a cordial of incredible virtue. Crossing a bare common, in snow puddles, at twilight, under a clouded sky, without having in my thoughts any occurrence of special good fortune, I have enjoyed a perfect exhilaration. I am glad to the brink of fear. In the woods, too, a man casts off his years, as the snake his slough, and at what period soever of life is always a child. In the woods is perpetual youth. Within these plantations of God, a decorum and sanctity reign, a perennial festival is dressed, and the guest sees not how he should tire of them in a thousand years. In the woods, we return to reason and faith. There I feel that nothing can befall me in life, — no disgrace, no calamity (leaving me my eyes), which nature cannot repair. Standing on the bare ground, — my head bathed by the blithe air and uplifted into infinite space, — all mean egotism vanishes. I become a transparent eyeball; I am nothing; I see all; the currents of the Universal Being circulate through me; I am part or parcel of God. The name of the nearest friend sounds then foreign and accidental: to be brothers, to be acquaintances, master or servant, is then a trifle and a disturbance. I am the lover of uncontained and immortal beauty. In the wilderness, I find something more dear and connate than in streets or villages. In the tranquil landscape, and especially in the distant line of the horizon, man beholds somewhat as beautiful as his own nature.

The greatest delight which the fields and woods minister is the suggestion of an occult relation between man and the vegetable. I am not alone and unacknowledged. They nod to me, and I to them. The waving of the boughs in the storm is new to me and old. It takes me by surprise, and yet is not unknown. Its effect is like that of a higher thought or a better emotion coming over me, when I deemed I was thinking justly or doing right.

Yet it is certain that the power to produce this delight does not reside in nature, but in man, or in a harmony of both. It is necessary to use these pleasures with great temperance. For nature is not always tricked in holiday attire, but the same scene which yesterday breathed perfume and glittered as for the frolic of the nymphs is overspread with melancholy today. Nature always wears the colors of the spirit. To a man laboring under calamity, the heat of his own fire hath sadness in it. Then there is a kind of contempt of the landscape felt by him who has just lost by death a dear friend. The sky is less grand as it shuts down over less worth in the population.

contradict?

II. COMMODITY

WHOEVER considers the final cause [5] of the world will discern a multitude of uses that enter as parts into that result. They all admit of being thrown into one of the following classes: Commodity; Beauty; Language; and Discipline.

Under the general name of commodity, I rank all those advantages which our senses owe to nature. This, of course, is a benefit which is temporary and mediate, not ultimate, like its service to the soul. Yet although low, it is perfect in its kind, and is the only use of nature which all men apprehend. The misery of man appears like childish petulance, when we explore the steady and prodigal provision that has been made for his support and delight on this green ball which floats him through the heavens. What angels invented these splendid ornaments, these rich conveniences, this ocean of air above, this ocean of water beneath, this firmament of earth between? this zodiac of lights, this tent of dropping clouds, this striped coat of climates, this fourfold year? Beasts, fire, water, stones, and corn serve him. The field is at once his floor, his work-yard, his play-ground, his garden, and his bed.

> "More servants wait on man
> Than he'll take notice of."

NATURE serves man

Nature, in its ministry to man, is not only the material, but is also the process and the result. All the parts incessantly work into each other's hands for the profit of man. The wind sows the seed; the sun evaporates the sea; the wind blows the vapor to the field; the ice, on the other side of the planet, condenses rain on this; the rain feeds the plant; the plant feeds the animal; and thus the endless circulations of the divine charity nourish man.

The useful arts are reproductions or new combinations by the wit of man, of the same natural benefactors. He no longer

[5] Purpose.

waits for favoring gales, but by means of steam, he realizes the
fable of Aeolus's bag,[6] and carries the two and thirty winds in
the boiler of his boat. To diminish friction, he paves the road
with iron bars, and, mounting a coach with a ship-load of men,
animals, and merchandise behind him, he darts through the country, from town to town, like an eagle or a swallow through the
air. By the aggregate of these aids, how is the face of the world
changed, from the era of Noah to that of Napoleon! The private
poor man hath cities, ships, canals, bridges, built for him. He
goes to the post-office, and the human race run on his errands;
to the book-shop, and the human race read and write of all that
happens, for him; to the court-house, and nations repair his wrongs.
He sets his house upon the road, and the human race go forth
every morning, and shovel out the snow, and cut a path for
him.

But there is no need of specifying particulars in this class of
uses. The catalogue is endless, and the examples so obvious, that
I shall leave them to the reader's reflection, with the general remark, that this mercenary benefit is one which has respect to a
farther good. A man is fed, not that he may be fed, but that he
may work.

III. BEAUTY

A NOBLER want of man is served by nature, namely, the love of
Beauty.

The ancient Greeks called the world Κόσμος,[7] beauty. Such is
the constitution of all things, or such the plastic power of the
human eye, that the primary forms, as the sky, the mountain, the
tree, the animal, give us a delight *in and for themselves;* a pleasure
arising from outline, color, motion, and grouping. This seems
partly owing to the eye itself. The eye is the best of artists. By
the mutual action of its structure and of the laws of light, perspective is produced, which integrates every mass of objects, of
what character soever, into a well colored and shaded globe, so
that where the particular objects are mean and unaffecting, the
landscape which they compose is round and symmetrical. And as
the eye is the best composer, so light is the first of painters.
There is no object so foul that intense light will not make beautiful. And the stimulus it affords to the sense, and a sort of in-

---

[6] A bag which held the winds (Odyssey).
[7] Kosmos, order.

finitude which it hath, like space and time, make all matter gay.
Even the corpse has its own beauty. But besides this general
grace diffused over nature, almost all the individual forms are
agreeable to the eye, as is proved by our endless imitations of some
of them, as the acorn, the grape, the pine-cone, the wheat-ear,
the egg, the wings and forms of most birds, the lion's claw, the
serpent, the butterfly, sea-shells, flames, clouds, buds, leaves, and
the forms of many trees, as the palm.

For better consideration, we may distribute the aspects of
Beauty in a threefold manner.   "The Rhodora" p. 412

1. First, the simple perception of natural forms is a delight.
The influence of the forms and actions in nature is so needful
to man, that, in its lowest functions, it seems to lie on the confines of commodity and beauty. To the body and mind which
have been cramped by noxious work or company, nature is medicinal and restores their tone. The tradesman, the attorney comes
out of the din and craft of the street and sees the sky and the
woods, and is a man again. In their eternal calm, he finds himself.
The health of the eye seems to demand a horizon. We are never
tired, so long as we can see far enough.

But in other hours, Nature satisfies by its loveliness, and without
any mixture of corporeal benefit. I see the spectacle of morning
from the hilltop over against my house, from daybreak to sunrise, with emotions which an angel might share. The long slender
bars of cloud float like fishes in the sea of crimson light. From
the earth, as a shore, I look out into that silent sea. I seem
to partake its rapid transformations; the active enchantment
reaches my dust, and I dilate and conspire [8] with the morning
wind. How does Nature deify us with a few and cheap elements!
Give me health and a day, and I will make the pomp of emperors ridiculous. The dawn is my Assyria; the sunset and moon-
rise my Paphos, and unimaginable realms of faerie; broad noon
shall be my England of the senses and the understanding; the
night shall be my Germany of mystic philosophy and dreams.

Not less excellent, except for our less susceptibility in the afternoon, was the charm, last evening, of a January sunset. The
western clouds divided and subdivided themselves into pink
flakes modulated with tints of unspeakable softness, and the air
had so much life and sweetness that it was a pain to come within
doors. What was it that nature would say? Was there no meaning in the live repose of the valley behind the mill, and which

[8] Breathe together.

Homer or Shakespeare could not re-form for me in words? The leafless trees become spires of flame in the sunset, with the blue east for their background, and the stars of the dead calices of flowers, and every withered stem and stubble rimed with frost, contribute something to the mute music.

The inhabitants of cities suppose that the country landscape is pleasant only half the year. I please myself with the graces of the winter scenery, and believe that we are as much touched by it as by the genial influences of summer. To the attentive eye, each moment of the year has its own beauty, and in the same field, it beholds, every hour, a picture which was never seen before, and which shall never be seen again. The heavens change every moment, and reflect their glory or gloom on the plains beneath. The state of the crop in the surrounding farms alters the expression of the earth from week to week. The succession of native plants in the pastures and roadsides, which makes the silent clock by which time tells the summer hours, will make even the divisions of the day sensible to a keen observer. The tribes of birds and insects, like the plants punctual to their time, follow each other, and the year has room for all. By watercourses, the variety is greater. In July, the blue pontederia or pickerel-weed blooms in large beds in the shallow parts of our pleasant river, and swarms with yellow butterflies in continual motion. Art cannot rival this pomp of purple and gold. Indeed the river is a perpetual gala, and boasts each month a new ornament.

But this beauty of Nature which is seen and felt as beauty, is the least part. The shows of day, the dewy morning, the rainbow, mountains, orchards in blossom, stars, moonlight, shadows in still water, and the like, if too eagerly hunted, become shows merely, and mock us with their unreality. Go out of the house to see the moon, and 'tis mere tinsel; it will not please as when its light shines upon your necessary journey. The beauty that shimmers in the yellow afternoons of October, who ever could clutch it? Go forth to find it, and it is gone; 'tis only a mirage as you look from the windows of diligence.

2. The presence of a higher, namely, of the spiritual element is essential to its perfection. The high and divine beauty which can be loved without effeminacy, is that which is found in combination with the human will. Beauty is the mark God sets upon virtue. Every natural action is graceful. Every heroic act is also decent, [9] and causes the place and the bystanders to shine.

9 Comely, becoming.

We are taught by great actions that the universe is the property
of every individual in it. Every rational creature has all nature for
his dowry and estate. It is his, if he will. He may divest himself
of it; he may creep into a corner, and abdicate his kingdom, as
most men do, but he is entitled to the world by his constitution.
In proportion to the energy of his thought and will, he takes up
the world into himself. "All those things for which men plough,
build, or sail, obey virtue," said Sallust. "The winds and waves,"
said Gibbon, "are always on the side of the ablest navigators." So
are the sun and moon and all the stars of heaven. When a noble
act is done, — perchance in a scene of great natural beauty; when
Leonidas and his three hundred martyrs consume one day in
dying, and the sun and moon come each and look at them once
in the steep defile of Thermopylae; when Arnold Winkelried, in
the high Alps, under the shadow of the avalanche, gathers in his
side a sheaf of Austrian spears to break the line for his com-
rades; are not these heroes entitled to add the beauty of the scene
to the beauty of the deed? When the bark of Columbus nears
the shore of America; — before it the beach lined with savages,
fleeing out of all their huts of cane; the sea behind; and the purple mountains of the Indian Archipelago around, can we separate
the man from the living picture? Does not the New World clothe
his form with her palm-groves and savannahs as fit drapery? Ever
does natural beauty steal in like air, and envelope great actions.
When Sir Harry Vane [1] was dragged up the Tower-hill, sitting on
a sled, to suffer death as the champion of the English laws, one of
the multitude cried out to him, "You never sate on so glorious a
seat!" Charles II, to intimidate the citizens of London, caused the
patriot Lord Russell [2] to be drawn in an open coach through the
principal streets of the city on his way to the scaffold. "But," his
biographer says, "the multitude imagined they saw liberty and
virtue sitting by his side." In private places, among sordid objects, an act of truth or heroism seems at once to draw to itself the
sky as its temple, the sun as its candle. Nature stretches out her
arms to embrace man, only let his thoughts be of equal greatness.
Willingly does she follow his steps with the rose and the violet,
and bend her lines of grandeur and grace to the decoration
of her darling child. Only let his thoughts be of equal scope, and
the frame will suit the picture. A virtuous man is in unison with

---

[1] Fourth governor of Massachusetts; a leader of the Commonwealth, put to
death by Charles II.
[2] Lord William Russell, parliamentary opponent of Charles II.

her works, and makes the central figure of the visible sphere. Homer, Pindar, Socrates, Phocion, associate themselves fitly in our memory with the geography and climate of Greece. The visible heavens and earth sympathize with Jesus. And in common life whosoever has seen a person of powerful character and happy genius, will have remarked how easily he took all things along with him, — the persons, the opinions, and the day, and nature become ancillary to a man.

3. There is still another aspect under which the beauty of the world may be viewed, namely, as it becomes an object of the intellect. Beside the relation of things to virtue, they have a relation to thought. The intellect searches out the absolute order of things as they stand in the mind of God, and without the colors of affection. The intellectual and the active powers seem to succeed each other, and the exclusive activity of the one generates the exclusive activity of the other. There is something unfriendly in each to the other, but they are like the alternate periods of feeding and working in animals; each prepares and will be followed by the other. Therefore does beauty, which, in relation to actions, as we have seen, comes unsought, and comes because it is unsought, remain for the apprehension and pursuit of the intellect; and then again, in its turn, of the active power. Nothing divine dies. All good is eternally reproductive. The beauty of nature re-forms itself in the mind, and not for barren contemplation, but for new creation.

All men are in some degree impressed by the face of the world; some men even to delight. This love of beauty is Taste. Others have the same love in such excess, that, not content with admiring, they seek to embody it in new forms. The creation of beauty is Art.

The production of a work of art throws a light upon the mystery of humanity. A work of art is an abstract or epitome of the world. It is the result or expression of nature, in miniature. For although the works of nature are innumerable and all different, the result or the expression of them all is similar and single. Nature is a sea of forms radically alike and even unique. A leaf, a sunbeam, a landscape, the ocean, make an analogous impression on the mind. What is common to them all, — that perfectness and harmony, is beauty. The standard of beauty is the entire circuit of natural forms, — the totality of nature; which the Italians expressed by defining beauty "il più nell' uno." [3] Nothing is quite

[3] The many in one.

beautiful alone; nothing but is beautiful in the whole. A single object is only so far beautiful as it suggests this universal grace. The poet, the painter, the sculptor, the musician, the architect, seek each to concentrate this radiance of the world on one point, and each in his several work to satisfy the love of beauty which stimulates him to produce. Thus is Art a nature passed through the alembic of man. Thus in art does Nature work through the will of a man filled with the beauty of her first works.

The world thus exists to the soul to satisfy the desire of beauty. This element I call an ultimate end. No reason can be asked or given why the soul seeks beauty. Beauty, in its largest and profoundest sense, is one expression for the universe. God is the all-fair. Truth, and goodness, and beauty, are but different faces of the same All. But beauty in nature is not ultimate. It is the herald of inward and eternal beauty, and is not alone a solid and satisfactory good. It must stand as a part, and not as yet the last or highest expression of the final cause of Nature.

"Each and All"
P. 413

IV. LANGUAGE

LANGUAGE is a third use which Nature subserves to man. Nature is the vehicle of thought, and in a simple, double, and threefold degree.

1. Words are signs of natural facts.
2. Particular natural facts are symbols of particular spiritual facts.
3. Nature is the symbol of spirit.

1. Words are signs of natural facts. The use of natural history is to give us aid in supernatural history; the use of the outer creation, to give us language for the beings and changes of the inward creation. Every word which is used to express a moral or intellectual fact, if traced to its root, is found to be borrowed from some material appearance. *Right* means *straight*; *wrong* means *twisted*. *Spirit* primarily means *wind*; *transgression*, the *crossing of a line*; *supercilious*, the *raising of the eyebrow*. We say the *heart* to express emotion, the *head* to denote thought; and *thought* and *emotion* are words borrowed from sensible things, and now appropriated to spiritual nature. Most of the process by which this transformation is made, is hidden from us in the remote time when language was framed; but the same tendency may be daily observed in children. Children and savages use only nouns or

names of things, which they convert into verbs, and apply to analogous mental acts.

2. But this origin of all words that convey a spiritual import, — so conspicuous a fact in the history of language, — is our least debt to nature. It is not words only that are emblematic; it is things which are emblematic. Every natural fact is a symbol of some spiritual fact. Every appearance in nature corresponds to some state of the mind, and that state of the mind can only be described by presenting that natural appearance as its picture. An enraged man is a lion, a cunning man is a fox, a firm man is a rock, a learned man is a torch. A lamb is innocence; a snake is subtle spite; flowers express to us the delicate affections. Light and darkness are our familiar expression for knowledge and ignorance; and heat for love. Visible distance behind and before us, is respectively our image of memory and hope.

Who looks upon a river in a meditative hour and is not reminded of the flux of all things? Throw a stone into the stream, and the circles that propagate themselves are the beautiful type of all influence. Man is conscious of a universal soul within or behind his individual life, wherein, as in a firmament, the natures of Justice, Truth, Love, Freedom, arise and shine. This universal soul he calls Reason: it is not mine, or thine, or his, but we are its; we are its property and men. And the blue sky in which the private earth is buried, the sky with its eternal calm, and full of everlasting orbs, is the type of Reason. That which intellectually considered we call Reason, considered in relation to nature, we call Spirit. Spirit is the Creator. Spirit hath life in itself. And man in all ages and countries embodies it in his language as the FATHER.

It is easily seen that there is nothing lucky or capricious in these analogies, but that they are constant, and pervade nature. These are not the dreams of a few poets, here and there, but man is an analogist, and studies relations in all objects. He is placed in the center of beings, and a ray of relation passes from every other being to him. And neither can man be understood without these objects, nor these objects without man. All the facts in natural history taken by themselves, have no value, but are barren, like a single sex. But marry it to human history, and it is full of life. Whole floras, all Linnaeus' and Buffon's volumes, are dry catalogues of facts; but the most trivial of these facts, the habit of a plant, the organs, or work, or noise of an insect, applied to the illustration of a fact in intellectual philosophy, or in any way associated to human nature, affects us in the most lively and agreeable manner. The seed of a plant, — to what affecting analogies in the nature of man is that little fruit made use of, in all discourse, up to the voice of Paul, who calls the human corpse a seed, — "It is sown a natural body; it is raised a spiritual body." The motion of the earth round its axis and round the sun, makes the day and the year. These are certain amounts of brute light and heat. But is there no intent of an analogy between man's life and the seasons? And do the seasons gain no grandeur or pathos from that analogy? The instincts of the ant are very unimportant considered as the ant's; but the moment a ray of relation is seen to extend from it to man, and the little drudge is seen to be a monitor, a little body with a mighty heart, then all its habits, even that said to be recently observed, that it never sleeps, become sublime.

Because of this radical correspondence between visible things and human thoughts, savages, who have only what is necessary, converse in figures. As we go back in history, language becomes more picturesque, until its infancy, when it is all poetry; or all spiritual facts are represented by natural symbols. The same symbols are found to make the original elements of all languages. It has moreover been observed, that the idioms of all languages approach each other in passages of the greatest eloquence and power. And as this is the first language, so is it the last. This immediate dependence of language upon nature, this conversion of an outward phenomenon into a type of somewhat in human life, never loses its power to affect us. It is this which gives that piquancy to the conversation of a strong-natured farmer or back-woodsman, which all men relish.

A man's power to connect his thought with its proper symbol, and so to utter it, depends on the simplicity of his character, that is, upon his love of truth and his desire to communicate it without loss. The corruption of man is followed by the corruption of language. When simplicity of character and the sovereignty of ideas is broken up by the prevalence of secondary desires, — the desire of riches, of pleasure, of power, and of praise, — and duplicity and falsehood take place of simplicity and truth, the power over nature as an interpreter of the will is in a degree lost; new imagery ceases to be created, and old words are perverted to stand for things which are not; a paper currency is employed, when there is no bullion in the vaults. In due time the fraud is manifest, and words lose all power to stimulate the understanding or the affections. Hundreds of writers may be found in every long-civilized nation who for a short time believe and make others believe that they see and utter truths, who do not of themselves clothe one thought in its natural garment, but who feed unconsciously on the language created by the primary writers of the country, those, namely, who hold primarily on nature.

But wise men pierce this rotten diction and fasten words again to visible things; so that picturesque language is at once a commanding certificate that he who employs it is a man in alliance with truth and God. The moment our discourse rises above the ground line of familiar facts and is inflamed with passion or exalted by thought, it clothes itself in images. A man conversing in earnest, if he watch his intellectual processes, will find that a material image more or less luminous arises in his mind, contemporaneous with every thought, which furnishes the vestment of the thought. Hence, good writing and brilliant discourse are perpetual allegories. This imagery is spontaneous. It is the blending of experience with the present action of the mind. It is proper creation. It is the working of the Original Cause through the instruments he has already made.

These facts may suggest the advantage which the country-life possesses, for a powerful mind, over the artificial and curtailed life of cities. We know more from nature than we can at will communicate. Its light flows into the mind evermore, and we forget its presence. The poet, the orator, bred in the woods, whose senses have been nourished by their fair and appeasing changes, year after year, without design and without heed, — shall not lose their lesson altogether, in the roar of cities or the broil of politics. Long hereafter, amidst agitation and terror in national councils, — in the hour of revolution, — these solemn images shall reappear in their morning lustre, as fit symbols and words of the thoughts which the passing events shall awaken. At the call of a noble sentiment, again the woods wave, the pines murmur, the river rolls and shines, and the cattle low upon the mountains, as he saw and heard them in his infancy. And with these forms, the spells of persuasion, the keys of power are put into his hands.

3. We are thus assisted by natural objects in the expression of particular meanings. But how great a language to convey such pepper-corn informations! Did it need such noble races of creatures, this profusion of forms, this host of orbs in heaven, to furnish man with the dictionary and grammar of his municipal speech? Whilst we use this grand cipher to expedite the affairs

of our pot and kettle, we feel that we have not yet put it to its use, neither are able. We are like travelers using the cinders of a volcano to roast their eggs. Whilst we see that it always stands ready to clothe what we would say, we cannot avoid the question whether the characters are not significant of themselves. Have mountains, and waves, and skies, no significance but what we consciously give them when we employ them as emblems of our thoughts? The world is emblematic. Parts of speech are metaphors, because the whole of nature is a metaphor of the human mind. The laws of moral nature answer to those of matter as face to face in a glass. "The visible world and the relation of its parts, is the dial plate of the invisible." The axioms of physics translate the laws of ethics. Thus, "the whole is greater than its part"; "reaction is equal to action"; "the smallest weight may be made to lift the greatest, the difference of weight being compensated by time"; and many the like propositions, which have an ethical as well as physical sense. These propositions have a much more extensive and universal sense when applied to human life, than when confined to technical use.

In like manner, the memorable words of history and the proverbs of nations consist usually of a natural fact, selected as a picture or parable of a moral truth. Thus; A rolling stone gathers no moss; A bird in the hand is worth two in the bush; A cripple in the right way will beat a racer in the wrong; Make hay while the sun shines; 'Tis hard to carry a full cup even; Vinegar is the son of wine; The last ounce broke the camel's back; Long-lived trees make roots first; — and the like. In their primary sense these are trivial facts, but we repeat them for the value of their analogical import. What is true of proverbs, is true of all fables, parables, and allegories.

This relation between the mind and matter is not fancied by some poet, but stands in the will of God, and so is free to be known by all men. It appears to men, or it does not appear. When in fortunate hours we ponder this miracle, the wise man doubts if at all other times he is not blind and deaf;

> "Can such things be,
> And overcome us like a summer's cloud,
> Without our special wonder?"

for the universe becomes transparent, and the light of higher laws than its own shines through it. It is the standing problem which has exercised the wonder and the study of every fine genius since the world began; from the era of the Egyptians and the Brahmins to that of Pythagoras, of Plato, of Bacon, of Leibnitz, of Swedenborg. There sits the Sphinx at the road-side, and from age to age, as each prophet comes by, he tries his fortune at reading her riddle.[4] There seems to be a necessity in spirit to manifest itself in material forms; and day and night, river and storm, beast and bird, acid and alkali, preëxist in necessary Ideas in the mind of God, and are what they are by virtue of preceding affections in the world of spirit. A Fact is the end or last issue of spirit. The visible creation is the terminus or the circumference of the invisible world. "Material objects," said a French philosopher, "are necessarily kinds of *scoriae*[5] of the substantial thoughts of the Creator, which must always preserve an exact relation to their first origin; in other words, visible nature must have a spiritual and moral side."

This doctrine is abstruse, and though the images of "garment," "scoriae," "mirror," etc., may stimulate the fancy, we must summon the aid of subtler and more vital expositors to make it plain. "Every scripture is to be interpreted by the same spirit which gave it forth," — is the fundamental law of criticism. A life in harmony with Nature, the love of truth and of virtue, will purge the eyes to understand her text. By degrees we may come to know the primitive sense of the permanent objects of nature, so that the world shall be to us an open book, and every form significant of its hidden life and final cause.

A new interest surprises us, whilst, under the view now suggested, we contemplate the fearful extent and multitude of objects; since "every object rightly seen, unlocks a new faculty of the soul." That which was unconscious truth, becomes, when interpreted and defined in an object, a part of the domain of knowledge, — a new weapon in the magazine of power.

v. DISCIPLINE

IN view of the significance of nature, we arrive at once at a new fact, that nature is a discipline. This use of the world includes the preceding uses, as parts of itself.

Space, time, society, labor, climate, food, locomotion, the animals, the mechanical forces, give us sincerest lessons, day by day,

4 Cf. "The Sphinx" (p. 420).
5 Dross, slag.

whose meaning is unlimited. They educate both the Understanding and the Reason. Every property of matter is a school for the understanding, — its solidity or resistance, its inertia, its extension, its figure, its divisibility. The understanding adds, divides, combines, measures, and finds nutriment and room for its activity in this worthy scene. Meantime, Reason transfers all these lessons into its own world of thought, by perceiving the analogy that marries Matter and Mind.

1. Nature is a discipline of the understanding in intellectual truths. Our dealing with sensible objects is a constant exercise in the necessary lessons of difference, of likeness, of order, of being and seeming, of progressive arrangement; of ascent from particular to general; of combination to one end of manifold forces. Proportioned to the importance of the organ to be formed, is the extreme care with which its tuition is provided, — a care pretermitted in no single case. What tedious training, day after day, year after year, never ending, to form the common sense; what continual reproduction of annoyances, inconveniences, dilemmas; what rejoicing over us of little men; what disputing of prices, what reckonings of interest, — and all to form the Hand of the mind; — to instruct us that "good thoughts are no better than good dreams, unless they be executed!"

The same good office is performed by Property and its filial systems of debt and credit. Debt, grinding debt, whose iron face the widow, the orphan, and the sons of genius fear and hate; — debt, which consumes so much time, which so cripples and disheartens a great spirit with cares that seem so base, is a preceptor whose lessons cannot be foregone, and is needed most by those who suffer from it most. Moreover, property, which has been well compared to snow, — "if it fall level today, it will be blown into drifts tomorrow," — is the surface action of internal machinery, like the index on the face of a clock. Whilst now it is the gymnastics of the understanding, it is hiving, in the foresight of the spirit, experience in profounder laws.

The whole character and fortune of the individual are affected by the least inequalities in the culture of the understanding; for example, in the perception of differences. Therefore is Space, and therefore Time, that man may know that things are not huddled and lumped, but sundered and individual. A bell and a plough have each their use, and neither can do the office of the other. Water is good to drink, coal to burn, wool to wear; but wool cannot be drunk, nor water spun, nor coal eaten. The wise man shows his wisdom in separation, in gradation, and his scale of creatures and of merits is as wide as nature. The foolish have no range in their scale, but suppose every man is as every other man. What is not good they call the worst, and what is not hateful, they call the best.

In like manner, what good heed Nature forms in us! She pardons no mistakes. Her yea is yea, and her nay, nay.

The first steps in Agriculture, Astronomy, Zoölogy (those first steps which the farmer, the hunter, and the sailor take), teach that Nature's dice are always loaded; that in her heaps and rubbish are concealed sure and useful results.

How calmly and genially the mind apprehends one after another the laws of physics! What noble emotions dilate the mortal as he enters into the councils of the creation, and feels by knowledge the privilege to Be! His insight refines him. The beauty of nature shines in his own breast. Man is greater that he can see this, and the universe less, because Time and Space relations vanish as laws are known.

Here again we are impressed and even daunted by the immense Universe to be explored. "What we know is a point to what we do not know." Open any recent journal of science, and weigh the problems suggested concerning Light, Heat, Electricity, Magnetism, Physiology, Geology, and judge whether the interest of natural science is likely to be soon exhausted.

Passing by many particulars of the discipline of nature, we must not omit to specify two.

The exercise of the Will, or the lesson of power, is taught in every event. From the child's successive possession of his several senses up to the hour when he saith, "Thy will be done!" he is learning the secret that he can reduce under his will not only particular events but great classes, nay, the whole series of events, and so conform all facts to his character. Nature is thoroughly mediate. It is made to serve. It receives the dominion of man as meekly as the ass on which the Saviour rode. It offers all its kingdoms to man as the raw material which he may mold into what is useful. Man is never weary of working it up. He forges the subtile and delicate air into wise and melodious words, and gives them wing as angels of persuasion and command. One after another his victorious thought comes up with and reduces all things, until the world becomes at last only a realized will, — the double of the man.

2. Sensible objects conform to the premonitions of Reason and

reflect the conscience. All things are moral; and in their boundless changes have an unceasing reference to spiritual nature.
Therefore is nature glorious with form, color, and motion; that
every globe in the remotest heaven, every chemical change from
the rudest crystal up to the laws of life, every change of vegetation from the first principle of growth in the eye of a leaf, to
the tropical forest and antediluvian coal-mine, every animal function from the sponge up to Hercules, shall hint or thunder to
man the laws of right and wrong, and echo the Ten Commandments. Therefore is Nature ever the ally of Religion: lends all
her pomp and riches to the religious sentiment. Prophet and
priest, David, Isaiah, Jesus, have drawn deeply from this source.
This ethical character so penetrates the bone and marrow of nature, as to seem the end for which it was made. Whatever private
purpose is answered by any member or part, this is its public and
universal function, and is never omitted. Nothing in nature is
exhausted in its first use. When a thing has served an end to the
uttermost, it is wholly new for an ulterior service. In God, every
end is converted into a new means. Thus the use of commodity,
regarded by itself, is mean and squalid. But it is to the mind an
education in the doctrine of Use, namely, that a thing is good
only so far as it serves; that a conspiring of parts and efforts to
the production of an end is essential to any being. The first and
gross manifestation of this truth is our inevitable and hated
training in values and wants, in corn and meat.

It has already been illustrated, that every natural process is a
version of a moral sentence. The moral law lies at the center of
nature and radiates to the circumference. It is the pith and marrow of every substance, every relation, and every process. All
things with which we deal, preach to us. What is a farm but a
mute gospel? The chaff and the wheat, weeds and plants, blight,
rain, insects, sun, — it is a sacred emblem from the first furrow
of spring to the last stack which the snow of winter overtakes in
the fields. But the sailor, the shepherd, the miner, the merchant,
in their several resorts, have each an experience precisely parallel,
and leading to the same conclusion: because all organizations
are radically alike. Nor can it be doubted that this moral sentiment which thus scents the air, grows in the grain, and impreg-
nates the waters of the world, is caught by man and sinks into his
soul. The moral influence of nature upon every individual is that
amount of truth which it illustrates to him. Who can estimate
this? Who can guess how much firmness the sea-beaten rock has

taught the fisherman? how much tranquillity has been reflected
to man from the azure sky, over whose unspotted deeps the winds
forevermore drive flocks of stormy clouds, and leave no wrinkle
or stain? how much industry and providence and affection we
have caught from the pantomime of brutes? What a searching
preacher of self-command is the varying phenomenon of Health!

Herein is especially apprehended the unity of Nature, — the
unity in variety, — which meets us everywhere. All the endless
variety of things make an identical impression. Xenophanes
complained in his old age, that, look where he would, all things
hastened back to Unity. He was weary of seeing the same entity
in the tedious variety of forms. The fable of Proteus has a cordial [6] truth. A leaf, a drop, a crystal, a moment of time, is related
to the whole, and partakes of the perfection of the whole. Each
particle is a microcosm, and faithfully renders the likeness of the
world.

Not only resemblances exist in things whose analogy is obvious,
as when we detect the type of the human hand in the flipper of
the fossil saurus, but also in objects wherein there is great superficial unlikeness. Thus architecture is called "frozen music," by
De Staël and Goethe. Vitruvius thought an architect should be a
musician. "A Gothic church," said Coleridge, "is a petrified religion." Michael Angelo maintained, that, to an architect, a
knowledge of anatomy is essential. In Haydn's oratorios, the
notes present to the imagination not only motions, as of the
snake, the stag, and the elephant, but colors also; as the green
grass. The law of harmonic sounds reappears in the harmonic
colors. The granite is differenced in its laws only by the more or
less of heat from the river that wears it away. The river, as it flows,
resembles the air that flows over it; the air resembles the light
which traverses it with more subtle currents; the light resembles
the heat which rides with it through Space. Each creature is only
a modification of the other; the likeness in them is more than the
difference, and their radical law is one and the same. A rule of one
art, or a law of one organization, holds true throughout nature.
So intimate is this Unity, that, it is easily seen, it lies under the
undermost garment of Nature, and betrays its source in Universal
Spirit. For it pervades Thought also. Every universal truth
which we express in words, implies or supposes every other truth.
Omne verum vero consonat.[7] It is like a great circle on a sphere,

6 Vital.
7 All truth accords with truth.

comprising all possible circles; which, however, may be drawn and comprise it in like manner. Every such truth is the absolute Ens [8] seen from one side. But it has innumerable sides.

The central Unity is still more conspicuous in actions. Words are finite organs of the infinite mind. They cannot cover the dimensions of what is in truth. They break, chop, and impoverish it. An action is the perfection and publication of thought. A right action seems to fill the eye, and to be related to all nature. "The wise man, in doing one thing, does all; or, in the one thing he does rightly, he sees the likeness of all which is done rightly."

Words and actions are not the attributes of brute nature. They introduce us to the human form, of which all other organizations appear to be degradations. When this appears among so many that surround it, the spirit prefers it to all others. It says, "From such as this have I drawn joy and knowledge; in such as this have I found and beheld myself; I will speak to it; it can speak again; it can yield me thought already formed and alive." In fact, the eye, — the mind, — is always accompanied by these forms, male and female; and these are incomparably the richest informations of the power and order that lie at the heart of things. Unfortunately every one of them bears the marks as of some injury; is marred and superficially defective. Nevertheless, far different from the deaf and dumb nature around them, these all rest like fountain-pipes on the unfathomed sea of thought and virtue whereto they alone, of all organizations, are the entrances.

It were a pleasant inquiry to follow into detail their ministry to our education, but where would it stop? We are associated in adolescent and adult life with some friends, who, like skies and waters, are coextensive with our idea; who, answering each to a certain affection of the soul, satisfy our desire on that side; whom we lack power to put at such focal distance from us, that we can mend or even analyze them. We cannot choose but love them. When much intercourse with a friend has supplied us with a standard of excellence, and has increased our respect for the resources of God who thus sends a real person to outgo our ideal; when he has, moreover, become an object of thought, and, whilst his character retains all its unconscious effect, is converted in the mind into solid and sweet wisdom, — it is a sign to us that his office is closing, and he is commonly withdrawn from our sight in a short time.

8 Being.

VI. IDEALISM

THUS is the unspeakable but intelligible and practicable meaning of the world conveyed to man, the immortal pupil, in every
object of sense. To this one end of Discipline, all parts of nature
conspire.

A noble doubt perpetually suggests itself, — whether this end
be not the Final Cause of the Universe; and whether nature outwardly exists. It is a sufficient account of that Appearance we call
the World, that God will teach a human mind, and so makes it
the receiver of a certain number of congruent sensations, which
we call sun and moon, man and woman, house and trade. In my
utter impotence to test the authenticity of the report of my senses,
to know whether the impressions they make on me correspond
with outlying objects, what difference does it make, whether Orion
is up there in heaven, or some god paints the image in the firmament of the soul? The relations of parts and the end of the whole
remaining the same, what is the difference, whether land and sea
interact, and worlds revolve and intermingle without number or
end, — deep yawning under deep, and galaxy balancing galaxy,
throughout absolute space, — or whether, without relations of time
and space, the same appearances are inscribed in the constant faith
of man? Whether nature enjoy a substantial existence without, or
is only in the apocalypse of the mind, it is alike useful and alike
venerable to me. Be it what it may, it is ideal to me so long as I
cannot try the accuracy of my senses.

The frivolous make themselves merry with the Ideal theory, as if
its consequences were burlesque; as if it affected the stability of
nature. It surely does not. God never jests with us, and will not
compromise the end of nature by permitting any inconsequence in
its procession. Any distrust of the permanence of laws would para-
lyze the faculties of man. Their permanence is sacredly respected,
and his faith therein is perfect. The wheels and springs of man are
all set to the hypothesis of the permanence of nature. We are not
built like a ship to be tossed, but like a house to stand. It is a
natural consequence of this structure, that so long as the active
powers predominate over the reflective, we resist with indignation
any hint that nature is more short-lived or mutable than spirit. The
broker, the wheelwright, the carpenter, the tollman, are much displeased at the intimation.

But whilst we acquiesce entirely in the permanence of natural
laws, the question of the absolute existence of nature still remains

open. It is the uniform effect of culture on the human mind, not to shake our faith in the stability of particular phenomena, as of heat, water, azote; but to lead us to regard nature as a phenomenon, not a substance; to attribute necessary existence to spirit; to esteem nature as an accident and an effect.

To the senses and the unrenewed understanding, belongs a sort of instinctive belief in the absolute existence of nature. In their view man and nature are indissolubly joined. Things are ultimates, and they never look beyond their sphere. The presence of Reason mars this faith. The first effort of thought tends to relax this despotism of the senses which binds us to nature as if we were a part of it, and shows us nature aloof, and, as it were, afloat. Until this higher agency intervened, the animal eye sees, with wonderful accuracy, sharp outlines and colored surfaces. When the eye of Reason opens, to outline and surface are at once added grace and expression. These proceed from imagination and affection, and abate somewhat of the angular distinctness of objects. If the Reason be stimulated to more earnest vision, outlines and surfaces become transparent, and are no longer seen; causes and spirits are seen through them. The best moments of life are these delicious awakenings of the higher powers, and the reverential withdrawing of nature before its God.

Let us proceed to indicate the effects of culture.

1. Our first institution [9] in the Ideal philosophy is a hint from Nature herself.

Nature is made to conspire with spirit to emancipate us. Certain mechanical changes, a small alteration in our local position, apprizes us of a dualism. We are strangely affected by seeing the shore from a moving ship, from a balloon, or through the tints of an unusual sky. The least change in our point of view gives the whole world a pictorial air. A man who seldom rides, needs only to get into a coach and traverse his own town, to turn the street into a puppet-show. The men, the women, — talking, running, bartering, fighting, — the earnest mechanic, the lounger, the beggar, the boys, the dogs are unrealized [1] at once, or, at least, wholly detached from all relation to the observer, and seen as apparent, not substantial beings. What new thoughts are suggested by seeing a face of country quite familiar, in the rapid movement of the railroad car! Nay, the most wonted objects, (make a very slight change in the point of vision), please us most. In a camera ob-

[9] Instruction.
[1] Made unreal.

scura,[2] the butcher's cart, and the figure of one of our own family amuse us. So a portrait of a well-known face gratifies us. Turn the eyes upside down, by looking at the landscape through your legs, and how agreeable is the picture, though you have seen it any time these twenty years!

In these cases, by mechanical means, is suggested the difference between the observer and the spectacle — between man and nature. Hence arises a pleasure mixed with awe; I may say, a low degree of the sublime is felt, from the fact, probably, that man is hereby apprized that whilst the world is a spectacle, something in himself is stable.

2. In a higher manner the poet communicates the same pleasure. By a few strokes he delineates, as on air, the sun, the mountain, the camp, the city, the hero, the maiden, not different from what we know them, but only lifted from the ground and afloat before the eye. He unfixes the land and the sea, makes them revolve around the axis of his primary thought, and disposes them anew. Possessed himself by a heroic passion, he uses matter as symbols of it. The sensual man conforms thoughts to things; the poet conforms things to his thoughts. The one esteems nature as rooted and fast; the other, as fluid, and impresses his being thereon. To him, the refractory world is ductile and flexible; he invests dust and stones with humanity, and makes them the words of the Reason. The Imagination may be defined to be the use which the Reason makes of the material world. Shakespeare possesses the power of subordinating nature for the purposes of expression, beyond all poets. His imperial muse tosses the creation like a bauble from hand to hand, and uses it to embody any caprice of thought that is uppermost in his mind. The remotest spaces of nature are visited, and the farthest sundered things are brought together, by a subtile spiritual connection. We are made aware that magnitude of material things is relative, and all objects shrink and expand to serve the passion of the poet. Thus in his sonnets, the lays of birds, the scents and dyes of flowers he finds to be the *shadow* of his beloved; time, which keeps her from him, is his *chest*; the suspicion she has awakened, is her *ornament*;

> "The ornament of beauty is Suspect,
> A crow which flies in heaven's sweetest air."

His passion is not the fruit of chance; it swells, as he speaks, to a city, or a state.

[2] "Dark chamber"; in effect, a camera in which the image can be seen directly.

> "No, it was builded far from accident;
> It suffers not in smiling pomp, nor falls
> Under the brow of thralling discontent;
> It fears not policy, that heretic,
> That works on leases of short numbered hours,
> But all alone stands hugely politic."

In the strength of his constancy, the Pyramids seem to him recent and transitory. The freshness of youth and love dazzles him with its resemblance to morning;

> "Take those lips away
> Which so sweetly were forsworn;
> And those eyes, — the break of day,
> Lights that do mislead the morn."

The wild beauty of this hyperbole, I may say in passing, it would not be easy to match in literature.

This transfiguration which all material objects undergo through the passion of the poet, — this power which he exerts to dwarf the great, to magnify the small, — might be illustrated by a thousand examples from his Plays. I have before me the Tempest, and will cite only these few lines.

> "PROSPERO. The strong based promontory
> Have I made shake, and by the spurs plucked up
> The pine and cedar."

Prospero calls for music to soothe the frantic Alonzo, and his companions;

> "A solemn air, and the best comforter
> To an unsettled fancy, cure thy brains
> Now useless, boiled within thy skull."

Again;

> "The charm dissolves apace,
> And, as the morning steals upon the night,
> Melting the darkness, so their rising senses
> Begin to chase the ignorant fumes that mantle
> Their clearer reason.
> 　　　　　Their understanding
> Begins to swell: and the approaching tide
> Will shortly fill the reasonable shores
> That now lie foul and muddy."

The perception of real affinities between events (that is to say, of *ideal* affinities, for those only are real), enables the poet thus to make free with the most imposing forms and phenomena of the world, and to assert the predominance of the soul.

3. Whilst thus the poet animates nature with his own thoughts, he differs from the philsopher only herein, that the one proposes Beauty as his main end; the other Truth. But the philosopher, not less than the poet, postpones the apparent order and relations of things to the empire of thought. "The problem of philosophy," according to Plato, "is, for all that exists conditionally, to find a ground unconditioned and absolute." It proceeds on the faith that a law determines all phenomena, which being known, the phenomena can be predicted. That law, when in the mind, is an idea. Its beauty is infinite. The true philosopher and the true poet are one, and a beauty, which is truth, and a truth, which is beauty, is the aim of both. Is not the charm of one of Plato's or Aristotle's definitions strictly like that of the Antigone of Sophocles? It is, in both cases, that a spiritual life has been imparted to nature; that the solid seeming block of matter has been pervaded and dissolved by a thought; that this feeble human being has penetrated the vast masses of nature with an informing soul, and recognized itself in their harmony, that is, seized their law. In physics, when this is attained, the memory disburthens itself of its cumbrous catalogues of particulars, and carries centuries of observation in a single formula.

Thus even in physics, the material is degraded before the spiritual. The astronomer, the geometer, rely on their irrefragable analysis, and disdain the results of observation. The sublime remark of Euler on his law of arches, "This will be found contrary to all experience, yet is true"; had already transferred nature into the mind, and left matter like an outcast corpse.

4. Intellectual science has been observed to beget invariably a doubt of the existence of matter. Turgot said, "He that has never doubted the existence of matter, may be assured he has no aptitude for metaphysical inquiries." It fastens the attention upon immortal necessary uncreated natures, that is, upon Ideas; and in their presence we feel that the outward circumstance is a dream and a shade. Whilst we wait in this Olympus of gods, we think of nature as an appendix to the soul. We ascend into their region, and know that these are the thoughts of the Supreme Being. "These are they who were set up from everlasting, from the beginning, or ever the earth was. When he prepared the heavens, they were there; when he established the clouds above, when he strengthened

the fountains of the deep. Then they were by him, as one brought up with him. Of them took he counsel."

Their influence is proportionate. As objects of science they are accessible to few men. Yet all men are capable of being raised by piety or by passion, into their region. And no man touches these divine natures, without becoming, in some degree, himself divine. Like a new soul, they renew the body. We become physically nimble and lightsome; we tread on air; life is no longer irksome, and we think it will never be so. No man fears age or misfortune or death in their serene company, for he is transported out of the district of change. Whilst we behold unveiled the nature of Justice and Truth, we learn the difference between the absolute and the conditional or relative. We apprehend the absolute. As it were, for the first time, *we exist.* We become immortal, for we learn that time and space are relations of matter; that with a perception of truth or a virtuous will they have no affinity.

5. Finally, religion and ethics, which may be fitly called the practice of ideas, or the introduction of ideas into life, have an analogous effect with all lower culture, in degrading nature and suggesting its dependence on spirit. Ethics and religion differ herein; that the one is the system of human duties commencing from man; the other, from God. Religion includes the personality of God; Ethics does not. They are one to our present design. They both put nature under foot. The first and last lesson of religion is, "The things that are seen, are temporal; the things that are unseen, are eternal." It puts an affront upon nature. It does that for the unschooled, which philosophy does for Berkeley and Viasa.[3] The uniform language that may be heard in the churches of the most ignorant sects is, — "Contemn the unsubstantial shows of the world; they are vanities, dreams, shadows, unrealities; seek the realities of religion." The devotee flouts nature. Some theosophists have arrived at a certain hostility and indignation towards matter, as the Manichean and Plotinus. They distrusted in themselves any looking back to these flesh-pots of Egypt. Plotinus was ashamed of his body. In short, they might all say of matter, what Michael Angelo said of external beauty, "It is the frail and weary weed, in which God dresses the soul which he has called into time."

It appears that motion, poetry, physical and intellectual science, and religion, all tend to affect our convictions of the reality of the external world. But I own there is something ungrateful in ex-

3 Reputed author of the Hindu *Vedas.*

panding too curiously the particulars of the general proposition, that all culture tends to imbue us with idealism. I have no hostility to nature, but a child's love to it. I expand and live in the warm day like corn and melons. Let us speak her fair. I do not wish to fling stones at my beautiful mother, nor soil my gentle nest. I only wish to indicate the true position of nature in regard to man, wherein to establish man all right education tends; as the ground which to attain is the object of human life, that is, of man's connection with nature. Culture inverts the vulgar views of nature, and brings the mind to call that apparent which it uses to call real, and that real which it uses to call visionary. Children, it is true, believe in the external world. The belief that it appears only, is an afterthought, but with culture this faith will as surely arise on the mind as did the first.

The advantage of the ideal theory over the popular faith is this, that it presents the world in precisely that view which is most desirable to the mind. It is, in fact, the view which Reason, both speculative and practical, that is, philosophy and virtue take. For seen in the light of thought, the world always is phenomenal; and virtue subordinates it to the mind. Idealism sees the world in God. It beholds the whole circle of persons and things, of actions and events, of country and religion, not as painfully accumulated, atom after atom, act after act, in an aged creeping Past, but as one vast picture which God paints on the instant eternity for the contemplation of the soul. Therefore the soul holds itself off from a too trivial and microscopic study of the universal tablet. It respects the end too much to immerse itself in the means. It sees something more important in Christianity than the scandals of ecclesiastical history or the niceties of criticism; and, very incurious concerning persons or miracles, and not at all disturbed by chasms of historical evidence, it accepts from God the phenomenon, as it finds it, as the pure and awful form of religion in the world. It is not hot and passionate at the appearance of what it calls its own good or bad fortune, at the union or opposition of other persons. No man is its enemy. It accepts whatsoever befalls, as part of its lesson. It is a watcher more than a doer, and it is a doer, only that it may the better watch.

VII. SPIRIT

IT is essential to a true theory of nature and of man, that it should contain somewhat progressive. Uses that are exhausted or that may be, and facts that end in the statement, cannot be all that is true of this brave lodging wherein man is harbored, and wherein all his faculties find appropriate and endless exercise. And all the uses of nature admit of being summed in one, which yields the activity of man an infinite scope. Through all its kingdoms, to the suburbs and outskirts of things, it is faithful to the cause whence it had its origin. It always speaks of Spirit. It suggests the absolute. It is a perpetual effect. It is a great shadow pointing always to the sun behind us.

The aspect of Nature is devout. Like the figure of Jesus, she stands with bended head, and hands folded upon the breast. The happiest man is he who learns from nature the lesson of worship. Of that ineffable essence which we call Spirit, he that thinks most, will say least. We can foresee God in the coarse, and, as it were, distant phenomena of matter; but when we try to define and describe himself, both language and thought desert us, and we are as helpless as fools and savages. That essence refuses to be recorded in propositions, but when man has worshipped him intellectually, the noblest ministry of nature is to stand as the apparition of God. It is the organ through which the universal spirit speaks to the individual, and strives to lead back the individual to it.

When we consider Spirit, we see that the views already presented do not include the whole circumference of man. We must add some related thoughts.

Three problems are put by nature to the mind: What is matter? Whence is it? and Whereto? The first of these questions only, the ideal theory answers. Idealism saith: matter is a phenomenon, not a substance. Idealism acquaints us with the total disparity between the evidence of our own being and the evidence of the world's being. The one is perfect; the other, incapable of any assurance; the mind is a part of the nature of things; the world is a divine dream, from which we may presently awake to the glories and certainties of day. Idealism is a hypothesis to account for nature by other principles than those of carpentry and chemistry. Yet, if it only deny the existence of matter, it does not satisfy the demands of the spirit. It leaves God out of me. It leaves me in the splendid labyrinth of my perceptions, to wander without end. Then the heart resists it, because it balks the affections in denying substantive being to men and women. Nature is so pervaded with human life that there is something of humanity in all and in every particular. But this theory makes nature foreign to me, and does not account for that consanguinity which we acknowledge to it.

Let it stand then, in the present state of our knowledge, merely as a useful introductory hypothesis, serving to apprize us of the eternal distinction between the soul and the world.

But when, following the invisible steps of thought, we come to inquire, Whence is matter? and Whereto? many truths arise to us out of the recesses of consciousness. We learn that the highest is present to the soul of man; that the dread universal essence, which is not wisdom, or love, or beauty, or power, but all in one, and each entirely, is that for which all things exist, and that by which they are; that spirit creates; that behind nature, throughout nature, spirit is present; one and not compound it does not act upon us from without, that is, in space and time, but spiritually, or through ourselves: therefore, that spirit, that is, the Supreme Being, does not build up nature around us, but puts it forth through us, as the life of the tree puts forth new branches and leaves through the pores of the old. As a plant upon the earth, so a man rests upon the bosom of God; he is nourished by unfailing fountains, and draws at his need inexhaustible power. Who can set bounds to the possibilities of man? Once inhale the upper air, being admitted to behold the absolute natures of justice and truth, and we learn that man has access to the entire mind of the Creator, is himself the creator in the finite. This view, which admonishes me where the sources of wisdom and power lie, and points to virtue as to

> "The golden key
> Which opes the palace of eternity,"

carries upon its face the highest certificate of truth, because it animates me to create my own world through the purification of my soul.

The world proceeds from the same spirit as the body of man. It is a remoter and inferior incarnation of God, a projection of God in the unconscious. But it differs from the body in one important respect. It is not, like that, now subjected to the human will. Its serene order is inviolable by us. It is, therefore, to us, the present expositor of the divine mind. It is a fixed point whereby we may measure our departure. As we degenerate, the contrast between us and our house is more evident. We are as much strangers in nature as we are aliens from God. We do not understand the notes of birds. The fox and the deer run away from us; the bear and tiger rend us. We do not know the uses of more than a few plants, as corn and the apple, the potato and the vine. Is not the land-

scape, every glimpse of which hath a grandeur, a face of him? Yet
this may show us what discord is between man and nature, for you
cannot freely admire a noble landscape if laborers are digging in the
field hard by. The poet finds something ridiculous in his delight
until he is out of the sight of men.

VIII. PROSPECTS

IN inquiries respecting the laws of the world and the frame of
things, the highest reason is always the truest. That which seems
faintly possible, it is so refined, is often faint and dim because it is
deepest seated in the mind among the eternal verities. Empirical
science is apt to cloud the sight, and by the very knowledge of
functions and processes to bereave the student of the manly contemplation of the whole. The savant becomes unpoetic. But the
best read naturalist who lends an entire and devout attention to
truth, will see that there remains much to learn of his relation to
the world, and that it is not to be learned by any addition or sub-
traction or other comparison of known quantities, but is arrived
at by untaught sallies of the spirit, by a continual self-recovery, and
by entire humility. He will perceive that there are far more excellent qualities in the student than preciseness and infallibility;
that a guess is often more fruitful than an indisputable affirmation,
and that a dream may let us deeper into the secret of nature than
a hundred concerted experiments.

For the problems to be solved are precisely those which the
physiologist and the naturalist omit to state. It is not so pertinent
to man to know all the individuals of the animal kingdom, as it is
to know whence and whereto is this tyrannizing unity in his constitution, which evermore separates and classifies things, endeavoring to reduce the most diverse to one form. When I behold a rich
landscape, it is less to my purpose to recite correctly the order and
superposition of the strata, than to know why all thought of multitude is lost in a tranquil sense of unity. I cannot greatly honor
minuteness in details, so long as there is no hint to explain the relation between things and thoughts; no ray upon the *metaphysics*
of conchology, of botany, of the arts, to show the relation of the
forms of flowers, shells, animals, architecture, to the mind, and
build science upon ideas. In a cabinet of natural history, we become sensible of a certain occult recognition and sympathy in regard to the most unwieldly and eccentric forms of beast, fish, and

insect. The American who has been confined, in his own country, to the sight of buildings designed after foreign models, is surprised on entering York Minster or St. Peter's at Rome, by the feeling that these structures are imitations also, — faint copies of an invisible archetype. Nor has science sufficient humanity, so long as the naturalist overlooks that wonderful congruity which subsists between man and the world; of which he is lord, not because he is the most subtile inhabitant, but because he is its head and heart, and finds something of himself in every great and small thing, in every mountain stratum, in every new law of color, fact of astronomy, or atmospheric influence which observation or analysis lays open. A perception of this mystery inspires the muse of George Herbert, the beautiful psalmist of the seventeenth century. The following lines are part of his little poem on Man.

"Man is all symmetry,
Full of proportions, one limb to another,
And all to all the world besides.
Each part may call the farthest, brother;
For head with foot hath private amity,
And both with moons and tides.

"Nothing hath got so far
But man hath caught and kept it as his prey;
His eyes dismount the highest star:
He is in little all the sphere.
Herbs gladly cure our flesh, because that they
Find their acquaintance there.

"For us, the winds do blow,
The earth doth rest, heaven move, and fountains flow,
Nothing we see, but means our good,
As our delight, or as our treasure;
The whole is either our cupboard of food,
Or cabinet of pleasure.

"The stars have us to bed:
Night draws the curtain; which the sun withdraws.
Music and light attend our head.
All things unto our flesh are kind,
In their descent and being; to our mind,
In their ascent and cause.

"More servants wait on man
Than he'll take notice of. In every path,

> He treads down that which doth befriend him
> When sickness makes him pale and wan.
> Oh mighty love! Man is one world, and hath
> Another to attend him."

The perception of this class of truths makes the attraction which draws men to science, but the end is lost sight of in attention to the means. In view of this half-sight of science, we accept the sentence of Plato, that "poetry comes nearer to vital truth than history." Every surmise and vaticination of the mind is entitled to a certain respect, and we learn to prefer imperfect theories, and sentences which contain glimpses of truth, to digested systems which have no one valuable suggestion. A wise writer will feel that the ends of study and composition are best answered by announcing undiscovered regions of thought, and so communicating, through hope, new activity to the torpid spirit.

I shall therefore conclude this essay with some traditions of man and nature, which a certain poet sang to me; and which, as they have always been in the world, and perhaps reappear to every bard, may be both history and prophecy.

"The foundations of man are not in matter, but in spirit. But the element of spirit is eternity. To it, therefore, the longest series of events, the oldest chronologies are young and recent. In the cycle of the universal man, from whom the known individuals proceed, centuries are points, and all history is but the epoch of one degradation.

"We distrust and deny inwardly our sympathy with nature. We own and disown our relation to it, by turns. We are like Nebuchadnezzar, dethroned, bereft of reason, and eating grass like an ox. But who can set limits to the remedial force of spirit?

"A man is a god in ruins. When men are innocent, life shall be longer, and shall pass into the immortal as gently as we awake from dreams. Now, the world would be insane and rabid, if these disorganizations should last for hundreds of years. It is kept in check by death and infancy. Infancy is the perpetual Messiah, which comes into the arms of fallen men, and pleads with them to return to paradise.

"Man is the dwarf of himself. Once he was permeated and dissolved by spirit. He filled nature with his overflowing currents. Out from him sprang the sun and moon; from man the sun, from woman the moon. The laws of his mind, the periods of his actions externized themselves into day and night, into the year and the seasons. But, having made for himself this huge shell, his waters retired; he no longer fills the veins and veinlets; he is shrunk to a drop. He sees that the structure still fits him, but fits him colossally. Say, rather, once it fitted him, now it corresponds to him from far and on high. He adores timidly his own work. Now is man the follower of the sun, and woman the follower of the moon. Yet sometimes he starts in his slumber, and wonders at himself and his house, and muses strangely at the resemblance betwixt him and it. He perceives that if his law is still paramount, if still he have elemental power, if his word is sterling yet in nature, it is not conscious power, it is not inferior but superior to his will. It is instinct." Thus my Orphic poet sang.

At present, man applies to nature but half his force. He works on the world with his understanding alone. He lives in it and masters it by a penny-wisdom; and he that works most in it is but a half-man, and whilst his arms are strong and his digestion good, his mind is imbruted, and he is a selfish savage. His relation to nature, his power over it, is through the understanding, as by manure; the economic use of fire, wind, water, and the mariner's needle; steam, coal, chemical agriculture; the repairs of the human body by the dentist and the surgeon. This is such a resumption of power as if a banished king should buy his territories inch by inch, instead of vaulting at once into his throne. Meantime, in the thick darkness, there are not wanting gleams of a better light, — occasional examples of the action of man upon nature with his entire force, — with reason as well as understanding. Such examples are, the traditions of miracles in the earliest antiquity of all nations; the history of Jesus Christ; the achievements of a principle, as in religious and political revolutions, and in the abolition of the slave-trade; the miracles of enthusiasm, as those reported of Swedenborg, Hohenlohe,[4] and the Shakers; many obscure and yet contested facts, now arranged under the name of Animal Magnetism;[5] prayer; eloquence; self-healing; and the wisdom of children. These are examples of Reason's momentary grasp of the scepter; the exertions of a power which exists not in time or space, but an instantaneous in-streaming causing power. The difference between the actual and the ideal force of man is happily figured by the schoolmen, in saying, that the knowledge of man is an evening knowledge, *vespertina cognitio*, but that of God is a morning knowledge, *matutina cognitio*.

[4] German priest of Emerson's day, known for his miraculous cures.
[5] Hypnotism

The problem of restoring to the world original and eternal beauty is solved by the redemption of the soul. The ruin or the blank that we see when we look at nature, is in our own eye. The axis of vision is not coincident with the axis of things, and so they appear not transparent but opaque. The reason why the world lacks unity, and lies broken and in heaps, is because man is disunited with himself. He cannot be a naturalist until he satisfies all the demands of the spirit. Love is as much its demand as perception. Indeed, neither can be perfect without the other. In the uttermost meaning of the words, thought is devout, and devotion is thought. Deep calls unto deep. But in actual life, the marriage is not celebrated. There are innocent men who worship God after the tradition of their fathers, but their sense of duty has not yet extended to the use of all their faculties. And there are patient naturalists, but they freeze their subject under the wintry light of the understanding. Is not prayer also a study of truth, — a sally of the soul into the unfound infinite? No man ever prayed heartily without learning something. But when a faithful thinker, resolute to detach every object from personal relations and see it in the light of thought, shall, at the same time, kindle science with the fire of the holiest affections, then will God go forth anew into the creation.

It will not need, when the mind is prepared for study, to search for objects. The invariable mark of wisdom is to see the miraculous in the common. What is a day? What is a year? What is summer? What is woman? What is a child? What is sleep? To our blindness, these things seem unaffecting. We make fables to hide the baldness of the fact and conform it, as we say, to the higher law of the mind. But when the fact is seen under the light of an idea, the gaudy fable fades and shrivels. We behold the real higher law. To the wise, therefore, a fact is true poetry, and the most beautiful of fables. These wonders are brought to our own door. You also are a man. Man and woman and their social life, poverty, labor, sleep, fear, fortune, are known to you. Learn that none of these things is superficial, but that each phenomenon has its roots in the faculties and affections of the mind. Whilst the abstract question occupies your intellect, nature brings it in the concrete to be solved by your hands. It were a wise inquiry for the closet, to compare, point by point, especially at remarkable crises in life, our daily history with the rise and progress of ideas in the mind.

So shall we come to look at the world with new eyes. It shall answer the endless inquiry of the intellect, — What is truth? and

Build your own House; relation of man to nature

of the affections, — What is good? by yielding itself passive to the educated Will. Then shall come to pass what my poet said: "Nature is not fixed but fluid. Spirit alters, molds, makes it. The immobility or bruteness of nature is the absence of spirit; to pure spirit it is fluid, it is volatile, it is obedient. Every spirit builds itself a house, and beyond its house a world, and beyond its world a heaven. Know then that the world exists for you. For you is the phenomenon perfect. What we are, that only can we see. All that Adam had, all that Caesar could, you have and can do. Adam called his house, heaven and earth; Caesar called his house, Rome; you perhaps call yours, a cobbler's trade; a hundred acres of ploughed land; or a scholar's garret. Yet line for line and point for point your dominion is as great as theirs, though without fine names. Build therefore your own world. As fast as you conform your life to the pure idea in your mind, that will unfold its great proportions. A correspondent revolution in things will attend the influx of the spirit. So fast will disagreeable appearances, swine, spiders, snakes, pests, mad-houses, prisons, enemies, vanish; they are temporary and shall be no more seen. The sordor and filths of nature, the sun shall dry up and the wind exhale.[6] As when the summer comes from the south the snow-banks melt and the face of the earth becomes green before it, so shall the advancing spirit create its ornaments along its path, and carry with it the beauty it visits and the song which enchants it; it shall draw beautiful faces, warm hearts, wise discourse, and heroic acts, around its way, until evil is no more seen. The kingdom of man over nature, which cometh not with observation, — a dominion such as now is beyond his dream of God, — he shall enter without more wonder than the blind man feels who is gradually restored to perfect sight."

[6] Carry away.

1837–1838

Challenge

After *Nature* Emerson continued his quiet life of journal-keeping and lecturing, cheered by the birth of a son, Waldo, in October, 1836. In the winter of 1836–37 he gave a course of lectures in Boston on "The Philosophy of History," and the next winter one on "Human Culture"; three more series followed in succeeding winters. Each of these courses, like *Nature*, summed up his reflections to date on the main topics that concerned him: science, intellect, art, literature, society, greatness, ethics, religion, the times. Though he grew to hate the imperfection of these lectures, as he did of nearly everything he wrote, he found this regular task a useful stimulus; the lectures afterwards became the quarry for much of *Essays, First Series*.

His journals show that his quiet literary round covered an ardent inner life. A transforming greatness seemed very near to him then — he had only to reach out his hand; yet even as he felt his latent power he was haunted by a sense of incapacity, especially in relation to his enlarging circle of friends and visitors. The importunities of society bred a hearty wish to "hug the absolute being" of his privacy; the emptiness of solitude in turn required relief in society. Life was a queer alternation of contradictory states: he was all in all to himself; he was nothing he ought to be. From such sharp conflicts he swung away to the peace of contemplation and detachment; more typically in these years there welled up a fervent protest, expressed in earnest exhortations to himself and in radical challenges to society. The crash of the spring of 1837, for example, when all the banks in New York, Philadelphia, Baltimore and some in Boston suspended specie payments, stirred him to minatory thunder in his journals. In the same year he took advantage of an invitation to deliver the annual address to the

Phi Beta Kappa Society at Harvard to transform the conventional topic on such occasions, The American Scholar, into a ringing call to all thinking men to take the lead in the conversion of the world. The result was Emerson's most memorable performance. If grim elders disapproved, "the young men went out from it as if a prophet had been proclaiming to them, 'Thus saith the Lord.'" A year after this success he opened his heart once more in his address to the graduating class of the Harvard Divinity School — this time with a very different reception.[1]

⚔

September 30, 1836

Observe how strongly guarded is the Common Sense. If men were left to contemplation, if the contemplative life were practicable, to what subtilties, to what dreams and extravagancies would not all run! Laputa,[2] a court of love, a college of schoolmen, would be the result. How is this hindered? Poverty, Frost, Famine, Rain, Disease, are the beadles and guardsmen that hold us to Common Sense.

January 29, 1837

One has patience with every kind of living thing, but not with the dead alive. I, at least, hate to see persons of that lumpish class who are here they know not why, and ask not whereto, but live as the larva of the ant or the bee, to be lugged into the sun, and then lugged back into the cell, and then fed. The end of nature for such, is that they should be fatted. If mankind should pass a vote on the subject, I think they would throw them in sacks into the sea.

[February 16, 1837]

When the act of reflection takes place in the mind, when we look at ourselves in the light of thought, we discover that our life is embosomed in beauty. Behind us, as we go, all things assume pleasing forms, as clouds do far off. Not only things familiar and stale, but even the tragic and terrible are comely as they take their place in the pictures of memory. The river-bank, the weed at the water-side, the old house, the foolish person, however neglected in the passing, have a grace in the past. Even the corpse that has lain in the chambers has added a solemn ornament to the house.

[1] See pp. 97–121.
[2] Land of foolish pedants, in Swift's *Gulliver's Travels*.

The soul will not know either deformity or pain. If in the hours of
clear reason we should speak the severest truth, we should say that
we had never made a sacrifice. In these hours the mind seems so
great that nothing can be taken from us that seems much. All loss,
all pain, is particular; the universe remains to the heart unhurt.
Neither vexations nor calamities abate our trust. No man ever
stated his griefs as lightly as he might. Allow for exaggeration in
the most patient and sorely ridden hack that ever was driven. For
it is only the finite that has wrought and suffered; the infinite lies
stretched in smiling repose.

The intellectual life may be kept clean and healthful if man will
live the life of nature and not import into his mind difficulties
which are none of his. No man need be perplexed in his speculations. Let him do and say what strictly belongs to him, and
though very ignorant of books, his nature shall not yield him any
intellectual obstructions and doubts. Our young people are dis-
eased with the theological problems of original sin, origin of evil,
predestination and the like. These never presented a practical
difficulty to any man, — never darkened across any man's road who
did not go out of his way to seek them. These are the soul's
mumps and measles and whooping-coughs, and those who have
not caught them cannot describe their health or prescribe the cure.
A simple mind will not know these enemies. It is quite another
thing that he should be able to give account of his faith and ex-
pound to another the theory of his self-union and freedom. This
requires rare gifts. Yet without this self-knowledge there may be a
sylvan strength and integrity in that which he is. "A few strong
instincts and a few plain rules" suffice us.

From "Spiritual Laws"

March 14, 1837

Edward Taylor [3] came last night and gave us in the old church a
Lecture on Temperance. A wonderful man; I had almost said, a
perfect orator. The utter want and loss of all method, the ridicule
of all method, the bright chaos come again of his bewildering
oratory, certainly bereaves it of power, — but what splendor! what
sweetness! what richness! what depth! what cheer! How he con-
ciliates, how he humanizes! how he exhilarates and ennobles!
Beautiful philanthropist! Godly poet! the Shakespeare of the

[3] "Missionary in charge" of the Seamen's Bethel in Boston. His picturesque
nautical preaching was famous. He is supposed to be one of the originals for
Father Mapple in Melville's *Moby Dick*.

sailor and the poor. God has found one harp of divine melody to ring and sigh sweet music amidst caves and cellars.

He spent the night with me. He says he lives a monarch's life, he has none to control him, or to divide the power with him. His word is law for all his people and his coadjutors. He is a very charming object to me. I delight in his great personality, the way and sweep of the man which, like a frigate's way, takes up for the time the center of the ocean, paves it with a white street, and all the lesser craft

"Do curtsey to him, do him reverence."

Everybody plays a second part in his presence, and takes a deferential and apologetic tone. In the church, likewise, everybody, — the rich, the poor, the scoffer, the drunkard, the exquisite, and the populace, — acknowledge the man, and feel that to be right and lordly which he doth, — so that his prayer is a winged ship in which all are floated forward. The wonderful and laughing life of his illustration keeps us broad awake. A string of rockets all night. He described his bar-room gentry as "hanging like a half-dead bird over a counter." He describes Helen Loring as out on her errands of charity, and "running through the rain like a beach-bird." He speaks of poor ministers coming out of divinity schools, etc., as "Poor fellows hobbling out of Jerusalem." "We'll give you hypocrites for honest men, two for one, and trade all night." "The world is just large enough for the people. There is no room for a partition wall."

March 29, 1837

Noble paper of Carlyle on Mirabeau.[4] This piece will establish his kingdom, I forebode, in the mind of his countrymen. How he gropes with giant fingers into the dark of man, into the obscure recesses of power in human will, and we are encouraged by his word to feel the might that is in a man. . . . It seems to me his genius is the redolence of London, "the Great Metropolis." So vast, enormous, with endless details, and so related to all the world is he. It would seem as if no baker-shop, no mutton-stall, no academy, no church, no placard, no coronation, but he saw and sympathized with all, and took all up into his omnivorous memory, and hence his panoramic style, and this encyclopaediacal allusion to all knowables.

[4] French Revolutionary statesman. Carlyle's review-article on Mirabeau's *Mémoires* appeared in *The London and Westminster Review*, January, 1837.

Then he is a worshipper of strength, heedless much whether its present phase be divine or diabolic. Burns, George Fox, Luther, and those unclean beasts Diderot, Danton, Mirabeau, whose sinews are their own and who trample on the tutoring and conventions of society, he loves. For he believes that every noble nature was made by God, and contains, if savage passions, also fit checks and grand impulses within it, hath its own resources, and however erring, will return from far. Then he writes English and crowds meaning into all the nooks and corners of his sentences. Once read, he is but half read. . . .

I think he has seen, as no other in our time, how inexhaustible a mine is the language of Conversation. He does not use the *written* dialect of the time, in which scholars, pamphleteers and the clergy write, nor the Parliamentary dialect, in which the lawyer, the statesman, and the better newspapers write, but draws strength and mother-wit out of a poetic use of the spoken vocabulary, so that his paragraphs are all a sort of splendid conversation.

May 19, 1837

Society an imperfect union. — Is it not pathetic that the action of men on men is so partial? We never touch but at points. The most that I can have or be to my fellow man, is it the reading of his book, or the hearing of his project in conversation? I approach some Carlyle with desire and joy. I am led on from month to month with an expectation of some total embrace and oneness with a noble mind, and learn at last that it is only so feeble and remote and hiant action as reading a Mirabeau or a Diderot paper, and a few the like. This is all that can be looked for. More we shall not be to each other. Baulked soul! It is not that the sea and poverty and pursuit separate us. Here is Alcott [5] by my door, yet is the union more profound? No, the Sea, vocation, poverty, are seeming fences, but man is insular and cannot be touched. Every man is an infinitely repellent orb, and holds his individual being on that condition.

April 29 ?, 1837

How wild and mysterious our position as individuals to the Universe! Here is always a certain amount of truth lodged as intrinsic foundation in the depths of the soul, a certain perception of absolute being, as justice, love, and the like, natures which must be the God of God, and this is our capital stock, this is our centripetal

[5] See pp. 125–31.

force. We can never quite doubt, we can never be adrift, we can never be nothing, because of this Holy of Holies, out of sight of which we cannot go. Then, on the other side, all is to seek. We understand nothing; our ignorance is abysmal, the overhanging immensity staggers us, whither we go, what we do, who we are, we cannot even so much as guess. We stagger and grope.

May 26, 1837

The Individual. — Who shall define to me an Individual? I behold with awe and delight many illustrations of the One Universal Mind. I see my being imbedded in it. As a plant in the earth so I grow in God. I am only a form of him. He is the soul of me. . . . Yet why not always so? How came the Individual, thus armed and impassioned, to parricide thus murderously inclined, ever to traverse and kill the Divine Life? Ah, wicked Manichee! [6] Into that dim problem I cannot enter. A believer in Unity, a seer of Unity, I yet behold two. . . .

A certain wandering light comes to me which I instantly perceive to be the Cause of Causes. It transcends all proving. It is itself the ground of being; and I see that it is not one, and I another, but this is the life of my life. That is one fact then; that in certain moments I have known that I existed directly from God, and am, as it were, his organ, and in my ultimate consciousness am He. Then, secondly, the contradictory fact is familiar, that I am a surprised spectator and learner of all my life. This is the habitual posture of the mind — beholding. But whenever the day dawns, the great day of truth on the soul, it comes with awful invitation to me to accept it, to blend with its aurora.

Cannot I conceive the Universe without a contradiction?

May 21, 1837

I see a good in such emphatic and universal calamity as the times bring, that they dissatisfy me with society. Under common burdens we say there is much virtue in the world, and what evil co-exists is inevitable. I am not aroused to say, "I have sinned; I am in the gall of bitterness, and bond of iniquity"; but when these full measures come, it then stands confessed, — society has played out its last stake; it is check-mated. Young men have no hope. Adults stand like day-laborers idle in the streets. None calleth us to labor. The old wear no crown of warm life on their gray hairs. The present generation is bankrupt of principles and hope, as of prop-

[6] See p. 474.

erty. I see man is not what man should be. He is the treadle of a wheel. He is a tassel at the apron-string of society. He is a money-chest. He is the servant of his belly. This is the causal bankruptcy, this the cruel oppression, that the ideal should serve the actual; that the head should serve the feet. Then first, I am forced to inquire if the Ideal might not also be tried. Is it to be taken for granted that it is impracticable? Behold the boasted world has come to nothing. Prudence itself is at her wits' end. Pride, and Thrift, and Expediency, who jeered and chirped and were so well pleased with themselves, and made merry with the dream, as they termed it, of Philosophy and Love, — behold they are all flat, and here is the Soul erect and unconquered still. What answer is it now to say, It has always been so? I acknowledge that, as far back as I can see the widening procession of humanity, the marchers are lame and blind and deaf; but to the soul that whole past is but one finite series in its infinite scope. Deteriorating ever and now desperate. Let me begin anew. Let me teach the finite to know its master. Let me ascend above my fate and work down upon my world.

July 21, 1837

Courage consists in the conviction that they with whom you contend are no more than you. If we believed in the existence of strict *individuals*, natures, that is, not radically identical but unknown, immeasurable, we should never dare to fight.

The American Scholar

Mr. President and Gentlemen:

I greet you on the recommencement of our literary year. Our anniversary is one of hope, and, perhaps, not enough of labor. We do not meet for games of strength or skill, for the recitation of histories, tragedies, and odes, like the ancient Greeks; for parliaments of love and poesy, like the Troubadours; nor for the advancement of science, like our contemporaries in the British and European capitals. Thus far, our holiday has been simply a friendly sign of the survival of the love of letters amongst a people too busy to give to letters any more. As such it is precious as the sign of an indestructible instinct. Perhaps the time is already come when it ought to be, and will be, something else; when the sluggard intellect of this continent will look from under its iron lids and fill the postponed expectation of the world with something better than the exertions of mechanical skill. Our day of dependence, our long apprenticeship to the learning of other lands, draws to a close. The millions that around us are rushing into life, cannot always be fed on the sere remains of foreign harvests. Events, actions arise, that must be sung, that will sing themselves. Who can doubt that poetry will revive and lead in a new age, as the star in the constellation Harp, which now flames in our zenith, astronomers announce, shall one day be the polestar for a thousand years?

In this hope I accept the topic which not only usage but the nature of our association seem to prescribe to this day, — the AMERICAN SCHOLAR. Year by year we come up hither to read one more chapter of his biography. Let us inquire what light new days and events have thrown on his character and his hopes.

It is one of those fables which out of an unknown antiquity convey an unlooked-for wisdom, that the gods, in the beginning, divided Man into men, that he might be more helpful to himself; just as the hand was divided into fingers, the better to answer its end.

The old fable covers a doctrine ever new and sublime; that there is One Man, — present to all particular men only partially, or through one faculty; and that you must take the whole society to find the whole man. Man is not a farmer, or a professor, or an engineer, but he is all. Man is priest, and scholar, and statesman, and producer, and soldier. In the *divided* or social state these functions are parcelled out to individuals, each of whom aims to do his stint of the joint work, whilst each other performs his. The fable implies that the individual, to possess himself, must sometimes return from his own labor to embrace all the other laborers. But, unfortunately, this original unit, this fountain of power, has been so distributed to multitudes, has been so minutely subdivided and peddled out, that it is spilled into drops, and cannot be gathered. The state of society is one in which the members have suffered amputation from the trunk, and strut about so many walking monsters, — a good finger, a neck, a stomach, an elbow, but never a man.

Man is thus metamorphosed into a thing, into many things. The planter, who is Man sent out into the field to gather food, is seldom cheered by any idea of the true dignity of his ministry.

He sees his bushel and his cart, and nothing beyond, and sinks into the farmer, instead of Man on the farm. The tradesman scarcely ever gives an ideal worth to his work, but is ridden by the routine of his craft, and the soul is subject to dollars. The priest becomes a form; the attorney a statute-book; the mechanic a machine; the sailor a rope of the ship.

In this distribution of functions the scholar is the delegated intellect. In the right state he is *Man Thinking*. In the degenerate state, when the victim of society, he tends to become a mere thinker, or still worse, the parrot of other men's thinking.

In this view of him, as Man Thinking, the theory of his office is contained. Him Nature solicits with all her placid, all her monitory pictures; him the past instructs; him the future invites. Is not indeed every man a student, and do not all things exist for the student's behoof? And, finally, is not the true scholar the only true master? But the old oracle said, "All things have two handles: beware of the wrong one." In life, too often, the scholar errs with mankind and forfeits his privilege. Let us see him in his school, and consider him in reference to the main influences he receives.

I. The first in time and the first in importance of the influences upon the mind is that of nature. Every day, the sun; and, after sunset, Night and her stars. Ever the winds blow; ever the grass grows. Every day, men and women, conversing — beholding and beholden. The scholar is he of all men whom this spectacle most engages. He must settle its value in his mind. What is nature to him? There is never a beginning, there is never an end, to the inexplicable continuity of this web of God, but always circular power returning into itself. Therein it resembles his own spirit, whose beginning, whose ending, he never can find, — so entire, so boundless. Far too as her splendors shine, system on system shooting like rays, upward, downward, without center, without circumference, — in the mass and in the particle, Nature hastens to render account of herself to the mind. Classification begins. To the young mind every thing is individual, stands by itself. By and by, it finds how to join two things and see in them one nature; then three, then three thousand; and so, tyrannized over by its own unifying instinct, it goes on tying things together, diminishing anomalies, discovering roots running under ground whereby contrary and remote things cohere and flower out from one stem. It presently learns that since the dawn of history there has been a constant accumulation and classifying of facts. But what is classification but the perceiving that these objects are not chaotic, and are not foreign, but have a law which is also a law of the human mind? The astronomer discovers that geometry, a pure abstraction of the human mind, is the measure of planetary motion. The chemist finds proportions and intelligible method throughout matter; and science is nothing but the finding of analogy, identity, in the most remote parts. The ambitious soul sits down before each refractory fact; one after another reduces all strange constitutions, all new powers, to their class and their law, and goes on forever to animate the last fiber of organization, the outskirts of nature, by insight.

Thus to him, to this schoolboy under the bending dome of day, is suggested that he and it proceed from one root; one is leaf and one is flower; relation, sympathy, stirring in every vein. And what is that root? Is not that the soul of his soul? A thought too bold; a dream too wild. Yet when this spiritual light shall have revealed the law of more earthly natures, — when he has learned to worship the soul, and to see that the natural philosophy that now is, is only the first gropings of its gigantic hand, he shall look forward to an ever expanding knowledge as to a becoming creator. He shall see that nature is the opposite of the soul, answering to it part for part. One is seal and one is print. Its beauty is the beauty of his own mind. Its laws are the laws of his own mind. Nature then becomes to him the measure of his attainments. So much of nature as he is ignorant of, so much of his own mind does he not yet possess. And, in fine, the ancient precept, "Know thyself," and the modern precept, "Study nature," become at last one maxim.

II. The next great influence into the spirit of the scholar is the mind of the Past, — in whatever form, whether of literature, of art, of institutions, that mind is inscribed. Books are the best type of the influence of the past, and perhaps we shall get at the truth, — learn the amount of this influence more conveniently, — by considering their value alone.

The theory of books is noble. The scholar of the first age received into him the world around; brooded thereon; gave it the new arrangement of his own mind, and uttered it again. It came into him life; it went out from him truth. It came to him short-lived actions; it went out from him immortal thoughts. It came to him business; it went from him poetry. It was dead fact; now, it is quick thought. It can stand, and it can go. It now endures, it now flies, it now inspires. Precisely in proportion to the depth of mind from which it issued, so high does it soar, so long does it sing.

Or, I might say, it depends on how far the process had gone, of transmuting life into truth. In proportion to the completeness of the distillation, so will the purity and imperishableness of the product be. But none is quite perfect. As no air-pump can by any means make a perfect vacuum, so neither can any artist entirely exclude the conventional, the local, the perishable from his book, or write a book of pure thought, that shall be as efficient, in all respects, to a remote posterity, as to contemporaries, or rather to the second age. Each age, it is found, must write its own books; or rather, each generation for the next succeeding. The books of an older period will not fit this.

Yet hence arises a grave mischief. The sacrednesss which attaches to the act of creation, the act of thought, is transferred to the record. The poet chanting was felt to be a divine man: henceforth the chant is divine also. The writer was a just and wise spirit: henceforward it is settled the book is perfect; as love of the hero corrupts into worship of his statue. Instantly the book becomes noxious: the guide is a tyrant. The sluggish and perverted mind of the multitude, slow to open to the incursions of Reason, having once opened, having once received this book, stands upon it, and makes an outcry if it is disparaged. Colleges are built on it. Books are written on it by thinkers, not by Man Thinking; by men of talent, that is, who start wrong, who set out from accepted dogmas, not from their own sight of principles. Meek young men grow up in libraries, believing it their duty to accept the views which Cicero, which Locke, which Bacon, have given; forgetful that Cicero, Locke, and Bacon were only young men in libraries when they wrote these books.

Hence, instead of Man Thinking, we have the bookworm. Hence the book-learned class, who value books, as such; not as related to nature and the human constitution, but as making a sort of Third Estate [7] with the world and the soul. Hence the restorers of readings, the emendators, the bibliomaniacs of all degrees.

Books are the best of things, well used; abused, among the worst. What is the right use? What is the one end which all means go to effect? They are for nothing but to inspire. I had

[7] The medieval parliament was divided into three "estates" — nobility, clergy, and commons.

better never see a book than to be warped by its attraction clean out of my own orbit, and made a satellite instead of a system. The one thing in the world, of value, is the active soul. This every man is entitled to; this every man contains within him, although in almost all men obstructed and as yet unborn. The soul active sees absolute truth and utters truth, or creates. In this action it is genius; not the privilege of here and there a favorite, but the sound estate of every man. In its essence it is progressive. The book, the college, the school of art, the institution of any kind, stop with some past utterance of genius. This is good, say they, — let us hold by this. They pin me down. They look backward and not forward. But genius looks forward: the eyes of man are set in his forehead, not in his hindhead: man hopes: genius creates. Whatever talents may be, if the man create not, the pure efflux of the Deity is not his; — cinders and smoke there may be, but not yet flame. There are creative manners, there are creative actions, and creative words; manners, actions, words, that is, indicative of no custom or authority, but springing spontaneous from the mind's own sense of good and fair.

On the other part, instead of being its own seer, let it receive from another mind its truth, though it were in torrents of light, without periods of solitude, inquest, and self-recovery, and a fatal disservice is done. Genius is always sufficiently the enemy of genius by over-influence. The literature of every nation bears me witness. The English dramatic poets have Shakespearized now for two hundred years.

Undoubtedly there is a right way of reading, so it be sternly subordinated. Man Thinking must not be subdued by his instruments. Books are for the scholars' idle times. When he can read God directly, the hour is too precious to be wasted in other men's transcripts of their readings. But when the intervals of darkness come, as come they must, — when the sun is hid and the stars withdraw their shining, — we repair to the lamps which were kindled by their ray, to guide our steps to the East again, where the dawn is. We hear, that we may speak. The Arabian proverb says, "A fig tree, looking on a fig tree, becometh fruitful."

It is remarkable, the character of the pleasure we derive from the best books. They impress us with the conviction that one nature wrote and the same reads. We read the verses of one of the great English poets, of Chaucer, of Marvell, of Dryden, with the most modern joy, — with a pleasure, I mean, which is in great part caused by the abstraction of all *time* from their verses. There is some awe mixed with the joy of our surprise, when this poet, who lived in some past world, two or three hundred years ago, says that which lies close to my own soul, that which I also had well-nigh thought and said. But for the evidence thence afforded to the philosophical doctrine of the identity of all minds, we should suppose some preëstablished harmony, some foresight of souls that were to be, and some preparation of stores for their future wants, like the fact observed in insects, who lay up food before death for the young grub they shall never see.

I would not be hurried by any love of system, by any exaggeration of instincts, to underrate the Book. We all know, that as the human body can be nourished on any food, though it were boiled grass and the broth of shoes, so the human mind can be fed by any knowledge. And great and heroic men have existed who had almost no other information than by the printed page. I only would say that it needs a strong head to bear that diet. One must be an inventor to read well. As the proverb says, "He that would bring home the wealth of the Indies, must carry out the wealth of the Indies." There is then creative reading as well as creative writing. When the mind is braced by labor and invention, the page of whatever book we read becomes luminous with manifold allusion. Every sentence is doubly significant, and the sense of our author is as broad as the world. We then see, what is always true, that as the seer's hour of vision is short and rare among heavy days and months, so is its record, perchance, the least part of his volume. The discerning will read, in his Plato or Shakespeare, only that least part, — only the authentic utterances of the oracle; — all the rest he rejects, were it never so many times Plato's and Shakespeare's.

Of course there is a portion of reading quite indispensable to a wise man. History and exact science he must learn by laborious reading. Colleges, in like manner, have their indispensable office, — to teach elements. But they can only highly serve us when they aim not to drill, but to create; when they gather from far every ray of various genius to their hospitable halls, and by the concentrated fires, set the hearts of their youth on flame. Thought and knowledge are natures in which apparatus and pretension avail nothing. Gowns and pecuniary foundations, though of towns of gold, can never countervail the least sentence or syllable of wit. Forget this, and our American colleges will recede in their public importance, whilst they grow richer every year.

III. There goes in the world a notion that the scholar should

be a recluse, a valetudinarian, — as unfit for any handiwork or
public labor as a penknife for an axe. The so-called "practical
men" sneer at speculative men, as if, because they speculate or
see, they could do nothing. I have heard it said that the clergy,
— who are always, more universally than any other class, the
scholars of their day, — are addressed as women; that the rough,
spontaneous conversation of men they do not hear, but only a
mincing and diluted speech. They are often virtually disfran-
chised; and indeed there are advocates for their celibacy. As far as
this is true of the studious classes, it is not just and wise. Action
is with the scholar subordinate, but it is essential. Without it he
is not yet man. Without it thought can never ripen into truth.
Whilst the world hangs before the eye as a cloud of beauty, we
cannot even see its beauty. Inaction is cowardice, but there can
be no scholar without the heroic mind. The preamble of thought,
the transition through which it passes from the unconscious to the
conscious, is action. Only so much do I know, as I have lived.
Instantly we know whose words are loaded with life, and whose
not.

The world, — this shadow of the soul, or *other me*, — lies wide
around. Its attractions are the keys which unlock my thoughts
and make me acquainted with myself. I run eagerly into this
resounding tumult. I grasp the hands of those next me, and take
my place in the ring to suffer and to work, taught by an instinct
that so shall the dumb abyss be vocal with speech. I pierce its
order; I dissipate its fear; I dispose of it within the circuit of my
expanding life. So much only of life as I know by experience, so
much of the wilderness have I vanquished and planted, or so far
have I extended my being, my dominion. I do not see how any
man can afford, for the sake of his nerves and his nap, to spare
any action in which he can partake. It is pearls and rubies to his
discourse. Drudgery, calamity, exasperation, want, are instructors
in eloquence and wisdom. The true scholar grudges every opportunity of action past by, as a loss of power. It is the raw material
out of which the intellect molds her splendid products. A strange
process too, this by which experience is converted into thought,
as a mulberry leaf is converted into satin. The manufacture goes
forward at all hours.

The actions and events of our childhood and youth are now
matters of calmest observation. They lie like fair pictures in the
air. Not so with our recent actions, — with the business which
we now have in hand. On this we are quite unable to speculate.

Our affections as yet circulate through it. We no more feel or
know it than we feel the feet, or the hand, or the brain of our
body. The new deed is yet a part of life, — remains for a time
immersed in our unconscious life. In some contemplative hour it
detaches itself from the life like a ripe fruit, to become a thought
of the mind. Instantly it is raised, transfigured; the corruptible
has put on incorruption. Henceforth it is an object of beauty,
however base its origin and neighborhood. Observe too the impossibility of antedating this act. In its grub state, it cannot fly, it
cannot shine, it is a dull grub. But suddenly, without observation,
the selfsame thing unfurls beautiful wings, and is an angel of
wisdom. So is there no fact, no event, in our private history,
which shall not, sooner or later, lose its adhesive, inert form, and
astonish us by soaring from our body into the empyrean. Cradle
and infancy, school and playground, the fear of boys, and dogs, and
ferules, the love of little maids and berries, and many another
fact that once filled the whole sky, are gone already; friend and
relative, profession and party, town and country, nation and
world, must also soar and sing.

Of course, he who has put forth his total strength in fit actions
has the richest return of wisdom. I will not shut myself out of this
globe of action, and transplant an oak into a flower-pot, there to
hunger and pine; nor trust the revenue of some single faculty, and
exhaust one vein of thought, much like those Savoyards, who,
getting their livelihood by carving shepherds, shepherdesses, and
smoking Dutchmen, for all Europe, went out one day to the
mountain to find stock, and discovered that they had whittled up
the last of their pine trees. Authors we have, in numbers, who
have written out their vein, and who, moved by a commendable
prudence, sail for Greece or Palestine, follow the trapper into the
prairie, or ramble round Algiers, to replenish their merchantable
stock.

If it were only for a vocabulary, the scholar would be covetous
of action. Life is our dictionary. Years are well spent in country
labors; in town; in the insight into trades and manufactures; in
frank intercourse with many men and women; in science; in art;
to the one end of mastering in all their facts a language by which
to illustrate and embody our perceptions. I learn immediately
from any speaker how much he has already lived, through the
poverty or the splendor of his speech. Life lies behind us as the
quarry from whence we get tiles and copestones for the masonry
of today. This is the way to learn grammar. Colleges and books

only copy the language which the field and the work-yard made.

But the final value of action, like that of books, and better than books, is that it is a resource. That great principle of Undulation in nature, that shows itself in the inspiring and expiring of the breath; in desire and satiety; in the ebb and flow of the sea; in day and night; in heat and cold; and, as yet more deeply ingrained in every atom and every fluid, is known to us under the name of Polarity, — these "fits of easy transmission and reflection," as Newton called them, are the law of nature because they are the law of spirit.

The mind now thinks, now acts, and each fit reproduces the other. When the artist has exhausted his materials, when the fancy no longer paints, when thoughts are no longer apprehended and books are a weariness, — he has always the resource *to live*. Character is higher than intellect. Thinking is the function. Living is the functionary. The stream retreats to its source. A great soul will be strong to live, as well as strong to think. Does he lack organ or medium to impart his truths? He can still fall back on this elemental force of living them. This is a total act. Thinking is a partial act. Let the grandeur of justice shine in his affairs. Let the beauty of affection cheer his lowly roof. Those "far from fame," who dwell and act with him, will feel the force of his constitution in the doings and passages of the day better than it can be measured by any public and designed display. Time shall teach him that the scholar loses no hour which the man lives. Herein he unfolds the sacred germ of his instinct, screened from influence. What is lost in seemliness is gained in strength. Not out of those on whom systems of education have exhausted their culture, comes the helpful giant to destroy the old or to build the new, but out of unhandselled savage nature; out of terrible Druids and Berserkers come at last Alfred and Shakespeare.

I hear therefore with joy whatever is beginning to be said of the dignity and necessity of labor to every citizen. There is virtue yet in the hoe and the spade, for learned as well as for unlearned hands. And labor is everywhere welcome; always we are invited to work; only be this limitation observed, that a man shall not for the sake of wider activity sacrifice any opinion to the popular judgments and modes of action.

I have now spoken of the education of the scholar by nature, by books, and by action. It remains to say somewhat of his duties.

They are such as become Man Thinking. They may all be
comprised in self-trust. The office of the scholar is to cheer, to
raise, and to guide men by showing them facts amidst appearances. He plies the slow, unhonored, and unpaid task of observation. Flamsteed and Herschel, in their glazed observatories, may
catalogue the stars with the praise of all men, and the results being
splendid and useful, honor is sure. But he, in his private observa-
tory, cataloguing obscure and nebulous stars of the human mind,
which as yet no man has thought of as such, — watching days and
months sometimes for a few facts; correcting still his old records;
— must relinquish display and immediate fame. In the long
period of his preparation he must betray often an ignorance and
shiftlessness in popular arts, incurring the disdain of the able who
shoulder him aside. Long he must stammer in his speech; often
forego the living for the dead. Worse yet, he must accept — how
often! — poverty and solitude. For the ease and pleasure of tread-
ing the old road, accepting the fashions, the education, the religion of society, he takes the cross of making his own, and, of
course, the self-accusation, the faint heart, the frequent uncer-
tainty and loss of time, which are the nettles and tangling vines
in the way of the self-relying and self-directed; and the state of
virtual hostility in which he seems to stand to society, and
especially to educated society. For all this loss and scorn, what
offset? He is to find consolation in exercising the highest functions of human nature. He is one who raises himself from private
considerations and breathes and lives on public and illustrious
thoughts. He is the world's eye. He is the world's heart. He is to
resist the vulgar prosperity that retrogrades ever to barbarism, by
preserving and communicating heroic sentiments, noble biographies, melodious verse, and the conclusions of history. Whatsoever oracles the human heart, in all emergencies, in all solemn
hours, has uttered as its commentary on the world of actions, —
these he shall receive and impart. And whatsoever new verdict
Reason from her inviolable seat pronounces on the passing men
and events of today, — this he shall hear and promulgate.

These being his functions, it becomes him to feel all confidence
in himself, and to defer never to the popular cry. He and he only
knows the world. The world of any moment is the merest appearance. Some great decorum,[8] some fetish of a government, some
ephemeral trade, or war, or man, is cried up by half mankind and
cried down by the other half, as if all depended on this particular

[8] Code of propriety.

up or down. The odds are that the whole question is not worth
the poorest thought which the scholar has lost in listening to the
controversy. Let him not quit his belief that a popgun is a popgun, though the ancient and honorable of the earth affirm it to
be the crack of doom. In silence, in steadiness, in severe abstraction, let him hold by himself; add observation to observation,
patient of neglect, patient of reproach, and bide his own time, —
happy enough if he can satisfy himself alone that this day he has
seen something truly. Success treads on every right step. For the
instinct is sure, that prompts him to tell his brother what he
thinks. He then learns that in going down into the secrets of his
own mind he has descended into the secrets of all minds. He
learns that he who has mastered any law in his private thoughts,
is master to that extent of all men whose language he speaks, and
of all into whose language his own can be translated. The poet,
in utter solitude remembering his spontaneous thoughts and
recording them, is found to have recorded that which men in
crowded cities find true for them also. The orator distrusts at first
the fitness of his frank confessions, his want of knowledge of the
persons he addresses, until he finds that he is the complement of
his hearers; — that they drink his words because he fulfils for
them their own nature; the deeper he dives into his privatest,
secretest presentiment, to his wonder he finds this is the most
acceptable, most public, and universally true. The people delight
in it; the better part of every man feels, This is my music; this is
myself.

In self-trust all the virtues are comprehended. Free should the
scholar be, — free and brave. Free even to the definition of freedom, "without any hindrance that does not arise out of his own
constitution." Brave; for fear is a thing which a scholar by his
very function puts behind him. Fear always springs from ignorance. It is a shame to him if his tranquillity, amid dangerous
times, arise from the presumption that like children and women
his is a protected class; or if he seek a temporary peace by the
diversion of his thoughts from politics or vexed questions, hiding
his head like an ostrich in the flowering bushes, peeping into
microscopes, and turning rhymes, as a boy whistles to keep his
courage up. So is the danger a danger still; so is the fear worse.
Manlike let him turn and face it. Let him look into its eye and
search its nature, inspect its origin, — see the whelping of this
lion, — which lies no great way back; he will then find in himself
a perfect comprehension of its nature and extent; he will have

made his hands meet on the other side, and can henceforth defy it and pass on superior. The world is his who can see through its pretension. What deafness, what stone-blind custom, what overgrown error you behold is there only by sufferance, — by your sufferance. See it to be a lie, and you have already dealt it its mortal blow.

Yes, we are the cowed, — we the trustless. It is a mischievous notion that we are come late into nature; that the world was finished a long time ago. As the world was plastic and fluid in the hands of God, so it is ever to so much of his attributes as we bring to it. To ignorance and sin, it is flint. They adapt themselves to it as they may; but in proportion as a man has any thing in him divine, the firmament flows before him and takes his signet and form. Not he is great who can alter matter, but he who can alter my state of mind. They are the kings of the world who give the color of their present thought to all nature and all art, and persuade men by the cheerful serenity of their carrying the matter, that this thing which they do is the apple which the ages have desired to pluck, now at last ripe, and inviting nations to the harvest. The great man makes the great thing. Wherever Macdonald [9] sits, there is the head of the table. Linnaeus makes botany the most alluring of studies, and wins it from the farmer and the herb-woman; Davy, chemistry; Cuvier, fossils. The day is always his who works in it with serenity and great aims. The unstable estimates of men crowd to him whose mind is filled with a truth, as the heaped waves of the Atlantic follow the moon.

For this self-trust, the reason is deeper than can be fathomed, — darker than can be enlightened. I might not carry with me the feeling of my audience in stating my own belief. But I have already shown the ground of my hope, in adverting to the doctrine that man is one. I believe man has been wronged; he has wronged himself. He has almost lost the light that can lead him back to his prerogatives. Men are become of no account. Men in history, men in the world of today, are bugs, are spawn, and are called "the mass" and "the herd." In a century, in a millennium, one or two men; that is to say, one or two approximations to the right state of every man. All the rest behold in the hero or the poet their own green and crude being, — ripened; yes, and are content to be less, so *that* may attain to its full stature. What a testimony, full of grandeur, full of pity, is borne to the demands of his own

⁹ I.e., the head of the clan.

nature, by the poor clansman, the poor partisan, who rejoices in the glory of his chief. The poor and the low find some amends to their immense moral capacity, for their acquiescence in a political and social inferiority. They are content to be brushed like flies from the path of a great person, so that justice shall be done by him to that common nature which it is the dearest desire of all to see enlarged and glorified. They sun themselves in the great man's light, and feel it to be their own element. They cast the dignity of man from their downtrod selves upon the shoulders of a hero, and will perish to add one drop of blood to make that great heart beat, those giant sinews combat and conquer. He lives for us, and we live in him.

Men, such as they are, very naturally seek money or power; and power because it is as good as money, — the "spoils," so called, "of office." And why not? for they aspire to the highest, and this, in their sleep-walking, they dream is highest. Wake them and they shall quit the false good and leap to the true, and leave governments to clerks and desks. This revolution is to be wrought by the gradual domestication of the idea of Culture. The main enterprise of the world for splendor, for extent, is the upbuilding of a man. Here are the materials strewn along the ground. The private life of one man shall be a more illustrious monarchy, more formidable to its enemy, more sweet and serene in its influence to its friend, than any kingdom in history. For a man, rightly viewed, comprehendeth the particular natures of all men. Each philosopher, each bard, each actor has only done for me, as by a delegate, what one day I can do for myself. The books which once we valued more than the apple of the eye, we have quite exhausted. What is that but saying that we have come up with the point of view which the universal mind took through the eyes of one scribe; we have been that man, and have passed on. First, one, then another, we drain all cisterns, and waxing greater by all these supplies, we crave a better and more abundant food. The man has never lived that can feed us ever. The human mind cannot be enshrined in a person who shall set a barrier on any one side to this unbounded, unboundable empire. It is one central fire, which, flaming now out of the lips of Etna, lightens the capes of Sicily, and now out of the throat of Vesuvius, illuminates the towers and vineyards of Naples. It is one light which beams out of a thousand stars. It is one soul which animates all men.

But I have dwelt perhaps tediously upon this abstraction of the

Scholar. I ought not to delay longer to add what I have to say of nearer reference to the time and to this country.

Historically, there is thought to be a difference in the ideas which predominate over successive epochs, and there are data for marking the genius of the Classic, of the Romantic, and now of the Reflective or Philosophical age. With the views I have intimated of the oneness or the identity of the mind through all individuals, I do not much dwell on these differences. In fact, I believe each individual passes through all three. The boy is a Greek; the youth, romantic; the adult, reflective. I deny not, however, that a revolution in the leading idea may be distinctly enough traced.

Our age is bewailed as the age of Introversion. Must that needs be evil? We, it seems, are critical; we are embarrassed with second thoughts; we cannot enjoy any thing for hankering to know whereof the pleasure consists; we are lined with eyes; we see with our feet; the time is infected with Hamlet's unhappiness, —

> "Sicklied o'er with the pale cast of thought."

It is so bad then? Sight is the last thing to be pitied. Would we be blind? Do we fear lest we should outsee nature and God, and drink truth dry? I look upon the discontent of the literary class as a mere announcement of the fact that they find themselves not in the state of mind of their fathers, and regret the coming state as untried; as a boy dreads the water before he has learned that he can swim. If there is any period one would desire to be born in, is it not the age of Revolution; when the old and the new stand side by side and admit of being compared; when the energies of all men are searched by fear and by hope; when the historic glories of the old can be compensated by the rich possibilities of the new era? This time, like all times, is a very good one, if we but know what to do with it. *embrace the tumult*

I read with some joy of the auspicious signs of the coming days, as they glimmer already through poetry and art, through philosophy and science, through church and state.

One of these signs is the fact that the same movement which effected the elevation of what was called the lowest class in the state, assumed in literature a very marked and as benign an aspect. Instead of the sublime and beautiful, the near, the low, the common, was explored and poetized. That which had been negligently trodden under foot by those who were harnessing and provisioning themselves for long journeys into far countries, is

elevation of the common man

suddenly found to be richer than all foreign parts. The literature of the poor, the feelings of the child, the philosophy of the street, the meaning of household life, are the topics of the time. It is a great stride. It is a sign — is it not? — of new vigor when the extremities are made active, when currents of warm life run into the hands and the feet. I ask not for the great, the remote, the romantic; what is doing in Italy or Arabia; what is Greek art, or Provençal minstrelsy; I embrace the common, I explore and sit at the feet of the familiar, the low. Give me insight into today, and you may have the antique and future worlds. What would we really know the meaning of? The meal in the firkin; the milk in the pan; the ballad in the street; the news of the boat; the glance of the eye; the form and the gait of the body; — show me the ultimate reason of these matters; show me the sublime presence of the highest spiritual cause lurking, as always it does lurk, in these suburbs and extremities of nature; let me see every trifle bristling with the polarity that ranges it instantly on an eternal law; and the shop, the plough, and the ledger referred to the like cause by which light undulates and poets sing; — and the world lies no longer a dull miscellany and lumber-room, but has form and order; there is no trifle, there is no puzzle, but one design unites and animates the farthest pinnacle and the lowest trench.

This idea has inspired the genius of Goldsmith, Burns, Cowper, and, in a newer time, of Goethe, Wordsworth and Carlyle. This idea they have differently followed and with various success. In contrast with their writing, the style of Pope, of Johnson, of Gibbon, looks cold and pedantic. This writing is blood-warm. Man is surprised to find that things near are not less beautiful and wondrous than things remote. The near explains the far. The drop is a small ocean. A man is related to all nature. This perception of the worth of the vulgar is fruitful in discoveries. Goethe, in this very thing the most modern of the moderns, has shown us, as none ever did, the genius of the ancients.

There is one man of genius who has done much for this philosophy of life, whose literary value has never yet been rightly estimated; — I mean Emanuel Swedenborg. The most imaginative of men, yet writing with the precision of a mathematician, he endeavored to engraft a purely philosophical Ethics on the popular Christianity of his time. Such an attempt of course must have difficulty which no genius could surmount. But he saw and showed the connection between nature and the affections of the soul. He pierced the emblematic or spiritual character of the visible, audible, tangible world. Especially did his shade-loving muse hover over and interpret the lower parts of nature; he showed the mysterious bond that allies moral evil to the foul material forms, and has given in epical parables a theory of insanity, of beasts, of unclean and fearful things.

Another sign of our times, also marked by an analogous political movement, is the new importance given to the single person. Every thing that tends to insulate the individual, — to surround him with barriers of natural respect, so that each man shall feel the world is his, and man shall treat with man as a sovereign state with a sovereign state, — tends to true union as well as greatness. "I learned," said the melancholy Pestalozzi, "that no man in God's wide earth is either willing or able to help any other man." Help must come from the bosom alone. The scholar is that man who must take up into himself all the ability of the time, all the contributions of the past, all the hopes of the future. He must be an university of knowledges. If there be one lesson more than another which should pierce his ear, it is, The world is nothing, the man is all; in yourself is the law of all nature, and you know not yet how a globule of sap ascends; in yourself slumbers the whole of Reason; it is for you to know all; it is for you to dare all. Mr. President and Gentlemen, this confidence in the unsearched might of man belongs, by all motives, by all prophecy, by all preparation, to the American Scholar. We have listened too long to the courtly muses of Europe. The spirit of the American freeman is already suspected to be timid, imitative, tame. Public and private avarice make the air we breathe thick and fat. The scholar is decent, indolent, complaisant. See already the tragic consequence. The mind of this country, taught to aim at low objects, eats upon itself. There is no work for any but the decorous and the complaisant. Young men of the fairest promise, who begin life upon our shores, inflated by the mountain winds, shined upon by all the stars of God, find the earth below not in unison with these, but are hindered from action by the disgust which the principles on which business is managed inspire, and turn drudges, or die of disgust, some of them suicides. What is the remedy? They did not yet see, and thousands of young men as hopeful now crowding to the barriers for the career do not yet see, that if the single man plant himself indomitably on his instincts, and there abide, the huge world will come round to him. Patience, — patience; with the shades of all the good and great for company; and for solace the perspective of your own infinite life; and for work the study and the communication of principles, the making those instincts prevalent, the conversion of the world. Is it not the chief disgrace in the world, not to be an unit; — not to be reckoned one character; — not to yield that peculiar fruit which each man was created to bear, but to be reckoned in the gross, in the hundred, or the thousand, of the party, the section, to which we belong; and our opinion predicted geographically, as the north, or the south? Not so, brothers and friends — please God, ours shall not be so. We will walk on our own feet; we will work with our own hands; we will speak our own minds. The study of letters shall be no longer a name for pity, for doubt, and for sensual indulgence. The dread of man and the love of man shall be a wall of defence and a wreath of joy around all. A nation of men will for the first time exist, because each believes himself inspired by the Divine Soul which also inspires all men.

September 21, 1837

The autumnal equinox comes with sparkling stars and thoughtful days. I think the principles of the Peace party sublime, and that the opposers of this philanthropy do not sufficiently consider the positive side of the spiritualist, but only see his negative or abstaining side. But if a nation of men is exalted to that height of morals as to refuse to fight and choose rather to suffer loss of goods and loss of life than to use violence, they must be not helpless, but most effective and great men; they would overawe their invader, and make him ridiculous; they would communicate the contagion of their virtue and inoculate all mankind.

November 6?, 1837

Why yes, perhaps he said wisely who said that war is the natural state of man and the nurse of all virtues. I will not say man is to man a wolf, but man should be to man a hero.

October 2, 1837

The pagan theology of our churches treats Heaven as an inevitable evil, which, as there is no help against, the best way is to put the best face on the matter we can. "From whence," said the good preacher yesterday in his prayer, "we shall not be able to return." Truth will out.

October, 1837

The common complaint is of the dullness of life. I do not know but it must be confessed that the glance we give at the world in a leisure hour is melancholy: that melancholy cleaves to the English mind as to the Aeolian harp. But I maintain that all melancholy belongs to the exterior of man; I claim to be a part of the All. All exterior life declares interior life. I could not be, but that absolute life circulated in me, and I could not think this without being that absolute life. The constant warfare in each heart is betwixt Reason and Commodity. The victory is won as soon as any Soul has learned always to take sides with Reason against himself; to transfer his Me from his person, his name, his interest, back upon Truth and Justice, so that when he is disgraced and defeated and fretted and disheartened, and wasted by nothings, he bears it well, never one instant relaxing his watchfulness, and, as soon as he can get a respite from the insults or the sadness, records all these phenomena, pierces their beauty as phenomena, and, like a God, oversees himself. Thus he harvests his losses, and turns the dust of his shoes to gems. Keep the habit of the observer, and, as fast as you can, break off your association with your personality and identify yourself with the Universe. Be a football to time and chance, the more kicks, the better, so that you inspect the whole game and know its uttermost law. As true is this ethics for trivial as for calamitous days.

October, 1837

We are carried by destiny along our life's course, looking as grave and knowing as little as the infant who is carried in his wicker coach through the street.

October 13, 1837

With much to say, I put off writing until perhaps I shall have nothing in my memory. Now too soon, then too late. I must try the pen and make a beginning.

At Boston, Thursday, I found myself nearly alone in the Athenaeum,[1] and so dropt my book to gaze at the Laocoön. The main figure is great: the two youths work harmoniously on the eye, producing great admiration, so long as the eye is directed at the old man; but look at them, and they are slight and unaffecting statues. No miniature copy and no single busts can do justice to

[1] See p. 4.

this work. Its mass and its integrity are essential. At the Athenaeum, you cannot see it unless the room is nearly empty. For you must stand at the distance of nearly the whole hall to see it, and interposing bystanders eclipse the statue. How is time abolished by the delight I have in this old work, and, without a name, I receive it as a gift from the Universal Mind.

Then I read with great content the August number of the *Asiatic Journal*. Herein is always the piquancy of the meeting of civilization and barbarism. Calcutta or Canton are twilights where Night and Day contend. A very good paper is the narrative of Lord Napier's mission to China (who arrived at Macao 15 July, 1834, and died 11 October). There stand in close contrast the brief, wise English despatches, with the mountainous nonsense of the Chinese diplomacy. The "red permit" writ by the vermilion pencil of the emperor, the super-African ignorance with which England is disdained as out of the bounds of civilization, and her king called "reverently submissive," etc., etc. There is no farce in fiction better than this historical one of John Bull and the Yellow Man: albeit it ends tragically, as Lord Napier died of vexation apparently. I must get that book again.

Then I read an ascent of the Himmaleh mounts, and the terror of the cold, and the river seen bursting through caves of snow, and the traveler finding all over the desolate mountains bears' dung. Then a duel, —pistols for two, and coffee for the survivor. Then an escape from a tiger in a canebrake. Then, thinking of the trees which draw out of the air their food by their aerial roots the leaves, I mused on the strange versatility of the mind's appetite and food. Here were in the Reading Room some four or five men besides me, feeding on newspapers and journals, unfolding our being thereby. Secluded from war, from trade, and from tillage, we were making amends to ourselves by devouring the descriptions of these things, and atoning for the thinness by the quantity of our fare.

October 13, 1837

. . . I read with joy the life of Hampden, Pym, or Penn, of men conversant with governments and revolutions, and dilate in the swelling scene. Is not the delight I there find an intimation that not always in speculation, not always by the poetic imagination alone, shall the scholar, the private soul, be great, but one day in action also? When private men shall act with vast views, the lustre will be transferred from the actions of kings to those of gentlemen. It made my heart beat quicker to think that the gorgeous pictures which fill my imagination in reading the actions of Hampden, Pym, Falkland, are only a revelation to me how needlessly mean our life is; that we, by the depth of our living should deck it with more than regal or national splendor. Very coarse, very abhorrent to the imagination is the American White House. Because it has no historic lustre and natural growth out of feudalism, etc., like theirs, and is not, on the other hand, a new creation out of the soul, out of virtue and truth, outshining theirs, but is an imitation of their gaudiness, like a Negro gay with cast-off epaulettes and gold-laced hat of his master.

October 20, 1837

Wild man attracts. — As the contemporaries of Columbus hungered to see the wild man, so undoubtedly we should have the liveliest interest in a wild man, but men in society do not interest us because they are tame. We know all they will do, and man is like man as one steamboat is like another. Tame men are inexpressibly tedious, like the talking with a young Southerner who says, "Yes, sir," indifferently to every sort of thing you say, thinking Yes, sir, to mean nothing. . . .

October 28, 1837

The event of death is always astounding; our philosophy never reaches, never possesses it; we are always at the beginning of our catechism; always the definition is yet to be made. What is death?

I see nothing to help beyond observing what the mind's habit is in regard to that crisis. Simply I have nothing to do with it. It is nothing to me. After I have made my will and set my house in order, I shall do in the immediate expectation of death the same things I should do without it.

But more difficult is it to know the death of another. . . . In us there ought to be remedy. There ought to be, there can be nothing to which the soul is called, to which the soul is not equal. And I suppose that the roots of my relation to every individual are in my own constitution, and not less the causes of his disappearance from me.

Why should we lie so? A question is asked of the Understanding which lies in the province of the Reason, and we foolishly try to make an answer. Our constructiveness overpowers our love of truth. How noble is it when the mourner looks for comfort in your face to give only sympathy and confession; confession that it is a great grief, and the greater because the apprehension of its nature still loiters.

Who set you up for Professor of omniscience and *cicerone* [2] to the Universe? Why teach? Learn rather.

November 7 ?, 1837

"Miracles have ceased." Have they indeed? When? They had not ceased this afternoon when I walked into the wood and got into bright, miraculous sunshine, in shelter from the roaring wind. Who sees a pine-cone, or the turpentine exuding from the tree, or a leaf, the unit of vegetation, fall from its bough, as if it said, "the year is finished," or hears in the quiet, piny glen the titmouse chirping his cheerful note, or walks along the lofty promontory-like ridges which, like natural causeways, traverse the morass, or gazes upward at the rushing clouds, or downward at a moss or a stone and says to himself, "Miracles have ceased"? Tell me, good friend, when this hillock on which your foot stands swelled from the level of the sphere by volcanic force; pick up that pebble at your feet; look at its gray sides, its sharp crystal, and tell me what fiery inundation of the world melted the minerals like wax, and, as if the globe were one glowing crucible, gave this stone its shape. There is the truth-speaking pebble itself, to affirm to endless ages the thing was so. Tell me where is the manufactory of this air, so thin, so blue, so restless, which eddies around you, in which your life floats, of which your lungs are but an organ, and which you coin into musical words. I am agitated with curiosity to know the secret of nature. Why cannot geology, why cannot botany speak and tell me what has been, what is, as I run along the forest promontory, and ask when it rose like a blister on heated steel? Then I looked up and saw the sun shining in the vast sky, and heard the wind bellow above and the water glistened in the vale. These were the forces that wrought then and work now. Yes, there they grandly speak to all plainly, in proportion as we are quick to apprehend.

October 23, 1837

It seems to me as if the high idea of Culture as the end of existence, does not pervade the mind of the thinking people of our Community, the conviction that a discovery of human power, to which the trades and occupations they follow, the connections

2 Guide.

they form, and the motley tissue of their common experience are quite subordinate and auxiliary, — is the main interest of history. Could this be properly taught, I think it must provoke and over-master the young and ambitious, and yield rich fruits.

Culture, in the high sense, does not consist in polishing or varnishing, but in so presenting the attractions of nature that the slumbering attributes of man may burst their iron sleep and rush, full-grown, into day. Culture is not the trimming and turfing of gardens, but the showing the true harmony of the unshorn land-scape with horrid thickets and bald mountains and the balance of the land and sea.

March 4, 1838

Last night a remembering and remembering talk with Lidian. I went back to the first smile of Ellen on the door-stone at Con-cord. I went back to all that delicious relation to feel, as ever, how many shades, how much reproach. Strange is it that I can go back to no part of youth, no past relation, without shrinking and shrinking. Not Ellen, not Edward, not Charles. Infinite compunctions embitter each of those dear names, and all who surrounded them. Ah! could I have felt in the presence of the first, as now I feel, my own power and hope, and so have offered her in every word and look the heart of a man humble and wise, but resolved to be true and perfect with God, and not, as I fear it seemed, the uneasy, uncentered joy of one who received in her a good — a lovely good — out of all proportion to his deserts, I might haply have made her days longer and certainly sweeter, and at least have recalled her seraph smile without a pang. I con-sole myself with the thought that if Ellen, if Edward, if Charles, could have read my entire heart, they should have seen nothing but rectitude of purpose and generosity conquering the superficial coldness and prudence. But I ask now, Why was not I made like all these beatified mates of mine, *superficially* generous and noble, as well as *internally* so? They never needed to shrink at any re-membrance; — and I at so many sad passages that look to me now as if I [had] been blind and mad. Well, O God, I will try and learn from this sad memory to be brave and circumspect and true henceforth and weave now a web that will not shrink. This is the thorn in the flesh.

[*March 27, 1838*]

By Latin and English poetry we were born and bred in an oratorio of praises of nature, — flowers, birds, mountains, sun, and moon; — yet the naturalist of this hour finds that he knows nothing, by all their poems, of any of these fine things; that he has conversed with the mere surface and show of them all; and of their essence, or of their history, knowing nothing. Further inquiry will discover that nobody, — that not these chanting poets themselves, knew anything sincere of these handsome natures they so commended; that they contented themselves with the passing chirp of a bird, that they saw one or two mornings, and listlessly looked at sunsets, and repeated idly these few glimpses in their song. But go into the forest, you shall find all new and undescribed. The honking of the wild geese flying by night; the thin note of the companionable titmouse in the winter day; the fall of swarms of flies, in autumn, from combats high in the air, pattering down on the leaves like rain; the angry hiss of the wood-birds; the pine throwing out its pollen for the benefit of the next century; the turpentine exuding from the tree; — and indeed any vegetation, any animation, any and all, are alike unattempted. The man who stands on the seashore, or who rambles in the woods, seems to be the first man that ever stood on the shore, or entered a grove, his sensations and his world are so novel and strange. Whilst I read the poets, I think that nothing new can be said about morning and evening. But when I see the daybreak I am not reminded of these Homeric, or Shakespearian, or Miltonic, or Chaucerian pictures. No, but I feel perhaps the pain of an alien world; a world not yet subdued by the thought; or I am cheered by the moist, warm, glittering, budding, melodious hour, that takes down the narrow walls of my soul, and extends its life and pulsation to the very horizon. *That* is morning, to cease for a bright hour to be a prisoner of this sickly body, and to become as large as nature.   *From "Literary Ethics"*

April 26, 1838

Yesterday went the letter to Van Buren,[3] a letter hated of me, a deliverance that does not deliver the soul. What I do, be sure, is all that concerns my majesty and not what men great or small think of it. Yet I accept the Dartmouth College invitation to speak to the boys with great delight. I write my journal,

[3] An open letter to the President protesting the removal of the Cherokee Indians from the state of Georgia.

I read my lecture, with joy, but this stirring in the philanthropic mud gives me no peace. I will let the Republic alone until the Republic comes to me. I fully sympathize, be sure, with the sentiment I write, but I accept it rather from my friends than dictate it. It is not my impulse to say it, and therefore my genius deserts me. No muse befriends, no music of thought or of word accompanies. Bah!

As far as I notice what passes in philanthropic meetings and holy hurrahs there is very little depth of interest. The speakers warm each other's skin and lubricate each other's tongue, and the words flow and the superlatives thicken and the lips quiver and the eyes moisten, and an observer new to such scenes would say, Here was true fire; the assembly were all ready to be martyred, and the effect of such a spirit on the community would be irresistible; but they separate and go to the shop, to a dance, to bed, and an hour afterwards they care so little for the matter that on slightest temptation each one would disclaim the meeting. "Yes, he went, but they were for carrying it too far," etc., etc.

The lesson is, to know that men are superficially very inflammable, but that these fervors do not strike down and reach the action and habit of the man.

May 5, 1838

Last night E. H. described the apathy from which she suffers. I own I was at a loss to prescribe, as I did not sufficiently understand the state of mind she paints. . . .

I complain in my own experience of the feeble influence of thought on life, a ray as pale and ineffectual as that of the sun in our cold and bleak spring. They seem to lie — the actual life and the intellectual intervals — in parallel lines and never meet. Yet we doubt not they act and react ever, that one is even cause of the other; that one is causal and one servile, a mere vesture. Yet it takes a great deal of elevation of thought to produce a very little elevation of life. How slowly the highest raptures of the intellect break through the trivial forms of habit. Yet imperceptibly they do. Gradually, in long years, we bend our living toward our idea, but we serve seven years and twice seven for Rachel. If Mr. G., that old gander (I owned) should now stop at my gate, I should duck to him as to an angel, and waste all my time for him, etc., etc., instead of telling him, as truth seems to require, that his visit and his babble was an impertinence, and bidding him Begone. Just so, when Miss W. and Mrs.

G. and Miss M. come, I straightway sit glued to my chair, all thought, all action, all play, departed and paralyzed, and acquiesce, and become less than they are, instead of nodding slightly to them and treating them like shadows, and persisting in the whim of pathos, or the whim of fun, or the whim of poetry in which they found me, and constraining them to accept the law of this higher thought (also theirs) instead of kneeling to their triviality.

I'll tell you what to do; try to make humanity lovely unto them.[4]

May 6, 1838

Do not charge me with egotism and presumption. I see with awe the attributes of the farmers and villagers whom you despise. A man saluted me today in a manner which at once stamped him for a theist, a self-respecting gentleman, a lover of truth and virtue. How venerable are the manners often of the poor. . . .

May 11, 1838

Last night the moon rose behind four distinct pine-tree tops in the distant woods and the night at ten was so bright that I walked abroad. But the sublime light of night is unsatisfying, provoking; it astonishes but explains not. Its charm floats, dances, disappears, comes and goes, but palls in five minutes after you have left the house. Come out of your warm, angular house, resounding with few voices, into the chill, grand, instantaneous night, with such a Presence as a full moon in the clouds, and you are struck with poetic wonder. In the instant you leave far behind all human relations, wife, mother and child, and live only with the savages — water, air, light, carbon, lime, and granite. I think of Kuhleborn.[5] I become a moist, cold element. "Nature grows over me." Frogs pipe; waters far off tinkle; dry leaves hiss; grass bends and rustles, and I have died out of the human world and come to feel a strange, cold, aqueous, terraqueous, aerial, ethereal sympathy and existence. I sow the sun and moon for seeds.

---

[4] This sentence is faintly pencilled underneath, and very possibly was written by Mrs. Emerson. — E.W.E.

[5] A fierce spirit of the torrent or stormy mist in the once-popular tale of *Undine* (1811), by the German author Fouqué.

June 9, 1838

Why do we seek this lurking beauty in skies, in poems, in drawings? Ah! because there we are safe, there we neither sicken nor die. I think we fly to Beauty as an asylum from the terrors of finite nature. We are made immortal by this kiss, by the contemplation of beauty. . . . Whilst I behold the holy lights of the June sunset, last evening or tonight, I am raised instantly out of fear and out of time, and care not for the knell of this coughing body. — Strange the succession of humors that pass through this human spirit. Sometimes I am the organ of the Holy Ghost and sometimes of a vixen petulance. . . .

June, 1838

Alternation. — The Bath and the Battle of Pisa as drawn by Michael Angelo, exhibited the extremes of relaxation and strength. We like the girding belt; we like to be dissolved in liberty. When we have seen friends and talked for days until we are turned inside out, — then go lie down, then lock the study door; shut the shutters, then welcome fall the imprisoning rain, dear hermitage of nature. Recollect [6] the spirits. Close up the too expanded leaves.

June, 1838

This afternoon the foolishest preaching — which bayed at the moon. Go, hush, old man, whom years have taught no truth. The hardness and ignorance with which the threat that the Son of Man when he cometh in clouds will be ashamed of A. and B., because they are not members of Concord Church, must have suggested to them, "Be it so; then I also will be ashamed of Him." Such Moabitish [7] darkness, well typified in the perplexity about his glasses, reminded one of the squash-bugs, who stupid stare at you when you lift the rotten leaf of the vines.

June 18, 1838

C[aroline] S[turgis] protests. That is a good deal. In these times, you shall find a small number of persons of whom only that can be affirmed that they protest. Yet is it as divine to say no, as to say yes. You say they go too much alone. Yea, but they shun society to the end of finding society. They repudiate the false

---

6 Collect again.

7 The Moabites, near neighbors and near kin to Israel, are the target for many prophecies in the Old Testament.

out of love of the true. Extravagance is a good token. In an Extravagance,[8] there is hope; in Routine, none. . . .

[*June 18, 1838*]

This country has not fulfilled what seemed the reasonable expectation of mankind. Men looked, when all feudal straps and bandages were snapped asunder, that nature, too long the mother of dwarfs, should reimburse itself by a brood of Titans, who should laugh and leap in the continent, and run up the mountains of the West with the errand of genius and of love. But the mark of American merit in painting, in sculpture, in poetry, in fiction, in eloquence, seems to be a certain grace without grandeur, and itself not new but derivative, a vase of fair outline, but empty, — which whoso sees may fill with what wit and character is in him, but which does not, like the charged cloud, overflow with terrible beauty, and emit lightnings on all beholders. . . .

From "Literary Ethics"

June 21, 1838

Day creeps after day, each full of facts, dull, strange, despised things that we cannot enough despise, — call heavy, prosaic, and desart.[9] And presently the aroused intellect finds gold and gems in one of these scorned facts, then finds that the day of facts is a rock of diamonds, that a fact is an Epiphany of God, that on every fact of his life he should rear a temple of wonder, joy, and praise; that in going to eat meat, to buy, or sell, to meet a friend, or thwart an adversary, to communicate a piece of news, or buy a book, he celebrates the arrival of an inconceivably remote purpose and law at last on the shores of Being, and into the ripeness and term of nature. And because nothing chances, but all is locked and wheeled and chained in Law, in these motes and dust he can read the writing of the True Life and of a startling sublimity. ⁻

June 22, 1838

Conjure with the great name. Who forbade you to create? Fear. And who made fear? Sin; Inaction; Ignorance. What is this astounding greatness of other men that they should be as god to you? Why, it is two things: First, your littleness, which makes them seem so large; and, second, your identity with them,

---

[8] Leaving the beaten path.
[9] Cf. "Days," p. 451.

which makes them delightful to you as the colossal portrait of yourself. If society sleeps and snores, if there is no art, no poetry, no genius, no virtue, do not say that such things cannot be, but remember in your own sorrowful life the sin that is also in theirs, namely, the surrender of hope, the voluntary abdication that somewhere was, covered up now in the bushes and wilderness of so many years. When you said, — "As others do, so will I; I renounce — I am sorry for it — my early visions. I must eat the good of the land, and let learning and romantic expectations go until a more convenient season," — then died the man in you; then perished the buds of art and poetry and genius. Had you stood firm, had many stood firm, Oh God! had all, — we should no longer speak of society with cold disapproval, warning you against it, but we should see in it the half-gods, whose traces are not yet quite obliterated, careering in contest or in love, in the still grand remains of Greek art.

June 23, 1838

I hate goodies. I hate goodness that preaches. Goodness that preaches undoes itself. A little electricity of virtue lurks here and there in kitchens and among the obscure, chiefly women, that flashes out occasional light and makes the existence of the thing still credible. But one had as lief curse and swear as be guilty of this odious religion that watches the beef and watches the cider in the pitcher at table, that shuts the mouth hard at any remark it cannot twist nor wrench into a sermon, and preaches as long as itself and its hearer is awake. Goodies make us very bad. . . . We will almost sin to spite them. Better indulge yourself, feed fat, drink liquors, than go straitlaced for such cattle as these.

June 28, 1838

The moon and Jupiter side by side last night stemmed the sea of clouds and plied their voyage in convoy through the sublime Deep as I walked the old and dusty road. The snow and the enchantment of the moonlight make all landscapes alike, and the road that is so tedious and homely that I never take it by day, — by night is Italy or Palmyra. In these divine pleasures permitted to me of walks in the June night under moon and stars, I can put my life as a fact before me and stand aloof from its honor and shame.

September 1, 1838

Looked over S. G. Ward's portfolio of drawings and prints.[1]
In landscapes it ought to be that the painter should give us not
surely the enjoyment of a real landscape, — for air, light, motion,
life, dampness, heat, and actual infinite space he cannot give us,
— but the suggestion of a better, fairer creation than we know;
he should crowd a greater number of beautiful effects into his
picture than coexist in any real landscape. All the details, all the
prose of nature, he should omit, and give us only the spirit and
splendor. So that we should find his landscape more exalting to
the inner man than is Walden Pond or the Pays de Vaud. All
spiritual activity is abridgment, selection.

[October 9, 1838]

Van Burenism. — I passed by the shop and saw my spruce
neighbor, the dictator of our rural Jacobins,[2] teaching his little
circle of villagers their political lessons. And here, thought I, is
one who loves what I hate; here is one wholly reversing my code.
I hate persons who are nothing but persons. I hate numbers.
He cares for nothing but numbers and persons. All the quali-
ties of man, all his accomplishments, affections, enterprises, except solely the ticket he votes for, are nothing to this philosopher.
Numbers of majorities are all he sees in the newspaper. All of
North or South, all in Georgia, Alabama, Pennsylvania or New
England that this man considers is, What is the relation of Mr.
Clay, or of Mr. Van Buren, to those mighty mountain chains,
those vast, fruitful champaigns, those expanding nations of men.
What an existence is this, to have no home, no heart, but to feed
on the very refuse and old straw and chaff of men, the numbers
and names of voters!

One thing deserves the thought of the modern Jacobin. It
seems the relations of society, the position of classes, irk and sting
him, and he lends himself to each malignant party that assails
what is eminent. He will one day know that this is not remov-
able, but a distinction in the nature of things; that neither the
caucus, nor the newspaper, nor the Congress, nor the mob, nor
the guillotine, nor fire, nor all together, can avail to outlaw, cut
out, burn or destroy the offence of superiority in persons. The
manners, the pretension, which annoy me so much, are not superficial, but built on a real distinction in the nature of my com-

---

[1] Cf. "Art," p. 461.
[2] I.e., Democrats.

panion. The superiority in him is inferiority in me, and if this particular companion were wiped by a sponge out of Nature, my inferiority would still be made evident to me by other persons everywhere and every day.

October, 1838

Edward Palmer [3] asked me if I liked two services in a Sabbath. I told him, Not very well. If the sermon was good I wished to think of it; if it was bad, one was enough.

[*October 26, 1838*]

In common speech we refer all things to time, as we habitually refer the immensely sundered stars to one concave sphere. And so we say that the Judgment is distant or near, that the Millennium approaches, that a day of certain political, moral, social reforms is at hand, and the like, when we mean that in the nature of things one of the facts we contemplate is external and fugitive, and the other is permanent and connate with the soul. The things we now esteem fixed shall, one by one, detach themselves like ripe fruit from our experience, and fall. The wind shall blow them none knows whither. The landscape, the figures, Boston, London, are facts as fugitive as any institution past, or any whiff of mist or smoke, and so is society, and so is the world. The soul looketh steadily forwards, creating a world before her, leaving worlds behind her. She has no dates, nor rites, nor persons, nor specialties nor men. The soul knows only the soul; the web of events is the flowing robe in which she is clothed.

From "The Over-Soul"

October 26, 1838

Jones Very came hither, two days since, and gave occasion to many thoughts on his peculiar state of mind and his relation to society. His position accuses society as much as society names it false and morbid; and much of his discourse concerning society, the church, and the college was perfectly just. Entertain every thought, every character, that goes by with the hospitality of your soul. Give him the freedom of your inner house. He shall make you wise to the extent of his own uttermost receivings. Especially if one of these monotones, whereof, as my friends think, I have a savage society, like a menagerie of monsters, come to you, receive him. For the partial action of his mind in one direction is a tele-

[3] A traveling reformer who had given up the use of money.

scope for the objects on which it is pointed. And as we know that every path we take is but a radius of our sphere, and we may dive as deep in every other direction as we have in that, a far insight of one evil suggests instantly the immense extent of that revolution that must be wrought before He whose right it is shall reign, the All in All.

October 28, 1838

Jones Very says it is with him a day of hate; that he discerns the bad element in every person whom he meets, which repels him: he even shrinks a little to give the hand, — that sign of receiving. The institutions, the cities which men have built the world over, look to him like a huge blot of ink. His own only guard in going to see men is that he goes to do them good, else they would injure him (spiritually). He lives in the sight that he who made him, made the things he sees. . . .

He had the manners of a man, one, that is, to whom life was more than meat, the body than raiment. He felt it an honor, he said, to wash his face, being, as it was, the temple of the Spirit. And he is gone into the multitude as solitary as Jesus. In dismissing him I seem to have discharged an arrow into the heart of society. Wherever that young enthusiast goes he will astonish and disconcert men by dividing for them the cloud that covers the profound gulf that is in man.

October 30, 1838

I ought not to omit recording the astonishment which seized all the company when our brave saint,[4] the other day, fronted the presiding preacher. The preacher began to tower and dogmatize with many words. Instantly I foresaw that his doom was fixed; and as quick as he ceased speaking, the saint set him right and blew away all his words in an instant, — unhorsed him, I may say, and tumbled him along the ground in utter dismay, like my angel of Heliodorus. Never was discomfiture more complete. In tones of genuine pathos he "bid him wonder at the Love which suffered him to speak there in his chair, of things he knew nothing of; one might expect to see the book taken from his hands and him thrust out of the room, — and yet he was allowed to sit and talk, whilst every word he spoke was a step of departure from the truth, and of this he commanded himself to bear witness!"

4 Jones Very

November 3, 1838

I should not dare to tell all my story. A great deal of it I do not yet understand. How much of it is incomplete. In my strait and decorous way of living, native to my family and to my country, and more strictly proper to me, is nothing extravagant or flowing. I content myself with moderate, languid actions, and never transgress the staidness of village manners. Herein I consult the poorness of my powers. More culture would come out of great virtues and vices perhaps, but I am not up to that. Should I obey an irregular impulse, and establish every new relation that my fancy prompted with the men and women I see, I should not be followed by my faculties; they would play me false in making good their very suggestions. They delight in inceptions, but they warrant nothing else. I see very well the beauty of sincerity, and tend that way, but if I should obey the impulse so far as to say to my fashionable acquaintance, "you are a coxcomb, — I dislike your manners — I pray you avoid my sight," — I should not serve him nor me, and still less the truth; I should act quite unworthy of the truth, for I could not carry out the declaration with a sustained, even-minded frankness and love, which alone could save such a speech from rant and absurdity.

We must tend ever to the good life.

November 3, 1838

I told Jones Very that I had never suffered, that I could scarce bring myself to feel a concern for the safety and life of my nearest friends that would satisfy them; that I saw clearly that if my wife, my child, my mother, should be taken from me, I should still remain whole, with the same capacity of cheap enjoyment from all things. I should not grieve enough, although I love them. But could I make them feel what I feel, — the boundless resources of the soul, — remaining entire when particular threads of relation are snapped, — I should then dismiss forever the little remains of uneasiness I have in regard to them.

November 12, 1838

I could forgive your want of faith if you had any knowledge of the uttermost that man could be and do, if arithmetic could predict the last possibilities of instinct. But men are not made like boxes, a hundred or thousand to order, and all exactly alike, of known dimension, and all their properties known; but no, they come into nature through a nine months' astonishment, and of a character, each one, incalculable, and of extravagant possibilities; out of darkness and out of the awful Cause they come to be caught up into this vision of a seeing, partaking, acting and suffering life, not foreknown, not fore-estimable, but slowly or speedily they unfold new, unknown, mighty traits: not boxes, but these machines are alive, agitated, fearing, sorrowing.

1838

The Divinity School Address

The Address to the Harvard Divinity School Seniors occupies a special position among Emerson's lectures, both because of its background and its consequences. Though the Unitarians of his day, among whom he was still nominally numbered, had attacked the dogmatism of Calvinism in the name of liberal Christianity, they were not prepared to be liberal beyond a certain point. To them a Christian was one who accepted the divine commission of Christ, as attested by his miracles, and therefore the divine authority of his teachings; else Christianity ceased to be "the power of God unto salvation." As early as 1826 Emerson had come to suspect that faith could never be established in that historical way. By the time he gave up his post at the Second Church in 1832 he was filled with "the doctrine of man's moral nature" — his oneness with God — which swept away all petty quibbles about a special Revelation. In the succeeding years he had several times written out the substance of his gospel in long, strongly-felt entries in his journals.[1] His last sermons, notably "Religion and Society" (1833) and "The Miracle of Our Being" (1834) had been public statements of it, as had been in part a number of his lectures, particularly "Religion" (January, 1837). Already in 1835 he had resolved to "write and print a discourse upon Spiritual and Traditional Religion"; though restrained somewhat by a fear of unsettling the faith of good people not ready for his light, he was clearly going to accept the first fair opportunity to testify to his Truth. On July 15, 1838, that occasion came.

To proclaim the doctrine of the perpetual revelation in the very citadel of the faith he challenged was to fling down a gauntlet the Unitarian champions were not slow to pick up. On August 27,

[1] See pp. 10–11, 14–16, and 98–99, and also *Journals*, III, 235–40 and IV, 126–29.

shortly after the Address was published, a blast was printed in
The Boston Daily Advertiser by the Dexter Professor of Sacred
Literature at Harvard, Andrews Norton, an act so unprecedented,
Perry Miller has remarked, "that it could have been inspired by
nothing less than pure rage." The Hollis Professor of Theology,
Henry Ware, Jr., a gentler spirit and Emerson's former colleague
at the Second Church, preached a sermon on September 23 on
"The Personality of the Deity" which was designed to clear the
Divinity School of implication in Emerson's opinions. There was
considerable outcry in the newspapers about "infidelity," "panthe-
ism," and "atheism," and a lively pamphlet warfare of some years'
duration ensued. The direct consequences for Emerson were the
virtual end of his preaching career, a reputation among the conservative as a dangerous heretic, and a ban on further speaking
engagements at Harvard that held for over twenty years.

Although throughout this "storm in our washbowl" Emerson
remained outwardly unmoved, retracting nothing and defending
nothing, his journals show his inward agitation. In a series of
remarkable entries he declared himself untouched; acknowledged
that his shortcomings deserved worse trials; protested his irrespon-
sibility; and roundly promised to repeat the offense. Some years
later he reviewed the whole affair in an ironic allegory, his poem
"Uriel," in which he made clear his unrepentant delight in the
consternation his "treason" had caused; "I unsettle all things," he
warned in an essay. The most lasting effect of the episode, however, seems to have been to send him "into his cloud," to
strengthen his natural inclination to stay above the battle and
"mind thy rhyme."

December 29, 1834

To the music of the surly storm that thickens the darkness of
the night abroad, and rocks the walls and fans my cheek through
the chinks and cracks, I would sing my strain, though hoarse and
small. Yet, please God, it shall be lowly, affectionate and true. It
were worth trial whether the distinction between a spiritual and
traditional religion could not be made apparent to an ordinary
congregation. There are parts of faith so great, so self-evident,
that when the mind rests in them the pretensions of the most
illuminated, most pretending sect pass for nothing. . . .
But to show men the nullity of church-going compared with a

real exaltation of their being, I think might even promote parish objects and draw them to church. To show the reality and infinite depth of spiritual laws, that all the maxims of Christ are true to the core of the world; that there is not, can't be, any cheating of nature, might be apprehended.

Every spiritual law, I suppose, would be a contradiction to common sense. Thus I should begin with my old saws, that nothing can be given; everything is sold; love compels love; hatred, hatred; action and reaction always are equal; no evil in society but has its check which coexists; the moral, the physical, the social world is a *plenum*,[2] and any flood in one place produces equal ebb in another; nothing is free but the will of man, and that only to procure his own virtue: on every other side but that one he beats the air with his pompous action; that punishment not follows but accompanies crime.

They have said in churches in this age, "Mere Morality." O God, they know thee not who speak contemptuously of all that is grand. It is the distinction of Christianity, that it is moral. All that is personal in it is nought. When anyone comes who speaks with better insight into moral nature, he will be the new gospel; miracle or not, inspired or uninspired, he will be the Christ; persons are nothing. If I could tell you what you know not; could, by my knowledge of the divine being, put that within your grasp which now you dimly apprehend, and make you feel the moral sublime, you would never think of denying my inspiration. The whole power of Christianity resides in this fact, that it is more agreeable to the constitution of man than any other teaching. But from the constitution of man may be got better teaching still.

Morality requires purity, but purity is not it; requires justice, but justice is not that; requires beneficence, but is something better. Indeed there is a kind of descent and accommodation felt when we leave speaking of Moral Nature to urge a virtue it enjoins. For to the soul in her pure action all the virtues are natural, and not painfully acquired. Excite the soul, and it becomes suddenly virtuous. Touch the deep heart, and all these listless, stingy, beef-eating bystanders will see the dignity of a sentiment; will say, This is good, and all I have I will give for that. Excite the soul, and the weather and the town and your condition in the world all disappear; the world itself loses its solidity, nothing remains but the soul and the Divine Presence in which it lives. Youth and age are indifferent in this presence.

2 Filled space.

"Overturn, overturn, and overturn," said our aged priest,[3] "until he whose right it is to reign, shall come into his kingdom."

May 9, 1838

... You have good philosophy, and disdain the feeble routine and mere verbal learning and ritual virtue of the School and the Church. Well, beware of Antinomianism.[4] All men have a slight distrust of your novelties and think you do not esteem the old laws of true witness, just dealing, chaste conversing, as much as they. They have some reason. For as they make a bad use of their old truths, so we make a bad use of our new ones. They ... query whether the loss of the old checks will not sometimes be a temptation which the unripeness of the new will not countervail. ...

July 8, 1838

We shun to say that which shocks the religious ear of the people and to take away titles even of false honor from Jesus. But this fear is an impotency to commend the moral sentiment. For if I can so imbibe that wisdom as to utter it well, instantly love and awe take place. The reverence for Jesus is only reverence for this, and if you can carry this home to any man's heart, instantly he feels that all is made good and that God sits once more on the throne. But when I have as clear a sense as now that I am speaking simple truth without any bias, any foreign interest in the matter, — all railing, all unwillingness to hear, all danger of injury to the conscience, dwindles and disappears. I refer to the discourse now growing under my eye to the Divinity School.

Address

IN this refulgent summer, it has been a luxury to draw the breath of life. The grass grows, the buds burst, the meadow is spotted with fire and gold in the tint of flowers. The air is full of birds, and sweet with the breath of the pine, the balm-of-Gilead, and the new hay. Night brings no gloom to the heart with its welcome shade.

[3] Dr. Ripley.
[4] Literally, against-the-law-ism. A name given to any religious heresy that taught the adequacy of the inner experience of faith alone to attest salvation, with or without works.

Through the transparent darkness the stars pour their almost spiritual rays. Man under them seems a young child, and his huge globe a toy. The cool night bathes the world as with a river, and prepares his eyes again for the crimson dawn. The mystery of nature was never displayed more happily. The corn and the wine have been freely dealt to all creatures, and the never-broken silence with which the old bounty goes forward has not yielded yet one word of explanation. One is constrained to respect the perfection of this world in which our senses converse. How wide; how rich; what invitation from every property it gives to every faculty of man! In its fruitful soils; in its navigable sea; in its mountains of metal and stone; in its forests of all woods; in its animals; in its chemical ingredients; in the powers and path of light, heat, attraction and life, it is well worth the pith and heart of great men to subdue and enjoy it. The planters, the mechanics, the inventors, the astronomers, the builders of cities, and the captains, history delights to honor.

But when the mind opens and reveals the laws which traverse the universe and make things what they are, then shrinks the great world at once into a mere illustration and fable of this mind. What am I? and What is? asks the human spirit with a curiosity new-kindled, but never to be quenched. Behold these outrunning laws, which our imperfect apprehension can see tend this way and that, but not come full circle. Behold these infinite relations, so like, so unlike; many, yet one. I would study, I would know, I would admire forever. These works of thought have been the entertainments of the human spirit in all ages.

A more secret, sweet, and overpowering beauty appears to man when his heart and mind open to the sentiment of virtue. Then he is instructed in what is above him. He learns that his being is without bound; that to the good, to the perfect, he is born, low as he now lies in evil and weakness. That which he venerates is still his own, though he has not realized it yet. *He ought.* He knows the sense of that grand word, though his analysis fails to render account of it. When in innocency or when by intellectual perception he attains to say, — "I love the Right; Truth is beautiful within and without for evermore. Virtue, I am thine; save me; use me; thee will I serve, day and night, in great, in small, that I may be not virtuous, but virtue"; — then is the end of the creation answered, and God is well pleased.

The sentiment of virtue is a reverence and delight in the presence of certain divine laws. It perceives that this homely game of

life we play, covers, under what seem foolish details, principles
that astonish. The child amidst his baubles is learning the action
of light, motion, gravity, muscular force; and in the game of human
life, love, fear, justice, appetite, man, and God, interact. These
laws refuse to be adequately stated. They will not be written out
on paper, or spoken by the tongue. They elude our persevering
thought; yet we read them hourly in each other's faces, in each
other's actions, in our own remorse. The moral traits which are
all globed into every virtuous act and thought, — in speech we
must sever, and describe or suggest by painful enumeration of
many particulars. Yet, as this sentiment is the essence of all religion, let me guide your eye to the precise objects of the sentiment, by an enumeration of some of those classes of facts in which
this element is conspicuous.

The intuition of the moral sentiment is an insight of the perfection of the laws of the soul. These laws execute themselves. They
are out of time, out of space, and not subject to circumstance.
Thus in the soul of man there is a justice whose retributions are
instant and entire. He who does a good deed is instantly ennobled. He who does a mean deed is by the action itself con-
tracted. He who puts off impurity, thereby puts on purity. If a
man is at heart just, then in so far is he God; the safety of God,
the immortality of God, the majesty of God do enter into that
man with justice. If a man dissemble, deceive, he deceives himself, and goes out of acquaintance with his own being. A man in
the view of absolute goodness, adores, with total humility. Every
step so downward, is a step upward. The man who renounces himself, comes to himself.

See how this rapid intrinsic energy worketh everywhere, righting
wrongs, correcting appearances, and bringing up facts to a harmony
with thoughts. Its operation in life, though slow to the senses, is
at last as sure as in the soul. By it a man is made the Providence
to himself, dispensing good to his goodness, and evil to his sin.
Character is always known. Thefts never enrich; alms never impoverish; murder will speak out of stone walls. The least admix-
ture of a lie, — for example, the taint of vanity, any attempt to
make a good impression, a favorable appearance, — will instantly
vitiate the effect. But speak the truth, and all nature and all spirits
help you with unexpected furtherance. Speak the truth, and all
things alive or brute are vouchers, and the very roots of the grass
underground there do seem to stir and move to bear you witness.
See again the perfection of the Law as it applies itself to the affec-

tions, and becomes the law of society. As we are, so we associate. The good, by affinity, seek the good; the vile, by affinity, the vile. Thus of their own volition, souls proceed into heaven, into hell.

These facts have always suggested to man the sublime creed that the world is not the product of manifold power, but of one will, of one mind; and that one mind is everywhere active, in each ray of the star, in each wavelet of the pool; and whatever opposes that will is everywhere balked and baffled, because things are made so, and not otherwise. Good is positive. Evil is merely privative, not absolute: it is like cold, which is the privation of heat. All evil is so much death or nonentity. Benevolence is absolute and real. So much benevolence as a man hath, so much life hath he. For all things proceed out of this same spirit, which is differently named love, justice, temperance, in its different applications, just as the ocean receives different names on the several shores which it washes. All things proceed out of the same spirit, and all things conspire with it. Whilst a man seeks good ends, he is strong by the whole strength of nature. In so far as he roves from these ends, he bereaves himself of power, or auxiliaries; his being shrinks out of all remote channels, he becomes less and less, a mote a point, until absolute badness is absolute death.

The perception of this law of laws awakens in the mind a sentiment which we call the religious sentiment, and which makes our highest happiness. Wonderful is its power to charm and to command. It is a mountain air. It is the embalmer of the world. It is myrrh and storax, and chlorine and rosemary. It makes the sky and the hills sublime, and the silent song of the stars is it. By it is the universe made safe and habitable, not by science or power. Thought may work cold and intransitive in things, and find no end or unity; but the dawn of the sentiment of virtue on the heart, gives and is the assurance that Law is sovereign over all natures; and the worlds, time, space, eternity, do seem to break out into joy.

This sentiment is divine and deifying. It is the beatitude of man. It makes him illimitable. Through it, the soul first knows itself. It corrects the capital mistake of the infant man, who seeks to be great by following the great, and hopes to derive advantages *from another*, — by showing the fountain of all good to be in himself, and that he, equally with every man, is an inlet into the deeps of Reason. When he says, "I ought"; when love warms him; when he chooses, warned from on high, the good and great deed; then, deep melodies wander through his soul from Supreme Wisdom. — Then he can worship, and be enlarged by his worship; for he can never go behind this sentiment. In the sublimest flights of the soul, rectitude is never surmounted, love is never outgrown.

This sentiment lies at the foundation of society, and successively creates all forms of worship. The principle of veneration never dies out. Man fallen into superstition, into sensuality, is never quite without the visions of the moral sentiment. In like manner, all the expressions of this sentiment are sacred and permanent in proportion to their purity. The expressions of this sentiment affect us more than all other compositions. The sentences of the oldest time, which ejaculate this piety, are still fresh and fragrant. This thought dwelled always deepest in the minds of men in the devout and contemplative East; not alone in Palestine, where it reached its purest expression, but in Egypt, in Persia, in India, in China. Europe has always owed to oriental genius its divine impulses. What these holy bards said, all sane men found agreeable and true. And the unique impression of Jesus upon mankind, whose name is not so much written as ploughed into the history of this world, is proof of the subtle virtue of this infusion.

Meantime, whilst the doors of the temple stand open, night and day, before every man, and the oracles of this truth cease never, it is guarded by one stern condition; this, namely; it is an intuition. It cannot be received at second hand. Truly speaking, it is not instruction, but provocation, that I can receive from another soul. What he announces, I must find true in me, or reject; and on his word, or as his second, be he who he may, I can accept nothing. On the contrary, the absence of this primary faith is the presence of degradation. As is the flood, so is the ebb. Let this faith depart, and the very words it spake and the things it made become false and hurtful. Then falls the church, the state, art, letters, life. The doctrine of the divine nature being forgotten, a sickness infects and dwarfs the constitution. Once man was all; now he is an appendage, a nuisance. And because the indwelling Supreme Spirit cannot wholly be got rid of, the doctrine of it suffers this perversion, that the divine nature is attributed to one or two persons, and denied to all the rest, and denied with fury. The doctrine of inspiration is lost; the base doctrine of the majority of voices usurps the place of the doctrine of the soul. Miracles, prophecy, poetry, the ideal life, the holy life, exist as ancient history merely; they are not in the belief, nor in the aspiration of society; but, when suggested, seem ridiculous. Life is comic or pitiful as soon as the high ends

of being fade out of sight, and man becomes near-sighted, and can
only attend to what addresses the senses.

These general views, which, whilst they are general, none will
contest, find abundant illustration in the history of religion, and
especially in the history of the Christian church. In that, all of us
have had our birth and nurture. The truth contained in that, you,
my young friends, are now setting forth to teach. As the Cultus,
or established worship of the civilized world, it has great historical
interest for us. Of its blessed words, which have been the consolation of humanity, you need not that I should speak. I shall endeavor to discharge my duty to you on this occasion, by pointing
out two errors in its administration, which daily appear more gross
from the point of view we have just now taken.

Jesus Christ belonged to the true race of prophets. He saw with
open eye the mystery of the soul. Drawn by its severe harmony,
ravished with its beauty, he lived in it, and had his being there.
Alone in all history he estimated the greatness of man. One man
was true to what is in you and me. He saw that God incarnates
himself in man, and evermore goes forth anew to take possession
of his World. He said, in this jubilee of sublime emotion, "I am
divine. Through me, God acts; through me, speaks. Would you
see God, see me; or see thee, when thou also thinkest as I now
think." But what a distortion did his doctrine and memory suffer
in the same, in the next, and the following ages! There is no doctrine of the Reason which will bear to be taught by the Understanding. The understanding caught this high chant from the
poet's lips, and said, in the next age, "This was Jehovah come
down out of heaven. I will kill you, if you say he was a man." The
idioms of his language and the figures of his rhetoric have usurped
the place of his truth; and churches are not built on his principles,
but on his tropes. Christianity became a Mythus, as the poetic
teaching of Greece and of Egypt, before. He spoke of miracles;
for he felt that man's life was a miracle, and all that man doth,
and he knew that this daily miracle shines as the character ascends.
But the word Miracle, as pronounced by Christian churches, gives
a false impression; it is Monster. It is not one with the blowing
clover and the falling rain.

He felt respect for Moses and the prophets, but no unfit tenderness at postponing their initial revelations to the hour and the man
that now is; to the eternal revelation in the heart. Thus was he a
true man. Having seen that the law in us is commanding, he would
not suffer it to be commanded. Boldly, with hand, and heart, and

life, he declared it was God. Thus is he, as I think, the only soul in history who has appreciated the worth of man.

(7. In this point of view we become sensible of the first defect of historical Christianity. Historical Christianity has fallen into the error that corrupts all attempts to communicate religion. As it appears to us, and as it has appeared for ages, it is not the doctrine of the soul, but an exaggeration of the personal, the positive, the ritual. It has dwelt, it dwells, with noxious exaggeration about the *person* of Jesus. The soul knows no persons. It invites every man to expand to the full circle of the universe, and will have no preferences but those of spontaneous love. But by this eastern monarchy of a Christianity, which indolence and fear have built, the friend of man is made the injurer of man. The manner in which his name is surrounded with expressions which were once sallies of admiration and love, but are now petrified into official titles, kills all generous sympathy and liking. All who hear me, feel that the language that describes Christ to Europe and America is not the style of friendship and enthusiasm to a good and noble heart, but is appropriated and formal, — paints a demigod, as the Orientals or the Greeks would describe Osiris or Apollo. Accept the injurious impositions of our early catechetical instruction, and even honesty and self-denial were but splendid sins, if they did not wear the Christian name. One would rather be

"A pagan, suckled in a creed outworn,"

than to be defrauded of his manly right in coming into nature and finding not names and places, not land and professions, but even virtue and truth foreclosed and monopolized. You shall not be a man even. You shall not own the world; you shall not dare and live after the infinite Law that is in you, and in company with the infinite Beauty which heaven and earth reflect to you in all lovely forms; but you must subordinate your nature to Christ's nature; you must accept our interpretations, and take his portrait as the vulgar draw it.

That is always best which gives me to myself. The sublime is excited in me by the great stoical doctrine, Obey thyself. That which shows God in me, fortifies me. That which shows God out of me, makes me a wart and a wen. There is no longer a necessary reason for my being. Already the long shadows of untimely oblivion creep over me, and I shall decease forever.

The divine bards are the friends of my virtue, of my intellect, of my strength. They admonish me that the gleams which flash across

my mind are not mine, but God's; that they had the like, and were
not disobedient to the heavenly vision. So I love them. Noble
provocations go out from them, inviting me to resist evil; to subdue the world; and to Be. And thus, by his holy thoughts, Jesus
serves us, and thus only. To aim to convert a man by miracles is
a profanation of the soul. A true conversion, a true Christ, is now,
as always, to be made by the reception of beautiful sentiments. It
is true that a great and rich soul, like his, falling among the simple,
does so preponderate, that, as his did, it names the world. The
world seems to them to exist for him, and they have not yet drunk
so deeply of his sense as to see that only by coming again to themselves, or to God in themselves, can they grow forevermore. It
is a low benefit to give me something; it is a high benefit to enable me to do somewhat of myself. The time is coming when all
men will see that the gift of God to the soul is not a vaunting,
overpowering, excluding sanctity, but a sweet, natural goodness, a
goodness like thine and mine, and that so invites thine and mine to
be and to grow.

The injustice of the vulgar tone of preaching is not less flagrant
to Jesus than to the souls which it profanes. The preachers do not
see that they make his gospel not glad, and shear him of the locks
of beauty and the attributes of heaven. When I see a majestic
Epaminondas, or Washington; when I see among my contemporaries a true orator, an upright judge, a dear friend; when I vibrate to
the melody and fancy of a poem; I see beauty that is to be desired.
And so lovely, and with yet more entire consent of my human
being, sounds in my ear the severe music of the bards that have
sung of the true God in all ages. Now do not degrade the life and
dialogues of Christ out of the circle of this charm, by insulation
and peculiarity. Let them lie as they befell, alive and warm, part
of human life and of the landscape and of the cheerful day.

2. The second defect of the traditionary and limited way of using the mind of Christ is a consequence of the first; this, namely;
that the Moral Nature, that Law of laws whose revelations introduce greatness — yea, God himself — into the open soul, is not
explored as the fountain of the established teaching in society.
Men have come to speak of the revelation as somewhat long ago
given and done, as if God were dead. The injury to faith throttles
the preacher; and the goodliest of institutions becomes an uncertain and inarticulate voice.

It is very certain that it is the effect of conversation with the
beauty of the soul, to beget a desire and need to impart to others

the same knowledge and love. If utterance is denied, the thought lies like a burden on the man. Always the seer is a sayer. Somehow his dream is told; somehow he publishes it with solemn joy: sometimes with pencil on canvas, sometimes with chisel on stone, sometimes in towers and aisles of granite, his soul's worship is builded; sometimes in anthems of indefinite music; but clearest and most permanent, in words.

The man enamored of this excellency becomes its priest or poet. The office is coeval with the world. But observe the condition, the spiritual limitation of the office. The spirit only can teach. Not any profane man, not any sensual, not any liar, not any slave can teach, but only he can give, who has; he only can create, who is. The man on whom the soul descends, through whom the soul speaks, alone can teach. Courage, piety, love, wisdom, can teach; and every man can open his door to these angels, and they shall bring him the gift of tongues. But the man who aims to speak as books enable, as synods use, as the fashion guides, and as interest commands, babbles. Let him hush.

To this holy office you propose to devote yourselves. I wish you may feel your call in throbs of desire and hope. The office is the first in the world. It is of that reality that it cannot suffer the deduction of any falsehood. And it is my duty to say to you that the need was never greater of new revelation than now. From the views I have already expressed, you will infer the sad conviction, which I share, I believe, with numbers, of the universal decay and now almost death of faith in society. The soul is not preached. The Church seems to totter to its fall, almost all life extinct. On this occasion, any complaisance would be criminal which told you, whose hope and commission it is to preach the faith of Christ, that the faith of Christ is preached.

It is time that this ill-suppressed murmur of all thoughtful men against the famine of our churches; — this moaning of the heart because it is bereaved of the consolation, the hope, the grandeur that come alone out of the culture of the moral nature, — should be heard through the sleep of indolence, and over the din of routine. This great and perpetual office of the preacher is not discharged. Preaching is the expression of the moral sentiment in application to the duties of life. In how many churches, by how many prophets, tell me, is man made sensible that he is an infinite Soul; that the earth and heavens are passing into his mind; that he is drinking forever the soul of God? Where now sounds the persuasion, that by its very melody imparadises my heart, and so affirms its own origin in heaven? Where shall I hear words such as in elder ages drew men to leave all and follow, — father and mother, house and land, wife and child? Where shall I hear these august laws of moral being so pronounced as to fill my ear, and I feel ennobled by the offer of my uttermost action and passion? The test of the true faith, certainly, should be its power to charm and command the soul, as the laws of nature control the activity of the hands, — so commanding that we find pleasure and honor in obeying. The faith should blend with the light of rising and of setting suns, with the flying cloud, the singing bird, and the breath of flowers. But now the priest's Sabbath has lost the splendor of nature; it is unlovely; we are glad when it is done; we can make, we do make, even sitting in our pews, a far better, holier, sweeter, for ourselves.

Whenever the pulpit is usurped by a formalist, then is the worshipper defrauded and disconsolate. We shrink as soon as the prayers begin, which do not uplift, but smite and offend us. We are fain to wrap our cloaks about us, and secure, as best we can, a solitude that hears not. I once heard a preacher who sorely tempted me to say I would go to church no more. Men go, thought I, where they are wont to go, else had no soul entered the temple in the afternoon. A snow-storm was falling around us. The snow-storm was real, the preacher merely spectral, and the eye felt the sad contrast in looking at him, and then out of the window behind him into the beautiful meteor of the snow. He had lived in vain. He had no one word intimating that he had laughed or wept, was married or in love, had been commended, or cheated, or chagrined. If he had ever lived and acted, we were none the wiser for it. The capital secret of his profession, namely, to convert life into truth, he had not learned. Not one fact in all his experience had he yet imported into his doctrine. This man had ploughed and planted and talked and bought and sold; he had read books; he had eaten and drunken; his head aches, his heart throbs; he smiles and suffers; yet was there not a surmise, a hint, in all the discourse, that he had ever lived at all. Not a line did he draw out of real history. The true preacher can be known by this, that he deals out to the people his life, — life passed through the fire of thought. But of the bad preacher, it could not be told from his sermon what age of the world he fell in; whether he had a father or a child; whether he was a freeholder or a pauper; whether he was a citizen or a countryman; or any other fact of his biography. It seemed strange that the people should come to church. It seemed as if their houses were very unentertaining, that they should prefer this thoughtless clamor. It shows that there is a commanding attraction in the moral sentiment, that can lend a faint tint of light to dulness and ignorance coming in its name and place. The good hearer is sure he has been touched sometimes; is sure there is somewhat to be reached, and some word that can reach it. When he listens to these vain words, he comforts himself by their relation to his remembrance of better hours, and so they clatter and echo unchallenged.

I am not ignorant that when we preach unworthily, it is not always quite in vain. There is a good ear, in some men, that draws supplies to virtue out of very indifferent nutriment. There is poetic truth concealed in all the commonplaces of prayer and of sermons, and though foolishly spoken, they may be wisely heard; for each is some select expression that broke out in a moment of piety from some stricken or jubilant soul, and its excellency made it remembered. The prayers and even the dogmas of our church are like the zodiac of Denderah [5] and the astronomical monuments of the Hindus, wholly insulated from anything now extant in the life and business of the people. They mark the height to which the waters once rose. But this docility is a check upon the mischief from the good and devout. In a large portion of the community, the religious service gives rise to quite other thoughts and emotions. We need not chide the negligent servant. We are struck with pity, rather, at the swift retribution of his sloth. Alas for the unhappy man that is called to stand in the pulpit, and not give bread of life. Everything that befalls, accuses him. Would he ask contributions for the missions, foreign or domestic? Instantly his face is suffused with shame, to propose to his parish that they should send money a hundred or a thousand miles, to furnish such poor fare as they have at home and would do well to go the hundred or the thousand miles to escape. Would he urge people to a godly way of living; — and can he ask a fellow-creature to come to Sabbath meetings, when he and they all know what is the poor uttermost they can hope for therein? Will he invite them privately to the Lord's Supper? He dares not. If no heart warm this rite, the hollow, dry, creaking formality is too plain, than that he can face a man of wit and energy and put the invitation without terror. In the street, what has he to say to the bold village blasphemer? The village blasphemer sees fear in the face, form, and gait of the minister.

[5] Ancient Egyptian table of zodiacal signs.

Let me not taint the sincerity of this plea by any oversight of the claims of good men. I know and honor the purity and strict conscience of numbers of the clergy. What life the public worship retains, it owes to the scattered company of pious men, who minister here and there in the churches, and who, sometimes accepting with too great tenderness the tenet of the elders, have not accepted from others, but from their own heart, the genuine impulses of virtue, and so still command our love and awe, to the sanctity of character. Moreover, the exceptions are not so much to be found in a few eminent preachers, as in the better hours, the truer inspirations of all, — nay, in the sincere moments of every man. But, with whatever exception, it is still true that tradition characterizes the preaching of this country; that it comes out of the memory, and not out of the soul; that it aims at what is usual, and not at what is necessary and eternal; that thus historical Christianity destroys the power of preaching, by withdrawing it from the exploration of the moral nature of man; where the sublime is, where are the resources of astonishment and power. What a cruel injustice it is to that Law, the joy of the whole earth, which alone can make thought dear and rich; that Law whose fatal sureness the astronomical orbits poorly emulate; — that it is travestied and depreciated, that it is behooted and behowled, and not a trait, not a word of it articulated. The pulpit in losing sight of this Law, loses its reason, and gropes after it knows not what. And for want of this culture the soul of the community is sick and faithless. It wants nothing so much as a stern, high, stoical, Christian discipline, to make it know itself and the divinity that speaks through it. Now man is ashamed of himself; he skulks and sneaks through the world, to be tolerated, to be pitied, and scarcely in a thousand years does any man dare to be wise and good, and so draw after him the tears and blessings of his kind.

Certainly there have been periods when, from the inactivity of the intellect on certain truths, a greater faith was possible in names and persons. The Puritans in England and America found in the Christ of the Catholic Church and in the dogmas inherited from Rome, scope for their austere piety and their longings for civil freedom. But their creed is passing away, and none arises in its room. I think no man can go with his thoughts about him into one of our churches, without feeling that what hold the public worship had on men is gone, or going. It has lost its grasp on the affection of the good and the fear of the bad. In the country, neighborhoods, half parishes are *signing off*, to use the local term.

It is already beginning to indicate character and religion to withdraw from the religious meetings. I have heard a devout person,
who prized the Sabbath, say in bitterness of heart, "On Sundays,
it seems wicked to go to church." And the motive that holds the
best there is now only a hope and a waiting. What was once a
mere circumstance, that the best and the worst men in the parish,
the poor and the rich, the learned and the ignorant, young and old,
should meet one day as fellows in one house, in sign of an equal
right in the soul, has come to be a paramount motive for going
thither.

My friends, in these two errors, I think, I find the causes of a
decaying church and a wasting unbelief. And what greater calamity can fall upon a nation than the loss of worship? Then all things
go to decay. Genius leaves the temple to haunt the senate or the
market. Literature becomes frivolous. Science is cold. The eye
of youth is not lighted by the hope of other worlds, and age is
without honor. Society lives to trifles, and when men die we do
not mention them.

And now, my brothers, you will ask, What in these desponding
days can be done by us? The remedy is already declared in the
ground of our complaint of the Church. We have contrasted the
Church with the Soul. In the soul then let the redemption be
sought. Wherever a man comes, there comes revolution. The
old is for slaves. When a man comes, all books are legible, all
things transparent, all religions are forms. He is religious. Man
is the wonderworker. He is seen amid miracles. All men bless and
curse. He saith yea and nay, only. The stationariness of religion;
the assumption that the age of inspiration is past, that the Bible
is closed; the fear of degrading the character of Jesus by representing him as a man; — indicate with sufficient clearness the falsehood of our theology. It is the office of a true teacher to show
us that God is, not was; that He speaketh, not spake. The true
Christianity, — a faith like Christ's in the infinitude of man, —
is lost. None believeth in the soul of man, but only in some man
or person old and departed. Ah me! no man goeth alone. All
men go in flocks to this saint or that poet, avoiding the God who
seeth in secret. They cannot see in secret; they love to be blind
in public. They think society wiser than their soul, and know not
that one soul, and their soul, is wiser than the whole world. See
how nations and races flit by on the sea of time and leave no
ripple to tell where they floated or sunk, and one good soul shall
make the name of Moses, or of Zeno, or of Zoroaster, reverend

forever. None assayeth the stern ambition to be the Self of the nation and of nature, but each would be an easy secondary to some Christian scheme, or sectarian connection, or some eminent man. Once leave your own knowledge of God, your own sentiment, and take secondary knowledge, as St. Paul's, or George Fox's, or Swedenborg's, and you get wide from God with every year this secondary form lasts, and if, as now, for centuries, — the chasm yawns to that breadth, that men can scarcely be convinced there is in them anything divine.

Let me admonish you, first of all, to go alone; to refuse the good models, even those which are sacred in the imagination of men, and dare to love God without mediator or veil. Friends enough you shall find who will hold up to your emulation Wesleys and Oberlins, Saints and Prophets. Thank God for these good men, but say, "I also am a man." Imitation cannot go above its model. The imitator dooms himself to hopeless mediocrity. The inventor did it because it was natural to him, and so in him it has a charm. In the imitator something else is natural, and he bereaves himself of his own beauty, to come short of another man's.

Yourself a newborn bard of the Holy Ghost, cast behind you all conformity, and acquaint men at first hand with Deity. Look to it first and only, that fashion, custom, authority, pleasure, and money, are nothing to you, — are not bandages over your eyes, that you cannot see, — but live with the privilege of the immeasurable mind. Not too anxious to visit periodically all families and each family in your parish connection, — when you meet one of these men or women, be to them a divine man; be to them thought and virtue; let their timid aspirations find in you a friend; let their trampled instincts be genially tempted out in your atmosphere; let their doubts know that you have doubted, and their wonder feel that you have wondered. By trusting your own heart, you shall gain more confidence in other men. For all our penny-wisdom, for all our soul-destroying slavery to habit, it is not to be doubted that all men have sublime thoughts; that all men value the few real hours of life; they love to be heard; they love to be caught up into the vision of principles. We mark with light in the memory the few interviews we have had, in the dreary years of routine and of sin, with souls that made our souls wiser; that spoke what we thought; that told us what we knew; that gave us leave to be what we inly were. Discharge to men the priestly office, and, present or absent, you shall be followed with their love as by an angel.

And, to this end, let us not aim at common degrees of merit.

Can we not leave, to such as love it, the virtue that glitters for the commendation of society, and ourselves pierce the deep solitudes of absolute ability and worth? We easily come up to the standard of goodness in society. Society's praise can be cheaply secured, and almost all men are content with those easy merits; but the instant effect of conversing with God will be to put them away. There are persons who are not actors, not speakers, but influences; persons too great for fame, for display; who disdain eloquence; to whom all we call art and artist, seems too nearly allied to show and by-ends, to the exaggeration of the finite and selfish, and loss of the universal. The orators, the poets, the commanders encroach on us only as fair women do, by our allowance and homage. Slight them by preoccupation of mind, slight them, as you can well afford to do, by high and universal aims, and they instantly feel that you have right, and that it is in lower places that they must shine. They also feel your right; for they with you are open to the influx of the all-knowing Spirit, which annihilates before its broad noon the little shades and gradations of intelligence in the compositions we call wiser and wisest.

In such high communion let us study the grand strokes of rectitude: a bold benevolence, an independence of friends, so that not the unjust wishes of those who love us shall impair our freedom, but we shall resist for truth's sake the freest flow of kindness, and appeal to sympathies far in advance; and, — what is the highest form in which we know this beautiful element, — a certain solidity of merit, that has nothing to do with opinion, and which is so essentially and manifestly virtue, that it is taken for granted that the right, the brave, the generous step will be taken by it, and nobody thinks of commending it. You would compliment a coxcomb doing a good act, but you would not praise an angel. The silence that accepts merit as the most natural thing in the world, is the highest applause. Such souls, when they appear, are the Imperial Guard of Virtue, the perpetual reserve, the dictators of fortune. One needs not praise their courage, — they are the heart and soul of nature. O my friends, there are resources in us on which we have not drawn. There are men who rise refreshed on hearing a threat; men to whom a crisis which intimidates and paralyzes the majority, — demanding not the faculties of prudence and thrift, but comprehension, immovableness, the readiness of sacrifice, — comes graceful and beloved as a bride. Napoleon said of Massena, that he was not himself until the battle began to go against him; then, when the dead began to fall in ranks around

him, awoke his powers of combination, and he put on terror and
victory as a robe. So it is in rugged crises, in unwearieable endurance, and in aims which put sympathy out of question, that the
angel is shown. But these are heights that we can scarce remember and look up to without contrition and shame. Let us thank
God that such things exist.

And now let us do what we can to rekindle the smouldering,
nigh quenched fire on the altar. The evils of the church that now
is are manifest. The question returns, What shall we do? I confess,
all attempts to project and establish a Cultus with new rites and
forms, seem to me vain. Faith makes us, and not we it, and faith
makes its own forms. All attempts to contrive a system are as cold
as the new worship introduced by the French to the goddess of
Reason, — today, pasteboard and filigree, and ending tomorrow in
madness and murder. Rather let the breath of new life be breathed
by you through the forms already existing. For if once you are
alive, you shall find they shall become plastic and new. The
remedy to their deformity is first, soul, and second, soul, and
evermore, soul. A whole popedom of forms one pulsation of virtue
can uplift and vivify. Two inestimable advantages Christianity has
given us; first the Sabbath, the jubilee of the whole world, whose
light dawns welcome alike into the closet of the philosopher, into
the garret of toil, and into prison-cells, and everywhere suggests,
even to the vile, the dignity of spiritual being. Let it stand forevermore, a temple, which new love, new faith, new sight shall restore
to more than its first splendor to mankind. And secondly, the
institution of preaching, — the speech of man to men, — essentially the most flexible of all organs, of all forms. What hinders
that now, everywhere, in pulpits, in lecture-rooms, in houses, in
fields, wherever the invitation of men or your own occasions lead
you, you speak the very truth, as your life and conscience teach it,
and cheer the waiting, fainting hearts of men with new hope and
new revelation?

I look for the hour when that supreme Beauty which ravished
the souls of those Eastern men, and chiefly of those Hebrews, and
through their lips spoke oracles to all time, shall speak in the West
also. The Hebrew and Greek Scriptures contain immortal sentences, that have been bread of life to millions. But they have no
epical integrity; are fragmentary; are not shown in their order to
the intellect. I look for the new Teacher that shall follow so far
those shining laws that he shall see them come full circle; shall
see their rounding complete grace; shall see the world to be the

mirror of the soul; shall see the identity of the law of gravitation with purity of heart; and shall show that the Ought, that Duty, is one thing with Science, with Beauty, and with Joy.

August 31, 1838

Yesterday at Phi Beta Kappa anniversary. Steady, steady. I am convinced that if a man will be a true scholar, he shall have perfect freedom. The young people and the mature hint at odium, and aversion of faces to be presently encountered in society. I say, No: I fear it not. No scholar need fear it. For if it be true that he is merely an observer, a dispassionate reporter, no partisan, a singer merely for the love of music, his is a position of perfect immunity. . . .

Who are these murmurers, these haters, these revilers? Men of no knowledge, and therefore no stability. The scholar, on the contrary, is sure of his point, is fast-rooted, and can securely predict the hour when all this roaring multitude shall roar for him. Analyze the chiding opposition, and it is made up of such timidities, uncertainties and no opinions, that it is not worth dispersing.

September 30 ?, 1838

It seems as if a man should learn to fish, to plant, or to hunt, that he might secure his subsistence if he were cast out from society and not be painful to his friends and fellow men.

To Henry Ware, Jr.

October 8, 1838

. . . It strikes me very oddly and even a little ludicrously that the good and great men of Cambridge should think of raising me into an object of criticism. I have always been from my very incapacity of methodical writing a chartered libertine, free to worship and free to rail, lucky when I was understood but never esteemed near enough to the institutions and mind of society to deserve the notice of the masters of literature and religion. I have appreciated fully the advantage of my position, for I well knew that there was no scholar less willing or less able to be a polemic. I could not give account of myself if challenged. I could not possibly give you one of the "arguments" on which, as you cruelly hint, any position of mine stands. For I do not know, I confess, what arguments mean in reference to any expression of a thought.

I delight in telling what I think, but if you ask me how I dare say so or why it is so I am the most helpless of mortal men; I see not even that either of these questions admit of an answer. So that in the present droll posture of my affairs, when I see myself suddenly raised into the importance of a heretic, I am very uneasy if I advert to the supposed duties of such a personage, who is expected to make good his thesis against all comers. I therefore tell you plainly I shall do no such thing. I shall read what you and other good men write as I have always done, glad when you speak my thought and skipping the page that has nothing for me. I shall go on just as before, seeing whatever I can and telling what I see, and I suppose with the same fortune as has hitherto attended me, the joy of finding that my abler and better brothers, who work with the sympathy of society and love it, unexpectedly confirm my perceptions, and find my nonsense is only their own thought in motley.

October 8 ?, 1838

Compensation. — How soon the sunk spirits rise again, how quick the little wounds of fortune skin over and are forgotten. I am sensitive as a leaf to impressions from abroad, and under this night's beautiful heaven I have forgotten that ever I was *reviewed.* It is strange how superficial are our views of these matters, seeing we are all writers and philosophers. A man thinks it of importance what the great sheet or pamphlet of today proclaims of him to all the reading town; and if he sees graceful compliments, he relishes his dinner; and if he sees threatening paragraphs and odious nicknames, it becomes a solemn, depressing fact and sables his whole thoughts until bedtime. But in truth the effect of these paragraphs is mathematically measurable by their depth of thought. How much water do they draw? If they awaken you to think — if they lift you from your feet with the great voice of eloquence — then their effect is to be wide, slow, permanent over the minds of men: but if they instruct you not, they will die like flies in an hour.

October 10 ?, 1838

A *Fact.* — In our vulgar politics the knowing men have a good deal to say about the "moral effect" of a victory and a defeat. The fact that the city of New York has gone for the Whigs, though only by a slender majority, is of the utmost importance to the Whig party about to vote in a distant state. Why? be-

cause it is a fact, a presentable fact. States of mind we care not
for; we ignore them; but a mere fact, though proving a less favorable state of mind than we have a right to infer, we overvalue.
A man writes a book which displeases somebody, who writes an
angry paragraph about it in the next newspaper. That solitary
paragraph, whilst it stands unanswered, seems the voice of the
world. Hundreds of passive readers read it with such passiveness
that it becomes their voice. The man that made the book and
his friends are superstitious about it. They cannot put it out of
their heads. Their entire relations to society seem changed.
What was yesterday a warm, convenient, hospitable world, solicit-
ing all the talents of all its children, looks bleak and hostile, and
our native tendency to complete any view we take carries the imagination out at once to images of persecution, hatred and want.

In debate, the last speaker always carries with him such a prevailing air that all seems to be over and the question settled when
he concludes; so that, if a new man arise and state with nonchalance a new and opposite view, we draw our breath freely
and hear with a marked surprise this suspension of fate.

An election, the fact of having been elected to a conspicuous
office, as President, King, Governor, etc., even though we know
the paltry machinery by which it was brought about, is, notwithstanding, a certificate of value to the person in *all* men's eyes, ever
after.

The courage of men is shown in resisting this *fact* and preferring the *state of mind*. The poet must set over against the lam-
poon his conviction of divine light, the patriot his deep devotion
to the country against the mere hurrah of the boys in the street.

October 12, 1838

It seems not unfit that the scholar should deal plainly with society and tell them that he saw well enough before he spoke the
consequence of his speaking, that up there in his silent study, by
his dim lamp, he fore-heard this Babel of outcries. The nature
of man he knew, the insanity that comes of inaction and tradition, and knew well that when their dream and routine were
disturbed, like bats and owls and nocturnal beasts they would
howl and shriek and fly at the torch-bearer. But he saw plainly
that under this their distressing disguise of bird-form and beast-
form, the divine features of man were hidden, and he felt that
he would dare to be so much their friend as to do them this violence to drag them to the day and to the healthy air and water

of God, that the unclean spirits that had possessed them might be exorcised and depart. The taunts and cries of hatred and anger, the very epithets you bestow on me, are so familiar long ago in my reading that they sound to me ridiculously old and stale. The same thing has happened so many times over (that is, with the appearance of every original observer) that, if people were not very ignorant of literary history, they would be struck with the exact coincidence. I, whilst I see this, that you must have been shocked and must cry out at what I have said, I see too that we cannot easily be reconciled, for I have a great deal more to say that will shock you out of all patience. Every day I am struck with new particulars of the antagonism between your habits of thought and action, and the divine law of your being, and as fast as these become clear to me you may depend on my proclaiming them.

October 19, 1838

It is a poor-spirited age. The great army of cowards who bellow and bully from their bed-chamber windows have no confidence in truth or God. Truth will not maintain itself, they fancy, unless they bolster it up, and whip and stone the assailants; and the religion of God, the being of God, they seem to think dependent on what we say of it. The feminine vehemence with which the A[ndrews] N[orton] of the *Daily Advertiser* beseeches the dear people to whip that naughty heretic is the natural feeling in the mind whose religion is external. It cannot subsist; it suffers shipwreck if its faith is not confirmed by all surrounding persons. A believer, a mind whose faith is consciousness, is never disturbed because other persons do not yet see the fact which he sees.

It is plain that there are two classes in our educated community: first, those who confine themselves to the facts in their consciousness; and secondly, those who superadd sundry propositions. The aim of a true teacher now would be to bring men back to a trust in God and destroy before their eyes these idolatrous propositions: to teach the doctrine of the perpetual revelation.

October 20, 1838

Steady, steady! When this fog of good and evil affections falls, it is hard to see and walk straight.

. . . It is plain from all the noise that there is atheism somewhere; the only question is now, Which is the atheist?

October 30, 1838

There is no terror like that of being known. The world lies in night of sin. It hears not the cock crowing: it sees not the grey streak in the East. At the first entering ray of light, society is shaken with fear and anger from side to side. Who opened that shutter? they cry, Wo to him! They belie it, they call it darkness that comes in, affirming that they were in light before. Before the man who has spoken to them the dread word, they tremble and flee. They flee to new topics, to their learning, to the solid institutions about them, to their great men, to their windows, and look-out on the road and passengers, to their very furniture, and meats, and drinks, — anywhere, anyhow to escape the apparition. The wild horse has heard the whisper of the Tamer: the maniac has caught the glance of the Keeper. They try to forget the memory of the speaker, to put him down into the same obscure place he occupied in their minds before he spoke to them. It is all in vain. They even flatter themselves that they have killed and buried the enemy, when they have magisterially denied and denounced him. But vain, vain, all vain. It was but the first mutter of the distant storm they heard, — it was the first cry of the Revolution, — it was the touch, the palpitation that goes before the Earthquake. Even now society is shaken because a thought or two have been thrown into the midst. The sects, the colleges, the church, the statesmen all have forebodings. It now works only in a handful. What does State Street and Wall Street and the Royal Exchange and the Bourse at Paris care for these few thoughts and these few men? Very little; truly; most truly. But the doom of State Street, and Wall Street, of London, and France, of the whole world, is advertised by those thoughts; is in the procession of the Soul which comes after those few thoughts.

October 31, 1838

When I look at life, and see the snatches of thought, the gleams of goodness here and there amid the wide and wild madness, I seem to be a god dreaming; and when shall I awake and dissipate these fumes and phantoms? [6]

November 8, 1838

Let me never fall into the vulgar mistake of dreaming that I am persecuted, whenever I am contradicted. No man, I think, had ever a greater well-being with a less desert than I. I can

[6] The poem "Uriel" (p. 426), an allegorical comment on the *Address* and its reception, should be read in connection with these passages.

very well afford to be accounted bad or foolish by a few dozen
or a few hundred persons, — I who see myself greeted by the good
expectation of so many friends far beyond any power of thought
or communication of thought residing in me. Besides, I own, I
am often inclined to take part with those who say I am bad or
foolish, for I fear I am both. I believe and know there must be
a perfect compensation. I know too well my own dark spots. Not
having myself attained, not satisfied myself, far from a holy obedience, — how can I expect to satisfy others, to command their
love? A few sour faces, a few biting paragraphs, — is but a cheap
expiation for all these shortcomings of mine.

June 6, 1839

My life is a May game, I will live as I like. I defy your straitlaced, weary, social ways and modes. Blue is the sky, green the
fields and groves, fresh the springs, glad the rivers, and hospitable
the splendor of sun and star. I will play my game out. And if any
shall say me nay, shall come out with swords and staves against me
to prick me to death for their foolish laws, — come and welcome.
I will not look grave for such a fool's matter. I cannot lose my
cheer for such trumpery. Life is a May game still.

From SAADI [7]

Whispered the Muse in Saadi's cot:
"O gentle Saadi, listen not,
Tempted by thy praise of wit,
Or by thirst and appetite
For the talents not thine own,
To sons of contradiction.
Never, son of eastern morning,
Follow falsehood, follow scorning.
Denounce who will, who will deny,
And pile the hills to scale the sky;
Let theist, atheist, pantheist,
Define and wrangle how they list,
Fierce conserver, fierce destroyer, —
But thou, joy-giver and enjoyer,
Unknowing war, unknowing crime,
Gentle Saadi, mind thy rhyme;
Heed not what the brawlers say,
Heed thou only Saadi's lay. . . ."

1842

[7] A Persian poet. Here: the Poet.

1839–1840

Society and Solitude

Emerson asserted his solitude so often that we tend to overlook
his remarkable circle of friends. Not to speak of Carlyle and
Sterling overseas, it now included two of the most extraordinary
men in America, "my brave Henry" Thoreau and the unique
Bronson Alcott. Ellery Channing, also, sublimo-slipshod poet and
nephew to the great Unitarian leader, was a lively companion for
a walk. With Elizabeth Hoar, fair-minded daughter of his upright
neighbor, Samuel Hoar, and former fiancée of Charles, he had
formed a "beautiful relation." At a somewhat greater distance yet
more disturbing were the imperious Margaret Fuller and her
galaxy of friends, bright spirits like Ellen and Caroline Sturgis,
the beauty Anna Barker, who was to flutter the Transcendental
dovecotes by turning Catholic, and the brilliant man she married,
Samuel Gray Ward.

Emerson's observation of this "magic circle" was both warm
and acute. Though he never wrote his intended essay on Alcott,
a fine portrait can be put together from the journals: an extended sketch of him as he was before leaving for England
in 1842, comments on the tragi-comic fiasco at Fruitlands in 1843,
and tributes to his true greatness, which no one saw so well as
Emerson, for all the tedium and foolishness. A similar skill in
portraiture is shown in the comments on Margaret Fuller, as in
the later private comments on the death of Hawthorne, or the
public eulogy of Thoreau.[1]

But Emerson was no mere cold onlooker, though he may have
seemed so. He valued the life of the affections all the more because he was himself helplessly barred from it in face-to-face rela-

[1] See pp. 379 and 403.

tions. He found the necessary relief and consolation for his "shrinking" and "freezing" in an austerely platonic theory of friendship which held that love for persons was initial only, while the true object of love was "the eternal"; yet he was not satisfied so, but agitated himself writing "romances of letters" in which he opened some of his heart, as he rarely could in conversation. The essay "Friendship," apparently so lonely, is redolent with his troubled pleasure at these actual "thought-exchanges."

Beyond their immediate circle, Emerson and his friends found themselves caught up in a wider movement toward awakening and reform which acquired, no one knew quite how, the clumsy label Transcendentalism. Manifestations were the so-called Transcendental Club, a group of liberal thinkers, dissatisfied with the still reigning empiricism, rationalism, and realism, who met irregularly, sometimes at Emerson's, to discuss philosophic issues; the opening of Brook Farm in 1840 by George Ripley and others as a community where the routine and drudgery of ordinary life would be relieved and a happier combination of manual labor and intellectual culture be made possible for each; and the founding of The Dial in 1840 as a publication to speak for the new movement. Emerson wrote the preface to the first number, contributed often, and in 1843 took over the editorship from Margaret Fuller until it failed for want of support in 1844.

Meanwhile he continued to record his daily reflections in his journals and to report them in lectures. They proceed on lines previously laid down, for the most part, though a new awareness of flowing begins to make itself felt — the "onward" of nature, of time, of even the most stable thoughts. The enterprise of life, we begin to feel, is less to capture the Pegasus of our inner power and more to ride our whole nature, as equestrians in a circus balance on two horses at once. At the beginning of 1841 Emerson sent to press his first book of Essays, a distillation of his work of the past five years. A hint of the same shift of viewpoint is apparent between the essay "Self-Reliance," in great part an anthology of passages on this pole-star of his inner life from the earlier journals and lectures, and "Circles," largely written in 1840. To sketch arcs of a circle, as these essays do, is to define a starting point, he realizes, not a conclusion.

To Thomas Carlyle

May 10, 1838

. . . In aid of your friendliest purpose,[2] I will set down some of the facts. I occupy, or *improve*, as we Yankees say, two acres only of God's earth; on which is my house, my kitchen-garden, my orchard of thirty young trees, my empty barn. My house is now a very good one for comfort, and abounding in room. Besides my house, I have, I believe, $22,000, whose income in ordinary years is six per cent. I have no other tithe or glebe except the income of my winter lectures, which was last winter $800. Well, with this income, here at home, I am a rich man. I stay at home and go abroad at my own instance. I have food, warmth, leisure, books, friends. Go away from home, I am rich no longer. I never have a dollar to spend on a fancy. As no wise man, I suppose, ever was rich in the sense of *freedom to spend*, because of the inundation of claims, so neither am I, who am not wise. But at home, I am rich, — rich enough for ten brothers. My wife Lidian is an incarnation of Christianity, — I call her Asia, — and keeps my philosophy from Antinomianism; my mother, whitest, mildest, most conservative of ladies, whose only exception to her universal preference for old things is her son; my boy, a piece of love and sunshine, well worth my watching from morning to night; — these, and three domestic women, who cook and sew and run for us, make all my household. Here I sit and read and write, with very little system, and, as far as regards composition, with the most fragmentary result: paragraphs incompressible, each sentence an infinitely repellent particle.

In summer, with the aid of a neighbor, I manage my garden; and a week ago I set out on the west side of my house forty young pine trees to protect me or my son from the wind of January. The ornament of the place is the occasional presence of some ten or twelve persons, good and wise, who visit us in the course of the year. . . .

March 13, 1839

Conversation. — The office of conversation is to give me self-possession. I lie torpid as a clod. Virtue, wisdom, sound to me fabulous, — all cant. I am an unbeliever. Then comes by a safe and gentle spirit who spreads out in order before me his own life and aims, not as experience, but as the good and desirable. Straightway I feel the presence of a new and yet old, a genial, a

---

[2] Carlyle was talking of coming to America.

native element. I am like a Southerner, who, having spent the
winter in a polar climate, feels at last the south wind blow, the
rigid fibers relax, and his whole frame expands to the welcome
heats. In this bland, flowing atmosphere, I regain, one by one,
my faculties, my organs; life returns to a finger, a hand, a foot.
A new nimbleness — almost wings — unfold at my side, and I
see my right to the heaven as well as to the farthest fields of the
earth. The effect of the conversation resembles the effect of a
beautiful voice in a church choir . . . , which insinuates itself as
water into all chinks and cracks and presently floats the whole
discordant choir and holds it in solution in its melody. Well, I
too am a ship aground, and the bard directs a river to my shoals,
relieves me of these perilous rubs and strains, and at last fairly up-
lifts me on the waters, and I put forth my sails, and turn my head
to the sea. Alcott is the only majestic converser I now meet. He
gives me leave to be, more than all others. Alcott is so apprehensive that he does not need to be learned.

Amos Bronson Alcott[3]

May 19, 1837

Yesterday Alcott left me after three days spent here. I had
"lain down a man and waked up a bruise," by reason of a bad
cold, and was lumpish, tardy and cold. Yet could I see plainly
that I conversed with the most extraordinary man and the highest genius of the time. He is a Man. He is erect; he sees; let
whoever be overthrown or parasitic or blind. Life he would have,
and enact, and not nestle into any cast-off shell and form of the
old time; and now proposes to preach to the people, or to take
his staff and walk through the country conversing with the school-
teachers, and holding conversations in the villages. And so he
ought to go publishing through the land his gospel, like them of
old times. Wonderful is his vision; the steadiness and scope of
his eye at once rebukes all before it, and we little men creep about
ashamed. It is amusing even to see how this great visual orb rolls
round upon object after object, and threatens them all with annihilation, — seemeth to wither and scorch.

[3] The series of entries which follows brings together some of the materials
Emerson could have drawn on for his contemplated essay on Alcott. The title
is supplied by the editor.

Coldly he asks "whether Milton is to continue to meet the wants of the mind?" and so Bacon, and so of all. He is, to be sure, monotonous; you may say, one gets tired of the uniformity, — he will not be amused, he never cares for the pleasant side of things, but always truth and their origin he seeketh after.

Autumn, 1840

I shed all influences. A[lcott] is a tedious archangel. . . .

October 19, 1841 ?

. . . This noble genius discredits genius to me. I do not want any more such persons to exist.

March, 1842

Here prepares now the good Alcott to go to England, after so long and strict acquaintance as I have had with him for seven years. I saw him for the first time in Boston in 1835.

What shall we say of him to the wise Englishman?

He is a man of ideas, a man of faith. Expect contempt for all usages which are simply such. His social nature and his taste for beauty and magnificence will betray him into tolerance and indulgence, even, to men and to magnificence, but a statute or a practice he is condemned to measure by its essential wisdom or folly.

He delights in speculation, in nothing so much, and is very well endowed and weaponed for that work with a copious, accurate and elegant vocabulary; I may say poetic; so that I know no man who speaks such good English as he, and is so inventive withal. He speaks truth truly; or the expression is adequate. Yet he knows only this one language. He hardly needs an antagonist, — he needs only an intelligent ear. Where he is greeted by loving and intelligent persons, his discourse soars to a wonderful height, so regular, so lucid, so playful, so new and disdainful of all boundaries of tradition and experience, that the hearers seem no longer to have bodies or material gravity, but almost they can mount into the air at pleasure, or leap at one bound out of this poor solar system. I say this of his speech exclusively, for when he attempts to write, he loses, in my judgment, all his power, and I derive more pain than pleasure from the perusal. The *Boston Post* expresses the feeling of most readers in its rude joke, when it said of his *Orphic Sayings* [4] that they "resembled

4 Contributed to *The Dial*, July, 1840, and January, 1841.

a train of fifteen railroad cars with one passenger." He has moreover the greatest possession both of mind and of temper in his
discourse, so that the mastery and moderation and foresight, and
yet felicity, with which he unfolds his thought, are not to be sur-
passed. This is of importance to such a broacher of novelties as
he is, and to one baited, as he is very apt to be, by the sticklers
for old books or old institutions. He takes such delight in the
exercise of this faculty that he will willingly talk the whole of a
day, and most part of the night, and then again tomorrow, for
days successively, and if I, who am impatient of much speaking,
draw him out to walk in the woods or fields, he will stop at the
first fence and very soon propose either to sit down or to return.
He seems to think society exists for this function, and that all
literature is good or bad as it approaches colloquy, which is its
perfection. Poems and histories may be good, but only as adum-
brations of this; and the only true manner of writing the literature
of a nation would be to convene the best heads in the community,
set them talking, and then introduce stenographers to record
what they say. He so swiftly and naturally plants himself on the
moral sentiment in any conversation that no man will ever get
any advantage of him, unless he be a saint, as Jones Very [5] was.
Every one else Alcott will put in the wrong.

It must be conceded that it is speculation which he loves, and
not action. Therefore he dissatisfies everybody and disgusts many.
When the conversation is ended, all is over. He lives tomorrow,
as he lived today, for further discourse, not to begin, as he seemed
pledged to do, a new celestial life. . . . He has no vocation to
labor, and, although he strenuously preached it for a time, and
made some efforts to practise it, he soon found he had no genius
for it, and that it was a cruel waste of his time. It depressed his
spirits even to tears.

He is very noble in his carriage to all men, of a serene and lofty
aspect and deportment in the street and in the house. . . . Moreover, every man who converses with him is presently made sensible that, although this person has no faculty or patience for our
trivial hodiernal labors, yet if there were a great courage, a great
sacrifice, a self-immolation to be made, this and no other is the
man for a crisis, — and with such grandeur, yet with such temperance in his mien. . . .

He carries all his opinions and all his condition and manner
of life in his hand, and, whilst you talk with him, it is plain he

[5] See pp. 93–94.

has put out no roots, but is an air-plant, which can readily and without any ill consequence be transported to any place. He is quite ready at any moment to abandon his present residence and employment, his country, nay, his wife and children, on very short notice, to put any new dream into practice which has bubbled up in the effervescence of discourse. If it is so with his way of living, much more so is it with his opinions. He never remembers. He never affirms anything today because he has affirmed it before. You are rather astonished, having left him in the morning with one set of opinions, to find him in the evening totally escaped from all recollection of them, as confident of a new line of conduct and heedless of his old advocacy. . . .

This man entertained in his spirit all vast and magnificent problems. None came to him so much recommended as the most universal. He delighted in the fable of Prometheus; in all the dim, gigantic pictures of the most ancient mythology; in the Indian and Egyptian traditions; in the history of magic, of palmistry, of temperaments, of astrology, of whatever showed any impatience of custom and limits, any impulse to dare the solution of the total problem of man's nature, finding in every such experiment an implied pledge and prophecy of worlds of science and power yet unknown to us. He seems often to realize the pictures of the old alchemists: for he stood brooding on the edge of discovery of the Absolute from month to month, ever and anon affirming that it was within his reach, and nowise discomfited by uniform shortcomings. . . .

His vice, an intellectual vice, grew out of this constitution, and was that to which almost all spiritualists have been liable, — a certain brooding on the private thought which produces monotony in the conversation, and egotism in the character. Steadily subjective himself, the variety of facts which seem necessary to the health of most minds, yielded him no variety of meaning, and he quickly quitted the play on objects, to come to *the Subject*, which was always the same, viz., *Alcott in reference to the World of Today*. . . .

November 19, 1842

. . . I begged Alcott to paint out his project,[6] and he proceeded to say that there should be found a farm of a hundred acres in excellent condition, with good buildings, a good orchard, and grounds which admitted of being laid out with great beauty; and

6 For Fruitlands.

this should be purchased and given to them, in the first place. I replied, You ask too much. This is not solving the problem; there are hundreds of innocent young persons, whom, if you will thus stablish and endow and protect, will find it no hard matter to keep their innocency. And to see their tranquil household, after all this has been done for them, will in no wise instruct or strengthen me. But he will instruct and strengthen me, who, there where he is, unaided, in the midst of poverty, toil, and traffic, extricates himself from the corruptions of the same and builds on his land a house of peace and benefit, good customs, and free thoughts. But, replied Alcott, how is this to be done? How can I do it who have a wife and family to maintain? I answered that he was not the person to do it, or he would not ask the question. When he that shall come is born, he will not only see the thing to be done, but invent the life, invent the ways and means of doing it. . . .

This fatal fault in the logic of our friends still appears: Their whole doctrine is spiritual, but they always end with saying, Give us much land and money. If I should give them anything, it would be facility and not beneficence. Unless one should say after the maxims of the world, Let them drink their own error to saturation, and this will be the best hellebore. . . .

July 8, 1843

The sun and the evening sky do not look calmer than Alcott and his family at Fruitlands. They seemed to have arrived at the fact, to have got rid of the show, and so to be serene. Their manners and behavior in the house and in the field were those of superior men, of men at rest. What had they to conceal? What had they to exhibit? And it seemed so high an attainment that I thought, as often before, so now more, because they had a fit home or the picture was fitly framed, that these men ought to be maintained in their place by the country for its culture. Young men and young maidens, old men and women, should visit them and be inspired. I think there is as much merit in beautiful manners as in hard work. I will not prejudge them successful. They look well in July. We will see them in December. I know they are better for themselves than as partners. One can easily see that they have yet to settle several things. Their saying that things are clear, and they sane, does not make them so. If they will in very deed be lovers and not selfish; if they will serve the town of Harvard, and make their neighbors feel them as benefactors wherever they touch them, they are as safe as the sun.

April, 1844

Very sad, indeed, it was to see this half-god driven to the wall, reproaching men, and hesitating whether he should not reproach the gods. The world was not, on trial, a possible element for him to live in. A lover of law had tried whether law could be kept in this world, and all things answered, No. He had entertained the thought of leaving it, and going where freedom and an element could be found. And if he should be found tomorrow at the roadside, it would be the act of the world. We pleaded guilty to perceiving the inconvenience and the inequality of property, and he said, "I will not be a convict." Very tedious and prosing and egotistical and narrow he is, but a profound insight, a Power, a majestical man, looking easily along the centuries to explore *his contemporaries*, with a painful sense of being an orphan and a hermit here. I feel his statement to be partial and to have fatal omissions, but I think I shall never attempt to set him right any more. It is not for me to answer him: though I feel the limitations and exaggeration of his picture, and the wearisome personalities. His statement proves too much: it is a *reductio ad absurdum*. But I was quite ashamed to have just revised and printed last week the old paper denying the existence of tragedy, when this modern Prometheus was in the heat of his quarrel with the gods. . . .

October, 1848

Alcott is a certain fluid in which men of a certain spirit can easily expand themselves and swim at large, they who elsewhere found themselves confined. He gives them nothing but themselves. . . .

Me he has served now these twelve years in that way; he was the reasonable creature to speak to that I wanted.

January, 1853

It is a bitter satire on our social order, just at present, the . . . plight . . . of Mr. Alcott, the most refined and the most advanced soul we have had in New England, who makes all other souls appear slow and cheap and mechanical; a man of such a courtesy and greatness, that (in conversation) all others, even the intellectual, seem sharp and fighting for victory, and angry, — he has the unalterable sweetness of a muse, — yet because he cannot earn money by his pen or his talk, or by school-keeping or book-keeping or editing or any kind of meanness, — nay, for this very cause, that he is ahead of his contemporaries, — is higher than they, — and keeps himself out of the shop-condescensions and smug arts which they stoop to, or, unhappily, need not stoop to, but find themselves, as it were, born to, — therefore, it is the unanimous opinion of New England judges that this man must die; we shall all hear of his death with pleasure, and feel relieved that his board and clothes are saved! We do not adjudge him to hemlock, or to garroting, — we are much too hypocritical and cowardly for that, — but we not less surely doom him, by refusing to protest against this doom, or combine to save him, and to set him on employments fit for him and salutary to the State, or to the Senate of fine Souls, which is the heart of the state.

May ?, 1856

. . . For every opinion or sentence of Alcott, a reason may be sought and found, not in his will or fancy, but in the necessity of nature itself, which has daguerred that fatal impression on his susceptible soul. He is as good as a lens or a mirror, a beautiful susceptibility, every impression on which is not to be reasoned against, or derided, but to be accounted for, and until accounted for, registered as an addition to our catalogue of natural facts. There are defects in the lens, and errors of refraction and position, etc., to be allowed for, and it needs one acquainted with the lens by frequent use, to make these allowances; but 'tis the best instrument I have ever met with.

August 12, 1866

. . . The moral benefit of such a mind cannot be told. The world fades: men, reputations, politics shrivel: the interests, power, future of the soul beam a new dayspring. Faith becomes sight.

※※

October 21, 1839

How can I not record, though now with sleepy eye and flagging spirits, so fair a fact as the visit of Alcott and Margaret Fuller, who came hither yesterday and departed this morning? Very friendly influences these, each and both. Cold as I am, they are almost dear. I shall not, however, fill my page with the gifts or merits of either. They brought nothing but good spirits and good tidings with them of new literary plans here, and good fellowship and recognition abroad. And then to my private ear a chronicle of sweet romance, of love and nobleness which have inspired the beautiful and brave. What is good to make me happy is not however good to make me write. Life too near paralyzes art. Long these things refuse to be recorded except in the invisible colors of memory.

August 16, 1840

After seeing Anna Barker I rode with Margaret to the plains. She taxed me, as often before, so now more explicitly, with inhospitality of Soul. She and C[aroline] would gladly be my friends, yet our intercourse is not friendship, but literary gossip. I count and weigh, but do not love. They make no progress with me, but however often we have met, we still meet as strangers. They feel wronged in such relation and do not wish to be catechised and criticised. I thought of my experience with several persons which resembled this: and confessed that I would not converse with the divinest person more than one week. M. insisted that it was no friendship which was thus so soon exhausted, and that I ought to know how to be silent and companionable at the same moment. She would surprise me, — she would have me say and do what surprised myself. I confess to all this charge with humility unfeigned. I can better converse with George Bradford [7] than with any other. Elizabeth Hoar and I have a beautiful relation, not however quite free from the same hardness and fences. Yet would nothing be so grateful to me as to melt once for all these icy barriers, and unite with these lovers. But great is the law.

To Margaret Fuller

October, 1840?

None knows better than I — more's the pity — the gloomy inhospitality of the man, the want of power to meet and unite with even those whom he loves in his "flinty way." . . . Would you know more of his history? — Diffident, shy, proud, having settled it long ago in his mind that he and society must always

[7] An old friend from Divinity School days.

be nothing to each other — he received with astonishment the kind regards of such as, coming from the opposite quarter of the heavens, he now calls his friends — with surprise and when he dared to believe them, with delight. Can one be glad of an affection which he knows not how to return? I am. Humbly grateful for every expression of tenderness — which makes the day sweet and inspires unlimited hopes. I say this not to you only, but to the four persons who seemed to offer me love at the same time and draw to me and draw me to them. Yet I did not deceive myself with thinking that the old bars would suddenly fall. No, I knew that if I would cherish my dear romance, I must treat it gently, forbear it long, — worship, not use it, — and so at last by piety I might be tempered and annealed to bear contact and conversation as well-mixed natures should. Therefore, my friend, treat me always as a mute, not ungrateful though now incommunicable. . . .

December 8, 1839

. . . I woke this morn with devout thanksgiving for my friends, the old and the new. I think no man in the planet has a circle more noble. They have come to me unsought: the great God gave them to me. Will they separate themselves from me again, or some of them? I know not, but I fear it not, for my relation to them is so pure that we hold by simple affinity; and the Genius of my life being thus social, the same affinity will exert its energy on whosoever is as noble as these men and women, wherever I may be.

[December, 1839]

It is almost dangerous to me to "crush the sweet poison of misused wine" of the affections. A new person is to me a great event and hinders me from sleep. I have often had fine fancies about persons which have given me delicious hours; but the joy ends in the day; it yields no fruit. Thought is not born of it; my action is very little modified. . . .

It has seemed to me lately more possible than I knew, to carry a friendship greatly, on one side, without due correspondence on the other. Why should I cumber myself with regrets that the receiver is not capacious? It never troubles the sun that some of his rays fall wide and vain into ungrateful space, and only a small part on the reflecting planet. Let your greatness educate the crude and cold companion. If he is unequal, he will presently pass away;

but thou art enlarged by thy own shining, and no longer a mate for frogs and worms, dost soar and burn with the gods of the empyrean. It is thought a disgrace to love unrequited. But the great will see that true love cannot be unrequited. True love transcends the unworthy object and dwells and broods on the eternal, and when the poor interposed mask crumbles, it is not sad, but feels rid of so much earth and feels its independency the surer. Yet these things may hardly be said without a sort of treachery to the relation. The essence of friendship is entireness, a total magnanimity and trust. It must not surmise or provide for infirmity. It treats its object as a god, that it may deify both.

From "Friendship"

September 1, 1840

One fact the fine conversations of the last week — now already fast fading into oblivion — revealed to me, not without a certain shudder of joy, that I must thank what I am, and not what I do, for the love my friends bear me. I, conscious all the time of the shortcoming of my hands, haunted ever with a sense of beauty which makes all I do and say pitiful to me, and the occasion of perpetual apologies, assure myself to disgust those whom I admire, — and now suddenly it comes out that they have been loving me all this time, not at all thinking of my hands or my words, but only of that love of something more beautiful than the world, which, it seems, being in my heart, overflowed through my eyes or the tones of my speech. Gladly I learn that we have these subterranean, — say rather, these supersensuous channels of communication, and that spirits can meet in their pure upper sky without the help of organs.

❧❧

June, 1840

Now for near five years I have been indulged by the gracious Heaven in my long holiday in this goodly house of mine, entertaining and entertained by so many worthy and gifted friends, and all this time poor Nancy Barron, the mad-woman, has been screaming herself hoarse at the Poorhouse across the brook and I still hear her whenever I open my window.

May 19, 1839

At church today I felt how unequal is this match of words against things. Cease, O thou unauthorized talker, to prate of

consolation, and resignation, and spiritual joys, in neat and balanced sentences. For I know these men who sit below, and on
the hearing of these words look up. Hush, quickly: for care and
calamity are things to them. There is Mr. Tolman, the shoemaker,
whose daughter is gone mad, and he is looking up through his
spectacles to hear what you can offer for his case. Here is my
friend, whose scholars are all leaving him, and he knows not what
to turn his hand to, next. Here is my wife, who has come to church
in hope of being soothed and strengthened after being wounded
by the sharp tongue of a slut in her house. Here is the stage-driver
who has the jaundice, and cannot get well. Here is B. who failed
last week, and he is looking up. O speak things, then, or hold
thy tongue.

May 28, 1839

There is no history. There is only biography. The attempt to
perpetuate, to fix a thought or principle, fails continually. You
can only live for yourself; your action is good only whilst it is alive,
— whilst it is in you. The awkward imitation of it by your child
or your disciple is not a repetition of it, is not the same thing,
but another thing. The new individual must work out the whole
problem of science, letters and theology for himself; can owe his
fathers nothing. There is no history; only biography.

August 14, 1839

. . . It is the peculiarity of Truth that it must *live* every moment
in the beginning, in the middle, and onward forever in every stage
of statement. I cannot accept without qualification the most indisputable of your axioms. I see that they are not quite true.

[July 3, 1839]

In Boston yesterday and the day before, and saw the Allston
Gallery.[8] . . .
The landscapes pleased me well. I like them all: he is a fine
pastoral poet and invites us to come again and again. The drawing also of the figures is always pleasing, but they lack fire, and
the impression of the gallery, though bland, is faint in the memory.
Nothing haunts the memory from it. It never quickens a pulse
of virtue, it never causes an emulous throb. Herein perhaps it
resembles the genius of Spenser; and is, as I have said, Elysian.

[8] The American painter, Washington Allston, held an exhibition of his
paintings in Boston in the summer of 1839.

When I went to Europe, I fancied the great pictures were great strangers; some new unexperienced pomp and show; a foreign wonder, barbaric pearl and gold, like the spontoons and standards of the militia, which play such pranks in the eyes and imaginations of school-boys. I was to see and acquire I knew not what. When I came at last to Rome and saw with eyes the pictures, I found that genius left to novices the gay and fantastic and ostentatious, and itself pierced directly to the simple and true; that it was familiar and sincere; that it was the old, eternal fact I had met already in so many forms, — unto which I lived; that it was the plain *you and me* I knew so well, — had left at home in so many conversations. . . . It had traveled by my side; that which I fancied I had left in Boston was here in the Vatican, and again at Milan and at Paris, and made all traveling ridiculous as a treadmill. I now require this of all pictures, that they domesticate me, not that they dazzle me. Allston's St. Peter is not yet human enough for me. It is too picturesque, and like a bronzed cast of the Socrates or Venus.

September 14, 1839

Education. — . . . An education in things is not. We all are involved in the condemnation of words, an age of words. We are shut up in schools and college recitation rooms for ten or fifteen years, and come out at last with a bellyful of words and do not know a thing. We cannot use our hands, or our legs, or our eyes, or our arms. We do not know an edible root in the woods. We cannot tell our course by the stars, nor the hour of the day by the sun. It is well if we can swim and skate. We are afraid of a horse, of a cow, of a dog, of a cat, of a spider. Far better was the Roman rule to teach a boy nothing that he could not learn standing. Now here are my wise young neighbors [9] who, instead of getting, like the woodmen, into a railroad-car, where they have not even the activity of holding the reins, have got into a boat which they have built with their own hands, with sails which they have contrived to serve as a tent by night, and gone up the Merrimack to live by their wits on the fish of the stream and the berries of the wood. My worthy neighbor Dr. Bartlett expressed a true parental instinct when he desired to send his boy with them to learn something. The farm, the farm, is the right school. The reason of my deep respect for the farmer is that he is a realist, and not a dictionary. The farm is a piece of the world, the school-house is not. The

[9] John and Henry Thoreau.

farm, by training the physical, rectifies and invigorates the metaphysical and moral nature.

Now so bad we are that the world is stripped of love and of
terror. Here came the other night an Aurora [Borealis] so wonderful, a curtain of red and blue and silver glory, that in any other
age or nation it would have moved the awe and wonder of men
and mingled with the profoundest sentiments of religion and love,
and we all saw it with cold, arithmetical eyes, we knew how many
colors shone, how many degrees it extended, how many hours
it lasted, and of this heavenly flower we beheld nothing more: a
primrose by the brim of the river of time.

Shall we not wish back again the Seven Whistlers, the Flying
Dutchman, the lucky and unlucky days, and the terrors of the Day
of Doom?

September 14, 1839

I lament that I find in me no enthusiasm, no resources for the
instruction and guidance of the people, when they shall discover
that their present guides are blind. . . . I hate preaching, whether
in pulpits or in teachers' meetings. Preaching is a pledge, and I
wish to say what I think and feel today, with the proviso that
tomorrow perhaps I shall contradict it all. Freedom boundless I
wish. I will not pledge myself not to drink wine, not to drink ink,
not to lie, and not to commit adultery, lest I hanker tomorrow to
do these very things by reason of my having tied my hands. Besides, man is so poor he cannot afford to part with any advantages,
or bereave himself of the functions even of one hair. I do not
like to speak to the Peace Society, if so I am to restrain me in so
extreme a privilege as the use of the sword and bullet. For the
peace of the man who has forsworn the use of the bullet seems to
me not quite peace, but a canting impotence: but with knife and
pistol in my hands, if I, from greater bravery and honor, cast them
aside, then I know the glory of peace.

September 14, 1839

The mob are always interesting. We hate editors, preachers and
all manner of scholars, and fashionists. A blacksmith, a truckman,
a farmer, we follow into the bar-room and watch with eagerness
what they shall say, for such as they do not speak because they are
expected to, but because they have somewhat to say.

December, 1841

. . . When, in our discontent with the pedantry of scholars, we prefer farmers, and when, suspecting their conservatism, we hearken after the hard words of drovers and Irishmen, this is only subjective or relative criticism, this is alkali to our acid, or shade to our too much sunshine; but abide with these, and you will presently find they are the same men you left. A coat has cheated you.

September 28, 1839

I can be wise very well for myself, but not for another, nor among others. I smile and ignore woe, and if that which they call woe shall come to me I hope and doubt not to smile still. They smile never and think joy amiss. All their facts are tinged with gloom, and all my pains are edged with pleasure. But if I intermeddle, if I quit my divine island and seek to right them in particulars, if I look upon them as corrigible individuals and their fortunes curable, I grow giddy and skeptical presently in their company. Old age is a sad riddle which this stony Sphinx [1] reads us. . . . I can only solve this sad problem by esteeming it a slide in my lamp. It is a shade which adds splendor to the lights. But if I intermeddle, if I esteem it an entity, — already my own hair grizzles. . . .

But what is old age? what is the Fall? what Sin? what Death? lying as we do in this eternal Soul originating benefit forevermore. The dullest scholar learns the secret of Space and Time; learns that Time is infinite; that the instruments of God are all commensurate. Is not that lesson enough for a life? The Power that deals with us, the Power which we study and which we are to inherit as fast as we learn to use it, is, in sum, dazzling, terrific, inaccessible. It now benignly shows us in parts and atoms some arc of its magnificent circle, elements which are radically ours.

August 14, 1839

The way in which the doctrine of the immortality of the soul is taught and heard is false. It is Duration, but there is no warrant for teaching this. There is no promise to Aaron and Abner that Aaron and Abner shall live. It is only the Soul that, in rare awakenings, saith through all her being, I AM, and Time is below me; and the awkward Understanding translates the rapture into English prose, and saith, That voice came out of a mortal man, and he said that he should live a good many thousand years. . . .

[1] Cf. "The Sphinx" (p. 420).

October 18, 1839

Lectures. — In these golden days it behooves me once more to make my annual inventory of the world. For the five last years I have read each winter a new course of lectures in Boston, and each was my creed and confession of faith. Each told all I thought of the past, the present and the future. Once more I must renew my work, and I think only once in the same form, though I see that he who thinks he does something for the last time ought not to do it at all. Yet my objection is not to the thing, but with the form: and the concatenation of errors called *society* to which I still consent, until my plumes be grown, makes even a duty of this concession also. So I submit to sell tickets again.

But the form is neither here nor there. What shall be the substance of my shrift? Adam in the garden, I am to new name all the beasts in the field and all the gods in the sky. I am to invite men drenched in Time to recover themselves and come out of time, and taste their native immortal air. I am to fire with what skill I can the artillery of sympathy and emotion. I am to indicate constantly, though all unworthy, the Ideal and Holy Life, the life within life, the Forgotten Good, the Unknown Cause in which we sprawl and sin. I am to try the magic of sincerity, that luxury permitted only to kings and poets. I am to celebrate the spiritual powers in their infinite contrast to the mechanical powers and the mechanical philosophy of this time. I am to console the brave sufferers under evils whose end they cannot see by appeals to the great optimism, self-affirmed in all bosoms.

April 7 ?, 1840

In all my lectures, I have taught one doctrine, namely, the infinitude of the private man. This the people accept readily enough, and even with loud commendation, as long as I call the lecture Art, or Politics, or Literature, or the Household; but the moment I call it Religion, they are shocked, though it be only the application of the same truth which they receive everywhere else, to a new class of facts.

November 17, 1839

The Bible. — . . . The most original book in the world is the Bible. This old collection of the ejaculations of love and dread, of the supreme desires and contritions of men, proceeding out of the region of the grand and eternal, by whatsoever different mouths spoken, and through a wide extent of times and countries, seems the alphabet of the nations, and all posterior literature either the chronicle of facts under very inferior Ideas, or, when it rises to sentiment, the combinations, analogies or degradations of this.

It is in the nature of things that the highest originality must be moral. The only person who can be entirely independent of this fountain of literature and equal to it, must be a prophet in his own proper person. Shakespeare, the first literary genius of the world, leans on the Bible: his poetry supposes it. If we examine this brilliant influence, Shakespeare, as it lies in our minds, we shall find it reverent, deeply indebted to the traditional morality, — in short, compared with the tone of the prophets, *Secondary.* On the other hand, the Prophets do not imply the existence of Shakespeare or Homer, — advert to no books or arts, — only to dread Ideas and emotions. People imagine that the place which the Bible holds in the world, it owes to miracles. It owes it simply to the fact that it came out of a profounder depth of thought than any other book, and the effect must be precisely proportionate. . . .

I have used in the above remarks the Bible for the Ethical Revelation considered generally, including, that is, the Vedas,[2] the Sacred Writings of every nation, and not of the Hebrews alone; although these last, for the very reason I have given, precede all similar writings so far as to be commonly called *The Book*, or Bible, alone.

December 23 ?, 1839

Treat Things Poetically. — Everything should be treated poetically, — law, politics, housekeeping, money. A judge and a banker must drive their craft poetically as well as a dancer or a scribe. That is, they must exert that higher vision which causes the object to become fluid and plastic. Then they are inventive, they detect its capabilities. If they do not this, they have nothing that can be called success, but the work and the workman become blockish and near the point of everlasting congelation. All human affairs need the perpetual intervention of this elastic principle to preserve them supple and alive, as the earth needs the presence of caloric through its pores to resist the tendency to absolute solidity. If you would write a code, or logarithms, or a cookbook, you cannot spare the poetic impulse. We must not only have hydrogen in balloons, and steel springs under coaches, but we must have fire under the Andes at the core of the world. . . .

[2] The sacred writings of the Hindus.

June 27, 1839

Rhyme. — Rhyme; not tinkling rhyme, but grand Pindaric strokes, as firm as the tread of a horse. Rhyme that vindicates itself as an art, the stroke of the bell of a cathedral. Rhyme which knocks at prose and dullness with the stroke of a cannon ball. Rhyme which builds out into Chaos and old night a splendid architecture to bridge the impassable, and call aloud on all the children of morning that the Creation is recommencing. I wish to write such rhymes as shall not suggest a restraint, but contrariwise the wildest freedom.[3]

October 17, 1840

. . . I love spring water and wild air, and not the manufacture of the chemist's shop. I see in a moment, on looking into our new *Dial*, which is the wild poetry, and which the tame, and see that one wild line out of a private heart saves the whole book.

November 6, 1839

People hold to you as long as you please yourself with the Ideal life only as a pretty dream and concede a resistless force to the limitations of the same, to structure, or organization, and to society. But as quickly as you profess your unlimited allegiance to the first, so far as to be no longer contented with doing the best you can in the circumstances, but demand that these mountain circumstances should skip like rams and the little hills like lambs before the presence of the Soul, then they distrust your wisdom and defy your resolutions. And yet Nature is in earnest. . . . The moral nature is not a patch of light here, whilst the social world is a lump of darkness there, but tends incessantly to rectify and ennoble the whole circumference of facts.

Never was anything gained by admitting the omnipotence of limitations, but all immortal action is an overstepping of these busy rules. . . .

June 11, 1840

I finish this morning transcribing my old essay on Love, but I see well its inadequateness. I, cold because I am hot, — cold at the surface only as a sort of guard and compensation for the fluid tenderness of the core, — have much more experience than I have written there, more than I will, more than I can write. In silence we must wrap much of our life, because it is too fine for speech,

[3] Cf. "Merlin" (p. 447).

because also we cannot explain it to others, and because somewhat we cannot yet understand. We do not live as angels, eager to introduce each other to new perfections in our brothers and sisters, and frankly avowing our delight in each new trait of character, in the magic of each new eyebeam, but that which passes for love in the world gets official, and instead of embracing, hates all the divine traits that dare to appear in other persons. A better and holier society will mend this selfish cowardice, and we shall have brave ties of affection, not petrified by law, not dated or ordained by law to last for one year, for five years, or for life; but drawing their date, like all friendship, from itself only; brave as I said, because innocent, and religiously abstinent from the connubial endearments, being a higher league on a purely spiritual basis. This nobody believes possible who is not good. The good know it is possible. . . .[4]

[*November 21, 1840*]

[Swedenborg] exaggerates the circumstance of marriage; and though he finds false marriages on earth, fancies a wiser choice in heaven. But of progressive souls, all loves and friendships are momentary. *Do you love me?* means, Do you see the same truth? If you do, we are happy with the same happiness: but presently one of us passes into the perception of new truth; — we are divorced, and no tension in nature can hold us to each other. I know how delicious is this cup of love, — I existing for you, you existing for me; but it is a child's clinging to his toy; an attempt to eternize the fireside and nuptial chamber; to keep the picture-alphabet through which our first lessons are prettily conveyed. The Eden of God is bare and grand: like the out-door landscape remembered from the evening fireside, it seems cold and desolate whilst you cower over the coals, but once abroad again, we pity those who can forego the magnificence of nature for candle-light and cards. . . . For God is the bride or bridegroom of the soul. Heaven is not the pairing of two, but the communion of all souls. We meet, and dwell an instant under the temple of one thought, and part, as though we parted not, to join another thought in other fellowships of joy. So far from there being anything divine in the low and proprietary sense of *Do you love me?* it is only when you leave and lose me by casting yourself on a sentiment which is higher than both of us, that I draw near and find myself at your side; and I am repelled if you fix your eye on me and demand love. In fact, in the spiritual world we change sexes every moment. You

[4] Cf. "Give All to Love," p. 436.

love the worth in me; then I am your husband: but it is not me, but the worth, that fixes the love; and that worth is a drop of the ocean of worth that is beyond me. Meantime I adore the greater worth in another, and so become his wife. He aspires to a higher worth in another spirit, and is wife or receiver of that influence.

From "Swedenborg"

June, 1840

The Best are never demoniacal or magnetic, but all brutes are. The Democratic Party in this country is more magnetic than the Whig. Andrew Jackson is an eminent example of it. Van Buren is not, — but his masters are, who placed him in his house. Amos Kendall and [Levi] Woodbury.[5] Mr. Hoar is entirely destitute of this element. It is the prince of the power of the air. The lowest angel is better. It is the height of the animal; below the region of the divine.

June, 1840

Nature. — I think I must do these eyes of mine the justice to write a new chapter on Nature. This delight we all take in every show of night or day, of field or forest or sea or city, down to the lowest particulars, is not without sequel, though we be as yet only wishers and gazers, not at all knowing what we want. We are predominated herein, as elsewhere, by an upper wisdom, and resemble those great discoverers who are haunted for years, sometimes from infancy, with a passion for the fact or class of facts in which the secret lies which they are destined to unlock, and they let it not go until the blessing is won. So these sunsets and starlights, these swamps and rocks, these birdnotes and animal forms off which we cannot get our eyes and ears, but hover still, as moths, round a lamp, are no doubt a Sanscrit cipher covering the whole religious history of the universe, and presently we shall read it off into action and character. The pastures are full of ghosts for me, the morning woods full of angels. Now and then they give me a broad hint. Every natural fact is trivial until it becomes symbolical or moral.

July, 1840

We see the river glide below us, but we see not the river that glides over us and envelopes us in its floods. A month ago, I met myself, as I was speeding away from some trifle to chase a new one, and knew that I had eaten lotus and been a stranger from my home

[5] Democratic leaders.

all this time. And now I see that, with that word and thought in my mind, another wave took me and washed my remembrance away, and only now I regain myself a little and turn in my sleep.

To Samuel Gray Ward

July 18, 1840

. . . In the sleep of the great heats there was nothing for me but to read the Vedas, the bible of the tropics, which I find I come back upon every three or four years. It is sublime as heat and night and a breathless ocean. It contains every religious sentiment, all the grand ethics which visit in turn each noble and poetic mind, and nothing is easier than to separate what must have been the primeval inspiration from the endless ceremonial nonsense which caricatures and contradicts it through every chapter. It is of no use to put away the book: if I trust myself in the woods or in a boat upon the pond, nature makes a Brahmin of me presently: eternal necessity, eternal compensation, unfathomable power, unbroken silence, — this is her creed. Peace, she saith to me, and purity and absolute abandonment — these penances expiate all sin and bring you to the beatitude of the "Eight Gods." . . .

October 7, 1840

Circumstances are dreams, which, springing unawares from ourselves, amuse us whilst we doze and sleep, but when we wake, nothing but causes can content us. The life of man is the true romance which, when it is valiantly conducted and all the stops of the instrument opened, will go nigh to craze the reader with anxiety, wonder and love. I am losing all relish for books and for feats of skill in my delight in this Power. Do not accuse me of sloth. Do not ask me to your philanthropies, charities, and duties, as you term them; — mere circumstances; — flakes of the snow-cloud, leaves of the trees; — I sit at home with the cause, grim or glad. I think I may never do anything that you shall call a deed again. I have been writing with some pains Essays on various matters as a sort of apology to my country for my apparent idleness. But the poor work has looked poorer daily, as I strove to end it. My genius seemed to quit me in such a mechanical work, a seeming wise — a cold exhibition of dead thoughts. When I write a letter to anyone whom I love, I have no lack of words or thoughts. I am wiser than myself and read my paper with the pleasure of one who receives a letter, but what I write to fill up the gaps of a chapter is hard and cold, is grammar and logic; there is no magic in it; I do

not wish to see it again. Settle with yourself your accusations of
me. If I do not please you, ask me not to please you, but please
yourself. What you call my indolence, Nature does not accuse;
the twinkling leaves, the sailing fleets of water-flies, the deep sky,
like me well enough and know me for their own. With them I
have no embarrassments, diffidences or compunctions; with them
I mean to stay. You think it is because I have an income which
exempts me from your day-labor, that I waste (as you call it) my
time in sun-gazing and star-gazing. You do not know me. If my
debts, as they threaten, should consume what money I have, I
should live just as I do now: I should eat worse food, and wear a
coarser coat, and should wonder in a potato patch instead of in the
wood, — but it is I, and not my twelve hundred dollars a year, that
love God.

October 17, 1840

Yesterday George and Sophia Ripley, Margaret Fuller and Alcott discussed here the new Social Plans.[6] I wished to be convinced, to be thawed, to be made nobly mad by the kindlings before my eye of a new dawn of human piety. But this scheme was
arithmetic and comfort: this was a hint borrowed from the Tremont House and United States Hotel; a rage in our poverty and
politics to live rich and gentleman-like, an anchor to leeward
against a change of weather; a prudent forecast on the probable
issue of the great questions of Pauperism and Poverty. And not
once could I be inflamed, but sat aloof and thoughtless; my voice
faltered and fell. It was not the cave of persecution which is the
palace of spiritual power, but only a room in the Astor House hired
for the Transcendentalists. I do not wish to remove from my present prison to a prison a little larger. I wish to break all prisons. I
have not yet conquered my own house. It irks and repents me.
Shall I raise the siege of this hencoop, and march baffled away to
a pretended siege of Babylon? It seems to me that so to do were
to dodge the problem I am set to solve, and to hide my impotency
in the thick of a crowd. I can see too, afar, — that I should not find
myself more than now, — no, not so much, in that select, but not
by me selected, fraternity. Moreover, to join this body would be to
traverse all my long trumpeted theory, and the instinct which spoke
from it, that one man is a counterpoise to a city, — that a man is
stronger than a city, that his solitude is more prevalent and beneficent than the concert of crowds.

[6] For Brook Farm.

October 23, 1840

And must I go and do somewhat if I would learn new secrets of self-reliance? for my chapter is not finished. But self-reliance is precisely that secret, — to make your supposed deficiency redundancy. If I am true, the theory is, the very want of action, my very impotency, shall become a greater excellency than all skill and toil.

December ?, 1840

Nature ever flows; stands never still. Motion or change is her mode of existence. The poetic eye sees in Man the Brother of the River, and in Woman the Sister of the River. Their life is always transition. Hard blockheads only drive nails all the time; forever remember; which is fixing. Heroes do not fix, but flow, bend forward ever and invent a resource for every moment.

A man is a compendium of nature, an indomitable savage; take the smoothest curled courtier in London or Paris, as long as he has a temperament of his own, and a hair growing on his skin, a pulse beating in his veins, he has a physique which disdains all intrusion, all despotism; it lives, wakes, alters, by omnipotent modes, and is directly related there, amid essences and *billets doux*,[7] to Himmaleh mountain chains, wild cedar swamps, and the interior fires, the molten core of the globe.

January 1, 1841

I begin the year by sending my little book of Essays [8] to the press. What remains to be done to its imperfect chapters I will seek to do justly. I see no reason why we may not write with as much grandeur of spirit as we can serve or suffer. Let the page be filled with the character, not with the skill of the writer.

January 31 ?, 1841

All my thoughts are foresters. I have scarce a day-dream on which the breath of the pines has not blown, and their shadows waved. Shall I not then call my little book Forest Essays?

[7] Perfumes and love-letters.
[8] *Essays, First Series*, published in March.

Self-Reliance

"Ne te quaesiveris extra." **9**

"Man is his own star; and the soul that ca_
Render an honest and a perfect man,
Commands all light, all influence, all fate;
Nothing to him falls early or too late.
Our acts our angels are, or good or ill,
Our fatal shadows that walk by us still."

Epilogue to Beaumont and Fletcher's
Honest Man's Fortune

Cast the bantling on the rocks,
Suckle him with the she-wolf's teat,
Wintered with the hawk and fox,
Power and speed be hands and feet.

I READ the other day some verses written by an eminent painter
which were original and not conventional. The soul always hears
an admonition in such lines, let the subject be what it may. The
sentiment they instil is of more value than any thought they may
contain. To believe your own thought, to believe that what is
true for you in your private heart is true for all men, — that is
genius. Speak your latent conviction, and it shall be the universal
sense; for the inmost in due time becomes the outmost, and our
first thought is rendered back to us by the trumpets of the Last
Judgment. Familiar as the voice of the mind is to each, the highest
merit we ascribe to Moses, Plato and Milton is that they set at
naught books and traditions, and spoke not what men, but what
they thought. A man should learn to detect and watch that gleam
of light which flashes across his mind from within, more than the
lustre of the firmament of bards and sages. Yet he dismisses without notice his thought, because it is his. In every work of genius
we recognize our own rejected thoughts; they come back to us
with a certain alienated majesty. Great works of art have no more
affecting lesson for us than this. They teach us to abide by our
spontaneous impression with good-humored inflexibility then most
when the whole cry of voices is on the other side. Else tomorrow a
stranger will say with masterly good sense precisely what we have
thought and felt all the time, and we shall be forced to take with
shame our own opinion from another.

There is a time in every man's education when he arrives at the

9 Do not seek yourself outside yourself.

conviction that envy is ignorance; that imitation is suicide; that he must take himself for better for worse as his portion; that though the wide universe is full of good, no kernel of nourishing corn can come to him but through his toil bestowed on that plot of ground which is given to him to till. The power which resides in him is new in nature, and none but he knows what that is which he can do, nor does he know until he has tried. Not for nothing one face, one character, one fact, makes much impression on him, and another none. This sculpture in the memory is not without pre-established harmony. The eye was placed where one ray should fall, that it might testify of that particular ray. We but half express ourselves, and are ashamed of that divine idea which each of us represents. It may be safely trusted as proportionate and of good issues, so it be faithfully imparted, but God will not have his work made manifest by cowards. A man is relieved and gay when he has put his heart into his work and done his best; but what he has said or done otherwise shall give him no peace. It is a deliverance which does not deliver. In the attempt his genius deserts him; no muse befriends; no invention, no hope.

Trust thyself: every heart vibrates to that iron string. Accept the place the divine providence has found for you, the society of your contemporaries, the connection of events. Great men have always done so, and confided themselves childlike to the genius of their age, betraying their perception that the absolutely trustworthy was seated at their heart, working through their hands, predominating in all their being. And we are now men, and must accept in the highest mind the same transcendent destiny; and not minors and invalids in a protected corner, not cowards fleeing before a revolution, but guides, redeemers and benefactors, obeying the Almighty effort and advancing on Chaos and the Dark.

What pretty oracles nature yields us on this text in the face and behavior of children, babes, and even brutes! That divided and rebel mind, that distrust of a sentiment because our arithmetic has computed the strength and means opposed to our purpose, these have not. Their mind being whole, their eye is as yet unconquered, and when we look in their faces we are disconcerted. Infancy conforms to nobody; all conform to it; so that one babe commonly makes four or five out of the adults who prattle and play to it. So God has armed youth and puberty and manhood no less with its own piquancy and charm, and made it enviable and gracious and its claims not to be put by, if it will stand by itself. Do not think the youth has no force, because he cannot speak to you and me.

Hark! in the next room his voice is sufficiently clear and emphatic. It seems he knows how to speak to his contemporaries. Bashful or bold then, he will know how to make us seniors very unnecessary.

The nonchalance of boys who are sure of a dinner, and would disdain as much as a lord to do or say aught to conciliate one, is the healthy attitude of human nature. A boy is in the parlor what the pit is in the playhouse; independent, irresponsible, looking out from his corner on such people and facts as pass by, he tries and sentences them on their merits, in the swift, summary way of boys, as good, bad, interesting, silly, eloquent, troublesome. He cumbers himself never about consequences, about interests; he gives an independent, genuine verdict. You must court him; he does not court you. But the man is as it were clapped into jail by his consciousness. As soon as he has once acted or spoken with *éclat* he is a committed person, watched by the sympathy or the hatred of hundreds, whose affections must now enter into his account. There is no Lethe for this. Ah, that he could pass again into his neutrality! Who can thus avoid all pledges and, having observed, observe again from the same unaffected, unbiased, unbribable, unaffrighted innocence, — must always be formidable. He would utter opinions on all passing affairs, which being seen to be not private but necessary, would sink like darts into the ear of men and put them in fear.

These are the voices which we hear in solitude, but they grow faint and inaudible as we enter into the world. Society everywhere is in conspiracy against the manhood of every one of its members. Society is a joint-stock company, in which the members agree, for the better securing of his bread to each shareholder, to surrender the liberty and culture of the eater. The virtue in most request is conformity. Self-reliance is its aversion. It loves not realities and creators, but names and customs.

Whoso would be a man, must be a nonconformist. He who would gather immortal palms must not be hindered by the name of goodness, but must explore if it be goodness. Nothing is at last sacred but the integrity of your own mind. Absolve you to yourself, and you shall have the suffrage of the world. I remember an answer which when quite young I was prompted to make to a valued adviser who was wont to importune me with the dear old doctrines of the church. On my saying, "What have I to do with the sacredness of traditions, if I live wholly from within?" my friend suggested, — "But these impulses may be from below, not from above." I replied, "They do not seem to me to be such; but if I am the Devil's child, I will live then from the Devil." No law can be sacred to me but that of my nature. Good and bad are but names very readily transferable to that or this; the only right is what is after my constitution; the only wrong what is against it. A man is to carry himself in the presence of all opposition as if every thing were titular and ephemeral but he. I am ashamed to think how easily we capitulate to badges and names, to large societies and dead institutions. Every decent and well-spoken individual affects and sways me more than is right. I ought to go upright and vital, and speak the rude truth in all ways. If malice and vanity wear the coat of philanthropy, shall that pass? If an angry bigot assumes this bountiful cause of Abolition, and comes to me with his last news from Barbadoes, why should I not say to him, "Go love thy infant; love thy wood-chopper; be good-natured and modest; have that grace; and never varnish your hard, uncharitable ambition with this incredible tenderness for black folk a thousand miles off. Thy love afar is spite at home." Rough and graceless would be such greeting, but truth is handsomer than the affectation of love. Your goodness must have some edge to it, — else it is none. The doctrine of hatred must be preached, as the counteraction of the doctrine of love, when that pules and whines. I shun father and mother and wife and brother when my genius calls me. I would write on the lintels of the door-post, *Whim*. I hope it is somewhat better than whim at last, but we cannot spend the day in explanation. Expect me not to show cause why I seek or why I exclude company. Then again, do not tell me, as a good man did today, of my obligation to put all poor men in good situations. Are they *my* poor? I tell thee, thou foolish philanthropist, that I grudge the dollar, the dime, the cent I give to such men as do not belong to me and to whom I do not belong. There is a class of persons to whom by all spiritual affinity I am bought and sold; for them I will go to prison if need be; but your miscellaneous popular charities; the education at college of fools; the building of meeting-houses to the vain end to which many now stand; alms to sots, and the thousand-fold Relief Societies; — though I confess with shame I sometimes succumb and give the dollar, it is a wicked dollar, which by and by I shall have the manhood to withhold.

Virtues are, in the popular estimate, rather the exception than the rule. There is the man *and* his virtues. Men do what is called a good action, as some piece of courage or charity, much as they would pay a fine in expiation of daily non-appearance on parade.

Their works are done as an apology or extenuation of their living in the world, — as invalids and the insane pay a high board. Their virtues are penances. I do not wish to expiate, but to live. My life is for itself and not for a spectacle. I much prefer that it should be of a lower strain, so it be genuine and equal, than that it should be glittering and unsteady. I wish it to be sound and sweet, and not to need diet and bleeding. I ask primary evidence that you are a man, and refuse this appeal from the man to his actions. I know that for myself it makes no difference whether I do or forbear those actions which are reckoned excellent. I cannot consent to pay for a privilege where I have intrinsic right. Few and mean as my gifts may be, I actually am, and do not need for my own assurance or the assurance of my fellows any secondary testimony.

What I must do is all that concerns me, not what the people think. This rule, equally arduous in actual and in intellectual life, may serve for the whole distinction between greatness and mean-ness. It is the harder because you will always find those who think they know what is your duty better than you know it. It is easy in the world to live after the world's opinion; it is easy in solitude to live after our own; but the great man is he who in the midst of the crowd keeps with perfect sweetness the independence of soli-tude.

The objection to conforming to usages that have become dead to you is that it scatters your force. It loses your time and blurs the impression of your character. If you maintain a dead church, contribute to a dead Bible-society, vote with a great party either for the government or against it, spread your table like base house-keepers, — under all these screens I have difficulty to detect the precise man you are: and of course so much force is withdrawn from your proper life. But do your work, and I shall know you. Do your work, and you shall reinforce yourself. A man must con-sider what a blind-man's-buff is this game of conformity. If I know your sect I anticipate your argument. I hear a preacher announce for his text and topic the expediency of one of the institutions of his church. Do I not know beforehand that not possibly can he say a new and spontaneous word? Do I not know that with all this ostentation of examining the grounds of the institution he will do no such thing? Do I not know that he is pledged to himself not to look but at one side, the permitted side, not as a man, but as a parish minister? He is a retained attorney, and these airs of the bench are the emptiest affectation. Well, most men have bound their eyes with one or another handkerchief, and attached themselves to some one of these communities of opinion. This conformity makes them not false in a few particulars, authors of a few lies, but false in all particulars. Their every truth is not quite true. Their two is not the real two, their four not the real four; so that every word they say chagrins us and we know not where to begin to set them right. Meantime nature is not slow to equip us in the prison-uniform of the party to which we adhere. We come to wear one cut of face and figure, and acquire by degrees the gentlest asinine expression. There is a mortifying experience in particular, which does not fail to wreak itself also in the general history; I mean "the foolish face of praise," the forced smile which we put on in company where we do not feel at ease, in answer to conversation which does not interest us. The muscles, not spontaneously moved but moved by a low usurping wilfulness, grow tight about the outline of the face, with the most disagreeable sensation.

For nonconformity the world whips you with its displeasure. And therefore a man must know how to estimate a sour face. The by-standers look askance on him in the public street or in the friend's parlor. If this aversion had its origin in contempt and resistance like his own he might well go home with a sad countenance; but the sour faces of the multitude, like their sweet faces, have no deep cause, but are put on and off as the wind blows and a newspaper directs. Yet is the discontent of the multitude more formidable than that of the senate and the college. It is easy enough for a firm man who knows the world to brook the rage of the cultivated classes. Their rage is decorous and prudent, for they are timid, as being very vulnerable themselves. But when to their feminine rage the indignation of the people is added, when the ignorant and the poor are aroused, when the unintelligent brute force that lies at the bottom of society is made to growl and mow, it needs the habit of magnanimity and religion to treat it godlike as a trifle of no concernment.

The other terror that scares us from self-trust is our consistency; a reverence for our past act or word because the eyes of others have no other data for computing our orbit than our past acts, and we are loth to disappoint them.

But why should you keep your head over your shoulder? Why drag about this corpse of your memory, lest you contradict somewhat you have stated in this or that public place? Suppose you should contradict yourself; what then? It seems to be a rule of wisdom never to rely on your memory alone, scarcely even in acts of pure memory, but to bring the past for judgment into the thousand-eyed present, and live ever in a new day. In your metaphysics you have denied personality to the Deity, yet when the devout motions of the soul come, yield to them heart and life, though they should clothe God with shape and color. Leave your theory, as Joseph his coat in the hand of the harlot, and flee.

A foolish consistency is the hobgoblin of little minds, adored by little statesmen and philosophers and divines. With consistency a great soul has simply nothing to do. He may as well concern himself with his shadow on the wall. Speak what you think now in hard words and tomorrow speak what tomorrow thinks in hard words again, though it contradict every thing you said today. — "Ah, so you shall be sure to be misunderstood." — Is it so bad then to be misunderstood? Pythagoras was misunderstood, and Socrates, and Jesus, and Luther, and Copernicus, and Galileo, and Newton, and every pure and wise spirit that ever took flesh. To be great is to be misunderstood.

I suppose no man can violate his nature. All the sallies of his will are rounded in by the law of his being, as the inequalities of Andes and Himmaleh are insignificant in the curve of the sphere. Nor does it matter how you gauge and try him. A character is like an acrostic or Alexandrian stanza; — read it forward, backward, or across, it still spells the same thing. In this pleasing contrite woodlife which God allows me, let me record day by day my honest thought without prospect or retrospect, and, I cannot doubt, it will be found symmetrical, though I mean it not and see it not. My book should smell of pines and resound with the hum of insects. The swallow over my window should interweave that thread or straw he carries in his bill into my web also. We pass for what we are. Character teaches above our wills. Men imagine that they communicate their virtue or vice only by overt actions, and do not see that virtue or vice emit a breath every moment.

There will be an agreement in whatever variety of actions, so they be each honest and natural in their hour. For of one will, the actions will be harmonious, however unlike they seem. These varieties are lost sight of at a little distance, at a little height of thought. One tendency unites them all. The voyage of the best ship is a zigzag line of a hundred tacks. See the line from a sufficient distance, and it straightens itself to the average tendency. Your genuine action will explain itself and will explain your other genuine actions. Your conformity explains nothing. Act singly, and what you have already done singly will justify you now. Greatness appeals to the future. If I can be firm enough today to do

right and scorn eyes, I must have done so much right before as to
defend me now. Be it how it will, do right now. Always scorn appearances and you always may. The force of character is cumulative. All the foregone days of virtue work their health into this.
What makes the majesty of the heroes of the senate and the field,
which so fills the imagination? The consciousness of a train of
great days and victories behind. They shed a united light on the
advancing actor. He is attended as by a visible escort of angels.
That is it which throws thunder into Chatham's voice, and dignity
into Washington's port, and America into Adam's eye. Honor is
venerable to us because it is no ephemera. It is always ancient virtue. We worship it today because it is not of today. We love it
and pay it homage because it is not a trap for our love and homage,
but is self-dependent, self-derived, and therefore of an old im-
maculate pedigree, even if shown in a young person.

I hope in these days we have heard the last of conformity and
consistency. Let the words be gazetted and ridiculous henceforward. Instead of the gong for dinner, let us hear a whistle from
the Spartan fife. Let us never bow and apologize more. A great
man is coming to eat at my house. I do not wish to please him; I
wish that he should wish to please me. I will stand here for
humanity, and though I would make it kind, I would make it true.
Let us affront and reprimand the smooth mediocrity and squalid
contentment of the times, and hurl in the face of custom and
trade and office, the fact which is the upshot of all history, that
there is a great responsible Thinker and Actor working wherever
a man works; that a true man belongs to no other time or place,
but is the center of things. Where he is, there is nature. He measures you and all men and all events. Ordinarily, every body in
society reminds us of somewhat else, or of some other person. Character, reality, reminds you of nothing else; it takes place of the
whole creation. The man must be so much that he must make
all circumstances indifferent. Every true man is a cause, a country,
and an age; requires infinite spaces and numbers and time fully to
accomplish his design; — and posterity seem to follow his steps as
a train of clients. A man Caesar is born, and for ages after we have
a Roman Empire. Christ is born, and millions of minds so grow
and cleave to his genius that he is confounded with virtue and the
possible of man. An institution is the lengthened shadow of one
man; as, Monachism, of the Hermit Antony; the Reformation, of
Luther; Quakerism, of Fox; Methodism, of Wesley; Abolition, of

Clarkson.[1] Scipio, Milton called "the height of Rome"; and all history resolves itself very easily into the biography of a few stout and earnest persons.

Let a man then know his worth, and keep things under his feet. Let him not peep or steal, or skulk up and down with the air of a charity-boy, a bastard, or an interloper in the world which exists for him. But the man in the street, finding no worth in himself which corresponds to the force which built a tower or sculptured a marble god, feels poor when he looks on these. To him a palace, a statue, or a costly book have an alien and forbidding air, much like a gay equipage, and seem to say like that, "Who are you, Sir?" Yet they all are his, suitors for his notice, petitioners to his faculties that they will come out and take possession. The picture waits for my verdict; it is not to command me, but I am to settle its claims to praise. That popular fable of the sot who was picked up dead-drunk in the street, carried to the duke's house, washed and dressed and laid in the duke's bed, and, on his waking, treated with all obsequious ceremony like the duke, and assured that he had been insane, owes its popularity to the fact that it symbolizes so well the state of man, who is in the world a sort of sot, but now and then wakes up, exercises his reason and finds himself a true prince.

Our reading is mendicant and sycophantic. In history our imagination plays us false. Kingdom and lordship, power and estate, are a gaudier vocabulary than private John and Edward in a small house and common day's work; but the things of life are the same to both; the sum total of both is the same. Why all this deference to Alfred and Scanderbeg and Gustavus?[2] Suppose they were virtuous; did they wear out virtue? As great a stake depends on your private act today as followed their public and renowned steps. When private men shall act with original views, the lustre will be transferred from the actions of kings to those of gentlemen.

The world has been instructed by its kings, who have so magnetized the eyes of nations. It has been taught by this colossal symbol the mutual reverence that is due from man to man. The joyful loyalty with which men have everywhere suffered the king, the noble, or the great proprietor to walk among them by a law of his own, make his own scale of men and things and reverse theirs, pay for benefits not with money but with honor, and represent the law in his person, was the hieroglyphic by which they obscurely

---

[1] A leader of British Abolition.
[2] Saxon, Albanian, Swedish national heroes and rulers.

signified their consciousness of their own right and comeliness, the right of every man.

The magnetism which all original action exerts is explained when we inquire the reason of self-trust. Who is the Trustee? What is the aboriginal Self, on which a universal reliance may be grounded? What is the nature and power of that science-baffling star, without parallax, without calculable elements, which shoots a ray of beauty even into trivial and impure actions, if the least mark of independence appear? The inquiry leads us to that source, at once the essence of genius, of virtue, and of life, which we call Spontaneity or Instinct. We denote this primary wisdom as Intuition, whilst all later teachings are tuitions. In that deep force, the last fact behind which analysis cannot go, all things find their common origin. For the sense of being which in calm hours rises, we know not how, in the soul, is not diverse from things, from space, from light, from time, from man, but one with them and proceeds obviously from the same source whence their life and being also proceed. We first share the life by which things exist and afterwards see them as appearances in nature and forget that we have shared their cause. Here is the fountain of action and of thought. Here are the lungs of that inspiration which giveth man wisdom and which cannot be denied without impiety and atheism. We lie in the lap of immense intelligence, which makes us receivers of its truth and organs of its activity. When we discern justice, when we discern truth, we do nothing of ourselves, but allow a passage to its beams. If we ask whence this comes, if we seek to pry into the soul that causes, all philosophy is at fault. Its presence or its absence is all we can affirm. Every man discriminates between the voluntary acts of his mind and his involuntary perceptions, and knows that to his involuntary perceptions a perfect faith is due. He may err in the expression of them, but he knows that these things are so, like day and night, not to be disputed. My wilful actions and acquisitions are but roving; — the idlest reverie, the faintest native emotion, command my curiosity and respect. Thoughtless people contradict as readily the statement of perceptions as of opinions, or rather much more readily; for they do not distinguish between perception and notion. They fancy that I choose to see this or that thing. But perception is not whimsical, but fatal. If I see a trait, my children will see it after me, and in course of time all mankind, — although it may chance that no one has seen it before me. For my perception of it is as much a fact as the sun.

The relations of the soul to the divine spirit are so pure that it is profane to seek to interpose helps. It must be that when God speaketh he should communicate, not one thing, but all things; should fill the world with his voice; should scatter forth light, nature, time, souls, from the center of the present thought; and new date and new create the whole. Whenever a mind is simple and receives a divine wisdom, old things pass away, — means, teachers, texts, temples fall; it lives now, and absorbs past and future into the present hour. All things are made sacred by relation to it, — one as much as another. All things are dissolved to their center by their cause, and in the universal miracle petty and particular miracles disappear. If therefore a man claims to know and speak of God and carries you backward to the phraseology of some old moldered nation in another country, in another world, believe him not. Is the acorn better than the oak which is its fulness and completion? Is the parent better than the child into whom he has cast his ripened being? Whence then this worship of the past? The centuries are conspirators against the sanity and authority of the soul. Time and space are but physiological colors which the eye makes, but the soul is light: where it is, is day; where it was, is night; and history is an impertinence and an injury if it be any thing more than a cheerful apologue or parable of my being and becoming.

Man is timid and apologetic; he is no longer upright; he dares not say "I think," "I am," but quotes some saint or sage. He is ashamed before the blade of grass or the blowing rose. These roses under my window make no reference to former roses or to better ones; they are for what they are; they exist with God today. There is no time to them. There is simply the rose; it is perfect in every moment of its existence. Before a leaf-bud has burst, its whole life acts; in the full-blown flower there is no more; in the leafless root there is no less. Its nature is satisfied and it satisfies nature in all moments alike. But man postpones or remembers; he does not live in the present, but with reverted eye laments the past, or, heedless of the riches that surround him, stands on tiptoe to foresee the future. He cannot be happy and strong until he too lives with nature in the present, above time.

This should be plain enough. Yet see what strong intellects dare not yet hear God himself unless he speak the phraseology of I know not what David, or Jeremiah, or Paul. We shall not always set so great a price on a few texts, on a few lives. We are like children who repeat by rote the sentences of grandames and tutors, and, as they grow older, of the men of talents and character they chance to see, — painfully recollecting the exact words they spoke; afterwards, when they come into the point of view which those had who uttered these sayings, they understand them and are willing to let the words go; for at any time they can use words as good when occasion comes. If we live truly, we shall see truly. It is as easy for the strong man to be strong, as it is for the weak to be weak. When we have new perception, we shall gladly disburden the memory of its hoarded treasures as old rubbish. When a man lives with God, his voice shall be as sweet as the murmur of the brook and the rustle of the corn.

And now at last the highest truth on this subject remains unsaid; probably cannot be said; for all that we say is the far-off remembering of the intuition. That thought by what I can now nearest approach to say it, is this. When good is near you, when you have life in yourself, it is not by any known or accustomed way; you shall not discern the footprints of any other; you shall not see the face of man; you shall not hear any name; — the way, the thought, the good, shall be wholly strange and new. It shall exclude example and experience. You take the way from man, not to man. All persons that ever existed are its forgotten ministers. Fear and hope are alike beneath it. There is somewhat low even in hope. In the hour of vision there is nothing that can be called gratitude, nor properly joy. The soul raised over passion beholds identity and eternal causation, perceives the self-existence of Truth and Right, and calms itself with knowing that all things go well. Vast spaces of nature, the Atlantic Ocean, the South Sea; long intervals of time, years, centuries, are of no account. This which I think and feel underlay every former state of life and circumstances, as it does underlie my present, and what is called life and what is called death.

Life only avails, not the having lived. Power ceases in the instant of repose; it resides in the moment of transition from a past to a new state, in the shooting of the gulf, in the darting to an aim. This one fact the world hates; that the soul *becomes*; for that forever degrades the past, turns all riches to poverty, all reputation to a shame, confounds the saint with the rogue, shoves Jesus and Judas equally aside. Why then do we prate of self-reliance? Inasmuch as the soul is present there will be power not confident but agent. To talk of reliance is a poor external way of speaking. Speak rather of that which relies because it works and is. Who has more obedience than I masters me, though he should not raise his finger. Round him I must revolve by the gravitation of spirits. We fancy it rhetoric when we speak of eminent virtue. We do not yet see that virtue is Height, and that a man or a company of men, plastic and permeable to principles, by the law of nature must over-power and ride all cities, nations, kings, rich men, poets, who are not.

This is the ultimate fact which we so quickly reach on this, as on every topic, the resolution of all into the ever-blessed ONE. Self-existence is the attribute of the Supreme Cause, and it consti-tutes the measure of good by the degree in which it enters into all lower forms. All things real are so by so much virtue as they contain. Commerce, husbandry, hunting, whaling, war, eloquence, personal weight, are somewhat, and engage my respect as examples of its presence and impure action. I see the same law working in nature for conservation and growth. Power is, in nature, the es-sential measure of right. Nature suffers nothing to remain in her kingdoms which cannot help itself. The genesis and maturation of a planet, its poise and orbit, the bended tree recovering itself from the strong wind, the vital resources of every animal and vege-table, are demonstrations of the self-sufficing and therefore self-relying soul.

Thus all concentrates: let us not rove; let us sit at home with the cause. Let us stun and astonish the intruding rabble of men and books and institutions by a simple declaration of the divine fact. Bid the invaders take the shoes from off their feet, for God is here within. Let our simplicity judge them, and our docility to our own law demonstrate the poverty of nature and fortune beside our na-tive riches.

But now we are a mob. Man does not stand in awe of man, nor is his genius admonished to stay at home, to put itself in communi-cation with the internal ocean, but it goes abroad to beg a cup of water of the urns of other men. We must go alone. I like the silent church before the service begins, better than any preaching. How far off, how cool, how chaste the persons look, begirt each one with a precinct or sanctuary! So let us always sit. Why should we assume the faults of our friend, or wife, or father, or child, be-cause they sit around our hearth, or are said to have the same blood? All men have my blood and I all men's. Not for that will I adopt their petulance or folly, even to the extent of being ashamed of it. But your isolation must not be mechanical, but spiritual, that is, must be elevation. At times the whole world seems to be in conspiracy to importune you with emphatic trifles.

Friend, client, child, sickness, fear, want, charity, all knock at once
at thy closet door and say, — "Come out unto us." But keep thy
state; come not into their confusion. The power men possess to
annoy me I give them by a weak curiosity. No man can come near
me but through my act. "What we love that we have, but by
desire we bereave ourselves of the love."   *inconsistency*

If we cannot at once rise to the sanctities of obedience and faith,
let us at least resist our temptations; let us enter into the state of
war and wake Thor and Woden, courage and constancy, in our
Saxon breasts. This is to be done in our smooth times by speaking
the truth. Check this lying hospitality and lying affection. Live
no longer to the expectation of these deceived and deceiving people with whom we converse. Say to them, "O father, O mother, O
wife, O brother, O friend, I have lived with you after appearances
hitherto. Henceforward I am the truth's. Be it known unto you
that henceforward I obey no law less than the eternal law. I will
have no covenants but proximities. I shall endeavor to nourish my
parents, to support my family, to be the chaste husband of one
wife, — but these relations I must fill after a new and unprecedented way. I appeal from your customs. I must be myself. I cannot break myself any longer for you, or you. If you can love me for
what I am, we shall be the happier. If you cannot, I will still seek
to deserve that you should. I will not hide my tastes or aversions.
I will so trust that what is deep is holy, that I will do strongly before the sun and moon whatever inly rejoices me and the heart appoints. If you are noble, I will love you; if you are not, I will not
hurt you and myself by hypocritical attentions. If you are true,
but not in the same truth with me, cleave to your companions; I
will seek my own. I do this not selfishly but humbly and truly. It
is alike your interest, and mine, and all men's, however long we
have dwelt in lies, to live in truth. Does this sound harsh today?
You will soon love what is dictated by your nature as well as mine,
and if we follow the truth it will bring us out safe at last." — But
so may you give these friends pain. Yes, but I cannot sell my
liberty and my power, to save their sensibility. Besides, all persons
have their moments of reason, when they look out into the region
of absolute truth; then will they justify me and do the same thing.

The populace think that your rejection of popular standards is
a rejection of all standard, and mere antinomianism; and the bold
sensualist will use the name of philosophy to gild his crimes. But
the law of consciousness abides. There are two confessionals, in
one or the other of which we must be shriven. You may fulfil your

round of duties by clearing yourself in the *direct,* or in the *reflex*
way. Consider whether you have satisfied your relations to father,
mother, cousin, neighbor, town, cat and dog — whether any of
these can upbraid you. But I may also neglect this reflex standard
and absolve me to myself. I have my own stern claims and perfect
circle. It denies the name of duty to many offices that are called
duties. But if I can discharge its debts it enables me to dispense
with the popular code. If any one imagines that this law is lax, let
him keep its commandment one day.

And truly it demands something godlike in him who has cast off
the common motives of humanity and has ventured to trust himself for a taskmaster. High be his heart, faithful his will, clear his
sight, that he may in good earnest be doctrine, society, law, to himself, that a simple purpose may be to him as strong as iron necessity
is to others!

If any man consider the present aspects of what is called by distinction *society*, he will see the need of these ethics. The sinew
and heart of man seem to be drawn out, and we are become
timorous, desponding whimperers. We are afraid of truth, afraid
of fortune, afraid of death, and afraid of each other. Our age yields
no great and perfect persons. We want men and women who shall
renovate life and our social state, but we see that most natures are
insolvent, cannot satisfy their own wants, have an ambition out of
all proportion to their practical force and do lean and beg day and
night continually. Our housekeeping is mendicant, our arts, our
occupations, our marriages, our religion we have not chosen, but
society has chosen for us. We are parlor soldiers. We shun the
rugged battle of fate, where strength is born.

If our young men miscarry in their first enterprises they lose all
heart. If the young merchant fails, men say he is *ruined.* If the
finest genius studies at one of our colleges and is not installed in an
office within one year afterwards in the cities or suburbs of Boston
or New York, it seems to his friends and to himself that he is right
in being disheartened and in complaining the rest of his life. A
sturdy lad from New Hampshire or Vermont, who in turn tries all
the professions, who *teams it, farms it, peddles,* keeps a school,
preaches, edits a newspaper, goes to Congress, buys a township, and
so forth, in successive years, and always like a cat falls on his feet,
is worth a hundred of these city dolls. He walks abreast with his
days and feels no shame in not "studying a profession," for he does
not postpone his life, but lives already. He has not one chance, but
a hundred chances. Let a Stoic open the resources of man and tell

men they are not leaning willows, but can and must detach themselves; that with the exercise of self-trust, new powers shall appear; that a man is the word made flesh, born to shed healing to the nations; that he should be ashamed of our compassion, and that the moment he acts from himself, tossing the laws, the books, idolatries and customs out of the window, we pity him no more but thank and revere him; — and that teacher shall restore the life of man to splendor and make his name dear to all history.

It is easy to see that a greater self-reliance must work a revolution in all the offices and relations of men; in their religion; in their education; in their pursuits; their modes of living; their association; in their property; in their speculative views.

1. In what prayers do men allow themselves! That which they call a holy office is not so much as brave and manly. Prayer looks abroad and asks for some foreign addition to come through some foreign virtue, and loses itself in endless mazes of natural and supernatural, and mediatorial and miraculous. Prayer that craves a particular commodity, anything less than all good, is vicious. Prayer is the contemplation of the facts of life from the highest point of view. It is the soliloquy of a beholding and jubilant soul. It is the spirit of God pronouncing his works good. But prayer as a means to effect a private end is meanness and theft. It supposes dualism and not unity in nature and consciousness. As soon as the man is at one with God, he will not beg. He will then see prayer in all action. The prayer of the farmer kneeling in his field to weed it, the prayer of the rower kneeling with the stroke of his oar, are true prayers heard throughout nature, though for cheap ends. Caratach, in Fletcher's "Bonduca," when admonished to inquire the mind of the god Audate, replies, —

> "His hidden meaning lies in our endeavors;
> Our valors are our best gods."

Another sort of false prayers are our regrets. Discontent is the want of self-reliance: it is infirmity of will. Regret calamities if you can thereby help the sufferer; if not, attend your own work and already the evil begins to be repaired. Our sympathy is just as base. We come to them who weep foolishly and sit down and cry for company, instead of imparting to them truth and health in rough electric shocks, putting them once more in communication with their own reason. The secret of fortune is joy in our hands. Welcome evermore to gods and men is the self-helping man. For him all doors are flung wide; him all tongues greet, all honors crown, all

eyes follow with desire. Our love goes out to him and embraces
him because he did not need it. We solicitously and apologetically
caress and celebrate him because he held on his way and scorned
our disapprobation. The gods love him because men hated him.
"To the persevering mortal," said Zoroaster, "the blessed Im-
mortals are swift."

As men's prayers are a disease of the will, so are their creeds a
disease of the intellect. They say with those foolish Israelites, "Let
not God speak to us, lest we die. Speak thou, speak any man with
us, and we will obey." Everywhere I am hindered of meeting God
in my brother, because he has shut his own temple doors and re-
cites fables merely of his brother's, or his brother's brother's God.
Every new mind is a new classification. If it prove a mind of un-
common activity and power, a Locke, a Lavoisier, a Hutton, a
Bentham, a Fourier, it imposes its classification on other men, and
lo! a new system. In proportion to the depth of the thought, and
so to the number of the objects its touches and brings within
reach of the pupil, is his complacency. But chiefly is this apparent
in creeds and churches, which are also classifications of some
powerful mind acting on the elemental thought of duty and man's
relation to the Highest. Such is Calvinism, Quakerism, Sweden-
borgism. The pupil takes the same delight in subordinating every
thing to the new terminology as a girl who has just learned botany
in seeing a new earth and new seasons thereby. It will happen for
a time that the pupil will find his intellectual power has grown by
the study of his master's mind. But in all unbalanced minds the
classification is idolized, passes for the end and not for a speedily
exhaustible means, so that the walls of the system blend to their
eye in the remote horizon with the walls of the universe; the
luminaries of heaven seem to them hung on the arch their master
built. They cannot imagine how you aliens have any right to see,
— how you can see; "It must be somehow that you stole the light
from us." They do not yet perceive that light, unsystematic, indomitable, will break into any cabin, even into theirs. Let them
chirp awhile and call it their own. If they are honest and do well,
presently their neat new pinfold will be too strait and low, will
crack, will lean, will rot and vanish, and the immortal light, all
young and joyful, million-orbed, million-colored, will beam over
the universe as on the first morning.

2. It is for want of self-culture that the superstition of Traveling,
whose idols are Italy, England, Egypt, retains its fascination for all
educated Americans. They who made England, Italy, or Greece

venerable in the imagination, did so by sticking fast where they were, like an axis of the earth. In manly hours we feel that duty is our place. The soul is no traveler; the wise man stays at home, and when his necessities, his duties, on any occasion call him from his house, or into foreign lands, he is at home still and shall make men sensible by the expression of his countenance that he goes, the missionary of wisdom and virtue, and visits cities and men like a sovereign and not like an interloper or a valet.

I have no churlish objection to the circumnavigation of the globe for the purposes of art, of study, and benevolence, so that the man is first domesticated, or does not go abroad with the hope of finding somewhat greater than he knows. He who travels to be amused, or to get somewhat which he does not carry, travels away from himself, and grows old even in youth among old things. In Thebes, in Palmyra, his will and mind have become old and dilapidated as they. He carries ruins to ruins.

Traveling is a fool's paradise. Our first journeys discover to us the indifference of places. At home I dream that at Naples, at Rome, I can be intoxicated with beauty and lose my sadness. I pack my trunk, embrace my friends, embark on the sea and at last wake up in Naples, and there beside me is the stern fact, the sad self, unrelenting, identical, that I fled from. I seek the Vatican and the palaces. I affect to be intoxicated with sights and suggestions, but I am not intoxicated. My giant goes with me wherever I go.

3. But the rage of traveling is a symptom of a deeper unsoundness affecting the whole intellectual action. The intellect is vagabond, and our system of education fosters restlessness. Our minds travel when our bodies are forced to stay at home. We imitate; and what is imitation but the traveling of the mind? Our houses are built with foreign taste; our shelves are garnished with foreign ornaments; our opinions, our tastes, our faculties, lean, and follow the Past and the Distant. The soul created the arts wherever they have flourished. It was in his own mind that the artist sought his model. It was an application of his own thought to the thing to be done and the conditions to be observed. And why need we copy the Doric or the Gothic model? Beauty, convenience, grandeur of thought and quaint expression are as near to us as to any, and if the American artist will study with hope and love the precise thing to be done by him, considering the climate, the soil, the length of the day, the wants of the people, the habit and form of the government, he will create a house in which all these will find themselves fitted, and taste and sentiment will be satisfied also.

Insist on yourself; never imitate. Your own gift you can present every moment with the cumulative force of a whole life's cultivation; but of the adopted talent of another you have only an extemporaneous half possession. That which each can do best, none but his Maker can teach him. No man yet knows what it is, nor can, till that person has exhibited it. Where is the master who could have taught Shakespeare? Where is the master who could have instructed Franklin, or Washington, or Bacon, or Newton? Every great man is a unique. The Scipionism of Scipio is precisely that part he could not borrow. Shakespeare will never be made by the study of Shakespeare. Do that which is assigned you, and you cannot hope too much or dare too much. There is at this moment for you an utterance brave and grand as that of the colossal chisel of Phidias, or trowel of the Egyptians, or the pen of Moses or Dante, but different from all these. Not possibly will the soul, all rich, all eloquent, with thousand-cloven tongue, deign to repeat itself; but if you can hear what these patriarchs say, surely you can reply to them in the same pitch of voice; for the ear and the tongue are two organs of one nature. Abide in the simple and noble regions of thy life, obey thy heart, and thou shalt reproduce the Foreworld again.

4. As our Religion, our Education, our Art look abroad, so does our spirit of society. All men plume themselves on the improvement of society, and no man improves.

Society never advances. It recedes as fast on one side as it gains on the other. It undergoes continual changes; it is barbarous, it is civilized, it is christianized, it is rich, it is scientific; but this change is not amelioration. For every thing that is given something is taken. Society acquires new arts and loses old instincts. What a contrast between the well-clad, reading, writing, thinking American, with a watch, a pencil and a bill of exchange in his pocket, and the naked New Zealander, whose property is a club, a spear, a mat and an undivided twentieth of a shed to sleep under! But compare the health of the two men and you shall see that the white man has lost his aboriginal strength. If the traveler tell us truly, strike the savage with a broad-axe and in a day or two the flesh shall unite and heal as if you struck the blow into soft pitch, and the same blow shall send the white to his grave.

The civilized man has built a coach, but has lost the use of his feet. He is supported on crutches, but lacks so much support of muscle. He has a fine Geneva watch, but he fails of the skill to tell the hour by the sun. A Greenwich nautical almanac he has, and so being sure of the information when he wants it, the man in the street does not know a star in the sky. The solstice he does not observe; the equinox he knows as little; and the whole bright calendar of the year is without a dial in his mind. His note-books impair his memory; his libraries overload his wit; the insurance-office increases the number of accidents; and it may be a question whether machinery does not encumber; whether we have not lost by refinement some energy, by a Christianity, entrenched in establishments and forms, some vigor of wild virtue. For every Stoic was a Stoic; but in Christendom where is the Christian?

There is no more deviation in the moral standard than in the standard of height or bulk. No greater men are now than ever were. A singular equality may be observed between the great men of the first and of the last ages; nor can all the science, art, religion, and philosophy of the nineteenth century avail to educate greater men than Plutarch's heroes, three or four and twenty centuries ago. Not in time is the race progressive. Phocion, Socrates, Anaxagoras, Diogenes, are great men, but they leave no class. He who is really of their class will not be called by their name, but will be his own man, and in his turn the founder of a sect. The arts and inventions of each period are only its costume and do not invigorate men. The harm of the improved machinery may compensate its good. Hudson and Behring accomplished so much in their fishing-boats as to astonish Parry and Franklin, whose equipment exhausted the resources of science and art. Galileo, with an opera-glass, discovered a more splendid series of celestial phenomena than any one since. Columbus found the New World in an undecked boat. It is curious to see the periodical disuse and perishing of means and machinery which were introduced with loud laudation a few years or centuries before. The great genius returns to essential man. We reckoned the improvements of the art of war among the triumphs of science, and yet Napoleon conquered Europe by the bivouac, which consisted of falling back on naked valor and disencumbering it of all aids. The Emperor held it impossible to make a perfect army, says Las Cases, "without abolishing our arms, magazines, commissaries and carriages, until, in imitation of the Roman custom, the soldier should receive his supply of corn, grind it in his hand-mill and bake his bread himself."

Society is a wave. The wave moves onward, but the water of which it is composed does not. The same particle does not rise from the valley to the ridge. Its unity is only phenomenal. The persons who make up a nation today, next year die, and their experience dies with them.

And so the reliance on Property, including the reliance on governments which protect it, is the want of self-reliance. Men have looked away from themselves and at things so long that they have come to esteem the religious, learned and civil institutions as guards of property, and they deprecate assaults on these, because they feel them to be assaults on property. They measure their esteem of each other by what each has, and not by what each is. But a cultivated man becomes ashamed of his property, out of new respect for his nature. Especially he hates what he has if he see that it is accidental, — came to him by inheritance, or gift, or crime; then he feels that it is not having; it does not belong to him, has no root in him and merely lies there because no revolution or no robber takes it away. But that which a man is, does always by necessity acquire; and what the man acquires, is living property, which does not wait the beck of rulers, or mobs, or revolutions, or fire, or storm, or bankruptcies, but perpetually renews itself wherever the man breathes. "Thy lot or portion of life," said the Caliph Ali, "is seeking after thee; therefore be at rest from seeking after it." Our dependence on these foreign goods leads us to our slavish respect for numbers. The political parties meet in numerous conventions; the greater the concourse and with each new uproar of announcement, The delegation from Essex! The Democrats from New Hampshire! The Whigs of Maine! the young patriot feels himself stronger than before by a new thousand of eyes and arms. In like manner the reformers summon conventions and vote and resolve in multitude. Not so, O friends! will the God deign to enter and inhabit you, but by a method precisely the reverse. It is only as a man puts off all foreign support and stands alone that I see him to be strong and to prevail. He is weaker by every recruit to his banner. Is not a man better than a town? Ask nothing of men, and, in the endless mutation, thou only firm column must presently appear the upholder of all that surrounds thee. He who knows that power is inborn, that he is weak because he has looked for good out of him and elsewhere, and, so perceiving, throws himself unhesitatingly on his thought, instantly rights himself, stands in the erect position, commands his limbs, works miracles; just as a man who stands on his feet is stronger than a man who stands on his head.

So use all that is called Fortune. Most men gamble with her,

persons who make up a nation today, next year die, and their experience dies with them.

And so the reliance on Property, including the reliance on governments which protect it, is the want of self-reliance. Men have looked away from themselves and at things so long that they have come to esteem the religious, learned and civil institutions as guards of property, and they deprecate assaults on these, because they feel them to be assaults on property. They measure their esteem of each other by what each has, and not by what each is. But a cultivated man becomes ashamed of his property, out of new respect for his nature. Especially he hates what he has if he see that it is accidental, — came to him by inheritance, or gift, or crime; then he feels that it is not having; it does not belong to him, has no root in him and merely lies there because no revolution or no robber takes it away. But that which a man is, does always by necessity acquire; and what the man acquires, is living property, which does not wait the beck of rulers, or mobs, or revolutions, or fire, or storm, or bankruptcies, but perpetually renews itself wherever the man breathes. "Thy lot or portion of life," said the Caliph Ali, "is seeking after thee; therefore be at rest from seeking after it." Our dependence on these foreign goods leads us to our slavish respect for numbers. The political parties meet in numerous conventions; the greater the concourse and with each new uproar of announcement, The delegation from Essex! The Democrats from New Hampshire! The Whigs of Maine! the young patriot feels himself stronger than before by a new thousand of eyes and arms. In like manner the reformers summon conventions and vote and resolve in multitude. Not so, O friends! will the God deign to enter and inhabit you, but by a method precisely the reverse. It is only as a man puts off all foreign support and stands alone that I see him to be strong and to prevail. He is weaker by every recruit to his banner. Is not a man better than a town? Ask nothing of men, and, in the endless mutation, thou only firm column must presently appear the upholder of all that surrounds thee. He who knows that power is inborn, that he is weak because he has looked for good out of him and elsewhere, and, so perceiving, throws himself unhesitatingly on his thought, instantly rights himself, stands in the erect position, commands his limbs, works miracles; just as a man who stands on his feet is stronger than a man who stands on his head.

So use all that is called Fortune. Most men gamble with her.

and gain all, and lose all, as her wheel rolls. But do thou leave as unlawful these winnings, and deal with Cause and Effect, the chancellors of God. In the Will work and acquire, and thou hast chained the wheel of Chance, and shall sit hereafter out of fear from her rotations. A political victory, a rise of rents, the recovery of your sick or the return of your absent friend, or some other favorable event raises your spirits, and you think good days are preparing for you. Do not believe it. Nothing can bring you peace but yourself. Nothing can bring you peace but the triumph of principles.

rampant individualism

❋❋

Circles

Nature centers into balls,
And her proud ephemerals,
Fast to surface and outside,
Scan the profile of the sphere;
Knew they what that signified,
A new genesis were here.

THE eye is the first circle; the horizon which it forms is the second; and throughout nature this primary figure is repeated without end. It is the highest emblem in the cipher of the world. St. Augustine described the nature of God as a circle whose center was everywhere and its circumference nowhere. We are all our lifetime reading the copious sense of this first of forms. One moral we have already deduced in considering the circular or compensatory character of every human action. Another analogy we shall now trace, that every action admits of being outdone. Our life is an apprenticeship to the truth that around every circle another can be drawn; that there is no end in nature, but every end is a beginning; that there is always another dawn risen on mid-noon, and under every deep a lower deep opens.

This fact, as far as it symbolizes the moral fact of the Unattainable, the flying Perfect, around which the hands of man can never meet, at once the inspirer and the condemner of every success, may conveniently serve us to connect many illustrations of human power in every department.

There are no fixtures in nature. The universe is fluid and volatile. Permanence is but a word of degrees. Our globe seen by God is a transparent law, not a mass of facts. The law dissolves the fact and holds it fluid. Our culture is the predominance of an idea which draws after it this train of cities and institutions. Let us rise into another idea; they will disappear. The Greek sculpture is all melted away, as if it had been statues of ice; here and there a solitary figure or fragment remaining, as we see flecks and scraps of snow left in cold dells and mountain clefts in June and July. For the genius that created it creates now somewhat else. The Greek letters last a little longer, but are already passing under the same sentence and tumbling into the inevitable pit which the creation of new thought opens for all that is old. The new continents are built out of the ruins of an old planet; the new races fed out of the decomposition of the foregoing. New arts destroy the old. See the investment of capital in aqueducts, made useless by hydraulics; fortifications, by gunpowder; roads and canals, by railways; sails, by steam; steam by electricity.

You admire this tower of granite, weathering the hurts of so many ages. Yet a little waving hand built this huge wall, and that which builds is better than that which is built. The hand that built can topple it down much faster. Better than the hand and nimbler was the invisible thought which wrought through it; and thus ever, behind the coarse effect, is a fine cause, which, being narrowly seen, is itself the effect of a finer cause. Everything looks permanent until its secret is known. A rich estate appears to women a firm and lasting fact; to a merchant, one easily created out of any materials, and easily lost. An orchard, good tillage, good grounds, seem a fixture, like a gold mine, or a river, to a citizen; but to a large farmer, not much more fixed than the state of the crop. Nature looks provokingly stable and secular, but it has a cause like all the rest; and when once I comprehend that, will these fields stretch so immovably wide, these leaves hang so individually considerable? Permanence is a word of degrees. Every thing is medial. Moons are no more bounds to spiritual power than bat-balls.

The key to every man is his thought. Sturdy and defying though he look, he has a helm which he obeys, which is the idea after which all his facts are classified. He can only be reformed by showing him a new idea which commands his own. The life of man is a self-evolving circle, which, from a ring imperceptibly small, rushes on all sides outwards to new and larger circles, and that without end. The extent to which this generation of circles, wheel without wheel, will go, depends on the force or truth of the individual soul.

For it is the inert effort of each thought, having formed itself into a circular wave of circumstance, — as for instance an empire, rules of an art, a local usage, a religious rite, — to heap itself on that ridge and to solidify and hem in the life. But if the soul is quick and strong it bursts over that boundary on all sides and expands another orbit on the great deep, which also runs up into a high wave, with attempt again to stop and to bind. But the heart refuses to be imprisoned; in its first and narrowest pulses it already tends outward with a vast force and to immense and innumerable expansions.

Every ultimate fact is only the first of a new series. Every general law only a particular fact of some more general law presently to disclose itself. There is no outside, no inclosing wall, no circumference to us. The man finishes his story, — how good! how final! how it puts a new face on all things! He fills the sky. Lo! on the other side rises also a man and draws a circle around the circle we had just pronounced the outline of the sphere. Then already is our first speaker not man, but only a first speaker. His only redress is forthwith to draw a circle outside of his antagonist. And so men do by themselves. The result of today, which haunts the mind and cannot be escaped, will presently be abridged into a word, and the principle that seemed to explain nature will itself be included as one example of a bolder generalization. In the thought of tomorrow there is a power to upheave all thy creed, all the creeds, all the literatures of the nations, and marshal thee to a heaven which no epic dream has yet depicted. Every man is not so much a workman in the world as he is a suggestion of that he should be. Men walk as prophecies of the next age.

Step by step we scale this mysterious ladder; the steps are actions, the new prospect is power. Every several result is threatened and judged by that which follows. Every one seems to be contradicted by the new; it is only limited by the new. The new statement is always hated by the old, and, to those dwelling in the old, comes like an abyss of skepticism. But the eye soon gets wonted to it, for the eye and it are effects of one cause; then its innocency and benefit appear, and presently, all its energy spent, it pales and dwindles before the revelation of the new hour.

Fear not the new generalization. Does the fact look crass and material, threatening to degrade thy theory of spirit? Resist it not; it goes to refine and raise thy theory of matter just as much.

There are no fixtures to men, if we appeal to consciousness. Every man supposes himself not to be fully understood; and if there is any truth in him, if he rests at last on the divine soul, I see not how it can be otherwise. The last chamber, the last closet, he must feel was never opened; there is always a residuum unknown, un-analyzable. That is, every man believes that he has a greater pos-sibility.

Our moods do not believe in each other. Today I am full of thoughts and can write what I please. I see no reason why I should not have the same thought, the same power of expression, to-morrow. What I write, whilst I write it, seems the most natural thing in the world; but yesterday I saw a dreary vacuity in this direction in which now I see so much; and a month hence, I doubt not, I shall wonder who he was that wrote so many continuous pages. Alas for this infirm faith, this will not strenuous, this vast ebb of a vast flow! I am God in nature; I am a weed by the wall.

The continual effort to raise himself above himself, to work a pitch above his last height, betrays itself in a man's relations. We thirst for approbation, yet cannot forgive the approver. The sweet of nature is love; yet if I have a friend I am tormented by my im-perfections. The love of me accuses the other party. If he were high enough to slight me, then could I love him, and rise by my affection to new heights. A man's growth is seen in the successive choirs of his friends. For every friend whom he loses for truth, he gains a better. I thought as I walked in the woods and mused on my friends, why should I play with them this game of idolatry? I know and see too well, when not voluntarily blind, the speedy limits of persons called high and worthy. Rich, noble and great they are by the liberality of our speech, but truth is sad. O blessed Spirit, whom I forsake for these, they are not thou! Every personal consideration that we allow costs us heavenly state. We sell the thrones of angels for a short and turbulent pleasure.

How often must we learn this lesson? Men cease to interest us when we find their limitations. The only sin is limitation. As soon as you once come up with a man's limitations, it is all over with him. Has he talents? has he enterprise? has he knowledge? It boots not. Infinitely alluring and attractive was he to you yesterday, a great hope, a sea to swim in; now, you have found his shores, found it a pond, and you care not if you never see it again.

Each new step we take in thought reconciles twenty seemingly discordant facts, as expressions of one law. Aristotle and Plato are reckoned the respective heads of two schools. A wise man will see that Aristotle platonizes. By going one step farther back in thought, discordant opinions are reconciled by being seen to be two extremes of one principle, and we can never go so far back as to preclude a still higher vision.

Beware when the great God lets loose a thinker on this planet. Then all things are at risk. It is as when a conflagration has broken out in a great city, and no man knows what is safe, or where it will end. There is not a piece of science but its flank may be turned tomorrow; there is not any literary reputation, not the so-called eternal names of fame, that may not be revised and condemned. The very hopes of man, the thoughts of his heart, the religion of nations, the manners and morals of mankind are all at the mercy of a new generalization. Generalization is always a new influx of the divinity into the mind. Hence the thrill that attends it.

Valor consists in the power of self-recovery, so that a man cannot have his flank turned, cannot be out-generaled, but put him where you will, he stands. This can only be by his preferring truth to his past apprehension of truth, and his alert acceptance of it from whatever quarter; the intrepid conviction that his laws, his relations to society, his Christianity, his world, may at any time be superseded and decease.

There are degrees in idealism. We learn first to play with it academically, as the magnet was once a toy. Then we see in the heyday of youth and poetry that it may be true, that it is true in gleams and fragments. Then its countenance waxes stern and grand, and we see that it must be true. It now shows itself ethical and practical. We learn that God IS; that he is in me; and that all things are shadows of him. The idealism of Berkeley is only a crude statement of the idealism of Jesus, and that again is a crude statement of the fact that all nature is the rapid efflux of goodness executing and organizing itself. Much more obviously is history and the state of the world at any one time directly dependent on the intellectual classification then existing in the minds of men. The things which are dear to men at this hour are so on account of the ideas which have emerged on their mental horizon, and which cause the present order of things, as a tree bears its apples. A new degree of culture would instantly revolutionize the entire system of human pursuits.

Conversation is a game of circles. In conversation we pluck up the *termini* which bound the common of silence on every side. The parties are not to be judged by the spirit they partake and even express under this Pentecost.[3] Tomorrow they will have receded

---

[3] The day when the disciples of Jesus, fifty days after his resurrection, were filled with the Holy Ghost, which appeared as "cloven tongues like as of fire."

from this highwater mark. Tomorrow you shall find them stooping under the old pack-saddles. Yet let us enjoy the cloven flame whilst it glows on our walls. When each new speaker strikes a new light, emancipates us from the oppression of the last speaker to oppress us with the greatness and exclusiveness of his own thought, then yields us to another redeemer, we seem to recover our rights, to become men. O, what truths profound and executable only in ages and orbs, are supposed in the announcement of every truth! In common hours, society sits cold and statuesque. We all stand waiting, empty, — knowing, possibly, that we can be full, surrounded by mighty symbols which are not symbols to us, but prose and trivial toys. Then cometh the god and converts the statues into fiery men, and by a flash of his eye burns up the veil which shrouded all things, and the meaning of the very furniture, of cup and saucer, of chair and clock and tester, is manifest. The facts which loomed so large in the fogs of yesterday, — property, climate, breeding, personal beauty and the like, have strangely changed their proportions. All that we reckoned settled shakes and rattles; and literatures, cities, climates, religions, leave their foundations and dance before our eyes. And yet here again see the swift circumscription! Good as is discourse, silence is better, and shames it. The length of the discourse indicates the distance of thought betwixt the speaker and the hearer. If they were at a perfect understanding in any part, no words would be necessary thereon. If at one in all parts, no words would be suffered.

Literature is a point outside of our hodiernal circle through which a new one may be described. The use of literature is to afford us a platform whence we may command a view of our present life, a purchase by which we may move it. We fill ourselves with ancient learning, install ourselves the best we can in Greek, in Punic, in Roman houses, only that we may wiselier see French, English and American houses and modes of living. In like manner we see literature best from the midst of wild nature, or from the din of affairs, or from a high religion. The field cannot be well seen from within the field. The astronomer must have his diameter of the earth's orbit as a base to find the parallax of any star.

Therefore we value the poet. All the argument and all the wisdom is not in the encyclopaedia, or the treatise on metaphysics, or the Body of Divinity, but in the sonnet or the play. In my daily work I incline to repeat my old steps, and do not believe in remedial force, in the power of change and reform. But some Petrarch or Ariosto, filled with the new wine of his imagination, writes me *positive effect w/ effort*

an ode or a brisk romance, full of daring thought and action. He
smites and arouses me with his shrill tones, breaks up my whole
chain of habits, and I open my eye on my own possibilities. He
claps wings to the sides of all the solid old lumber of the world, and
I am capable once more of choosing a straight path in theory and
practice.

We have the same need to command a view of the religion of
the world. We can never see Christianity from the catechism: —
from the pastures, from a boat in the pond, from amidst the songs
of wood-birds we possibly may. Cleansed by the elemental light
and wind, steeped in the sea of beautiful forms which the field
offers us, we may chance to cast a right glance back upon biography. Christianity is rightly dear to the best of mankind; yet was
there never a young philosopher whose breeding had fallen into the
Christian church by whom that brave text of Paul's was not specially prized: "Then shall also the Son be subject unto Him who
put all things under him, that God may be all in all." Let the
claims and virtues of persons be never so great and welcome, the
instinct of man presses eagerly onward to the impersonal and illimitable, and gladly arms itself against the dogmatism of bigots
with this generous word out of the book itself.

The natural world may be conceived of as a system of concentric
circles, and we now and then detect in nature slight dislocations
which apprise us that this surface on which we now stand is not
fixed, but sliding. These manifold tenacious qualities, this chemistry and vegetation, these metals and animals, which seem to
stand there for their own sake, are means and methods only, —
are words of God, and as fugitive as other words. Has the naturalist or chemist learned his craft, who has explored the gravity of
atoms and the elective affinities, who has not yet discerned the
deeper law whereof this is only a partial or approximate statement,
namely that like draws to like, and that the goods which belong
to you gravitate to you and need not be pursued with pains and
cost? Yet is that statement approximate also, and not final. Omnipresence is a higher fact. Not through subtle subterranean channels need friend and fact be drawn to their counterpart, but,
rightly considered, these things proceed from the eternal generation of the soul. Cause and effect are two sides of one fact.

The same law of eternal procession ranges all that we call the
virtues, and extinguishes each in the light of a better. The great
man will not be prudent in the popular sense; all his prudence will
be so much deduction from his grandeur. But it behooves each

to see, when he sacrifices prudence, to what god he devotes it; if to ease and pleasure, he had better be prudent still; if to a great trust, he can well spare his mule and panniers who has a winged chariot instead. Geoffrey draws on his boots to go through the woods, that his feet may be safer from the bite of snakes; Aaron never thinks of such a peril. In many years neither is harmed by such an accident. Yet it seems to me that with every precaution you take against such an evil you put yourself into the power of the evil. I suppose that the highest prudence is the lowest prudence. Is this too sudden a rushing from the center to the verge of our orbit? Think how many times we shall fall back into pitiful calculations before we take up our rest in the great sentiment, or make the verge of today the new center. Besides, your bravest sentiment is familiar to the humblest men. The poor and the low have their way of expressing the last facts of philosophy as well as you. "Blessed be nothing" and "The worse things are, the better they are" are proverbs which express the transcendentalism of common life.

relativism

One man's justice is another's injustice; one man's beauty another's ugliness; one man's wisdom another's folly, as one beholds the same objects from a higher point. One man thinks justice consists in paying debts, and has no measure in his abhorrence of another who is very remiss in this duty and makes the creditor wait tediously. But that second man has his own way of looking at things; asks himself Which debt must I pay first, the debt to the rich, or the debt to the poor? the debt of money, or the debt of thought to mankind, of genius to nature? For you, O broker, there is no other principle but arithmetic. For me, commerce is of trivial import; love, faith, truth of character, the aspiration of man, these are sacred; nor can I detach one duty, like you, from all other duties, and concentrate my forces mechanically on the payment of moneys. Let me live onward; you shall find that, though slower, the progress of my character will liquidate all these debts without injustice to higher claims. If a man should dedicate himself to the payment of notes, would not this be injustice? Does he owe no debt but money? And are all claims on him to be postponed to a landlord's or a banker's?

There is no virtue which is final; all are initial. The virtues of society are vices of the saint. The terror of reform is the discovery that we must cast away our virtues, or what we have always esteemed such, into the same pit that has consumed our grosser vices: —

> "Forgive his crimes, forgive his virtues too,
> Those smaller faults, half converts to the right."

It is the highest power of divine moments that they abolish our contritions also. I accuse myself of sloth and unprofitableness day by day; but when these waves of God flow into me I no longer reckon lost time. I no longer poorly compute my possible achievement by what remains to me of the month or the year; for these moments confer a sort of omnipresence and omnipotence which asks nothing of duration, but sees that the energy of the mind is commensurate with the work to be done, without time.

And thus, O circular philosopher, I hear some reader exclaim, you have arrived at a fine Pyrrhonism,[4] at an equivalence and indifference of all actions, and would fain teach us that *if we are true*, forsooth, our crimes may be lively stones out of which we shall construct the temple of the true God!

I am not careful to justify myself. I own I am gladdened by seeing the predominance of the saccharine principle throughout vegetable nature, and not less by beholding in morals that unrestrained inundation of the principle of good into every chink and hole that selfishness has left open, yea into selfishness and sin itself; so that no evil is pure, nor hell itself without its extreme satisfactions. But lest I should mislead any when I have my own head and obey my whims, let me remind the reader that I am only an experimenter. Do not set the least value on what I do, or the least discredit on what I do not, as if I pretended to settle any thing as true or false. I unsettle all things. No facts are to me sacred; none are profane; I simply experiment, an endless seeker with no Past at my back.

Yet this incessant movement and progression which all things partake could never become sensible to us but by contrast to some principle of fixture or stability in the soul. Whilst the eternal generation of circles proceeds, the eternal generator abides. That central life is somewhat superior to creation, superior to knowledge and thought, and contains all its circles. Forever it labors to create a life and thought as large and excellent as itself, but in vain, for that which is made instructs how to make a better.

Thus there is no sleep, no pause, no preservation, but all things renew, germinate and spring. Why should we import rags and relics into the new hour? Nature abhors the old, and old age seems the only disease; all others run into this one. We call it

---

4 Comprehensive skepticism.

by many names, — fever, intemperance, insanity, stupidity and crime; they are all forms of old age; they are rest, conservatism, appropriation, inertia; not newness, not the way onward. We grizzle every day. I see no need of it. Whilst we converse with what is above us, we do not grow old, but grow young. Infancy, youth, receptive, aspiring, with religious eye looking upward, counts itself nothing and abandons itself to the instruction flowing from all sides. But the man and woman of seventy assume to know all, they have outlived their hope, they renounce aspiration, accept the actual for the necessary and talk down to the young. Let them then become organs of the Holy Ghost; let them be lovers; let them behold truth; and their eyes are uplifted, their wrinkles smoothed, they are perfumed again with hope and power. This old age ought not to creep on a human mind. In nature every moment is new; the past is always swallowed and forgotten; the coming only is sacred. Nothing is secure but life, transition, the energizing spirit. No love can be bound by oath or covenant to secure it against a higher love. No truth so sublime but it may be trivial tomorrow in the light of new thoughts. People wish to be settled; only as far as they are unsettled is there any hope for them.

Life is a series of surprises. We do not guess today the mood, the pleasure, the power of tomorrow, when we are building up our being. Of lower states, of acts of routine and sense, we can tell somewhat; but the masterpieces of God, the total growths and universal movements of the soul, he hideth; they are incalculable. I can know that truth is divine and helpful; but how it shall help me I can have no guess, for *so to be* is the sole inlet of *so to know*. The new position of the advancing man has all the powers of the old, yet has them all new. It carries in its bosom all the energies of the past, yet is itself an exhalation of the morning. I cast away in this new moment all my once hoarded knowledge, as vacant and vain. Now for the first time seem I to know any thing rightly. The simplest words, — we do not know what they mean except when we love and aspire.

The difference between talents and character is adroitness to keep the old and trodden round, and power and courage to make a new road to new and better goals. Character makes an overpowering present; a cheerful, determined hour, which fortifies all the company by making them see that much is possible and excellent that was not thought of. Character dulls the impression of particular events. When we see the conqueror we do not think much of any one battle or success. We see that we had exaggerated the difficulty. It was easy to him. The great man is not convulsible or tormentable; events pass over him without much impression. People say sometimes, "See what I have overcome; see how cheerful I am; see how completely I have triumphed over these black events." Not if they still remind me of the black event. True conquest is the causing the calamity to fade and disappear as an early cloud of insignificant result in a history so large and advancing.

The one thing which we seek with insatiable desire is to forget ourselves, to be surprised out of our propriety, to lose our sempiternal memory and to do something without knowing how or why; in short to draw a new circle. Nothing great was ever achieved without enthusiasm. The way of life is wonderful; it is by abandonment. The great moments of history are the facilities of performance through the strength of ideas, as the works of genius and religion. "A man," said Oliver Cromwell, "never rises so high as when he knows not whither he is going." Dreams and drunkenness, the use of opium and alcohol are the semblance and counterfeit of this oracular genius, and hence their dangerous attraction for men. For the like reason they ask the aid of wild passions, as in gaming and war, to ape in some manner these flames and generosities of the heart.

1841–1843

Lords of Life

With the publication of Essays, First Series the quality of Emerson's life underwent a subtle change of which he himself did not become fully aware for some time. His writing and speaking ceased to be what he did to earn his bread while "waiting" — for what he could hardly have said — and became his life. The prophet of moral revolution faded into the light of common day and he became a professional author. Though he continued to deplore his lack of "performance," he found increasingly in his "distinct vocation" of observing and reporting "the great felicity of my lot."

Even in his last revolutionary manifesto, the lecture on "Man the Reformer" in January of 1841, the tone was less prophetic and more dramatic than before. So in his lecture series on "The Times," the next winter, which he described as a "portrait gallery," the lecture on "The Transcendentalist" paints sympathetically a portrait to which the painter himself is clearly not committed. Emerson's disengagement in part reflects a progressive disillusionment with man the reformer, when more nearly seen. The reform he looked for was personal — "self-union" — but the many reform movements of the time evaded this aim to seek some social goal. With violence or with gentle irony he rejected them all for "the sacredness of private integrity." At the same time the stream of his life began increasingly to feel its banks as it cut a deeper channel. Even while he continued to affirm the power of the inspired will to remake the self and the world, he was also forced to concede the dominion of Necessity. The result was a dramatic alternation of moods as his sense of truth swung between the opposing principles of Power and Fate.

In politics, to which he now paid more attention, his transcendental vision of the "wise man" who would make the State unnecessary confronted the strong case for conservatism in the "very low state of the world" that exists in fact. In the private experience, his sharpened "double consciousness" prompted various attempts at resolution: the ideal of Character, for example, a persisting and immovable probity and competence; or again, encouraged by his reading in the Hindu scriptures, a mood of total abandonment in which the whole scene of action dissolved into "the terrific Unity" behind all particulars. From this "drowsy sense of being dragged easily somewhere by that locomotive Destiny" — clearly the product of recurrent low vitality — he swung in turn to a reaffirmation of his "distinct vocation," as notably in the extensive ideal portrait of the Poet that now took shape in prose and verse. In the Poet's "potent song," if anywhere, he felt, man could win at least a momentary release from the tyranny of fate.

The sharpest blow fate dealt him in these years was the loss of his first son, Waldo, in 1842. For a time his faith was shaken, and the note of morbid self-criticism which marked his early journals reappeared with his grief. He found some relief in the distressed outpouring of his "Threnody," to which some time later, when his "efficient faith" had in a measure returned, he added an answer from his God — one in which the words are those of a consoling Father but the voice is that which silenced Job. Meanwhile he found distraction in work. He wrote much poetry; and a lecture tour to Washington, Baltimore, Philadelphia, and New York in 1843 was followed by the preparation of a second series of Essays, published in October, 1844.

⚔ ⚔

[January 17, 1841]

. . . These continent, persisting, immovable persons who are scattered up and down for the blessing of the world, howsoever named, Osiris or Washington or Samuel Hoar, have in this phlegm or gravity of their nature a quality which answers to the fly-wheel in a mill, which distributes the motion equably over all the wheels and hinders it from falling unequally and suddenly in destructive shocks. It is better that joy should be spread over all the day in the form of strength, than that it should be concentrated into ecstasies, full of danger and followed by reactions. There is a sublime prudence which is the very highest that we know of man, which, believing in a vast future, — sure of more to come than is yet seen, — postpones always the present hour to the whole life; postpones talent to genius, and special results to character. As the merchant gladly takes money from his income to add to his capital, so is the great man very willing to lose particular powers and talents, so that he gain in the elevation of his life.

May 17, 1840

In architecture, height and mass have a wonderful effect because they suggest immediately a relation to the sphere on which the structure stands, and so to the gravitating system. This tower which with such painful solidity soars like an arrow to heaven apprizes me in an unusual manner of that law of gravitation, by its truth to which it can rear aloft into the atmosphere those dangerous masses of granite, and keep them there for ages as easily as if it were a feather or a scrap of down. . . .

February 1 ?, 1842

Masses again. — If you go near to the White Mountains, you cannot see them; you must go off thirty or forty miles to get a good view. Well, so is it with men, and with all that is high in our life, it is a total and distant effect, a *mass* effect, that instructs us, and not the first apprehension of them. . . .

Will is a particular, Habit a massive force; Speech a particular, Manners a mass.

[April 13 ?, 1841]

I read alternately in Doctor Nichol and in Saint-Simon,[1] that is, in the Heavens and in the Earth, and the effect is grotesque enough. When we have spent our wonder in computing this wasteful hospitality with which boon Nature turns off new firmaments without end into her wide common, as fast as the madrepores make coral, — suns and planets hospitable to souls, — and then shorten the sight to look into this court of Louis Quatorze, and see the game that is played there, — duke and marshal, abbé and madame, — a gambling table where each is laying traps for the other, where the end is ever by some lie or fetch to outwit your rival and ruin him with this solemn fop in wig and stars, — the king; — one can hardly help asking if this planet is a fair specimen of the so gen-

---

[1] John Pringle Nichol, *Views of the Architecture of the Heavens* (repub. New York, 1840); Louis de Rouvroy, Duc de Saint-Simon, *Mémoires* (1739-51) of the court of Louis XIV.

erous astronomy, and if so, whether the experiment have not failed, and whether it be quite worth while to make more, and glut the innocent space with so poor an article.

But there are many answers at hand to the poor cavil. And all doubt is ribald. An answer, — certainly not the highest, — the astronomy itself may furnish, namely, that all grows, all is nascent, infant. When we are dizzied with the arithmetic of the savant toiling to compute the length of her line, the return of her curve, we are steadied by the perception that a great deal is doing; that all seems just begun; remote aims are in active accomplishment. We can point nowhere to anything final; but tendency appears on all hands: planet, system, constellation, total nature is growing like a field of maize in July; is becoming somewhat else; is in rapid metamorphosis. The embryo does not more strive to be man, than yonder burr of light we call a nebula tends to be a ring, a comet, a globe, and parent of new stars. Why should not then these messieurs of Versailles strut and plot for tabourets and ribbons, for a season, without prejudice to their faculty to run on better errands by and by?

Yet the whole code of nature's laws may be written on the thumbnail, or the signet of a ring. The whirling bubble on the surface of a brook admits us to the secret of the mechanics of the sky. Every shell on the beach is a key to it. A little water made to rotate in a cup explains the formation of the simpler shells; the addition of matter from year to year arrives at last at the most complex forms; and yet so poor is nature with all her craft, that from the beginning to the end of the universe she has but one stuff, — but one stuff with its two ends, to serve up all her dream-like variety. Compound it how she will, star, sand, fire, water, tree, man, it is still one stuff, and betrays the same properties to the anointed eye; and every marshal that bristles, every valet that grimaces in the French Court is related bodily to that heaven which Lagrange has been searching and works every moment by the same laws we thought so grand up there.

But the true answer to the cavil ... is of course that the cavil only reaches the ear; it does never sink into the heart. I am of the Maker not of the Made. The vastness of the Universe, the portentous year of Mizar and Alcor are no vastness, no longevity to me. In the eternity of truth, in the almightiness of love, I slight these monsters. Through all the running sea of forms, I am truth, I am love, and immutable I transcend form as I do time and space.

April 23, 1841

Do not cast about for reasons among their shop of reasons, but adduce yourself as the only reason. We forget daily our high call to be discoverers — we forget that we are embarked on a holy, unknown sea in whose blue recesses we have a secret warrant that we shall yet arrive at the Fortunate Isles [2] hid from men; and at each saucy wood-craft or revenue cutter or rum-boat that hails us, we are astonished, and put off from our purpose, and ready to return to the rotten towns we have left, and quit our seeking of the Virgin Shore. . . .

To Margaret Fuller

March 14, 1841

. . . I know but one solution to my nature and relations, which I find in the remembering the joy with which in my boyhood I caught the first hint of the Berkleian philosophy, and which I certainly never lost sight of afterwards. There is a foolish man who goes up and down the country giving lectures on electricity; — this one secret he has, to draw a spark out of every object, from desk, and lamp, and wooden log, and the farmer's blue frock, and by this he gets his living: for paupers and Negroes will pay to see this celestial emanation from their own basket and their own body. Well, I was not an electrician, but an Idealist. I could see that there was a cause behind every stump and clod, and by the help of some fine words could make every old wagon and woodpile and stone wall oscillate a little and threaten to dance; nay, give me fair field, — and the Selectmen of Concord and the Reverend Doctor Poundmedown himself began to look unstable and vaporous. . . . Now there is this difference between the electrician — Mr. Quimby, is his name? (I never saw him) — and the Idealist, namely, that the spark is to that philosopher a toy, but the dance is to the Idealist terror and beauty, life and light. . . . This Insight is so precious to society that where the least glimmer of it appears all men should befriend and protect it for its own sake. . . . You and those others who are dear to me should be so rightly my friends as never to suffer me for a moment to attempt the game of wits and fashionists, no nor even that of those you call friends; no, but by expecting of me a song of laws and causes only, should make me noble and the encourager of your nobility. . . .

[2] Legendary Isles of the Blest where heroes dwelt after death. Cf. Tennyson's "Ulysses."

To ———

July 3, 1841

... I am, like you, a seeker of the perfect and admirable Good. My creed is very simple, that Goodness is the only Reality, that to Goodness alone can we trust, to that we may trust all and always; beautiful and blessed and blessing is it, even though it should seem to slay me.

Beyond this I have no knowledge, no intelligence of methods; I know no steps, no degrees, no favorite means, no detached rules. Itself is gate and road and leader and march. Only trust it, be of it, be it, and it shall be well with us forever. It will be and govern in its own transcendent way, and not in ways that arithmetic and mortal experience can measure....

To Samuel Gray Ward

Nantasket Beach, July, 1841.

... But is it the picture of the unbounded sea, or is it the lassitude of this Syrian summer, that more and more draws the cords of Will out of my thought and leaves me nothing but perpetual observation, perpetual acquiescence and perpetual thankfulness? Shall I not be Turk and fatalist before today's sun shall set? and in this thriving New England too, full of din and snappish activity and invention and wilfulness. Can you not save me, dip me into ice water, find me some girding belt, that I glide not away into a stream or a gas, and decease in infinite diffusion? Reinforce me, I entreat you, with showing me some man, work, aim or fact under the *angle of practice*, that I may see you as an elector and rejector, an agent, an antagonist and a commander. I have seen enough of the obedient sea wave forever lashing the obedient shore. I find no emblems here that speak any other language than the sleep and abandonment of my woods and blueberry pastures at home. If you know the ciphers of rudder and direction, communicate them to me without delay. Noah's flood and the striae which the good geologist finds on every mountain and rock seem to me the records of a calamity less universal than this metaphysical flux which threatens every enterprise, every thought and every thinker. How high will this Nile, this Mississippi, this Ocean, rise, and will ever the waters be stayed? ...

[*July, 1841*]

... Yet we care for individuals, not for the waste universality. It is the same ocean everywhere, but it has no character until seen with the shore or the ship. Who would value any number of miles of Atlantic brine bounded by lines of latitude and longitude? Confine it by granite rocks, let it wash a shore where wise men dwell, and it is filled with expression; and the point of greatest interest is where the land and water meet.

Summer, 1841

The metamorphosis of Nature shows itself in nothing more than this, that there is no word in our language that cannot become typical to us of Nature by giving it emphasis. The world is a Dancer; it is a Rosary; it is a Torrent; it is a Boat; a Mist; a Spider's Snare; it is what you will; and the metaphor will hold, and it will give the imagination keen pleasure. Swifter than light the world converts itself into that thing you name, and all things find their right place under this new and capricious classification. There is nothing small or mean to the soul. It derives as grand a joy from symbolizing the Godhead or his universe under the form of a moth or a gnat as of a Lord of Hosts. Must I call the heaven and the earth a maypole and country fair with booths, or an anthill, or an old coat, in order to give you the shock of pleasure which the imagination loves and the sense of spiritual greatness? Call it a blossom, a rod, a wreath of parsley, a tamarisk-crown, a cock, a sparrow, the ear instantly hears and the spirit leaps to the trope....

September 1?, 1841

Every gardener can change his flowers and leaves into fruit and so is the genius that today can upheave and balance and toss every object in Nature for his metaphor, capable in his next manifestation of playing such a game with his hands instead of his brain. An instinctive suspicion that this may befal, seems to have crept into the mind of men. What would happen to us who live on the surface, if this fellow in some new transmigration should have acquired power to do what he now delights to say? He must be watched.

December?, 1841

All writing is by the grace of God. People do not deserve to have good writing, they are so pleased with bad. In these sentences that you show me, I can find no beauty, for I see death in every clause and every word. There is a fossil or a mummy character which pervades this book. The best sepulchres, the vastest catacombs, Thebes and Cairo Pyramids are sepulchres to me. I like gardens and nurseries. Give me initiative, spermatic, prophesying, man-making words.

[*April 9, 1842*]

I have sometimes thought that he would render the greatest service to modern criticism, who should draw the line of relation that subsists between Shakespeare and Swedenborg. The human mind stands ever in perplexity, demanding intellect, demanding sanctity, impatient equally of each without the other. The reconciler has not yet appeared. If we tire of the saints, Shakespeare is our city of refuge. Yet the instincts presently teach that the problem of essence must take precedence of all others; — the questions of Whence? What? and Whither? and the solution of these must be in a life, and not in a book. A drama or poem is a proximate or oblique reply; but Moses, Menu,[3] Jesus, work directly on this problem. *From "Swedenborg"*

September 21, 1841

Dr. Ripley died this morning. The fall of this oak of ninety years makes some sensation in the forest, old and doomed as it was. He has identified himself with the forms at least of the old church of the New England Puritans, his nature was eminently loyal, not in the least adventurous or democratical; and his whole being leaned backward on the departed, so that he seemed one of the rear-guard of this great camp and army which have filled the world with fame, and with him passes out of sight almost the last banner and guidon flag of a mighty epoch. For these Puritans, however in our last days they have declined into ritualists, solemnized the heyday of their strength by the planting and the liberating of America.

Great, grim, earnest men, I belong by natural affinity to other thoughts and schools than yours, but my affection hovers respectfully about your retiring footprints, your unpainted churches, strict platforms, and sad offices; the iron-gray deacon and the wearisome prayer rich with the diction of ages. Well, the new is only the seed of the old. What is this abolition and non-resistance and temperance but the continuation of Puritanism, though it operate inevitably the destruction of the church in which it grew, as the new is always making the old superfluous? . . .

[3] Legendary author of the Hindu scripture, *The Laws of Menu*.

He looks like a sachem fallen in the forest, or rather like "a warrior taking his rest with his martial cloak around him." I carried Waldo to see him, and he testified neither repulsion nor surprise, but only the quietest curiosity. . . .

July 7 ?, 1839

Reform. — The past has baked my loaf, and in the strength of its bread I break up the old oven.

October, 1841

. . . I told Henry Thoreau that his freedom is in the form, but he does not disclose new matter. I am very familiar with all his thoughts, — they are my own quite originally drest. But if the question be, what new ideas has he thrown into circulation, he has not yet told what that is which he was created to say. I said to him what I often feel, I only know three persons who seem to me fully to see this law of reciprocity or compensation, — himself, Alcott, and myself: and 'tis odd that we should all be neighbors, for in the wide land or the wide earth I do not know another who seems to have it as deeply and originally as these three Gothamites.

October, 1841

. . . I am not such a fool but that I taste the joy which comes from a new and prodigious person, from Dante, from Rabelais, from Piranesi, flinging wide to me the doors of new modes of existence, and even if . . . the basis of this joy is at last the instinct, that I am only let into my own estate, that the poet and his book and his story are only fictions and semblances in which my thought is pleased to dress itself, I do not the less yield myself to the keen delight of difference and newness.

October ?, 1841

There is a great destiny which comes in with this as with every age, which is colossal in its traits, terrible in its strength, which cannot be tamed, or criticised, or subdued. It is shared by every man and woman of the time, for it is by it they live. As a vast, solid phalanx the generation comes on, they have the same features, and their pattern is new in the world. All wear the same expression, but it is that which they do not detect in each other. . . . Feeble persons are occupied with themselves, — with what they have knowingly done, and what they propose to do, and they talk much hereof with modesty and fear. The strong persons look at themselves as facts, in which the involuntary part is so much as to fill all their wonder, and leave them no countenance to say anything of what is so trivial as their private thinking and doing. I can well speak of myself as a figure in a panorama so absorbing.

[October, 1841]

Exaggeration is a law of Nature. As we have not given a peck of apples or potatoes, until we have heaped the measure, so Nature sends no creature, no man into the world without adding a small excess of his proper quality. Given the planet, it is still necessary to add the impulse; so to every creature nature added a little violence of direction in its proper path, a shove to put it on its way; in every instance a slight generosity, a drop too much. Without electricity the air would rot, and without this violence of direction which men and women have, without a spice of bigot and fanatic, no excitement, no efficiency. We aim above the mark to hit the mark. Every sentence hath some falsehood of exaggeration in it. For the infinite diffuseness refuses to be epigrammatized, the world to be shut in a word. The thought being spoken in a sentence becomes by mere detachment falsely emphatic.

[March, 1844]

Art, in the artist, is proportion, or a habitual respect to the whole by an eye loving beauty in details. And the wonder and charm of it is the sanity in insanity which it denotes. Proportion is almost impossible to human beings. There is no one who does not exaggerate. In conversation, men are encumbered with personality, and talk too much. In modern sculpture, picture and poetry, the beauty is miscellaneous; the artist works here and there and at all points, adding and adding, instead of unfolding the unit of his thought. Beautiful details we must have, or no artist; but they must be means and never other. The eye must not lose sight for a moment of the purpose. Lively boys write to their ear and eye, and the cool reader finds nothing but sweet jingles in it. When they grow older, they respect the argument.

From "Nominalist and Realist"

October 7?, 1841

... There are two directions in which souls move: one is trust, religion, consent to be nothing for eternity, entranced waiting, the worship of Ideas: the other is activity, the busybody, the following of that practical talent which we have, in the belief that what is so natural, easy, and pleasant to us and desirable to others will surely lead us out safely: in this direction lies usefulness, comfort, society, low power of all sorts. The other is solitary, grand, secular. I see not but these diverge from every moment, and that either may be chosen.... Whether does Love reconcile these two divergencies? for it is certain that every impulse of that sentiment exalts, and yet it brings all practical power into play. Here I am in a dark corner again. We have no one example of the poetic life realized, therefore all we say seems bloated.

If life is sad and do not content us, if the heavens are brass, and rain no sweet thoughts on us, and especially we have nothing to say to shipwrecked and self-tormenting and young-old people, let us hold our tongues.... Patience and truth, patience with our own frosts and negations, and few words must serve.... Perhaps all that is not performance is preparation, or performance that shall be....

October 23, 1841

...I think Society has the highest interest in seeing that this movement called the Transcendental is no boys' play or girls' play, but has an interest very near and dear to him; that it has a necessary place in history, is a Fact not to be overlooked, not possibly to be prevented, and, however discredited to the heedless and to the moderate and conservative persons by the foibles or inadequacy of those who partake the movement, yet is it the pledge and the herald of all that is dear to the human heart, grand and inspiring to human faith.

I think the genius of this age more philosophical than any other has been, righter in its aims, truer, with less fear, less fable, less mixture of any sort.

October 26?, 1841

Society ought to be forgiven if it do not love its rude unmaskers. The Council of Trent did not love Father Paul Sarpi.[4] "But I show you," says the philosopher, "the leprosy which is covered by these gay coats." "Well, I had rather see the handsome mask than the unhandsome skin," replies Beacon Street. Do you not know that this is a masquerade? Did you suppose I took these harlequins for the kings and queens, the gods and goddesses they represent? I am not such a child. There is a terrific skepticism at the bottom of the determined conservers.

[4] His *History of the Council of Trent* (1619) exposed it as an instrument of papal policy.

[December, 1841]

... As we take our stand on Necessity, or on Ethics, shall we go
for the conservative, or for the reformer. If we read the world historically, we shall say, Of all the ages, the present hour and circumstance is the cumulative result; this is the best throw of the
dice of nature that has yet been, or that is yet possible. If we see
it from the side of Will, or the Moral Sentiment, we shall accuse
the Past and the Present, and require the impossible of the Future.

From "The Conservative"

August 22, 1841

Society may well value measure, for all its law and order is nothing else. There is a combat of opposite instincts and the golden
mean, that is Right. What is the argument for marriage but this?
What for a church, a state, or any existing institution, but just this
— We must have a mean, some mean?

October 24?, 1841

I told Garrison [5] that I thought he must be a very young man, or
his time hang very heavy on his hands, who can afford to think
much and talk much about the foibles of his neighbors, or *"denounce,"* and play "the son of thunder" as he called it. I am one
who believe all times to be pretty much alike, and yet I sympathize so keenly with this. We want to be expressed, yet you take
from us War, that great opportunity which allowed the accumulations of electricity to stream off from both poles, the positive and
the negative, — well, now you take from us our cup of alcohol, as
before you took our cup of wrath. We had become canting moths
of peace, our helm was a skillet, and now we must become temperance water-sops. You take away, but what do you give me? ...
Good vent or bad we must have for our nature, somewhere we
must let out all the length of all the reins. Make love a crime, and
we shall have lust. If you cannot contrive to raise us up to the
love of science and make brute matter our antagonist which we
shall have joy in handling, mastering, penetrating, condensing to
adamant, dissolving to light, then we must brawl, carouse, gamble,
or go to bull-fights. If we can get no full demonstration of our
heart and mind, we feel wronged and incarcerated: the philosophers and divines we shall hate most, as the upper turnkeys. We
wish to take the gas which allows us to break through your weari-

[5] Reformer and militant Abolitionist.

some proprieties, to plant the foot, to set the teeth, to fling abroad the arms, and dance and sing.

October 24?, 1841

In the republic must always happen what happened here, that the steamboats and stages and hotels vote one way and the nation votes the other: and it seems to every meeting of readers and writers as if it were intolerable that Broad Street Paddies and bar-room politicians, the sots and loafers and all manner of ragged and unclean and foul-mouthed persons without a dollar in their pocket should control the property of the country and make the lawgiver and the law. But is that any more than their share whilst you hold property selfishly? They are opposed to you: yes, but first you are opposed to them: they, to be sure, malevolently, menacingly, with songs and rowdies and mobs; you cunningly, plausibly, and well-bred; you cheat and they strike; you sleep and eat at their expense; they vote and threaten and sometimes throw stones, at yours.

[October 28?, 1841]

Wealth. — Conversation, character, were the avowed ends; wealth was good as it appeased the animal cravings, cured the smoky chimney, silenced the creaking door, brought friends together in a warm and quiet room, and kept the children and the dinner-table in a different apartment. Thought, virtue, beauty, were the ends; but it was known that men of thought and virtue sometimes had the headache, or wet feet, or could lose good time whilst the room was getting warm in winter days. Unluckily, in the exertions necessary to remove these inconveniences, the main attention has been diverted to this object; the old aims have been lost sight of, and to remove friction has come to be the end. That is the ridicule of rich men; and Boston, London, Vienna, and now the governments generally of the world, are cities and governments of the rich; and the masses are not men, but *poor men*, that is, men who would be rich; this is the ridicule of the class, that they arrive with pains and sweat and fury nowhere; when all is done, it is for nothing. They are like one who has interrupted the conversation of a company to make his speech, and now has forgotten what he went to say. . . . Hence the appearance which everywhere strikes the eye of an aimless society, an aimless nation, an aimless world. The earth is sick with that sickness. The man was made for activity, and action to any end has some health and pleasure for him.

November, 1841

Great causes are never tried, assaulted, or defended on their merits: they need so long perspective, and the habits of the race are marked with so strong a tendency to particulars. The stake is Europe or Asia, and the battle is for some contemptible village or dog-hutch. A man shares the new light that irradiates the world and promises the establishment of the Kingdom of Heaven, and ends with champing unleavened bread or devoting himself to the nourishment of a beard, or making a fool of himself about his hat or his shoes. A man is furnished with this superb case of instruments, the senses, and perceptive and executive faculties, and they betray him every day. He transfers his allegiance from Instinct and God to this adroit little committee. A man is an exaggerator. In every conversation see how the main end is still lost sight of by all but the best, and with slight apology or none, a digression made to a creaking door or a buzzing fly. What heavenly eloquence could hold the ear of an audience if a child cried? A man with a truth to express is caught by the beauty of his own words and ends with being a rhymester or critic. And Genius is sacrificed to talent every day.

November 12 ?, 1841

... "But bad thoughts," said M., "Who could dare to uncover all the thoughts of a single hour?" Indeed! is it so bad? I own that to a witness worse than myself and less intelligent, I should not willingly put a window into my breast, but to a witness more intelligent and virtuous than I, or to one precisely as intelligent and well intentioned, I have no objection to uncover my heart. ...

※※

The Transcendentalist

THE first thing we have to say respecting what are called *new views* here in New England, at the present time, is, that they are not new, but the very oldest of thoughts cast into the mold of these new times. The light is always identical in its composition, but it falls on a great variety of objects, and by so falling is first revealed to us, not in its own form, for it is formless, but in theirs; in like manner, thought only appears in the objects it classifies. What is popularly called Transcendentalism among us, is Idealism; Idealism as it appears in 1842. As thinkers, mankind have ever divided into two sects, Materialists and Idealists; the first class founding on experience, the second on consciousness; the first class beginning to think from the data of the senses, the second class perceive that the senses are not final, and say, The senses give us representations of things, but what are the things themselves, they cannot tell. The materialist insists on facts, on history, on the force of circumstances and the animal wants of man; the idealist on the power of Thought and of Will, on inspiration, on miracle, on individual culture. These two modes of thinking are both natural, but the idealist contends that his way of thinking is in higher nature. He concedes all that the other affirms, admits the impressions of sense, admits their coherency, their use and beauty, and then asks the materialist for his grounds of assurance that things are as his senses represent them. But I, he says, affirm facts not affected by the illusions of sense, facts which are of the same nature as the faculty which reports them, and not liable to doubt; facts which in their first appearance to us assume a native superiority to material facts, degrading these into a language by which the first are to be spoken; facts which it only needs a retirement from the senses to discern. Every materialist will be an idealist; but an idealist can never go backward to be a materialist.

The idealist, in speaking of events, sees them as spirits. He does not deny the sensuous fact: by no means; but he will not see that alone. He does not deny the presence of this table, this chair, and the walls of this room, but he looks at these things as the reverse side of the tapestry, as the *other end*, each being a sequel or completion of a spiritual fact which nearly concerns him. This manner of looking at things transfers every object in nature from an independent and anomalous position without there, into the consciousness. Even the materialist Condillac, perhaps the most logical expounder of materialism, was constrained to say, "Though we should soar into the heavens, though we should sink into the abyss, we never go out of ourselves; it is always our own thought that we perceive." What more could an idealist say?

The materialist, secure in the certainty of sensation, mocks at fine-spun theories, at star-gazers, and dreamers, and believes that his life is solid, that he at least takes nothing for granted, but knows where he stands, and what he does. Yet how easy it is to show him that he also is a phantom walking and working amid phantoms, and that he need only ask a question or two beyond his daily questions to find his solid universe growing dim and impalpable before his sense. The sturdy capitalist, no matter how

deep and square on blocks of Quincy granite he lays the foundations of his banking-house or Exchange, must set it, at last, not on
a cube corresponding to the angles of his structure, but on a mass
of unknown materials and solidity, red-hot or white-hot perhaps at
the core, which rounds off to an almost perfect sphericity, and lies
floating in soft air, and goes spinning away, dragging bank and
banker with it at a rate of thousands of miles the hour, he knows
not whither, — a bit of bullet, now glimmering, now darkling
through a small cubic space on the edge of an unimaginable pit of
emptiness. And this wild balloon, in which his whole venture is
embarked, is a just symbol of his whole state and faculty. One
thing at least, he says, is certain, and does not give me the headache, that figures do not lie; the multiplication table has been
hitherto found unimpeachable truth; and, moreover, if I put a gold
eagle in my safe, I find it again tomorrow; — but for these thoughts,
I know not whence they are. They change and pass away. But ask
him why he believes that an uniform experience will continue uniform, or on what grounds he founds his faith in his figures, and he
will perceive that his mental fabric is built up on just as strange and
quaking foundations as his proud edifice of stone.

In the order of thought, the materialist takes his departure from
the external world, and esteems a man as one product of that. The
idealist takes his departure from his consciousness, and reckons the
world an appearance. The materialist respects sensible masses,
Society, Government, social art and luxury, every establishment,
every mass, whether majority of numbers, or extent of space,
or amount of objects, every social action. The idealist has another measure, which is metaphysical, namely the *rank* which
things themselves take in his consciousness; not at all the size
or appearance. Mind is the only reality, of which men and all
other natures are better or worse reflectors. Nature, literature, history, are only subjective phenomena. Although in his action overpowered by the laws of action, and so, warmly coöperating with
men, even preferring them to himself, yet when he speaks scien-
tifically, or after the order of thought, he is constrained to degrade
persons into representatives of truths. He does not respect labor, or
the products of labor, namely property, otherwise than as a manifold symbol, illustrating with wonderful fidelity of details the laws
of being; he does not respect government, except as far as it re-
iterates the law of his mind; nor the church, nor charities, nor arts,
for themselves; but hears, as at a vast distance, what they say, as if

his consciousness would speak to him through a pantomimic scene. His thought, — that is the Universe. His experience inclines him to behold the procession of facts you call the world, as flowing perpetually outward from an invisible, unsounded center in himself, center alike of him and of them, and necessitating him to regard all things as having a subjective or relative existence, relative to that aforesaid Unknown Center of him.

From this transfer of the world into the consciousness, this beholding of all things in the mind, follow easily his whole ethics. It is simpler to be self-dependent. The height, the deity of man is to be self-sustained, to need no gift, no foreign force. Society is good when it does not violate me, but best when it is likest to solitude. Everything real is self-existent. Everything divine shares the self-existence of Deity. All that you call the world is the shadow of that substance which you are, the perpetual creation of the powers of thought, of those that are dependent and of those that are independent of your will. Do not cumber yourself with fruitless pains to mend and remedy remote effects; let the soul be erect, and all things will go well. You think me the child of my circumstances: I make my circumstance. Let any thought or motive of mine be different from that they are, the difference will transform my condition and economy. I — this thought which is called I — is the mold into which the world is poured like melted wax. The mold is invisible, but the world betrays the shape of the mold. You call it the power of circumstance, but it is the power of me. Am I in harmony with myself? my position will seem to you just and commanding. Am I vicious and insane? my fortunes will seem to you obscure and descending. As I am, so shall I associate, and so shall I act; Caesar's history will paint out Caesar. Jesus acted so, because he thought so. I do not wish to overlook or to gainsay any reality; I say I make my circumstance; but if you ask me, Whence am I? I feel like other men my relation to that Fact which cannot be spoken, or defined, nor even thought, but which exists, and will exist.

The Transcendentalist adopts the whole connection of spiritual doctrine. He believes in miracle, in the perpetual openness of the human mind to new influx of light and power; he believes in inspiration, and in ecstasy. He wishes that the spiritual principle should be suffered to demonstrate itself to the end, in all possible applications to the state of man, without the admission of anything unspiritual; that is, any thing positive, dogmatic, personal.

Thus the spiritual measure of inspiration is the depth of the thought, and never, who said it? And so he resists all attempts to palm other rules and measures on the spirit than its own.

In action he easily incurs the charge of antinomianism by his avowal that he, who has the Law-giver, may with safety not only neglect, but even contravene every written commandment. In the play of Othello, the expiring Desdemona absolves her husband of the murder, to her attendant Emilia. Afterwards, when Emilia charges him with the crime, Othello exclaims,

> "You heard her say herself it was not I."

Emilia replies,

> "The more angel she, and thou the blacker devil."

Of this fine incident, Jacobi, the Transcendental moralist, makes use, with other parallel instances, in his reply to Fichte. Jacobi, refusing all measure of right and wrong except the determinations of the private spirit, remarks that there is no crime but has sometimes been a virtue. "I," he says, "am that atheist, that godless person who, in opposition to an imaginary doctrine of calculation, would lie as the dying Desdemona lied; would lie and deceive, as Pylades when he personated Orestes; would assassinate like Timoleon; would perjure myself like Epaminondas and John de Witt; I would resolve on suicide like Cato; I would commit sacrilege with David; yea, and pluck ears of corn on the Sabbath, for no other reason than that I was fainting for lack of food. For I have assurance in myself that in pardoning these faults according to the letter, man exerts the sovereign right which the majesty of his being confers on him; he sets the seal of his divine nature to the grace he accords."

In like manner, if there is anything grand and daring in human thought or virtue, any reliance on the vast, the unknown; any presentiment, any extravagance of faith, the spiritualist adopts it as most in nature. The oriental mind has always tended to this largeness. Buddhism is an expression of it. The Buddhist, who thanks no man, who says, "Do not flatter your benefactors," but who, in his conviction that every good deed can by no possibility escape its reward, will not deceive the benefactor by pretending that he has done more than he should, is a Transcendentalist.

You will see by this sketch that there is no such thing as a Transcendental *party*; that there is no pure Transcendentalist; that we know of none but prophets and heralds of such a philosophy; that all who by strong bias of nature have leaned to the spiritual side in doctrine, have stopped short of their goal. We have had many harbingers and forerunners; but of a purely spiritual life, history has afforded no example. I mean we have yet no man who has leaned entirely on his character, and eaten angels' food; who, trusting to his sentiments, found life made of miracles; who, working for universal aims, found himself fed, he knew not how; clothed, sheltered, and weaponed, he knew not how, and yet it was done by his own hands. Only in the instinct of the lower animals we find the suggestion of the methods of it, and something higher than our understanding. The squirrel hoards nuts and the bee gathers honey, without knowing what they do, and they are thus provided for without selfishness or disgrace.

Shall we say then that Transcendentalism is the Saturnalia [6] or excess of Faith; the presentiment of a faith proper to man in his integrity, excessive only when his imperfect obedience hinders the satisfaction of his wish? Nature is transcendental, exists primarily, necessarily, ever works and advances, yet takes no thought for the morrow. Man owns the dignity of the life which throbs around him, in chemistry, and tree, and animal, and in the involuntary functions of his own body; yet he is balked when he tries to fling himself into this enchanted circle, where all is done without degradation. Yet genius and virtue predict in man the same absence of private ends and of condescension to circumstances, united with every trait and talent of beauty and power.

This way of thinking, falling on Roman times, made Stoic philosophers; falling on despotic times, made patriot Catos and Brutuses; falling on superstitious times, made prophets and apostles; on popish times, made protestants and ascetic monks, preachers of Faith against the preachers of Works; on prelatical times, made Puritans and Quakers; and falling on Unitarian and commercial times, makes the peculiar shades of Idealism which we know.

It is well known to most of my audience that the Idealism of the present day acquired the name of Transcendental from the use of that term by Immanuel Kant, of Königsberg, who replied to the skeptical philosophy of Locke, which insisted that there was nothing in the intellect which was not previously in the experience of the senses, by showing that there was a very important class of ideas or imperative forms, which did not come by experience, but through which experience was acquired; that these were intuitions of the mind itself; and he denominated them *Transcendental*

6 Roman feast-time.

forms. The extraordinary profoundness and precision of that man's thinking have given vogue to his nomenclature, in Europe and America, to that extent that whatever belongs to the class of intuitive thought is popularly called at the present day *Transcendental.*

Although, as we have said, there is no pure Transcendentalist, yet the tendency to respect the intuitions and to give them, at least in our creed, all authority over our experience, has deeply colored the conversation and poetry of the present day; and the history of genius and of religion in these times, though impure, and as yet not incarnated in any powerful individual, will be the history of this tendency.

It is a sign of our times, conspicuous to the coarsest observer, that many intelligent and religious persons withdraw themselves from the common labors and competitions of the market and the caucus, and betake themselves to a certain solitary and critical way of living, from which no solid fruit has yet appeared to justify their separation. They hold themselves aloof: they feel the disproportion between their faculties and the work offered them, and they prefer to ramble in the country and perish of ennui, to the degradation of such charities and such ambitions as the city can propose to them. They are striking work, and crying out for somewhat worthy to do! What they do is done only because they are overpowered by the humanities that speak on all sides; and they consent to such labor as is open to them, though to their lofty dream the writing of Iliads or Hamlets, or the building of cities or empires seems drudgery.

Now every one must do after his kind, be he asp or angel, and these must. The question which a wise man and a student of modern history will ask, is, what that kind is? And truly, as in ecclesiastical history we take so much pains to know what the Gnostics, what the Essenes, what the Manichees, and what the Reformers believed, it would not misbecome us to inquire nearer home, what these companions and contemporaries of ours think and do, at least so far as these thoughts and actions appear to be not accidental and personal, but common to many, and the inevitable flower of the Tree of Time. Our American literature and spiritual history are, we confess, in the optative mood; but whoso knows these seething brains, these admirable radicals, these unsocial worshippers, these talkers who talk the sun and moon away, will believe that this heresy cannot pass away without leaving its mark.

They are lonely; the spirit of their writing and conversation is

lonely; they repel influences; they shun general society; they incline
to shut themselves in their chamber in the house, to live in the
country rather than in the town, and to find their tasks and amusements in solitude. Society, to be sure, does not like this very well,
it saith, Whoso goes to walk alone, accuses the whole world; he
declares all to be unfit to be his companions; it is very uncivil, nay,
insulting; Society will retaliate. Meantime, this retirement does
not proceed from any whim on the part of these separators; but if
any one will take pains to talk with them, he will find that this part
is chosen both from temperament and from principle; with some
unwillingness too, and as a choice of the less of two evils; for these
persons are not by nature melancholy, sour, and unsocial, — they
are not stockish or brute, — but joyous, susceptible, affectionate;
they have even more than others a great wish to be loved. Like the
young Mozart, they are rather ready to cry ten times a day, "But
are you sure you love me?" Nay, if they tell you their whole
thought, they will own that love seems to them the last and highest
gift of nature; that there are persons whom in their hearts they
daily thank for existing, — persons whose faces are perhaps unknown to them, but whose fame and spirit have penetrated their
solitude, — and for whose sake they wish to exist. To behold the
beauty of another character, which inspires a new interest in our
own; to behold the beauty lodged in a human being, with such
vivacity of apprehension that I am instantly forced home to inquire
if I am not deformity itself; to behold in another the expression of a
love so high that it assures itself, — assures itself also to me against
every possible casualty except my unworthiness; — these are degrees on the scale of human happiness to which they have ascended; and it is a fidelity to this sentiment which has made common association distasteful to them. They wish a just and even
fellowship, or none. They cannot gossip with you, and they do not
wish, as they are sincere and religious, to gratify any mere curiosity
which you may entertain. Like fairies, they do not wish to be
spoken of. Love me, they say, but do not ask who is my cousin and
my uncle. If you do not need to hear my thought, because you can
read it in my face and behavior, then I will tell it you from sunrise
to sunset. If you cannot divine it, you would not understand what
I say. I will not molest myself for you. I do not wish to be pro-
faned.

   And yet, it seems as if this loneliness, and not this love, would
prevail in their circumstances, because of the extravagant demand
they make on human nature. That, indeed, constitutes a new

feature in their portrait, that they are the most exacting and ex-
tortionate critics. Their quarrel with every man they meet is not
with his kind, but with his degree. There is not enough of him, —
that is the only fault. They prolong their privilege of childhood
in this wise; of doing nothing, but making immense demands on
all the gladiators in the lists of action and fame. They make us
feel the strange disappointment which overcasts every human
youth. So many promising youths, and never a finished man! The
profound nature will have a savage rudeness; the delicate one will
be shallow, or the victim of sensibility; the richly accomplished
will have some capital absurdity; and so every piece has a crack.
'Tis strange, but this masterpiece is the result of such an extreme
delicacy that the most unobserved flaw in the boy will neutralize
the most aspiring genius, and spoil the work. Talk with a seaman
of the hazards to life in his profession and he will ask you, "Where
are the old sailors? Do you not see that all are young men?" And
we, on this sea of human thought, in like manner inquire, Where
are the old idealists? where are they who represented to the last
generation that extravagant hope which a few happy aspirants suggest to ours? In looking at the class of counsel, and power, and
wealth, and at the matronage of the land, amidst all the prudence
and all the triviality, one asks, Where are they who represented
genius, virtue, the invisible and heavenly world, to these? Are they
dead, — taken in early ripeness to the gods, — as ancient wisdom
foretold their fate? Or did the high idea die out of them, and leave
their unperfumed body as its tomb and tablet, announcing to all
that the celestial inhabitant, who once gave them beauty, had departed? Will it be better with the new generation? We easily predict a fair future to each new candidate who enters the lists, but
we are frivolous and volatile, and by low aims and ill example do
what we can to defeat this hope. Then these youths bring us a
rough but effectual aid. By their unconcealed dissatisfaction they
expose our poverty and the insignificance of man to man. A man is
a poor limitary benefactor. He ought to be a shower of benefits —
a great influence, which should never let his brother go, but should
refresh old merits continually with new ones; so that though absent
he should never be out of my mind, his name never far from my
lips; but if the earth should open at my side, or my last hour were
come, his name should be the prayer I should utter to the Universe. But in our experience, man is cheap and friendship wants its
deep sense. We affect to dwell with our friends in their absence,
but we do not; when deed, word, or letter comes not, they let us

go. These exacting children advertise us of our wants. There is no
compliment, no smooth speech with them; they pay you only this
one compliment, of insatiable expectation; they aspire, they se-
verely exact, and if they only stand fast in this watch-tower, and
persist in demanding unto the end, and without end, then are they
terrible friends, whereof poet and priest cannot choose but stand
in awe; and what if they eat clouds, and drink wind, they have not
been without service to the race of man.

With this passion for what is great and extraordinary, it cannot
be wondered at that they are repelled by vulgarity and frivolity in
people. They say to themselves, It is better to be alone than in bad
company. And it is really a wish to be met, — the wish to find society for their hope and religion, — which prompts them to shun
what is called society. They feel that they are never so fit for
friendship as when they have quitted mankind and taken themselves to friend. A picture, a book, a favorite spot in the hills or
the woods which they can people with the fair and worthy creation of the fancy, can give them often forms so vivid that these for
the time shall seem real, and society the illusion.

But their solitary and fastidious manners not only withdraw
them from the conversation, but from the labors of the world;
they are not good citizens, not good members of society; unwillingly they bear their part of the public and private burdens; they
do not willingly share in the public charities, in the public religious rites, in the enterprises of education, of missions foreign and
domestic, in the abolition of the slave-trade, or in the temperance
society. They do not even like to vote. The philanthropists inquire whether Transcendentalism does not mean sloth: they had as
lief hear that their friend is dead, as that he is a Transcendentalist;
for then is he paralyzed, and can never do anything for humanity.
What right, cries the good world, has the man of genius to retreat
from work, and indulge himself? The popular literary creed seems
to be, "I am a sublime genius; I ought not therefore to labor." But
genius is the power to labor better and more availably. Deserve
thy genius: exalt it. The good, the illuminated, sit apart from the
rest, censuring their dulness and vices, as if they thought that by
sitting very grand in their chairs, the very brokers, attorneys, and
congressmen would see the error of their ways, and flock to them.
But the good and wise must learn to act, and carry salvation to the
combatants and demagogues in the dusty arena below.

On the part of these children it is replied that life and their
faculty seem to them gifts too rich to be squandered on such trifles

as you propose to them. What you call your fundamental institutions, your great and holy causes, seem to them great abuses, and, when nearly seen, paltry matters. Each "cause" as it is called, — say Abolition, Temperance, say Calvinism, or Unitarianism, — becomes speedily a little shop, where the article, let it have been at first never so subtle and ethereal, is now made up into portable and convenient cakes, and retailed in small quantities to suit purchasers. You make very free use of these words "great" and "holy," but few things appear to them such. Few persons have any magnificence of nature to inspire enthusiasm, and the philanthropies and charities have a certain air of quackery. As to the general course of living, and the daily employments of men, they cannot see much virtue in these, since they are parts of this vicious circle; and as no great ends are answered by the men, there is nothing noble in the arts by which they are maintained. Nay, they have made the experiment and found that from the liberal professions to the coarsest manual labor, and from the courtesies of the academy and the college to the conventions of the cotillon-room and the morning call, there is a spirit of cowardly compromise and seeming which intimates a frightful skepticism, a life without love, and an activity without an aim.

Unless the action is necessary, unless it is adequate, I do not wish to perform it. I do not wish to do one thing but once. I do not love routine. Once possessed of the principle, it is equally easy to make four or forty thousand applications of it. A great man will be content to have indicated in any the slightest manner his perception of the reigning Idea of his time, and will leave to those who like it the multiplication of examples. When he has hit the white, the rest may shatter the target. Every thing admonishes us how needlessly long life is. Every moment of a hero so raises and cheers us that a twelvemonth is an age. All that the brave Xanthus brings home from his wars is the recollection that at the storming of Samos, "in the heat of the battle, Pericles smiled on me, and passed on to another detachment." It is the quality of the moment, not the number of days, of events, or of actors, that imports.

New, we confess, and by no means happy, is our condition: if you want the aid of our labor, we ourselves stand in greater want of the labor. We are miserable with inaction. We perish of rest and rust: but we do not like your work.

"Then," says the world, "show me your own."

"We have none."

"What will you do, then?" cries the world.

"We will wait."

"How long?"

"Until the Universe beckons and calls us to work."

"But whilst you wait, you grow old and useless."

"Be it so: I can sit in a corner and *perish* (as you call it), but I will not move until I have the highest command. If no call should come for years, for centuries, then I know that the want of the Universe is the attestation of faith by my abstinence. Your virtuous projects, so called, do not cheer me. I know that which shall come will cheer me. If I cannot work, at least I need not lie. All that is clearly due today is not to lie. In other places other men have encountered sharp trials, and have behaved themselves well. The martyrs were sawn asunder, or hung alive on meat-hooks. Cannot we screw our courage to patience and truth, and without complaint, or even with good-humor, await our turn of action in the Infinite Counsels?"

But to come a little closer to the secret of these persons, we must say that to them it seems a very easy matter to answer the objections of the man of the world, but not so easy to dispose of the doubts and objections that occur to themselves. They are exercised in their own spirit with queries which acquaint them with all adversity, and with the trials of the bravest heroes. When I asked them concerning their private experience, they answered somewhat in this wise: It is not to be denied that there must be some wide difference between my faith and other faith; and mine is a certain brief experience, which surprised me in the highway or in the market, in some place, at some time, — whether in the body or out of the body, God knoweth, — and made me aware that I had played the fool with fools all this time, but that law existed for me and for all; that to me belonged trust, a child's trust and obedience, and the worship of ideas, and I should never be fool more. Well, in the space of an hour probably, I was let down from this height; I was at my old tricks, the selfish member of a selfish society. My life is superficial, takes no root in the deep world; I ask, When shall I die and be relieved of the responsibility of seeing a Universe I do not use? I wish to exchange this flash-of-lightning faith for continuous daylight, this fever-glow for a benign climate.

These two states of thought diverge every moment, and stand in wild contrast. To him who looks at his life from these moments of illumination, it will seem that he skulks and plays a mean, shiftless and subaltern part in the world. That is to be done which he has not skill to do, or to be said which others can say better, and he lies by, or occupies his hands with some plaything, until his houi comes again. Much of our reading, much of our labor, seems mere waiting: it was not that we were born for. Any other could do it as well or better. So little skill enters into these works, so little do they mix with the divine life, that it really signifies little what we do, whether we turn a grindstone, or ride, or run, or make fortunes, or govern the state. The worst feature of this double consciousness is, that the two lives, of the understanding and of the soul, which we lead, really show very little relation to each other; never meet and measure each other: one prevails now, all buzz and din; and the other prevails then, all infinitude and paradise; and, with the progress of life, the two discover no greater disposition to reconcile themselves. Yet, what is my faith? What am I? What but a thought of serenity and independence, an abode in the deep blue sky? Presently the clouds shut down again; yet we retain the belief that this pretty web we weave will at last be overshot and reticulated with veins of the blue, and that the moments will characterize the days. Patience, then, is for us, is it not? Patience, and still patience. When we pass, as presently we shall, into some new infinitude, out of this Iceland of negations, it will please us to reflect that though we had few virtues or consolations, we bore with our indigence, nor once strove to repair it with hypocrisy or false heat of any kind.

But this class are not sufficiently characterized if we omit to add that they are lovers and worshippers of Beauty. In the eternal trinity of Truth, Goodness, and Beauty, each in its perfection including the three, they prefer to make Beauty the sign and head. Something of the same taste is observable in all the moral movements of the time, in the religious and benevolent enterprises. They have a liberal, even an aesthetic spirit. A reference to Beauty in action sounds, to be sure, a little hollow and ridiculous in the ears of the old church. In politics, it has often sufficed, when they treated of justice, if they kept the bounds of selfish calculation. If they granted restitution, it was prudence which granted it. But the justice which is now claimed for the black, and the pauper, and the drunkard, is for Beauty, — is for a necessity to the soul of the agent, not of the beneficiary. I say this is the tendency, not yet the realization. Our virtue totters and trips, does not yet walk firmly. Its representatives are austere; they preach and denounce; their rectitude is not yet a grace. They are still liable to that slight taint of burlesque which in our strange world attaches to the zealot. A saint should be as dear as the apple of the eye. Yet we are tempted to smile, and we flee from the working to the speculative reformer, to escape that same slight ridicule. Alas for these days of derision and criticism! We call the Beautiful the highest, because it appears to us the golden mean, escaping the dowdiness of the good and the heartlessness of the true. They are lovers of nature also, and find an indemnity in the inviolable order of the world for the violated order and grace of man.

There is, no doubt, a great deal of well-founded objection to be spoken or felt against the sayings and doings of this class, some of whose traits we have selected; no doubt they will lay themselves open to criticism and to lampoons, and as ridiculous stories will be to be told of them as of any. There will be cant and pretension; there will be subtilty and moonshine. These persons are of unequal strength, and do not all prosper. They complain that everything around them must be denied; and if feeble, it takes all their strength to deny, before they can begin to lead their own life. Grave seniors insist on their respect to this institution and that usage; to an obsolete history; to some vocation, or college, or etiquette, or beneficiary, or charity, or morning or evening call, which they resist as what does not concern them. But it costs such sleepless nights, alienations and misgivings, — they have so many moods about it; these old guardians never change *their* minds; they have but one mood on the subject, namely, that Antony is very perverse, — that it is quite as much as Antony can do to assert his rights, abstain from what he thinks foolish, and keep his temper. He cannot help the reaction of this injustice in his own mind. He is braced-up and stilted; all freedom and flowing genius, all sallies of wit and frolic nature are quite out of the question; it is well if he can keep from lying, injustice, and suicide. This is no time for gaiety and grace. His strength and spirits are wasted in rejection. But the strong spirits overpower those around them without effort. Their thought and emotion comes in like a flood, quite withdraws them from all notice of these carping critics; they surrender themselves with glad heart to the heavenly guide, and only by implication reject the clamorous nonsense of the hour. Grave seniors talk to the deaf, — church and old book mumble and ritualize to an unheeding, preoccupied and advancing mind, and thus they by happiness of greater momentum lose no time, but take the right road at first.

But all these of whom I speak are not proficients; they are novices; they only show the road in which man should travel, when the soul has greater health and prowess. Yet let them feel the dignity of their charge, and deserve a larger power. Their heart is the ark in which the fire is concealed which shall burn in a broader and universal flame. Let them obey the Genius then most when his impulse is wildest; then most when he seems to lead to uninhabitable deserts of thought and life; for the path which the hero travels alone is the highway of health and benefit to mankind. What is the privilege and nobility of our nature but its persistency, through its power to attach itself to what is permanent?

Society also has its duties in reference to this class, and must behold them with what charity it can. Possibly some benefit may yet accrue from them to the state. In our Mechanics' Fair, there must be not only bridges, ploughs, carpenters' planes, and baking troughs, but also some few finer instruments, — rain-gauges, thermometers, and telescopes; and in society, besides farmers, sailors, and weavers, there must be a few persons of purer fire kept specially as gauges and meters of character; persons of a fine, detecting instinct, who note the smallest accumulations of wit and feeling in the bystander. Perhaps too there might be room for the exciters and monitors; collectors of the heavenly spark, with power to convey the electricity to others. Or, as the storm-tossed vessel at sea speaks the frigate or "line packet" to learn its longitude, so it may not be without its advantage that we should now and then encounter rare and gifted men, to compare the points of our spiritual compass, and verify our bearings from superior chronometers.

Amidst the downward tendency and proneness of things, when every voice is raised for a new road or another statute or a subscription of stock; for an improvement in dress, or in dentistry; for a new house or a larger business; for a political party, or the division of an estate; — will you not tolerate one or two solitary voices in the land, speaking for thoughts and principles not marketable or perishable? Soon these improvements and mechanical inventions will be superseded; these modes of living lost out of memory; these cities rotted, ruined by war, by new inventions, by new seats of trade, or the geologic changes: — all gone, like the shells which sprinkle the sea-beach with a white colony today, forever renewed to be forever destroyed. But the thoughts which these few hermits strove to proclaim by silence as well as by speech, not only by what they did, but by what they forbore to do, shall abide in beauty and strength, to reorganize themselves in nature, to invest themselves anew in other, perhaps higher endowed and happier mixed clay than ours, in fuller union with the surrounding system.

Spring, 1844

In general, I am pained by observing the indigence of Nature in this American Commonwealth. Ellen H[ooper] said she sympathized with the Transcendental Movement, but she sympathized even more with the objectors. I replied that, when I saw how little kernel there was to that comet which had shed terror from its flaming hair on the nations, how few and what cinders of genius, I was rather struck with surprise at the largeness of the effect, and drew a favorable inference as to the intellectual and spiritual tendencies of our people. For there had not yet appeared one man among us of a great talent. If two or three persons should come with a high spiritual aim and with great powers, the world would fall into their hands like a ripe peach.

January 28, 1842

Yesterday night, at fifteen minutes after eight, my little Waldo ended his life.

January 30, 1842

. . . The boy had his full swing in this world; never, I think, did a child enjoy more; he had been thoroughly respected by his parents and those around him, and not interfered with; and he had been the most fortunate in respect to the influences near him, for his Aunt Elizabeth had adopted him from his infancy and treated him ever with that plain and wise love which belongs to her and, as she boasted, had never given him sugarplums. So he was won to her, and always signalized her arrival as a visit to him, and left playmates, playthings, and all to go to her. Then Mary Russell had been his friend and teacher for two summers, with true love and wisdom. Then Henry Thoreau had been one of the family for the last year, and charmed Waldo by the variety of toys, whistles, boats, popguns, and all kinds of instruments which he could make and mend; and possessed his love and respect by the gentle firmness with which he always treated him. Margaret Fuller and Caroline Sturgis had also marked the boy and caressed and conversed with him whenever they were here. Meantime every day his grandmother gave him his reading-lesson and had by patience taught him to read and spell; by patience and by love, for she loved him dearly.

Sorrow makes us all children again, — destroys all differences of intellect. The wisest knows nothing. . . .

To Caroline Sturgis

February 4, 1842

The days of our mourning ought, no doubt, to be accomplished ere this, and the innocent and beautiful should not be sourly and gloomily lamented, but with music and fragrant thoughts and sportive recollections. Alas! I chiefly grieve that I cannot grieve; that this fact takes no more deep hold than other facts, is as dreamlike as they; a lambent flame that will not burn playing on the surface of my river. Must every experience — those that promised to be dearest and most penetrative, — only kiss my cheek like the wind and pass away? I think of Ixion and Tantalus and Kehama.[7] Dear Boy, too precious and unique a creation to be huddled aside into the waste and prodigality of things! . . . Calm and wise, calmly and wisely happy, the beautiful Creative power looked out from him and spoke of anything but chaos and interruption; signified strength and unity — and gladdening, all-uniting life. . . .

March 20 ?, 1842

I comprehend. nothing of this fact but its bitterness. Explanation I have none, consolation none that rises out of the fact itself; only diversion; only oblivion of this and pursuit of new objects.

April, 1842

The history of Christ is the best document of the power of Character which we have. A youth who owed nothing to fortune and who was "hanged at Tyburn," — by the pure quality of his nature has shed this epic splendor around the facts of his death which has transfigured every particular into a grand universal symbol for the eyes of all mankind ever since.

He did well. This great Defeat is hitherto the highest fact we have. But he that shall come shall do better. The mind requires a far higher exhibition of character, one which shall make itself good to the senses as well as to the soul; a success to the senses as well as to the soul. This was a great Defeat; we demand Victory. More character will convert judge and jury, soldier and king; will rule human and animal and mineral nature; will command irresistibly and blend with the course of Universal Nature.

In short, there ought to be no such thing as Fate. As long as we

7 See p. 491.

use this word, it is a sign of our impotence and that we are not yet ourselves. There is now a sublime revelation in each of us which makes us so strangely aware and certain of our riches that although I have never since I was born for so much as one moment expressed the truth, and although I have never heard the expression of it from any other, I know that the whole is here, — the wealth of the Universe is for me, everything is explicable and practicable for me. And yet whilst I adore this ineffable life which is at my heart, it will not condescend to gossip with me, it will not announce to me any particulars of science, it will not enter into the details of my biography, and say to me why I have a son and daughters born to me, or why my son dies in his sixth year of joy. Herein, then, I have this latent omniscience coexistent with omni-ignorance. Moreover, whilst this Deity glows at the heart, and by his unlimited presentiments gives me all Power, I know that to-morrow will be as this day, I am a dwarf, and I remain a dwarf. That is to say, I believe in Fate. As long as I am weak, I shall talk of Fate; whenever the God fills me with his fulness, I shall see the disappearance of Fate.

I am *Defeated* all the time; yet to Victory I am born.

April 14, 1842

If I should write an honest diary, what should I say? Alas, that life has halfness, shallowness. I have almost completed thirty-nine years, and I have not yet adjusted my relation to my fellows on the planet, or to my own work. Always too young or too old, I do not satisfy myself; how can I satisfy others?

April 28, 1842

Q. Why not great and good?

Ans. Because I am not what I ought to be.

Q. But why not what you ought?

Ans. The Deity still solicits me, but this self, this individuality, this will resists.

Q. Well for you that it does: if it did yield, you would die, as it is called. But why does it resist?

Ans. I can only reply, God is great: it is the will of God. When he wills, he enters: when he does not will, he enters not.

June, 1842

Charles King Newcomb took us all captive. He had grown so fast that I told him I should not show him the many things I had

bribed him with. Why tease him with multitude? Multitude is
for children. I should let him alone. His criticism in his "Book-
Journal" was captivating and in its devotion to the author, whether
Aeschylus, Dante, Shakespeare, Austin, or Scott, as feeling that he
had a stake in that book, — "who touches that, touches me"; —
and in the total solitude of the critic, the Patmos of thought from
which he writes, in total unconsciousness of any eyes that shall
ever read this writing, he reminds me of Aunt Mary. Charles is a
Religious Intellect. Let it be his praise that when I carried his
manuscript story to the woods, and read it in the armchair of the
upturned root of a pine tree, I felt for the first time since Waldo's
death some efficient faith again in the repairs of the Universe, some
independency of natural relations whilst spiritual affinities can be
so perfect and compensating.[8]

[March, 1842]
[Fourier and the Socialists.] — We had an opportunity of learning something of these Socialists and their theory, from the indefatigable apostle of the sect in New York, Albert Brisbane. Mr.
Brisbane pushed his doctrine with all the force of memory, talent,
honest faith and importunacy. As we listened to his exposition it
appeared to us the sublime of mechanical philosophy; for the system was the perfection of arrangement and contrivance. . . .
Society, concert, coöperation, is the secret of the coming Paradise.
By reason of the isolation of men at the present day, all work is
drudgery. By concert and the allowing each laborer to choose his
own work, it becomes pleasure. . . . It takes sixteen hundred and
eighty men to make one Man, complete in all the faculties; that
is, to be sure that you have got a good joiner, a good cook, a barber,
a poet, a judge, an umbrella-maker, a mayor and alderman, and so
on. Your community should consist of two thousand persons, to
prevent accidents of omission; and each community should take
up six thousand acres of land. Now fancy the earth planted with
fifties and hundreds of these phalanxes side by side, — what tillage,
what architecture, what refectories, what dormitories, what read-
ing-rooms, what concerts, what lectures, what gardens, what
baths! . . .
Our feeling was that Fourier had skipped no fact but one,
namely Life. He treats man as a plastic thing, something that may
be put up or down, ripened or retarded, molded, polished, made

[8] The poem "Threnody" (p. 428), an elegy for Waldo, should be read
in connection with these passages.

into solid or fluid or gas, at the will of the leader; or perhaps as a vegetable, from which, though now a poor crab, a very good peach can by manure and exposure be in time produced, — but skips the faculty of life, which spawns and scorns system and system-makers; which eludes all conditions; which makes or supplants a thousand phalanxes and New Harmonies with each pulsation. There is an order in which in a sound mind the faculties always appear, and which, according to the strength of the individual, they seek to realize in the surrounding world. The value of Fourier's system is that it is a statement of such an order externized, or carried outward into its correspondence in facts. The mistake is that this particular order and series is to be imposed, by force or preaching and votes, on all men, and carried into rigid execution. But what is true and good must not only be begun by life, but must be conducted to its issues by life. Could not the conceiver of this design have also believed that a similar model lay in every mind, and that the method of each associate might be trusted, as well as that of his particular Committee and General Office, No. 200 Broadway? . . .   *From "Life and Letters in New England"*

November 5, 1845
Yesterday evening, saw Robert Owen [9] at Mr. Alcott's. His *Four Elements* are Production, Distribution, Formation of Character, and Local and General Governing. His *Three Errors*, on which society has always been based, and is now, are, (1) that we form ourselves; (2) that we form our opinions; (3) that we form our feelings. The *Three Truths* with which he wishes to replace these, are, (1) that we proceed from a creating power; (2) that our opinions come from conviction; (3) that our feelings come from our instincts.

The *Five Evils* which proceed from our *Three Errors*, and which make the misery of life, are, (1) religious perplexities; (2) disappointment in affections; (3) pecuniary difficulties; (4) intemperance; (5) anxiety for offspring. He also requires a Transitional State. . . .

You are very external with your evils, Mr. Owen: let me give you some real mischiefs: Living for show; losing the whole in the particular; indigence of vital power. I am afraid these will appear in a phalanstery, or in a tub.

We were agreed, that Mr. Owen was right in imputing despotism to circumstances, and that the priest and poet are right in at-

[9] British socialist reformer and founder of New Harmony, Indiana.

tributing responsibility to men. Owen was a better man than he knew, and his love of men made us forget his "Three Errors." . . .

April 1 ?, 1842

What room for Fourier phalanxes, for large and remote schemes of happiness, when I may be in any moment surprised by contentment?

April 1 ?, 1842

What for the visions of the night? Our life is so safe and regular that we hardly know the emotion of terror. Neither public nor private violence, neither natural catastrophes, as earthquake, volcano, or deluge; nor the expectation of supernatural agents in the form of ghosts, or of purgatory and devils and hell fire, disturb the sleepy circulations of our blood in these calm, well-spoken days. And yet dreams acquaint us with what the day omits. . . . Let me consider: I found myself in a garret disturbed by the noise of some one sawing wood. On walking towards the sound, I saw lying in a crib an insane person whom I very well knew, and the noise instantly stopped: there was no saw, a mere stirring among several trumpery matters, fur muffs and empty baskets that lay on the floor. As I tried to approach, the muffs swelled themselves a little, as with wind, and whirled off into a corner of the garret, as if alive, and a kind of animation appeared in all the objects in that corner. Seeing this, and instantly aware that here was Witchcraft, that here was a devilish Will which signified itself plainly enough in the stir and the sound of the wind, I was unable to move; my limbs were frozen with fear; I was bold and would go forward, but my limbs I could not move; I mowed the defiance I could not articulate, and woke with the ugly sound I made. After I woke and recalled the impressions, my brain tingled with repeated vibrations of terror; and yet was the sensation pleasing, as it was a sort of rehearsal of a Tragedy.

August 20 ?, 1842

In talking with W. Ellery Channing on Greek mythology as it was believed at Athens, I could not help feeling how fast the key to such possibilities is lost, the key to the faith of men perishes with the faith. A thousand years hence it will seem less monstrous that those acute Greeks believed in the fables of Mercury and Pan, than that these learned and practical nations of modern Europe and America, these physicians, metaphysicians, mathematicians, critics, and merchants, believed this Jewish apologue of the poor Jewish boy, and how they contrived to attach that accidental history to the religious idea, and this famous dogma of the Triune God, etc., etc. Nothing more facile, so long as the detachment is not made; nothing so wild and incredible the moment after that shall happen.

November 15?, 1841

I am for preserving all those religious writings which were in their origin poetic, ecstatic expressions which the first user of did not know what he said, but they were spoken through him and from above, not from his level; things which seemed a happy casualty, but which were no more random than the human race are a random formation. "It is necessary," says Iamblichus,[1] "that ancient prayers, like sacred *asyla*, should be preserved invariably the same, neither taking anything from them nor adding anything to them which is elsewhere derived."

This is the reason, doubtless, why Homer declares that Jove loved the Ethiopians. And Iamblichus in answer to the query, "Why of significant names we prefer such as are barbaric to our own?" says, among other reasons: "Barbarous names have much emphasis, great conciseness, and less ambiguity, variety, and multitude"; and then afterwards: "But the Barbarians are stable in their manners, and firmly continue to employ the same words. Hence they are dear to the gods, and proffer words which are grateful to them." And the ancients spoke of the Egyptians and Chaldaeans as "sacred nations."

Now the words "God," "Grace," "Prayer," "Heaven," "Hell," are these barbarous and sacred words, to which we must still return, whenever we would speak an ecstatic and universal sense. There are objections to them, no doubt, for academical use, but when the professor's gown is taken off, Man will come back to them.

September, 1842

Nathaniel Hawthorne's reputation as a writer is a very pleasing fact, because his writing is not good for anything, and this is a tribute to the man.

[1] Fourth-century Neoplatonist, a pupil of Porphyry.

September 30 ?, 1842

September 27 was a fine day, and Hawthorne and I set forth
on a walk. . . . The day was full of sunshine, and it was a luxury to
walk in the midst of all this warm and colored light. The days of
September are so rich that it seems natural to walk to the end of
one's strength, and then fall prostrate, saturated with the fine
floods, and cry, *Nunc dimittis me.*[2] Fringed gentians, a thornbush
with red fruit, wild apple trees whose fruit hung like berries, and
grapevines were the decorations of the path. We scarcely encountered man or boy in our road nor saw any in the fields. This
depopulation lasted all day. But the outlines of the landscape were
so gentle that it seemed as if we were in a very cultivated country,
and elegant persons must be living just over yonder hills. Three or
four times, or oftener, we saw the entrance to their lordly park.[3]
But nothing in the farms or in the houses made this good. And it
is to be considered that when any large brain is born in these
towns, it is sent, at sixteen or twenty years, to Boston or New York,
and the country is tilled only by the inferior class of the people, by
the second crop or *rowan* of the Men. Hence all these shiftless
poverty-struck pig-farms. In Europe, where society has an aristocratic structure, the land is full of men of the best stock, and the
best culture, whose interest and pride it is to remain half of the
year at least on their estates and to fill these with every convenience
and ornament. Of course these make model-farms and model-
architecture, and are a constant education to the eye and hand of
the surrounding population.

Our walk had no incidents. It needed none, for we were in excellent spirits, had much conversation, for we were both old collectors who had never had opportunity before to show each other
our cabinets, so that we could have filled with matter much longer
days. . . . After noon we reached Stow, and dined, and then continued our journey towards Harvard, making our day's walk, according to our best computation, about twenty miles. The last
mile, however, we rode in a wagon, having been challenged by a
friendly, fatherly gentleman, who knew my name, and my father's
name and history, and who insisted on doing the honors of his
town to us, and of us to his townsmen; for he fairly installed us at
the tavern, introduced us to the Doctor, and to General ——, and
bespoke the landlord's best attention to our wants. We get the
view of the Nashua River Valley from the top of Oak Hill, as we

[2] Now let thy servant depart.
[3] Cf. "Forerunners," p. 425.

enter Harvard village. Next morning we began our walk at 6:30 o'clock for the Shaker Village, distant three and a half miles. Whilst the good Sisters were getting ready our breakfast, we had a conversation with Seth Blanchard and Cloutman of the Brethren, who gave an honest account, by yea and by nay, of their faith and practice. They were not stupid, like some whom I have seen of their Society, and not worldly like others. The conversation on both parts was frank enough; with the downright I will be downright, thought I, and Seth showed some humor. I doubt not we should have had our own way with them to a good extent (not quite after the manner of Hayraddin Maugrabin with the Monks of Liège)[4] if we could have stayed twenty-four hours; although my powers of persuasion were crippled by a disgraceful barking cold, and Hawthorne inclined to play Jove more than Mercurius.[5] After breakfast Cloutman showed us the farm, vineyard, orchard, barn, herb room, pressing-room, etc. The vineyard contained two noble arcades of grapes, both white and Isabella, full of fruit; the orchard, fine varieties of pears and peaches and apples.

They have fifteen hundred acres here, a tract of woodland in Ashburnham, and a sheep pasture somewhere else, enough to supply the wants of the two hundred souls in this family. They are in many ways an interesting society, but at present have an additional importance as an experiment of socialism which so falls in with the temper of the times. What improvement is made is made forever; this capitalist is old and never dies, his subsistence was long ago secured, and he has gone on now for long scores of years in adding easily compound interests to his stock. Moreover, this settlement is of great value in the heart of the country as a model-farm, in the absence of that rural nobility we talked of yesterday. Here are improvements invented, or adopted from the other Shaker communities, which the neighboring farmers see and copy. From the Shaker Village we came to Littleton and thence to Acton, still in the same redundance of splendor. It was like a day of July, and from Acton we sauntered leisurely homeward, to finish the nineteen miles of our second day before four in the afternoon. . . .

[November, 1842]

The world is awaking to the idea of union, and these experiments show what it is thinking of. It is and will be magic. Men will live and communicate, and plough, and reap, and govern, as

---

[4] In Scott's *Quentin Durward*. Hayraddin, a gypsy, got them drunk.
[5] I.e., to be pontifical rather than persuasive.

by added ethereal power, when once they are united; as in a celebrated experiment, by expiration and respiration exactly together, four persons lift a heavy man from the ground by the little finger only, and without sense of weight. But this union must be inward, and not one of covenants, and is to be reached by a reverse of the methods they use. The union is only perfect when all the uniters are isolated. It is the union of friends who live in different streets or towns. Each man, if he attempts to join himself to others, is on all sides cramped and diminished of his proportion; and the stricter the union the smaller and the more pitiful he is. But leave him alone, to recognize in every hour and place the secret soul; he will go up and down doing the works of a true member, and, to the astonishment of all, the work will be done with concert, though no man spoke. Government will be adamantine without any governor. The union must be ideal in actual individualism.

From "New England Reformers."

November, 1842

Do not gloze and prate and mystify. Here is our dear, grand Alcott says, You shall dig in my field for a day and I will give you a dollar when it is done, and it shall not be a business transaction! It makes me sick. Whilst money is the measure *really* adopted by us all as the most convenient measure of all material values, let us not affectedly disuse the name, and mystify ourselves and others; let us not "say no, and take it." We may very well and honestly have theoretical and practical objections to it; if they are fatal to the use of money and barter, let us disuse them; if they are less grave than the inconvenience of abolishing traffic, let us not pretend to have done with it, whilst we eat and drink and wear and breathe it.

Autumn, 1843

People came, it seems, to my lectures with expectation that I was to realize the Republic I described, and ceased to come when they found this reality no nearer. They mistook me. I am and always was a painter. I paint still with might and main, and choose the best subjects I can. Many have I seen come and go with false hopes and fears, and dubiously affected by my pictures. But I paint on. I count this distinct vocation which never leaves me in doubt what to do, but in all times, places, and fortunes gives me an open future, to be the great felicity of my lot. . . .

December 31, 1843

Belief and Unbelief. — . . . The two parties in life are the believers and unbelievers, variously named. The believer is poet, saint, democrat, theocrat, free-trade, no church, no capital punishment, idealist. The unbeliever supports the church, education, the fine arts, etc., as *amusements*. . . .

But the unbelief is very profound: Who can escape it? I am nominally a believer: yet I hold on to property: I eat my bread with unbelief. I approve every wild action of the experimenters. I say what they say concerning celibacy, or money, or community of goods, and my only apology for not doing their work is preoccupation of mind. I have a work of my own which I know I can do with some success. It would leave that undone if I should undertake with them, and I do not see in myself any vigor equal to such an enterprise. My genius loudly calls me to stay where I am, even with the degradation of owning bank-stock and seeing poor men suffer, whilst the Universal Genius apprises me of this disgrace and beckons me to the martyr's and redeemer's office.

This is belief, too, this debility of practice, this staying by our work. For the obedience to a man's genius is the *particular* of Faith: by and by, shall come the *universal* of Faith.

November 26?, 1842

Conservatism stands on this, that a man cannot jump out of his skin; and well for him that he cannot, for his skin is the world; and the stars of heaven do hold him there: in the folly of men glitters the wisdom of God.

To Margaret Fuller

Baltimore, January 8, 1843

. . . This morning I went to the Cathedral to hear mass with much content. It is so dignified to come where the priest is nothing, and the people nothing, and an idea for once excludes these impertinences. The chanting priest, the pictured walls, the lighted altar, the surpliced boys, the swinging censer, every whiff of which I inhaled, brought all Rome again to mind. And Rome can smell so far! It is a dear old church, the Roman I mean, and today I detest the Unitarians and Martin Luther and all the parliament of Barebones.[6] We understand so well the joyful adhesion of the Winckelmanns and Tiecks and Schlegels; [7] just as we seize with

6 Puritan parliament under Cromwell.
7 German scholars and authors, all Catholic converts.

joy the fine romance and toss the learned Heeren [8] out of the window; unhappily with the same sigh as belongs to the romance: "Ah! that one word of it were true!" . . .

To Margaret Fuller
Washington, January 13, 1843

. . . The Capitol deserves its name and singularly pleases by its mass, — in this country where we never have the satisfaction of seeing large buildings; satisfies too, by its commanding position, and fine entrances. The interior passages are inconveniently small from the doors to the Rotunda and from thence to the legislative chambers, but the Rotunda I admire. Night before last I went thither to see the Washington, which Greenough [9] was endeavoring to show by torchlight. It was his private experiment merely to see if it were practicable to show it so, for now in the daylight it is a statue in a cave. The experiment did not turn out well: a sufficiently powerful light could not be shed on the whole of so great a figure, but it must be shown part by part by removing the light, — which is not easy, as there are no fixtures to which the sconce could be attached, excepting a standing pole which had been erected and rigged for the purpose. . . . It happened that night that our sconce did not succeed very well, for it soon set on fire the wooden case which held the lamps and was let down rapidly, lamps melting and exploding and brilliant balls of light falling on the floor. By the time it was fairly down it was a brilliant bonfire and it was necessary, in order not to fill the rotunda (picture hung) with smoke, to drag it out of the doors on to the piazza, where it drew together a rabble from all parts. — Afterwards with a humbler contrivance the details of the figure, which are of great beauty, were successively brought out. — But the two hours I spent here were very pleasant. I sat on the stone floor in all parts of this grand area and watched the statue with its great limbs and the colossal shadows of the five or six persons who were moving about; the great height above, and the moonlight looking in at the skylight and the resonance of every word and footstep and the electric air of this place, the political center of the continent, made it a very fanciful and exhilarating spot. — John C. Calhoun was one of the company. . . .

[8] Historian of the ancient world.
[9] Horatio Greenough, American sculptor. Congress had commissioned him to do a statue of Washington for the Capitol.

To Margaret Fuller

New York, February 2, 1843

. . . I admire the merchants; I think they shame the scholars. They understand and do their work greatly better than these do theirs. They take up and consume a great deal more vital force, and the conversations of the hotels are much better exhibitions of manly power than any that I hear in libraries. I admire their manners and their docility: so many scholars are made of buckram in mind as well as body, and these men, I mean the good of the class, are ductile, ample, liberal natures. . . .

April ?, 1843

Much poor talk concerning woman, which at least had the effect of revealing the true sex of several of the party who usually go disguised in the form of the other sex. Thus Mrs. B. is a man. The finest people marry the two sexes in their own person. Hermaphrodite is then the symbol of the finished soul. It was agreed that in every act should appear the married pair: the two elements should mix in every act.

To me it sounded hoarsely, the attempt to prescribe didactically to woman her duties. Man can never tell woman what her duties are: he will certainly end in describing a man in female attire, as Harriet Martineau, a masculine woman, solved her problem of woman. No, woman only can tell the heights of feminine nature, and the only way in which man can help her, is by observing woman reverently, and whenever she speaks from herself, and catches him in inspired moments up to a heaven of honor and religion, to hold her to that point by reverential recognition of the divinity that speaks through her.

I can never think of woman without gratitude for the bright revelations of her best nature which have been made to me, unworthy. The angel who walked with me in younger days shamed my ambition and prudence by her generous love in our first interview. I described my prospects. She said, I do not wish to hear of your prospects.

June 14, 1842

A highly endowed man with good intellect and good conscience is a Man-woman and does not so much need the complement of woman to his being as another. Hence his relations to the sex are somewhat dislocated and unsatisfactory. He asks in woman, sometimes the woman, sometimes the man.

May 2 ?, 1843

In America, out-of-doors all seems a market, in-doors an airtight stove of conventionalism. Everybody who comes into the house savors of these precious habits: the men, of the market; the women, of the custom. In every woman's conversation and total influence, mild or acid, lurks the *conventional devil*. They look at your carpet, they look at your cap, at your salt-cellar, at your cook and waiting-maid, conventionally, — to see how close they square with the customary cut in Boston and Salem and New Bedford. But Aunt Mary and Elizabeth [Hoar] do not bring into a house with them a platoon of conventional devils.

May 18, 1843

Extremes meet: there is no straight line. Machinery and Transcendentalism agree well. Stage-Coach and Railroad are bursting the old legislation like green withes.

May 20, 1843

Walked with Ellery [Channing]. In the landscape felt the magic of color; the world is all opal, and those ethereal tints the mountains wear have the finest effects of music on us. Mountains are great poets, and one glance at this fine cliff scene undoes a great deal of prose, and reinstates us wronged men in our rights. All life, all society begins to get illuminated and transparent, and we generalize boldly and well. Space is felt as a great thing. There is some pinch and narrowness to us, and we laugh and leap to see the world, and what amplitudes it has of meadow, stream, upland, forest, and sea, which yet are but lanes and crevices to the great Space in which the world swims like a cockboat in the sea. A little canoe with three figures put out from a creek into the river and sailed downstream to the Bridge, and we rejoiced in the Blessed Water inviolable, magical, whose nature is Beauty, which instantly began to play its sweet games, all circles and dimples and lovely gleaming motions, — always Ganges, the Sacred River, and which cannot be desecrated or made to forget itself. But there below are these farms, yet are the farmers unpoetic. The life of labor does not make men, but drudges. Pleasant it is, as the habits of all poets may testify, to think of great proprietors, to reckon this grove we walk in a park of the noble; but a continent cut up into ten-acre farms is not desirable to the imagination. The Farmer is an enchanted laborer, and after toiling his brains out, sacrificing thought, religion, taste, love, hope, courage at the shrine of toil, turns out a bankrupt as well as the merchant. It is time to have the thing looked into, and with a transpiercing criticism settled whether life is worth having on such terms. If not, let us eat less food and less, and clear ourselves of such a fool's universe. I will not stay, for one, longer than I am contented. Ellery thinks that very few men carry the world in their thoughts. But the actual of it is thus, that every man of mediocre health stands there for the support of fourteen or fifteen sick; and though it were easy to get his own bread with little labor, yet the other fourteen damn him to toil. See this great shovel-handed Irish race who precede everywhere the civilization of America, and grade the road for the rest! . . .

September, 1843

Fear haunts the building railroad, but it will be American power and beauty, when it is done. And these peaceful shovels are better, dull as they are, than pikes in the hands of these Kernes; and this stern day's work of fifteen or sixteen hours, though deplored by all the humanity of the neighborhood, and, though all Concord cries Shame! on the contractors, is a better police than the sheriff and his deputies to let off the peccant humors.

May 21 ?, 1843

Man sheds grief as his skin sheds rain. A preoccupied mind an immense protection. There is a great concession on all hands to the ideal decorum in grief, as well as joy, but few hearts are broken.

To Margaret Fuller

June 7, 1843

. . . I love life — never little, — and now, I think, more and more, entertained and puzzled though I be by this lubricity of it, and inaccessibleness of its pith and heart. The variety of our vital game delights me. I seem in the bosom of all possibility and have never tried but one or two trivial experiments. In happy hours it seems as if one could not lie too lightly on it and like a cloud it would buoy him up and convey him anywhither. But by infirm faith we lose our delicate balance, flounder about and come into the realms and under the laws of mud and stones. The depth of the notes which we accidentally sound on the strings of nature are out of all proportion to our taught and ascertained power and teach us what strangers and novices we are in nature, vagabond in this universe of pure power to which we have not the smallest key. I will at least be glad of my days — I who have so many of them —

and having been informed by God though in the casualest manner that my funds are inexhaustible I will believe it with all my heart. . . .

The Poet

A moody child and wildly wise
Pursued the game with joyful eyes,
Which chose, like meteors, their way,
And rived the dark with private ray:
They overleapt the horizon's edge,
Searched with Apollo's privilege;
Through man, and woman, and sea, and star
Saw the dance of nature forward far;
Through worlds, and races, and terms, and times
Saw musical order, and pairing rhymes.

Olympian bards who sung
Divine ideas below,
Which always find us young,
And always keep us so.

THOSE who are esteemed umpires of taste are often persons who have acquired some knowledge of admired pictures or sculptures, and have an inclination for whatever is elegant; but if you inquire whether they are beautiful souls, and whether their own acts are like fair pictures, you learn that they are selfish and sensual. Their cultivation is local, as if you should rub a log of dry wood in one spot to produce fire, all the rest remaining cold. Their knowledge of the fine arts is some study of rules and particulars, or some limited judgment of color or form, which is exercised for amusement or for show. It is a proof of the shallowness of the doctrine of beauty as it lies in the minds of our amateurs, that men seem to have lost the perception of the instant dependence of form upon soul. There is no doctrine of forms in our philosophy. We were put into our bodies, as fire is put into a pan to be carried about; but there is no accurate adjustment between the spirit and the organ, much less is the latter the germination of the former. So in regard to other forms, the intellectual men do not believe in any essential dependence of the material world on thought and volition. Theologians think it a pretty air-castle to talk of the spiritual meaning of a ship or a cloud, of a city or a contract, but they prefer to come again to the solid ground of historical evidence; and even the poets are contented with a civil and conformed manner of living, and to write poems from the fancy, at a safe distance from their own experience. But the highest minds of the world have never ceased to explore the double meaning, or shall I say the quadruple or the centuple or much more manifold meaning, of every sensuous fact; Orpheus, Empedocles, Heraclitus, Plato, Plutarch, Dante, Swedenborg, and the masters of sculpture, picture and poetry. For we are not pans and barrows, nor even porters of the fire and torch-bearers, but children of the fire, made of it, and only the same divinity transmuted and at two or three removes, when we know least about it. And this hidden truth, that the fountains whence all this river of Time and its creatures floweth are intrinsically ideal and beautiful, draws us to the consideration of the nature and functions of the Poet, or the man of Beauty; to the means and materials he uses, and to the general aspect of the art in the present time.

The breadth of the problem is great, for the poet is representative. He stands among partial men for the complete man, and apprises us not of his wealth, but of the common wealth. The young man reveres men of genius, because, to speak truly, they are more himself than he is. They receive of the soul as he also receives, but they more. Nature enhances her beauty, to the eye of loving men, from their belief that the poet is beholding her shows at the same time. He is isolated among his contemporaries by truth and by his art, but with this consolation in his pursuits, that they will draw all men sooner or later. For all men live by truth and stand in need of expression. In love, in art, in avarice, in politics, in labor, in games, we study to utter our painful secret. The man is only half himself, the other half is his expression.

Notwithstanding this necessity to be published, adequate expression is rare. I know not how it is that we need an interpreter, but the great majority of men seem to be minors, who have not yet come into possession of their own, or mutes, who cannot report the conversation they have had with nature. There is no man who does not anticipate a supersensual utility in the sun and stars, earth and water. These stand and wait to render him a peculiar service. But there is some obstruction or some excess of phlegm in our constitution, which does not suffer them to yield the due effect. Too feeble fall the impressions of nature on us to make us artists Every touch should thrill. Every man should be so much an artist that he could report in conversation what had befallen him. Yet, in our experience, the rays or appulses have sufficient force to ar-

rive at the senses, but not enough to reach the quick and compel
the reproduction of themselves in speech. The poet is the person
in whom these powers are in balance, the man without impediment, who sees and handles that which others dream of, traverses
the whole scale of experience, and is representative of man, in virtue of being the largest power to receive and to impart.

For the Universe has three children, born at one time, which reappear under different names in every system of thought, whether
they be called cause, operation and effect; or, more poetically, Jove,
Pluto, Neptune; or, theologically, the Father, the Spirit and the
Son; but which we will call here the Knower, the Doer and the
Sayer. These stand respectively for the love of truth, for the love
of good, and for the love of beauty. These three are equal. Each
is that which he is, essentially, so that he cannot be surmounted or
analyzed, and each of these three has the power of the others latent
in him and his own, patent.

The poet is the sayer, the namer, and represents beauty. He is
a sovereign, and stands on the center. For the world is not painted
or adorned, but is from the beginning beautiful; and God has not
made some beautiful things, but Beauty is the creator of the universe. Therefore the poet is not any permissive potentate, but is
emperor in his own right. Criticism is infested with a cant of
materialism, which assumes that manual skill and activity is the
first merit of all men, and disparages such as say and do not, over-
looking the fact that some men, namely poets, are natural sayers,
sent into the world to the end of expression, and confounds them
with those whose province is action but who quit it to imitate the
sayers. But Homer's words are as costly and admirable to Homer
as Agamemnon's victories are to Agamemnon. The poet does
not wait for the hero or the sage, but, as they act and think primarily, so he writes primarily what will and must be spoken,
reckoning the others, though primaries also, yet, in respect to him,
secondaries and servants; as sitters or models in the studio of a
painter, or as assistants who bring building-materials to an architect.

For poetry was all written before time was, and whenever we
are so finely organized that we can penetrate into that region
where the air is music, we hear those primal warblings and attempt
to write them down, but we lose ever and anon a word or a verse
and substitute something of our own, and thus miswrite the
poem. The men of more delicate ear write down these cadences
more faithfully, and these transcripts, though imperfect, become

the songs of the nations. For nature is as truly beautiful as it is
good, or as it is reasonable, and must as much appear as it must
be done, or be known. Words and deeds are quite indifferent
modes of the divine energy. Words are also actions, and actions
are a kind of words.

The sign and credentials of the poet are that he announces that
which no man foretold. He is the true and only doctor; [1] he knows
and tells; he is the only teller of news, for he was present and
privy to the appearance which he describes. He is a beholder of
ideas and an utterer of the necessary and causal. For we do not
speak now of men of poetical talents, or of industry and skill in
meter, but of the true poet. I took part in a conversation the other
day concerning a recent writer of lyrics, a man of subtle mind,
whose head appeared to be a music-box of delicate tunes and
rhythms, and whose skill and command of language we could not
sufficiently praise. But when the question arose whether he was
not only a lyrist but a poet, we were obliged to confess that he is
plainly a contemporary, not an eternal man. He does not stand out
of our low limitations, like a Chimborazo under the line, running
up from a torrid base through all the climates of the globe, with
belts of the herbage of every latitude on its high and mottled sides;
but this genius is the landscape-garden of a modern house, adorned
with fountains and statues, with well-bred men and women standing and sitting in the walks and terraces. We hear, through all
the varied music, the ground-tone of conventional life. Our poets
are men of talents who sing, and not the children of music. The
argument is secondary, the finish of the verses is primary.

For it is not meters, but a meter-making argument that makes
a poem, — a thought so passionate and alive that like the spirit
of a plant or an animal it has an architecture of its own, and
adorns nature with a new thing. The thought and the form are
equal in the order of time, but in the order of genesis the thought
is prior to the form. The poet has a new thought; he has a whole
new experience to unfold; he will tell us how it was with him,
and all men will be the richer in his fortune. For the experience
of each new age requires a new confession, and the world seems
always waiting for its poet. I remember when I was young how
much I was moved one morning by tidings that genius had appeared in a youth who sat near me at table. He had left his
work and gone rambling none knew whither, and had written
hundreds of lines, but could not tell whether that which was in

[1] Teacher.

him was therein told; he could tell nothing but that all was changed, — man, beast, heaven, earth and sea. How gladly we listened! how credulous! Society seemed to be compromised. We sat in the aurora of a sunrise which was to put out all the stars. Boston seemed to be at twice the distance it had the night before, or was much farther than that. Rome, — what was Rome? Plutarch and Shakespeare were in the yellow leaf, and Homer no more should be heard of. It is much to know that poetry has been written this very day, under this very roof, by your side. What! that wonderful spirit has not expired! These stony moments are still sparkling and animated! I had fancied that the oracles were all silent, and nature had spent her fires; and behold! all night, from every pore, these fine auroras have been streaming. Every one has some interest in the advent of the poet, and no one knows how much it may concern him. We know that the secret of the world is profound, but who or what shall be our interpreter, we know not. A mountain ramble, a new style of face, a new person, may put the key into our hands. Of course the value of genius to us is in the veracity of its report. Talent may frolic and juggle; genius realizes and adds. Mankind in good earnest have availed so far in understanding themselves and their work, that the foremost watchman on the peak announces his news. It is the truest word ever spoken, and the phrase will be the fittest, most musical, and the unerring voice of the world for that time.

All that we call sacred history attests that the birth of a poet is the principal event in chronology. Man, never so often deceived, still watches for the arrival of a brother who can hold him steady to a truth until he has made it his own. With what joy I begin to read a poem which I confide in as an inspiration! And now my chains are to be broken; I shall mount above these clouds and opaque airs in which I live, — opaque, though they seem transparent, — and from the heaven of truth I shall see and comprehend my relations. That will reconcile me to life and renovate nature, to see trifles animated by a tendency, and to know what I am doing. Life will no more be a noise; now I shall see men and women, and know the signs by which they may be discerned from fools and satans. This day shall be better than my birthday: then I became an animal; now I am invited into the science of the real. Such is the hope, but the fruition is postponed. Oftener it falls that this winged man, who will carry me into the heaven, whirls me into mists, then leaps and frisks about with me as it were from cloud to cloud, still affirming that he is bound heavenward; and I, being

myself a novice, am slow in perceiving that he does not know the
way into the heavens, and is merely bent that I should admire his
skill to rise like a fowl or a flying fish, a little way from the ground
or the water; but the all-piercing, all-feeding and ocular air of
heaven that man shall never inhabit. I tumble down again soon
into my old nooks, and lead the life of exaggerations as before,
and have lost my faith in the possibility of any guide who can lead
me thither where I would be.

But, leaving these victims of vanity, let us, with new hope, observe how nature, by worthier impulses, has insured the poet's
fidelity to his office of announcement and affirming, namely by the
beauty of things, which becomes a new and higher beauty when
expressed. Nature offers all her creatures to him as a picture-lan-
guage. Being used as a type, a second wonderful value appears in
the object, far better than its old value; as the carpenter's stretched
cord, if you hold your ear close enough, is musical in the breeze.
"Things more excellent than every image," says Jamblichus, "are
expressed through images." Things admit of being used as symbols because nature is a symbol, in the whole, and in every part.
Every line we can draw in the sand has expression; and there is
no body without its spirit or genius. All form is an effect of character; all condition, of the quality of the life; all harmony, of health;
and for this reason a perception of beauty should be sympathetic,
or proper only to the good. The beautiful rests on the foundations
of the necessary. The soul makes the body, as the wise Spenser
teaches: —

> "So every spirit, as it is more pure,
> And hath in it the more of heavenly light,
> So it the fairer body doth procure
> To habit in, and it more fairly dight,
> With cheerful grace and amiable sight.
> For, of the soul, the body form doth take,
> For soul is form, and doth the body make."

Here we find ourselves suddenly not in a critical speculation but in
a holy place, and should go very warily and reverently. We stand
before the secret of the world, there where Being passes into Appearance and Unity into Variety.

The Universe is the externization of the soul. Wherever the
life is, that bursts into appearance around it. Our science is sensual, and therefore superficial. The earth and the heavenly bodies,
physics and chemistry, we sensually treat, as if they were self-existent; but these are the retinue of that Being we have. "The

mighty heaven," said Proclus, "exhibits, in its transfigurations, clear
images of the splendor of intellectual perceptions; being moved in
conjunction with the unapparent periods of intellectual natures."
Therefore science always goes abreast with the just elevation of the
man, keeping step with religion and metaphysics; or the state of
science is an index of our self-knowledge. Since every thing in nature answers to a moral power, if any phenomenon remains brute
and dark it is because the corresponding faculty in the observer is
not yet active.

No wonder then, if these waters be so deep, that we hover over
them with a religious regard. The beauty of the fable proves the
importance of the sense; to the poet, and to all others; or, if you
please, every man is so far a poet as to be susceptible of these enchantments of nature; for all men have the thoughts whereof the
universe is the celebration. I find that the fascination resides in the
symbol. Who loves nature? Who does not? Is it only poets, and
men of leisure and cultivation, who live with her? No; but also
hunters, farmers, grooms and butchers, though they express their
affection in their choice of life and not in their choice of words.
The writer wonders what the coachman or the hunter values in
riding, in horses and dogs. It is not superficial qualities. When
you talk with him he holds these at as slight a rate as you. His
worship is sympathetic; he has no definitions, but he is commanded
in nature by the living power which he feels to be there present.
No imitation or playing of these things would content him; he
loves the earnest of the north wind, of rain, of stone and wood and
iron. A beauty not explicable is dearer than a beauty which we
can see to the end of. It is nature the symbol, nature certifying
the supernatural, body overflowed by life which he worships with
coarse but sincere rites.

The inwardness and mystery of this attachment drive men of
every class to the use of emblems. The schools of poets and philosophers are not more intoxicated with their symbols than the populace with theirs. In our political parties, compute the power of
badges and emblems. See the great ball which they roll from Baltimore to Bunker Hill! In the political processions, Lowell goes in a
loom, and Lynn in a shoe, and Salem in a ship. Witness the cider-
barrel, the log-cabin, the hickory-stick, the palmetto, and all the
cognizances of party. See the power of national emblems. Some
stars, lilies, leopards, a crescent, a lion, an eagle, or other figure
which came into credit God knows how, on an old rag of bunting,
blowing in the wind on a fort at the ends of the earth, shall make

the blood tingle under the rudest or the most conventional exterior. The people fancy they hate poetry, and they are all poets and mystics!

Beyond this universality of the symbolic language, we are apprised of the divineness of this superior use of things, whereby the world is a temple whose walls are covered with emblems, pictures and commandments of the Deity, — in this, that there is no fact in nature which does not carry the whole sense of nature; and the distinctions which we make in events and in affairs, of low and high, honest and base, disappear when nature is used as a symbol. Thought makes everything fit for use. The vocabulary of an omniscient man would embrace words and images excluded from polite conversation. What would be base, or even obscene, to the obscene, becomes illustrious, spoken in a new connection of thought. The piety of the Hebrew prophets purges their grossness. The circumcision is an example of the power of poetry to raise the low and offensive. Small and mean things serve as well as great symbols. The meaner the type by which a law is expressed, the more pungent it is, and the more lasting in the memories of men; just as we choose the smallest box or case in which any needful utensil can be carried. Bare lists of words are found suggestive to an imaginative and excited mind, as it is related of Lord Chatham that he was accustomed to read in Bailey's Dictionary when he was preparing to speak in Parliament. The poorest experience is rich enough for all the purposes of expressing thought. Why covet a knowledge of new facts? Day and night, house and garden, a few books, a few actions, serve us as well as would all trades and all spectacles. We are far from having exhausted the significance of the few symbols we use. We can come to use them yet with a terrible simplicity. It does not need that a poem should be long. Every word was once a poem. Every new relation is a new word. Also we use defects and deformities to a sacred purpose, so expressing our sense that the evils of the world are such only to the evil eye. In the old mythology, mythologists observe, defects are ascribed to divine natures, as lameness to Vulcan, blindness to Cupid, and the like, — to signify exuberances.

For as it is dislocation and detachment from the life of God that makes things ugly, the poet, who re-attaches things to nature and the Whole, — re-attaching even artificial things and violation of nature, to nature, by a deeper insight, — disposes very easily of the most disagreeable facts. Readers of poetry see the factory-village and the railway, and fancy that the poetry of the landscape is broken up by these; for these works of art are not yet consecrated in their reading; but the poet sees them fall within the great Order not less than the beehive or the spider's geometrical web. Nature adopts them very fast into her vital circles, and the gliding train of cars she loves like her own. Besides, in a centered mind, it signifies nothing how many mechanical inventions you exhibit. Though you add millions, and never so surprising, the fact of mechanics has not gained a grain's weight. The spiritual fact remains unalterable, by many or by few particulars; as no mountain is of any appreciable height to break the curve of the sphere. A shrewd country-boy goes to the city for the first time, and the complacent citizen is not satisfied with his little wonder. It is not that he does not see all the fine houses and know that he never saw such before, but he disposes of them as easily as the poet finds place for the railway. The chief value of the new fact is to enhance the great and constant fact of Life, which can dwarf any and every circumstance, and to which the belt of wampum and the commerce of America are alike.

The world being thus put under the mind for verb and noun, the poet is he who can articulate it. For though life is great, and fascinates and absorbs; and though all men are intelligent of the symbols through which it is named; yet they cannot originally use them. We are symbols and inhabit symbols; workmen, work, and tools, words and things, birth and death, all are emblems; but we sympathize with the symbols, and being infatuated with the economical uses of things, we do not know that they are thoughts. The poet, by an ulterior intellectual perception, gives them a power which makes their old use forgotten, and puts eyes and a tongue into every dumb and inanimate object. He perceives the independence of the thought on the symbol, the stability of the thought, the accidency and fugacity of the symbol. As the eyes of Lyncaeus were said to see through the earth, so the poet turns the world to glass, and shows us all things in their right series and procession. For through that better perception he stands one step nearer to things, and sees the flowing or metamorphosis; perceives that thought is multiform; that within the form of every creature is a force impelling it to ascend into a higher form; and following with his eyes the life, uses the forms which express that life, and so his speech flows with the flowing of nature. All the facts of the animal economy, sex, nutriment, gestation, birth, growth, are symbols of the passage of the world into the soul of man, to suffer there a change and reappear a new and higher fact. He uses forms according to the life, and not according to the form. This is true science. The poet alone knows astronomy, chemistry, vegetation and animation, for he does not stop at these facts, but employs them as signs. He knows why the plain or meadow of space was strown with these flowers we call suns and moons and stars; why the great deep is adorned with animals, with men, and gods; for in every word he speaks he rides on them as the horses of thought.

By virtue of this science the poet is the Namer or Language-maker, naming things sometimes after their appearance, sometimes after their essence, and giving to every one its own name and not another's, thereby rejoicing the intellect, which delights in detachment or boundary. The poets made all the words, and therefore language is the archives of history, and, if we must say it, a sort of tomb of the muses. For though the origin of most of our words is forgotten, each word was at first a stroke of genius, and obtained currency because for the moment it symbolized the world to the first speaker and to the hearer. The etymologist finds the deadest word to have been once a brilliant picture. Language is fossil poetry. As the limestone of the continent consists of infinite masses of the shells of animalcules, so language is made up of images or tropes, which now, in their secondary use, have long ceased to remind us of their poetic origin. But the poet names the thing because he sees it, or comes one step nearer to it than any other. This expression or naming is not art, but a second nature, grown out of the first, as a leaf out of a tree. What we call nature is a certain self-regulated motion or change; and nature does all things by her own hands, and does not leave another to baptize her but baptizes herself; and this through the metamorphosis again. I remember that a certain poet described it to me thus: —

Genius is the activity which repairs the decays of things, whether wholly or partly of a material and finite kind. Nature, through all her kingdoms, insures herself. Nobody cares for planting the poor fungus; so she shakes down from the gills of one agaric countless spores, any one of which, being preserved, transmits new billions of spores tomorrow or next day. The new agaric of this hour has a chance which the old one had not. This atom of seed is thrown into a new place, not subject to the accidents which destroyed its parent two rods off. She makes a man; and having brought him to ripe age, she will no longer run the risk of losing this wonder at a blow, but she detaches from him a new self, that the kind may be safe from accidents to which the individual is exposed. So when the soul of the poet has come to ripeness of thought, she detaches and sends away from it its poems or songs, — a fearless, sleepless, deathless progeny, which is not exposed to the accidents of the weary kingdom of time; a fearless, vivacious offspring, clad with wings (such was the virtue of the soul out of which they came) which carry them fast and far, and infix them irrecoverably into the hearts of men. These wings are the beauty of the poet's soul. The songs, thus flying immortal from their mortal parent, are pursued by clamorous flights of censures, which swarm in far greater numbers and threaten to devour them; but these last are not winged. At the end of a very short leap they fall plump down and rot, having received from the souls out of which they came no beautiful wings. But the melodies of the poet ascend and leap and pierce into the deeps of infinite time.

So far the bard taught me, using his freer speech. But nature has a higher end, in the production of new individuals, than security, namely *ascension*, or the passage of the soul into higher forms. I knew in my younger days the sculptor who made the statue of the youth which stands in the public garden. He was, as I remember, unable to tell directly what made him happy or unhappy, but by wonderful indirections he could tell. He rose one day, according to his habit, before the dawn, and saw the morning break, grand as the eternity out of which it came, and for many days after, he strove to express this tranquillity, and lo! his chisel had fashioned out of marble the form of a beautiful youth, Phosphorus, whose aspect is such that it is said all persons who look on it become silent. The poet also resigns himself to his mood, and that thought which agitated him is expressed, but *alter idem*,[2] in a manner totally new. The expression is organic, or the new type which things themselves take when liberated. As, in the sun, objects paint their images on the retina of the eye, so they, sharing the aspiration of the whole universe, tend to paint a far more delicate copy of their essence in his mind. Like the metamorphosis of things into higher organic forms is their change into melodies. Over everything stands its daemon or soul, and, as the form of the thing is reflected by the eye, so the soul of the thing is reflected by a melody. The sea, the mountain-ridge, Niagara, and every flower-bed, pre-exist, or super-exist, in pre-cantations, which sail like odors in the air, and when any man goes by with an ear sufficiently fine, he overhears them and endeavors to write down the

2 The same yet different.

notes without diluting or depraving them. And herein is the legitimation of criticism, in the mind's faith that the poems are a corrupt version of some text in nature with which they ought to be made to tally. A rhyme in one of our sonnets should not be less pleasing than the iterated nodes of a seashell, or the resembling difference of a group of flowers. The pairing of the birds is an idyl, not tedious as our idyls are; a tempest is a rough ode, without falsehood or rant; a summer, with its harvest sown, reaped and stored, is an epic song, subordinating how many admirably executed parts. Why should not the symmetry and truth that modulate these, glide into our spirits, and we participate the invention of nature?

This insight, which expresses itself by what is called Imagination, is a very high sort of seeing, which does not come by study, but by the intellect being where and what it sees; by sharing the path or circuit of things through forms, and so making them translucid to others. The path of things is silent. Will they suffer a speaker to go with them? A spy they will not suffer; a lover, a poet, is the transcendency of their own nature, — him they will suffer. The condition of true naming, on the poet's part, is his resigning himself to the divine *aura* which breathes through forms, and accompanying that.

It is a secret which every intellectual man quickly learns, that beyond the energy of his possessed and conscious intellect he is capable of a new energy (as of an intellect doubled on itself), by abandonment to the nature of things; that beside his privacy of power as an individual man, there is a great public power on which he can draw, by unlocking, at all risks, his human doors, and suffering the ethereal tides to roll and circulate through him; then he is caught up into the life of the Universe, his speech is thunder, his thought is law, and his words are universally intelligible as the plants and animals. The poet knows that he speaks adequately then only when he speaks somewhat wildly, or "with the flower of the mind"; not with the intellect used as an organ, but with the intellect released from all service and suffered to take its direction from its celestial life; or as the ancients were wont to express themselves, not with intellect alone but with the intellect inebriated by nectar. As the traveler who has lost his way throws his reins on his horse's neck and trusts to the instinct of the animal to find his road, so must we do with the divine animal who carries us through this world. For if in any manner we can stimulate this instinct, new passages are opened for us into nature; the mind flows into and through things hardest and highest, and the metamorphosis is possible.

This is the reason why bards love wine, mead, narcotics, coffee, tea, opium, the fumes of sandalwood and tobacco, or whatever other procurers of animal exhilaration. All men avail themselves of such means as they can, to add this extraordinary power to their normal powers; and to this end they prize conversation, music, pictures, sculpture, dancing, theaters, traveling, war, mobs, fires, gaming, politics, or love, or science, or animal intoxication, — which are several coarser or finer *quasi*-mechanical substitutes for the true nectar, which is the ravishment of the intellect by coming nearer to the fact. These are auxiliaries to the centrifugal tendency of a man, to his passage out into free space, and they help him to escape the custody of that body in which he is pent up, and of that jail-yard of individual relations in which he is enclosed. Hence a great number of such as were professionally expressers of Beauty, as painters, poets, musicians and actors, have been more than others wont to lead a life of pleasure and indulgence; all but the few who received the true nectar; and, as it was a spurious mode of attaining freedom, as it was an emancipation not into the heavens but into the freedom of baser places, they were punished for that advantage they won, by a dissipation and deterioration. But never can any advantage be taken of nature by a trick. The spirit of the world, the great calm presence of the Creator, comes not forth to the sorceries of opium or of wine. The sublime vision comes to the pure and simple soul in a clean and chaste body. That is not an inspiration, which we owe to narcotics, but some counterfeit excitement and fury. Milton says that the lyric poet may drink wine and live generously, but the epic poet, he who shall sing of the gods and their descent unto men, must drink water out of a wooden bowl. For poetry is not "Devil's wine," but God's wine. It is with this as it is with toys. We fill the hands and nurseries of our children with all manner of dolls, drums and horses; withdrawing their eyes from the plain face and sufficing objects of nature, the sun and moon, the animals, the water and stones, which should be their toys. So the poet's habit of living should be set on a key so low that the common influences should delight him. His cheerfulness should be the gift of the sunlight; the air should suffice for his inspiration, and he should be tipsy with water. That spirit which suffices quiet hearts, which seems to come forth to such from every dry knoll of sere grass, from every pine stump and half-imbedded stone on which the dull March sun shines, comes forth to the poor and hungry, and such as are of simple taste. If thou fill thy brain with Boston and New York, with fashion and covetousness, and wilt stimulate thy jaded senses with wine and French coffee, thou shalt find no radiance of wisdom in the lonely waste of the pine woods.

If the imagination intoxicates the poet, it is not inactive in other men. The metamorphosis excites in the beholder an emotion of joy. The use of symbols has a certain power of emancipation and exhilaration for all men. We seem to be touched by a wand which makes us dance and run about happily, like children. We are like persons who come out of a cave or cellar into the open air. This is the effect on us of tropes, fables, oracles and all poetic forms. Poets are thus liberating gods. Men have really got a new sense, and found within their world another world, or nest of worlds; for, the metamorphosis once seen, we divine that it does not stop. I will not now consider how much this makes the charm of algebra and the mathematics, which also have their tropes, but it is felt in every definition; as when Aristotle defines *space* to be an immovable vessel in which things are contained; — or when Plato defines a *line* to be a flowing point; or *figure* to be a bound of solid; and many the like. What a joyful sense of freedom we have when Vitruvius announces the old opinion of artists that no architect can build any house well who does not know something of anatomy. When Socrates, in Charmides, tells us that the soul is cured of its maladies by certain incantations, and that these incantations are beautiful reasons, from which temperance is generated in souls; when Plato calls the world an animal, and Timaeus affirms that the plants also are animals; or affirms a man to be a heavenly tree, growing with his root, which is his head, upward; and, as George Chapman, following him, writes,

> "So in our tree of man, whose nervie root
> Springs in his top;" —

when Orpheus speaks of hoariness as "that white flower which marks extreme old age"; when Proclus calls the universe the statue of the intellect; when Chaucer, in his praise of "Gentilesse," compares good blood in mean condition to fire, which, though carried to the darkest house betwixt this and the mount of Caucasus, will yet hold its natural office and burn as bright as if twenty thousand men did it behold; when John saw, in the Apocalypse, the ruin of the world through evil, and the stars fall from heaven as the fig tree casteth her untimely fruit; when Aesop reports the whole catalogue of common daily relations through the masquerade of birds and beasts; — we take the cheerful hint of the immortality of our essence and its versatile habit and escapes, as when the gypsies say of themselves "it is in vain to hang them, they cannot die."

The poets are thus liberating gods. The ancient British bards had for the title of their order, "Those who are free throughout the world." They are free, and they make free. An imaginative book renders us much more service at first, by stimulating us through its tropes, than afterward when we arrive at the precise sense of the author. I think nothing is of any value in books excepting the transcendental and extraordinary. If a man is inflamed and carried away by his thought, to that degree that he forgets the authors and the public and heeds only this one dream which holds him like an insanity, let me read his paper, and you may have all the arguments and histories and criticism. All the value which attaches to Pythagoras, Paracelsus, Cornelius Agrippa, Cardan, Kepler, Swedenborg, Schelling, Oken, or any other who introduces questionable facts into his cosmogony, as angels, devils, magic, astrology, palmistry, mesmerism, and so on, is the certificate we have of departure from routine, and that here is a new witness. That also is the best success in conversation, the magic of liberty, which puts the world like a ball in our hands. How cheap even the liberty then seems; how mean to study, when an emotion communicates to the intellect the power to sap and upheave nature; how great the perspective! nations, times, systems, enter and disappear like threads in tapestry of large figure and many colors; dream delivers us to dream, and while the drunkenness lasts we will sell our bed, our philosophy, our religion, in our opulence.

There is good reason why we should prize this liberation. The fate of the poor shepherd, who, blinded and lost in the snowstorm, perishes in a drift within a few feet of his cottage door, is an emblem of the state of man. On the brink of the waters of life and truth, we are miserably dying. The inaccessibleness of every thought but that we are in, is wonderful. What if you come near to it; you are as remote when you are nearest as when you are farthest. Every thought is also a prison; every heaven is also a prison. Therefore we love the poet, the inventor, who in any form, whether in an ode or in an action or in looks and behavior, has yielded us a new thought. He unlocks our chains and admits us to a new scene.

This emancipation is dear to all men, and the power to impart it, as it must come from greater depth and scope of thought, is a measure of intellect. Therefore all books of the imagination endure, all which ascend to that truth that the writer sees nature beneath him, and uses it as his exponent. Every verse or sentence possessing this virtue will take care of its own immortality. The religions of the world are the ejaculations of a few imaginative men.

But the quality of the imagination is to flow, and not to freeze. The poet did not stop at the color or the form, but read their meaning; neither may he rest in this meaning, but he makes the same objects exponents of his new thought. Here is the difference betwixt the poet and the mystic, that the last nails a symbol to one sense, which was a true sense for a moment, but soon becomes old and false. For all symbols are fluxional; all language is vehicular and transitive, and is good, as ferries and horses are, for conveyance, not as farms and houses are, for homestead. Mysticism consists in the mistake of an accidental and individual symbol for an universal one. The morning-redness happens to be the favorite meteor to the eyes of Jacob Behmen, and comes to stand to him for truth and faith; and, he believes, should stand for the same realities to every reader. But the first reader prefers as naturally the symbol of a mother and child, or a gardener and his bulb, or a jeweler polishing a gem. Either of these, or of a myriad more, are equally good to the person to whom they are significant. Only they must be held lightly, and be very willingly translated into the equivalent terms which others use. And the mystic must be steadily told, — All that you say is just as true without the tedious use of that symbol as with it. Let us have a little algebra, instead of this trite rhetoric, — universal signs, instead of these village symbols, — and we shall both be gainers. The history of hierarchies seems to show that all religious error consisted in making the symbol too stark and solid, and was at last nothing but an excess of the organ of language.

Swedenborg, of all men in the recent ages, stands eminently for the translator of nature into thought. I do not know the man in history to whom things stood so uniformly for words. Before him the metamorphosis continually plays. Everything on which his eye rests, obeys the impulses of moral nature. The figs become grapes whilst he eats them. When some of his angels affirmed a truth, the laurel twig which they held blossomed in their hands. The noise which at a distance appeared like gnashing and thumping, on coming nearer was found to be the voice of disputants. The men in one of his visions, seen in heavenly light, appeared like dragons, and seemed in darkness; but to each other they appeared as men, and when the light from heaven shone into their cabin, they complained of the darkness, and were compelled to shut the window that they might see.

There was this perception in him which makes the poet or seer an object of awe and terror, namely that the same man or society of men may wear one aspect to themselves and their companions, and a different aspect to higher intelligences. Certain priests, whom he describes as conversing very learnedly together, appeared to the children who were at some distance, like dead horses; and many the like misappearances. And instantly the mind inquires whether these fishes under the bridge, yonder oxen in the pasture, those dogs in the yard, are immutably fishes, oxen and dogs, or only so appear to me, and perchance to themselves appear upright men; and whether I appear as a man to all eyes. The Brahmins and Pythagoras propounded the same question, and if any poet has witnessed the transformation he doubtless found it in harmony with various experiences. We have all seen changes as considerable in wheat and caterpillars. He is the poet and shall draw us with love and terror, who sees through the flowing vest the firm nature, and can declare it.

I look in vain for the poet whom I describe. We do not with sufficient plainness or sufficient profoundness address ourselves to life, nor dare we chaunt our own times and social circumstance. If we filled the day with bravery, we should not shrink from celebrating it. Time and nature yield us many gifts, but not yet the timely man, the new religion, the reconciler, whom all things await. Dante's praise is that he dared to write his autobiography in colossal cipher, or into universality. We have yet had no genius in America, with tyrannous eye, which knew the value of our incomparable materials, and saw, in the barbarism and materialism of the times, another carnival of the same gods whose picture he so much admires in Homer; then in the Middle Age; then in Calvinism. Banks and tariffs, the newspaper and caucus, Methodism and Unitarianism, are flat and dull to dull people, but rest on the same foundations of wonder as the town of Troy and the temple of Delphi, and are as swiftly passing away. Our log-rolling, our stumps and their politics, our fisheries, our Negroes and Indians, our boats and our repudiations, the wrath of rogues and the pusillanimity of honest men, the northern trade, the southern planting, the western clearing, Oregon and Texas, are yet unsung. Yet America is a poem in our eyes; its ample geography dazzles the imagination, and it will not wait long for meters. If I have not found that excellent combination of gifts in my countrymen which

I seek, neither could I aid myself to fix the idea of the poet by
reading now and then in Chalmers's collection of five centuries of
English poets. These are wits more than poets, though there have
been poets among them. But when we adhere to the ideal of the
poet, we have our difficulties even with Milton and Homer. Milton is too literary, and Homer too literal and historical.

But I am not wise enough for a national criticism, and must use
the old largeness a little longer, to discharge my errand from the
muse to the poet concerning his art.

Art is the path of the creator to his work. The paths or methods
are ideal and eternal, though few men ever see them; not the artist
himself for years, or for a lifetime, unless he come into the conditions. The painter, the sculptor, the composer, the epic rhapsodist,
the orator, all partake one desire, namely to express themselves
symmetrically and abundantly, not dwarfishly and fragmentarily.
They found or put themselves in certain conditions, as, the painter
and sculptor before some impressive human figures; the orator
into the assembly of the people; and the others in such scenes as
each has found exciting to his intellect; and each presently feels
the new desire. He hears a voice, he sees a beckoning. Then he
is apprised, with wonder, what herds of daemons hem him in.
He can no more rest; he says, with the old painter, "By God it is
in me and must go forth of me." He pursues a beauty, half seen,
which flies before him. The poet pours out verses in every solitude.
Most of the things he says are conventional, no doubt; but by and
by he says something which is original and beautiful. That charms
him. He would say nothing else but such things. In our way of
talking we say "That is yours, this is mine"; but the poet knows
well that it is not his; that it is as strange and beautiful to him as
to you; he would fain hear the like eloquence at length. Once
having tasted this immortal ichor,[3] he cannot have enough of it,
and as an admirable creative power exists in these intellections, it
is of the last importance that these things get spoken. What a
little of all we know is said! What drops of all the sea of our
science are baled up! and by what accident it is that these are exposed, when so many secrets sleep in nature! Hence the necessity
of speech and song; hence these throbs and heart-beatings in the
orator, at the door of the assembly, to the end namely that thought
may be ejaculated as Logos, or Word.

Doubt not, O poet, but persist. Say "It is in me, and shall out."

---

[3] Blood of the gods (Greek). The shades in Hades had to drink blood
before they could speak.

Stand there, balked and dumb, stuttering and stammering, hissed and hooted, stand and strive, until at last rage draw out of thee that *dream*-power which every night shows thee is thine own; a power transcending all limit and privacy, and by virtue of which a man is the conductor of the whole river of electricity. Nothing walks, or creeps, or grows, or exists, which must not in turn arise and walk before him as exponent of his meaning. Comes he to that power, his genius is no longer exhaustible. All the creatures by pairs and by tribes pour into his mind as into a Noah's ark, to come forth again to people a new world. This is like the stock of air for our respiration or for the combustion of our fireplace; not a measure of gallons, but the entire atmosphere if wanted. And therefore the rich poets, as Homer, Chaucer, Shakespeare, and Raphael, have obviously no limits to their works except the limits of their lifetime, and resemble a mirror carried through the street, ready to render an image of every created thing.

O poet! a new nobility is conferred in groves and pastures, and not in castles or by the sword-blade any longer. The conditions are hard, but equal. Thou shalt leave the world, and know the muse only. Thou shalt not know any longer the times, customs, graces, politics, or opinions of men, but shalt take all from the muse. For the time of towns is tolled from the world by funereal chimes, but in nature the universal hours are counted by succeeding tribes of animals and plants, and by growth of joy on joy. God wills also that thou abdicate a manifold and duplex life, and that thou be content that others speak for thee. Others shall be thy gentlemen and shall represent all courtesy and worldly life for thee; others shall do the great and resounding actions also. Thou shalt lie close hid with nature, and canst not be afforded to the Capitol or the Exchange. The world is full of renunciations and apprenticeships, and this is thine; thou must pass for a fool and a churl for a long season. This is the screen and sheath in which Pan has protected his well-beloved flower, and thou shalt be known only to thine own, and they shall console thee with tenderest love. And thou shalt not be able to rehearse the names of thy friends in thy verse, for an old shame before the holy ideal. And this is the reward; that the ideal shall be real to thee, and the impressions of the actual world shall fall like summer rain, copious, but not troublesome to thy invulnerable essence. Thou shalt have the whole land for thy park and manor, the sea for thy bath and navigation, without tax and without envy; the woods and the rivers thou shalt own, and thou shalt possess that wherein others are only tenants and boarders. Thou true land-lord! sea-lord! air-lord! Wherever snow falls or water flows or birds fly, wherever day and night meet in twilight, wherever the blue heaven is hung by clouds or sown with stars, wherever are forms with transparent boundaries, wherever are outlets into celestial space, wherever is danger, and awe, and love, — there is Beauty, plenteous as rain, shed for thee, and though thou shouldst walk the world over, thou shalt not be able to find a condition inopportune or ignoble.

Politics

Gold and iron are good
To buy iron and gold;
All earth's fleece and food
For their like are sold.
Boded Merlin wise,
Proved Napoleon great,
Nor kind nor coinage buys
Aught above its rate.
Fear, Craft and Avarice
Cannot rear a State.
Out of dust to build
What is more than dust, —
Walls Amphion piled
Phoebus stablish must.
When the Muses nine
With the Virtues meet,
Find to their design
An Atlantic seat,
By green orchard boughs
Fended from the heat,
Where the statesman ploughs
Furrow for the wheat, —
When the Church is social worth,
When the state-house is the hearth,
Then the perfect State is come,
The republican at home.

IN dealing with the State we ought to remember that its institutions are not aboriginal, though they existed before we were born; that they are not superior to the citizen; that every one of them was once the act of a single man; every law and usage was a man's expedient to meet a particular case; that they all are imitable, all alterable; we may make as good, we may make better. Society is an illusion to the young citizen. It lies before him in rigid repose,

with certain names, men and institutions rooted like oak-trees to
the center, round which all arrange themselves the best they can.
But the old statesman knows that society is fluid; there are no
such roots and centers, but any particle may suddenly become the
center of the movement and compel the system to gyrate round
it; as every man of strong will, like Pisistratus or Cromwell, does
for a time, and every man of truth, like Plato or Paul, does forever. But politics rest on necessary foundations, and cannot be
treated with levity. Republics abound in young civilians who believe that the laws make the city, that grave modifications of the
policy and modes of living and employments of the population,
that commerce, education and religion may be voted in or out;
and that any measure, though it were absurd, may be imposed on
a people if only you can get sufficient voices to make it a law. But
the wise know that foolish legislation is a rope of sand which
perishes in the twisting;[4] that the State must follow and not lead
the character and progress of the citizen; the strongest usurper is
quickly got rid of; and they only who build on Ideas, build for
eternity; and that the form of government which prevails is the
expression of what cultivation exists in the population which permits it. The law is only a memorandum. We are superstitious, and
esteem the statute somewhat: so much life as it has in the character of living men is its force. The statute stands there to say, Yesterday we agreed so and so, but how feel ye this article today? Our
statute is a currency which we stamp with our own portrait: it
soon becomes unrecognizable, and in process of time will return to
the mint. Nature is not democratic, nor limited-monarchical, but
despotic, and will not be fooled or abated of any jot of her authority by the pertest of her sons; and as fast as the public mind is
opened to more intelligence, the code is seen to be brute and
stammering. It speaks not articulately, and must be made to.
Meantime the education of the general mind never stops. The
reveries of the true and simple are prophetic. What the tender
poetic youth dreams, and prays, and paints today, but shuns the
ridicule of saying aloud, shall presently be the resolutions of public
bodies; then shall be carried as grievance and bill of rights through
conflict and war, and then shall be triumphant law and establishment for a hundred years, until it gives place in turn to new prayers
and pictures. The history of the State sketches in coarse outline

[4] Students of the Black Art held that demons could be kept out of
mischief by setting them at hopeless tasks, such as making ropes out of
sand. — E.W.E.

the progress of thought, and follows at a distance the delicacy of
culture and of aspiration.

The theory of politics which has possessed the mind of men,
and which they have expressed the best they could in their laws
and in their revolutions, considers persons and property as the two
objects for whose protection government exists. Of persons, all
have equal rights, in virtue of being identical in nature. This interest of course with its whole power demands a democracy.
Whilst the rights of all as persons are equal, in virtue of their
access to reason, their rights in property are very unequal. One
man owns his clothes, and another owns a county. This accident,
depending primarily on the skill and virtue of the parties, of which
there is every degree, and secondarily on patrimony, falls unequally,
and its rights of course are unequal. Personal rights, universally
the same, demand a government framed on the ratio of the census;
property demands a government framed on the ratio of owners
and of owning. Laban, who has flocks and herds, wishes them
looked after by an officer on the frontiers, lest the Midianites shall
drive them off; and pays a tax to that end. Jacob has no flocks or
herds and no fear of the Midianites, and pays no tax to the officer.
It seemed fit that Laban and Jacob should have equal rights to
elect the officer who is to defend their persons, but that Laban
and not Jacob should elect the officer who is to guard the sheep and
cattle. And if question arise whether additional officers or watch-
towers should be provided, must not Laban and Isaac, and those
who must sell part of their herds to buy protection for the rest,
judge better of this, and with more right, than Jacob, who, because he is a youth and a traveler, eats their bread and not his own?

In the earliest society the proprietors made their own wealth,
and so long as it comes to the owners in the direct way, no other
opinion would arise in any equitable community than that property should make the law for property, and persons the law for
persons.

But property passes through donation or inheritance to those
who do not create it. Gift, in one case, makes it as really the new
owner's, as labor made it the first owner's: in the other case, of
patrimony, the law makes an ownership which will be valid in each
man's view according to the estimate which he sets on the public
tranquillity.

It was not, however, found easy to embody the readily admitted
principle that property should make law for property, and persons
for persons; since persons and property mixed themselves in every

transaction. At last it seemed settled that the rightful distinction
was that the proprietors should have more elective franchise than
non-proprietors, on the Spartan principle of "calling that which is
just, equal; not that which is equal, just."

That principle no longer looks so self-evident as it appeared in
former times, partly because doubts have arisen whether too much
weight had not been allowed in the laws to property, and such a
structure given to our usages as allowed the rich to encroach on the
poor, and to keep them poor; but mainly because there is an instinctive sense, however obscure and yet inarticulate, that the
whole constitution of property, on its present tenures, is injurious,
and its influence on persons deteriorating and degrading; that truly
the only interest for the consideration of the State is persons; that
property will always follow persons; that the highest end of government is the culture of men; and that if men can be educated,
the institutions will share their improvement and the moral sentiment will write the law of the land.

If it be not easy to settle the equity of this question, the peril
is less when we take note of our natural defenses. We are kept by
better guards than the vigilance of such magistrates as we commonly elect. Society always consists in greatest part of young and
foolish persons. The old, who have seen through the hypocrisy
of courts and statesmen, die and leave no wisdom to their sons.
They believe their own newspaper, as their fathers did at their age.
With such an ignorant and deceivable majority, States would soon
run to ruin, but that there are limitations beyond which the folly
and ambition of governors cannot go. Things have their laws,
as well as men; and things refuse to be trifled with. Property will be
protected. Corn will not grow unless it is planted and manured;
but the farmer will not plant or hoe it unless the chances are a
hundred to one that he will cut and harvest it. Under any forms,
persons and property must and will have their just sway. They
exert their power, as steadily as matter its attraction. Cover up a
pound of earth never so cunningly, divide and subdivide it; melt it
to liquid, convert it to gas; it will always weigh a pound; it will always attract and resist other matter by the full virtue of one pound
weight: — and the attributes of a person, his wit and his moral
energy, will exercise, under any law or extinguishing tyranny, their
proper force, — if not overtly, then covertly; if not for the law,
then against it; if not wholesomely, then poisonously; with right,
or by might.

The boundaries of personal influence it is impossible to fix, as

persons are organs of moral or supernatural force. Under the
dominion of an idea which possesses the minds of multitudes, as
civil freedom, or the religious sentiment, the powers of persons are
no longer subjects of calculation. A nation of men unanimously
bent on freedom or conquest can easily confound the arithmetic of
statists, and achieve extravagant actions, out of all proportion to
their means; as the Greeks, the Saracens, the Swiss, the Americans,
and the French have done.

In like manner to every particle of property belongs its own attraction. A cent is the representative of a certain quantity of corn
or other commodity. Its value is in the necessities of the animal
man. It is so much warmth, so much bread, so much water, so
much land. The law may do what it will with the owner of property; its just power will still attach to the cent. The law may in a
mad freak say that all shall have power except the owners of property; they shall have no vote. Nevertheless, by a higher law, the
property will, year after year, write every statute that respects
property. The non-proprietor will be the scribe of the proprietor.
What the owners wish to do, the whole power of property will do,
either through the law or else in defiance of it. Of course I speak
of all the property, not merely of the great estates. When the rich
are outvoted, as frequently happens, it is the joint treasury of the
poor which exceeds their accumulations. Every man owns something, if it is only a cow, or a wheelbarrow, or his arms, and so has
that property to dispose of.

The same necessity which secures the rights of person and property against the malignity or folly of the magistrate, determines the
form and methods of governing, which are proper to each nation
and to its habit of thought, and nowise transferable to other states
of society. In this country we are very vain of our political institutions, which are singular in this, that they sprung, within the memory of living men, from the character and condition of the people,
which they still express with sufficient fidelity, — and we ostentatiously prefer them to any other in history. They are not better,
but only fitter for us. We may be wise in asserting the advantage
in modern times of the democratic form, but to other states of
society, in which religion consecrated the monarchical, that and
not this was expedient. Democracy is better for us, because the
religious sentiment of the present time accords better with it. Born
democrats, we are nowise qualified to judge of monarchy, which, to
our fathers living in the monarchical idea, was also relatively right.
But our institutions, though in coincidence with the spirit of the

age, have not any exemption from the practical defects which have discredited other forms. Every actual State is corrupt. Good men must not obey the laws too well. What satire on government can equal the severity of censure conveyed in the word *politic*, which now for ages has signified *cunning*, intimating that the State is a trick?

The same benign necessity and the same practical abuse appear in the parties, into which each State divides itself, of opponents and defenders of the administration of the government. Parties are also founded on instincts, and have better guides to their own humble aims than the sagacity of their leaders. They have nothing perverse in their origin, but rudely mark some real and lasting relation. We might as wisely reprove the east wind or the frost, as a political party, whose members, for the most part, could give no account of their position, but stand for the defense of those interests in which they find themselves. Our quarrel with them begins when they quit this deep natural ground at the bidding of some leader, and obeying personal considerations, throw themselves into the maintenance and defense of points nowise belonging to their system. A party is perpetually corrupted by personality. Whilst we absolve the association from dishonesty, we cannot extend the same charity to their leaders. They reap the rewards of the docility and zeal of the masses which they direct. Ordinarily our parties are parties of circumstance, and not of principle; as the planting interest in conflict with the commercial; the party of capitalists and that of operatives: parties which are identical in their moral character, and which can easily change ground with each other in the support of many of their measures. Parties of principle, as, religious sects, or the party of free-trade, of universal suffrage, of abolition of slavery, of abolition of capital punishment, — degenerate into personalities, or would inspire enthusiasm. The vice of our leading parties in this country (which may be cited as a fair specimen of these societies of opinion) is that they do not plant themselves on the deep and necessary grounds to which they are respectively entitled, but lash themselves to fury in the carrying of some local and momentary measure, nowise useful to the commonwealth. Of the two great parties which at this hour almost share the nation between them, I should say that one has the best cause, and the other contains the best men. The philosopher, the poet, or the religious man, will of course wish to cast his vote with the democrat, for free-trade, for wide suffrage, for the abolition of legal cruelties in the penal code, and for facilitating in every manner the access of the young and the poor to the sources of wealth and power. But he can rarely accept the persons whom the so-called popular party propose to him as representatives of these liberalities. They have not at heart the ends which give to the name of democracy what hope and virtue are in it. The spirit of our American radicalism is destructive and aimless: it is not loving; it has no ulterior and divine ends, but is destructive only out of hatred and selfishness. On the other side, the conservative party, composed of the most moderate, able and cultivated part of the population, is timid, and merely defensive of property. It vindicates no right, it aspires to no real good, it brands no crime, it proposes no generous policy; it does not build, nor write, nor cherish the arts, nor foster religion, nor establish schools, nor encourage science, nor emancipate the slave, nor befriend the poor, or the Indian, or the immigrant. From neither party, when in power, has the world any benefit to expect in science, art, or humanity, at all commensurate with the resources of the nation.

I do not for these defects despair of our republic. We are not at the mercy of any waves of chance. In the strife of ferocious parties, human nature always finds itself cherished; as the children of the convicts at Botany Bay are found to have as healthy a moral sentiment as other children. Citizens of feudal states are alarmed at our democratic institutions lapsing into anarchy, and the older and more cautious among ourselves are learning from Europeans to look with some terror at our turbulent freedom. It is said that in our license of construing the Constitution, and in the despotism of public opinion, we have no anchor; and one foreign observer thinks he has found the safeguard in the sanctity of Marriage among us; and another thinks he has found it in our Calvinism. Fisher Ames expressed the popular security more wisely, when he compared a monarchy and a republic, saying that a monarchy is a merchantman, which sails well, but will sometimes strike on a rock and go to the bottom; whilst a republic is a raft, which would never sink, but then your feet are always in water. No forms can have any dangerous importance whilst we are befriended by the laws of things. It makes no difference how many tons' weight of atmosphere presses on our heads, so long as the same pressure resists it within the lungs. Augment the mass a thousand-fold, it cannot begin to crush us, as long as reaction is equal to action. The fact of two poles, of two forces, centripetal and centrifugal, is universal, and each force by its own activity develops the other. Wild liberty develops iron conscience. Want of liberty, by strengthening law and decorum, stupefies conscience. "Lynch-law" prevails only where there is greater hardihood and self-subsistency in the leaders. A mob cannot be a permanency; everybody's interest requires that it should not exist, and only justice satisfies all.

We must trust infinitely to the beneficent necessity which shines through all laws. Human nature expresses itself in them as characteristically as in statues, or songs, or railroads; and an abstract of the codes of nations would be a transcript of the common conscience. Governments have their origin in the moral identity of men. Reason for one is seen to be reason for another, and for every other. There is a middle measure which satisfies all parties, be they never so many or so resolute for their own. Every man finds a sanction for his simplest claims and deeds, in decisions of his own mind, which he calls Truth and Holiness. In these decisions all the citizens find a perfect agreement, and only in these; not in what is good to eat, good to wear, good use of time, or what amount of land or of public aid each is entitled to claim. This truth and justice men presently endeavor to make application of to the measuring of land, the apportionment of service, the protection of life and property. Their first endeavors, no doubt, are very awkward. Yet absolute right is the first governor; or, every government is an impure theocracy. The idea after which each community is aiming to make and mend its law, is the will of the wise man. The wise man it cannot find in nature, and it makes awkward but earnest efforts to secure his government by contrivance; as by causing the entire people to give their voices on every measure; or by a double choice to get the representation of the whole; or by a selection of the best citizens; or to secure the advantages of efficiency and internal peace by confiding the government to one, who may himself select his agents. All forms of government symbolize an immortal government, common to all dynasties and independent of numbers, perfect where two men exist, perfect where there is only one man.

Every man's nature is a sufficient advertisement to him of the character of his fellows. My right and my wrong is their right and their wrong. Whilst I do what is fit for me, and abstain from what is unfit, my neighbor and I shall often agree in our means, and work together for a time to one end. But whenever I find my dominion over myself not sufficient for me, and undertake the direction of him also, I overstep the truth, and come into false relations to him. I may have so much more skill or strength than he that he cannot express adequately his sense of wrong, but it is a lie, and hurts like a lie both him and me. Love and nature cannot maintain the assumption; it must be executed by a practical lie, namely by force. This undertaking for another is the blunder which stands in colossal ugliness in the governments of the world. It is the same thing in numbers, as in a pair, only not quite so intelligible. I can see well enough a great difference between my setting myself down to a self-control, and my going to make somebody else act after my views; but when a quarter of the human race assume to tell me what I must do, I may be too much disturbed by the circumstances to see so clearly the absurdity of their command. Therefore all public ends look vague and quixotic beside private ones. For any laws but those which men make for themselves are laughable. If I put myself in the place of my child, and we stand in one thought and see that things are thus or thus, that perception is law for him and me. We are both there, both act. But if, without carrying him into the thought, I look over into his plot, and, guessing how it is with him, ordain this or that, he will never obey me. This is the history of governments, — one man does something which is to bind another. A man who cannot be acquainted with me, taxes me; looking from afar at me ordains that a part of my labor shall go to this or that whimsical end, — not as I, but as he happens to fancy. Behold the consequence. Of all debts men are least willing to pay the taxes. What a satire is this on government! Everywhere they think they get their money's worth, except for these.

Hence the less government we have the better, — the fewer laws, and the less confided power. The antidote to this abuse of formal government is the influence of private character, the growth of the Individual; the appearance of the principal to supersede the proxy; the appearance of the wise man; of whom the existing government is, it must be owned, but a shabby imitation. That which all things tend to educe; which freedom, cultivation, intercourse, revolutions, go to form and deliver, is character; that is the end of Nature, to reach unto this coronation of her king. To educate the wise man the State exists, and with the appearance of the wise man the State expires. The appearance of character makes the State unnecessary. The wise man is the State. He needs no army, fort, or navy, — he loves men too well; no bribe, or feast, or palace, to draw friends to him; no vantage ground, no favorable circumstance. He needs no library, for he has not done thinking; no church, for he is a prophet; no statute-book, for he has the lawgiver; no money, for he is value; no road, for he is at home where he is; no experience, for the life of tne creator shoots through him, and looks from his eyes. He has no personal friends, for he who has the spell to draw the prayer and piety of all men unto him needs not husband and educate a few to share with him a select and poetic life. His relation to men is angelic; his memory is myrrh to them; his presence, frankincense and flowers.

We think our civilization near its meridian, but we are yet only at the cock-crowing and the morning star. In our barbarous society the influence of character is in its infancy. As a political power, as the rightful lord who is to tumble all rulers from their chairs, its presence is hardly yet suspected. Malthus and Ricardo quite omit it; the Annual Register is silent; in the Conversations' Lexicon it is not set down; the President's Message, the Queen's Speech, have not mentioned it; and yet it is never nothing. Every thought which genius and piety throw into the world, alters the world. The gladiators in the lists of power feel, through all their frocks of force and simulation, the presence of worth. I think the very strife of trade and ambition is confession of this divinity; and successes in those fields are the poor amends, the fig-leaf with which the shamed soul attempts to hide its nakedness. I find the like unwilling homage in all quarters. It is because we know how much is due from us that we are impatient to show some petty talent as a substitute for worth. We are haunted by a conscience of this right to grandeur of character, and are false to it. But each of us has some talent, can do somewhat useful, or graceful, or formidable, or amusing, or lucrative. That we do, as an apology to others and to ourselves for not reaching the mark of a good and equal life. But it does not satisfy *us*, whilst we thrust it on the notice of our companions. It may throw dust in their eyes, but does not smooth our own brow, or give us the tranquillity of the strong when we walk abroad. We do penance as we go. Our talent is a sort of expiation, and we are constrained to reflect on our splendid moment with a certain humiliation, as somewhat too fine, and not as one act of many acts, a fair expression of our permanent energy. Most persons of ability meet in society with a kind of tacit appeal. Each seems to say, "I am not all here." Senators and presidents have climbed so high with pain enough, not because they think the place specially agreeable, but as an apology for real worth, and to vindicate their manhood in our eyes. This conspicuous chair is their compensation to themselves for being of a poor, cold, hard nature. They must do what they can. Like one class of forest animals, they have nothing but a prehensile tail;

climb they must, or crawl. If a man found himself so rich-natured that he could enter into strict relations with the best persons and make life serene around him by the dignity and sweetness of his behavior, could he afford to circumvent the favor of the caucus and the press, and covet relations so hollow and pompous as those of a politician? Surely nobody would be a charlatan who could afford to be sincere.

The tendencies of the times favor the idea of self-government, and leave the individual, for all code, to the rewards and penalties of his own constitution; which work with more energy than we believe whilst we depend on artificial restraints. The movement in this direction has been very marked in modern history. Much has been blind and discreditable, but the nature of the revolution is not affected by the vices of the revolters; for this is a purely moral force. It was never adopted by any party in history, neither can be. It separates the individual from all party, and unites him at the same time to the race. It promises a recognition of higher rights than those of personal freedom, or the security of property. A man has a right to be employed, to be trusted, to be loved, to be revered. The power of love, as the basis of a State, has never been tried. We must not imagine that all things are lapsing into confusion if every tender protestant be not compelled to bear his part in certain social conventions; nor doubt that roads can be built, letters carried, and the fruit of labor secured, when the government of force is at an end. Are our methods now so excellent that all competition is hopeless? could not a nation of friends even devise better ways? On the other hand, let not the most conservative and timid fear anything from a premature surrender of the bayonet and the system of force. For, according to the order of nature, which is quite superior to our will, it stands thus; there will always be a government of force where men are selfish; and when they are pure enough to abjure the code of force they will be wise enough to see how these public ends of the post-office, of the highway, of commerce and the exchange of property, of museums and libraries, of institutions of art and science can be answered.

We live in a very low state of the world, and pay unwilling tribute to governments founded on force. There is not, among the most religious and instructed men of the most religious and civil nations, a reliance on the moral sentiment and a sufficient belief in the unity of things, to persuade them that society can be maintained without artificial restraints, as well as the solar system; or that the private citizen might be reasonable and a good neighbor, without the hint of a jail or a confiscation. What is strange too, there never was in any man sufficient faith in the power of rectitude to inspire him with the broad design of renovating the State on the principle of right and love. All those who have pretended this design have been partial reformers, and have admitted in some manner the supremacy of the bad State. I do not call to mind a single human being who has steadily denied the authority of the laws, on the simple ground of his own moral nature. Such designs, full of genius and full of faith as they are, are not entertained except avowedly as air-pictures. If the individual who exhibits them dare to think them practicable, he disgusts scholars and churchmen; and men of talent and women of superior sentiments cannot hide their contempt. Not the less does nature continue to fill the heart of youth with suggestions of this enthusiasm, and there are now men, — if indeed I can speak in the plural number, — more exactly, I will say, I have just been conversing with one man, to whom no weight of adverse experience will make it for a moment appear impossible that thousands of human beings might exercise towards each other the grandest and simplest sentiments, as well as a knot of friends, or a pair of lovers.

Skepticism

Sometime near the end of 1843 Emerson "set his heart on honesty" and wrote out an essay on "Life." "I am not the novice I was fourteen, nor yet seven years ago," he wrote at its conclusion; and its tone was no longer the confident exhortation of "The American Scholar." Five of the seven "lords of life" the essay distinguished were conditions that operated to make inspiration by the Divine Soul impossible. He contrived to rescue his old hope from his new skepticism, the resulting shock of opposites making "Experience," as he finally called it, probably his strongest essay. From this time on, however, he habitually assumed the enigmatic nature of his world and the inherent absurdity of that ever-losing winner, man.

About two years later this same mood of exploration and suspended judgment found expression in a lecture; this time he distrustfully called it "Skepticism" and ascribed it to one of his favorite authors, Michel de Montaigne. Though he made his own final rejection of skepticism very clear, the lecture summed up much of the new Emerson, just as "The American Scholar" had summed up much of the old. "What is the use of pretending to powers we have not?" he asks, in view of the "little conceited vulnerable popinjay that a man is," after all. All questions are open: "There is much to say on all sides." His skepticism is an answer to the vast claims of his transcendentalism, forced on him by their contradiction of the facts. He never repudiates them; they are facts too, none greater; but the naïve rhapsodist who wrote Nature is gone for good. To marry faith and skepticism has become his settled aim as an author.

One reason for this development, as we can see in the journal entries between these two essays, is a growing awareness of the vast age and power of nature, and a growing acceptance of the idea of a long evolution of species, with the implication the idea encouraged both of a natural progress in the human race and society as a whole and of the present insignificance of the individual. More immediately, the political events of 1844 and 1845 pushed him toward skepticism. His lecture course in the winter of 1846 — "Representative Men" — reflected a similar shift in position. Every man was an exaggerator, held by his insanity to the one end which nature had at heart in creating him. Though the men Emerson chose to describe represented types of human performance, they did not include a Reformer, such as he had described five years before. For all man's dancing possibilities, he was an organic part, if possibly a central one, of one evolving whole.

Experience

The lords of life, the lords of life, —
I saw them pass
In their own guise,
Like and unlike,
Portly and grim, —
Use and Surprise,
Surface and Dream,
Succession swift and spectral **Wrong**,
Temperament without a tongue,
And the inventor of the game
Omnipresent without name; —
Some to see, some to be guessed,
They marched from east to west:
Little man, least of all,
Among the legs of his guardians tall,
Walked about with puzzled look.
Him by the hand dear Nature took;
Dearest Nature, strong and kind,
Whispered, "Darling, never mind!
Tomorrow they will wear another face,
The founder thou; these are thy race!"

WHERE do we find ourselves? In a series of which we do not know the extremes, and believe that it has none. We wake and find ourselves on a stair; there are stairs below us, which we seem to have ascended; there are stairs above us, many a one, which go upward and out of sight. But the Genius which according to the old belief stands at the door by which we enter, and gives us the lethe to drink, that we may tell no tales, mixed the cup too strongly, and we cannot shake off the lethargy now at noonday. Sleep lingers all our lifetime about our eyes, as night hovers all day in the boughs of the fir-tree. All things swim and glitter. Our life is not so much threatened as our perception. Ghostlike we glide through nature, and should not know our place again. Did our birth fall in some fit of indigence and frugality in nature, that she was so sparing of her fire and so liberal of her earth that it appears to us that we lack the affirmative principle, and though we have health and reason, yet we have no superfluity of spirit for new creation? We have enough to live and bring the year about, but not an ounce to impart or to invest. Ah that our Genius were a little more of a genius! We are like millers on the lower levels of a stream, when the factories above them have exhausted the water. We too fancy that the upper people must have raised their dams.

If any of us knew what we were doing, or where we are going, then when we think we best know! We do not know today whether we are busy or idle. In times when we thought ourselves indolent, we have afterwards discovered that much was accomplished and much was begun in us. All our days are so unprofitable while they pass, that 'tis wonderful where or when we ever got anything of this which we call wisdom, poetry, virtue. We never got it on any dated calendar day. Some heavenly days must have been intercalated somewhere, like those that Hermes won with dice of the Moon, that Osiris might be born. It is said all martyrdoms looked mean when they were suffered. Every ship is a romantic object, except that we sail in. Embark, and the romance quits our vessel and hangs on every other sail in the horizon. Our life looks trivial, and we shun to record it. Men seem to have learned of the horizon the art of perpetual retreating and reference. "Yonder uplands are rich pasturage, and my neighbor has fertile meadow, but my field," says the querulous farmer, "only holds the world together." I quote another man's saying; unluckily that other withdraws himself in the same way, and quotes me. 'Tis the trick of nature thus to degrade today; a good deal of buzz, and somewhere a result slipped magically in. Every roof is agreeable to the eye until it is lifted; then we find tragedy and moaning women and hard-eyed husbands and deluges of lethe, and the men ask, "What's the news?" as if the old were so bad. How many individuals can we count in society? how many actions? how many opinions? So much of our time is preparation, so much is routine, and so much retrospect, that the pith of each man's genius contracts itself to a very few hours. The history of literature — take the net result of Tiraboschi, Warton, or Schlegel — is a sum of very few ideas and of very few original tales; all the rest being variation of these. So in this great society wide lying around us, a critical analysis would find very few spontaneous actions. It is almost all custom and gross sense. There are even few opinions, and these seem organic in the speakers, and do not disturb the universal necessity.

What opium is instilled into all disaster! It shows formidable as we approach it, but there is at last no rough rasping friction, but the most slippery sliding surfaces; we fall soft on a thought; *Ate Dea* is gentle, —

> "Over men's heads walking aloft,
> With tender feet treading so soft."

People grieve and bemoan themselves, but it is not half so bad with them as they say. There are moods in which we court suffering, in the hope that here at least we shall find reality, sharp peaks and edges of truth. But it turns out to be scene-painting and counterfeit. The only thing grief has taught me is to know how shallow it is. That, like all the rest, plays about the surface, and never introduces me into the reality, for contact with which we would even pay the costly price of sons and lovers. Was it Boscovich who found out that bodies never come in contact? Well, souls never touch their objects. An innavigable sea washes with silent waves between us and the things we aim at and converse with. Grief too will make us idealists. In the death of my son, now more than two years ago, I seem to have lost a beautiful estate, — no more. I cannot get it nearer to me. If tomorrow I should be informed of the bankruptcy of my principal debtors, the loss of my property would be a great inconvenience to me, perhaps, for many years; but it would leave me as it found me, — neither better nor worse. So is it with this calamity; it does not touch me; something which I fancied was a part of me, which could not be torn away without tearing me nor enlarged without enriching me, falls off from me and leaves no scar. It was caducous. I grieve that grief can teach me nothing, nor carry me one step into real nature. The Indian who was laid under a curse that the wind should not blow on him, nor water flow to him, nor fire burn him, is a type of us all. The dearest events are summer-rain, and we the Para coats that shed every drop. Nothing is left us now but death. We look to that with a grim satisfaction, saying, There at least is reality that will not dodge us.

I take this evanescence and lubricity of all objects, which lets them slip through our fingers then when we clutch hardest, to be the most unhandsome part of our condition. Nature does not like to be observed, and likes that we should be her fools and playmates. We may have the sphere for our cricket-ball, but not a berry for our philosophy. Direct strokes she never gave us power to make; all our blows glance, all our hits are accidents. Our relations to each other are oblique and casual. *cynicism and skepticism have seemed to set in*

Dream delivers us to dream, and there is no end to illusion. Life is a train of moods like a string of beads, and as we pass through them they prove to be many-colored lenses which paint the world their own hue, and each shows only what lies in its focus. From the mountain you see the mountain. We animate what we can, and we see only what we animate. Nature and books belong to the eyes that see them. It depends on the mood of the man whether he shall see the sunset or the fine poem. There are always sunsets, and there is always genius; but only a few hours so serene that we can relish nature or criticism. The more or less depends on structure or temperament. Temperament is the iron wire on which the beads are strung. Of what use is fortune or talent to a cold and defective nature? Who cares what sensibility or discrimination a man has at some time shown, if he falls asleep in his chair? or if he laugh and giggle? or if he apologize? or is infected with egotism? or thinks of his dollar? or cannot go by food? or has gotten a child in his boyhood? Of what use is genius, if the organ is too convex or too concave and cannot find a focal distance within the actual horizon of human life? Of what use, if the brain is too cold or too hot, and the man does not care enough for results to stimulate him to experiment, and hold him up in it? or if the web is too finely woven, too irritable by pleasure and pain, so that life stagnates from too much reception without due outlet? Of what use to make heroic vows of amendment, if the same old law-breaker is to keep them? What cheer can the religious sentiment yield, when that is suspected to be secretly dependent on the seasons of the year and the state of the blood? I knew a witty physician who found the creed in the biliary duct, and used to affirm that if there was disease in the liver, the man became a Calvinist, and if that organ was sound, he became a Unitarian. Very mortifying is the reluctant experi-

futility

ence that some unfriendly excess or imbecility neutralizes the promise of genius. We see young men who owe us a new world, so readily and lavishly they promise, but they never acquit the debt; they die young and dodge the account; or if they live they lose themselves in the crowd.

Temperament also enters fully into the system of illusions and shuts us in a prison of glass which we cannot see. There is an optical illusion about every person we meet. In truth they are all creatures of given temperament, which will appear in a given character, whose boundaries they will never pass; but we look at them, they seem alive, and we presume there is impulse in them. In the moment it seems impulse; in the year, in the lifetime, it turns out to be a certain uniform tune which the revolving barrel of the music-box must play. Men resist the conclusion in the morning, but adopt it as the evening wears on, that temper prevails over everything of time, place and condition, and is inconsumable in the flames of religion. Some modifications the moral sentiment avails to impose, but the individual texture holds its dominion, if not to bias the moral judgments, yet to fix the measure of activity and of enjoyment.

I thus express the law as it is read from the platform of ordinary life, but must not leave it without noticing the capital exception. For temperament is a power which no man willingly hears any one praise but himself. On the platform of physics we cannot resist the contracting influences of so-called science. Temperament puts all divinity to rout. I know the mental proclivity of physicians. I hear the chuckle of the phrenologists. Theoretic kidnappers and slave-drivers, they esteem each man the victim of another, who winds him round his finger by knowing the law of his being; and, by such cheap signboards as the color of his beard or the slope of his occiput, reads the inventory of his fortunes and character. The grossest ignorance does not disgust like this impudent knowingness. The physicians say they are not materialists; but they are: — Spirit is matter reduced to an extreme thinness: O so thin! — But the definition of spiritual should be, that which is its own evidence. What notions do they attach to love! what to religion! One would not willingly pronounce these words in their hearing, and give them the occasion to profane them. I saw a gracious gentleman who adapts his conversation to the form of the head of the man he talks with! I had fancied that the value of life lay in its inscrutable possibilities; in the fact that I never know, in addressing myself to a new individual, what may befall me. I carry the keys of my castle in my hand, ready to throw them at the feet of my lord, whenever and in what disguise soever he shall appear. I know he is in the neighborhood, hidden among vagabonds. Shall I preclude my future by taking a high seat and kindly adapting my conversation to the shape of heads? When I come to that, the doctors shall buy me for a cent. — "But, sir, medical history; the report to the Institute; the proven facts!" — I distrust the facts and the inferences. Temperament is the veto or limitation-power in the constitution, very justly applied to restrain an opposite excess in the constitution, but absurdly offered as a bar to original equity. When virtue is in presence, all subordinate powers sleep. On its own level, or in view of nature, temperament is final. I see not, if one be once caught in this trap of so-called sciences, any escape for the man from the links of the chain of physical necessity. Given such an embryo, such a history must follow. On this platform one lives in a sty of sensualism, and would soon come to suicide. But it is impossible that the creative power should exclude itself. Into every intelligence there is a door which is never closed, through which the creator passes. The intellect, seeker of absolute truth, or the heart, lover of absolute good, intervenes for our succor, and at one whisper of these high powers we awake from ineffectual struggles with this nightmare. We hurl it into its own hell, and cannot again contract ourselves to so base a state.

many disregard call of the lover, the seeker

The secret of the illusoriness is in the necessity of a succession of moods or objects. Gladly we would anchor, but the anchorage is quicksand. This onward trick of nature is too strong for us: *Pero si muove.*[1] When at night I look at the moon and stars, I seem stationary, and they to hurry. Our love of the real draws us to permanence, but health of body consists in circulation, and sanity of mind in variety or facility of association. We need change of objects. Dedication to one thought is quickly odious. We house with the insane, and must humor them; then conversation dies out. Once I took such delight in Montaigne that I thought I should not need any other book; before that, in Shakespeare; then in Plutarch; then in Plotinus; at one time in Bacon; afterwards in Goethe; even in Bettine;[2] but now I turn the pages of either of them languidly, whilst I still cherish their genius. So with pictures;

[1] "Still, it moves." Galileo's remark just after recanting his heresy that the earth moved round the sun.

[2] Elizabeth (Brentano) von Arnim, in whose supposed correspondence with Goethe Emerson delighted in 1839.

each will bear an emphasis of attention once, which it cannot retain, though we fain would continue to be pleased in that manner. How strongly I have felt of pictures that when you have seen one well, you must take your leave of it; you shall never see it again. I have had good lessons from pictures which I have since seen without emotion or remark. A deduction must be made from the opinion which even the wise express on a new book or occurrence. Their opinion gives me tidings of their mood, and some vague guess at the new fact, but is nowise to be trusted as the lasting relation between that intellect and that thing. The child asks, "Mamma, why don't I like the story as well as when you told it me yesterday?" Alas! child, it is even so with the oldest cherubim of knowledge. But will it answer thy question to say, Because thou wert born to a whole and this story is a particular? The reason of the pain this discovery causes us (and we make it late in respect to works of art and intellect) is the plaint of tragedy which murmurs from it in regard to persons, to friendship and love.

That immobility and absence of elasticity which we find in the arts, we find with more pain in the artist. There is no power of expansion in men. Our friends early appear to us as representatives of certain ideas which they never pass or exceed. They stand on the brink of the ocean of thought and power, but they never take the single step that would bring them there. A man is like a bit of Labrador spar, which has no lustre as you turn it in your hand until you come to a particular angle; then it shows deep and beautiful colors. There is no adaptation or universal applicability in men, but each has his special talent, and the mastery of successful men consists in adroitly keeping themselves where and when that turn shall be oftenest to be practised. We do what we must, and call it by the best names we can, and would fain have the praise of having intended the result which ensues. I cannot recall any form of man who is not superfluous sometimes. But is not this pitiful? Life is not worth the taking, to do tricks in.

Of course it needs the whole society to give the symmetry we seek. The party-colored wheel must revolve very fast to appear white. Something is earned too by conversing with so much folly and defect. In fine, whoever loses, we are always of the gaining party. Divinity is behind our failures and follies also. The plays of children are nonsense, but very educative nonsense. So it is with the largest and solemnest things, with commerce, government, church, marriage, and so with the history of every man's bread, and the ways by which he is to come by it. Like a bird which alights nowhere, but hops perpetually from bough to bough, is the Power which abides in no man and in no woman, but for a moment speaks from this one, and for another moment from that one.

But what help from these fineries or pedantries? What help from thought? Life is not dialectics. We, I think, in these times, have had lessons enough of the futility of criticism. Our young people have thought and written much on labor and reform, and for all that they have written, neither the world nor themselves have got on a step. Intellectual tasting of life will not supersede muscular activity. If a man should consider the nicety of the passage of a piece of bread down his throat, he would starve. At Education Farm the noblest theory of life sat on the noblest figures of young men and maidens, quite powerless and melancholy. It would not rake or pitch a ton of hay; it would not rub down a horse; and the men and maidens it left pale and hungry.[3] A political orator wittily compared our party promises to western roads, which opened stately enough, with planted trees on either side to tempt the traveler, but soon became narrow and narrower and ended in a squirrel-track and ran up a tree. So does culture with us; it ends in headache. Unspeakably sad and barren does life look to those who a few months ago were dazzled with the splendor of the promise of the times. "There is now no longer any right course of action nor any self-devotion left among the Iranis." Objections and criticism we have had our fill of. There are objections to every course of life and action, and the practical wisdom infers an indifferency, from the omnipresence of objection. The whole frame of things preaches indifferency. Do not craze yourself with thinking, but go about your business anywhere. Life is not intellectual or critical, but sturdy. Its chief good is for well-mixed people who can enjoy what they find, without question. Nature hates peeping, and our mothers speak her very sense when they say, "Children, eat your victuals, and say no more of it." To fill the hour, — that is happiness; to fill the hour and leave no crevice for a repentance or an approval. We live amid surfaces, and the true art of life is to skate well on them. Under the oldest moldiest conventions a man of native force prospers just as well as in the newest world, and that by skill of handling and treatment. He can take hold anywhere. Life itself is a mixture of power and form, and will not bear the least excess of either. To finish the moment, to find the journey's end in every step of the road, to live the great-

[3] An allusion to one of the problems of Brook Farm (see pp. 480–81).

est number of good hours, is wisdom. It is not the part of men, but
of fanatics, or of mathematicians if you will, to say that, the short-
ness of life considered, it is not worth caring whether for so short
a duration we were sprawling in want or sitting high. Since our
office is with moments, let us husband them. Five minutes of
today are worth as much to me as five minutes in the next millennium. Let us be poised, and wise, and our own, today. Let us treat
the men and women well; treat them as if they were real; perhaps
they are. Men live in their fancy, like drunkards whose hands are
too soft and tremulous for successful labor. It is a tempest of
fancies, and the only ballast I know is a respect to the present hour.
Without any shadow of doubt, amidst this vertigo of shows and
politics, I settle myself ever the firmer in the creed that we should
not postpone and refer and wish, but do broad justice where we
are, by whomsoever we deal with, accepting our actual companions
and circumstances, however humble or odious, as the mystic
officials to whom the universe has delegated its whole pleasure for
us. If these are mean and malignant, their contentment, which is
the last victory of justice, is a more satisfying echo to the heart than
the voice of poets and the casual sympathy of admirable persons.
I think that however a thoughtful man may suffer from the defects and absurdities of his company, he cannot without affectation
deny to any set of men and women a sensibility to extraordinary
merit. The coarse and frivolous have an instinct of superiority, if
they have not a sympathy, and honor it in their blind capricious
way with sincere homage.

The fine young people despise life, but in me, and in such as
with me are free from dyspepsia, and to whom a day is a sound and
solid good, it is a great excess of politeness to look scornful and to
cry for company. I am grown by sympathy a little eager and senti-
mental, but leave me alone and I should relish every hour and what
it brought me, the potluck of the day, as heartily as the oldest
gossip in the bar-room. I am thankful for small mercies. I compared notes with one of my friends who expects everything of the
universe and is disappointed when anything is less than the best,
and I found that I begin at the other extreme, expecting nothing,
and am always full of thanks for moderate goods. I accept the
clangor and jangle of contrary tendencies. I find my account in
sots and bores also. They give a reality to the circumjacent picture
which such a vanishing meteorous appearance can ill spare. In the
morning I awake and find the old world, wife, babes and mother,
Concord and Boston, the dear old spiritual world and even the

dear old devil not far off. If we will take the good we find, asking
no questions, we shall have heaping measures. The great gifts are
not got by analysis. Everything good is on the highway. The middle region of our being is the temperate zone. We may climb into
the thin and cold realm of pure geometry and lifeless science, or
sink into that of sensation. Between these extremes is the equator
of life, of thought, of spirit, of poetry, — a narrow belt. Moreover,
in popular experience everything good is on the highway. A collector peeps into all the picture-shops of Europe for a landscape
of Poussin, a crayon-sketch of Salvator; but the Transfiguration, the
Last Judgment, the Communion of Saint Jerome, and what are as
transcendent as these, are on the walls of the Vatican, the Uffizi, or
the Louvre, where every footman may see them; to say nothing of
Nature's pictures in every street, of sunsets and sunrises every day,
and the sculpture of the human body never absent. A collector
recently bought at public auction, in London, for one hundred and
fifty-seven guineas, an autograph of Shakespeare; but for nothing
a school-boy can read Hamlet and can detect secrets of highest
concernment yet unpublished therein. I think I will never read any
but the commonest books, — the Bible, Homer, Dante, Shakespeare and Milton. Then we are impatient of so public a life and
planet, and run hither and thither for nooks and secrets. The imagination delights in the woodcraft of Indians, trappers and bee-
hunters. We fancy that we are strangers, and not so intimately
domesticated in the planet as the wild man and the wild beast and
bird. But the exclusion reaches them also; reaches the climbing,
flying, gliding, feathered and four-footed man. Fox and woodchuck, hawk and snipe and bittern, when nearly seen, have no
more root in the deep world than man, and are just such superficial
tenants of the globe. Then the new molecular philosophy shows
astronomical interspaces betwixt atom and atom, shows that the
world is all outside; it has no inside.

The mid-world is best. Nature, as we know her, is no saint. The
lights of the church, the ascetics, Gentoos and corn-eaters, she does
not distinguish by any favor. She comes eating and drinking and
sinning. Her darlings, the great, the strong, the beautiful, are not
children of our law; do not come out of the Sunday School, nor
weigh their food, nor punctually keep the commandments. If we
will be strong with her strength we must not harbor such disconsolate consciences, borrowed too from the consciences of other
nations. We must set up the strong present tense against all the
rumors of wrath, past or to come. So many things are unsettled

which it is of the first importance to settle; — and, pending their settlement, we will do as we do. Whilst the debate goes forward on the equity of commerce, and will not be closed for a century or two, New and Old England may keep shop. Law of copyright and international copyright is to be discussed, and in the interim we will sell our books for the most we can. Expediency of literature, reason of literature, lawfulness of writing down a thought, is questioned; much is to say on both sides, and, while the fight waxes hot, thou, dearest scholar, stick to thy foolish task, add a line every hour, and between whiles add a line. Right to hold land, right of property, is disputed, and the conventions convene, and before the vote is taken, dig away in your garden, and spend your earnings as a waif or godsend to all serene and beautiful purposes. Life itself is a bubble and a skepticism, and a sleep within a sleep. Grant it, and as much more as they will, — but thou, God's darling! heed thy private dream; thou wilt not be missed in the scorning and skepticism; there are enough of them; stay there in thy closet and toil until the rest are agreed what to do about it. Thy sickness, they say, and thy puny habit require that thou do this or avoid that, but know that thy life is a flitting state, a tent for a night, and do thou, sick or well, finish that stint. Thou art sick, but shalt not be worse, and the universe, which holds thee dear, shall be the better.

Human life is made up of the two elements, power and form, and the proportion must be invariably kept if we would have it sweet and sound. Each of these elements in excess makes a mischief as hurtful as its defect. Everything runs to excess; every good quality is noxious if unmixed, and, to carry the danger to the edge of ruin, nature causes each man's peculiarity to superabound. Here, among the farms, we adduce the scholars as examples of this treachery. They are nature's victims of expression. You who see the artist, the orator, the poet, too near, and find their life no more excellent than that of mechanics or farmers, and themselves victims of partiality, very hollow and haggard, and pronounce them failures, not heroes, but quacks, — conclude very reasonably that these arts are not for man, but are disease. Yet nature will not bear you out. Irresistible nature made men such, and makes legions more of such, every day. You love the boy reading in a book, gazing at a drawing or a cast; yet what are these millions who read and behold, but incipient writers and sculptors? Add a little more of that quality which now reads and sees, and they will seize the pen and chisel. And if one remembers how innocently he began to be an artist, he perceives that nature joined with his enemy. A man is a golden impossibility. The line he must walk is a hair's breadth. The wise through excess of wisdom is made a fool.

How easily, if fate would suffer it, we might keep forever these beautiful limits, and adjust ourselves, once for all, to the perfect calculation of the kingdom of known cause and effect. In the street and in the newspapers, life appears so plain a business that manly resolution and adherence to the multiplication-table through all weathers will insure success. But ah! presently comes a day, or is it only a half-hour, with its angel-whispering, — which discomfits the conclusions of nations and of years! Tomorrow again every thing looks real and angular, the habitual standards are reinstated, common-sense is as rare as genius, — is the basis of genius, and experience is hands and feet to every enterprise; — and yet, he who should do his business on this understanding would be quickly bankrupt. Power keeps quite another road than the turnpikes of choice and will; namely the subterranean and invisible tunnels and channels of life. It is ridiculous that we are diplomatists, and doctors, and considerate people; there are no dupes like these. Life is a series of surprises, and would not be worth taking or keeping if it were not. God delights to isolate us every day, and hide from us the past and the future. We would look about us, but with grand politeness he draws down before us an impenetrable screen of purest sky, and another behind us of purest sky. "You will not remember," he seems to say, "and you will not expect." All good conversation, manners and action come from a spontaneity which forgets usages and makes the moment great. Nature hates calculators; her methods are saltatory and impulsive. Man lives by pulses; our organic movements are such; and the chemical and ethereal agents are undulatory and alternate; and the mind goes antagonizing on, and never prospers but by fits. We thrive by casualties.[4] Our chief experiences have been casual. The most attractive class of people are those who are powerful obliquely and not by the direct stroke; men of genius, but not yet accredited; one gets the cheer of their light without paying too great a tax. Theirs is the beauty of the bird or the morning light, and not of art. In the thought of genius there is always a surprise; and the moral sentiment is well called "the newness," for it is never other; as new to the oldest intelligence as to the young child; — "the kingdom that cometh without observation." In like manner, for practical success, there must not be too much design. A man will not be observed in doing that which he can do best. There is a

4 Chance occurrences.

certain magic about his properest action which stupefies your
powers of observation, so that though it is done before you, you
wist not of it. The art of life has a pudency, and will not be exposed. Every man is an impossibility until he is born; every thing
impossible until we see a success. The ardors of piety agree at last
with the coldest skepticism, — that nothing is of us or our works,
— that all is of God. Nature will not spare us the smallest leaf of
laurel. All writing comes by the grace of God, and all doing and
having. I would gladly be moral and keep due metes and bounds,
which I dearly love, and allow the most to the will of man; but I
have set my heart on honesty in this chapter, and I can see nothing
at last, in success or failure, than more or less of vital force supplied
from the Eternal. The results of life are uncalculated and un-
calculable. The years teach much which the days never know. The
persons who compose our company converse, and come and go,
and design and execute many things, and somewhat comes of it all,
but an unlooked-for result. The individual is always mistaken. He
designed many things, and drew in other persons as coadjutors,
quarreled with some or all, blundered much, and something is
done; all are a little advanced, but the individual is always mistaken. It turns out somewhat new and very unlike what he promised himself.

The ancients, struck with this irreducibleness of the elements of
human life to calculation, exalted Chance into a divinity; but that
is to stay too long at the spark, which glitters truly at one point,
but the universe is warm with the latency of the same fire. The
miracle of life which will not be expounded but will remain a
miracle, introduces a new element. In the growth of the embryo,
Sir Everard Home I think noticed that the evolution was not from
one central point, but coactive from three or more points. Life has
no memory. That which proceeds in succession might be remembered, but that which is coexistent, or ejaculated from a
deeper cause, as yet far from being conscious, knows not its own
tendency. So is it with us, now skeptical or without unity, because
immersed in forms and effects all seeming to be of equal yet hostile
value, and now religious, whilst in the reception of spiritual law.
Bear with these distractions, with this coetaneous growth of the
parts; they will one day be *members*, and obey one will. On that
one will, on that secret cause, they nail our attention and hope.
Life is hereby melted into an expectation or a religion. Underneath the inharmonious and trivial particulars, is a musical per-

fection; the Ideal journeying always with us, the heaven without
rent or seam. Do but observe the mode of our illumination. When
I converse with a profound mind, or if at any time being alone I
have good thoughts, I do not at once arrive at satisfactions, as
when, being thirsty, I drink water; or go to the fire, being cold; no!
but I am at first apprised of my vicinity to a new and excellent
region of life. By persisting to read or to think, this region gives
further sign of itself, as it were in flashes of light, in sudden discoveries of its profound beauty and repose, as if the clouds that
covered it parted at intervals and showed the approaching traveler
the inland mountains, with the tranquil eternal meadows spread
at their base, whereon flocks graze and shepherds pipe and dance.
But every insight from this realm of thought is felt as initial, and
promises a sequel. I do not make it; I arrive there, and behold what
was there already. I make! O no! I clap my hands in infantine joy
and amazement before the first opening to me of this august
magnificence, old with the love and homage of innumerable ages,
young with the life of life, the sunbright Mecca of the desert. And
what a future it opens! I feel a new heart beating with the love of
the new beauty. I am ready to die out of nature and be born again
into this new yet unapproachable America I have found in the
West: —

> "Since neither now nor yesterday began
> These thoughts, which have been ever, nor yet can
> A man be found who their first entrance knew."

If I have described life as a flux of moods, I must now add that
there is that in us which changes not and which ranks all sensations
and states of mind. The consciousness in each man is a sliding
scale, which identifies him now with the First Cause, and now with
the flesh of his body; life above life, in infinite degrees. The sentiment from which it sprung determines the dignity of any deed, and
the question ever is, not what you have done or forborne, but at
whose command you have done or forborne it.

Fortune, Minerva, Muse, Holy Ghost, — these are quaint
names, too narrow to cover this unbounded substance. The baffled
intellect must still kneel before this cause, which refuses to be
named, — ineffable cause, which every fine genius has essayed to
represent by some emphatic symbol, as, Thales by water, Anaximenes by air, Anaxagoras by (Νοῦς) thought, Zoroaster by fire,
Jesus and the moderns by love; and the metaphor of each has become a national religion. The Chinese Mencius has not been the

least successful in his generalization. "I fully understand language," he said, "and nourish well my vast-flowing vigor." — "I beg to ask what you call vast-flowing vigor?" said his companion. "The explanation," replied Mencius, "is difficult. This vigor is supremely great, and in the highest degree unbending. Nourish it correctly and do it no injury, and it will fill up the vacancy between heaven and earth. This vigor accords with and assists justice and reason, and leaves no hunger." — In our more correct writing we give to this generalization the name of Being, and thereby confess that we have arrived as far as we can go. Suffice it for the joy of the universe that we have not arrived at a wall, but at interminable oceans. Our life seems not present so much as prospective; not for the affairs on which it is wasted, but as a hint of this vast-flowing vigor. Most of life seems to be mere advertisement of faculty; information is given us not to sell ourselves cheap; that we are very great. So, in particulars, our greatness is always in a tendency or direction, not in an action. It is for us to believe in the rule, not in the exception. The noble are thus known from the ignoble. So in accepting the leading of the sentiments, it is not what we believe concerning the immortality of the soul or the like, but *the universal impulse to believe*, that is the material circumstance and is the principal fact in the history of the globe. Shall we describe this cause as that which works directly? The spirit is not helpless or needful of mediate organs. It has plentiful powers and direct effects. I am explained without explaining, I am felt without acting, and where I am not. Therefore all just persons are satisfied with their own praise. They refuse to explain themselves, and are content that new actions should do them that office. They believe that we communicate without speech and above speech, and that no right action of ours is quite unaffecting to our friends, at whatever distance; for the influence of action is not to be measured by miles. Why should I fret myself because a circumstance has occurred which hinders my presence where I was expected? If I am not at the meeting, my presence where I am should be as useful to the commonwealth of friendship and wisdom, as would be my presence in that place. I exert the same quality of power in all places. Thus journeys the mighty Ideal before us; it never was known to fall into the rear. No man ever came to an experience which was satiating, but his good is tidings of a better. Onward and onward! In liberated moments we know that a new picture of life and duty is already possible; the elements already exist in many minds around you of a doctrine of life which shall transcend any written record we have. The new statement will comprise the skepticisms as well as the faiths of society, and out of unbeliefs a creed shall be formed. For skepticisms are not gratuitous or lawless, but are limitations of the affirmative statement, and the new philosophy must take them in and make affirmations outside of them, just as much as it must include the oldest beliefs.

It is very unhappy, but too late to be helped, the discovery we have made that we exist. That discovery is called the Fall of Man. *original sin* Ever afterwards we suspect our instruments. We have learned that we do not see directly, but mediately, and that we have no means of correcting these colored and distorting lenses which we are, or of computing the amount of their errors. Perhaps these subject-lenses have a creative power; perhaps there are no objects. Once we lived in what we saw; now, the rapaciousness of this new power, which threatens to absorb all things, engages us. Nature, art, persons, letters, religions, objects, successively tumble in, and God is but one of its ideas. Nature and literature are subjective phenomena; every evil and every good thing is a shadow which we cast. The street is full of humiliations to the proud. As the fop contrived to dress his bailiffs in his livery and make them wait on his guests at table, so the chagrins which the bad heart gives off as bubbles, at once take form as ladies and gentlemen in the street, shopmen or bar-keepers in hotels, and threaten or insult whatever is threatenable and insultable in us. 'Tis the same with our idolatries. People forget that it is the eye which makes the horizon, and the rounding mind's eye which makes this or that man a type or representative of humanity, with the name of hero or saint. Jesus, the "providential man," is a good man on whom many people are agreed that these optical laws shall take effect. By love on one part and by forbearance to press objection on the other part, it is for a time settled that we will look at him in the center of the horizon, and ascribe to him the properties that will attach to any man so seen. But the longest love or aversion has a speedy term. The great and crescive self, rooted in absolute nature, supplants all relative existence and ruins the kingdom of mortal friendship and love. Marriage (in what is called the spiritual world) is impossible, because of the inequality between every subject and every object. The subject is the receiver of Godhead, and at every comparison must feel his being enhanced by that cryptic might. Though not in energy, yet by presence, this magazine of substance cannot be otherwise than felt; nor can any force of intellect attribute to the

object the proper deity which sleeps or wakes forever in every subject. Never can love make consciousness and ascription equal in
force. There will be the same gulf between every me and thee as
between the original and the picture. The universe is the bride of
the soul. All private sympathy is partial. Two human beings are
like globes, which can touch only in a point, and whilst they remain in contact all other points of each of the spheres are inert;
their turn must also come, and the longer a particular union lasts
the more energy of appetency the parts not in union acquire.

Life will be imaged, but cannot be divided nor doubled. Any
invasion of its unity would be chaos. The soul is not twin-born
but the only begotten, and though revealing itself as child in
time, child in appearance, is of a fatal and universal power, admitting no co-life. Every day, every act betrays the ill-concealed
deity. We believe in ourselves as we do not believe in others. We
permit all things to ourselves, and that which we call sin in others
is experiment for us. It is an instance of our faith in ourselves that
men never speak of crime as lightly as they think; or every man
thinks a latitude safe for himself which is no wise to be indulged
to another. The act looks very differently on the inside and on
the outside; in its quality and in its consequences. Murder in the
murderer is no such ruinous thought as poets and romancers will
have it; it does not unsettle him or fright him from his ordinary
notice of trifles; it is an act quite easy to be contemplated; but
in its sequel it turns out to be a horrible jangle and confounding
of all relations. Especially the crimes that spring from love seem
right and fair from the actor's point of view, but when acted are
found destructive of society. No man at last believes that he can
be lost, or that the crime in him is as black as in the felon. Because the intellect qualifies in our own case the moral judgments.
For there is no crime to the intellect. That is antinomian or hyper-
nomian, and judges law as well as fact. "It is worse than a crime,
it is a blunder," said Napoleon, speaking the language of the intellect. To it, the world is a problem in mathematics or the science
of quantity, and it leaves out praise and blame and all weak emotions. All stealing is comparative. If you come to absolutes, pray
who does not steal? Saints are sad, because they behold sin (even
when they speculate) from the point of view of the conscience,
and not of the intellect; a confusion of thought. Sin, seen from
the thought, is a diminution, or *less*; seen from the conscience or
will, it is pravity or *bad*. The intellect names it shade, absence of
light, and no essence. The conscience must feel it as essence.

essential evil. This it is not; it has an objective existence, but no subjective.

Thus inevitably does the universe wear our color, and every object fall successively into the subject itself. The subject exists, the subject enlarges; all things sooner or later fall into place. As I am, so I see; use what language we will, we can never say anything but what we are; Hermes, Cadmus, Columbus, Newton, Bonaparte, are the mind's ministers. Instead of feeling a poverty when we encounter a great man, let us treat the new-comer like a traveling geologist who passes through our estate and shows us good slate, or limestone, or anthracite, in our brush pasture. The partial action of each strong mind in one direction is a telescope for the objects on which it is pointed. But every other part of knowledge is to be pushed to the same extravagance, ere the soul attains her due sphericity. Do you see that kitten chasing so prettily her own tail? If you could look with her eyes you might see her surrounded with hundreds of figures performing complex dramas, with tragic and comic issues, long conversations, many characters, many ups and downs of fate, — and meantime it is only puss and her tail. How long before our masquerade will end its noise of tambourines, laughter and shouting, and we shall find it was a solitary performance? A subject and an object, — it takes so much to make the galvanic circuit complete, but magnitude adds nothing. What imports it whether it is Kepler and the sphere, Columbus and America, a reader and his book, or puss with her tail?

It is true that all the muses and love and religion hate these developments, and will find a way to punish the chemist who publishes in the parlor the secrets of the laboratory. And we cannot say too little of our constitutional necessity of seeing things under private aspects, or saturated with our humors. And yet is the God the native of these bleak rocks. That need makes in morals the capital virtue of self-trust. We must hold hard to this poverty, however scandalous, and by more vigorous self-recoveries, after the sallies of action, possess our axis more firmly. The life of truth is cold and so far mournful; but it is not the slave of tears, contritions and perturbations. It does not attempt another's work, nor adopt another's facts. It is a main lesson of wisdom to know your own from another's. I have learned that I cannot dispose of other people's facts; but I possess such a key to my own as persuades me, against all their denials, that they also have a key to theirs. A sympathetic person is placed in the dilemma of a swimmer among drowning men, who all catch at him, and if he give so much as a leg or a finger they will drown him. They wish to be saved from the mischiefs of their vices, but not from their vices. Charity would be wasted on this poor waiting on the symptoms. A wise and hardy physician will say, *Come out of that,* as the first condition of advice.

In this our talking America we are ruined by our good nature and listening on all sides. This compliance takes away the power of being greatly useful. A man should not be able to look other than directly and forthright. A preoccupied attention is the only answer to the importunate frivolity of other people; an attention, and to an aim which makes their wants frivolous. This is a divine answer, and leaves no appeal and no hard thoughts. In Flaxman's drawing of the Eumenides of Aeschylus, Orestes supplicates Apollo, whilst the Furies sleep on the threshold. The face of the god expresses a shade of regret and compassion, but is calm with the conviction of the irreconcilableness of the two spheres. He is born into other politics, into the eternal and beautiful. The man at his feet asks for his interest in turmoils of the earth, into which his nature cannot enter. And the Eumenides there lying express pictorially this disparity. The god is surcharged with his divine destiny.

Illusion, Temperament, Succession, Surface, Surprise, Reality, Subjectiveness, — these are threads on the loom of time, these are the lords of life. I dare not assume to give their order, but I name them as I find them in my way. I know better than to claim any completeness for my picture. I am a fragment, and this is a fragment of me. I can very confidently announce one or another law, which throws itself into relief and form, but I am too young yet by some ages to compile a code. I gossip for my hour concerning the eternal politics. I have seen many fair pictures not in vain. A wonderful time I have lived in. I am not the novice I was fourteen, nor yet seven years ago. Let who will ask, Where is the fruit? I find a private fruit sufficient. This is a fruit, — that I should not ask for a rash effect from meditations, counsels and the hiving of truths. I should feel it pitiful to demand a result on this town and county, an overt effect on the instant month and year. The effect is deep and secular as the cause. It works on periods in which mortal lifetime is lost. All I know is reception; I am and I have: but I do not get, and when I have fancied I had gotten anything, I found I did not. I worship with wonder the great Fortune. My reception has been so large, that I am not annoyed by receiving this or that superabundantly. I say to the Genius, if he will pardon the proverb, *In for a mill, in for a million.* When I receive a new gift, I do not macerate my body to make the account square, for if I should die I could not make the account square. The benefit overran the merit the first day, and has overrun the merit ever since. The merit itself, so-called, I reckon part of the receiving.

Also that hankering after an overt or practical effect seems to me an apostasy. In good earnest I am willing to spare this most unnecessary deal of doing. Life wears to me a visionary face. Hardest roughest action is visionary also. It is but a choice between soft and turbulent dreams. People disparage knowing and the intellectual life, and urge doing. I am very content with knowing, if only I could know. That is an august entertainment, and would suffice me a great while. To know a little would be worth the expense of this world. I hear always the law of Adrastia, "that every soul which had acquired any truth, should be safe from harm until another period."

I know that the world I converse with in the city and in the farms, is not the world I *think.* I observe that difference, and shall observe it. One day I shall know the value and law of this discrepance. But I have not found that much was gained by manipular attempts to realize the world of thought. Many eager persons successively make an experiment in this way, and make themselves ridiculous. They acquire democratic manners, they foam at the mouth, they hate and deny. Worse, I observe that in the history of mankind there is never a solitary example of success, — taking their own tests of success. I say this polemically, or in reply to the inquiry, Why not realize your world? But far be from me the despair which prejudges the law by a paltry empiricism; — since there never was a right endeavor but it succeeded. Patience and patience, we shall win at the last. We must be very suspicious of the deceptions of the element of time. It takes a good deal of time to eat or to sleep, or to earn a hundred dollars, and a very little time to entertain a hope and an insight which becomes the light of our life. We dress our garden, eat our dinners, discuss the household with our wives, and these things make no impression, are forgotten next week; but, in the solitude to which every man is always returning, he has a sanity and revelations which in his passage into new worlds he will carry with him. Never mind the ridicule, never mind the defeat; up again, old heart! — it seems to say, — there is victory yet for all justice; and the true romance which the world exists to realize will be the transformation of genius into practical power.

⚔ ⚔

To Thomas Carlyle

December 31, 1844

. . . Thanks to you for the kind thought of a "Notice," [5] and for its friendly wit. You shall not do this thing again, if I should send you any more books. A Preface from you is a sort of banner or oriflamme, a little too splendid for my occasion, and misleads. I fancy my readers to be a very quiet, plain, even obscure class, — men and women of some religious culture and aspirations, young, or else mystical, and by no means including the great literary and fashionable army, which no man can count, who now read your books. If you introduce me, your readers and the literary papers try to read me, and with false expectations. I had rather have fewer readers and only such as belong to me.

I doubt not your stricture on the book [6] as sometimes unconnected and inconsecutive is just. Your words are very gentle. I should describe it much more harshly. My knowledge of the defects of these things I write is all but sufficient to hinder me from writing at all. I am only a sort of lieutenant here in the deplorable absence of captains, and write the laws ill as thinking it a better homage than universal silence. You Londoners know little of the dignities and duties of country lyceums. But of what you say now and heretofore respecting the remoteness of my writing and thinking from real life, though I hear substantially the same criticism made by my countrymen, I do not know what it means. If I can at any time express the law and the ideal right, that should satisfy me without measuring the divergence from it of the last act of Congress. And though I sometimes accept a popular call, and preach on Temperance or the Abolition of Slavery, as lately on the 1st of August,[7] I am sure to feel, before I have done with it, what an intrusion it is into another sphere, and so much loss of virtue in my own. . . .

---

[5] Carlyle had written a brief preface for the English edition of *Essays, Second Series,* as he had for the first series.

[6] In a private letter.

[7] See pp. 277–78.

February ?, 1844

That bread which we ask of Nature is that she should entrance us, but amidst her beautiful or her grandest pictures I cannot escape the *second thought*. I walked this P.M. in the woods, but there too the snowbanks were sprinkled with tobacco-juice. We have the wish to forget night and day, father and mother, food and ambition, but we never lose our dualism. Blessed, wonderful Nature, nevertheless! without depth, but with immeasurable lateral spaces. If we look before us, if we compute our path, it is very short. Nature has only the thickness of a shingle or a slate: we come straight to the extremes; but sidewise, and at unawares, the present moment opens into other moods and moments, rich, prolific, leading onward without end. . . .

[July, 1844]

Geology has initiated us into the secularity [8] of Nature, and taught us to disuse our dame-school measures, and exchange our Mosaic and Ptolemaic schemes for her large style. We knew nothing rightly, for want of perspective. Now we learn what patient periods must round themselves before the rock is formed; then before the rock is broken, and the first lichen race has disintegrated the thinnest external plate into soil, and opened the door for the remote Flora, Fauna, Ceres, and Pomona to come in. How far off yet is the trilobite! how far the quadruped! how inconceivably remote is man! All duly arrive, and then race after race of men. It is a long way from granite to the oyster; farther yet to Plato and the preaching of the immortality of the soul. Yet all must come, as surely as the first atom has two sides.

From "Nature"

August 19 ?, 1845

There are always two histories of man in literature contending for our faith. One is the scientific or skeptical, and derives his origin from the gradual composition, subsidence, and refining, — from the Negro, from the ape, progressive from the animalcule savages of the waterdrop, from *volvox globator*, up to the wise man of the nineteenth century. The other is the believer's, the poet's, the faithful history, always testified by the mystic and the devout, the history of the Fall, of a descent from a superior and pure race, attested in actual history by the grand remains of elder ages, of a

[8] Great age.

science in the East unintelligible to the existing population; Cyclopean architecture in all quarters of the world. . . . The faithful dogma assumes that the other is an optical show, but that the universe was long already complete through law; and that the tiger and the midge are only penal forms, the Auburn and Sing-Sing of nature; men, men, all and everywhere.

Autumn, 1845

> Herbs gladly cure our flesh because that they
> Find their acquaintance there.
>   HERBERT, *"Man"*

This is mystically true. The master can do his great deed, the desire of the world, — say to find his way between azote and oxygen, detect the secret of the new rock superposition, find the law of the curves, — because he has just come out of Nature, or from being a part of that thing. As if one went into the mesmeric state to find the way of Nature in some function, and then sharing it, came out into the normal state and repeated the trick. He knows the laws of azote because just now he was azote. Man is only a piece of the universe made alive. Man active can do what just now he suffered.

Autumn, 1845

. . . Metamorphosis is the law of the universe. All forms are fluent, and as the bird alights on the bough and pauses for rest, then plunges into the air again on its way, so the thoughts of God pause but for a moment in any form, but pass into a new form, as if by touching the earth again in burial, to acquire new energy. A wise man is not deceived by the pause: he knows that it is momentary: he already foresees the new departure, and departure after departure, in long series. Dull people think they have traced the matter far enough if they have reached the history of one of these temporary forms, which they describe as fixed and final.

Winter, 1844

The question of the annexation of Texas is one of those which look very differently to the centuries and to the years. It is very certain that the strong British race, which have now overrun so much of this continent, must also overrun that tract, and Mexico

and Oregon also, and it will in the course of ages be of small import by what particular occasions and methods it was done. It is a secular question. It is quite necessary and true to our New England character that we should consider the question in its local and temporary bearings, and resist the annexation with tooth and nail.

It is a measure which goes not by right, nor by wisdom, but by feeling. It would be a pity to dissolve the Union and so diminish immensely every man's personal importance. We are just beginning to feel our oats.

[July, 1844]

... Our planet, before the age of written history, had its races of savages, like the generations of sour paste, or the animalcules that wiggle and bite in a drop of putrid water. Who cares for these or for their wars? We do not wish a world of bugs or of birds; neither afterward of Scythians, Caraibs or Feejees. The grand style of Nature, her great periods, is all we observe in them. Who cares for oppressing whites, or oppressed blacks, twenty centuries ago, more than for bad dreams? Eaters and food are in the harmony of Nature; and there too is the germ forever protected, unfolding gigantic leaf after leaf, a newer flower, a richer fruit, in every period, yet its next product is never to be guessed. It will only save what is worth saving; and it saves not by compassion, but by power. It appoints no police to guard the lion but his teeth and claws; no fort or city for the bird but his wings; no rescue for flies and mites but their spawning numbers, which no ravages can overcome. It deals with men after the same manner. If they are rude and foolish, down they must go. When at last in a race a new principle appears, an idea, — *that* conserves it; ideas only save races. If the black man is feeble and not important to the existing races, not on a parity with the best race, the black man must serve, and be exterminated. But if the black man carries in his bosom an indispensable element of a new and coming civilization; for the sake of that element, no wrong nor strength nor circumstance can hurt him: he will survive and play his part. So now, the arrival in the world of such men as Toussaint, and the Haytian heroes, or of the leaders of their race in Barbadoes and Jamaica, outweighs in good omen all the English and American humanity. The anti-slavery of the whole world is dust in the balance before this, — is a poor squeamishness and nervousness: the might and the right are here: here is the anti-slave: here is man: and if you have man, black or white is an insignificance.... I say to you, you must save yourself,

black or white, man or woman; other help is none. I esteem the
occasion of this jubilee to be the proud discovery that the black
race can contend with the white: that in the great anthem which
we call history, a piece of many parts and vast compass, after playing a long time a very low and subdued accompaniment, they perceive the time arrived when they can strike in with effect and take
a master's part in the music. . . .[9]

From "Emancipation in the West Indies"

March, 1845

A despair has crept over the Whig party in this country.[1] They,
the active, enterprising, intelligent, well-meaning, and wealthy
part of the people, the real love and strength of the American
people, find themselves paralyzed and defeated everywhere by the
hordes of ignorant and deceivable natives and the armies of foreign
voters who fill Pennsylvania, New York, and New Orleans, and by
those unscrupulous editors and orators who have assumed to lead
these masses. The creators of wealth, and conscientious rational
and responsible persons, those whose names are given in as fit for
jurors, for referees, for offices of trust, those whose opinion is public opinion, find themselves degraded into observers, and violently
turned out of all share in the action and counsels of the nation.

What is the difference between the Abolitionist and the Locofoco? this only, that the one knows the facts in this iniquity, and
the other does not. One has informed himself of the slave laws
of the Southern States, and the other has not; but both suffer the
whole damnable mischief to go on.

March, 1845

How many degrees of power! That which we exert political,
social, intellectual, moral is most superficial. We talk and work
half asleep. Between us and our last energy lie terrific social, and
then sublime solitary exertions. Let our community rise *en masse*,
the undrilled original militia; or let the private man put off the
citizen, and make the hero; then is one a match for a nation.

[9] Cf. "Ode to Channing," p. 439.
[1] James K. Polk, a Democrat, had just been inaugurated as President. He
had defeated the Whigs in a close election, largely as a result of votes siphoned
off by an Abolitionist third party. "Locofoco," in 1845, was simply an anti-
Democrat epithet.

March, 1845

You no longer see Phoenixes; men are not divine individuals; but you learn to revere their social and representative character. They are not gods, but the spirit of God sparkles on and about them.

April ?, 1845

Conservatism has in the present society every advantage. All are on its side. Of those who pretend to ideas, all are really and in practice on the side of the state. They know that, if they should persist in actualizing their theories, it would be all convulsion and plunging. Their talk is the mere brag of liberalism. Yet, yet, they like to feel their wings. The soul, with Plato in *Phaedrus*, likes to feel its wings; and they indulge themselves with this religious luxury, assured that, though the lion is as yet only half disengaged from the soil,[2] the dream of today is prophetic of the experience of tomorrow.

April ?, 1845

The lesson [Bonaparte] teaches is that which vigor always teaches, that there is always room for it. He would not take "No" for an answer. . . . He found impediments that would have stopped anybody else, but he saw what gibbering, quaking ghosts they were, and he put his hand through them. . . . There is always room for a man of force, and not only so, but he makes room for many. . . .
    Yet a bully cannot lead the age.

April ?, 1845

The puny race of Scholars in this country have no counsel to give, and are not felt. Every wretched partisan, every village brawler, every man with talents for contention, every clamorous place-hunter makes known what he calls his opinion, all over the country, that is, as loud as he can scream. Really, no opinions are given; only the wishes of each side are expressed, of the spoils party, that is, and of the malcontents. But the voice of the intelligent and the honest, of the unconnected and independent, the voice of truth and equity, is suppressed. In England, it is not so. You can always find in their journals and newspapers a better and a best sense, as well as the low, coarse party cries.

2 As portrayed in some pictures of Genesis.

March, 1845

The only use which the country people can imagine of a scholar, the only compliment they can think of to pay him, is, to ask him to deliver a temperance lecture, or to be a member of the school committee.

Autumn, 1845

Native Americans. — I hate the narrowness of the Native American Party. It is the dog in the manger. It is precisely opposite to all the dictates of love and magnanimity: and therefore, of course, opposite to true wisdom.... Man is the most composite of all creatures.... Well, as in the old burning of the Temple at Corinth, by the melting and intermixture of silver and gold and other metals a new compound more precious than any, called the Corinthian brass, was formed; so in this continent, — asylum of all nations, — the energy of Irish, Germans, Swedes, Poles, and Cossacks, and all the European tribes, — of the Africans, and of the Polynesians, — will construct a new race, a new religion, a new state, a new literature, which will be as vigorous as the new Europe which came out of the smelting-pot of the Dark Ages, or that which earlier emerged from the Pelasgic and Etruscan barbarism.

La Nature aime les croisements.[3]

August 19?, 1845

The near-sighted people have much to say about action. But ... it is by no means action which is the essential point, but some middle quality indifferent both to poet and to actor, and which we call reality. So that we have reality and necessity, it is equivalent in a word or in a blow. The election of the will is the crisis; that is celebrated often by Yea or Nay: the following action is only the freight train. Not action, not speculation imports, but a middle essence common to both.

I believe in the sovereign virtue, or, shall I say, virulence, of probity, against all arithmetic. Arithmetic is the science of surfaces, probity that of essences. The most private will be the most public, if it be only real....

August, 1845

See how many cities of refuge we have. Skepticism, and again skepticism? Well, let abyss open under abyss, they are all con-

[3] **Nature** loves cross-breedings.

tained and bottomed at last, and I have only to endure. I am here to be worked upon.

August, 1845

Honor among thieves, let there be truth among skeptics. Are any or all of the institutions so valuable as to be lied for? Learn to esteem all things symptomatic, — no more.

September, 1845

We sidle towards the problem. If we could speak the direct, solving word, it would solve us too; we should die, or be liberated as the gas in the great gas of the atmosphere.

Autumn, 1845

Skepticism. — There are many skepticisms. The universe is like an infinite series of planes, each of which is a false bottom, and when we think our feet are planted now at last on the adamant, the slide is drawn out from under us.

Value of the skeptic is the resistance to premature conclusions. If he prematurely conclude, his conclusion will be shattered, and he will become malignant. But he must limit himself with the anticipation of law in the mutations, — flowing law.

June?, 1845

Men go through the world each musing on a great fable, dramatically pictured and rehearsed before him. If you speak to the man, he turns his eyes from his own scene, and slower or faster endeavors to comprehend what you say. When you have done speaking, he returns to his private music. Men generally attempt early in life to make their brothers first, afterwards their wives, acquainted with what is going forward in their private theatre, but they soon desist from the attempt, on finding that they also have some farce, or perhaps some ear and heart-rending tragedy forward on their secret boards, on which they are intent, and all parties acquiesce at last in a private box with the whole play performed before himself *solus.*

[September, 1845]

Cement of Inertia. — Is it not a rare contrivance that lodged the due inertia in every creature, the conserving, resisting energy, the anger at being waked or changed? Altogether independent of the intellectual force in each is the pride of opinion, the security that we are right. Not the feeblest grandame, not a mowing idiot, but uses what spark of perception and faculty is left, to chuckle and triumph in his or her opinion over the absurdities of all the rest. Difference from me is the measure of absurdity. Not one has a misgiving of being wrong. Was it not a bright thought that made things cohere with this bitumen, fastest of cements?

It is the bulwark of individualism.

October 27 ?, 1845

Fate. — The Indian system is full of fate, the Greek not. The Greek uses the word, indeed, but in his mind the Fates are three respectable old women who spin and shear a symbolic thread, — so narrow, so limitary is the sphere allowed them, and it is with music. We are only at a more beautiful opera, or at private theatricals. But in India, it is the dread reality, it is the cropping-out in our planted gardens of the core of the world: it is the abysmal Force, untameable and immense. They who wrestle with Hari see their doom in his eye before the fight begins.

November 1 ?, 1845

My dear friend,[4] standing on his mountains of fact whose strata, chemistry, meteors, landscape, counties, towns, meridian, magnetism, and what not he knows, asks me how all goes with me floating in obscure questions, musing on this and that metaphysical riddle? Well, it is even so. I stay where I can, and am peaceful and satisfied enough as long as no sentinel challenges me. I use no election of the questions that occupy me. No doubt, I should feel a humiliation if I were wont to task myself for men, or to compute in any manner of political economy my day's work, but well assured that this Questioner who brings me so many problems will bring the answers also in due time. Very rich, very potent, cheerful giver that he is, — he shall have it all his own way for me.

Autumn, 1845

A great man is he who answers questions which I have not skill to put.

One man all his lifetime answers a question which none of his contemporaries put: he is therefore isolated. . . .

[4] Carlyle.

November ?, 1845

Wisdom consists in keeping the soul liquid, or, in resisting the tendency to too rapid petrifaction.

November ?, 1845

There must be the Abyss, Nox and Chaos, out of which all come, and they must never be far off. Cut off the connection between any of our works and this dread origin, and the work is shallow and unsatisfying. That is the strength and excellence of the people, that they lean on this, and the mob is not quite so bad an argument as we are apt to represent it, for it has this divine side.

There is a moment in the history of every nation when, proceeding out of this brute youth, the perceptive powers reach with delight their greatest strength and have not yet become microscopic, so that the man at that instant extends across the entire scale, and, with his feet still planted on the immense forces of Night, converses by his eyes and brain with solar and stellar creation. That is the moment of perfect health, the culmination of their star of Empire.

Ah, let the twilight linger! We love the morning spread abroad among the mountains, but too fast comes on the broad noon blaze, only exposing the poverty and barrenness of our globe, the listlessness and meanness of its inhabitants.

December ?, 1845

Men also representative. — Swedenborg and Behmen saw that things were representative. They did not sufficiently see that men were. But we cannot, as we say, be in two places at once. My doing my office entitles me to the benefit of your doing yours. This is the secret after which the Communists [5] are coarsely and externally striving. Work in thy place with might and health, and thy secretion to the spiritual body is made. I in mine will do the like. Thus imperceptibly and most happily, genially and triumphantly doing that we delight in, behold we are communists, brothers, members one of another.

[5] I.e., men like Fourier, Owen, George Ripley, or other advocates of communities.

Montaigne; or, The Skeptic

Every fact is related on one side to sensation, and on the other to morals. The game of thought is, on the appearance of one of these two sides, to find the other: given the upper, to find the under side. Nothing so thin but has these two faces, and when the observer has seen the obverse, he turns it over to see the reverse. Life is a pitching of this penny, — heads or tails. We never tire of this game, because there is still a slight shudder of astonishment at the exhibition of the other face, at the contrast of the two faces. A man is flushed with success, and bethinks himself what this good luck signifies. He drives his bargain in the street; but it occurs that he also is bought and sold. He sees the beauty of a human face, and searches the cause of that beauty, which must be more beautiful. He builds his fortunes, maintains the laws, cherishes his children; but he asks himself, Why? and whereto? This head and this tail are called, in the language of philosophy, Infinite and Finite; Relative and Absolute; Apparent and Real; and many fine names beside.

Each man is born with a predisposition to one or the other of these sides of nature; and it will easily happen that men will be found devoted to one or the other. One class has the perception of difference, and is conversant with facts and surfaces, cities and persons, and the bringing certain things to pass; — the men of talent and action. Another class have the perception of identity, and are men of faith and philosophy, men of genius.

Each of these riders drives too fast. Plotinus believes only in philosophers; Fenelon,[6] in saints; Pindar and Byron, in poets. Read the haughty language in which Plato and the Platonists speak of all men who are not devoted to their own shining abstractions: other men are rats and mice. The literary class is usually proud and exclusive. The correspondence of Pope and Swift describes mankind around them as monsters; and that of Goethe and Schiller, in our own time, is scarcely more kind.

It is easy to see how this arrogance comes. The genius is a genius by the first look he casts on any object. Is his eye creative? Does he not rest in angles and colors, but beholds the design? — he will presently undervalue the actual object. In powerful moments, his thought has dissolved the works of art and nature into

[6] Seventeenth-century French theologian, defender of Quietism.

their causes, so that the works appear heavy and faulty. He has a conception of beauty which the sculptor cannot embody. Picture, statue, temple, railroad, steam-engine, existed first in an artist's mind, without flaw, mistake, or friction, which impair the executed models. So did the Church, the State, college, court, social circle, and all the institutions. It is not strange that these men, remembering what they have seen and hoped of ideas, should affirm disdainfully the superiority of ideas. Having at some time seen that the happy soul will carry all the arts in power, they say, Why cumber ourselves with superfluous realizations? and like dreaming beggars they assume to speak and act as if these values were already substantiated.

On the other part, the men of toil and trade and luxury, — the animal world, including the animal in the philosopher and poet also, and the practical world, including the painful drudgeries which are never excused to philosopher or poet any more than to the rest, — weigh heavily on the other side. The trade in our streets believes in no metaphysical causes, thinks nothing of the force which necessitated traders and a trading planet to exist: no, but sticks to cotton, sugar, wool and salt. The ward meetings, on election days, are not softened by any misgiving of the value of these ballotings. Hot life is streaming in a single direction. To the men of this world, to the animal strength and spirits, to the men of practical power, whilst immersed in it, the man of ideas appears out of his reason. They alone have reason.

Things always bring their own philosophy with them, that is, prudence. No man acquires property without acquiring with it a little arithmetic also. In England, the richest country that ever existed, property stands for more, compared with personal ability, than in any other. After dinner, a man believes less, denies more: verities have lost some charm. After dinner, arithmetic is the only science: ideas are disturbing, incendiary, follies of young men, repudiated by the solid portion of society: and a man comes to be valued by his athletic and animal qualities. Spence relates that Mr. Pope was with Sir Godfrey Kneller one day, when his nephew, a Guinea trader, came in. "Nephew," said Sir Godfrey, "you have the honor of seeing the two greatest men in the world." "I don't know how great men you may be," said the Guinea man, "but I don't like your looks. I have often bought a man much better than both of you, all muscles and bones, for ten guineas." Thus the men of the senses revenge themselves on the professors and repay scorn for scorn. The first had leaped to conclusions not yet ripe, and say more than is true; the others make themselves merry with the philosopher, and weigh man by the pound. They believe that mustard bites the tongue, that pepper is hot, friction-matches incendiary, revolvers are to be avoided, and suspenders hold up pantaloons; that there is much sentiment in a chest of tea; and a man will be eloquent, if you give him good wine. Are you tender and scrupulous, — you must eat more mince-pie. They hold that Luther had milk in him when he said, —

"Wer nicht liebt Wein, Weiber, Gesang,
Der bleibt ein Narr sein Leben lang;" — [7]

and when he advised a young scholar, perplexed with fore-ordination and free-will, to get well drunk. "The nerves," says Cabanis, "they are the man." My neighbor, a jolly farmer, in the tavern bar-room, thinks that the use of money is sure and speedy spending. For his part, he says, he puts his down his neck and gets the good of it.

The inconvenience of this way of thinking is that it runs into indifferentism and then into disgust. Life is eating us up. We shall be fables presently. Keep cool: it will be all one a hundred years hence. Life's well enough, but we shall be glad to get out of it, and they will all be glad to have us. Why should we fret and drudge? Our meat will taste tomorrow as it did yesterday, and we may at last have had enough of it. "Ah," said my languid gentleman at Oxford, "there's nothing new or true, — and no matter."

With a little more bitterness, the cynic moans; our life is like an ass led to market by a bundle of hay being carried before him; he sees nothing but the bundle of hay. "There is so much trouble in coming into the world," said Lord Bolingbroke, "and so much more, as well as meanness, in going out of it, that 'tis hardly worth while to be here at all." I knew a philosopher of this kidney who was accustomed briefly to sum up his experience of human nature in saying, "Mankind is a damned rascal": and the natural corollary is pretty sure to follow, — "The world lives by humbug, and so will I."

The abstractionist and the materialist thus mutually exasperating each other, and the scoffer expressing the worst of materialism, there arises a third party to occupy the middle ground between these two, the skeptic, namely. He finds both wrong by being in extremes. He labors to plant his feet, to be the beam of

[7] Who does not love wine, women, song.
Remains a fool his whole life long.

the balance. He will not go beyond his card. He sees the one-sidedness of these men of the street; he will not be a Gibeonite; he stands for the intellectual faculties, a cool head and whatever serves to keep it cool; no unadvised industry, no unrewarded self-devotion, no loss of the brains in toil. Am I an ox, or a dray? — You are both in extremes, he says. You that will have all solid, and a world of pig-lead, deceive yourselves grossly. You believe your-selves rooted and grounded on adamant; and yet, if we uncover the last facts of our knowledge, you are spinning like bubbles in a river, you know not whither or whence, and you are bottomed and capped and wrapped in delusions. Neither will he be betrayed to a book and wrapped in a gown. The studious class are their own victims; they are thin and pale, their feet are cold, their heads are hot, the night is without sleep, the day a fear of interruption, — pallor, squalor, hunger and egotism. If you come near them and see what conceits they entertain, — they are abstractionists, and spend their days and nights in dreaming some dream; in expecting the homage of society to some precious scheme, built on a truth, but destitute of proportion in its presentment, of justness in its application, and of all energy of will in the schemer to embody and vitalize it.

But I see plainly, he says, that I cannot see. I know that human strength is not in extremes, but in avoiding extremes. I, at least, will shun the weakness of philosophizing beyond my depth. What is the use of pretending to powers we have not? What is the use of pretending to assurances we have not, respecting the other life? Why exaggerate the power of virtue? Why be an angel before your time? These strings, wound up too high, will snap. If there is a wish for immortality, and no evidence, why not say just that? If there are conflicting evidences, why not state them? If there is not ground for a candid thinker to make up his mind, yea or nay, — why not suspend the judgment? I weary of these dogmatizers. I tire of these hacks of routine, who deny the dogmas. I neither affirm nor deny. I stand here to try the case. I am here to con-sider, σκοπεῖν, [8] to consider how it is. I will try to keep the balance true. Of what use to take the chair and glibly rattle off theories of society, religion and nature, when I know that practical objections lie in the way, insurmountable by me and by my mates? Why so talkative in public, when each of my neighbors can pin me to my seat by arguments I cannot refute? Why pretend that life is so simple a game, when we know how subtle and elusive the Proteus

[8] Skopein, to look out.

is? Why think to shut up all things in your narrow coop, when we know there are not one or two only, but ten, twenty, a thousand things, and unlike? Why fancy that you have all the truth in your keeping? There is much to say on all sides.

Who shall forbid a wise skepticism, seeing that there is no practical question on which any thing more than an approximate solution can be had? Is not marriage an open question, when it is alleged, from the beginning of the world, that such as are in the institution wish to get out, and such as are out wish to get in? And the reply of Socrates, to him who asked whether he should choose a wife, still remains reasonable, that "whether he should choose one or not, he would repent it." Is not the State a question? All society is divided in opinion on the subject of the State. Nobody loves it; great numbers dislike it and suffer conscientious scruples to allegiance; and the only defense set up, is the fear of doing worse in disorganizing. Is it otherwise with the Church? Or, to put any of the questions which touch mankind nearest, — shall the young man aim at a leading part in law, in politics, in trade? It will not be pretended that a success in either of these kinds is quite coincident with what is best and inmost in his mind. Shall he then, cutting the stays that hold him fast to the social state, put out to sea with no guidance but his genius? There is much to say on both sides. Remember the open question between the present order of "competition" and the friends of "attractive and associated labor." The generous minds embrace the proposition of labor shared by all; it is the only honesty; nothing else is safe. It is from the poor man's hut alone that strength and virtue come: and yet, on the other side, it is alleged that labor impairs the form and breaks the spirit of man, and the laborers cry unanimously, "We have no thoughts." Culture, how indispensable! I cannot forgive you the want of accomplishments; and yet culture will instantly impair that chiefest beauty of spontaneousness. Excellent is culture for a savage; but once let him read in the book, and he is no longer able not to think of Plutarch's heroes. In short, since true fortitude of understanding consists "in not letting what we know be embarrassed by what we do not know," we ought to secure those advantages which we can command, and not risk them by clutching after the airy and unattainable. Come, no chimeras! Let us go abroad; let us mix in affairs; let us learn and get and have and climb. "Men are a sort of moving plants, and, like trees, receive a great part of their nourishment from the air. If they keep too much at home, they pine." Let us have a robust, manly life; let us know what we know, for certain; what we have, let it be solid and seasonable and our own. A world in the hand is worth two in the bush. Let us have to do with real men and women, and not with skipping ghosts.

This then is the right ground of the skeptic, — this of consideration, of self-containing; not at all of unbelief; not at all of universal denying, nor of universal doubting, — doubting even that he doubts; least of all of scoffing and profligate jeering at all that is stable and good. These are no more his moods than are those of religion and philosophy. He is the considerer, the prudent, taking in sail, counting stock, husbanding his means, believing that a man has too many enemies than that he can afford to be his own foe; that we cannot give ourselves too many advantages in this unequal conflict, with powers so vast and unweariable ranged on one side, and this little conceited vulnerable popinjay that a man is, bobbing up and down into every danger, on the other. It is a position taken up for better defense, as of more safety, and one that can be maintained; and it is one of more opportunity and range: as, when we build a house, the rule is to set it not too high nor too low, under the wind, but out of the dirt.

The philosophy we want is one of fluxions and mobility. The Spartan and Stoic schemes are too stark and stiff for our occasion. A theory of Saint John,[9] and of non-resistance, seems, on the other hand, too thin and aerial. We want some coat woven of elastic steel, stout as the first and limber as the second. We want a ship in these billows we inhabit. An angular, dogmatic house would be rent to chips and splinters in this storm of many elements. No, it must be tight, and fit to the form of man, to live at all; as a shell must dictate the architecture of a house founded on the sea. The soul of man must be the type of our scheme, just as the body of man is the type after which a dwelling-house is built. Adaptiveness is the peculiarity of human nature. We are golden averages, volitant stabilities, compensated or periodic errors, houses founded on the sea. The wise skeptic wishes to have a near view of the best game and the chief players; what is best in the planet; art and nature, places and events; but mainly men. Every thing that is excellent in mankind, — a form of grace, an arm of iron, lips of persuasion, a brain of resources, every one skilful to play and win, — he will see and judge.

The terms of admission to this spectacle are, that he have a certain solid and intelligible way of living of his own; some method of

9 Teacher of Love.

answering the inevitable needs of human life; proof that he has played with skill and success; that he has evinced the temper, stoutness and the range of qualities which, among his contemporaries and countrymen, entitle him to fellowship and trust. For the secrets of life are not shown except to sympathy and likeness. Men do not confide themselves to boys, or coxcombs, or pedants, but to their peers. Some wise limitation, as the modern phrase is; some condition between the extremes, and having, itself, a positive quality; some stark and suffcient man, who is not salt or sugar, but sufficiently related to the world to do justice to Paris or London, and, at the same time, a vigorous and original thinker, whom cities can not overawe, but who uses them, — is the fit person to occupy this ground of speculation.

These qualities meet in the character of Montaigne. And yet, since the personal regard which I entertain for Montaigne may be unduly great, I will, under the shield of this prince of egotists, offer, as an apology for electing him as the representative of skepticism, a word or two to explain how my love began and grew for this admirable gossip.

A single odd volume of Cotton's translation of the Essays remained to me from my father's library, when a boy. It lay long neglected, until, after many years, when I was newly escaped from college, I read the book, and procured the remaining volumes. I remember the delight and wonder in which I lived with it. It seemed to me as if I had myself written the book, in some former life, so sincerely it spoke to my thought and experience. It happened, when in Paris, in 1833, that, in the cemetery of Père Lachaise, I came to a tomb of Auguste Collignon, who died in 1830, aged sixty-eight years, and who, said the monument, "lived to do right, and had formed himself to virtue on the Essays of Montaigne." Some years later, I became acquainted with an accomplished English poet, John Sterling; and, in prosecuting my correspondence, I found that, from a love of Montaigne, he had made a pilgrimage to his chateau, still standing near Castellan, in Périgord, and, after two hundred and fifty years, had copied from the walls of his library the inscriptions which Montaigne had written there. That Journal of Mr. Sterling's, published in the Westminster Review, Mr. Hazlitt has reprinted in the *Prolegomena* to his edition of the Essays. I heard with pleasure that one of the newly-discovered autographs of William Shakespeare was in a copy of Florio's translation of Montaigne. It is the only book which we certainly know to have been in the poet's library. And, oddly enough, the duplicate copy of Florio, which the British Museum purchased with a view of protecting the Shakespeare autograph (as I was informed in the Museum), turned out to have the autograph of Ben Jonson in the fly-leaf. Leigh Hunt relates of Lord Byron, that Montaigne was the only great writer of past times whom he read with avowed satisfaction. Other coincidences, not needful to be mentioned here, concurred to make this old Gascon still new and immortal for me.

In 1571, on the death of his father, Montaigne, then thirty-eight years old, retired from the practice of law at Bordeaux, and settled himself on his estate. Though he had been a man of pleasure and sometimes a courtier, his studious habits now grew on him, and he loved the compass,[1] staidness and independence of the country gentleman's life. He took up his economy in good earnest, and made his farms yield the most. Downright and plain-dealing, and abhorring to be deceived or to deceive, he was esteemed in the country for his sense and probity. In the civil wars of the League,[2] which converted every house into a fort, Montaigne kept his gates open and his house without defense. All parties freely came and went, his courage and honor being universally esteemed. The neighboring lords and gentry brought jewels and papers to him for safe-keeping. Gibbon reckons, in these bigoted times, but two men of liberality in France, — Henry IV and Montaigne.

Montaigne is the frankest and honestest of all writers. His French freedom runs into grossness; but he has anticipated all censure by the bounty of his own confessions. In his times, books were written to one sex only, and almost all were written in Latin; so that in a humorist a certain nakedness of statement was permitted, which our manners, of a literature addressed equally to both sexes, do not allow. But though a biblical plainness coupled with a most uncanonical levity may shut his pages to many sensitive readers, yet the offence is superficial. He parades it: he makes the most of it: nobody can think or say worse of him than he does. He pretends to most of the vices; and, if there be any virtue in him, he says, it got in by stealth. There is no man, in his opinion, who has not deserved hanging five or six times; and he pretends no exception in his own behalf. "Five or six as ridiculous stories," too, he says, "can be told of me, as of any man living." But, with all this really superfluous frankness, the opinion of an invincible probity grows into every reader's mind. "When I the most strictly

[1] Moderate bounds.
[2] Against Protestants; then turned against Henry IV.

and religiously confess myself, I find that the best virtue I have has·in it some tincture of vice; and I, who am as sincere and perfect a lover of virtue of that stamp as any other whatever, am afraid that Plato, in his purest virtue, if he had listened and laid his ear close to himself, would have heard some jarring sound of human mixture; but faint and remote and only to be perceived by himself."

Here is an impatience and fastidiousness at color or pretence of any kind. He has been in courts so long as to have conceived a furious disgust at appearances; he will indulge himself with a little cursing and swearing; he will talk with sailors and gipsies, use flash and street ballads; he has stayed in-doors till he is deadly sick; he will to the open air, though it rain bullets. He has seen too much of gentlemen of the long robe, until he wishes for cannibals; and is so nervous, by factitious life, that he thinks the more barbarous man is, the better he is. He likes his saddle. You may read theology, and grammar, and metaphysics elsewhere. Whatever you get here shall smack of the earth and of real life, sweet, or smart, or stinging. He makes no hesitation to entertain you with the records of his disease, and his journey to Italy is quite full of that matter. He took and kept this position of equilibrium. Over his name he drew an emblematic pair of scales, and wrote *Que sçais je?* [3] under it. As I look at his effigy opposite the title-page, I seem to hear him say, "You may play old Poz,[4] if you will; you may rail and exaggerate, — I stand here for truth, and will not, for all the states and churches and revenues and personal reputations of Europe, overstate the dry fact, as I see it; I will rather mumble and prose about what I certainly know, — my house and barns; my father, my wife and my tenants; my old lean bald pate; my knives and forks; what meats I eat and what drinks I prefer, and a hundred straws just as ridiculous, — than I will write, with a fine crowquill, a fine romance. I like gray days, and autumn and winter weather. I am gray and autumnal myself, and think an undress and old shoes that do not pinch my feet, and old friends who do not constrain me, and plain topics where I do not need to strain myself and pump my brains, the most suitable. Our condition as men is risky and ticklish enough. One cannot be sure of himself and his fortune an hour, but he may be whisked off into some pitiable or ridiculous plight. Why should I vapor and play the philosopher, instead of ballasting, the best I can, this dancing balloon? So, at least, I live within compass, keep myself ready for action, and can

---

[3] What do I know?
[4] One sure of all his opinions.

shoot the gulf at last with decency. If there be anything farcical in such a life, the blame is not mine: let it lie at fate's and nature's door."

The Essays, therefore, are an entertaining soliloquy on every random topic that comes into his head; treating every thing without ceremony, yet with masculine sense. There have been men with deeper insight; but, one would say, never a man with such abundance of thoughts: he is never dull, never insincere, and has the genius to make the reader care for all that he cares for.

The sincerity and marrow of the man reaches to his sentences. I know not anywhere the book that seems less written. It is the language of conversation transferred to a book. Cut these words, and they would bleed; they are vascular and alive. One has the same pleasure in it that he feels in listening to the necessary speech of men about their work, when any unusual circumstance gives momentary importance to the dialogue. For blacksmiths and teamsters do not trip in their speech; it is a shower of bullets. It is Cambridge men who correct themselves and begin again at every half sentence, and, moreover, will pun, and refine too much, and swerve from the matter to the expression. Montaigne talks with shrewdness, knows the world and books and himself, and uses the positive degree; never shrieks, or protests, or prays: no weakness, no convulsion, no superlative: does not wish to jump out of his skin, or play any antics, or annihilate space or time, but is stout and solid; tastes every moment of the day; likes pain because it makes him feel himself and realize things; as we pinch ourselves to know that we are awake. He keeps the plain; he rarely mounts or sinks; likes to feel solid ground and the stones underneath. His writing has no enthusiasms, no aspiration; contented, self-respecting and keeping the middle of the road. There is but one exception, — in his love for Socrates. In speaking of him, for once his cheek flushes and his style rises to passion.

Montaigne died of a quinsy, at the age of sixty, in 1592. When he came to die he caused the mass to be celebrated in his chamber. At the age of thirty-three, he had been married. "But," he says, "might I have had my own will, I would not have married Wisdom herself, if she would have had me: but 'tis to much purpose to evade it, the common custom and use of life will have it so. Most of my actions are guided by example, not choice." In the hour of death, he gave the same weight to custom. *Que sçais je?* What do I know?

This book of Montaigne the world has endorsed by translating it into all tongues and printing seventy-five editions of it in Europe; and that, too, a circulation somewhat chosen, namely among courtiers, soldiers, princes, men of the world and men of wit and generosity.

Shall we say that Montaigne has spoken wisely, and given the right and permanent expression of the human mind, on the conduct of life?

We are natural believers. Truth, or the connection between cause and effect, alone interests us. We are persuaded that a thread runs through all things: all worlds are strung on it, as beads; and men, and events, and life, come to us only because of that thread: they pass and repass only that we may know the direction and continuity of that line. A book or statement which goes to show that there is no line, but random and chaos, a calamity out of nothing, a prosperity and no account of it, a hero born from a fool, a fool from a hero, — dispirits us. Seen or unseen, we believe the tie exists. Talent makes counterfeit ties; genius finds the real ones. We hearken to the man of science, because we anticipate the sequence in natural phenomena which he uncovers. We love whatever affirms, connects, preserves; and dislike what scatters or pulls down. One man appears whose nature is to all men's eyes conserving and constructive; his presence supposes a well-ordered society, agriculture, trade, large institutions and empire. If these did not exist, they would begin to exist through his endeavors. Therefore he cheers and comforts men, who feel all this in him very readily. The noncomformist and the rebel say all manner of unanswerable things against the existing republic, but discover to our sense no plan of house or state of their own. Therefore, though the town and state and way of living, which our counsellor contemplated, might be a very modest or musty prosperity, yet men rightly go for him, and reject the reformer so long as he comes only with axe and crowbar.

But though we are natural conservers and causationists, and reject a sour, dumpish unbelief, the skeptical class, which Montaigne represents, have reason, and every man, at some time, belongs to it. Every superior mind will pass through this domain of equilibration, — I should rather say, will know how to avail himself of the checks and balances in nature, as a natural weapon against the exaggeration and formalism of bigots and blockheads.

Skepticism is the attitude assumed by the student in relation to the particulars which society adores, but which he sees to be reverend only in their tendency and spirit. The ground occupied by the skeptic is the vestibule of the temple. Society does not like to have any breath of question blown on the existing order. But the interrogation of custom at all points is an inevitable stage in the growth of every superior mind, and is the evidence of its perception of the flowing power which remains itself in all changes.

The superior mind will find itself equally at odds with the evils of society and with the projects that are offered to relieve them. The wise skeptic is a bad citizen; no conservative, he sees the selfishness of property and the drowsiness of institutions. But neither is he fit to work with any democratic party that ever was constituted; for parties wish every one committed, and he penetrates the popular patriotism. His politics are those of the "Soul's Errand" of Sir Walter Raleigh; or of Krishna, in the Bhagavat,[5] "There is none who is worthy of my love or hatred"; whilst he sentences law, physic, divinity, commerce and custom. He is a reformer; yet he is no better member of the philanthropic association. It turns out that he is not the champion of the operative, the pauper, the prisoner, the slave. It stands in his mind that our life in this world is not of quite so easy interpretation as churches and schoolbooks say. He does not wish to take ground against these benevolences, to play the part of devil's attorney, and blazon every doubt and sneer that darkens the sun for him. But he says, There are doubts.

I mean to use the occasion, and celebrate the calendar-day of our Saint Michel de Montaigne, by counting and describing these doubts or negations. I wish to ferret them out of their holes and sun them a little. We must do with them as the police do with old rogues, who are shown up to the public at the marshal's office. They will never be so formidable when once they have been identified and registered. But I mean honestly by them, — that justice shall be done to their terrors. I shall not take Sunday objections, made up on purpose to be put down. I shall take the worst I can find, whether I can dispose of them or they of me.

I do not press the skepticism of the materialist. I know the quadruped opinion will not prevail. 'Tis of no importance what bats and oxen think. The first dangerous symptom I report is, the levity of intellect; as if it were fatal to earnestness to know much. Knowledge is the knowing that we can not know. The dull pray; the geniuses are light mockers. How respectable is earnestness on

---

5 *Bhagavad-Gita*, a Hindu scripture. Cf. "Brahma" (p. 451).

every platform! but intellect kills it. Nay, San Carlo,[6] my subtle
and admirable friend, one of the most penetrating of men, finds
that all direct ascension, even of lofty piety, leads to this ghastly insight and sends back the votary orphaned. My astonishing San
Carlo thought the lawgivers and saints infected. They found the
ark empty; saw, and would not tell; and tried to choke off their approaching followers, by saying, "Action, action, my dear fellows, is
for you!" Bad as was to me this detection by San Carlo, this frost
in July, this blow from a bride, there was still a worse, namely the
cloy or satiety of the saints. In the mount of vision, ere they have
yet risen from their knees, they say, "We discover that this our
homage and beatitude is partial and deformed: we must fly for
relief to the suspected and reviled Intellect, to the Understanding,
the Mephistopheles, to the gymnastics of talent."

This is hobgoblin the first; and though it has been the subject
of much elegy in our nineteenth century, from Byron, Goethe and
other poets of less fame, not to mention many distinguished private observers, — I confess it is not very affecting to my imagination; for it seems to concern the shattering of baby-houses and
crockery-shops. What flutters the Church of Rome, or of England,
or of Geneva, or of Boston, may yet be very far from touching any
principle of faith. I think that the intellect and moral sentiment
are unanimous; and that though philosophy extirpates bugbears,
yet it supplies the natural checks of vice, and polarity to the soul.
I think that the wiser a man is, the more stupendous he finds the
natural and moral economy, and lifts himself to a more absolute
reliance.

There is the power of moods, each setting at nought all but its
own tissue of facts and beliefs. There is the power of complexions,
obviously modifying the dispositions and sentiments. The beliefs
and unbeliefs appear to be structural; and as soon as each man attains the poise and vivacity which allow the whole machinery to
play, he will not need extreme examples, but will rapidly alternate
all opinions in his own life. Our life is March weather, savage and
serene in one hour. We go forth austere, dedicated, believing in
the iron links of Destiny, and will not turn on our heel to save our
life: but a book, or a bust, or only the sound of a name, shoots a
spark through the nerves, and we suddenly believe in will: my
finger-ring shall be the seal of Solomon; fate is for imbeciles; all is
possible to the resolved mind. Presently a new experience gives a
new turn to our thoughts: common sense resumes its tyranny; we

[6] "St. Charles": Charles K. Newcomb (cf. pp. 209–10).

say, "Well, the army, after all, is the gate to fame, manners and poetry: and, look you, — on the whole, selfishness plants best, prunes best, makes the best commerce and the best citizen." Are the opinions of a man on right and wrong, on fate and causation, at the mercy of a broken sleep or an indigestion? Is his belief in God and Duty no deeper than a stomach evidence? And what guaranty for the permanence of his opinions? I like not the French celerity, — a new Church and State once a week. This is the second negation; and I shall let it pass for what it will. As far as it asserts rotation of states of mind, I suppose it suggests its own remedy, namely in the record of larger periods. What is the mean of many states; of all the states? Does the general voice of ages affirm any principle, or is no community of sentiment discoverable in distant times and places? And when it shows the power of self-interest, I accept that as part of the divine law and must reconcile it with aspiration the best I can.

The word Fate, or Destiny, expresses the sense of mankind, in all ages, that the laws of the world do not always befriend, but often hurt and crush us. Fate, in the shape of *Kinde* or nature, grows over us like grass. We paint Time with a scythe; Love and Fortune, blind; and Destiny, deaf. We have too little power of resistance against this ferocity which champs us up. What front can we make against these unavoidable, victorious, maleficent forces? What can I do against the influence of Race, in my history? What can I do against hereditary and constitutional habits; against scrofula, lymph, impotence? against climate, against barbarism, in my country? I can reason down or deny every thing, except this perpetual Belly: feed he must and will, and I cannot make him respectable.

But the main resistance which the affirmative impulse finds, and one including all others, is in the doctrine of the Illusionists. There is a painful rumor in circulation that we have been practiced upon in all the principal performances of life, and free agency is the emptiest name. We have been sopped and drugged with the air, with food, with woman, with children, with sciences, with events, which leave us exactly where they found us. The mathematics, 'tis complained, leave the mind where they find it: so do all sciences; and so do all events and actions. I find a man who has passed through all the sciences, the churl he was; and, through all the offices, learned, civil and social, can detect the child. We are not the less necessitated to dedicate life to them. In fact we may come to

accept it as the fixed rule and theory of our state of education, that
God is a substance, and his method is illusion. The Eastern sages
owned the goddess Yoganidra, the great illusory energy of Vishnu,
by whom, as utter ignorance, the whole world is beguiled.

Or shall I state it thus? — The astonishment of life is the absence of any appearance of reconciliation between the theory and
practice of life. Reason, the prized reality, the Law, is apprehended, now and then, for a serene and profound moment amidst
the hubbub of cares and works which have no direct bearing on it;
— is then lost for months or years, and again found for an interval,
to be lost again. If we compute it in time, we may, in fifty years,
have half a dozen reasonable hours. But what are these cares and
works the better? A method in the world we do not see, but this
parallelism of great and little, which never react on each other,
nor discover the smallest tendency to converge. Experiences, fortunes, governings, readings, writings, are nothing to the purpose;
as when a man comes into the room it does not appear whether he
has been fed on yams or buffalo, — he has contrived to get so much
bone and fiber as he wants, out of rice or out of snow. So vast is
the disproportion between the sky of law and the pismire of performance under it, that whether he is a man of worth or a sot is
not so great a matter as we say. Shall I add, as one juggle of this
enchantment, the stunning non-intercourse law which makes co-
operation impossible? The young spirit pants to enter society. But
all the ways of culture and greatness lead to solitary imprisonment.
He has been often balked. He did not expect a sympathy with his
thought from the village, but he went with it to the chosen and
intelligent, and found no entertainment for it, but mere misap-
prehension, distaste and scoffing. Men are strangely mistimed and
misapplied; and the excellence of each is an inflamed individualism
which separates him more.

There are these, and more than these diseases of thought, which
our ordinary teachers do not attempt to remove. Now shall we, because a good nature inclines us to virtue's side, say, There are no
doubts, — and lie for the right? Is life to be led in a brave or in a
cowardly manner? and is not the satisfaction of the doubts essential
to all manliness? Is the name of virtue to be a barrier to that which
is virtue? Can you not believe that a man of earnest and burly
habit may find small good in tea, essays and catechism, and want a
rougher instruction, want men, labor, trade, farming, war, hunger,
plenty, love, hatred, doubt and terror to make things plain to him;

and has he not a right to insist on being convinced in his own way? When he is convinced, he will be worth the pains.

Belief consists in accepting the affirmations of the soul; unbelief, in denying them. Some minds are incapable of skepticism. The doubts they profess to entertain are rather a civility or accommodation to the common discourse of their company. They may well give themselves leave to speculate, for they are secure of a return. Once admitted to the heaven of thought, they see no relapse into night, but infinite invitation on the other side. Heaven is within heaven, and sky over sky, and they are encompassed with divinities. Others there are to whom the heaven is brass, and it shuts down to the surface of the earth. It is a question of temperament, or of more or less immersion in nature. The last class must needs have a reflex or parasite faith; not a sight of realities, but an instinctive reliance on the seers and believers of realities. The manners and thoughts of believers astonish them and convince them that these have seen something which is hid from themselves. But their sensual habit would fix the believer to his last position, whilst he as inevitably advances; and presently the unbeliever, for love of belief, burns the believer.

Great believers are always reckoned infidels, impracticable, fantastic, atheistic, and really men of no account. The spiritualist finds himself driven to express his faith by a series of skepticisms. Charitable souls come with their projects and ask his coöperation. How can he hesitate? It is the rule of mere comity and courtesy to agree where you can, and to turn your sentence with something auspicious, and not freezing and sinister. But he is forced to say, "O, these things will be as they must be: what can you do? These particular griefs and crimes are the foliage and fruit of such trees as we see growing. It is vain to complain of the leaf or the berry; cut it off, it will bear another just as bad. You must begin your cure lower down." The generosities of the day prove an intractable element for him. The people's questions are not his; their methods are not his; and against all the dictates of good nature he is driven to say he has no pleasure in them.

Even the doctrines dear to the hope of man, of the divine Providence and of the immortality of the soul, his neighbors can not put the statement so that he shall affirm it. But he denies out of more faith, and not less. He denies out of honesty. He had rather stand charged with the imbecility of skepticism, than with untruth. I believe, he says, in the moral design of the universe; it exists hospitably for the weal of souls; but your dogmas seem to me caricatures: why should I make believe them? Will any say, This is cold and infidel? The wise and magnanimous will not say so. They will exult in his far-sighted good-will that can abandon to the adversary all the ground of tradition and common belief, without losing a jot of strength. It sees to the end of all transgression. George Fox saw that there was "an ocean of darkness and death; but withal an infinite ocean of light and love which flowed over that of darkness."

The final solution in which skepticism is lost, is in the moral sentiment, which never forfeits its supremacy. All moods may be safely tried, and their weight allowed to all objections: the moral sentiment as easily outweighs them all, as any one. This is the drop which balances the sea. I play with the miscellany of facts, and take those superficial views which we call skepticism; but I know that they will presently appear to me in that order which makes skepticism impossible. A man of thought must feel the thought that is parent of the universe; that the masses of nature do undulate and flow.

This faith avails to the whole emergency of life and objects. The world is saturated with deity and with law. He is content with just and unjust, with sots and fools, with the triumph of folly and fraud. He can behold with serenity the yawning gulf between the ambition of man and his power of performance, between the demand and supply of power, which makes the tragedy of all souls.

Charles Fourier announced that "the attractions of man are proportioned to his destinies"; in other words, that every desire predicts its own satisfaction. Yet all experience exhibits the reverse of this; the incompetency of power is the universal grief of young and ardent minds. They accuse the divine Providence of a certain parsimony. It has shown the heaven and earth to every child and filled him with a desire for the whole; a desire raging, infinite; a hunger, as of space to be filled with planets; a cry of famine, as of devils for souls. Then for the satisfaction, — to each man is administered a single drop, a bead of dew of vital power, *per day*, — a cup as large as space, and one drop of the water of life in it. Each man woke in the morning with an appetite that could eat the solar system like a cake; a spirit for action and passion without bounds; he could lay his hand on the morning star; he could try conclusions with gravitation or chemistry; but, on the first motion to prove his strength, — hands, feet, senses, gave way and would not serve him. He was an emperor deserted by his states, and left to whistle by himself, or thrust into a mob of emperors, all whistling: and still the sirens sang, "The attractions are proportioned to the destinies." In every house, in the heart of each maiden and of each boy, in the soul of the soaring saint, this chasm is found, — between the largest promise of ideal power, and the shabby experience.

The expansive nature of truth comes to our succor, elastic, not to be surrounded. Man helps himself by larger generalizations. The lesson of life is practically to generalize; to believe what the years and the centuries say, against the hours; to resist the usurpation of particulars; to penetrate to their catholic sense. Things seem to say one thing, and say the reverse. The appearance is immoral; the result is moral. Things seem to tend downward, to justify despondency, to promote rogues, to defeat the just; and by knaves as by martyrs the just cause is carried forward. Although knaves win in every political struggle, although society seems to be delivered over from the hands of one set of criminals into the hands of another set of criminals, as fast as the government is changed, and the march of civilization is a train of felonies, — yet, general ends are somehow answered. We see, now, events forced on which seem to retard or retrograde the civility of ages. But the world-spirit is a good swimmer, and storms and waves cannot drown him. He snaps his finger at laws: and so, throughout history, heaven seems to affect low and poor means. Through the years and the centuries, through evil agents, through toys and atoms, a great and beneficent tendency irresistibly streams.

Let a man learn to look for the permanent in the mutable and fleeting; let him learn to bear the disappearance of things he was wont to reverence without losing his reverence; let him learn that he is here, not to work but to be worked upon; and that, though abyss open under abyss, and opinion displace opinion, all are at last contained in the Eternal Cause:—

"If my bark sink. 'tis to another sea."

Fate

The years after 1845 brought a steady expansion of horizons. At Christmas time, 1846, the publication of a volume of poems revealed the unsuspected extent of his "rhyming mania" in the last decade.[1] The next event of importance was a second trip to Europe in 1847–48, mainly to lecture in England, also briefly to visit France, shortly after the Revolution of 1848. He saw Carlyle again and extended his acquaintance widely among the notables of his day. On his return he revised and published his old work of the thirties and forties in Nature; Addresses and Lectures (1849) and Representative Men (1850) and proceeded to write or refurbish a new repertoire of lectures, the chief of which were finally published in The Conduct of Life (1860). His finances made it necessary for him to take his lectures on wider and wider tours. He saw the Mississippi for the first time in 1850, was in Buffalo and Pittsburgh in 1851, went to Montreal in 1852, was back in St. Louis, Cincinnati, and the Middle West in 1853, and from then on each season was likely to see him braving the hardships of winter travel in the North and West to peddle his "intellectual notions." In 1871 he even reached California and the Far West.

Meanwhile his thought enlarged in scope and his style grew in force. "You have grown older, more pungent, piercing," Carlyle wrote him of The Conduct of Life: "I never read from you before such lightning-gleams of meaning as are to be found here." As the United States stumbled from the Mexican War to the Fugitive Slave Law, the journals acquired an acerbity partly toned down in the essays. He now expected very little from the mass of his countrymen: "We live in Lilliput," he concluded. He cherished men of grasp and competence because he found so few of them;

[1] See pp. 407–450.

one reason for his wrath at Webster's Seventh of March speech in 1850 was his assumption that in Webster the cause of the right lost one of the few superior men America could show. But men, even the best, were not of great importance — dwellers in tents, outlines in chalk, eggs and tadpoles. All that mattered at last was instinct, tendency, the "ethereal currents" and the imagination that could see and share them.

The themes of his lectures and journals were naturally often "old thrums," central beliefs he came back and back to. The change these years brought was not so much in ideas as in perspective. He stepped back from the "too rapid unity" of his earlier visions and the skepticism their clash with fact awakened until he could look out over this and all merely personal problems with relative equanimity as organic parts of a huge cosmic drama. The gain to his writing in ease and grasp is palpable; the loss in involvement was made up for by a new "longanimity." His conception of Nature had become a far cry from the "last thing of the soul" he had analyzed in 1836: a rushing metamorphosis, inconceivably vast in space and time, controlled by a supernal "breath of Will" that pressed on, using a few simple means, toward a grand end far beyond man's grasp. All creatures and most men were merely her raw materials, the "corallines" by which she built the world of the future. Only now and then some superior man, by his gift of thought, could merge his will with hers and for an expansive moment share her freedom. In other hours, he would seek health, probity, cheerfulness, proportion, the society of superior men, and always the work, grounding all on a constant trust in the Law behind life's snowstorm of illusions.

April, 1846

He or That which in despair of naming aright, some have called the *Newness*, — as the Hebrews did not like to pronounce the word, — he lurks, he hides, he who is success, reality, joy, power, — that which constitutes Heaven, which reconciles impossibilities, atones for shortcomings, expiates sins or makes them virtues, buries in oblivion the crowded historical past, sinks religions, philosophies, nations, persons to legends; reverses the scale of opinion, of fame; reduces sciences to opinion, and makes the thought of the moment the key to the universe, and the egg of history to come.

. . . 'Tis all alike, — astronomy, metaphysics, sword, spade, pencil, or instruments and arts yet to be invented, — this is the inventor, the worth-giver, the worth. This is He that shall come; or, if He come not, nothing comes: He that disappears in the moment when we go to celebrate Him. If we go to burn those that blame our celebration, He appears in them. The Divine Newness. Hoe and spade, sword and pen, cities, pictures, gardens, laws, bibles, are prized only because they were means He sometime used. So with astronomy, music, arithmetic, castes, feudalism, — we kiss with devotion these hems of his garment, — we mistake them for Him; they crumble to ashes on our lips.

April, 1846

I like man, but not men. Instincts, tendencies, — they do no wrong: they are beautiful, and may be confided in and obeyed. Though they slay us, let us trust them. Why should eggs and tadpoles talk? All is mere sketch, symptomatic, possible, or probable, for us, — we dwellers in tents, we outlines in chalk, we jokes and buffooneries, why should we be talking? Let us have the grace to be abstemious. The etiquette of society should guard and consecrate a poet; he should not be visited, nor be shown at dinner-tables: too costly to be seen except on high holidays. He should be relieved of visits and trivial correspondence. His time is the time of his nation.

Yes, we want a poet, the genuine poet of our time, no parrot, and no child. The poets that we praise, or try to, the Brownings, Barretts, Bryants, Tennysons, — are all abortive Homers; they at least show tendency, the direction of Nature to the star in Lyra. Boys still whistle, and every newspaper and girl's album attest the ineradicable appetite for melody. Oh, no, we have not done with music, nor must console ourselves with prose poets. We wish the undrawn line of tendency to be drawn for us. Where is the Euclid who can sum up these million errors, and compute the beautiful mean? We do not wish to make believe be instructed; we wish to be ravished, inspired, and taught.

[November 1?, 1845]

We are very clumsy writers of history. We tell the chronicle of parentage, birth, birth-place, schooling, school-mates, earning of money, marriage, publication of books, celebrity, death; and when we have come to an end of this gossip, no ray of relation appears between it and the goddess-born; and it seems as if, had we dipped at random into the "Modern Plutarch," and read any other life

there, it would have fitted the poems as well. It is the essence of
poetry to spring, like the rainbow daughter of Wonder, from the
invisible, to abolish the past and refuse all history. Malone, War-
burton, Dyce, and Collier [2] have wasted their oil. The famed
theaters, Covent Garden, Drury Lane, the Park and Tremont have
vainly assisted. Betterton, Garrick, Kemble, Kean, and Macready [3]
dedicate their lives to this genius; him they crown, elucidate, obey
and express. The genius knows them not. The recitation begins;
one golden word leaps out immortal from all this painted pedantry
and sweetly torments us with invitations to its own inaccessible
homes. I remember I went once to see the Hamlet of a famed
performer, the pride of the English stage; and all I then heard and
all now remember of the tragedian was that in which the tragedian
had no part; simply Hamlet's question to the ghost: —

> "What may this mean,
> That thou, dead corse, again in complete steel
> Revisit'st thus the glimpses of the moon?"

That imagination which dilates the closet he writes in to the
world's dimension, crowds it with agents in rank and order,
quickly reduces the big reality to be the glimpses of the moon.
These tricks of his magic spoil for us the illusions of the green-
room. Can any biography shed light on the localities into which
the Midsummer Night's Dream admits me? Did Shakespeare confide to any notary or parish recorder, sacristan, or surrogate in
Stratford, the genesis of that delicate creation? The forest of
Arden, the nimble air of Scone Castle, the moonlight of Portia's
villa, "the antres vast and desarts idle" of Othello's captivity, —
where is the third cousin, or grand-nephew, the chancellor's file of
accounts, or private letter, that has kept one word of those transcendent secrets? In fine, in this drama, as in all great works of
art, — in the Cyclopean architecture of Egypt and India, in the
Phidian sculpture, the Gothic minsters, the Italian painting, the
Ballads of Spain and Scotland, — the Genius draws up the ladder
after him, when the creative age goes up to heaven, and gives way
to a new age, which sees the works and asks in vain for a history.

From "Shakespeare"

April, 1846

Byron is no poet: what did he know of the world and its law
and Lawgiver? What moment had he of that mania which molds

[2] Editors.   [3] Actors.

history and man, and tough circumstance, — like wax? He had declamation; he had music, juvenile and superficial music. Even this is very rare, and we delight in it so much that Byron has obtained great fame by this fluency and music. It is delicious. All the "Hebrew Melodies" are examples.

"Warriors and chiefs! should the shaft or the sword,"

— how neat, how clever, how roundly it rolls off the tongue — but what poetry is here? It is the sublime of schoolboy verse. How many volumes of such jingle must we go through before we can be filled, sustained, taught, renewed?

[*June ?, 1846*]

Eloquence. — We go to the bar, the senate, the shop, the study, as peaceful professions, but you cannot escape the demand for courage, no, not in the shrine of Peace itself. Certainly there is no true orator who is not a hero. His attitude in the rostrum, on the platform, requires that he counterbalance his auditory. He is challenger, and must answer all comers. The orator must ever stand with forward foot, in the attitude of advancing. His speech must be just ahead of the assembly, ahead of the whole human race, or it is superfluous. His speech is not to be distinguished from action. It is the electricity of action. It is action, as the general's word of command or chart of battle is action. I must feel that the speaker compromises himself to his auditory, comes for something, — it is a cry on the perilous edge of the fight, — or let him be silent.

[Parker] Pillsbury, whom I heard last night, is the very gift from New Hampshire which we have long expected, a tough oak stick of a man not to be silenced or insulted or intimidated by a mob, because he is more mob than they; he mobs the mob. John Knox is come at last, on whom neither money nor politeness nor hard words nor rotten eggs nor kicks and brickbats make the slightest impression. He is fit to meet the bar-room wits and bullies; he is a wit and a bully himself and something more; he is a graduate of the plough and the cedar swamp and the snowbank, and has nothing new to learn of labor or poverty or the rough of farming. His hard head, too, had gone through in boyhood all the drill of Calvinism, with text and mortification, so that he stands in the New England assembly a purer bit of New England than any, and flings his sarcasms right and left, sparing no name or person or party or presence. . . .

June ?, 1846

The scrupulous and law-abiding become Whigs, the unscrupulous and energetic are Locofocos. The people are no worse since they invaded Mexico than they were before, only they have given their will a deed.

Every reform is only a mask under cover of which a more terrible reform, which dares not yet name itself, advances. Slavery and anti-slavery is the question of property and no property, rent and anti-rent; and anti-slavery dare not yet say that every man must do his own work, or, at least, receive no interest for money. Yet that is at last the upshot.

The United States will conquer Mexico, but it will be as the man swallows the arsenic, which brings him down in turn. Mexico will poison us.

The Southerner is cool and insolent. "We drive you to the wall, and will again." Yes, gentlemen, but do you know why Massachusetts and New York are so tame? — it is because we own you, and are very tender of our mortgages which cover all your property.

July, 1846

The State is a poor, good beast who means the best: it means friendly. A poor cow who does well by you, — do not grudge it its hay.[4] It cannot eat bread, as you can; let it have without grudge a little grass for its four stomachs. It will not stint to yield you milk from its teat. You, who are a man walking cleanly on two feet, will not pick a quarrel with a poor cow. Take this handful of clover and welcome. But if you go to hook me when I walk in the fields, then, poor cow, I will cut your throat.

Don't run amuck against the world. Have a good case to try the question on. It is the part of a fanatic to fight out a revolution on the shape of a hat or surplice, on paedo-baptism, or altar-rails, or fish on Friday. As long as the state means you well, do not refuse your pistareen. You have a tottering cause: ninety parts of the pistareen it will spend for what you think also good: ten parts for mischief. You cannot fight heartily for a fraction. But wait until you have a good difference to join issue upon. Thus Socrates was told he should not teach. "Please God, but I will." And he could

[4] Thoreau had just refused to pay his poll-tax.

die well for that. And Jesus had a cause. You will get one by and by. But now I have no sympathy. . . .

Alcott thought he could find as good a ground for quarrel in the state tax as Socrates did in the edict of the Judges. Then I say, Be consistent, and never more put an apple or a kernel of corn into your mouth. Would you feed the devil? Say boldly, "There is a sword sharp enough to cut sheer between flesh and spirit, and I will use it, and not any longer belong to this double-faced, equivocating, mixed, Jesuitical universe."

The Abolitionists should resist, because they are literalists; they know exactly what they object to, and there is a government possible which will content them. Remove a few specified grievances, and this present commonwealth will suit them. They are the new Puritans, and as easily satisfied. But you, nothing will content. No government short of a monarchy consisting of one king and one subject, will appease you. Your objection, then, to the State of Massachusetts is deceptive. Your true quarrel is with the state of Man.

In the particular, it is worth considering that refusing payment of the state tax does not reach the evil so nearly as many other methods within your reach. The state tax does not pay the Mexican War. Your coat, your sugar, your Latin and French and German book, your watch does. Yet these you do not stick at buying.

But really a scholar has too humble an opinion of the population, of their possibilities, of their future, to be entitled to go to war with them, as with equals.

This prison is one step to suicide.

He knows that nothing they can do will ever please him. Why should he poorly pound on some one string of discord, when all is jangle? [5]

April, 1846

Costume. — We must accept without criticism or modification the costume of our times, and be glad we have one care less on our hands, — dress, money, language, railroads, taxation, and the civilization generally. The custom of the country will do so much for us. Let it, and be thankful. . . .

[5] Cf. "Ode to Channing," p. 439.

[*July 31, 1846*]

Webster knows what is done in the shops, and remembers and uses it in the Senate. . . . He is a ship that finds the thing where it is cheap, and carries it where it is dear. Knowledge is of some use in the best company. But the grasp is the main thing. Most men's minds do not grasp anything. All slips through their fingers, like the paltry brass grooves that in most country houses are used to raise or drop the curtain, but are made to sell, and will not hold any curtain but cobwebs. I have heard that idiot children are known from their birth by the circumstance that their hands do not close round anything. Webster naturally and always grasps, and therefore retains something from every company and circumstance.

One of these tenacities, it is no matter where it goes. It gets an education in a shanty, in an alehouse, over a cigar or in a fishing boat, as good as it could find in Germany or in Sais: for the world is unexpectedly rich, and everywhere tells the same things. The grasp is much, but not quite all. The juggle of commerce never loses its power to astonish and delight us, namely, the unlooked-for union that cannot but be of things.

[*September ?, 1846*]

Greatness. Man of the World. — A man of the world, I wish to see, not such men as are called of the world, who more properly are men of a pistareen, men of a quart jar, men of a wine-glass; whose report reaches about as far as the pop of a champagne cork, and who are dumb as soon as they stray beyond that genial circle. I wish catholic men, who by their science and skill are at home in every latitude and longitude, who carry the world in their thoughts; men of universal politics, who are interested in things in proportion to their truth and magnitude; who know the beauty of animals and the laws of their nature, whom the mystery of botany allures, and the mineral laws; who see general effects and are not too learned to love the Imagination, the power and the spirits of Solitude; — men who see the dance in men's lives as well as in a ball-room, and can feel and convey the sense which is only collectively or totally expressed by a population; men who are charmed by the beautiful Nemesis as well as by the dire Nemesis, and dare trust their inspiration for their welcome. . . .

May 1 ?, 1847

The name of Washington City in the newspapers is every day
of blacker shade. All the news from that quarter being of a sadder
type, more malignant. It seems to be settled that no act of honor
or benevolence or justice is to be expected from the American
government, but only this, that they will be as wicked as they dare.
No man now can have any sort of success in politics without a
streak of infamy crossing his name. . . .

We live in Lilliput. The Americans are free-willers, fussy, self-
asserting, buzzing all round creation. But the Asiatics believe it is
writ on the iron leaf, and will not turn on their heel to save them
from famine, plague, or sword. That is great, gives a great air to
the people. . . .

June ?, 1847

Alas for America, as I must so often say, the ungirt, the diffuse,
the profuse, procumbent, — one wide ground juniper, out of which
no cedar, no oak will rear up a mast to the clouds! It all runs to
leaves, to suckers, to tendrils, to miscellany. The air is loaded with
poppy, with imbecility, with dispersion and sloth.

Eager, solicitous, hungry, rabid, busy-bodied America attempting
many things, vain, ambitious to feel thy own existence, and convince others of thy talent, by attempting and hastily accomplishing
much; yes, catch thy breath and correct thyself, and failing here,
prosper out there; speed and fever are never greatness; but reliance
and serenity and waiting and perseverance, heed of the work, and
negligence of the effect.

Great country, diminutive minds.

America is formless, has no terrible and no beautiful condensation. Genius, always anthropomorphist, runs every idea into a
fable, constructs, finishes, as the plastic [6] Italian cannot build a
post or a pump-handle but it terminates in a human head.

July ?, 1847

An American in this ardent climate gets up early some morning
and buys a river; and advertises for twelve or fifteen hundred
Irishmen; digs a new channel for it, brings it to his mills, and has
a head of twenty-four feet of water; then, to give him an appetite
for his breakfast, he raises a house; then carves out, within doors, a
quarter township into streets and building lots, tavern, school, and
Methodist meeting-house — sends up an engineer into New

[6] Creative.

Hampshire, to see where his water comes from, and, after advising with him, sends a trusty man of business to buy of all the farmers such mill-privileges as will serve him among their waste hill and pasture lots, and comes home with great glee announcing that he is now owner of the great Lake Winnipisogee, as reservoir for his Lowell mills at midsummer.

They are an ardent race, and are as fully possessed with that hatred of labor, which is the principle of progress in the human race, as any other people. They must and will have the enjoyment without the sweat. So they buy slaves, where the women will permit it; where they will not, they make the wind, the tide, the waterfall, the steam, the cloud, the lightning, do the work, by every art and device their cunningest brain can achieve.

August 24?, 1847

We go to Europe to see aristocratic society with as few abatements as possible. We go to be Americanized, to import what we can. This country has its proper glory, though now shrouded and unknown. We will let it shine. Patriotism is balderdash. Our side, our state, our town, is boyish enough. But it is true that every foot of soil has its proper quality, that the grape on either side of the same fence has its own flavor, and so every acre on the globe, every group of people, every point of climate, has its own moral meaning whereof it is the symbol. For such a patriotism let us stand. . . .

[September, 1847]

Not the phrenologist but the philosopher may well say, Let me see his brain, and I will tell you if he shall be poet, king, founder of cities, rich, magnetic, of a secure hand, of a scientific memory, a right classifier; or whether he shall be a bungler, driveler, unlucky, heavy and tedious.

It were to dispute against the sun, to deny this difference of brain. I see well enough that when I bring one man into an estate, he sees vague capabilities, what others might, could, would or should do with it. If I bring another, he sees what *he* should do with it. He appreciates the water-privilege, land fit for orchard, tillage, pasturage, wood-lot, cranberry-meadow; but just as easily he foresees all the means, all the steps of the process, and could lay his hand as readily on one as on another point in that series which opens the capability to the last point. The poet sees wishfully enough the result; the well-built head supplies all the steps, one as perfect as the other, in the series. Seeing this working head in him, it becomes to me as certain that he will have the direction of estates, as that there are estates. If we see tools in a magazine, as a file, an anchor, a plough, a pump, a paint-brush, a cider-press, a diving-bell, we can predict well enough their destination; and the man's associations, fortunes, love, hatred, residence, rank, the books he will buy, the roads he will traverse are predetermined in his organism. Men will need him, and he is rich and eminent by nature. That man cannot be too late or too early. Let him not hurry or hesitate. Though millions are already arrived, his seat is reserved. Though millions attend, they only multiply his friends and agents. It never troubles the Senator what multitudes crack the benches and bend the galleries to hear. He who understands the art of war, reckons the hostile battalions and cities, opportunities and spoils.

An aristocracy could not exist unless it were organic. Men are born to command, and — it is even so — "come into the world booted and spurred to ride." The blood royal never pays, we say. It obtains service, gifts, supplies, furtherance of all kinds from the love and joy of those who feel themselves honored by the service they render.

Dull people think it Fortune that makes one rich and another poor. Is it? Yes, but the fortune was earlier than they think, namely, in the balance or adjustment between devotion to what is agreeable today and the forecast of what will be valuable tomorrow.

From "Aristocracy"

October ?, 1847

Religion. — The Catholic religion respects masses of men and ages. If it elects, it is yet by millions, as when it divides the heathen and Christian. The Protestant, on the contrary, with its hateful "private judgment," brings parishes, families, and at last individual doctrinaires and schismatics, and, verily, at last, private gentlemen into play and notice, which to the gentle musing poet is to the last degree disagreeable. This of course their respective arts and artists must build and paint. The Catholic Church is ethnical, and every way superior. It is in harmony with Nature, which loves the race and ruins the individual. The Protestant has his pew, which of course is only the first step to a church for every individual citizen — a church apiece.

[*March?*, 1848]

There will be a new church founded on moral science; at first cold and naked, a babe in a manger again, the algebra and mathematics of ethical law, the church of men to come, without shawms, or psaltery, or sackbut; but it will have heaven and earth for its beams and rafters; science for symbol and illustration; it will fast enough gather beauty, music, picture, poetry. Was never stoicism so stern and exigent as this shall be. It shall send man home to his central solitude, shame these social, supplicating manners, and make him know that much of the time he must have himself to his friend. He shall expect no coöperation, he shall walk with no companion. The nameless Thought, the nameless Power, the superpersonal Heart, — he shall repose alone on that. . . .

From "Worship"

[*London, October 29?*, 1847]

I found at Liverpool, after a couple of days, a letter which had been seeking me, from Carlyle, addressed to "R. W. E. on the instant when he lands in England," conveying the heartiest welcome and urgent invitation to house and hearth. And finding that I should not be wanted for a week in the lecture rooms, I came down to London, on Monday, and at ten at night the door was opened to me by Jane Carlyle, and the man himself was behind her with a lamp in the hall. They were very little changed from their old selves of fourteen years ago (in August) when I left them at Craigenputtock. "Well," said Carlyle, "here we are, shovelled together again!" The floodgates of his talk are quickly opened, and the river is a plentiful stream. We had a wide talk that night until nearly one o'clock, and at breakfast next morning again. At noon or later we walked forth to Hyde Park, and the palaces, about two miles from here, to the National Gallery, and to the Strand, Carlyle melting all Westminster and London into his talk and laughter, as he goes. . . . An immense talker, and, altogether, as extraordinary in that as in his writing; I think even more so. . . . My few hours' discourse with him, long ago, in Scotland, gave me not enough knowledge of him; and I have now, at last, been taken by surprise by him.

He is not mainly a scholar, like the most of my acquaintances, but a very practical Scotchman, such as you would find in any saddler's or iron-dealer's shop, and then only accidentally and by a surprising addition the admirable scholar and writer he is. . . . He has, too, the strong religious tinge you sometimes find in burly people. That, and all his qualities, have a certain virulence, coupled though it be in his case with the utmost impatience of Christendom and Jewdom and all existing presentments of the good old story. He talks like a very unhappy man, — profoundly solitary, displeased and hindered by all men and things about him, and, biding his time, meditating how to undermine and explode the whole world of nonsense which torments him. He is obviously greatly respected by all sorts of people, understands his own value quite as well as Webster, of whom his behavior sometimes reminds me, and can see society on his own terms. . . .

To Lidian Emerson
Manchester, December 1, 1847

. . . Ah, perhaps you should see the tragic spectacles which these streets show, these Manchester and those Liverpool streets, by day and by night, to know how much of happiest circumstance, how much of safety, of dignity, and of opportunity belongs to us so easily that is ravished from this population. Woman is cheap and vile in England — it is tragical to see. Childhood, too, I see oftenest in the state of absolute beggary. My dearest little Edie, to tell you the truth, costs me many a penny, day by day. I cannot go up the street but I shall see some woman in rags with a little creature just of Edie's age and size, but in coarsest ragged clothes, and barefooted, stepping beside her, and I look curiously into *her* Edie's face, with some terror lest it should resemble *mine*, and the far-off Edie wins from me the halfpence for this near one. Bid Ellen and Edie thank God that they were born in New England, and bid them speak the truth and do the right forever and ever; and I hope they and theirs will not stand barefooted in the mud on a bridge in the rain all day to beg of passengers. But beggary is only the beginning and the sign of sorrow and evil here. . . .

To Lidian Emerson
London, March 8, 1848

. . . Ah, you still ask me for that unwritten letter always due, it seems, always unwritten, from year to year, by me to you, dear Lidian, — I fear too more widely true than you mean, — always due and unwritten by me to every sister and brother of the human race. I have only to say that I also bemoan myself daily for the same cause, that I cannot write this letter, that I have not stamina and constitution enough to mind the two functions of seraph and cherub — oh no, let me not use such great words, rather say that a photometer cannot be a stove. It must content you for the time, that I truly acknowledge a poverty of nature, and have really no proud defence at all to set up, but ill-health, puniness, and Stygian limitation. . . .

To Lidian Emerson
London, April 20, 1848

. . . You wrote me the kindest and best account of your reading in the precious file of letters. Your feeling was just and noble. And they deserved all you have said. For they came out of a heart which nature and destiny conspired to keep as inviolate, as are still those three children of whom you send me such happy accounts. But I am deeply gratified by your pleasure and sympathy in them. Ah, how we wander from goal to goal of our life, and often it seems as if one thread of consciousness did not tie the far parts together. Who am I that roam these desarts, and knew this and that in old years? But you should have seen Ellen. When she left this world, I valued everybody who had seen her, and disliked to meet those who had not. . . .

London, April, 1848

The objection, the loud denial, not less proves the reality and conquests of an idea than the friends and advocates it finds. Thus communism now is eagerly attacked,[7] and all its weak points acutely pointed out by British writers and talkers; which is all so much homage to the Idea, whose first inadequate expressions interest them so deeply, and with which they feel their fate to be mingled. If the French should set out to prove that three was four, would British journalism bestir itself to contradict them? The Geologic Society and the Stock Exchange would have no time to spare it.

London, April, 1848

For the matter of Socialism, there are no oracles. The oracle is dumb. When we would pronounce anything truly of man, we retreat instantly on the individual. We are authorized to say much on the destinies of one, nothing on those of many. . . .

[7] British conservatives were alarmed at the French revolution abroad, in which socialists were active, and at Chartist agitations at home. A much-feared demonstration in London, imminent as Emerson wrote, turned out to be a fiasco.

London, April 6?, 1848

People here expect a revolution. There will be no revolution, none that deserves to be called so. There may be a scramble for money. But as all the people we see want the things we now have, and not better things, it is very certain that they will, under whatever change of forms, keep the old system. When I see changed men, I shall look for a changed world. Whoever is skilful in heaping money now will be skilful in heaping money again. . . .

There must be a relation between power and probity. We seem already to have more [power] than we can be trusted with. And this preparation for a superior race is a higher omen of revolution than any other I have seen. Except to better men, the augmented science is a mere chemic experiment of the quickest poison.

What wrong road have we taken that all the improvements of machinery have helped everybody but the operative? Him they have incurably hurt.

London, May?, 1848

I saw Tennyson, first, at the house of Coventry Patmore, where we dined together. His friend Brookfield was also of the party. I was contented with him, at once. He is tall, scholastic-looking, no dandy, but a great deal of plain strength about him, and though cultivated, quite unaffected; quiet, sluggish sense and strength, refined, as all English are, and good-humored. The print of his head in Horne's book is too rounded and handsome. There is in him an air of general superiority, that is very satisfactory. He lives very much with his college set, — Spedding, Brookfield, Hallam, Rice, and the rest, — and has the air of one who is accustomed to be petted and indulged by those he lives with, like George Bradford. Take away Hawthorne's bashfulness, and let him talk easily and fast, and you would have a pretty good Tennyson. . . .

Carlyle describes him as staying in London through a course of eight o'clock dinners every night for months until he is thoroughly fevered: then, notice is given to one of his friends, as lately to Aubrey de Vere, who has a fine estate in Ireland, thirty miles from Limerick, to come and carry him off bodily. Tennyson had capitulated, on three conditions: first, that he should not hear anything about Irish distress; second, that he should not come downstairs to breakfast; third, that he might smoke in the house. I think these were the three. So poor Tennyson, who had been in the worst way, but had not force enough to choose where to go, and so sat still, was now disposed of.

Tennyson was in plain black suit and wears glasses. Carlyle thinks him the best man in England to smoke a pipe with, and used to see him much; had a place in his little garden, on the wall, where Tennyson's pipe was laid up. He has other brothers, I believe, besides Tennyson Turner, the elder; and, I remember, Carlyle told me with glee some story of one of them, who looked like Alfred, and whom some friend, coming in, found lying on the sofa and addressed him, "Ah, Alfred, I am glad to see you," and he said, "I am not Alfred, I am Septimus; I am the most morbid of all the Tennysons."

I suppose he is self-indulgent and a little spoiled and selfish by the warm and universal favor he has found. Lady Duff Gordon told me that the first day she saw him he lay his whole length on the carpet, and rolled himself to her feet and said, "Will you please to put your feet on me for a stool." Coventry Patmore described him as very capricious and as once spending the evening with a dozen friends, "not, to be sure, his equals, but as nearly his equals as any that could be collected." Yet Tennyson would not say a word, but sat with his pipe, silent, and at last said, "I am going to Cheltenham; I have had a glut of men." When he himself proposed, one day, to read Tennyson a poem which he had just finished, that Tennyson might tell him of anything which his taste would exclude, Tennyson replied, "Mr. Patmore, you can have no idea how many applications of this sort are made to me." . . .

※ ※

Concord, August ?, 1848

After much experience, we find literature the best thing, and men of thought, if still thinking, the best company. I went to England, and after allowing myself freely to be dazzled by the various brilliancy of men of talent; — in calm hours, I found myself no way helped, my sequins were all yellow leaves. I said, I have valued days, and must still, by the number of clear insights I get, and I must estimate my company so. Then I found I had scarcely had a good conversation, a solid dealing man with man, in England. Only in such passages is a reason for human life given; and every such meeting puts a mortal affront on kings and governments, by showing them to be of no account. Of course, these people, these and no others, interest us, — the dear and beautiful beings, who are absorbed in their own dream. Let us, then, have that told: let us have a record of friendship among six, or four, or two, if there be only two, of those who delight in each other only because both delight in the Eternal laws: who forgive nothing to each other: who, by their joy and homage to these laws, are made incapable of conceit, which destroys the fine wits. Any other affection between men than this geometric one of relation to the same thing is a mere mush of materialism.

November, 1848

. . . Cram people with your books, furnish them with a constant river of books and journals, and you may be sure they will remember as little as if they read none.

July, 1849

I think, if I were professor of Rhetoric, — teacher of the art of writing well to young men, — I should use Dante for my textbook. Come hither, youth, and learn how the brook that flows at the bottom of your garden, or the farmer who ploughs the adjacent field, your father and mother, your debts and credits, and your web of habits are the very best basis of poetry, and the material which you must work up. Dante knew how to throw the weight of his body into each act, and is, like Byron, Burke, and Carlyle, the Rhetorician. I find him full of the *nobil volgare eloquenza;* [8] that he knows "God damn," and can be rowdy if he please, and he does please. Yet is not Dante reason or illumination and that essence we were looking for, but only a new exhibition of the possibilities of genius. Here is an imagination that rivals in closeness and precision the senses. But we must prize him as we do a rainbow, we can appropriate nothing of him.

Summer, 1867

. . . But Dante still appears to me, as ever, an exceptional mind, a prodigy of imaginative function, executive rather than contemplative or wise. . . . Undeniable force of a peculiar kind, a prodigy, but not like Shakespeare, or Socrates, or Goethe, a beneficent humanity. His fames and infamies are so capriciously distributed, — what odd reasons for putting his men in inferno! The somnambulic genius of Dante is dream strengthened to the tenth power, — dream so fierce that it grasps all the details of the phan-

8 Noble eloquence of the people.

tom spectacle, and, in spite of itself, clutches and conveys them into the waking memory, and can recite what every other would forget. What pitiless minuteness of horrible details! He is a curiosity like the mastodon, but one would not desire such for friends and contemporaries, abnormal throughout like Swedenborg. But at a frightful cost these obtain their fame. Dante a man to put in a museum, but not in your house. Indeed I never read him, nor regret that I do not.

September ?, 1849

. . . it seems as if this Plato's power of grading or ranking all that offers itself at sight was as good as a duration of a thousand years. The reason why life is short is, because we are confounded by the dazzle of new things, and by the seeming equality which custom sheds on great and small, and we are obliged to spend a large part of life in corrections which we should save, if our judgment was sure when we first beheld things. Plato is like those tamers who have charmed down the ferocity of vicious animals, or who by some virulence or ferocity in their own nature have terrified frantic madmen. He looks through things at a glance, and they fly into place, and he walks in life with the security of a god. It seems as if the winds of ages swept through this universal thinking, so wide, so just, yet so minute, that it is impossible that an air of such calmness and long maturity can belong to the hasty, crude, experimental blotting of one lifetime.

September ?, 1849

Today, carpets; yesterday, the aunts; the day before, the funeral of poor S.; and every day, the remembrance in the library of the rope of work which I must spin; — in this way life is dragged down and confuted. We try to listen to the hymn of gods, and must needs hear this perpetual *cock-a-doodle-doo*, and *ke-tar-kut* right under the library windows. They, the gods, ought to respect a life, you say, whose objects are their own. But steadily they throw mud and eggs at us, roll us in the dirt, and jump on us.

Autumn, 1849

For the skeptic, yes, we may give ourselves what allowance we will, for once admitted to the heaven of thought, we see no relapse into night, but infinite invitation on the other side. Heaven is within heaven, and sky over sky, and we are encompassed with divinities. To what purpose dark ages and barbarous Irish, if I know, as I know, five or six men, without hardly going out of my village, to whom and with whom all is possible, who restore to me Plato, Shakespeare, Montaigne, Hindu cosmology, yea, Buddh himself, with their audacious intellectual adventure? We are as elastic as the gas of gunpowder, and small and tame as we walk here with our hands in our pockets, an imaginative book sets free our fancy, and in a moment our head is bathed in the galaxy, and our feet tread on the hells. Our indeterminate size is the delicious secret which books of imagination reveal to us.

O endless ends, O living child! how can you fail! To you I open the ill-kept secret that you are Hari, divine and invincible, — cousin to the four elements and the four hundred gods. . . . It is time you should show yourself. Fate is in your eye. You will yet be a horse, a lizard, a dragonfly, and a swamp full of alligators, but time and space are cheap to you, Hari; you can afford to be multiplied and divided, to bite and to be bitten, to be a bankrupt tradesman, or an acre of sand; divided you will reunite, and you thrive by dying; do not care, O Hari, for the speech of men, do not care for a shabby appearance!

December, 1849

Culture, the height of culture, highest behavior consist in the identification of the Ego with the universe, so that when a man says I think, I hope, I find, — he might properly say, the human race thinks, hopes, finds, he states a fact which commands the understandings and affections of all the company, and yet, at the same time, he shall be able continually to keep sight of his biographical Ego, — I had an ague, I had a fortune; my father had black hair, etc., as rhetoric, fun, or footman, to his grand and public Ego, without impertinence or ever confounding them.

January, 1850

The two Statements, or Bipolarity. — My geometry cannot span the extreme points which I see.

I affirm melioration, — which Nature teaches in pears, in the domesticated animals, and in her secular geology and this development of complex races. I affirm also the self-equality of Nature; or that only that is true which is always true; and that, in California, or in Greece, or in Jewry, or in Arcadia, existed the same amounts of private power, as now, and the same deductions, however differently distributed. But I cannot reconcile these two statements. I affirm the sacredness of the individual, the infinite reliance that may be put on his determination. I see also the benefits of cities, and the plausibility of phalansteries. But I cannot reconcile these oppositions.

I affirm the divinity of man; but as I know well how much is my debt to bread and coffee and flannel and heated room, I shun to be Tartuffe, and do affirm also with emphasis the value of these fomentations. But I cannot reconcile that absolute with this conditional. . . .

Winter, 1850

The English journals snub my new book; [9] as, indeed, they have all its foregoers. Only now they say that this has less vigor and originality than the others. Where, then, was the degree of merit that entitled my books to their notice? They have never admitted the claims of either of them. The fate of my books is like the impression of my face. My acquaintances, as long back as I can remember, have always said, "Seems to me you look a little thinner than when I saw you last."

February, 1850

Superlative. — The talent sucks the substance of the man. How often we repeat the disappointment of inferring general ability from conspicuous particular ability. But the accumulation on one point has drained the trunk. Blessed are those who have no talent! The expressors are the gods of the world, — Shakespeare and the rest, — but the same men whom these expressors revere are the solid, balanced, undemonstrative citizens who make the reserved guard, the central sense of the world.

'Tis because he is not well mixed that he needs to do some feat by way of fine or expiation.

April, 1850

The badness of the times is making death attractive.

To Lidian Emerson

St. Louis, June 16, 1850

. . . Cairo, you know, is a tongue of low land which separates the Ohio and Mississippi. Many years ago it was seized upon by speculators as a point that must necessarily be a depot of immense importance. The land for ten miles from the point was bought and lots were laid out and the biggest city of the world was to

[9] *Representative Men.*

be here. The Rothschilds are or have been owners or mortgagees of the property. But the river during a large part of the year keeps the whole of it under water, and the houses that were built by the Companies are now wide open to every pedlar and boatman to enter and take possession, if he will. The only habitable place seemed to be (what is often seen in these rivers) an old steamboat whose engine has been taken out and the boat moored and fitted up into the dirtiest of Ann-street boarding-houses. Here we took in wood, and tinkered at our engine — an operation, this last, almost as frequent in my recent experience as the first. The boats are very cheaply and poorly built, no "palaces" at all, just made to keep above water from port to port, and generally disabled of one wheel. Well, we got away from Cairo, its sailor-shops, tenpin-alleys, and faro-tables, still on the green and almost transparent Ohio, which now seemed so broad that the yellow line in front for which we were steering, looked hopelessly narrow; but [the] yellow line widened as we drew nigh, and at last we reached and crossed the perfectly-marked line of green on one side, and mud-hue on the other, and entered the Mississippi. It is one of the great river landscapes of the world — wide, wide eddying waters, low shores. The great river takes in the Ohio which had grown so large, turns it all to its own mud color, and does not become perceptibly larger.

The great sweeps of the Mississippi, the number of its large islands made and unmade in short periods, your distance from either shore, and the unvarying character of the green wilderness on either side from hour to hour, from day to day, — the loneliest river — no towns, no houses, no dents in the forest, no boats almost, — we met I believe but one steam-boat in the first hundred miles; — now and then we notice a flat wood-boat lying under the shore, blow our whistle, ring our bell, and near the land then out of some log-shed appear black or white men, and hastily put out their boat, a large mud-scow, loaded with corded wood. "How do you sell your wood?" cries the captain. "A dollar and a half." "Well, uncle, you'll help the men." So the scow is made fast to the boat, which immediately puts on steam again, and both go up the river amicably, till the negroes and sailors have got all the wood on board; then the scow is let go, and floats down stream home again. . . . Then there were planters traveling, one with his family of slaves (6 blacks); peaceable-looking, farmer-like men who, when they stretch themselves in the pauses of conversation, disclose the butts of their pistols in their breast-pockets.

Then a knot of gamblers playing quite ostentatiously on the cabin-tables, and large sums changing owners rapidly, and, as we Yankees fancied, with some glances of hope aimed at us that we should sit down with these amiable gentlemen who professed to be entire strangers to each other, and, if asked any question respecting the river, "had never been on these waters before." . . .

September, 1850

Yesterday took that secluded Marlboro' road with Channing in a wagon. Every rock was painted "Marlboro'," and we proposed to take the longest day in the year and ride to Marlboro', — that flying Italy. We went to Willis's Pond in Sudbury and paddled across it, and took a swim in its water, colored like sugar-baker's molasses. Nature, Ellery thought, is less interesting. Yesterday Thoreau told me it was more so, and persons less. I think it must always combine with man. Life is ecstatical, and we radiate joy and honor and gloom on the days and landscapes we converse with.

But I must remember a real or imagined period in my youth when they who spoke to me of Nature were religious, and made it so, and made it deep: now it is to the young sentimentalists frippery, and a milliner's shop has as much reason and worth.

February, 1851

The difference between Americans and English in the love of money, is, that, in the first, ambition unites with it, and they mean to be powerful, as well as rich. But nothing can be more foolish than this reproach, which goes from nation to nation, of the love of dollars. It is like oxen taxing each other with eating grass, or a society of borers in an oak tree accusing one another of eating wood; or, in a great society of cheese-mites, if one should begin making insinuations that the other was eating cheese.

February, 1851

Women carry sail, and men rudders. Women look very grave sometimes, and effect to steer, but their pretended rudder is only a masked sail. The rudder of the rudder is not there.

February, 1851

Genial heat. Imagination. — There is and must be a little air-chamber, a sort of tiny Bedlam in even the naturalist's or mathe-matician's brain who arrives at great results. They affect a sticking to facts; they repudiate all imagination and affection, as they would disown stealing. But Cuvier, Oken, Geoffroy Saint-Hilaire, Owen, Agassiz, Audubon, must all have this spark of fanaticism. . . . If you have never so much faculty of detail without this explosive gas, it makes the Dr. Prichards and Dr. Worcesters and Dr. Warrens, men that hold hard to facts, Dr. Dryasdusts, the most tedious and dreaded of mankind. But add this fanaticism, and you have Buffons and Davys. . . .

June?, 1851

Wealth. — The world is babyish, and the use of wealth is: it is made a toy. Men of sense esteem wealth to be the assimilation of Nature to themselves, the converting the sap and juices of the planet to the nutriment and incarnation of their design. Power is what they want, not candy, and they will pay any prices. Power for what? Power to execute their idea, — which, in any well-constituted man, of course, appears the end to which the universe exists and all its resources might be well applied. Each of the elm trees that you see over the land sends its roots far and wide; every great one to some river or watercourse; its roots will run a mile; and the education of each vascular man goes on well in proportion as his masculine roots draw from all the natures around him their tribute.

May, 1851

This floor holds us up by a fight with agencies that go to pull us down. The whole world is a series of balanced antagonisms.

[May?, 1851]

Every god is there sitting in his sphere. The young mortal enters the hall of the firmament; there is he alone with them alone, they pouring on him benedictions and gifts, and beckoning him up to their thrones. On the instant, and incessantly, fall snow-storms of illusions. He fancies himself in a vast crowd which sways this way and that and whose movement and doings he must obey: he fancies himself poor, orphaned, insignificant. The mad crowd drives hither and thither, now furiously commanding this thing to be done, now that. What is he that he should resist their will, and think or act for himself? Every moment new changes and new showers of deceptions to baffle and distract him. And when, by and by, for an instant, the air clears and the cloud lifts a little, there are the gods still sitting around him on their thrones, — they alone with him alone.   *From "Illusions"*

Summer, 1851

The ancients most truly and poetically represented the incarnation or descent into Nature of Pythagoras, his condescension to be born, as his first virtue.

It is indeed a perilous adventure, this serious act of venturing into mortality, swimming in a sea strewn with wrecks, where none indeed go undamaged. It is as bad as going to Congress; none comes back innocent.

Those who conquer, — the victory was born with them. They may well be serene. They seem to fight, but their lives are insured and their victories. You like better to hear what they say. Well you may, for they announce this success in every syllable.

As Vishnu in the Vedas pursues Maya in all forms, . . . so our metaphysics should be able to follow the flying force through all transformations, and name the new pair, identical through all variety. For Memory, Imagination, Reason, Sense are only masks of one power, as physical and spiritual laws are only new phases of limitation. The poet is the lover loving; the critic is the lover advised.

For the rest of man remains only the stoic resignation. They bridge up by their dying bodies the path of their successors. They are the corallines who make the new world, theater of new Redemption, and find their wages in an immense faith. . . .

[*August ?, 1851*]

Autobiography. — I am never beaten until I know that I am beaten. I meet powerful, brutal people to whom I have no skill to reply. They think they have defeated me. It is so published in society, in the journals; I am defeated in this fashion, in all men's sight, perhaps on a dozen different lines. My ledger may show that I am in debt, cannot yet make my ends meet and vanquish the enemy so. My race may not be prospering; we are sick, ugly, obscure, unpopular. My children may be worsted. I seem to fail in my friends and clients, too. That is to say, in all the encounters that have yet chanced, I have not been weaponed for that particular occasion, and have been historically beaten; and yet I know all the time that I have never been beaten; have never yet fought, shall certainly fight when my hour comes, and shall beat.   *From "Worship"*

August ?, 1851

Alcott thinks the American mind a little superior to English, German, Greek, or any other. It is a very amiable opinion and deserves encouragement; and certainly that is best which recommends his home and the present hour to every man.

Shall I say it has the confirmation of having been held of his own country by every son of Adam?

June 1, 1852

The belief of some of our friends in their duration suggests one of those musty householders who keep every broomstick and old grate, put in a box every old tooth that falls out of their heads, preserve [the] ancient frippery of their juvenile wardrobe, and they think God saves all the old souls which he has used up. What does he save them for?

June, 1852

. . . There is such an obvious accumulation of dexterity in the use of tools in the old scholar and thinker that it is not to be believed Nature will be such a spendthrift as to sponge all this out, like figures from a slate. . . .

Spring ?, 1855

A man of thought is willing to die, willing to live; I suppose because he has seen the thread on which the beads are strung, and perceived that it reaches up and down, existing quite independently of the present illusions. A man of affairs is afraid to die, is pestered with terrors, because he has not this vision. Yet the first cannot explain it to the second.

July, 1855

Sleepy Hollow.[1] — The blazing evidence of immortality is our dissatisfaction with any other solution.

All great natures love stability.

Our fear of death is like our fear that summer will be short, but when we have had our swing of pleasure, our fill of fruit, and our swelter of heat, we say we have had our day; and rest of brain and affection please.

[1] Cemetery at Concord.

June, 1852

Miss Bridge, a mantuamaker in Concord, became a "Medium," and gave up her old trade for this new one; and is to charge a pistareen a spasm, and nine dollars for a fit. This is the Rat-revelation, the gospel that comes by taps in the wall, and thumps in the table-drawer. The spirits make themselves of no reputation. They are rats and mice of society. And one of the demure disciples of the rat-tat-too, the other day, remarked that "this, like every other communication from the spiritual world, began very low." It was not ill said; for Christianity began in a manger, and the knuckle dispensation in a rat-hole.

July 6, 1852

The head of Washington hangs in my dining-room for a few days past, and I cannot keep my eyes off of it. It has a certain Appalachian strength, as if it were truly the first-fruits of America, and expressed the country. The heavy, leaden eyes turn on you, as the eyes of an ox in a pasture. And the mouth has a gravity and depth of quiet, as if this MAN had absorbed all the serenity of America, and left none for his restless, rickety, hysterical countrymen. Noble, aristocratic head, with all kinds of elevation in it, that come out by turns. Such majestical ironies, as he hears the day's politics, at table. We imagine him hearing the letter of General Cass, the letter of General Scott, the letter of Mr. Pierce,[2] the effronteries of Mr. Webster recited. This man listens like a god to these low conspirators.

July, 1852

A man avails much to us, like a point of departure to the seaman, or his stake and stones to the surveyor. I am my own man more than most men, yet the loss of a few persons would be most impoverishing; — a few persons who give flesh to what were, else, mere thoughts, and which now I am not at liberty to slight, or in any manner treat as fictions. It were too much to say that the Platonic world I might have learned to treat as cloud-land, had I not known Alcott, who is a native of that country, yet I will say that he makes it as solid as Massachusetts to me; and Thoreau gives me, in flesh and blood and pertinacious Saxon belief, my own ethics. He is far more real, and daily practically obeying them, than I; and fortifies my memory at all times with an affirmative experience which refuses to be set aside.

---

[2] Respectively, a Democratic politician, the Whig candidate for President in 1852, the Democratic candidate.

July, 1852

I live a good while and acquire as much skill in literature as an old carpenter does in wood. It occurs, then, what pity! that now, when you know something, have at least learned so much good omission, your organs should fail you; your eyes, health, fire, and zeal of work, should decay daily. Then I remember that it is the mind of the world which is the good carpenter, the good scholar, sailor, or blacksmith, thousand-handed, versatile, all-applicable, in all these indifferent channels entering with wild vigor, excited by novelty, in that untried channel, confined by dikes of pedantry; works out the proper results of that to the end, and surprises all with perfect consent, *alter et idem*,[3] to every other excellence; lexicography or Aristotelian logic being found consentaneous with music, with astronomy, with roses, with love. In you, this rich soul has peeped, despite your horny, muddy eyes, at books and poetry. Well, it took you up, and showed you something to the purpose; that there was something there. Look, look, old mole! there, straight up before you, is the magnificent Sun. If only for the instant, you see it. Well, in this way it educates the youth of the universe; in this way warms, suns, refines every particle; then it drops the little channel or canal, through which the Life rolled beatific, like a fossil to the ground, thus touched and educated, by a moment of sunshine, to be the fairer material for future channels and canals, through which the old Glory shall dart again, in new directions, until the Universe shall have been shot through and through, *tilled* with light. "Saxon self-disparagement" — yes, it is rather wider, rather a human trick, but there remain unbroken by our defects the old laws, upspringing like the arch of the sky, or like sunlight, which all the wind in the universe cannot blow away; high, old laws, round, unremovable; self-executing; it is noble, it is poetic, and makes poets, only to have seen them, — to have computed their curve. . . .

July, 1852

Souls with a certain quantity of light are in excess, and irrevocably belong to the moral class, — what animal force they may retain, to the contrary, notwithstanding. Souls with less light, it is chemically impossible that they be moral, — what talent or good they have, to the contrary, notwithstanding; and these belong to the world of Fate, or animal good: the youth of the universe; not yet twenty-one; not yet voters; not yet robed in the *toga virilis*.[4]

[3] The same yet different.   [4] Toga of manhood.

Nor is it permitted to any soul, of the free or of the apprentice class, that is, to the free, or to the fated, to cast a vote for the other. The world wants so much alum, and so much saccharine; so much iron, and so much hemp; so much paper, and so much mahogany: nor could any rebellion or arbitrament be suffered in its atoms, without chaos: if a particle of lead were to prefer to mask its properties, and exert the energies of cork or of vitriol; if coal should undertake to be a lemon; or feathers, turpentine; we should have a pretty ruin, to be sure.

But the laws use azote, oxygen, carbon, lime, magnesia, and so forth, as their means; and these very excesses and defects in you, these determinations to the moral or the animal, are the very means by which high Nature works, and cannot afford to want. Be her footmen, her Fates, her couriers, muses, and angels.

To Caroline Sturgis Tappan

July 22, 1853

. . . Friends are few, thoughts are few, facts few — only one; one only fact, now tragically, now tenderly, now exultingly illustrated in sky, in earth, in men and women, Fate, Fate. The universe is all chemistry, with a certain hint of a magnificent *Whence* or *Whereto* gilding or opalizing every angle of the old salt-acid acid-salt, endlessly reiterated and masqueraded through all time and space and form. The addition of that hint everywhere, saves things. Heavy and loathsome is the bounded world, bounded everywhere. An immense Boston or Hanover Street with mountains of ordinary women, trains and trains of mean, leathern men all immoveably bounded, no liquidity of hope or genius. But they are made chemically good, like oxen. In the absence of religion, they are polarized to decorum, which is its blockhead;[5] — thrown mechanically into parallelism with the high *Whence* and *Whither*, which makes mountains of rubbish reflect the morning sun and the evening star. And we all are privy counsellors to that Hint which homeopathically doses the system, and can co-operate with the slow and secular escape of these oxen and semi-oxen from their quadruped estate, and invite them to be men and hail them such. I do not know — now that Stoicism and Christianity have for two millenniums preached liberty, somewhat fulsomely — but it is the turn of Fatalism. And it has great conveniences for a public creed. Fatalism, foolish and flippant, is as bad as Unitarianism or Mormonism. But Fatalism held by an intelli-

5 The wooden head on which a hat was shaped.

gent soul who knows how to humor and obey the infinitesimal pulses of spontaneity, is by much the truest theory in use. All the great would call their thought fatalism, or concede that ninety-nine parts are nature and one part power, though that hundredth is elastic, miraculous, and, whenever it is in energy, dissolving all the rest.

Fate

Delicate omens traced in air,
To the lone bard true witness bare;
Birds with auguries on their wings
Chanted undeceiving things,
Him to beckon, him to warn;
Well might then the poet scorn
To learn of scribe or courier
Hints writ in vaster character;
And on his mind, at dawn of day,
Soft shadows of the evening lay.
For the prevision is allied
Unto the thing so signified;
Or say, the foresight that awaits
Is the same Genius that creates.

IT chanced during one winter a few years ago, that our cities were bent on discussing the theory of the Age. By an odd coincidence, four or five noted men were each reading a discourse to the citizens of Boston or New York, on the Spirit of the Times. It so happened that the subject had the same prominence in some remarkable pamphlets and journals issued in London in the same season. To me, however, the question of the times resolved itself into a practical question of the conduct of life. How shall I live? We are incompetent to solve the times. Our geometry cannot span the huge orbits of the prevailing ideas, behold their return and reconcile their opposition. We can only obey our own polarity. 'Tis fine for us to speculate and elect our course, if we must accept an irresistible dictation.

In our first steps to gain our wishes we come upon immovable limitations. We are fired with the hope to reform men. After many experiments we find that we must begin earlier, — at school. But the boys and girls are not docile; we can make nothing of them. We decide that they are not of good stock. We must be-

gin our reform earlier still, — at generation: that is to say, there
is Fate, or laws of the world.

But if there be irresistible dictation, this dictation understands
itself. If we must accept Fate, we are not less compelled to affirm
liberty, the significance of the individual, the grandeur of duty,
the power of character. This is true, and that other is true. But
our geometry cannot span these extreme points and reconcile
them. What to do? By obeying each thought frankly, by harping,
or, if you will, pounding on each string, we learn at last its power.
By the same obedience to other thoughts we learn theirs, and then
comes some reasonable hope of harmonizing them. We are sure
that, though we know not how, necessity does comport with liberty, the individual with the world, my polarity with the spirit of
the times. The riddle of the age has for each a private solution.
If one would study his own time, it must be by this method of
taking up in turn each of the leading topics which belong to our
scheme of human life, and by firmly stating all that is agreeable
to experience on one, and doing the same justice to the opposing
facts in the others, the true limitations will appear. Any excess of
emphasis on one part would be corrected, and a just balance would
be made.

But let us honestly state the facts. Our America has a bad
name for superficialness. Great men, great nations, have not been
boasters and buffoons, but perceivers of the terror of life, and have
manned themselves to face it. The Spartan, embodying his religion in his country, dies before its majesty without a question.
The Turk, who believes his doom is written on the iron leaf in the
moment when he entered the world, rushes on the enemy's
saber with undivided will. The Turk, the Arab, the Persian, accepts the foreordained fate: —

> "On two days, it steads not to run from thy grave,
>   The appointed, and the unappointed day;
> On the first, neither balm nor physician can save,
>   Nor thee, on the second, the Universe slay."

The Hindu under the wheel is as firm. Our Calvinists in the last
generation had something of the same dignity. They felt that the
weight of the Universe held them down to their place. What
could *they* do? Wise men feel that there is something which cannot be talked or voted away, — a strap or belt which girds the
world: —

"The Destinee, ministre general,
That executeth in the world over al,
The purveiance that God hath seen beforne,
So strong it is, that though the world had sworne
The contrary of a thing by yea or nay,
Yet sometime it shall fallen on a day
That falleth not oft in a thousand yeer;
For certainly, our appetités here,
Be it of warre, or pees, or hate, or love,
All this is ruled by the sight above."
CHAUCER: *The Knighte's Tale*.

The Greek Tragedy expressed the same sense. "Whatever is fated that will take place. The great immense mind of Jove is not to be transgressed."

Savages cling to a local god of one tribe or town. The broad ethics of Jesus were quickly narrowed to village theologies, which preach an election or favoritism. And now and then an amiable parson, like Jung Stilling or Robert Huntington, believes in a pistareen-Providence, which, whenever the good man wants a dinner, makes that somebody shall knock at his door and leave a half-dollar. But Nature is no sentimentalist, — does not cosset or pamper us. We must see that the world is rough and surly, and will not mind drowning a man or a woman, but swallows your ship like a grain of dust. The cold, inconsiderate of persons, tingles your blood, benumbs your feet, freezes a man like an apple. The diseases, the elements, fortune, gravity, lightning, respect no persons. The way of Providence is a little rude. The habit of snake and spider, the snap of the tiger and other leapers and bloody jumpers, the crackle of the bones of his prey in the coil of the anaconda, — these are in the system, and our habits are like theirs. You have just dined, and however scrupulously the slaughter-house is concealed in the graceful distance of miles, there is complicity, expensive races, — race living at the expense of race. The planet is liable to shocks from comets, perturbations from planets, rendings from earthquake and volcano, alterations of climate, precessions of equinoxes. Rivers dry up by opening of the forest. The sea changes its bed. Towns and counties fall into it. At Lisbon an earthquake killed men like flies. At Naples three years ago ten thousand persons were crushed in a few minutes. The scurvy at sea, the sword of the climate in the west of Africa, at Cayenne, at Panama, at New Orleans, cut off men like a massacre. Our western prairie shakes with fever and ague. The cholera, the small-pox, have proved as mortal to some tribes as a frost to the crickets, which, having filled the summer with noise, are silenced by a fall of the temperature of one night. Without uncovering what does not concern us, or counting how many species of parasites hang on a bombyx,[6] or groping after intestinal parasites or infusory biters, or the obscurities of alternate generation, — the forms of the shark, the *labrus*,[7] the jaw of the sea-wolf paved with crushing teeth, the weapons of the grampus, and other warriors hidden in the sea, are hints of ferocity in the interiors of nature. Let us not deny it up and down. Providence has a wild, rough, incalculable road to its end, and it is of no use to try to whitewash its huge, mixed instrumentalities, or to dress up that terrific benefactor in a clean shirt and white neckcloth of a student in divinity.

Will you say, the disasters which threaten mankind are exceptional, and one need not lay his account for cataclysms every day? Aye, but what happens once may happen again, and so long as these strokes are not to be parried by us they must be feared.

But these shocks and ruins are less destructive to us than the stealthy power of other laws which act on us daily. An expense of ends to means is fate; — organization tyrannizing over character. The menagerie, or forms and powers of the spine, is a book of fate; the bill of the bird, the skull of the snake, determines tyrannically its limits. So is the scale of races, of temperaments; so is sex; so is climate; so is the reaction of talents imprisoning the vital power in certain directions. Every spirit makes its house; but afterwards the house confines the spirit.

The gross lines are legible to the dull; the cabman is phrenologist so far, he looks in your face to see if his shilling is sure. A dome of brow denotes one thing, a pot-belly another; a squint, a pugnose, mats of hair, the pigment of the epidermis, betray character. People seem sheathed in their tough organization. Ask Spurzheim,[8] ask the doctors, ask Quetelet[9] if temperaments decide nothing? — or if there be anything they do not decide? Read the description in medical books of the four temperaments and you will think you are reading your own thoughts which you had not yet told. Find the part which black eyes and which blue eyes play severally in the company. How shall a man escape from his ancestors, or draw off from his veins the black drop which he drew from his father's or his mother's life? It often appears in a family as if all the qualities of the progenitors were potted in several jars,

[6] Moth of the silkworm.
[7] Species of predatory fish.
[8] Phrenologist.　　　　　[9] Statistician.

—some ruling quality in each son or daughter of the house; and sometimes the unmixed temperament, the rank unmitigated elixir, the family vice is drawn off in a separate individual and the others are proportionally relieved. We sometimes see a change of expression in our companion and say his father or his mother comes to the windows of his eyes, and sometimes a remote relative. In different hours a man represents each of several of his ancestors, as if there were seven or eight of us rolled up in each man's skin, — seven or eight ancestors at least; and they constitute the variety of notes for that new piece of music which his life is. At the corner of the street you read the possibility of each passenger in the facial angle, in the complexion, in the depth of his eye. His parentage determines it. Men are what their mothers made them. You may as well ask a loom which weaves huckabuck why it does not make cashmere, as expect poetry from this engineer, or a chemical discovery from that jobber. Ask the digger in the ditch to explain Newton's laws; the fine organs of his brain have been pinched by overwork and squalid poverty from father to son for a hundred years. When each comes forth from his mother's womb, the gate of gifts closes behind him. Let him value his hands and feet, he has but one pair. So he has but one future, and that is already predetermined in his lobes and described in that little fatty face, pig-eye, and squat form. All the privilege and all the legislation of the world cannot meddle or help to make a poet or a prince of him.

Jesus said, "When he looketh on her, he hath committed adultery." But he is an adulterer before he has yet looked on the woman, by the superfluity of animal and the defect of thought in his constitution. Who meets him, or who meets her, in the street, sees that they are ripe to be each other's victim.

In certain men digestion and sex absorb the vital force, and the stronger these are, the individual is so much weaker. The more of these drones perish, the better for the hive. If, later, they give birth to some superior individual, with force enough to add to this animal a new aim and a complete apparatus to work it out, all the ancestors are gladly forgotten. Most men and most women are merely one couple more. Now and then one has a new cell or camarilla opened in his brain, — an architectural, a musical, or a philological knack; some stray taste or talent for flowers, or chemistry, or pigments, or story-telling; a good hand for drawing, a good foot for dancing, an athletic frame for wide journeying, etc. — which skill nowise alters rank in the scale of nature, but serves to pass the time; the life of sensation going on as before. At last these hints and tendencies are fixed in one or in a succession. Each absorbs so much food and force as to become itself a new center. The new talent draws off so rapidly the vital force that not enough remains for the animal functions, hardly enough for health; so that in the second generation, if the like genius appear, the health is visibly deteriorated and the generative force impaired.

People are born with the moral or with the material bias; — uterine brothers with this diverging destination; and I suppose, with high magnifiers, Mr. Frauenhofer or Dr. Carpenter might come to distinguish in the embryo, at the fourth day, — this is a Whig, and that a Free-soiler.

It was a poetic attempt to lift this mountain of Fate, to reconcile this despotism of race with liberty, which led the Hindus to say, "Fate is nothing but the deeds committed in a prior state of existence." I find the coincidence of the extremes of Eastern and Western speculation in the daring statement of Schelling,[1] "There is in every man a certain feeling that he has been what he is from all eternity, and by no means became such in time." To say it less sublimely, — in the history of the individual is always an account of his condition, and he knows himself to be a party to his present estate.

A good deal of our politics is physiological. Now and then a man of wealth in the heyday of youth adopts the tenet of broadest freedom. In England there is always some man of wealth and large connection, planting himself, during all his years of health, on the side of progress, who, as soon as he begins to die, checks his forward play, calls in his troops and becomes conservative. All conservatives are such from personal defects. They have been effeminated by position or nature, born halt and blind, through luxury of their parents, and can only, like invalids, act on the defensive. But strong natures, backwoodsmen, New Hampshire giants, Napoleons, Burkes, Broughams, Websters, Kossuths, are inevitable patriots, until their life ebbs and their defects and gout, palsy and money, warp them.

The strongest idea incarnates itself in majorities and nations, in the healthiest and strongest. Probably the election goes by avoirdupois weight, and if you could weigh bodily the tonnage of any hundred of the Whig and the Democratic party in a town on the Dearborn balance, as they passed the hay-scales, you could predict with certainty which party would carry it. On the whole it

[1] German Idealistic philosopher.

would be rather the speediest way of deciding the vote, to put the selectmen or the mayor and aldermen at the hay-scales.

In science we have to consider two things: power and circumstance. All we know of the egg, from each successive discovery, is, *another vesicle*; and if, after five hundred years you get a better observer or a better glass, he finds, within the last observed, another. In vegetable and animal tissue it is just alike, and all that the primary power or spasm operates is still vesicles, vesicles. Yes, — but the tyrannical Circumstance! A vesicle in new circumstances, a vesicle lodged in darkness, Oken thought, became animal; in light, a plant. Lodged in the parent animal, it suffers changes which end in unsheathing miraculous capability in the unaltered vesicle, and it unlocks itself to fish, bird, or quadruped, head and foot, eye and claw. The Circumstance is Nature. Nature is what you may do. There is much you may not. We have two things, — the circumstance, and the life. Once we thought positive power was all. Now we learn that negative power, or circumstance, is half. Nature is the tyrannous circumstance, the thick skull, the sheathed snake, the ponderous, rock-like jaw; necessitated activity; violent direction; the conditions of a tool, like the locomotive, strong enough on its track, but which can do nothing but mischief off of it; or skates, which are wings on the ice but fetters on the ground.

The book of Nature is the book of Fate. She turns the gigantic pages, — leaf after leaf, — never re-turning one. One leaf she lays down, a floor of granite; then a thousand ages, and a bed of slate; a thousand ages, and a measure of coal; a thousand ages, and a layer of marl and mud: vegetable forms appear; her first misshapen animals, zoöphyte, trilobium, fish; then, saurians, — rude forms, in which she has only blocked her future statue, concealing under these unwieldy monsters the fine type of her coming king. The face of the planet cools and dries, the races meliorate, and man is born. But when a race has lived its term, it comes no more again.

The population of the world is a conditional population; not the best, but the best that could live now; and the scale of tribes, and the steadiness with which victory adheres to one tribe and defeat to another, is as uniform as the superposition of strata. We know in history what weight belongs to race. We see the English, French, and Germans planting themselves on every shore and market of America and Australia, and monopolizing the commerce of these countries. We like the nervous and victorious habit of our own branch of the family. We follow the step of the Jew, of the Indian, of the Negro. We see how much will has been expended to extinguish the Jew, in vain. Look at the unpalatable conclusions of Knox, in his Fragment of Races; — a rash and unsatisfactory writer, but charged with pungent and unforgetable truths. "Nature respects race, and not hybrids." "Every race has its own *habitat*." "Detach a colony from the race, and it deteriorates to the crab." See the shades of the picture. The German and Irish millions, like the Negro, have a great deal of guano in their destiny. They are ferried over the Atlantic and carted over America, to ditch and to drudge, to make corn cheap and then to lie down prematurely to make a spot of green grass on the prairie.

One more fagot of these adamantine bandages is the new science of Statistics. It is a rule that the most casual and extraordinary events, if the basis of population is broad enough, become matter of fixed calculation. It would not be safe to say when a captain like Bonaparte, a singer like Jenny Lind, or a navigator like Bowditch would be born in Boston; but, on a population of twenty or two hundred millions, something like accuracy may be had.

'Tis frivolous to fix pedantically the date of particular inventions. They have all been invented over and over fifty times. Man is the arch machine of which all these shifts drawn from himself are toy models. He helps himself on each emergency by copying or duplicating his own structure, just so far as the need is. 'Tis hard to find the right Homer, Zoroaster, or Menu; harder still to find the Tubal Cain, or Vulcan, or Cadmus, or Copernicus, or Fust, or Fulton; the indisputable inventor. There are scores and centuries of them. "The air is full of men." This kind of talent so abounds, this constructive tool-making efficiency, as if it adhered to the chemic atoms; as if the air he breathes were made of Vaucansons, Franklins, and Watts.

Doubtless in every million there will be an astronomer, a mathematician, a comic poet, a mystic. No one can read the history of astronomy without perceiving that Copernicus, Newton, Laplace, are not new men, or a new kind of men, but that Thales, Anaximenes, Hipparchus, Empedocles, Aristarchus, Pythagoras, Oenipodes, had anticipated them; each had the same tense geometrical brain, apt for the same vigorous computation and logic; a mind parallel to the movement of the world. The Roman mile probably rested on a measure of a degree of the meridian. Mahometan and Chinese know what we know of leap-year, of the Gregorian calendar, and of the precession of the equinoxes. As in every barrel of cowries [2] brought to New Bedford there shall be one *orangia*, so there will, in a dozen millions of Malays and Mahometans, be one or two astronomical skulls. In a large city, the most casual things, and things whose beauty lies in their casuality, are produced as punctually and to order as the baker's muffin for breakfast. Punch makes exactly one capital joke a week; and the journals contrive to furnish one good piece of news every day.

And not less work the laws of repression, the penalties of violated functions. Famine, typhus, frost, war, suicide and effete races must be reckoned calculable parts of the system of the world.

These are pebbles from the mountains, hints of the terms by which our life is walled up, and which show a kind of mechanical exactness, as of a loom or mill in what we call casual or fortuitous events.

[margin note: something controls nature, a pattern not as erratic as once thought]

The force with which we resist these torrents of tendency looks so ridiculously inadequate that it amounts to little more than a criticism or protest made by a minority of one, under compulsion of millions. I seemed in the height of a tempest to see men overboard struggling in the waves, and driven about here and there. They glanced intelligently at each other, but 'twas little they could do for one another; 'twas much if each could keep afloat alone. Well, they had a right to their eye-beams, and all the rest was Fate.   *Melville-like*

We cannot trifle with this reality, this cropping-out in our planted gardens of the core of the world. No picture of life can have any veracity that does not admit the odious facts. A man's power is hooped in by a necessity which, by many experiments, he touches on every side until he learns its arc.

The element running through entire nature, which we popularly call Fate, is known to us as limitation. Whatever limits us we call Fate. If we are brute and barbarous, the fate takes a brute and dreadful shape. As we refine, our checks become finer. If we rise to spiritual culture, the antagonism takes a spiritual form. In the Hindu fables, Vishnu follows Maya through all her ascending changes, from insect and crawfish up to elephant; whatever form she took, he took the male form of that kind, until she became at last woman and goddess, and he a man and a god. The limitations refine as the soul purifies, but the ring of necessity is always perched at the top.

[2] Shells.

When the gods in the Norse heaven were unable to bind the Fenris Wolf with steel or with weight of mountains, — the one he snapped and the other he spurned with his heel, — they put round his foot a limp band softer than silk or cobweb, and this held him; the more he spurned it the stiffer it drew. So soft and so stanch is the ring of Fate. Neither brandy, nor nectar, nor sulphuric ether, nor hell-fire, nor ichor, nor poetry, nor genius, can get rid of this limp band. For if we give it the high sense in which the poets use it, even thought itself is not above Fate; that too must act according to eternal laws, and all that is wilful and fantastic in it is in opposition to its fundamental essence.

And last of all, high over thought, in the world of morals, Fate appears as vindicator, leveling the high, lifting the low, requiring justice in man, and always striking soon or late when justice is not done. What is useful will last, what is hurtful will sink. "The doer must suffer," said the Greeks; "you would soothe a Deity not to be soothed." "God himself cannot procure good for the wicked," said the Welsh triad. "God may consent, but only for a time," said the bard of Spain. The limitation is impassable by any insight of man. In its last and loftiest ascensions, insight itself and the freedom of the will is one of its obedient members. But we must not run into generalizations too large, but show the natural bounds or essential distinctions, and seek to do justice to the other elements as well.

Thus we trace Fate in matter, mind, and morals; in race, in retardations of strata, and in thought and character as well. It is everywhere bound or limitation. But Fate has its lord; limitation its limits, — is different seen from above and from below, from within and from without. For though Fate is immense, so is Power, which is the other fact in the dual world, immense. If Fate follows and limits Power, Power attends and antagonizes Fate. We must respect Fate as natural history, but there is more than natural history. For who and what is this criticism that pries into the matter? Man is not order of nature, sack and sack, belly and members, link in a chain, nor any ignominious baggage; but a stupendous antagonism, a dragging together of the poles of the Universe. He betrays his relation to what is below him, — thick-skulled, small-brained, fishy, quadrumanous, quadruped ill-disguised, hardly escaped into biped, — and has paid for the new powers by loss of some of the old ones. But the lightning which explodes and fashions planets, maker of planets and suns, is in

him. On one side elemental order, sandstone and granite, rock-
ledges, peat-bog, forest, sea and shore; and on the other part
thought, the spirit which composes and decomposes nature, —
here they are, side by side, god and devil, mind and matter, king
and conspirator, belt and spasm, riding peacefully together in the
eye and brain of every man.

Nor can he blink the freewill. To hazard the contradiction, —
freedom is necessary. If you please to plant yourself on the side
of Fate, and say, Fate is all; then we say, a part of Fate is the freedom of man. Forever wells up the impulse of choosing and acting
in the soul. Intellect annuls Fate. So far as a man thinks, he is
free. And though nothing is more disgusting than the crowing
about liberty by slaves, as most men are, and the flippant mistaking
for freedom of some paper preamble like a Declaration of Independence or the statute right to vote, by those who have never
dared to think or to act, — yet it is wholesome to man to look not
at Fate, but the other way: the practical view is the other. His
sound relation to these facts is to use and command, not to cringe
to them. "Look not on Nature, for her name is fatal," said the
oracle. The too much contemplation of these limits induces
meanness. They who talk much of destiny, their birth-star, etc.,
are in a lower dangerous plane, and invite the evils they fear.

I cited the instinctive and heroic races as proud believers in
Destiny. They conspire with it; a loving resignation is with the
event. But the dogma makes a different impression when it is
held by the weak and lazy. 'Tis weak and vicious people who cast
the blame on Fate. The right use of Fate is to bring up our conduct to the loftiness of nature. Rude and invincible except by
themselves are the elements. So let man be. Let him empty his
breast of his windy conceits, and show his lordship by manners
and deeds on the scale of nature. Let him hold his purpose as
with the tug of gravitation. No power, no persuasion, no bribe
shall make him give up his point. A man ought to compare ad-
vantageously with a river, an oak, or a mountain. He shall have
not less the flow, the expansion, and the resistance of these.

'Tis the best use of Fate to teach a fatal courage. Go face the
fire at sea, or the cholera in your friend's house, or the burglar in
your own, or what danger lies in the way of duty, — knowing you
are guarded by the cherubim of Destiny. If you believe in Fate to
your harm, believe it at least for your good.

For if Fate is so prevailing, man also is part of it, and can con-
front fate with fate. If the Universe have these savage accidents.

our atoms are as savage in resistance. We should be crushed by the atmosphere, but for the reaction of the air within the body. A tube made of a film of glass can resist the shock of the ocean if filled with the same water. If there be omnipotence in the stroke, there is omnipotence of recoil.

1. But Fate against Fate is only parrying and defence: there are also the noble creative forces. The revelation of Thought takes man out of servitude into freedom. We rightly say of ourselves, we were born and afterward we were born again, and many times. We have successive experiences so important that the new forgets the old, and hence the mythology of the seven or the nine heavens. The day of days, the great day of the feast of life, is that in which the inward eye opens to the Unity in things, to the omnipresence of law: — sees that what is must be and ought to be, or is the best. This beatitude dips from on high down on us and we see. It is not in us so much as we are in it. If the air come to our lungs, we breathe and live; if not, we die. If the light come to our eyes, we see; else not. And if truth come to our mind we suddenly expand to its dimensions, as if we grew to worlds. We are as lawgivers; we speak for Nature; we prophesy and divine.

This insight throws us on the party and interest of the Universe, against all and sundry; against ourselves as much as others. A man speaking from insight affirms of himself what is true of the mind: seeing its immortality, he says, I am immortal; seeing its invincibility, he says, I am strong. It is not in us, but we are in it. It is of the maker, not of what is made. All things are touched and changed by it. This uses and is not used. It distances those who share it from those who share it not. Those who share it not are flocks and herds. It dates from itself; not from former men or better men, gospel, or constitution, or college, or custom. Where it shines, Nature is no longer intrusive, but all things make a musical or pictorial impression. The world of men show like a comedy without laughter: populations, interests, government, history; 'tis all toy figures in a toy house. It does not overvalue particular truths. We hear eagerly every thought and word quoted from an intellectual man. But in his presence our own mind is roused to activity, and we forget very fast what he says, much more interested in the new play of our own thought than in any thought of his. 'Tis the majesty into which we have suddenly mounted, the impersonality, the scorn of egotisms, the sphere of laws, that engage us. Once we were stepping a little this way and a little that way; now we are as men in a balloon, and do not think so much of the point we have left, or the point we would make, as of the liberty and glory of the way.

Just as much intellect as you add, so much organic power. He who sees through the design, presides over it, and must will that which must be. We sit and rule, and, though we sleep, our dream will come to pass. Our thought, though it were only an hour old, affirms an oldest necessity, not to be separated from thought, and not to be separated from will. They must always have coexisted. It apprises us of its sovereignty and godhead, which refuse to be severed from it. It is not mine or thine, but the will of all mind. It is poured into the souls of all men, as the soul itself which constitutes them men. I know not whether there be, as is alleged, in the upper region of our atmosphere, a permanent westerly current which carries with it all atoms which rise to that height, but I see that when souls reach a certain clearness of perception they accept a knowledge and motive above selfishness. A breath of will blows eternally through the universe of souls in the direction of the Right and Necessary. It is the air which all intellects inhale and exhale, and it is the wind which blows the worlds into order and orbit.

Thought dissolves the material universe by carrying the mind up into a sphere where all is plastic. Of two men, each obeying his own thought, he whose thought is deepest will be the strongest character. Always one man more than another represents the will of Divine Providence to the period.

2. If thought makes free, so does the moral sentiment. The mixtures of spiritual chemistry refuse to be analyzed. Yet we can see that with the perception of truth is joined the desire that it shall prevail; that affection is essential to will. Moreover, when a strong will appears, it usually results from a certain unity of organization, as if the whole energy of body and mind flowed in one direction. All great force is real and elemental. There is no manufacturing a strong will. There must be a pound to balance a pound. Where power is shown in will, it must rest on the universal force. Alaric and Bonaparte must believe they rest on a truth, or their will can be bought or bent. There is a bribe possible for any finite will. But the pure sympathy with universal ends is an infinite force, and cannot be bribed or bent. Whoever has had experience of the moral sentiment cannot choose but believe in unlimited power. Each pulse from that heart is an oath from the Most High. I know not what the word *sublime* means, if it be not the intimations, in this infant, of a terrific force. A text of heroism, a name

and anecdote of courage, are not arguments but sallies of freedom. One of these is the verse of the Persian Hafiz, " 'Tis written on the gate of Heaven, 'Woe unto him who suffers himself to be betrayed by Fate!' " Does the reading of history make us fatalists? What courage does not the opposite opinion show! A little whim of will to be free gallantly contending against the universe of chemistry.

But insight is not will, nor is affection will. Perception is cold, and goodness dies in wishes. As Voltaire said, 'tis the misfortune of worthy people that they are cowards; "un des plus grands malheurs des honnêtes gens c'est qu'ils sont des lâches." There must be a fusion of these two to generate the energy of will. There can be no driving force except through the conversion of the man into his will, making him the will, and the will him. And one may say boldly that no man has a right perception of any truth who has not been reacted on by it so as to be ready to be its martyr.

The one serious and formidable thing in nature is a will. Society is servile from want of will, and therefore the world wants saviours and religions. One way is right to go; the hero sees it, and moves on that aim, and has the world under him for root and support. He is to others as the world. His approbation is honor; his dissent, infamy. The glance of his eye has the force of sunbeams. A personal influence towers up in memory only worthy, and we gladly forget numbers, money, climate, gravitation, and the rest of Fate.

We can afford to allow the limitation, if we know it is the meter of the growing man. We stand against Fate, as children stand up against the wall in their father's house and notch their height from year to year. But when the boy grows to man, and is master of the house, he pulls down that wall and builds a new and bigger. 'Tis only a question of time. Every brave youth is in training to ride and rule this dragon. His science is to make weapons and wings of these passions and retarding forces. Now whether, seeing these two things, fate and power, we are permitted to believe in unity? The bulk of mankind believe in two gods. They are under one dominion here in the house, as friend and parent, in social circles, in letters, in art, in love, in religion; but in mechanics, in dealing with steam and climate, in trade, in politics, they think they come under another; and that it would be a practical blunder to transfer the method and way of working of one sphere into the other. What good, honest, generous men at home, will be wolves and foxes on 'Change! What pious men in the parlor will vote for what reprobates at the polls! To a certain point, they believe themselves the care of a Providence. But in a steamboat, in an epidemic, in war, they believe a malignant energy rules.

But relation and connection are not somewhere and sometimes, but everywhere and always. The divine order does not stop where their sight stops. The friendly power works on the same rules in the next farm and the next planet. But where they have not experience they run against it and hurt themselves. Fate then is a name for facts not yet passed under the fire of thought; for causes which are unpenetrated.

But every jet of chaos which threatens to exterminate us is convertible by intellect into wholesome force. Fate is unpenetrated causes. The water drowns ship and sailor like a grain of dust. But learn to swim, trim your bark, and the wave which drowned it will be cloven by it and carry it like its own foam, a plume and a power. The cold is inconsiderate of persons, tingles your blood, freezes a man like a dewdrop. But learn to skate, and the ice will give you a graceful, sweet, and poetic motion. The cold will brace your limbs and brain to genius, and make you foremost men of time. Cold and sea will train an imperial Saxon race, which nature cannot bear to lose, and after cooping it up for a thousand years in yonder England, gives a hundred Englands, a hundred Mexicos. All the bloods it shall absorb and domineer: and more than Mexicos, the secrets of water and steam, the spasms of electricity, the ductility of metals, the chariot of the air, the ruddered balloon are awaiting you.

The annual slaughter from typhus far exceeds that of war; but right drainage destroys typhus. The plague in the sea-service from scurvy is healed by lemon juice and other diets portable or procurable; the depopulation by cholera and small-pox is ended by drainage and vaccination; and every other pest is not less in the chain of cause and effect, and may be fought off. And whilst art draws out the venom, it commonly extorts some benefit from the vanquished enemy. The mischievous torrent is taught to drudge for man; the wild beasts he makes useful for food, or dress, or labor; the chemic explosions are controlled like his watch. These are now the steeds on which he rides. Man moves in all modes, by legs of horses, by wings of wind, by steam, by gas of balloon, by electricity, and stands on tiptoe threatening to hunt the eagle in his own element. There's nothing he will not make his carrier.

Steam was till the other day the devil which we dreaded. Every pot made by any human potter or brazier had a hole in its cover, to let off the enemy, lest he should lift pot and roof and carry the house away. But the Marquis of Worcester, Watt, and Fulton bethought themselves that where was power was not devil, but was God; that it must be availed of, and not by any means let off and wasted. Could he lift pots and roofs and houses so handily? He was the workman they were in search of. He could be used to lift away, chain and compel other devils far more reluctant and dangerous, namely, cubic miles of earth, mountains, weight or resistance of water, machinery, and the labors of all men in the world; and time he shall lengthen, and shorten space.

It has not fared much otherwise with higher kinds of steam. The opinion of the million was the terror of the world, and it was attempted either to dissipate it, by amusing nations, or to pile it over with strata of society, — a layer of soldiers, over that a layer of lords, and a king on the top; with clamps and hoops of castles, garrisons, and police. But sometimes the religious principle would get in and burst the hoops and rive every mountain laid on top of it. The Fultons and Watts of politics, believing in unity, saw that it was a power, and by satisfying it (as justice satisfies everybody), through a different disposition of society, — grouping it on a level instead of piling it into a mountain, — they have contrived to make of this terror the most harmless and energetic form of a State.

Very odious, I confess, are the lessons of Fate. Who likes to have a dapper phrenologist pronouncing on his fortunes? Who likes to believe that he has, hidden in his skull, spine, and pelvis, all the vices of a Saxon or Celtic race, which will be sure to pull him down, — with what grandeur of hope and resolve he is fired, — into a selfish, huckstering, servile, dodging animal? A learned physician tells us the fact is invariable with the Neapolitan, that when mature he assumes the forms of the unmistakable scoundrel. That is a little overstated, — but may pass.

But these are magazines and arsenals. A man must thank his defects, and stand in some terror of his talents. A transcendent talent draws so largely on his forces as to lame him; a defect pays him revenues on the other side. The sufferance which is the badge of the Jew, has made him, in these days, the ruler of the rulers of the earth. If Fate is ore and quarry, if evil is good in the making, if limitation is power that shall be, if calamities, oppositions, and weights are wings and means, — we are reconciled.

Fate involves the melioration. No statement of the Universe can have any soundness which does not admit its ascending effort.

The direction of the whole and of the parts is toward benefit, and in proportion to the health. Behind every individual closes organization; before him opens liberty, — the Better, the Best. The first and worse races are dead. The second and imperfect races are dying out, or remain for the maturing of higher. In the latest race, in man, every generosity, every new perception, the love and praise he extorts from his fellows, are certificates of advance out of fate into freedom. Liberation of the will from the sheaths and clogs of organization which he has outgrown, is the end and aim of this world. Every calamity is a spur and valuable hint; and where his endeavors do not yet fully avail, they tell as tendency. The whole circle of animal life — tooth against tooth, devouring war, war for food, a yelp of pain and a grunt of triumph, until at last the whole menagerie, the whole chemical mass is mellowed and refined for higher use — pleases at a sufficient perspective.

But to see how fate slides into freedom and freedom into fate, observe how far the roots of every creature run, or find if you can a point where there is no thread of connection. Our life is consentaneous and far-related. This knot of nature is so well tied that nobody was ever cunning enough to find the two ends. Nature is intricate, overlapped, interweaved and endless. Christopher Wren said of the beautiful King's College chapel, that "if anybody would tell him where to lay the first stone, he would build such another." But where shall we find the first atom in this house of man, which is all consent, inosculation and balance of parts?

The web of relation is shown in *habitat*, shown in hibernation. When hibernation was observed, it was found that whilst some animals became torpid in winter, others were torpid in summer: hibernation then was a false name. The *long sleep* is not an effect of cold, but is regulated by the supply of food proper to the animal. It becomes torpid when the fruit or prey it lives on is not in season, and regains its activity when its food is ready.

Eyes are found in light; ears in auricular air; feet on land; fins in water; wings in air; and each creature where it was meant to be, with a mutual fitness. Every zone has its own *Fauna*. There is adjustment between the animal and its food, its parasite, its enemy. Balances are kept. It is not allowed to diminish in numbers, nor to exceed. The like adjustments exist for man. His food is cooked when he arrives; his coal in the pit; the house ventilated; the mud of the deluge dried; his companions arrived at the same hour, and awaiting him with love, concert, laughter and tears. These are coarse adjustments, but the invisible are not less. There are more belongings to every creature than his air and his food. His instincts must be met, and he has predisposing power that bends and fits what is near him to his use. He is not possible until the invisible things are right for him, as well as the visible. Of what changes then in sky and earth, and in finer skies and earths, does the appearance of some Dante or Columbus apprise us!

How is this effected? Nature is no spendthrift, but takes the shortest way to her ends. As the general says to his soldiers, "If you want a fort, build a fort," so nature makes every creature do its own work and get its living, — is it planet, animal or tree. The planet makes itself. The animal cell makes itself; — then, what it wants. Every creature, wren or dragon, shall make its own lair. As soon as there is life, there is self-direction and absorbing and using of material. Life is freedom, — life in the direct ratio of its amount. You may be sure the new-born man is not inert. Life works both voluntarily and supernaturally in its neighborhood. Do you suppose he can be estimated by his weight in pounds, or that he is contained in his skin, — this reaching, radiating, jaculating fellow? The smallest candle fills a mile with its rays, and the papillae of a man run out to every star.

When there is something to be done, the world knows how to get it done. The vegetable eye makes leaf, pericarp, root, bark, or thorn, as the need is; the first cell converts itself into stomach, mouth, nose, or nail, according to the want; the world throws its life into a hero or a shepherd, and puts him where he is wanted. Dante and Columbus were Italians, in their time; they would be Russians or Americans today. Things ripen, new men come. The adaptation is not capricious. The ulterior aim, the purpose beyond itself, the correlation by which planets subside and crystallize, then animate beasts and men, — will not stop but will work into finer particulars, and from finer to finest.

The secret of the world is the tie between person and event. Person makes event, and event person. The "times," "the age," what is that but a few profound persons and a few active persons who epitomize the times? — Goethe, Hegel, Metternich, Adams, Calhoun, Guizot, Peel, Cobden, Kossuth, Rothschild, Astor, Brunel, and the rest. The same fitness must be presumed between a man and the time and event, as between the sexes, or between a race of animals and the food it eats, or the inferior races it uses. He thinks his fate alien, because the copula is hidden. But the soul contains the event that shall befall it; for the event is only the actualization of its thoughts, and what we pray to ourselves for is always granted. The event is the print of your form. It fits you like your skin. What each does is proper to him. Events are the children of his body and mind. We learn that the soul of Fate is the soul of us, as Hafiz sings, —

> "Alas! till now I had not known,
> My guide and fortune's guide are one."

All the toys that infatuate men and which they play for, — houses, land, money, luxury, power, fame, are the selfsame thing, with a new gauze or two of illusion overlaid. And of all the drums and rattles by which men are made willing to have their heads broke, and are led out solemnly every morning to parade, — the most admirable is this by which we are brought to believe that events are arbitrary and independent of actions. At the conjuror's, we detect the hair by which he moves his puppet, but we have not eyes sharp enough to descry the thread that ties cause and effect.

Nature magically suits the man to his fortunes, by making these the fruit of his character. Ducks take to the water, eagles to the sky, waders to the sea margin, hunters to the forest, clerks to counting-rooms, soldiers to the frontier. Thus events grow on the same stem with persons; are sub-persons. The pleasure of life is according to the man that lives it, and not according to the work or the place. Life is an ecstasy. We know what madness belongs to love, — what power to paint a vile object in hues of heaven. As insane persons are indifferent to their dress, diet, and other accommodations, and as we do in dreams, with equanimity, the most absurd acts, so a drop more of wine in our cup of life will reconcile us to strange company and work. Each creature puts forth from itself its own condition and sphere, as the slug sweats out its slimy house on the pear-leaf, and the woolly aphides on the apple perspire their own bed, and the fish its shell. In youth we clothe ourselves with rainbows and go as brave as the zodiac. In age we put out another sort of perspiration, — gout, fever, rheumatism, caprice, doubt, fretting and avarice.

A man's fortunes are the fruit of his character. A man's friends are his magnetisms. We go to Herodotus and Plutarch for examples of Fate; but we are examples. *"Quisque suos patimur manes."* [3] The tendency of every man to enact all that is in his constitution is expressed in the old belief that the efforts which we make to escape from our destiny only serve to lead us into it: and I have noticed a man likes better to be complimented on his

---

[3] Each of us suffers his own spirit.

position, as the proof of the last or total excellence, than on his merits.

A man will see his character emitted in the events that seem to meet, but which exude from and accompany him. Events expand with the character. As once he found himself among toys, so now he plays a part in colossal systems, and his growth is declared in his ambition, his companions and his performance. He looks like a piece of luck, but is a piece of causation; the mosaic, angulated and ground to fit into the gap he fills. Hence in each town there is some man who is, in his brain and performance, an explanation of the tillage, production, factories, banks, churches, ways of living and society of that town. If you do not chance to meet him, all that you see will leave you a little puzzled; if you see him it will become plain. We know in Massachusetts who built New Bedford, who built Lynn, Lowell, Lawrence, Clinton, Fitchburg, Holyoke, Portland, and many another noisy mart. Each of these men, if they were transparent, would seem to you not so much men as walking cities, and wherever you put them they would build one.

History is the action and reaction of these two, — Nature and Thought; two boys pushing each other on the curbstone of the pavement. Everything is pusher or pushed; and matter and mind are in perpetual tilt and balance, so. Whilst the man is weak, the earth takes up him. He plants his brain and affections. By and by he will take up the earth, and have his gardens and vineyards in the beautiful order and productiveness of his thought. Every solid in the universe is ready to become fluid on the approach of the mind, and the power to flux it is the measure of the mind. If the wall remain adamant, it accuses the want of thought. To a subtle force it will stream into new forms, expressive of the character of the mind. What is the city in which we sit here, but an aggregate of incongruous materials which have obeyed the will of some man? The granite was reluctant, but his hands were stronger, and it came. Iron was deep in the ground and well combined with stone, but could not hide from his fires. Wood, lime, stuffs, fruits, gums, were dispersed over the earth and sea, in vain. Here they are, within reach of every man's day-labor, — what he wants of them. The whole world is the flux of matter over the wires of thought to the poles or points where it would build. The races of men rise out of the ground preoccupied with a thought which rules them, and divided into parties ready armed and angry to fight for this metaphysical abstraction. The quality of the thought differences the Egyptian and the Roman, the Austrian and the American. The men who come on the stage at one period are all found to be related to each other. Certain ideas are in the air. We are all impressionable, for we are made of them; all impressionable, but some more than others, and these first express them. This explains the curious contemporaneousness of inventions and discoveries. The truth is in the air, and the most impressionable brain will announce it first, but all will announce it a few minutes later. So women, as most susceptible, are the best index of the coming hour. So the great man, that is, the man most imbued with the spirit of the time, is the impressionable man; — of a fiber irritable and delicate, like iodine to light. He feels the infinitesimal attractions. His mind is righter than others because he yields to a current so feeble as can be felt only by a needle delicately poised.

The correlation is shown in defects. Möller, in his Essay on Architecture, taught that the building which was fitted accurately to answer its end would turn out to be beautiful though beauty had not been intended. I find the like unity in human structures rather virulent and pervasive; that a crudity in the blood will appear in the argument; a hump in the shoulder will appear in the speech and handiwork. If his mind could be seen, the hump would be seen. If a man has a see-saw in his voice, it will run into his sentences, into his poem, into the structure of his fable, into his speculation, into his charity. And as every man is hunted by his own daemon, vexed by his own disease, this checks all his activity.

So each man, like each plant, has his parasites. A strong, astringent, bilious nature has more truculent enemies than the slugs and moths that fret my leaves. Such an one has curculios, borers, knife-worms; a swindler ate him first, then a client, then a quack, then smooth, plausible gentlemen, bitter and selfish as Moloch.[4]

This correlation really existing can be divined. If the threads are there, thought can follow and show them. Especially when a soul is quick and docile, as Chaucer sings: —

> "Or if the soule of proper kind
> Be so parfite as men find,
> That it wot what is to come,
> And that he warneth all and some
> Of everiche of hir aventures,
> By avisions or figures;
> But that our flesh hath no might
> To understand it aright
> For it is warned too derkely."

4 Idol to which children were sacrificed.

Some people are made up of rhyme, coincidence, omen, periodicity, and presage: they meet the person they seek; what their companion prepares to say to them, they first say to him; and a hundred signs apprise them of what is about to befall.

Wonderful intricacy in the web, wonderful constancy in the design this vagabond life admits. We wonder how the fly finds its mate, and yet year after year, we find two men, two women, without legal or carnal tie, spend a great part of their best time within a few feet of each other. And the moral is that what we seek we shall find; what we flee from flees from us; as Goethe said, "what we wish for in youth, comes in heaps on us in old age," too often cursed with the granting of our prayer: and hence the high caution, that since we are sure of having what we wish, we beware to ask only for high things.

One key, one solution to the mysteries of human condition, one solution to the old knots of fate, freedom, and foreknowledge, exists; the propounding, namely, of the double consciousness. A man must ride alternately on the horses of his private and his public nature, as the equestrians in the circus throw themselves nimbly from horse to horse, or plant one foot on the back of one and the other foot on the back of the other. So when a man is the victim of his fate, has sciatica in his loins and cramp in his mind; a club-foot and a club in his wit; a sour face and a selfish temper; a strut in his gait and a conceit in his affection; or is ground to powder by the vice of his race; — he is to rally on his relation to the Universe, which his ruin benefits. Leaving the daemon [5] who suffers, he is to take sides with the Deity who secures universal benefit by his pain.

To offset the drag of temperament and race, which pulls down, learn this lesson, namely, that by the cunning co-presence of two elements, which is throughout nature, whatever lames or paralyzes you draws in with it the divinity, in some form, to repay. A good intention clothes itself with sudden power. When a god wishes to ride, any chip or pebble will bud and shoot out winged feet and serve him for a horse.

Let us build altars to the Blessed Unity which holds nature and souls in perfect solution, and compels every atom to serve an universal end. I do not wonder at a snow-flake, a shell, a summer landscape, or the glory of the stars; but at the necessity of beauty under which the universe lies; that all is and must be pictorial; that the rainbow and the curve of the horizon and the arch of the

[5] Personal spirit (cf. p. 480).

blue vault are only results from the organism of the eye. There is
no need for foolish amateurs to fetch me to admire a garden of
flowers, or a sun-gilt cloud, or a waterfall, when I cannot look
without seeing splendor and grace. How idle to choose a random
sparkle here or there, when the indwelling necessity plants the
rose of beauty on the brow of chaos, and discloses the central intention of Nature to be harmony and joy.

Let us build altars to the Beautiful Necessity. If we thought
men were free in the sense that in a single exception one fantastical
will could prevail over the law of things, it were all one as if a child's
hand could pull down the sun. If in the least particular one could
derange the order of nature, — who would accept the gift of life?

Let us build altars to the Beautiful Necessity, which secures
that all is made of one piece; that plaintiff and defendant, friend
and enemy, animal and planet, food and eater are of one kind. In
astronomy is vast space but no foreign system; in geology, vast
time but the same laws as today. Why should we be afraid of
Nature, which is no other than "philosophy and theology em-
bodied"? Why should we fear to be crushed by savage elements,
we who are made up of the same elements? Let us build to the
Beautiful Necessity, which makes man brave in believing that he
cannot shun a danger that is appointed, nor incur one that is not;
to the Necessity which rudely or softly educates him to the perception that there are no contingencies; that Law rules throughout existence; a Law which is not intelligent but intelligence; —
not personal nor impersonal — it disdains words and passes understanding; it dissolves persons; it vivifies nature; yet solicits the pure
in heart to draw on all its omnipotence.

1853–1860

Crisis

The increasing demand for Emerson's wares, at home and abroad, was a conspicuous testimony to his growing fame and stature. From the time of his second trip to England on, the sense and the demands of success blunted the edge of his private problems. His circle of friends and acquaintances grew to include, it seemed, nearly everyone of importance in the literary world in England and America, with some in France and Germany. Coming more and more to value convivial occasions with his chosen peers, he helped Alcott to organize the short-lived Town and Country Club in 1849 and was a founder in 1856 of the successful Saturday Club. The solitary dissenter of 1837 became the "courteous and bland" gentleman memorialized by that soul of the Saturday Club, Oliver Wendell Holmes, Sr.

His lectures in the 1850's show the variety of the practiced professional. Along with the philosopher who expounds such views as he did in "Fate," we find the inspirational preacher who speaks in "Worship" (1851) or "Morals" (1859) or many others. Another important class of lectures were national portraits like "France, or Urbanity" (1854), "England" (1848), or "Anglo-Saxon" (1853). Those on England grew into English Traits (1856), the most readable of his volumes, where for all his criticism he revealed once more, as in the welcome he gave Whitman's Leaves of Grass in 1855, his temperamental bias toward any commanding vitality. And we encounter also the informal essayist who discusses with unassuming good sense the practical conduct of life, as he does in "Considerations by the Way" (1856) and "Works and Days" (1857). The latter illustrates well his now habitual method: to begin "low" — in this case so very low that the early pages have lost their interest — and then to carry the subject by stages as high as he believes he can take his often simple audiences with him. Though this popular counsellor is not the most memorable Emerson, he was highly thought of by his contemporaries and should not be unduly slighted. When the topic is close to him his easy mastery of thought and medium has its own distinction.

The journals of the time show a continuing drift toward a large "acquiescence" in his speculations. In sharp contrast came the shocks of the mounting national conflict over slavery. Though Emerson on the whole disliked abolitionists and preferred to hold himself out of the arena, he was deeply stirred and troubled, to the point of feeling that the badness of the times made death attractive. Since a selection made one hundred years later must largely omit the evidence, it is important to stress that his busy scholar's and lecturer's life in the 1850's was conducted under the darkening shadow of a crisis in which he was more and more actively involved. The Fugitive Slave Law jarred him to the core of his moral being, and thereafter he took his stand on every appropriate occasion with the uncompromising anti-slavery side. He made two major speeches against the Fugitive Slave Law; he spoke at a protest meeting for Sumner, at a relief meeting for Kansas, twice in praise of John Brown, and on many other occasions. His private activities for the cause were also many. When war finally struck, he was ready.

⚔

Spring, 1851

Bad Times. — We wake up with painful auguring, and, after exploring a little to know the cause, find it is the odious news in each day's paper, the infamy that has fallen on Massachusetts, that clouds the daylight and takes away the comfort out of every hour. We shall never feel well again until that detestable law [1] is nullified in Massachusetts and until the Government is assured that once for all it cannot and shall not be executed here. All I have and all I can do shall be given and done in opposition to the execution of the law.

Spring, 1851

There can never be peace whilst this **devilish** seed of war [2] is in our soil. Root it out, burn it up, pay for the damage, and let us

[1] The Fugitive Slave Law.
[2] Slavery.

have done with it. It costs a hundred millions. Twice so much were cheap for it. Boston is a little city, and yet is worth near two hundred millions. Boston itself would pay a large fraction of the sum, to be clean of it. I would pay a little of my estate with joy; for this calamity darkens my days. It is a local, accidental distemper, and the vast interests of a continent cannot be sacrificed for it.

[*Spring?, 1851*]

We are glad at last to get a clear case, one on which no shadow of doubt can hang. This is not meddling with other people's affairs: this is hindering other people from meddling with us. This is not going crusading into Virginia and Georgia after slaves, who, it is alleged, are very comfortable where they are: — that amiable argument falls to the ground: but this is befriending in our own State, on our own farms, a man who has taken the risk of being shot, or burned alive, or cast into the sea, or starved to death, or suffocated in a wooden box, to get away from his driver: and this man who has run the gauntlet of a thousand miles for his freedom, the statute says, you men of Massachusetts shall hunt, and catch, and send back again to the dog-hutch he fled from. And this filthy enactment was made in the nineteenth century, by people who could read and write. I will not obey it, by God.

August, 1852

I waked at night, and bemoaned myself, because I had not thrown myself into this deplorable question of Slavery, which seems to want nothing so much as a few assured voices. But then, in hours of sanity, I recover myself, and say, "God must govern his own world, and knows his way out of this pit, without my desertion of my post, which has none to guard it but me. I have quite other slaves to free than those negroes, to wit, imprisoned spirits, imprisoned thoughts, far back in the brain of man, — far retired in the heaven of invention, and which, important to the republic of Man, have no watchman, or lover, or defender, but I."

Autumn, 1852

The church is there for check of trade. But on examination all the deacons, ministers, and saints of this church are steering with all their sermons and prayers in the direction of the Trade. If the city says, "Freedom and no tax," they say so, and hunt up plenty of texts. But if the city says, "Freedom is a humbug. We prefer a strong government," the pulpit says the same, and finds a new set of applicable texts. But presently Trade says, "Slavery too has been misunderstood: it is not so bad; nay, it is good; on the whole, it is the best possible thing." The dear pulpit and deacons must turn over a new leaf, and find a new string of texts, which they are forward to do. And Sampson Reed, and Orville Dewey, and Moses Stewart, and Park Street, and Andover,[3] will get up the new march of the hypocrites to pudding for the occasion.

December, 1853

Of Phillips, Garrison,[4] and others I have always the feeling that they may wake up some morning and find that they have made a capital mistake, and are not the persons they took themselves for. Very dangerous is this thoroughly social and related life, whether antagonistic or coöperative. In a lonely world, or a world with half a dozen inhabitants, these would find nothing to do.

The first discovery I made of Phillips was, that while I admired his eloquence, I had not the faintest wish to meet the man. He had only a *platform*-existence, and no personality. Mere mouthpieces of a party; take away the party and they shrivel and vanish.

They are inestimable for workers on audiences; but for a private conversation, one to one, I must prefer to take my chance with that boy in the corner. . . .

February, 1855

Philip Randolph was surprised to find me speaking to the politics of anti-slavery, in Philadelphia. I suppose, because he thought me a believer in general laws, and that it was a kind of distrust of my own general teachings to appear in active sympathy with these temporary heats.

He is right so far as that it is becoming in the scholar to insist on central soundness, rather than on superficial applications. I am to give a wise and just ballot, though no man else in the republic doth. I am not to compromise or mix or accommodate. I am to demand the absolute right, affirm that, and do that; but not push Boston into a false, showy, and theatrical attitude, endeavoring to persuade her she is more virtuous than she is. Thereby

[3] Respectively, a Swedenborgian layman and public official (cf. p. 471), a Unitarian minister and distant kinsman, a Biblical scholar, a Boston church, a theological seminary.

[4] Abolitionist orators.

I am robbing myself, more than I am enriching the public. After twenty, fifty, a hundred years, it will be quite easy to discriminate who stood for the right, and who for the expedient.

The vulgar, comprising ranks on ranks of fine gentlemen, clergymen, college presidents and professors, and great Democratic statesmen bellowing for Liberty, will of course go for safe degrees of liberty, — that is, will side with property against the Spirit, subtle and absolute, which keeps no terms.

Spring?, 1855

Opposition is our belt and tonic. No opinion will pass, but must stand the tug of war.

Men wish to pay homage to courage and perseverance, to a man whose steps have no choice, but are planted, each one. We know the austere law of liberty, — that it must be reconquered day by day, that it subsists in a state of war, that it is always slipping away from those who boast it, to those who fight for it.

To Oliver Wendell Holmes

March, 1856

. . . I have not seen a true report of your speech [5] and confess to have drawn my sad thoughts about it from the comments of the journals. I am relieved to know that they misreported you, and the more they misreported or the wider you are from their notion of you, the better I shall be pleased. I divide men as aspirants and desperants. A scholar need not be cynical to feel that the vast multitude are almost on all fours; that the rich always vote after their fears; that cities, churches, colleges all go for the quadruped interest; and it is against this coalition that the pathetically small minority of disengaged or thinking men stand for the ideal right, for man as he should be, and (what is essential to any sane maintenance of his own right) for the right of every other as for his own. When masses then as cities or churches go for things as they are, we take no note of it, we expected as much. We leave them to the laws of repression, to the checks nature puts on beasts of prey, as mutual destruction, blind staggers, delirium tremens, or whatever else; but when a scholar (or disengaged man) seems to throw himself on the dark a cry of grief is heard from the aspirants' side exactly proportioned in its intensity to his believed spiritual rank. . . .

[5] Holmes, according to the newspapers, had "denounced the abolitionists of New England in good round terms as 'traitors to the Union.'"

The cant of Union, like the cant of extending the area of liberty by the annexing Texas and Mexico, is too transparent for its most impudent repeater to hope to deceive you. And for the Union with Slavery no manly person will suffer a day to go by without discrediting, disintegrating and finally exploding it. The "Union" they talk of is dead and rotten. The real union, that is, the will to keep and renew union, is like the will to keep and renew life, and this alone gives any tension to the dead letter and . . . when we have broken every several inch of the old wooden hoop will still hold us staunch.

[June ?, 1859]

Very little reliance must be put on the common stories that circulate of Mr. Webster's or Mr. Choate's [6] learning, their Greek, or their varied literature. That ice won't bear. Reading! — do you mean that this senator or this lawyer, who stood by and allowed the passage of infamous laws, was a reader of Greek books? That is not the question; but to what purpose did they read? I allow them the merit of that reading which appears in their opinions, tastes, beliefs and practice. They read that they might know, did they not? Well, these men did not know. They blundered; they were utterly ignorant of that which every boy or girl of fifteen knows perfectly, — the rights of men and women. And this bigmouthed talker, among his dictionaries and Leipzig editions of Lysias, had lost his knowledge. But the President of the Bank nods to the President of the Insurance Office, and relates that at Virginia Springs this idol of the forum exhausted a trunkful of classic authors. There is always the previous question, How came you on that side? You are a very elegant writer, but you can't write up what gravitates down.

October, 1859

Courage charms us, because it indicates that a man loves an idea better than all things in the world, that he is thinking neither of his bed, nor his dinner, nor his money, but will venture all to put in act the invisible thought of his mind.[7]

October, 1859

Ideas make real societies and states. My countryman is surely not James Buchanan, nor Caleb Cushing, nor Barnum, nor Gov-

---

[6] Rufus Choate, lawyer and orator.
[7] Written shortly after John Brown's raid on Harpers Ferry.

ernor Gardner, nor Mrs. Gardner the poisoner, nor Lot Poole, nor
Fernando Wood; [8] but Thoreau and Alcott and Sumner, and whoever lives in the same love and worship as I; every just person,
every man or woman who knows what truth means.

It will always be so. Every principle is a war-note. Whoever attempts to carry out the rule of right and love and freedom must
take his life in his hand.

※ ※

June, 1853

In Belgium and other countries, I have seen reports of model
farms; they begun with downs or running sands, — it makes no difference what bottom, mere land to lay their basket of loam down
upon; — then, they proceed from beach grass, or whatever, and
rye and clover, manuring all the time, until they have formed a
soil fourteen inches deep. Well, so I conceive, it is in national
genericulture, as in agriculture. You must manage to set up a
national will. You must find a land like England, where temperate
and sharp northern breezes blow, to keep that will alive and alert;
markets on every possible side, because it is an island; the people
tasked and kept at the top of their condition by the continual activity of seafaring and the exciting nature of sea-risks, and the deep
stimulus of gain: the land not large enough, the population not
large enough, to glut the market and depress one another; but so
proportioned is it to the size of Europe and of the world, that it
keeps itself healthy and bright, and, like an immense manufactory,
it yields, with perfect security and ease, incredible results.

Many things conduce to this. Over them all works a sort of
Anima mundi [9] or soul of the island, — the aggregation by time,
experience, and demand and supply, of a great many personalities,
— which fits them to each other, and enables them to keep step
and time, coöperate as harmoniously and punctually as the parts of
a human body. . . .

December 15?, 1849

England. — The dinner, the wine, the homes of England look
attractive to the traveler, but they are the poor utmost that il-

[8] Respectively, the President of the United States, a supporter of Breckin-
ridge, a showman, a Know-Nothing Governor of Massachusetts, a murderess,
an unidentified person, a Tammany politician.
[9] World-Soul.

liberal wealth can perform. Alas! the halls of England are musty, the land is full of coal-smoke and carpet-smell: not a breath of mountain air dilates the languishing lungs, — and the Englishman gets his amends by weaving his web very fine. He is bold and absolute in his narrow circle; he is versed in all his routine, sure and elegant; his stories are good, his sentences solid, and all his statesmen, lawyers, men of letters, and poets, finished and solid as the pavement.

September, 1853

What Englishman has idealism enough to lift the horizon of brass which shuts down like an umbrella close around his body? When did he ever pierce his fogs to see the awful spinners and weavers that spin and weave and cut so short his web of rank and money and politics, and interrogate the vital powers that make him man? Since Shakespeare, never one; and Shakespeare only for amusement of the playhouse.

The power of Fate, the dynastic oppression of Submind.

Cape Cod, September 5, 1853

Went to Yarmouth Sunday, 3d; to Orleans Monday, 4th; to Nauset Light on the back side of Cape Cod. Collins, the keeper, told us he found obstinate resistance on Cape Cod to the project of building a lighthouse on this coast, as it would injure the wrecking business. He had to go to Boston, and obtain the strong recommendation of the Port Society. From the high hill in the rear of Higgins's, in Orleans, I had a good view of the whole Cape and the sea on both sides. The Cape looks like one of the Newfoundland Banks just emerged, a huge tract of sand half-covered with poverty grass and beach grass, and for trees, abele and locust and plantations of pitch pine. Some good oak, and in Dennis and Brewster were lately good trees for ship lumber, and [they] still are well wooded on the east side. But the view I speak of looked like emaciated Orkneys, — Mull, Islay, and so forth, — made of salt dust, gravel, and fish bones. They say the wind makes the roads, and, as at Nantucket, a large part of the real estate was freely moving back and forth in the air. I heard much of the coming railroad which is about to reach Yarmouth and Hyannis, and they hope will come to Provincetown. I fancied the people were only waiting for the railroad to reach them in order to evacuate the country. For the stark nakedness of the country could not be exaggerated. But no; nothing was less true. They are all attached to what they call *the soil*. Mr. Collins had been as far as Indiana; but, he said, hill on hill, — he felt stifled, and "longed for the Cape, where he could see out." And whilst I was fancying that they would gladly give away land to anybody that would come and live there, and be a neighbor: no, they said, all real estate had risen, all over the Cape, and you could not buy land at less than fifty dollars per acre. And, in Provincetown, a lot on the Front Street of forty feet square would cost five or six hundred dollars.

Still, I saw at the Cape, as at Nantucket, they are a little tender about your good opinion: for if a gentleman at breakfast says he don't like Yarmouth, all real estate seems to them at once depreciated two or three per cent.

They are very careful to give you directions what road you shall take from town to town; but, as the country has the shape of a piece of tape, it is not easy to lose your way. For the same reason it behooves everybody who goes on to the Cape to behave well, as he must stop on his return at all the same houses, unless he takes the packet at Provincetown for Boston, six hours in good weather, and a week in bad.

February, 1855

Common Fame. — I trust a good deal to common fame, as we all must. If a man has good corn, or wood, or boards, or pigs, to sell, or can make better chairs or knives, crucibles or church organs, than anybody else, you will find a broad hard-beaten road to his house, though it be in the woods. And if a man knows the law, people find it out, though he live in a pine shanty, and resort to him. And if a man can pipe or sing, so as to wrap the prisoned soul in an elysium; or can paint landscape, and convey into oils and ochres all the enchantments of Spring or Autumn; or can liberate or intoxicate all people who hear him with delicious songs and verses; 'tis certain that the secret cannot be kept: the first witness tells it to a second, and men go by fives and tens and fifties to his door.

Well, it is still so with a thinker. If he proposes to show me any high secret, if he profess to have found the profoundly secret pass that leads from Fate to Freedom, all good heads and all mankind aspiringly and religiously wish to know it, and, though it sorely and unusually taxes their poor brain, they find out at last whether they have made the transit or no. If they have, they will know it; and his fame will surely be bruited abroad. If they come away unsatisfied, though it be easy to impute it (even in their belief) to their dulness in not being able to keep step with his snowshoes on the icy mountain paths, — I suspect it is because the transit has not been made. . . .

Spring?, 1855

It is on the completeness with which metrical forms have covered the whole circle of routinary experience that improvisation is possible to a rhymer familiar with this cyclus of forms, and quick and dexterous in combining them. Most poetry, stock poetry we call it, that we see in the magazines, is nothing but this mosaic-work done slowly.

But whether is improvisation of poetry possible, as well as this ballad-mongering?

Yes, no doubt, since geniuses have existed, we will not be disloyal or hopeless. But beside the strange power implied of passing at will into the state of vision and of utterance, is required huge means, vast health, vigor and celerity. . . .

To Walt Whitman

July 21, 1855

I am not blind to the worth of the wonderful gift of *Leaves of Grass*. I find it the most extraordinary piece of wit and wisdom that America has yet contributed. I am very happy in reading it, as great power makes us happy. It meets the demand I am always making of what seemed the sterile and stingy Nature, as if too much handiwork, or too much lymph in the temperament, were making our Western wits fat and mean.

I give you joy of your free and brave thought. I have great joy in it. I find incomparable things said incomparably well, as they must be. I find the courage of treatment which so delights us, and which large perception only can inspire.

I greet you at the beginning of a great career, which yet must have had a long foreground somewhere, for such a start. I rubbed my eyes a little, to see if this sunbeam were no illusion; but the solid sense of the book is a sober certainty. It has the best merits, namely, of fortifying and encouraging. . . .

August, 1855

Out upon scholars with their pale, sickly, etiolated indoor thoughts. Give me the out-of-door thoughts of sound men, — the thoughts, all fresh, blooming, [whiskered, and with the tan on!]

For the great poets, like the Greek artists, elaborated their designs, but slighted their finish, and it is the office of poets to suggest a vast wealth, a background, a divinity, out of which all this and much more readily springs; and if this religion is in the poetry, it raises us to some purpose, and we can well afford some staidness or gravity in the verses.

To Thomas Carlyle

May 6, 1856

. . . One book, last summer, came out in New York, a nondescript monster which yet had terrible eyes and buffalo strength, and was indisputably American, — which I thought to send you; but the book throve so badly with the few to whom I showed it, and wanted good morals so much, that I never did. Yet I believe now again, I shall. It is called *Leaves of Grass*, — was written and printed by a journeyman printer in Brooklyn, New York, named Walter Whitman; and after you have looked into it, if you think, as you may, that it is only an auctioneer's inventory of a warehouse, you can light your pipe with it. . . .

June, 1855

A scholar is a man with this inconvenience, that, when you ask him his opinion of any matter, he must go home and look up his manuscripts to know.

August ?, 1855

The melioration in pears, or in sheep and horses, is the only hint we have that suggests the creation of man. Everything has a family likeness to him. All natural history from the first fossil points at him. The resemblances approach very near in the satyr, to the Negro, or lowest man, and food, climate, and concurrence of happy stars, a guided fortune, will have at last piloted the poor quadrumanous [1] over the awful bar that separates the fixed beast from the versatile man. In no other direction have we any hint of the *modus* in which the infant man could be preserved. The fixity or unpassableness or inconvertibility of races, as we see them, is a feeble argument, since all the historical period is but a point to the duration in which Nature was wrought. Any the least and solitariest fact in our natural history has the worth of a power in the opportunity of geologic periods. All our apples came from the little crab.

[1] Four-handed.

Classic and Romantic. — The classic art was the art of necessity: modern romantic art bears the stamp of caprice and chance. One is the product of inclination, of caprice, of haphazard; the other carries its law and necessity within itself.

The politics of monarchy, when all hangs on the accidents of life and temper of a single person, may be called romantic politics. The democratic, when the power proceeds organically from the people and is responsible to them, are classic politics.

Republics run into romance when they lose sight of the inner necessity and organism that must be in their laws, and act from whim.

Wagner made music again classic. Goethe says, "I call classic the sound, and romantic the sick." . . .

Madame George Sand, though she writes fast and miscellaneously, is yet fundamentally classic and necessitated: and I, who tack things strangely enough together, and consult my ease rather than my strength, and often write *on the other side,* am yet an adorer of the *One.*

To be classic, then, *de rigueur,* is the prerogative of a vigorous mind who is able to execute what he conceives.

The classic unfolds: the romantic adds. . . .

Illinois, January 9 ?, 1856

This climate and people are a new test for the wares of a man of letters. All his thin, watery matter freezes; 'tis only the smallest portion of alcohol that remains good. At the lyceum, the stout Illinoian, after a short trial, walks out of the hall. The Committee tell you that the people want a hearty laugh, and Stark, and Saxe, and Park Benjamin, who give them that, are heard with joy. Well, I think with Governor Reynolds, the people are always right (in a sense), and that the man of letters is to say, These are the new conditions to which I must conform. The architect, who is asked to build a house to go upon the sea, must not build a Parthenon, or a square house, but a ship. And Shakespeare, or Franklin, or Aesop, coming to Illinois, would say, I must give my wisdom a comic form, instead of tragics or elegiacs, and well I know to do it, and he is no master who cannot vary his forms, and carry his own end triumphantly through the most difficult.

Spring, 1856

On further consideration of this practical quality, by which our people are proud to be marked, I concede its excellence; but practice or practicalness consists in the consequent or logical following out of a good theory. Here are they practical, i.e., they confound the means with the ends, and lose the ends thereby out of sight — freedom, worth, and beauty of life.

FROM Works and Days

[*In the early pages of this essay, Emerson first praises and then criticizes "Works," the marvellous "artillery of tools" accumulated by man in the nineteenth century, concluding: " 'Tis too plain that with the material power the moral progress has not kept pace. It appears that we have not made a judicious investment. Works and days were offered us, and we took works." He then turns to days.*]

. . . Hesiod wrote a poem which he called Works and Days, in which he marked the changes of the Greek year, instructing the husbandman at the rising of what constellation he might safely sow, when to reap, when to gather wood, when the sailor might launch his boat in security from storms, and what admonitions of the planets he must heed. It is full of economies for Grecian life, noting the proper age for marriage, the rules of household thrift and of hospitality. The poem is full of piety as well as prudence, and is adapted to all meridians by adding the ethics of works and of days. But he has not pushed his study of days into such inquiry and analysis as they invite.

A farmer said "he should like to have all the land that joined his own." Bonaparte, who had the same appetite, endeavored to make the Mediterranean a French lake. Czar Alexander was more expansive, and wished to call the Pacific *my ocean*; and the Americans were obliged to resist his attempts to make it a close sea. But if he had the earth for his pasture and the sea for his pond, he would be a pauper still. He only is rich who owns the day. There is no king, rich man, fairy or demon who possesses such power as that. The days are ever divine as to the first Aryans. They are of the least pretension and of the greatest capacity of anything that exists. They come and go like muffled and veiled figures, sent from a distant friendly party; but they say nothing, and if we do not use the gifts they bring, they carry them as silently away.[2]

How the day fits itself to the mind, winds itself round it like a fine drapery, clothing all its fancies! Any holiday communicates to us its color. We wear its cockade and favors in our humor. Remember what boys think in the morning of "Election day," of the Fourth of July, of Thanksgiving or Christmas. The very stars in their courses wink to them of nuts and cakes, bonbons, presents and fire-works. Cannot memory still descry the old school-house and its porch, somewhat hacked by jack-knives, where you spun tops and snapped marbles; and do you not recall that life was then calendared by moments, threw itself into nervous knots or glittering hours, even as now, and not spread itself abroad an equable felicity? In college terms, and in years that followed, the young graduate, when the Commencement anniversary returned, though he were in a swamp, would see a festive light and find the air faintly echoing with plausive academic thunders. In solitude and in the country, what dignity distinguishes the holy time! The old Sabbath, or Seventh Day, white with the religions of unknown thousands of years, when this hallowed hour dawns out of the deep, — a clean page, which the wise may inscribe with truth, whilst the savage scrawls it with fetishes, — the cathedral music of history breathes through it a psalm to our solitude.

So, in the common experience of the scholar, the weathers fit his moods. A thousand tunes the variable wind plays, a thousand spectacles it brings, and each is the frame or dwelling of a new spirit. I used formerly to choose my time with some nicety for each favorite book. One author is good for winter, and one for the dog-days. The scholar must look long for the right hour for Plato's Timaeus. At last the elect morning arrives, the early dawn, — a few lights conspicuous in the heaven, as of a world just created and still becoming, — and in its wide leisures we dare open that book.

There are days when the great are near us, when there is no frown on their brow, no condescension even; when they take us by the hand, and we share their thought. There are days which are the carnival of the year. The angels assume flesh, and repeatedly become visible. The imagination of the gods is excited and rushes on every side into forms. Yesterday not a bird peeped; the world was barren, peaked and pining: today 'tis inconceivably populous; creation swarms and meliorates.

[2] Cf. "Days" (p. 451).

The days are made on a loom whereof the warp and woof are past and future time. They are majestically dressed, as if every god brought a thread to the skyey web. 'Tis pitiful the things by which we are rich or poor, — a matter of coins, coats and carpets, a little more or less stone, or wood, or paint, the fashion of a cloak or hat; like the luck of naked Indians, of whom one is proud in the possession of a glass bead or a red feather, and the rest miserable in the want of it. But the treasures which Nature spent itself to amass, — the secular, refined, composite anatomy of man, which all strata go to form, which the prior races, from infusory and saurian, existed to ripen; the surrounding plastic natures; the earth with its foods; the intellectual, temperamenting air; the sea with its invitations; the heaven deep with worlds; and the answering brain and nervous structure replying to these; the eye that looketh into the deeps, which again look back to the eye, abyss to abyss; — these, not like a glass bead, or the coins or carpets, are given immeasurably to all.

This miracle is hurled into every beggar's hands. The blue sky is a covering for a market and for the cherubim and seraphim. The sky is the varnish or glory with which the Artist has washed the whole work, — the verge or confines of matter and spirit. Nature could no farther go. Could our happiest dream come to pass in solid fact, — could a power open our eyes to behold "millions of spiritual creatures walk the earth," — I believe I should find that mid-plain on which they moved floored beneath and arched above with the same web of blue depth which weaves itself over me now, as I trudge the streets on my affairs.

It is singular that our rich English language should have no word to denote the face of the world. *Kinde* was the old English term, which, however, filled only half the range of our fine Latin word, with its delicate future tense, — *natura, about to be born,* or what German philosophy denotes as a *becoming.* But nothing expresses that power which seems to work for beauty alone. The Greek *Kosmos* did; and therefore, with great propriety, Humboldt entitles his book, which recounts the last results of science, *Cosmos.*

Such are the days, — the earth is the cup, the sky is the cover, of the immense bounty of Nature which is offered us for our daily aliment; but what a force of *illusion* begins life with us and attends us to the end! We are coaxed, flattered and duped from morn to eve, from birth to death; and where is the old eye that ever saw through the deception? The Hindus represent Maia, the illusory energy of Vishnu, as one of his principal attributes. As if, in this gale of warring elements which life is, it was necessary to bind souls to human life as mariners in a tempest lash themselves to the mast and bulwarks of a ship, and Nature employed certain illusions as her ties and straps, — a rattle, a doll, an apple, for a child; skates, a river, a boat, a horse, a gun, for the growing boy; and I will not begin to name those of the youth and adult, for they are numberless. Seldom and slowly the mask falls and the pupil is permitted to see that all is one stuff, cooked and painted under many counterfeit appearances. Hume's doctrine was that the circumstances vary, the amount of happiness does not; that the beggar cracking fleas in the sunshine under a hedge, and the duke rolling by in his chariot; the girl equipped for her first ball, and the orator returning triumphant from the debate, had different means, but the same quantity of pleasant excitement.

This element of illusion lends all its force to hide the values of present time. Who is he that does not always find himself doing something less than his best task? "What are you doing?" "O, nothing; I have been doing thus, or I shall do so or so, but now I am only — " Ah! poor dupe, will you never slip out of the web of the master juggler, — never learn that as soon as the irrecoverable years have woven their blue glory between today and us these passing hours shall glitter and draw us as the wildest romance and the homes of beauty and poetry? How difficult to deal erect with them! The events they bring, their trade, entertainments and gossip, their urgent work, all throw dust in the eyes and distract attention. He is a strong man who can look them in the eye, see through this juggle, feel their identity, and keep his own; who can know surely that one will be like another to the end of the world, nor permit love, or death, or politics, or money, war or pleasure to draw him from his task.

The world is always equal to itself, and every man in moments of deeper thought is apprised that he is repeating the experiences of the people in the streets of Thebes or Byzantium. An everlasting Now reigns in Nature, which hangs the same roses on our bushes which charmed the Roman and the Chaldaean in their hanging-gardens. "To what end, then," he asks, "should I study languages, and traverse countries, to learn so simple truths?"

History of ancient art, excavated cities, recovery of books and incriptions, — yes, the works were beautiful, and the history worth knowing; and academies convene to settle the claims of the old schools. What journeys and measurements, — Niebuhr and Müller and Layard, — to identify the plain of Troy and Nimroud town!

And your homage to Dante costs you so much sailing; and to as-
certain the discoveries of America needs as much voyaging as the
discovery cost. Poor child! that flexile clay of which these old
brothers molded their admirable symbols was not Persian, nor
Memphian, nor Teutonic, nor local at all, but was common lime
and silex and water and sunlight, the heat of the blood and the
heaving of the lungs; it was that clay which thou heldest but now
in thy foolish hands, and threwest away to go and seek in vain in
sepulchres, mummy-pits and old book-shops of Asia Minor, Egypt
and England. It was the deep today which all men scorn; the rich
poverty which men hate; the populous, all-loving solitude which
men quit for the tattle of towns. He lurks, *he* hides, — *he* who is
success, reality, joy and power. One of the illusions is that the
present hour is not the critical, decisive hour. Write it on your
heart that every day is the best day in the year. No man has
learned anything rightly until he knows that every day is Dooms-
day. 'Tis the old secret of the gods that they come in low disguises.
'Tis the vulgar great who come dizened with gold and jewels. Real
kings hide away their crowns in their wardrobes, and affect a plain
and poor exterior. In the Norse legend of our ancestors, Odin
dwells in a fisher's hut and patches a boat. In the Hindu legends,
Hari dwells a peasant among peasants. In the Greek legend, Apollo
lodges with the shepherds of Admetus, and Jove liked to rusticate
among the poor Ethiopians. So, in our history, Jesus is born in a
barn, and his twelve peers are fishermen. 'Tis the very principle of
science that Nature shows herself best in leasts; it was the maxim of
Aristotle and Lucretius; and, in modern times, of Swedenborg and
of Hahnemann.[3] The order of changes in the egg determines the
age of fossil strata. So it was the rule of our poets, in the legends of
fairy lore, that the fairies largest in power were the least in size. In
the Christian graces, humility stands highest of all, in the form of
the Madonna; and in life, this is the secret of the wise. We owe
to genius always the same debt, of lifting the curtain from the common, and showing us that divinities are sitting disguised in the
seeming gang of gypsies and pedlars. In daily life, what distinguishes the master is the using those materials he has, instead of
looking about for what are more renowned, or what others have
used well. "A general," said Bonaparte, "always has troops enough,
if he only knows how to employ those he has, and bivouacs with
them." Do not refuse the employment which the hour brings you,
for one more ambitious. The highest heaven of wisdom is alike

[3] Founder of the homeopathic school of medicine.

near from every point, and thou must find it, if at all, by methods native to thyself alone.

That work is ever the more pleasant to the imagination which is not now required. How wistfully, when we have promised to attend the working committee, we look at the distant hills and their seductions!

The use of history is to give value to the present hour and its duty. That is good which commends to me my country, my climate, my means and materials, my associates. I knew a man in a certain religious exaltation who "thought it an honor to wash his own face." He seemed to me more sane than those who hold themselves cheap.

Zoölogists may deny that horse-hairs in the water change to worms, but I find that whatever is old corrupts, and the past turns to snakes. The reverence for the deeds of our ancestors is a treacherous sentiment. Their merit was not to reverence the old, but to honor the present moment; and we falsely make them excuses of the very habit which they hated and defied.

Another illusion is that there is not time enough for our work. Yet we might reflect that though many creatures eat from one dish, each, according to its constitution, assimilates from the elements what belongs to it, whether time, or space, or light, or water, or food. A snake converts whatever prey the meadow yields him into snake; a fox, into fox; and Peter and John are working up all existence into Peter and John. A poor Indian chief of the Six Nations of New York made a wiser reply than any philosopher, to some one complaining that he had not enough time. "Well," said Red Jacket, "I suppose you have all there is."

A third illusion haunts us, that a long duration, as a year, a decade, a century, is valuable. But an old French sentence says, "God works in moments," — "En peu d'heure Dieu labeure." We ask for long life, but 'tis deep life, or grand moments, that signify. Let the measure of time be spiritual, not mechanical. Life is unnecessarily long. Moments of insight, of fine personal relation, a smile, a glance, — what ample borrowers of eternity they are! Life culminates and concentrates; and Homer said, "The gods ever give to mortals their apportioned share of reason only on one day."

I am of the opinion of the poet Wordsworth, that "there is no real happiness in this life but in intellect and virtue." I am of the opinion of Pliny that "whilst we are musing on these things, we are adding to the length of our lives." I am of the opinion of

Glaucon, who said, "The measure of life, O Socrates, is, with the wise, the speaking and hearing such discourses as yours."

He only can enrich me who can recommend to me the space between sun and sun. 'Tis the measure of a man, — his apprehension of a day. For we do not listen with the best regard to the verses of a man who is only a poet, nor to his problems if he is only an algebraist; but if a man is at once acquainted with the geometric foundations of things and with their festal splendor, his poetry is exact and his arithmetic musical. And him I reckon the most learned scholar, not who can unearth for me the buried dynasties of Sesostris and Ptolemy, the Sothiac era, the Olympiads and consulships, but who can unfold the theory of this particular Wednesday. Can he uncover the ligaments concealed from all but piety, which attach the dull men and things we know to the First Cause? These passing fifteen minutes, men think, are time, not eternity; are low and subaltern, are but hope or memory; that is, the way *to* or the way *from* welfare, but not welfare. Can he show their tie? That interpreter shall guide us from a menial and eleemosynary existence into riches and stability. He dignifies the place where he is. This mendicant America, this curious, peering, itinerant, imitative America, studious of Greece and Rome, of England and Germany, will take off its dusty shoes, will take off its glazed traveler's-cap and sit at home with repose and deep joy on its face. The world has no such landscape, the aeons of history no such hour, the future no equal second opportunity. Now let poets sing! now let arts unfold!

One more view remains. But life is good only when it is magical and musical, a perfect timing and consent, and when we do not anatomize it. You must treat the days respectfully, you must be a day yourself, and not interrogate it like a college professor. The world is enigmatical, — everything said, and everything known or done, — and must not be taken literally, but genially. We must be at the top of our condition to understand anything rightly. You must hear the bird's song without attempting to render it into nouns and verbs. Cannot we be a little abstemious and obedient? Cannot we let the morning be?

Everything in the universe goes by indirection. There are no straight lines. I remember well the foreign scholar who made a week of my youth happy by his visit. "The savages in the islands," he said, "delight to play with the surf, coming in on the top of the rollers, then swimming out again, and repeat the delicious manoeuvre for hours. Well, human life is made up of such transits. There can be no greatness without abandonment. But here your very astronomy is an espionage. I dare not go out of doors and see the moon and stars, but they seem to measure my tasks, to ask how many lines or pages are finished since I saw them last. Not so, as I told you, was it in Belleisle. The days at Belleisle were all different, and only joined by a perfect love of the same object. Just to fill the hour, — that is happiness. Fill my hour, ye gods, so that I shall not say, whilst I have done this, 'Behold, also, an hour of my life is gone,' — but rather, 'I have lived an hour.' "

We do not want factitious men, who can do any literary or professional feat, as, to write poems, or advocate a cause, or carry a measure, for money; or turn their ability indifferently in any particular direction by the strong effort of will. No, what has been best done in the world, — the works of genius, — cost nothing. There is no painful effort, but it is the spontaneous flowing of the thought. Shakespeare made his Hamlet as a bird weaves its nest. Poems have been written between sleeping and waking, irresponsibly. Fancy defines herself: —

> "Forms that men spy
> With the half-shut eye
> In the beams of the setting sun, am I."

The masters painted for joy, and knew not that virtue had gone out of them. They could not paint the like in cold blood. The masters of English lyric wrote their songs so. It was a fine efflorescence of fine powers; as was said of the letters of the Frenchwoman, — "the charming accident of their more charming existence." Then the poet is never the poorer for his song. A song is no song unless the circumstance is free and fine. If the singer sing from a sense of duty or from seeing no way of escape, I had rather have none. Those only can sleep who do not care to sleep; and those only write or speak best who do not too much respect the writing or the speaking.

The same rule holds in science. The savant is often an amateur. His performance is a memoir to the Academy on fish-worms, tadpoles, or spiders' legs; he observes as other academicians observe; he is on stilts at a microscope, and his memoir finished and read and printed, he retreats into his routinary existence, which is quite separate from his scientific. But in Newton, science was as easy as breathing; he used the same wit to weigh the moon that he used to buckle his shoes; and all his life was simple, wise and majestic. So was it in Archimedes, — always self-same, like the sky. In Linnaeus, in Franklin, the like sweetness and equality, — no stilts, no tiptoe; and their results are wholesome and memorable to all men.

In stripping time of its illusions, in seeking to find what is the heart of the day, we come to the quality of the moment, and drop the duration altogether. It is the depth at which we live and not at all the surface extension that imports. We pierce to the eternity, of which time is the flitting surface; and, really, the least acceleration of thought and the least increase of power of thought, make life to seem and to be of vast duration. We call it time; but when that acceleration and that deepening take effect, it acquires another and a higher name.

There are people who do not need much experimenting; who, after years of activity, say, We knew all this before; who love at first sight and hate at first sight; discern the affinities and repulsions; who do not care so much for conditions as others, for they are always in one condition and enjoy themselves; who dictate to others and are not dictated to; who in their consciousness of deserving success constantly slight the ordinary means of attaining it; who have self-existence and self-help; who are suffered to be themselves in society; who are great in the present; who have no talents, or care not to have them, — being that which was before talent, and shall be after it, and of which talent seems only a tool: this is character, the highest name at which philosophy has arrived.

'Tis not important how the hero does this or this, but what he is. What he is will appear in every gesture and syllable. In this way the moment and the character are one.

It is a fine fable for the advantage of character over talent, the Greek legend of the strife of Jove and Phoebus. Phoebus challenged the gods, and said, "Who will outshoot the far-darting Apollo?" Zeus said, "I will." Mars shook the lots in his helmet, and that of Apollo leaped out first. Apollo stretched his bow and shot his arrow into the extreme west. Then Zeus rose, and with one stride cleared the whole distance, and said, "Where shall I shoot? there is no space left." So the bowman's prize was adjudged to him who drew no bow.

And this is the progress of every earnest mind; from the works of man and the activity of the hands to a delight in the faculties which rule them; from a respect to the works to a wise wonder at this mystic element of time in which he is conditioned; from local skills and the economy which reckons the amount of production *per* hour to the finer economy which respects the quality of what is done, and the right we have to the work, or the fidelity with which it flows from ourselves; then to the depth of thought it betrays, looking to its universality, or that its roots are in eternity, not in time. Then it flows from character, that sublime health which values one moment as another, and makes us great in all conditions, and is the only definition we have of freedom and power.

Spring, 1857

Because our education is defective, because we are superficial and ill-read, we were forced to make the most of that position, of ignorance; to idealize ignorance. Hence America is a vast know-nothing party, and we disparage books, and cry up intuition. With a few clever men we have made a reputable thing of that, and denouncing libraries and severe culture, and magnifying the mother-wit swagger of bright boys from the country colleges, we have even come so far as to deceive everybody, except ourselves, into an admiration of un-learning and inspiration, forsooth.

June, 1857

Scholar and Times. — Could I make you feel your indispensableness, — and yet it behooves first to show you the joy of your high place. You have the keys. You deal with design and the methods. Here lies this wide aboriginal Nature, old beyond figures, yet new and entire, the silver flame which flashes up the sky, — no aeons can date it, yet there it burns as delicately as the passing cinder of the firefly with the lightness of a new petal. Here you rest and work in this element of Space, whose bewildering circuits make all the universe a dot on its margin, — dwarfing the gods.

To teach us the first lesson of humility, God set down man in these two vastitudes of Space and Time, yet is he such an incorrigible peacock that he thinks them only a perch to show his dirty feathers on.

September ?, 1857

Naïveté. — Uses of Nature, to be sure! — Why, this is foremost. What we value, all we value, is the *naturel,* or peculiar quality of each man; and, in a large, healthy individual, this is the antagonist of gravitation, vegetation, chemistry, nay, of matter itself, and as good at least as they. This is the saliency,[4] the principle of levity,

4 Leaping quality.

the *sal volatile,* which is the balance, or offset, to the mountains and masses. This is forever a surprise, and engaging, and a man is therefore and thus wonderful and lovely. Now Homer, Shakespeare, Burns, Scott, Voltaire, Rabelais, Montaigne, Hafiz, have these spirits or intuitions, and are magnetic, or interesting to all men. We are curious about them, can't be satisfied with watching the primal springs, and their movements, wish to know their law, if we could. Well, every man has the like potency in him, more or less. This wit is related to the secret of the world, to the primitive power, the incessant creation. It is in harmony with gravity, and the orbit of stars, and the growth of grass, and the angles of crystals. There is no luck or choice about it, but law in it, from first to last. It is the next finer ascent or metamorphosis of gravity, chemistry, vegetation, animal life, the same thing, on the next higher plane; as the *morale* [5] is a still higher ascent or metamorphosis, and kindred to it. But the essence of it is, that it be native and intuitive. . . .

April, 1859

. . . An English speculator shows the wonder of electricity, and talks of its leaving poetry far behind, etc., or, perhaps, that it will yet show poetry new materials, etc. Yet poetry is in Nature just as much as carbon is: love and wonder and the delight in suddenly seen analogy exist as necessarily as space, or heat, or Canada thistles; and have their legitimate functions: and where they have no play, the impatience of the mind betrays precisely the distance from the truth, — the truth which satisfies the mind and affections, and leaves the real and the ideal in equilibrium, which constitutes happiness.

April, 1859

I have now for more than a year, I believe, ceased to write in my Journal, in which I formerly wrote almost daily. I see few intellectual persons, and even those to no purpose, and sometimes believe that I have no new thoughts, and that my life is quite at an end. But the magnet that lies in my drawer, for years, may believe it has no magnetism, and, on touching it with steel, it knows the old virtue; and, this morning, came by a man with knowledge and interests like mine, in his head, and suddenly I had thoughts again.

[5] Moral.

April, 1859

I am a natural reader, and only a writer in the absence of natural writers. In a true time, I should never have written.

April, 1859

I have been writing and speaking what were once called novelties, for twenty-five or thirty years, and have not now one disciple. Why? Not that what I said was not true; not that it has not found intelligent receivers; but because it did not go from any wish in me to bring men to me, but to themselves. I delight in driving them from me. What could I do, if they came to me? — they would interrupt and encumber me. This is my boast that I have no school follower. I should account it a measure of the impurity of insight, if it did not create independence.

May ?, 1859

Now and then, rarely, comes a stout man like Luther, Montaigne, Pascal, Herbert, who utters a thought or feeling in a virile manner, and it is unforgettable. Then follow any number of spiritual eunuchs and women, who talk about that thought, imply it, in pages and volumes. . . . Great bands of female souls who only receive the spermatic *aura* and brood on the same but add nothing.

Do not spend one moment on the last; they are mere publishers and diluters and critics.

May ?, 1859

People live like these boys who watch for a sleigh-ride and mount on the first that passes, and when they meet another that they know, swing themselves on to that, and ride in another direction, until a third passes, and they change again; 'tis no matter where they go, as long as there is snow and company.

May, 1859

Our doctrine must begin with the necessary and eternal, and discriminate Fate from the necessary. There is no limitation about the Eternal. Thought, Will, is co-eternal with the world; and, as soon as intellect is awaked in any man, it shares so far of the eternity, — is of the maker, not of the made. But Fate is the name we give to the action of that one eternal, all-various necessity on the brute myriads, whether in things, animals, or in men in whom the intellect pure is not yet opened. To such it is only a burning wall which hurts those who run against it.

The great day in the man is the birth of perception, which instantly throws him on the party of the Eternal. He sees what must be, and that it is not more that which must be, than it is that which should be, or what is best. To be then becomes the infinite good, and breath is jubilation. A breath of Will blows through the universe eternally in the direction of the right or necessary; it is the air which all intellects inhale and exhale, and all things are blown or moved by it in order and orbit. . . .

August, 1859

Beatitudes of Intellect. — Am I not, one of these days, to write consecutively of the beatitude of intellect? It is too great for feeble souls, and they are over-excited. The wineglass shakes, and the wine is spilled. What then? The joy which will not let me sit in my chair, which brings me bolt upright to my feet, and sends me striding around my room, like a tiger in his cage, and I cannot have composure and concentration enough even to set down in English words the thought which thrills me — is not that joy a certificate of the elevation? What if I never write a book or a line? for a moment, the eyes of my eyes were opened, the affirmative experience remains, and consoles through all suffering.

1861–1882

The War and After

When the Civil War began, Emerson was fifty-eight years old. The relief of a righteous cause after long shame seemed to rejuvenate him: "Ah! sometimes gunpowder smells good," he exclaimed. Too old to fight, he threw himself into work behind the lines: he spoke at rallies, he helped Concord do her bit, he lectured on the issues of the war and wrote poems about them, he served on a committee of visitation for West Point, he corresponded with Washington and visited there, meeting Lincoln and most of his Cabinet; in 1862 he pressed for the extreme Abolitionist position, at Appomattox he feared Grant's terms were too easy, and afterwards he deprecated Lincoln's lenient policy of reconstruction. Though he once confessed that "this mad war has made us all mad," all his truly formidable reserves of Puritan-bred moral indignation, all his still-latent protest against the "slavish Actual" was thrown into the furnace of this holy war; when it burnt out, his work was almost over too.

Not all these long four years were spent on war-matters. In 1862 Thoreau, once so much the more robust of the two, died at the early age of forty-four and Emerson forgot the war to speak the eulogy of his friend from earlier days. In 1864 Hawthorne followed and Emerson also began to feel his years. His last major undertaking was a course of lectures at Harvard in 1870 and 1871 on "Natural History of the Intellect." The invitation was a gratifying one and the topic an old favorite — he gave a series with the same title in England in 1848; the published portion of these lectures contains impressively modern insights that still reward study. Nevertheless, the course made him feel his inability to meet such demands any more; thereafter he did little new work. The shock of a fire in his home in 1872 hastened his decline, which another year in Europe did not do enough to arrest. With the progressive failure of his memory, he passed quietly into a long and on the whole serene retirement. Death came in 1882.

᯾

Thoreau

HENRY David Thoreau was the last male descendant of a French ancestor who came to this country from the Isle of Guernsey. His character exhibited occasional traits drawn from this blood, in singular combination with a very strong Saxon genius.

He was born in Concord, Massachusetts, on the 12th of July, 1817. He was graduated at Harvard College in 1837, but without any literary distinction. An iconoclast in literature, he seldom thanked colleges for their service to him, holding them in small esteem, whilst yet his debt to them was important. After leaving the University, he joined his brother in teaching a private school, which he soon renounced. His father was a manufacturer of lead-pencils, and Henry applied himself for a time to this craft, believing he could make a better pencil than was then in use. After completing his experiments, he exhibited his work to chemists and artists in Boston, and having obtained their certificates to its excellence and to its equality with the best London manufacture, he returned home contented. His friends congratulated him that he had now opened his way to fortune. But he replied that he should never make another pencil. "Why should I? I would not do again what I have done once." He resumed his endless walks and miscellaneous studies, making every day some new acquaintance with Nature, though as yet never speaking of zoölogy or botany, since, though very studious of natural facts, he was incurious of technical and textual science.

At this time, a strong, healthy youth, fresh from college, whilst all his companions were choosing their profession, or eager to begin some lucrative employment, it was inevitable that his thoughts should be exercised on the same question, and it required rare decision to refuse all the accustomed paths and keep his solitary freedom at the cost of disappointing the natural expectations of his family and friends: all the more difficult that he had a perfect probity, was exact in securing his own independence, and in holding every man to the like duty. But Thoreau never faltered. He was a born protestant. He declined to give up his large ambition of knowledge and action for any narrow craft or profession, aiming at a much more comprehensive calling, the art of living well. If he slighted and defied the opinions of others, it was only that he was more intent to reconcile his practice with his own belief. Never idle or self-indulgent, he preferred, when he wanted money, earning it by some piece of manual labor agreeable to him, as building a boat or a fence, planting, grafting, surveying or other short work, to any long engagements. With his hardy habits and few wants, his skill in wood-craft, and his powerful arithmetic, he was very competent to live in any part of the world. It would cost him less time to supply his wants than another. He was therefore secure of his leisure.

A natural skill for mensuration, growing out of his mathematical knowledge and his habit of ascertaining the measures and distances of objects which interested him, the size of trees, the depth and extent of ponds and rivers, the height of mountains and the airline distance of his favorite summits, — this, and his intimate knowledge of the territory about Concord, made him drift into the profession of land-surveyor. It had the advantage for him that it led him continually into new and secluded grounds, and helped his studies of Nature. His accuracy and skill in this work were readily appreciated, and he found all the employment he wanted.

He could easily solve the problems of the surveyor, but he was daily beset with graver questions, which he manfully confronted. He interrogated every custom, and wished to settle all his practice on an ideal foundation. He was a protestant *à outrance*,[1] and few lives contain so many renunciations. He was bred to no profession; he never married; he lived alone; he never went to church; he never voted; he refused to pay a tax to the State; he ate no flesh, he drank no wine, he never knew the use of tobacco; and, though a naturalist, he used neither trap nor gun. He chose, wisely no doubt for himself, to be the bachelor of thought and Nature. He had no talent for wealth, and knew how to be poor without the least hint of squalor or inelegance. Perhaps he fell into his way of living without forecasting it much, but approved it with later wisdom. "I am often reminded," he wrote in his journal, "that if I had bestowed on me the wealth of Croesus, my aims must be still the same, and my means essentially the same." He had no temptations to fight against, — no appetites, no passions, no taste for elegant trifles. A fine house, dress, the manners and talk of highly

[1] To the limit.

cultivated people were all thrown away on him. He much preferred a good Indian, and considered these refinements as impediments to conversation, wishing to meet his companion on the simplest terms. He declined invitations to dinner-parties, because there each was in every one's way, and he could not meet the individuals to any purpose. "They make their pride," he said, "in making their dinner cost much; I make my pride in making my dinner cost little." When asked at table what dish he preferred, he answered, "The nearest." He did not like the taste of wine, and never had a vice in his life. He said, — "I have a faint recollection of pleasure derived from smoking dried lily-stems, before I was a man. I had commonly a supply of these. I have never smoked anything more noxious."

He chose to be rich by making his wants few, and supplying them himself. In his travels, he used the railroad only to get over so much country as was unimportant to the present purpose, walking hundreds of miles, avoiding taverns, buying a lodging in farmers' and fishermen's houses, as cheaper, and more agreeable to him, and because there he could better find the men and the information he wanted.

There was somewhat military in his nature, not to be subdued, always manly and able, but rarely tender, as if he did not feel himself except in opposition. He wanted a fallacy to expose, a blunder to pillory, I may say required a little sense of victory, a roll of the drum, to call his powers into full exercise. It cost him nothing to say No; indeed he found it much easier than to say Yes. It seemed as if his first instinct on hearing a proposition was to controvert it, so impatient was he of the limitations of our daily thought. This habit, of course, is a little chilling to the social affections; and though the companion would in the end acquit him of any malice or untruth, yet it mars conversation. Hence, no equal companion stood in affectionate relations with one so pure and guileless. "I love Henry," said one of his friends, "but I cannot like him; and as for taking his arm, I should as soon think of taking the arm of an elm-tree."

Yet, hermit and stoic as he was, he was really fond of sympathy, and threw himself heartily and childlike into the company of young people whom he loved, and whom he delighted to entertain, as he only could, with the varied and endless anecdotes of his experiences by field and river: and he was always ready to lead a huckleberry-party or a search for chestnuts or grapes. Talking, one day, of a public discourse, Henry remarked that whatever succeeded with the audience was bad. I said, "Who would not like to write something which all can read, like Robinson Crusoe? and who does not see with regret that his page is not solid with a right materialistic treatment, which delights everybody?" Henry objected, of course, and vaunted the better lectures which reached only a few persons. But, at supper, a young girl, understanding that he was to lecture at the Lyceum, sharply asked him, "Whether his lecture would be a nice, interesting story, such as she wished to hear, or whether it was one of those old philosophical things that she did not care about." Henry turned to her, and bethought himself, and, I saw, was trying to believe that he had matter that might fit her and her brother, who were to sit up and go to the lecture, if it was a good one for them.

He was a speaker and actor of the truth, born such, and was ever running into dramatic situations from this cause. In any circumstance it interested all bystanders to know what part Henry would take, and what he would say; and he did not disappoint expectation, but used an original judgment on each emergency. In 1845 he built himself a small framed house on the shores of Walden Pond, and lived there two years alone, a life of labor and study. This action was quite native and fit for him. No one who knew him would tax him with affectation. He was more unlike his neighbors in his thought than in his action. As soon as he had exhausted the advantages of that solitude, he abandoned it. In 1847, not approving some uses to which the public expenditure was applied, he refused to pay his town tax, and was put in jail. A friend paid the tax for him, and he was released. The like annoyance was threatened the next year. But as his friends paid the tax, notwithstanding his protest, I believe he ceased to resist. No opposition or ridicule had any weight with him. He coldly and fully stated his opinion without affecting to believe that it was the opinion of the company. It was of no consequence if every one present held the opposite opinion. On one occasion he went to the University Library to procure some books. The librarian refused to lend them. Mr. Thoreau repaired to the President, who stated to him the rules and usages, which permitted the loan of books to resident graduates, to clergymen who were alumni, and to some others resident within a circle of ten miles' radius from the College. Mr. Thoreau explained to the President that the railroad had destroyed the old scale of distances, — that the library was useless, yes, and President and College useless, on the terms of his rules, — that the one benefit he owed to the College was its library, — that, at this moment, not only his want of books was imperative, but he wanted a large number of books, and assured him that he, Thoreau, and not the librarian, was the proper custodian of these. In short, the President found the petitioner so formidable, and the rules getting to look so ridiculous, that he ended by giving him a privilege which in his hands proved unlimited thereafter.

No truer American existed than Thoreau. His preference of his country and condition was genuine, and his aversation from English and European manners and tastes almost reached contempt. He listened impatiently to news or *bonmots* gleaned from London circles; and though he tried to be civil, these anecdotes fatigued him. The men were all imitating each other, and on a small mold. Why can they not live as far apart as possible, and each be a man by himself? What he sought was the most energetic nature; and he wished to go to Oregon, not to London. "In every part of Great Britain," he wrote in his diary, "are discovered traces of the Romans, their funereal urns, their camps, their roads, their dwellings. But New England, at least, is not based on any Roman ruins. We have not to lay the foundations of our houses on the ashes of a former civilization."

But idealist as he was, standing for abolition of slavery, abolition of tariffs, almost for abolition of government, it is needless to say he found himself not only unrepresented in actual politics, but almost equally opposed to every class of reformers. Yet he paid the tribute of his uniform respect to the Anti-Slavery party. One man, whose personal acquaintance he had formed, he honored with exceptional regard. Before the first friendly word had been spoken for Captain John Brown, he sent notices to most houses in Concord that he would speak in a public hall on the condition and character of John Brown, on Sunday evening, and invited all people to come. The Republican Committee, the Abolitionist Committee, sent him word that it was premature and not advisable. He replied, — "I did not send to you for advice, but to announce that I am to speak." The hall was filled at an early hour by people of all parties, and his earnest eulogy of the hero was heard by all respectfully, by many with a sympathy that surprised themselves.

It was said of Plotinus that he was ashamed of his body, and 'tis very likely he had good reason for it, — that his body was a bad servant, and he had not skill in dealing with the material world, as happens often to men of abstract intellect. But Mr. Thoreau was equipped with a most adapted and serviceable body. He was of short stature, firmly built, of light complexion, with strong, serious blue eyes, and a grave aspect, — his face covered in the late years with a becoming beard. His senses were acute, his frame well-knit and hardy, his hands strong and skilful in the use of tools. And there was a wonderful fitness of body and mind. He could pace sixteen rods more accurately than another man could measure them with rod and chain. He could find his path in the woods at night, he said, better by his feet than his eyes. He could estimate the measure of a tree very well by his eye; he could estimate the weight of a calf or a pig, like a dealer. From a box containing a bushel or more of loose pencils, he could take up with his hands fast enough just a dozen pencils at every grasp. He was a good swimmer, runner, skater, boatman, and would probably outwalk most countrymen in a day's journey. And the relation of body to mind was still finer than we have indicated. He said he wanted every stride his legs made. The length of his walk uniformly made the length of his writing. If shut up in the house he did not write at all.

He had a strong common sense, like that which Rose Flammock, the weaver's daughter in Scott's romance, commends in her father, as resembling a yardstick, which, whilst it measures dowlas and diaper, can equally well measure tapestry and cloth of gold. He had always a new resource. When I was planting forest trees, and had procured half a peck of acorns, he said that only a small portion of them would be sound, and proceeded to examine them and select the sound ones. But finding this took time, he said, "I think if you put them all into water the good ones will sink"; which experiment we tried with success. He could plan a garden or a house or a barn; would have been competent to lead a "Pacific Exploring Expedition"; could give judicious counsel in the gravest private or public affairs.

He lived for the day, not cumbered and mortified by his memory. If he brought you yesterday a new proposition, he would bring you today another not less revolutionary. A very industrious man, and setting, like all highly organized men, a high value on his time, he seemed the only man of leisure in town, always ready for any excursion that promised well, or for conversation prolonged into late hours. His trenchant sense was never stopped by his rules of daily prudence, but was always up to the new occasion. He liked and used the simplest food, yet, when some one urged a vegetable diet, Thoreau thought all diets a very small matter, saying that "the man who shoots the buffalo lives better than the man who boards at the Graham House." He said, — "You can sleep near the railroad, and never be disturbed: Nature knows very well what sounds are worth attending to, and has made up her mind not to hear the railroad-whistle. But things respect the devout mind, and a mental ecstasy was never interrupted." He noted what repeatedly befell him, that, after receiving from a distance a rare plant, he would presently find the same in his own haunts. And those pieces of luck which happen only to good players happened to him. One day, walking with a stranger, who inquired where Indian arrow-heads could be found, he replied, "Every where," and, stooping forward, picked one on the instant from the ground. At Mount Washington, in Tuckerman's Ravine, Thoreau had a bad fall, and sprained his foot. As he was in the act of getting up from his fall, he saw for the first time the leaves of the *Arnica mollis*.[2]

His robust common sense, armed with stout hands, keen perceptions and strong will, cannot yet account for the superiority which shone in his simple and hidden life. I must add the cardinal fact, that there was an excellent wisdom in him, proper to a rare class of men, which showed him the material world as a means and symbol. This discovery, which sometimes yields to poets a certain casual and interrupted light, serving for the ornament of their writing, was in him an unsleeping insight; and whatever faults or obstructions of temperament might cloud it, he was not disobedient to the heavenly vision. In his youth, he said, one day, "The other world is all my art; my pencils will draw no other; my jack-knife will cut nothing else; I do not use it as a means." This was the muse and genius that ruled his opinions, conversation, studies, work and course of life. This made him a searching judge of men. At first glance he measured his companion, and, though insensible to some fine traits of culture, could very well report his weight and calibre. And this made the impression of genius which his conversation sometimes gave.

He understood the matter in hand at a glance, and saw the limitations and poverty of those he talked with, so that nothing seemed concealed from such terrible eyes. I have repeatedly known young men of sensibility converted in a moment to the belief that this was the man they were in search of, the man of men, who could tell them all they should do. His own dealing with them was never affectionate, but superior, didactic, scorning their petty ways, — very slowly conceding, or not conceding at all, the promise of his

[2] Plant medicinal for sprains.

society at their houses, or even at his own. "Would he not walk with them?" "He did not know. There was nothing so important to him as his walk; he had no walks to throw away on company." Visits were offered him from respectful parties, but he declined them. Admiring friends offered to carry him at their own cost to the Yellowstone River, — to the West Indies, — to South America. But though nothing could be more grave or considered than his refusals, they remind one, in quite new relations, of that fop Brummel's reply to the gentleman who offered him his carriage in a shower, "But where will *you* ride, then?" — and what accusing silences, and what searching and irresistible speeches, battering down all defenses, his companions can remember!

Mr. Thoreau dedicated his genius with such entire love to the fields, hills and waters of his native town, that he made them known and interesting to all reading Americans, and to people over the sea. The river on whose banks he was born and died he knew from its springs to its confluence with the Merrimack. He had made summer and winter observations on it for many years, and at every hour of the day and night. The result of the recent survey of the Water Commissioners appointed by the State of Massachusetts he had reached by his private experiments, several years earlier. Every fact which occurs in the bed, on the banks or in the air over it; the fishes, and their spawning and nests, their manners, their food; the shad-flies which fill the air on a certain evening once a year, and which are snapped at by the fishes so ravenously that many of these die of repletion; the conical heaps of small stones on the river-shallows, the huge nests of small fishes, one of which will sometimes overfill a cart; the birds which frequent the stream, heron, duck, sheldrake, loon, osprey; the snake, muskrat, otter, woodchuck and fox, on the banks; the turtle, frog, hyla and cricket, which make the banks vocal, — were all known to him, and, as it were, townsmen and fellow creatures; so that he felt an absurdity or violence in any narrative of one of these by itself apart, and still more of its dimensions on an inch-rule, or in the exhibition of its skeleton, or the specimen of a squirrel or a bird in brandy. He liked to speak of the manners of the river, as itself a lawful creature, yet with exactness, and always to an observed fact. As he knew the river, so the ponds in this region.

One of the weapons he used, more important to him than microscope or alcohol-receiver to other investigators, was a whim which grew on him by indulgence, yet appeared in gravest statement, namely, of extolling his own town and neighborhood as the most

favored center for natural observation. He remarked that the Flora
of Massachusetts embraced almost all the important plants of
America, — most of the oaks, most of the willows, the best pines,
the ash, the maple, the beech, the nuts. He returned Kane's Arctic
Voyage to a friend of whom he had borrowed it, with the remark,
that "Most of the phenomena noted might be observed in Concord." He seemed a little envious of the Pole, for the coincident
sunrise and sunset, or five minutes' day after six months: a splendid
fact, which Annursnuc had never afforded him. He found red snow
in one of his walks, and told me that he expected to find yet the
Victoria regia in Concord. He was the attorney of the indigenous
plants, and owned to a preference of the weeds to the imported
plants, as of the Indian to the civilized man, and noticed, with
pleasure, that the willow bean-poles of his neighbor had grown
more than his beans. "See these weeds," he said, "which have been
hoed at by a million farmers all spring and summer, and yet have
prevailed, and just now come out triumphant over all lanes, pastures, fields and gardens, such is their vigor. We have insulted
them with low names, too, — as Pigweed, Wormwood, Chickweed,
Shad-blossom." He says, "They have brave names, too, — Am-
brosia, Stellaria, Amelanchier, Amaranth, etc."

I think his fancy for referring everything to the meridian of
Concord did not grow out of any ignorance or depreciation of
other longitudes or latitudes, but was rather a playful expression
of his conviction of the indifferency of all places, and that the
best place for each is where he stands. He expressed it once in
this wise: "I think nothing is to be hoped from you, if this bit of
mold under your feet is not sweeter to you to eat than any other in
this world, or in any world."

The other weapon with which he conquered all obstacles in
science was patience. He knew how to sit immovable, a part of the
rock he rested on, until the bird, the reptile, the fish, which had
retired from him, should come back and resume its habits, nay,
moved by curiosity, should come to him and watch him.

It was a pleasure and a privilege to walk with him. He knew the
country like a fox or a bird, and passed through it as freely by paths
of his own. He knew every track in the snow or on the ground,
and what creature had taken this path before him. One must submit abjectly to such a guide, and the reward was great. Under his
arm he carried an old music-book to press plants; in his pocket, his
diary and pencil, a spy-glass for birds, microscope, jack-knife and
twine. He wore a straw hat, stout shoes, strong gray trousers, to

brave scrub-oaks and smilax, and to climb a tree for a hawk's or a squirrel's nest. He waded into the pool for the water-plants, and his strong legs were no insignificant part of his armor. On the day I speak of he looked for the Menyanthes, detected it across the wide pool, and, on examination of the florets, decided that it had been in flower five days. He drew out of his breast-pocket his diary, and read the names of all the plants that should bloom on this day, whereof he kept account as a banker when his notes fall due. The Cypripedium not due till tomorrow. He thought that, if waked up from a trance, in this swamp, he could tell by the plants what time of the year it was within two days. The redstart was flying about, and presently the fine grosbeaks, whose brilliant scarlet "makes the rash gazer wipe his eye," and whose fine clear note Thoreau compared to that of a tanager which has got rid of its hoarseness. Presently he heard a note which he called that of the night-warbler, a bird he had never identified, had been in search of twelve years, which always, when he saw it, was in the act of diving down into a tree or bush, and which it was vain to seek; the only bird which sings indifferently by night and by day. I told him he must beware of finding and booking it, lest life should have nothing more to show him. He said, "What you seek in vain for, half your life, one day you come full upon, all the family at dinner. You seek it like a dream, and as soon as you find it you become its prey."

His interest in the flower or the bird lay very deep in his mind, was connected with Nature, — and the meaning of Nature was never attempted to be defined by him. He would not offer a memoir of his observations to the Natural History Society. "Why should I? To detach the description from its connections in my mind would make it no longer true or valuable to me: and they do not wish what belongs to it." His power of observation seemed to indicate additional senses. He saw as with microscope, heard as with ear-trumpet, and his memory was a photographic register of all he saw and heard. And yet none knew better than he that it is not the fact that imports, but the impression or effect of the fact on your mind. Every fact lay in glory in his mind, a type of the order and beauty of the whole.

His determination on Natural History was organic. He confessed that he sometimes felt like a hound or a panther, and, if born among Indians, would have been a fell hunter. But, restrained by his Massachusetts culture, he played out the game in this mild form of botany and ichthyology. His intimacy with animals suggested what Thomas Fuller records of Butler the apiologist, that "either he had told the bees things or the bees had told him." Snakes coiled round his legs; the fishes swam into his hand, and he took them out of the water; he pulled the woodchuck out of its hole by the tail, and took the foxes under his protection from the hunters. Our naturalist had perfect magnanimity; he had no secrets: he would carry you to the heron's haunt, or even to his most prized botanical swamp, — possibly knowing that you could never find it again, yet willing to take his risks.

No college ever offered him a diploma, or a professor's chair; no academy made him its corresponding secretary, its discoverer or even its member. Perhaps these learned bodies feared the satire of his presence. Yet so much knowledge of Nature's secret and genius few others possessed; none in a more large and religious synthesis. For not a particle of respect had he to the opinions of any man or body of men, but homage solely to the truth itself; and as he discovered everywhere among doctors some leaning of courtesy, it discredited them. He grew to be revered and admired by his townsmen, who had at first known him only as an oddity. The farmers who employed him as a surveyor soon discovered his rare accuracy and skill, his knowledge of their lands, of trees, of birds, of Indian remains and the like, which enabled him to tell every farmer more than he knew before of his own farm; so that he began to feel a little as if Mr. Thoreau had better rights in his land than he. They felt, too, the superiority of character which addressed all men with a native authority.

Indian relics abound in Concord, — arrow-heads, stone chisels, pestles and fragments of pottery; and on the river-bank, large heaps of clam-shells and ashes mark spots which the savages frequented. These, and every circumstance touching the Indian, were important in his eyes. His visits to Maine were chiefly for love of the Indian. He had the satisfaction of seeing the manufacture of the bark canoe, as well as of trying his hand in its management on the rapids. He was inquisitive about the making of the stone arrow-head, and in his last days charged a youth setting out for the Rocky Mountains to find an Indian who could tell him that: "It was well worth a visit to California to learn it." Occasionally, a small party of Penobscot Indians would visit Concord, and pitch their tents for a few weeks in summer on the river-bank. He failed not to make acquaintance with the best of them; though he well knew that asking questions of Indians is like catechizing beavers and rabbits. In his last visit to Maine he had great satisfaction from Joseph Polis, an intelligent Indian of Oldtown, who was his guide for some weeks.

He was equally interested in every natural fact. The depth of his perception found likeness of law throughout Nature, and I know not any genius who so swiftly inferred universal law from the single fact. He was no pedant of a department. His eye was open to beauty, and his ear to music. He found these, not in rare conditions, but wheresoever he went. He thought the best of music was in single strains; and he found poetic suggestion in the humming of the telegraph-wire.

His poetry might be bad or good; he no doubt wanted a lyric facility and technical skill, but he had the source of poetry in his spiritual perception. He was a good reader and critic, and his judgment on poetry was to the ground of it. He could not be deceived as to the presence or absence of the poetic element in any composition, and his thirst for this made him negligent and perhaps scornful of superficial graces. He would pass by many delicate rhythms, but he would have detected every live stanza or line in a volume and knew very well where to find an equal poetic charm in prose. He was so enamoured of the spiritual beauty that he held all actual written poems in very light esteem in the comparison. He admired Aeschylus and Pindar; but when some one was commending them, he said that Aeschylus and the Greeks, in describing Apollo and Orpheus, had given no song, or no good one. "They ought not to have moved trees, but to have chanted to the gods such a hymn as would have sung all their old ideas out of their heads, and new ones in." His own verses are often rude and defective. The gold does not yet run pure, is drossy and crude. The thyme and marjoram are not yet honey. But if he want lyric fineness and technical merits, if he have not the poetic temperament, he never lacks the causal thought, showing that his genius was better than his talent. He knew the worth of the Imagination for the uplifting and consolation of human life, and liked to throw every thought into a symbol. The fact you tell is of no value, but only the impression. For this reason his presence was poetic, always piqued the curiosity to know more deeply the secrets of his mind. He had many reserves, an unwillingness to exhibit to profane eyes what was still sacred in his own, and knew well how to throw a poetic veil over his experience. All readers of Walden will remember his mythical record of his disappointments: —

"I long ago lost a hound, a bay horse and a turtle-dove, and am still on their trail. Many are the travelers I have spoken concern-

ing them, describing their tracks, and what calls they answered to.
I have met one or two who have heard the hound, and the tramp
of the horse, and even seen the dove disappear behind a cloud;
and they seemed as anxious to recover them as if they had lost
them themselves."

His riddles were worth the reading, and I confide that if at any
time I do not understand the expression, it is yet just. Such was
the wealth of his truth that it was not worth his while to use words
in vain. His poem entitled "Sympathy" reveals the tenderness
under that triple steel of stoicism, and the intellectual subtility it
could animate. His classic poem on "Smoke" suggests Simonides,
but is better than any poem of Simonides. His biography is in
his verses. His habitual thought makes all his poetry a hymn
to the Cause of causes, the Spirit which vivifies and controls his
own: —

> "I hearing get, who had but ears,
> And sight, who had but eyes before;
> I moments live, who lived but years,
> And truth discern, who knew but learning's lore."

And still more in these religious lines: —

> "Now chiefly is my natal hour,
> And only now my prime of life;
> I will not doubt the love untold,
> Which not my worth nor want have bought,
> Which wooed me young, and wooes me old,
> And to this evening hath me brought."

Whilst he used in his writings a certain petulance of remark in
reference to churches or churchmen, he was a person of a rare,
tender and absolute religion, a person incapable of any profanation,
by act or by thought. Of course, the same isolation which belonged
to his original thinking and living detached him from the social
religious forms. This is neither to be censured nor regretted.
Aristotle long ago explained it, when he said, "One who surpasses
his fellow citizens in virtue is no longer a part of the city. Their
law is not for him, since he is a law to himself."

Thoreau was sincerity itself, and might fortify the convictions
of prophets in the ethical laws by his holy living. It was an affirmative experience which refused to be set aside. A truth-speaker he,
capable of the most deep and strict conversation; a physician to
the wounds of any soul; a friend, knowing not only the secret of

friendship, but almost worshipped by those few persons who resorted to him as their confessor and prophet, and knew the deep value of his mind and great heart. He thought that without religion or devotion of some kind nothing great was ever accomplished: and he thought that the bigoted sectarian had better bear this in mind.

His virtues, of course, sometimes ran into extremes. It was easy to trace to the inexorable demand on all for exact truth that austerity which made this willing hermit more solitary even than he wished. Himself of a perfect probity, he required not less of others. He had a disgust at crime, and no worldly success would cover it. He detected paltering as readily in dignified and prosperous persons as in beggars, and with equal scorn. Such dangerous frankness was in his dealing that his admirers called him "that terrible Thoreau," as if he spoke when silent, and was still present when he had departed. I think the severity of his ideal interfered to deprive him of a healthy sufficiency of human society.

The habit of a realist to find things the reverse of their appearance inclined him to put every statement in a paradox. A certain habit of antagonism defaced his earlier writings, — a trick of rhetoric not quite outgrown in his later, of substituting for the obvious word and thought its diametrical opposite. He praised wild mountains and winter forests for their domestic air, in snow and ice he would find sultriness, and commended the wilderness for resembling Rome and Paris. "It was so dry, that you might call it wet."

The tendency to magnify the moment, to read all the laws of Nature in the one object or one combination under your eye, is of course comic to those who do not share the philosopher's perception of identity. To him there was no such thing as size. The pond was a small ocean; the Atlantic, a large Walden Pond. He referred every minute fact to cosmical laws. Though he meant to be just, he seemed haunted by a certain chronic assumption that the science of the day pretended completeness, and he had just found out that the *savans* [3] had neglected to discriminate a particular botanical variety, had failed to describe the seeds or count the sepals. "That is to say," we replied, "the blockheads were not born in Concord; but who said they were? It was their unspeakable misfortune to be born in London, or Paris, or Rome; but, poor fellows, they did what they could, considering that they never saw

[3] Learned.

Bateman's Pond, or Nine-Acre Corner, or Becky Stow's Swamp; besides, what were you sent into the world for, but to add this observation?"

Had his genius been only contemplative, he had been fitted to his life, but with his energy and practical ability he seemed born for great enterprise and for command; and I so much regret the loss of his rare powers of action, that I cannot help counting it a fault in him that he had no ambition. Wanting this, instead of engineering for all America, he was the captain of a huckleberry-party. Pounding beans is good to the end of pounding empires one of these days; but if, at the end of years, it is still only beans!

But these foibles, real or apparent, were fast vanishing in the incessant growth of a spirit so robust and wise, and which effaced its defeats with new triumphs. His study of Nature was a perpetual ornament to him, and inspired his friends with curiosity to see the world through his eyes, and to hear his adventures. They possessed every kind of interest.

He had many elegancies of his own, whilst he scoffed at conventional elegance. Thus, he could not bear to hear the sound of his own steps, the grit of gravel; and therefore never willingly walked in the road, but in the grass, on mountains and in woods. His senses were acute, and he remarked that by night every dwelling-house gives out bad air, like a slaughter-house. He liked the pure fragrance of melilot.[4] He honored certain plants with special regard, and, over all, the pond-lily, — then, the gentian, and the *Mikania scandens*, and "life-everlasting," and a bass-tree which he visited every year when it bloomed, in the middle of July. He thought the scent a more oracular inquisition than the sight, — more oracular and trustworthy. The scent, of course, reveals what is concealed from the other senses. By it he detected earthiness. He delighted in echoes, and said they were almost the only kind of kindred voices that he heard. He loved Nature so well, was so happy in her solitude, that he became very jealous of cities and the sad work which their refinements and artifices made with man and his dwelling. The axe was always destroying his forest. "Thank God," he said, "they cannot cut down the clouds!" "All kinds of figures are drawn on the blue ground with this fibrous white paint."

I subjoin a few sentences taken from his unpublished manuscripts, not only as records of his thought and feeling, but for their power of description and literary excellence: —

４ Sweet clover.

"Some circumstantial evidence is very strong, as when you find a trout in the milk."

"The chub is a soft fish, and tastes like boiled brown paper salted."

"The youth gets together his materials to build a bridge to the moon, or, perchance, a palace or temple on the earth, and, at length the middle-aged man concludes to build a wood-shed with them."

"The locust z-ing."

"Devil's-needles zigzagging along the Nut-Meadow brook."

"Sugar is not so sweet to the palate as sound to the healthy ear."

"I put on some hemlock-boughs, and the rich salt crackling of their leaves was like mustard to the ear, the crackling of uncountable regiments. Dead trees love the fire."

"The bluebird carries the sky on his back."

"The tanager flies through the green foliage as if it would ignite the leaves."

"If I wish for a horse-hair for my compass-sight I must go to the stable; but the hair-bird, with her sharp eyes, goes to the road."

"Immortal water, alive even to the superficies."

"Fire is the most tolerable third party."

"Nature made ferns for pure leaves, to show what she could do in that line."

"No tree has so fair a bole and so handsome an instep as the beech."

"How did these beautiful rainbow-tints get into the shell of the fresh-water clam, buried in the mud at the bottom of our dark river?"

"Hard are the times when the infant's shoes are second-foot."

"We are strictly confined to our men to whom we give liberty."

"Nothing is so much to be feared as fear. Atheism may comparatively be popular with God himself."

"Of what significance the things you can forget? A little thought is sexton to all the world."

"How can we expect a harvest of thought who have not had a seed-time of character?"

"Only he can be trusted with gifts who can present a face of bronze to expectations."

"I ask to be melted. You can only ask of the metals that they be tender to the fire that melts them. To nought else can they be tender."

There is a flower known to botanists, one of the same genus with our summer plant called "Life-Everlasting," a *Gnaphalium* like that, which grows on the most inaccessible cliffs of the Tyrolese mountains, where the chamois dare hardly venture, and which the hunter, tempted by its beauty, and by his love (for it is immensely valued by the Swiss maidens), climbs the cliffs to gather, and is sometimes found dead at the foot, with the flower in his hand. It is called by botanists the *Gnaphalium leontopodium,* but by the Swiss *Edelweisse,* which signifies *Noble Purity.* Thoreau seemed to me living in the hope to gather this plant, which belonged to him of right. The scale on which his studies proceeded was so large as to require longevity, and we were the less prepared for his sudden disappearance. The country knows not yet, or in the least part, how great a son it has lost. It seems an injury that he should leave in the midst his broken task which none else can finish, a kind of indignity to so noble a soul that he should depart out of Nature before yet he has been really shown to his peers for what he is. But he, at least, is content. His soul was made for the noblest society; he had in a short life exhausted the capabilities of this world; wherever there is knowledge, wherever there is virtue, wherever there is beauty, he will find a home.

February, 1861

Do the duty of the day. Just now, the supreme public duty of all thinking men is to assert freedom. Go where it is threatened, and say, "I am for it, and do not wish to live in the world a moment longer than it exists." Phillips has the supreme merit in this time, that he and he alone stands in the gap and breach against the assailants. Hold up his hands. He did me the honor to ask me to come to the meeting [5] at Tremont Temple, and, esteeming such invitation a command, though sorely against my inclination and habit, I went, and, though I had nothing to say, showed myself. If I were dumb, yet I would have gone and mowed and muttered or made signs. The mob roared whenever I attempted to speak, and after several beginnings, I withdrew.

February, 1861

Liberty, like religion, is a short and hasty fruit of rare and happy conditions.

May, 1861

Men delight in being well governed. When two men meet, one of them usually offers his vacant helm to the hands of the other.

The country is cheerful and jocund in the belief that it has a government at last. The men in search of a party, parties in search of a principle, interests and dispositions that could not fuse for

[5] Of the Anti-Slavery Society of Massachusetts.

want of some base, — all joyfully unite in this great Northern party, on the basis of Freedom. What a healthy tone exists! I suppose when we come to fighting, and many of our people are killed, it will yet be found that the bills of mortality in the country will show a better result of this year than the last, on account of the general health; no dyspepsia, no consumption, no fevers, where there is so much electricity, and conquering heart and mind. . . .

January 31, 1862

At Washington, January 31, February 1, 2, and 3, saw Sumner, who, on the 2d, carried me to Mr. Chase, Mr. Bates, Mr. Stanton, Mr. Welles, Mr. Seward, Lord Lyons, and President Lincoln. The President impressed me more favorably than I had hoped. A frank, sincere, well-meaning man, with a lawyer's habit of mind, good clear statement of his fact; correct enough, not vulgar, as described, but with a sort of boyish cheerfulness, or that kind of sincerity and jolly good meaning that our class meetings on Commencement Days show, in telling our old stories over. When he has made his remark, he looks up at you with great satisfaction, and shows all his white teeth, and laughs. He argued to Sumner the whole case of Gordon, the slave-trader, point by point, and added that he was not quite satisfied yet, and meant to refresh his memory by looking again at the evidence. All this showed a fidelity and conscientiousness very honorable to him.

When I was introduced to him, he said, "Oh, Mr. Emerson, I once heard you say in a lecture, that a Kentuckian seems to say by his air and manners, 'Here am I; if you don't like me, the worse for you.' " . . .

Autumn, 1863

Lincoln. — We must accept the results of universal suffrage, and not try to make it appear that we can elect fine gentlemen. We shall have coarse men, with a fair chance of worth and manly ability, but not men to please the English or French.

You cannot refine Mr. Lincoln's taste, or extend his horizon; he will not walk dignifiedly through the traditional part of the President of America, but will pop out his head at each railroad station and make a little speech, and get into an argument with Squire A. and Judge B. He will write letters to Horace Greeley, and any editor or reporter or saucy party committee that writes to him, and cheapen himself.

But this we must be ready for, and let the clown appear, and hug ourselves that we are well off, if we have got good nature, honest meaning, and fidelity to public interest, with bad manners, — instead of an elegant *roué* and malignant self-seeker.

November, 1862

When we build, our first care is to find good foundation. If the surface be loose, or sandy, or springy, we clear it away, and dig down to the hard pan, or, better, to the living rock, and bed our courses in that. So will we do with the State. The war is serving many good purposes. It is no respecter of respectable persons or of worn-out party platforms. War is a realist, shatters everything flimsy and shifty, sets aside all false issues, and breaks through all that is not real as itself; comes to organic opinions and parties, resting on the necessities of man; like its own cannonade, comes crashing in through party walls that have stood fifty or sixty years as if they were solid. The screaming of leaders, the votes by acclamation of conventions, are all idle wind. They cry for mercy, but they cry to one who never knew the word. He is the arm of the Fates, and, as has been said, "Nothing prevails against God but God." Everything must perish except that which must live.

Well, this is the task before us, to accept the benefit of the War; it has not created our false relations, they have created it. It simply demonstrates the rottenness it found. We watch its course as we did the cholera, which goes where predisposition already existed, took only the susceptible, set its seal on every putrid spot, and on none other; followed the limestone, and left the granite. So the War. Anxious statesmen try to rule it, to slacken it here and let it rage there, to not exasperate, to keep the black man out of it; to keep it well in hand, nor let it ride over old party lines, nor much molest trade, and to confine it to the frontier of the two sections. Why need Cape Cod, why need Casco Bay, why need Lake Superior, know anything of it? But the Indians have been bought, and they came down on Lake Superior; Boston and Portland are threatened by the pirate; more than that, Secession unexpectedly shows teeth in Boston; our parties have just shown you that the War is already in Massachusetts, as in Richmond.

Let it search, let it grind, let it overturn, and, like the fire when it finds no more fuel, it burns out. The War will show, as all wars do, what wrong is intolerable, what wrong makes and breeds all this bad blood. I suppose that it shows two incompatible states of society, Freedom and Slavery. If a part of this country is civilized up to a clean insight of Freedom, and of its necessity, and another part is not so far civilized, then I suppose that the same difficulties will continue; the War will not be extinguished; no treaties, no peace, no constitution can paper over the lips of that red crater. Only when, at last, so many parts of the country as can combine on an equal and moral contract, — not to protect each other in polygamy, or in kidnapping, or in eating men, but in humane and just activities, — only so many can combine firmly and durably.

I speak the speech of an idealist. I say let the rule be right. If the theory is right, it is not so much matter about the facts. If the plan of your fort is right, it is not so much matter that you have got a rotten beam or a cracked gun somewhere; they can by and by be replaced by better without tearing your fort to pieces. But if the plan is wrong, then all is rotten, and every step adds to the ruin; every screw is loose, and all the machine crazy. The question stands thus. Reconstruction is no longer matter of doubt. All our action now is new and unconstitutional, and necessarily so. To bargain or treat at all with the rebels, to make arrangements with them about exchange of prisoners, or hospitals, or truces to bury the dead, all unconstitutional and enough to drive a strict constructionist out of his wits. Much more in our future action touching peace, any and every arrangement short of forcible subjugation of the rebel country, will be flat disloyalty, on our part.

Then how to reconstruct. I say, this time, go to work right. Go down to the pan. See that your works turn on a jewel. Do not make an impossible mixture. Do not lay your cornerstone on a shaking morass that will let down the superstructure into a bottomless pit again.

Leave Slavery out. Since (unfortunately as some may think) God is God, and nothing gratifies all men but justice, let us have that, and let us stifle our prejudices against common sense and humanity, and agree that every man shall have what he honestly earns, and, if he is a sane and innocent man, have an equal vote in the state, and a fair chance in society.

And I, speaking in the interest of no man and no party, but simply as a geometer of his forces, say that the smallest beginning, so that it is just, is better and stronger than the largest that is not quite just. This time, no compromises, no concealments, no crimes that cannot be called by name shall be tucked in under another name, like "persons held to labor," meaning persons stolen, and "held," meaning held by handcuffs, when they are not under whips. Now the smallest state so formed will and must be strong, the interest and the affection of every man will make it strong by his entire strength, and it will mightily persuade every other man, and every neighboring territory to make it larger, and it will not reach its limits until it comes to people who think that they are a little cunninger than the Maker of this world and of the consciences of men.

November, 1863

[The English] write better, but we read more out of their books than they do. They have better blowpipe; we have not yet narrowed our heat to a focus, — [having] a continent full of coal. England possesses drastic skill, always better artists than we: Carlyle a better writer, Gladstone or Bright a better debater, I suppose, than any of ours. Tennyson a better poet; but is the scope as high? Is the material of Tennyson better, or does not our dumb muse see stars and horizons they do not? In England, in France, in Germany, is the popular sentiment as illuminated as here? As I wrote the other day, — our native politics are ideal. These women, old wives sitting by the chimneyside here, shrill their exclamations of impatience and indignation, shame on Mr. Seward, shame on the Senate, etc., for their want of humanity, of mere morality; they stand on the ground of simple morality, and not on the class feeling which narrows the perception of English, French, German people, at home. We are affirmative; they live under obstructions and negations. England's six points of Chartism are still postponed. They have all been granted here to begin with. England has taken in more partners, stands better on its legs than once, but still has huge load to carry. See how this moderates the ferocity incident elsewhere to political changes. We, in the midst of a great Revolution, still enacting the sentiment of the Puritans, and the dreams of young people thirty years ago; we, passing out of the old remainders of barbarism into pure Christianity and humanity, into freedom of thought, of religion, of speech, of the press, and of trade, and of suffrage, or political right; and working through this tremendous ordeal, which elsewhere went by beheadings, and massacre, and reigns of terror, — passing through all this and through states and territories, like a sleep, and drinking our tea the while. 'Tis like a brick house moved from its old foundations and place, and passing through our streets, whilst all the family are pursuing their domestic work inside.

I hate to have the egotism thrust in with such effrontery. This revolution is the work of no man, but the effervescence of Nature

It never did not work. But nothing that has occurred but has been a surprise, and as much to the leaders as to the hindmost. And not an Abolitionist, not an idealist, can say without effrontery, I did it. It is the fly in the coach, again. Go boost the globe, or scotch the globe, to accelerate or retard it in its orb! It is elemental, it is the old eternal gravitations: beware of the swing and of the recoil! Who knows, or has computed, the periods? A little earlier, and you would have been burned or crazed; a little later, you are unnecessary. . . .

Spring, 1864

The cannon will not suffer any other sound to be heard for miles and for years around it. Our chronology has lost all old distinctions in one date, — *Before the War, and since.*

July, 1865

. . . I think it a singular and marked result that [the War] has established a conviction in so many minds that the right will get done; has established a chronic hope for a chronic despair.

This victory the most decisive. This will stay put. It will show your enemies that what has now been so well done will be surely better and quicker done, if need be, again.

November 5, 1865

We hoped that in the peace, after such a war, a great expansion would follow in the mind of the country; grand views in every direction, — true freedom in politics, in religion, in social science, in thought. But the energy of the nation seems to have expended itself in the war, and every interest is found as sectional and timorous as before. . . .

February, 1861

What came over me with delight as I sat on the ledge in the warm light of last Sunday was the memory of young days at College, the delicious sensibility of youth, how the air rings to it! how all light is festal to it! how it at any moment extemporizes a holiday! I remember how boys riding out together on a fine day looked to me! ah, there was a romance! How sufficing was mere melody! The thought, the meaning, was insignificant; the whole joy was in the melody. For that I read poetry, and wrote it; and in the light of that memory I ought to understand the doctrine of musicians, that the words are nothing, the air is all. What a joy I found, and still can find, in the Aeolian harp! What a youth find I still in Collins's "Ode to Evening," and in Gray's "Eton College"! What delight I owed to Moore's insignificant but melodious poetry.

That is the merit of Clough's "Bothie," that the joy of youth is in it. Ah the power of the spring! and, ah, the voice of the bluebird! And the witchcraft of the Mount Auburn dell, in those days! I shall be a Squire Slender [6] for a week.

February, 1862

The old school of Boston citizens whom I remember in my childhood had great vigor, great noisy bodies; I think a certain sternutatory vigor the like whereof I have not heard again. When Major B. or old Mr. T. H. took out their pocket handkerchiefs at church, it was plain they meant business; they would snort and roar through their noses, like the lowing of an ox, and make all ring again. Ah, it takes a Northender to do that!

January, 1862

Cannot we let people be themselves, and enjoy life in their own way? You are trying to make that man another *you*. One's enough.

July ?, 1862

Benefit of conceit. — When you next write on conceit, have the good nature to see it as it is, a balsam, a sugar on the lip of the cup to sweeten the sad potation to all mortals.

How kind this keeping the eyes shut! The little rhymester is just as much pleased with his *vers de société* as the poet with his images that electrify us; on the whole is happier, for he thinks they are good, and the poet is always wretched at his shortcomings.

August, 1861

I am at a loss to understand why people hold Miss Austen's novels at so high a rate, which seem to me vulgar in tone, sterile in artistic invention, imprisoned in the wretched conventions of English society, without genius, wit, or knowledge of the world.

[6] Emerson means Justice Shallow, the tedious old reminiscer in Shakespeare's *Henry IV, Part 2*. Slender is his silly young protégé in *Merry Wives of Windsor*

Never was life so pinched and narrow. The one problem in the mind of the writer in both the stories I have read, *Persuasion*, and *Pride and Prejudice*, is marriageableness. All that interests in any character introduced is still this one, Has he or she money to marry with, and conditions conforming? 'Tis "the nympholepsy [7] of a fond despair," say, rather, of an English boarding-house. Suicide is more respectable.

June, 1863

In reading Henry Thoreau's journal, I am very sensible of the vigor of his constitution. That oaken strength which I noted whenever he walked, or worked, or surveyed wood-lots, the same unhesitating hand with which a field-laborer accosts a piece of work, which I should shun as a waste of strength, Henry shows in his literary task. He has muscle, and ventures on and performs feats which I am forced to decline. In reading him, I find the same thought, the same spirit that is in me, but he takes a step beyond, and illustrates by excellent images that which I should have conveyed in a sleepy generality. 'Tis as if I went into a gymnasium, and saw youths leap, climb, and swing with a force unapproachable, — though their feats are only continuations of my initial grapplings and jumps.

April, 1864

When I read Shakespeare, as lately, I think the criticism and study of him to be in their infancy. The wonder grows of his long obscurity; how could you hide the only man that ever wrote from all men who delight in reading? Then, the courage with which, in each play, he accosts the main issue, the highest problem, never dodging the difficult or impossible, but addressing himself instantly to that, — so conscious of his secret competence; and, at once, like an aeronaut fills his balloon with a whole atmosphere of hydrogen that will carry him over Andes, if Andes be in his path.

I must say that in reading the plays, I am a little shy where I begin; for the interest of the story is sadly in the way of poetry. It is safer, therefore, to read the play backwards. To know the beauty of Shakespeare's level tone, one should read a few passages of what passes for good tragedy in other writers, and then try the opening of *Merchant of Venice*, Antonio's first speech. . . .

7 Frenzy.

May 24, 1864

Yesterday, May 23, we buried Hawthorne in Sleepy Hollow, in a pomp of sunshine and verdure, and gentle winds. James Freeman Clarke read the service in the church and at the grave. Long-fellow, Lowell, Holmes, Agassiz, Hoar, Dwight, Whipple, Norton, Alcott, Hillard, Fields, Judge Thomas, and I attended the hearse as pallbearers. Franklin Pierce was with the family. The church was copiously decorated with white flowers delicately arranged. The corpse was unwillingly shown, — only a few moments to this company of his friends. But it was noble and serene in its aspect, — nothing amiss, — a calm and powerful head. A large company filled the church and the grounds of the cemetery. All was so bright and quiet that pain or mourning was hardly suggested, and Holmes said to me that it looked like a happy meeting.

Clarke in the church said that Hawthorne had done more justice than any other to the shades of life, shown a sympathy with the crime in our nature, and, like Jesus, was the friend of sinners.

I thought there was a tragic element in the event, that might be more fully rendered, — in the painful solitude of the man, which, I suppose, could not longer be endured, and he died of it.

I have found in his death a surprise and disappointment. I thought him a greater man than any of his works betray, that there was still a great deal of work in him, and that he might one day show a purer power. Moreover, I have felt sure of him in his neighborhood, and in his necessities of sympathy and intelligence, — that I could well wait his time, — his unwillingness and caprice, — and might one day conquer a friendship. It would have been a happiness, doubtless to both of us, to have come into habits of un-reserved intercourse. It was easy to talk with him, — there were no barriers, — only, he said so little, that I talked too much, and stopped only because, as he gave no indications, I feared to exceed. He showed no egotism or self-assertion, rather a humility, and, at one time, a fear that he had written himself out. One day, when I found him on the top of his hill, in the woods, he paced back the path to his house, and said, "This path is the only remembrance of me that will remain." Now it appears that I waited too long.

Lately he had removed himself the more by the indignation his perverse politics and unfortunate friendship for that paltry Frank-lin Pierce awakened, though it rather moved pity for Hawthorne, and the assured belief that he would outlive it, and come right at last.

June ?, 1864

The grief of old age is, that, now, only in rare moments, and by happiest combinations or consent of the elements, can we attain those enlargements and that intellectual *élan*, [8] which were once a daily gift.

June ?, 1864

Old age brings along with its uglinesses the comfort that you will soon be out of it, — which ought to be a substantial relief to such discontented pendulums as we are. To be out of the war, out of debt, out of the drouth, out of the blues, out of the dentist's hands, out of the second thoughts, mortifications, and remorses that inflict such twinges and shooting pains, — out of the next winter, and the high prices, and company below your ambition, — surely these are soothing hints. And, harbinger of this, what an alleviator is sleep, which muzzles all these dogs for me every day?

June ?, 1864

Within, I do not find wrinkles and used heart, but unspent youth.

April ?, 1865

Immortality. — The path of spirits is in silence and hidden from sense. Who knows where or how the soul has existed, before it was incarnated in mortal body? Who knows where or how it thinks and works when it drops its fleshly frame? Like those asteroids, which we call shooting stars, which revolve forever in space, but sweeping for a moment through some arc of our atmosphere and heated by the friction, give out a dazzling gleam, then pass out of it again on their endless orbit invisible.

May, 1865

It should be easy to say what I have always felt, that Stanley's *Lives of the Philosophers*, or Marcus Antoninus, are agreeable and suggestive books to me, whilst St. Paul or St. John are not, and I should never think of taking up these to start me on my task, as I often have used Plato or Plutarch. It is because the Bible wears black cloth. It comes with a certain official claim against which the mind revolts. The book has its own nobilities — might well be charming, if it was left simply on its merits, as the others; but this "you must," — "it is your duty," repels. . . .

8 Vigor

September ?, 1866

... The fancy carries out all the sentiments into form, and makes angels in the sky, and organizes remorse into a Judgment Day, and the universe at court; and so we have painted out our heaven and hell.

But I do not know but the sad realist has an equal or better content in keeping his hard nut. He sees the eternal symmetry, the world persisting to be itself, the unstooping morals of Nature, and says, "I can trust it." There is no fancy in my innate, uniform essential perception of Right, unique though million-formed or -faced. Through all processes, through all enemies, the result is Benefit, Beauty, the aim is the Best. I can well omit this parish propensity of casting it in small, in creeds, in *Punch* pictures, as the popular religions do, into Westminster Catechisms; Athanasian creeds; Egyptian, Christian, Mahometan or Hindu paradises and hells. I will not be the fool of fancy, nor a child with toys.

The positive degree is manly, and suits me better: the truth is stranger and grander than the gayest fable. I cling to astronomy, botany, zoölogy, as read by the severe Intellect, and will live and die assured that I cannot go out of the Power and Deity which rule in all my experience, whether sensuous or spiritual.

September, 1866

As Parry, as [others], in their several explorations in the Arctic, came out each on the SEA, so the independent thinkers, like Behmen, like Spinoza, came out each on an adamantine Necessity: the theories of the students were weathercocks, but this inevitable result was final.

September, 1866

There may be two or three or four steps, according to the genius of each, but for every seeing soul there are two absorbing facts, — I *and the Abyss.*

To *Emma Lazarus*

July 22, 1876

I send you warm thanks for your kind letter and invitation; — but an old man fears most his best friends. It is not them that he is willing to distress with his perpetual forgetfulness of the right word for the name of book or fact or person he is eager to recall, but which refuses to come. I have grown silent to my own household under this vexation, and cannot afflict dear friends with my

tied tongue. Happily this embargo does not reach to the eyes, and
I read with unbroken pleasure. . . .

Autumn, 1845

It is the largest part of a man that is not inventoried. He has
many enumerable parts: he is social, professional, political, sectarian, literary, and is this or that set and corporation. But after
the most exhausting census has been made, there remains as much
more which no tongue can tell. And this remainder is that which
interests. This is that which the preacher and the poet and the
musician speak to. This is that which the strong genius works
upon; the region of destiny, of aspiration, of the unknown. Ah,
they have a secret persuasion that as little as they pass for in the
world, they are immensely rich in expectancy and power. Nobody
has ever yet dispossessed this adhesive self to arrive at any glimpse
or guess of the awful Life that lurks under it.

Far the best part, I repeat, of every mind is not that which he
knows, but that which hovers in gleams, suggestions, tantalizing,
unpossessed, before him. His firm recorded knowledge soon loses
all interest for him. But this dancing chorus of thoughts and hopes
is the quarry of his future, is his possibility, and teaches him that
his man's life is of a ridiculous brevity and meanness, but that it
is his first age and trial only of his young wings, [and] that vast
revolutions, migrations, and gyres on gyres in the celestial societies
invite him.

Poems[1]

"I am a bard least of bards. I cannot, like them, make lofty arguments in stately, continuous verse, constraining the rocks, trees, animals, and the periodic stars to say my thoughts, — for that is the gift of great poets; but I am a bard because I stand near them, and apprehend all they utter, and with pure joy hear that which I also would say, and, moreover, I speak interruptedly words and half stanzas which have the like scope and aim. . . ." (*Journals*, 1862).

Almost as soon as he could hold a pen Emerson was scribbling verses; to him poetry was always the literary art. The publication of a volume of poems in 1846 was thus a kind of coming of age in his literary career. Yet the plain fact is that, measured by the only standard he would have had, the best, Emerson was seldom a very good poet. When he wrote in 1835 that his singing was "very husky" he was characteristically modest but not far wrong. In spite of which fact, these cross-grained verses, like trees on the timber line, toughly cling to life and will not be forgotten or dismissed. As he said of Thoreau, his genius was better than his talent.

From one point of view, the poems justify the judgment that they "are a more brief and condensed form of the Essays" — that is to say, the thought remains the main source of interest, heightened though that may be by the concentration of the verse. Emerson's first concern was to get something said, if not with art then without it. In this he is representative of "the American way of poetry," which has typically inclined to rate "sincerity" above polish. His poems, like those of Americans from Taylor to Frost, ask the reader to share as equal and friend in a process of invention,

[1] Poems to be found elsewhere in this anthology are as follows:
A bit of early journal verse (p. 11).
A short selection from "Saadi" (p. 121).
The mottoes to the essays (pp. 21, 147, 168, 222, 241, 254, and 330).
In the Notes, "Fate," "Northman," and an early draft of "Merlin" (pp. 495, 496, and 506).

rather than invite his admiration for the completed work of a master.

From another point of view, however, such an approach is quite inadequate. A poetic personality — Emerson called him "Saadi" or "Seyd" or "Osman" — struggles for expression here who is largely silent in the essays (the "Orphic poet" in Nature is an exception). His major concern is not thought in any ordinary sense, but insight and power. He is, in intention, a potent liberating (and liberated) god, who frees our own powers by making us "see beyond the range of sight," using for this the primary means of any poet, metaphor and music. His problem, intensified by a provincial and isolated position, is also that of any poet, an adequate form. Emerson's poetic practice is marked, one might say scarred, by a confused, never quite successful, yet seminal search for his proper style.

Formally speaking, these varied poems tend to fall into the rough categories of the regular and the free, the poems of character and the poems of power. Generally the former are more successful, the latter more interesting. His most unequivocal successes are all regular and all short: "The Snow-Storm," "Concord Hymn," "Brahma," "Days." A distinguishing mark of these poems is their dignified yet flexible speaking voice; the "low tones that decide" were Emerson's best mode. Regularity did not, however, guarantee him success. He shared the weakness of his day for diffuse length, and like his contemporaries he was apt to add rhyme and meter to his thought as one might add water to wine. In general, the most regular poems are deliberate treatments of subjects chosen to be worked up into verse and do not suggest the spontaneous overflow of powerful feelings.

Not so the "free" poems, which tend, indeed, to overflow altogether too much. The speaker in these poems is not a contemporary of Young and Bryant, but rather of the legendary Welsh Merlin, an inspired bard whose mighty line can bereave a tyrant of his will, still tempests, and "bring in poetic peace." As vehicle for such power Emerson envisioned the natural or organic poem he described in "The Poet," the poem that showed "the instant dependence of form upon soul," the product of "a thought so passionate and alive that like the spirit of a plant or an animal it has an architecture of its own, and adorns nature with a new thing." Unlike a natural object, however, such a "new thing" in fact drew its life from its evocative power. Its soul was the soul of the Whole, siphoned for a creative moment into this particular symbol; even while as an objective utterance it was deathless — unlike the insight it sprang from — yet it lived only as it communicated the larger life which animated it. The bardic poem should be a kind of electrical circuit whereby disconnected men could be reunited for a pulse or two with the living truth.

Emerson's overmastering concern with "the active soul" led directly to his emphasis on the poet's symbol-making power, his magical faculty of seeing the idea in the thing and the image in the idea. Poetry — one might well say life — began and ended, he felt, in the moment of insight when the inner and outer worlds fuse together. His account of the poet's creative psychology is now attracting fresh attention in its modern emphasis on knowing as an organic activity and truth as a functional metaphor.

The results in his practice were mixed. On the one hand he moved toward the poem that accepts the adequacy of the symbol for meaning and structure and thus adumbrated one main development in modern poetry. Poems like "The Humble-Bee" and "Bacchus," it has been pointed out, are "wholly symbolic and allusive" in method. On the other hand, though his pioneering deserves recognition, he hardly solved the serious problems such poetry presents. Since he felt so strongly that poetic symbols should reveal one kind of meaning, he undervalued both their concreteness and their variety. Consequently, his poems tend to slide off quickly from the fact to the idea — the cloying literariness of too much of his imagery and diction seems to represent an unsuccessful attempt to make up this deficiency of the sensuous in his verse — and they typically lack the organic, musical structure of the modern symbolist poem, since that can result only from playing off one symbol or meaning against another in a pattern of contraries. Emerson's structures, when they exist, are usually simple rational containers rather than anything determined from within the poem and often provide no strong reason why a given passage should be included or should be where it is. The "structure" of "May-Day" or "Initial, Daemonic, and Celestial Love" was reached partly by a consultation of editors.

So runs the indictment of Emerson as a symbolist. Justified, surely — yet he is a poet of surprises: "The Snow-Storm" is built on as neat a paradox as either Brooks or Warren could wish; the structure of imagery in "Uriel" will repay the closest analysis. Furthermore, symbolic structure is only one kind of structure, and not without its limitations; as current criticism discovers other kinds we may see more in Emerson. Is there no place for the

poem — "Forerunners" is a good example — which gives the effect
of a loose improvisation on a single theme? Any two or four lines
could be omitted without apparent loss; yet it is odd how the concluding four lines do seem to round off a whole. Such a cumulative
effect is common in these poems, notably in the long, apparently
aimless essays in verse like "Monadnoc" or "Woodnotes."

Sudden concentrations of force, also, can flood without warning into any poem. Certain favorite themes — divine or god-given
energy, for example; certain classes of image, like the expansive,
mind-freeing natural image — mountain, ocean and river, sky and
astronomical imagery, large geologic images, the thawing heat of
spring: — when these or such as these fully engage Emerson's
austere imagination a passage can reach an incandescence not
quite like anything else in literature. Criticism will come back to
Emerson.

When it does it will have to deal with his most conspicuous
liability, his "huskiness" as a singer. What are we to make of a
poet who could and did habitually confess, "I think, and my
friends think, that I lack the rhythmical faculty"? In view of his
rhythmical successes we cannot take this self-analysis at face value.
The trouble was not so much with his skill as that he was basically
uncertain of what he wanted to do. On the one hand he sought
the sweeping effect of the inspired improvisation which would rise
above "the coil of rhythm and number" and "ring as blows the
breeze." For this purpose a certain roughness and carelessness in
particulars was positively desirable, to call attention away from the
parts to the "grand design"; when Whitman sent him the first
edition of Leaves of Grass he recognized the large bardic manner
he had been working toward. On the other hand he sought the
electric moment when the spark jumps from the words of the poet
to the mind of the hearer; each line should be a hammerblow,
striking past conventional attention to the life of the imagination.
Clearly from this point of view the part is all-important and the
whole little more than a collection of "strokes of fate."

The conflict appears in his use of rhymes. He wrote little
rhymeless verse (except blank verse) because he felt rhyme essential to the melody which was in turn essential to the power of
poetry. Yet he tended in practice both to exploit the epigrammatic
force of rhyme, often with an effect of gnomic concentration, and
to permit himself various kinds of off-rhyme to create an effect of
natural freedom; one tendency worked at cross-purposes with the
other and neither helped his melody. It must be added that, with

all his over-fondness for frequent rhymes, he was not an easy rhymer and his effect is often more clumsy than careless.

It was once the fashion to attack Emerson for his irregularities in form. In the light of the much more radical practices of modern poetry we can see that the true point of attack is not his mild innovations but his lack of sufficient art and system in using them — a lack made evident only because he attempted so much more than the "jingle men" who condescended to him. Much the same thing can be said of his peculiarities of diction. Even here, again, we must be careful. His "lack of ear" is intermittent and sometimes can be the critic's. Parts of "Merlin," for instance, one of his freest poems, have a rightness any poet might envy.

Emerson as a poet, in sum, must be looked on as a transitional and divided figure — partly holding to a discursive regular verse, partly moving toward a free symbolic verse. The longing to sing freely and powerfully as a liberating god was crossed by some inhibiting decorum which largely prevented him from realizing the freedom he could describe. But Emerson is a dangerous man to pigeonhole. Just as we have closed the drawer on this harmless object, it explodes and leaves the desk a ruin. Emerson's verse is a piece of Labrador spar which will flash only as we turn it the right way to the light —

> The hand that rounded Peter's dome
> And groined the aisles of Christian Rome —
>
> Or Music pours on mortals
> Its beautiful disdain —
>
> And the lone seaman all the night
> Sails, astonished, amid stars —
>
> Or teach thou, Spring! the grand recoil
> Of life resurgent from the soil —
>
> Subtle rhymes, with ruin rife,
> Murmur in the house of life,
> Sung by the sisters as they spin;
> In perfect time and measure they
> Build and unbuild our echoing clay,
> As the two twilights of the day
> Fold us music-drunken in.

The poet who could strike these notes will survive all criticism.

religion?

GRACE

How much, preventing God, how much I owe
To the defenses thou hast round me set;
Example, custom, fear, occasion slow, —
These scornéd bondmen were my parapet.
I dare not peep over this parapet   5
To gauge with glance the roaring gulf below,
The depths of sin to which I had descended,
Had not these me against myself defended.
1833   *1842*

COMPENSATION

Why should I keep holiday
    When other men have none?
Why but because, when these are gay,
    I sit and mourn alone?

And why, when mirth unseals all tongues,   5
    Should mine alone be dumb?
Ah! late I spoke to silent throngs,
    And now their hour is come.
1834   *1846*

beauty in "Nature" P. 2?

THE RHODORA *must*

On Being Asked, Whence Is the Flower?

In May, when sea-winds pierced our solitudes,
I found the fresh Rhodora in the woods,
Spreading its leafless blooms in a damp nook,
To please the desert and the sluggish brook.
The purple petals, fallen in the pool,   5
Made the black water with their beauty gay;
Here might the red-bird come his plumes to cool,
And court the flower that cheapens his array.
Rhodora! if the sages ask thee why

This charm is wasted on the earth and sky,   10
Tell them, dear, that if eyes were made for seeing,
Then Beauty is its own excuse for being:
Why thou wert there, O rival of the rose!
I never thought to ask, I never knew:
But, in my simple ignorance, suppose   15
The self-same Power that brought me there brought you.

1834   1839

EACH AND ALL

Little thinks, in the field, yon red-cloaked clown
Of thee from the hill-top looking down;
The heifer that lows in the upland farm,
Far-heard, lows not thine ear to charm;
The sexton, tolling his bell at noon,
Deems not that great Napoleon
Stops his horse, and lists with delight,
Whilst his files sweep round yon Alpine height;
Nor knowest thou what argument
Thy life to thy neighbor's creed has lent.
All are needed by each one;
Nothing is fair or good alone.
I thought the sparrow's note from heaven,
Singing at dawn on the alder bough;
I brought him home, in his nest, at even;   15
He sings the song, but it cheers not now,
For I did not bring home the river and sky; —
He sang to my ear, — they sang to my eye.
The delicate shells lay on the shore;
The bubbles of the latest wave   20
Fresh pearls to their enamel gave,
And the bellowing of the savage sea
Greeted their safe escape to me.
I wiped away the weeds and foam,
I fetched my sea-born treasures home;   25
But the poor, unsightly, noisome things
Had left their beauty on the shore
With the sun and the sand and the wild uproar.
The lover watched his graceful maid,
As 'mid the virgin train she strayed,   30

Nor knew her beauty's best attire
Was woven still by the snow-white choir.
At last she came to his hermitage,
Like the bird from the woodlands to the cage; —
The gay enchantment was undone,   35
A gentle wife, but fairy none.
Then I said, "I covet truth;
Beauty is unripe childhood's cheat;
I leave it behind with the games of youth:" —
As I spoke, beneath my feet   40
The ground-pine curled its pretty wreath,
Running over the club-moss burrs;
I inhaled the violet's breath;
Around me stood the oaks and firs;
Pine-cones and acorns lay on the ground;   45
Over me soared the eternal sky,
Full of light and of deity;
Again I saw, again I heard,
The rolling river, the morning bird;—
Beauty through my senses stole;   50
I yielded myself to the perfect whole.
1834   1839

THE SNOW-STORM

Announced by all the trumpets of the sky,
Arrives the snow, and, driving o'er the fields,
Seems nowhere to alight: the whited air
Hides hills and woods, the river, and the heaven,
And veils the farm-house at the garden's end.   5
The sled and traveler stopped, the courier's feet
Delayed, all friends shut out, the housemates sit
Around the radiant fireplace, enclosed
In a tumultuous privacy of storm.

Come see the north wind's masonry.   10
Out of an unseen quarry evermore
Furnished with tile, the fierce artificer
Curves his white bastions with projected roof
Round every windward stake, or tree, or door.
Speeding, the myriad-handed, his wild work   15

So fanciful, so savage, nought cares he
For number or proportion. Mockingly,
On coop or kennel he hangs Parian wreaths;
A swan-like form invests the hidden thorn;
Fills up the farmer's lane from wall to wall,   20
Maugre the farmer's sighs; and at the gate
A tapering turret overtops the work.
And when his hours are numbered, and the world
Is all his own, retiring, as he were not,
Leaves, when the sun appears, astonished Art   25
To mimic in slow structures, stone by stone,
Built in an age, the mad wind's night-work,
The frolic architecture of the snow.
1835   *1841*

CONCORD HYMN

*Sung at the Completion of the Battle
Monument, July 4, 1837*

By the rude bridge that arched the flood,
    Their flag to April's breeze unfurled,
Here once the embattled farmers stood
    And fired the shot heard round the world.

The foe long since in silence slept;   5
    Alike the conqueror silent sleeps;
And Time the ruined bridge has swept
    Down the dark stream which seaward creeps.

On this green bank, by this soft stream,
    We set today a votive stone;   10
That memory may their deed redeem,
    When, like our sires, our sons are gone.

Spirit, that made those heroes dare
    To die, and leave their children free,
Bid Time and Nature gently spare   15
    The shaft we raise to them and thee.
1837   *1837*

THE HUMBLE-BEE

Burly, dozing humble-bee,
Where thou art is clime for me.
Let them sail for Porto Rique,
Far-off heats through seas to seek,
I will follow thee alone,   5
Thou animated torrid-zone!
Zigzag steerer, desert cheerer,
Let me chase thy waving lines;
Keep me nearer, me thy hearer,
Singing over shrubs and vines.   10

Insect lover of the sun,
Joy of thy dominion!
Sailor of the atmosphere;
Swimmer through the waves of air;
Voyager of light and noon;   15
Epicurean of June;
Wait, I prithee, till I come
Within earshot of thy hum, —
All without is martyrdom.

When the south wind, in May days,   20
With a net of shining haze
Silvers the horizon wall,
And with softness touching all,
Tints the human countenance
With a color of romance,   25
And infusing subtle heats,
Turns the sod to violets,
Thou, in sunny solitudes,
Rover of the underwoods,
The green silence dost displace   30
With thy mellow, breezy bass.

Hot midsummer's petted crone,
Sweet to me thy drowsy tone
Tells of countless sunny hours,
Long days, and solid banks of flowers;   35
Of gulfs of sweetness without bound
In Indian wildernesses found;

Of Syrian peace, immortal leisure,
Firmest cheer, and bird-like pleasure.

Aught unsavory or unclean   40
Hath my insect never seen;
But violets and bilberry bells,
Maple-sap and daffodels,
Grass with green flag half-mast high,
Succory to match the sky,   45
Columbine with horn of honey,
Scented fern, and agrimony,
Clover, catchfly, adder's-tongue
And brier-roses, dwelt among;
All beside was unknown waste,   50
All was picture as he passed.

Wiser far than human seer,
Yellow-breeched philosopher!
Seeing only what is fair,
Sipping only what is sweet,   55
Thou dost mock at fate and care,
Leave the chaff, and take the wheat.
When the fierce northwestern blast
Cools sea and land so far and fast,
Thou already slumberest deep;   60
Woe and want thou canst outsleep;
Want and woe, which torture us,
Thy sleep makes ridiculous.
1837   1846

THE PROBLEM

I like a church; I like a cowl;
I love a prophet of the soul;
And on my heart monastic aisles
Fall like sweet strains, or pensive smiles;
Yet not for all his faith can see   5
Would I that cowléd churchman be.

Why should the vest on him allure,
Which I could not on me endure?

Not from a vain or shallow thought
His awful Jove young Phidias brought;   10
Never from lips of cunning fell
The thrilling Delphic oracle;
Out from the heart of nature rolled
The burdens of the Bible old;
The litanies of nations came,   15
Like the volcano's tongue of flame,
Up from the burning core below, —
The canticles of love and woe:
The hand that rounded Peter's dome
And groined the aisles of Christian Rome   20
Wrought in a sad sincerity;
Himself from God he could not free;
He builded better than he knew; —
The conscious stone to beauty grew.

Know'st thou what wove yon woodbird's nest   25
Of leaves, and feathers from her breast?
Or how the fish outbuilt her shell,
Painting with morn each annual cell?
Or how the sacred pine-tree adds
To her old leaves new myriads?   30
Such and so grew these holy piles,
Whilst love and terror laid the tiles.
Earth proudly wears the Parthenon,
As the best gem upon her zone,
And Morning opes with haste her lids   35
To gaze upon the Pyramids;
O'er England's abbeys bends the sky,
As on its friends, with kindred eye;
For out of Thought's interior sphere
These wonders rose to upper air;   40
And Nature gladly gave them place,
Adopted them into her race,
And granted them an equal date
With Andes and with Ararat.

These temples grew as grows the grass;   45
Art might obey, but not surpass.
The passive Master lent his hand
To the vast soul that o'er him planned;

And the same power that reared the shrine
Bestrode the tribes that knelt within.   50
Ever the fiery Pentecost
Girds with one flame the countless host,
Trances the heart through chanting choirs,
And through the priest the mind inspires.
The word unto the prophet spoken   55
Was writ on tables yet unbroken;
The word by seers or sibyls told,
In groves of oak, or fanes of gold,
Still floats upon the morning wind,
Still whispers to the willing mind.   60
One accent of the Holy Ghost
The heedless world hath never lost.
I know what say the fathers wise, —
The Book itself before me lies,
Old *Chrysostom*, best Augustine,   65
And he who blent both in his line,
The younger *Golden Lips* or mines,
Taylor, the Shakespeare of divines.
His words are music in my ear,
I see his cowléd portrait dear;   70
And yet, for all his faith could see,
I would not the good bishop be.
1839   *1840*

From WOODNOTES, I

2

And such I knew, a forest seer,
A minstrel of the natural year,
Foreteller of the vernal ides,
Wise harbinger of spheres and tides,
A lover true, who knew by heart   5
Each joy the mountain dales impart;
It seemed that Nature could not raise
A plant in any secret place,
In quaking bog, on snowy hill,
Beneath the grass that shades the rill,   10
Under the snow, between the rocks,

In damp fields known to bird and fox,
But he would come in the very hour
It opened in its virgin bower,
As if a sunbeam showed the place,   15
And tell its long-descended race.
It seemed as if the breezes brought him;
It seemed as if the sparrows taught him;
As if by secret sight he knew
Where, in far fields, the orchis grew.   20
Many haps fall in the field
Seldom seen by wishful eyes,
But all her shows did Nature yield,
To please and win this pilgrim wise.
He saw the partridge drum in the woods;   25
He heard the woodcock's evening hymn;
He found the tawny thrushes' broods;
And the shy hawk did wait for him;
What others did at distance hear,
And guessed within the thicket's gloom,   30
Was shown to this philosopher,
And at his bidding seemed to come.

1840

THE SPHINX

The Sphinx is drowsy,
    Her wings are furled:
Her ear is heavy,
    She broods on the world.
"Who'll tell me my secret,   5
    The ages have kept? —
I awaited the seer
    While they slumbered and slept: —

"The fate of the man-child,
    The meaning of man;   10
Known fruit of the unknown;
    Daedalian plan; [2]
Out of sleeping a waking,
    Out of waking a sleep;

[2] Daedalus built the labyrinth.

Life death overtaking;   15
  Deep underneath deep?

"Erect as a sunbeam,
  Upspringeth the palm;
The elephant browses,
  Undaunted and calm;   20
In beautiful motion
  The thrush plies his wings;
Kind leaves of his covert,
  Your silence he sings.

"The waves, unashaméd,   25
  In difference sweet,
Play glad with the breezes,
  Old playfellows meet;
The journeying atoms,
  Primordial wholes,   30
Firmly draw, firmly drive,
  By their animate poles.

"Sea, earth, air, sound, silence,
  Plant, quadruped, bird,
By one music enchanted,   35
  One deity stirred, —
Each the other adorning,
  Accompany still;
Night veileth the morning,
  The vapor the hill.   40

"The babe by its mother
  Lies bathéd in joy;
Glide its hours uncounted, —
  The sun is its toy;
Shines the peace of all being,   45
  Without cloud, in its eyes;
And the sum of the world
  In soft miniature lies.

"But man crouches and blushes,
  Absconds and conceals;   50

He creepeth and peepeth,
 He palters and steals;
Infirm, melancholy,
 Jealous glancing around,
An oaf, an accomplice,   55
 He poisons the ground.

"Out spoke the great mother,
 Beholding his fear; —
At the sound of her accents
 Cold shuddered the sphere: — 60
'Who has drugged my boy's cup?
 Who has mixed my boy's bread?
Who, with sadness and madness,
 Has turned my child's head?' "

I heard a poet answer   65
 Aloud and cheerfully,
"Say on, sweet Sphinx! thy dirges
 Are pleasant songs to me.
Deep love lieth under
 These pictures of time;   70
They fade in the light of
 Their meaning sublime.

"The fiend that man harries
 Is love of the Best;
Yawns the pit of the Dragon, 75
 Lit by rays from the Blest.
The Lethe of Nature
 Can't trance him again,
Whose soul sees the perfect,
 Which his eyes seek in vain. 80

"To vision profounder,
 Man's spirit must dive;
His aye-rolling orb
 At no goal will arrive;
The heavens that now draw him 85
 With sweetness untold,
Once found, — for new heavens
 He spurneth the old.

"Pride ruined the angels,
  Their shame them restores;
Lurks the joy that is sweetest
  In stings of remorse.
Have I a lover
  Who is noble and free? —
I would he were nobler
  Than to love me.

"Eterne alternation
  Now follows, now flies;
And under pain, pleasure, —
  Under pleasure, pain lies.
Love works at the center,
  Heart-heaving alway;
Forth speed the strong pulses
  To the borders of day.

"Dull Sphinx, Jove keep thy five wits;
  Thy sight is growing blear;
Rue, myrrh and cummin for the Sphinx,
  Her muddy eyes to clear!"
The old Sphinx bit her thick lip, —
  Said, "Who taught thee me to name?
I am thy spirit, yoke-fellow;
  Of thine eye I am eyebeam.

"Thou art the unanswered question;
  Couldst see thy proper eye,
Alway it asketh, asketh;
  And each answer is a lie.
So take thy quest through nature,
  It through thousand natures ply;
Ask on, thou clothed eternity;
  Time is the false reply."

Uprose the merry Sphinx,
  And crouched no more in stone;
She melted into purple cloud,
  She silvered in the moon;
She spired into a yellow flame;
  She flowered in blossoms red;

90

95

100

105

110

115

120

125

She flowed into a foaming wave:
  She stood Monadnoc's head.

Through a thousand voices
  Spoke the universal dame;   130
"Who telleth one of my meanings
  Is master of all I am."

                    1841

MEROPS [3]

What care I, so they stand the same, —
  Things of the heavenly mind, —
How long the power to give them name
  Tarries yet behind?

Thus far today your favors reach,   5
  O fair, appeasing presences!
Ye taught my lips a single speech,
  And a thousand silences.

Space grants beyond his fated road
  No inch to the god of day;   10
And copious language still bestowed
  One word, no more, to say.

                    1846

THE APOLOGY

Think me not unkind and rude
  That I walk alone in grove and glen;
I go to the god of the wood
  To fetch his word to men.

Tax not my sloth that I   5
  Fold my arms beside the brook;
Each cloud that floated in the sky
  Writes a letter in my book.

[3] Articulate speech.

Chide me not, laborious band,
  For the idle flowers I brought;   10
Every aster in my hand
  Goes home loaded with a thought.

There was never mystery
  But 'tis figured in the flowers;
Was never secret history   15
  But birds tell it in the bowers.

One harvest from thy field
  Homeward brought the oxen strong;
A second crop thine acres yield,
  Which I gather in a song.   20

              1846

SUUM CUIQUE [4]

The rain has spoiled the farmer's day;
Shall sorrow put my books away?
  Thereby two days are lost:
Nature shall mind her own affairs;
I will attend my proper cares,   5
  In rain, or sun, or frost.

              1841

FORERUNNERS

Long I followed happy guides,
I could never reach their sides;
Their step is forth, and, ere the day
Breaks up their leaguer, and away.
Keen my sense, my heart was young,   5
Right good-will my sinews strung,
But no speed of mine avails
To hunt upon their shining trails.
On and away, their hasting feet
Make the morning proud and sweet;   10
Flowers they strew, — I catch the scent;

4 To each his own.

Or tone of silver instrument
Leaves on the wind melodious trace;
Yet I could never see their face.
On eastern hills I see their smokes,   15
Mixed with mist by distant lochs.
I met many travelers
Who the road had surely kept;
They saw not my fine revelers, —
These had crossed them while they slept.   20
Some had heard their fair report,
In the country or the court.
Fleetest couriers alive
Never yet could once arrive,
As they went or they returned,   25
At the house where these sojourned.
Sometimes their strong speed they slacken,
Though they are not overtaken;
In sleep their jubilant troop is near, —
I tuneful voices overhear;   30
It may be in wood or waste, —
At unawares 'tis come and past.
Their near camp my spirit knows
By signs gracious as rainbows.
I thenceforward and long after   35
Listen for their harp-like laughter,
And carry in my heart, for days,
Peace that hallows rudest ways.

1846

URIEL [5]

It fell in the ancient periods
   Which the brooding soul surveys,
· Or ever the wild Time coined itself
   Into calendar months and days.

This was the lapse of Uriel,   5
Which in Paradise befell.
Once, among the Pleiads walking,

[5] Uriel is the name given in Milton's *Paradise Lost* to the archangel of the sun.

Seyd [6] overheard the young gods talking;
And the treason, too long pent,
To his ears was evident. 10
The young deities discussed
Laws of form, and meter just,
Orb, quintessence, and sunbeams,
What subsisteth, and what seems.
One, with low tones that decide, 15
And doubt and reverend use defied,
With a look that solved the sphere,
And stirred the devils everywhere,
Gave his sentiment divine
Against the being of a line. 20
"Line in nature is not found;
Unit and universe are round;
In vain produced, all rays return;
Evil will bless, and ice will burn."
As Uriel spoke with piercing eye, 25
A shudder ran around the sky;
The stern old war-gods shook their heads,
The seraphs frowned from myrtle-beds;
Seemed to the holy festival
The rash word boded ill to all; 30
The balance-beam of Fate was bent;
The bounds of good and ill were rent;
Strong Hades could not keep his own,
But all slid to confusion.

A sad self-knowledge, withering, fell 35
On the beauty of Uriel;
In heaven once eminent, the god
Withdrew, that hour, into his cloud;
Whether doomed to long gyration
In the sea of generation, 40
Or by knowledge grown too bright
To hit the nerve of feebler sight.
Straightway, a forgetting wind
Stole over the celestial kind,
And their lips the secret kept, 45
If in ashes the fire-seed slept.
But now and then, truth-speaking things

[6] The Poet.

Shamed the angels' veiling wings;
And, shrilling from the solar course,
Or from fruit of chemic force,   **50**
Procession of a soul in matter,
Or the speeding change of water,
Or out of the good of evil born,
Came Uriel's voice of cherub scorn,
And a blush tinged the upper sky,   **55**
And the gods shook, they knew not why.

                                   1846

SR: To be great is to be misunderstood

THRENODY

The South-wind brings
Life, sunshine and desire,
And on every mount and meadow
Breathes aromatic fire;
But over the dead he has no power,   **5**
The lost, the lost, he cannot restore;
And, looking over the hills, I mourn
The darling who shall not return.

I see my empty house,
I see my trees repair their boughs;   **10**
And he, the wondrous child,
Whose silver warble wild
Outvalued every pulsing sound
Within the air's cerulean round, —
The hyacinthine boy, for whom   **15**
Morn well might break and April bloom,
The gracious boy, who did adorn
The world whereinto he was born,
And by his countenance repay
The favor of the loving Day, —   **20**
Has disappeared from the Day's eye;
Far and wide she cannot find him;
My hopes pursue, they cannot bind him.
Returned this day, the South-wind searches,
And finds young pines and budding birches;   **25**
But finds not the budding man;
Nature, who lost, cannot remake him;

Fate let him fall, Fate can't retake him;
Nature, Fate, men, him seek in vain.

And whither now, my truant wise and sweet, 30
O, whither tend thy feet?
I had the right, few days ago,
Thy steps to watch, thy place to know:
How have I forfeited the right?
Hast thou forgot me in a new delight? 35
I hearken for thy household cheer,
O eloquent child!
Whose voice, an equal messenger,
Conveyed thy meaning mild.
What though the pains and joys 40
Whereof it spoke were toys
Fitting his age and ken,
Yet fairest dames and bearded men,
Who heard the sweet request,
So gentle, wise and grave, 45
Bended with joy to his behest
And let the world's affairs go by,
A while to share his cordial game,
Or mend his wicker wagon-frame,
Still plotting how their hungry ear 50
That winsome voice again might hear;
For his lips could well pronounce
Words that were persuasions.

Gentlest guardians marked serene
His early hope, his liberal mien; 55
Took counsel from his guiding eyes
To make this wisdom earthly wise.
Ah, vainly do these eyes recall
The school-march, each day's festival,
When every morn my bosom glowed 60
To watch the convoy on the road;
The babe in willow wagon closed,
With rolling eyes and face composed;
With children forward and behind,
Like Cupids studiously inclined; 65
And he the chieftain paced beside,
The center of the troop allied,

With sunny face of sweet repose,
To guard the babe from fancied foes.
The little captain innocent   70
Took the eye with him as he went;
Each village senior paused to scan
And speak the lovely caravan.
From the window I look out
To mark thy beautiful parade,   75
Stately marching in cap and coat
To some tune by fairies played; —
A music heard by thee alone
To works as noble led thee on.

Now Love and Pride, alas! in vain,   80
Up and down their glances strain.
The painted sled stands where it stood;
The kennel by the corded wood;
His gathered sticks to stanch the wall
Of the snow-tower, when snow should fall;   85
The ominous hole he dug in the sand,
And childhood's castles built or planned;
His daily haunts I well discern, —
The poultry-yard, the shed, the barn, —
And every inch of garden ground   90
Paced by the blessed feet around,
From the roadside to the brook
Whereinto he loved to look.
Step the meek fowls where erst they ranged;
The wintry garden lies unchanged;   95
The brook into the stream runs on;
But the deep-eyed boy is gone.

On that shaded day,
Dark with more clouds than tempests are,
When thou didst yield thy innocent breath   100
In birdlike heavings unto death,
Night came, and Nature had not thee;
I said, "We are mates in misery."
The morrow dawned with needless glow;
Each snowbird chirped, each fowl must crow;   105
Each tramper started; but the feet
Of the most beautiful and sweet

Of human youth had left the hill
And garden, — they were bound and still.
There's not a sparrow or a wren,   110
There's not a blade of autumn grain,
Which the four seasons do not tend
And tides of life and increase lend;
And every chick of every bird,
And weed and rock-moss is preferred.   115
O ostrich-like forgetfulness!
O loss of larger in the less!
Was there no star that could be sent,
No watcher in the firmament,
No angel from the countless host   120
That loiters round the crystal coast,
Could stoop to heal that only child,
Nature's sweet marvel undefiled,
And keep the blossom of the earth,
Which all her harvests were not worth?   125
Not mine, — I never called thee mine,
But Nature's heir, — if I repine,
And seeing rashly torn and moved
Not what I made, but what I loved,
Grow early old with grief that thou   130
Must to the wastes of Nature go, —
'Tis because a general hope
Was quenched, and all must doubt and grope.
For flattering planets seemed to say
This child should ills of ages stay,   135
By wondrous tongue, and guided pen,
Bring the flown Muses back to men.
Perchance not he but Nature ailed,
The world and not the infant failed.
It was not ripe yet to sustain   140
A genius of so fine a strain,
Who gazed upon the sun and moon
As if he came unto his own,
And, pregnant with his grander thought,
Brought the old order into doubt.   145
His beauty once their beauty tried;
They could not feed him, and he died,
And wandered backward as in scorn,
To wait an aeon to be born.

Ill day which made this beauty waste, 150
Plight broken, this high face defaced!
Some went and came about the dead;
And some in books of solace read;
Some to their friends the tidings say;
Some went to write, some went to pray; 155
One tarried here, there hurried one;
But their heart abode with none.
Covetous death bereaved us all,
To aggrandize one funeral.
The eager fate which carried thee 160
Took the largest part of me:
For this losing is true dying;
This is lordly man's down-lying,
This his slow but sure reclining,
Star by star his world resigning. 165

O child of paradise,
Boy who made dear his father's home,
In whose deep eyes
Men read the welfare of the times to come,
I am too much bereft. 170
The world dishonored thou hast left.
O truth's and nature's costly lie!
O trusted broken prophecy!
O richest fortune sourly crossed!
Born for the future, to the future lost! 175

The deep Heart answered, "Weepest thou?
Worthier cause for passion wild
If I had not taken the child.
And deemest thou as those who pore,
With aged eyes, short way before, — 180
Think'st Beauty vanished from the coast
Of matter, and thy darling lost?
Taught he not thee — the man of eld,
Whose eyes within his eyes beheld
Heaven's numerous hierarchy span 185
The mystic gulf from God to man?
To be alone wilt thou begin
When worlds of lovers hem thee in?
Tomorrow, when the masks shall fall

That dizen Nature's carnival,   190
The pure shall see by their own will,
Which overflowing Love shall fill,
'Tis not within the force of fate
The fate-conjoined to separate.
But thou, my votary, weepest thou?   195
I gave thee sight — where is it now?
I taught thy heart beyond the reach
Of ritual, bible, or of speech;
Wrote in thy mind's transparent table,
As far as the incommunicable;   200
Taught thee each private sign to raise
Lit by the supersolar blaze.
Past utterance, and past belief,
And past the blasphemy of grief,
The mysteries of Nature's heart;   205
And though no Muse can these impart,
Throb thine with Nature's throbbing breast,
And all is clear from east to west.

"I came to thee as to a friend;
Dearest, to thee I did not send   210
Tutors, but a joyful eye,
Innocence that matched the sky,
Lovely locks, a form of wonder,
Laughter rich as woodland thunder,
That thou might'st entertain apart   215
The richest flowering of all art:
And, as the great all-loving Day
Through smallest chambers takes its way,
That thou might'st break thy daily bread
With prophet, savior and head;   220
That thou might'st cherish for thine own
The riches of sweet Mary's Son,
Boy-Rabbi, Israel's paragon.
And thoughtest thou such guest
Would in thy hall take up his rest?   225
Would rushing life forget her laws,
Fate's glowing revolution pause?
High omens ask diviner guess;
Not to be conned to tediousness
And know my higher gifts unbind   230

The zone that girds the incarnate mind.
When the scanty shores are full
With Thought's perilous, whirling pool;
When frail Nature can no more,
Then the Spirit strikes the hour: 235
My servant Death, with solving rite,
Pours finite into infinite.
Wilt thou freeze love's tidal flow,
Whose streams through Nature circling go?
Nail the wild star to its track   240
On the half-climbed zodiac?
Light is light which radiates,
Blood is blood which circulates,
Life is life which generates,
And many-seeming life is one, —   245
Wilt thou transfix and make it none?
Its onward force too starkly pent
In figure, bone and lineament?
Wilt thou, uncalled, interrogate,
Talker! the unreplying Fate?   250
Nor see the genius of the whole
Ascendant in the private soul,
Beckon it when to go and come,
Self-announced its hour of doom?
Fair the soul's recess and shrine,   255
Magic-built to last a season;
Masterpiece of love benign;
Fairer that expansive reason
Whose omen 'tis, and sign.
Wilt thou not ope thy heart to know   260
What rainbows teach, and sunsets show?
Verdict which accumulates
From lengthening scroll of human fates,
Voice of earth to earth returned,
Prayers of saints that inly burned, —   256
Saying, *What is excellent,*
As God lives, is permanent;
Hearts are dust, hearts' loves remain;
Heart's love will meet thee again.
Revere the Maker; fetch thine eye   270
Up to his style, and manners of the sky.
Not of adamant and gold

Built he heaven stark and cold;
No, but a nest of bending reeds,
Flowering grass and scented weeds; 275
Or like a traveler's fleeing tent,
Or bow above the tempest bent;
Built of tears and sacred flames,
And virtue reaching to its aims;
Built of furtherance and pursuing, 280
Not of spent deeds, but of doing.
Silent rushes the swift Lord
Through ruined systems still restored,
Broadsowing, bleak and void to bless,
Plants with worlds the wilderness; 285
Waters with tears of ancient sorrow
Apples of Eden ripe tomorrow.
House and tenant go to ground,
Lost in God, in Godhead found."

    1846

THINE EYES STILL SHINED [7]

Thine eyes still shined for me, though far
 I lonely roved the land or sea:
As I behold yon evening star,
 Which yet beholds not me.

This morn I climbed the misty hill 5
 And roamed the pastures through;
How danced thy form before my path
 Amidst the deep-eyed dew!

When the redbird spread his sable wing,
 And showed his side of flame; 10
When the rosebud ripened to the rose,
 In both I read thy name.

1829?   1846

[7] Addressed to Ellen.

EROS

The sense of the world is short, —
Long and various the report, —
　To love and be beloved;
Men and gods have not outlearned it;
And, how oft soe'er they've turned it,   5
　Not to be improved.

　　　　　　　　1844

GIVE ALL TO LOVE

Give all to love;
Obey thy heart;
Friends, kindred, days,
Estate, good-fame,
Plans, credit and the Muse, —   5
Nothing refuse.

'Tis a brave master;
Let it have scope:
Follow it utterly,
Hope beyond hope: 10
High and more high
It dives into noon,
With wing unspent,
Untold intent;
But it is a god,   15
Knows its own path
And the outlets of the sky.

It was never for the mean;
It requireth courage stout.
Souls above doubt,   20
Valor unbending,
It will reward, —
They shall return
More than they were,
And every ascending.   25

Leave all for love;
Yet, hear me, yet,
One word more thy heart behoved,
One pulse more of firm endeavor,
Keep thee today,   30
Tomorrow, forever,
Free as an Arab
Of thy beloved.

Cling with life to the maid;
But when the surprise,   35
First vague shadow of surmise
Flits across her bosom young,
Of a joy apart from thee,
Free be she, fancy-free;
Nor thou detain her vesture's hem,   40
Nor the palest rose she flung
From her summer diadem.

Though thou loved her as thyself,
As a self of purer clay,
Though her parting dims the day,   45
Stealing grace from all alive;
Heartily know,
When half-gods go,
The gods arrive.

                                        1846

HAMATREYA [8]

Bulkeley, Hunt, Willard, Hosmer, Meriam, Flint,
Possessed the land which rendered to their toil
Hay, corn, roots, hemp, flax, apples, wool and wood.
Each of these landlords walked amidst his farm,
Saying, " 'Tis mine, my children's and my name's.   5
How sweet the west wind sounds in my own trees!
How graceful climb those shadows on my hill!
I fancy these pure waters and the flags
Know me, as does my dog: we sympathize;
And, I affirm, my actions smack of the soil."   10

[8] A variant on Maitreya, a Hindu proper name.

Where are these men? Asleep beneath their grounds:
And strangers, fond as they, their furrows plough.
Earth laughs in flowers, to see her boastful boys
Earth-proud, proud of the earth which is not theirs;
Who steer the plough, but cannot steer their feet   15
Clear of the grave.
They added ridge to valley, brook to pond,
And sighed for all that bounded their domain;
"This suits me for a pasture; that's my park;
We must have clay, lime, gravel, granite-ledge,   20
And misty lowland, where to go for peat.
The land is well, — lies fairly to the south.
'Tis good, when you have crossed the sea and back,
To find the sitfast acres where you left them."
Ah! the hot owner sees not Death, who adds   25
Him to his land, a lump of mold the more.
Hear what the Earth says:

EARTH-SONG

"Mine and yours;
Mine, not yours.
Earth endures;   30
Stars abide —
Shine down in the old sea;
Old are the shores;
But where are old men?
I who have seen much,   35
Such have I never seen.

"The lawyer's deed
Ran sure,
In tail,
To them, and to their heirs   40
Who shall succeed,
Without fail,
Forevermore.

"Here is the land,
Shaggy with wood,   45
With its old valley,
Mound and flood.

But the heritors? —
Fled like the flood's foam.
The lawyer, and the laws,   50
And the kingdom,
Clean swept herefrom.

"'They called me theirs,
Who so controlled me;
Yet every one   55
Wished to stay, and is gone,
How am I theirs,
If they cannot hold me,
But I hold them?"

When I heard the Earth-song   60
I was no longer brave;
My avarice cooled
Like lust in the chill of the grave.

                                        1846

ODE

Inscribed to W. H. Channing

Though loath to grieve
The evil time's sole patriot,
I cannot leave
My honied thought
For the priest's cant,   5
Or statesman's rant.

If I refuse
My study for their politique,
Which at the best is trick,
The angry Muse   10
Puts confusion in my brain.

But who is he that prates
Of the culture of mankind,
Of better arts and life?
Go, blindworm, go,   15

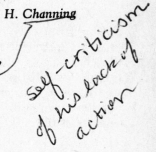

Behold the famous States   *Mexican War*
Harrying Mexico   *E. opposed*
With rifle and with knife!

Or who, with accent bolder,
Dare praise the freedom-loving mountaineer?   20
I found by thee, O rushing Contoocook!
And in thy valleys, Agiochook!
The jackals of the negro-holder.

The God who made New Hampshire
Taunted the lofty land   25
With little men; —
Small bat and wren
House in the oak: —
If earth-fire cleave
The upheaved land, and bury the folk,   30
The southern crocodile would grieve.
Virtue palters; Right is hence;
Freedom praised, but hid;
Funeral eloquence
Rattles the coffin-lid.   35

What boots thy zeal,
O glowing friend,
That would indignant rend
The northland from the south?
Wherefore? to what good end?   40
Boston Bay and Bunker Hill
Would serve things still;
Things are of the snake.

The horseman serves the horse,
The neatherd serves the neat,   45
The merchant serves the purse,
The eater serves his meat;
'Tis the day of the chattel,
Web to weave, and corn to grind;
Things are in the saddle,   50
And ride mankind.

There are two laws discrete,
Not reconciled, —

Law for man, and law for thing;
The last builds town and fleet, 55
But it runs wild,
And doth the man unking.

'Tis fit the forest fall,
The steep be graded,
The mountain tunneled, 60
The sand shaded,
The orchard planted,
The glebe tilled,
The prairie granted,
The steamer built. 65

Let man serve law for man;
Live for friendship, live for love,
For truth's and harmony's behoof;
The state may follow how it can,
As Olympus follows Jove. 70

  Yet do not I implore
The wrinkled shopman to my sounding woods,
Nor bid the unwilling senator
Ask votes of thrushes in the solitudes.
Every one to his chosen work; — 75
Foolish hands may mix and mar;
Wise and sure the issues are.
Round they roll till dark is light,
Sex to sex, and even to odd; —
The over-god 80
Who marries Right to Might,
Who peoples, unpeoples, —
He who exterminates
Races by stronger races,
Black by white faces, — 85
Knows to bring honey
Out of the lion;
Grafts gentlest scion
On pirate and Turk.

The Cossack eats Poland, 90
Like stolen fruit;

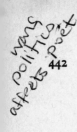

was
politics
affects poet

politics can't be
separated from
poet sort

Her last noble is ruined,
Her last poet mute:
Straight, into double band
The victors divide;   95
Half for freedom strike and stand; —
The astonished Muse finds thousands at her side.

                                                    1846

THE WORLD-SOUL

Thanks to the morning light,
  Thanks to the foaming sea,
To the uplands of New Hampshire,
  To the green-haired forest free;
Thanks to each man of courage,   5
  To the maids of holy mind,
To the boy with his games undaunted
  Who never looks behind.

Cities of proud hotels,
  Houses of rich and great,   10
Vice nestles in your chambers,
  Beneath your roofs of slate.
It cannot conquer folly, —
  Time-and-space-conquering steam, —
And the light-outspeeding telegraph   15
  Bears nothing on its beam.

The politics are base;
  The letters do not cheer;
And 'tis far in the deeps of history,
  The voice that speaketh clear.   20
Trade and the streets ensnare us,
  Our bodies are weak and worn;
We plot and corrupt each other,
  And we despoil the unborn.

Yet there in the parlor sits   25
  Some figure of noble guise, —
Our angel, in a stranger's form,
  Or woman's pleading eyes;

Or only a flashing sunbeam
  In at the window-pane;
Or Music pours on mortals
  Its beautiful disdain.

30

The inevitable morning
  Finds them who in cellars be;
And be sure the all-loving Nature
  Will smile in a factory.
Yon ridge of purple landscape,
  Yon sky between the walls,
Hold all the hidden wonders
  In scanty intervals.

35

40

Alas! the Sprite that haunts us
  Deceives our rash desire;
It whispers of the glorious gods,
  And leaves us in the mire.
We cannot learn the cipher
  That's writ upon our cell;
Stars taunt us by a mystery
  Which we could never spell.

45

If but one hero knew it,
  The world would blush in flame;
The sage, till he hit the secret,
  Would hang his head for shame.
Our brothers have not read it,
  Not one has found the key;
And henceforth we are comforted, —
  We are but such as they.

50

55

Still, still the secret presses;
  The nearing clouds draw down;
The crimson morning flames into
  The fopperies of the town.
Within, without the idle earth,
  Stars weave eternal rings;
The sun himself shines heartily,
  And shares the joy he brings.

60

And what if Trade sow cities   65
    Like shells along the shore,
And thatch with towns the prairie broad
    With railways ironed o'er? —
They are but sailing foam-bells
    Along Thought's causing stream,   70
And take their shape and sun-color
    From him that sends the dream.

For Destiny never swerves
    Nor yields to men the helm;
He shoots his thought, by hidden nerves,   75
    Throughout the solid realm.
The patient Daemon sits,
    With roses and a shroud;
He has his way, and deals his gifts, —
    But ours is not allowed.   80

He is no churl nor trifler,
    And his viceroy is none, —
Love-without-weakness, —
    Of Genius sire and son.
And his will is not thwarted;   85
    The seeds of land and sea
Are the atoms of his body bright,
    And his behest obey.

He serveth the servant,
    The brave he loves amain;   90
He kills the cripple and the sick,
    And straight begins again;
For gods delight in gods,
    And thrust the weak aside;
To him who scorns their charities   95
    Their arms fly open wide.

When the old world is sterile
    And the ages are effete,
He will from wrecks and sediment
    The fairer world complete.   100
He forbids to despair;
    His cheeks mantle with mirth;

And the unimagined good of men
   Is yeaning at the birth.

Spring still makes spring in the mind   105
   When sixty years are told;
Love wakes anew this throbbing heart,
   And we are never old;
Over the winter glaciers
   I see the summer glow,   110
And through the wild-piled snow-drift
   The warm rosebuds below.

              1846

INSIGHT

Power that by obedience grows,
Knowledge which its source not knows,
Wave which severs whom it bears
From the things which he compares,[9]
Adding wings through things to range,
To his own blood harsh and strange.

              1904

BACCHUS

Bring me wine, but wine which never grew
In the belly of the grape,
Or grew on vine whose tap-roots, reaching through
Under the Andes to the Cape,
Suffer no savor of the earth to scape.   5

Let its grapes the morn salute
From a nocturnal root,
Which feels the acrid juice
Of Styx and Erebus;
And turns the woe of Night,   10
By its own craft, to a more rich delight.

[9] Is like, is equal to.

We buy ashes for bread;
We buy diluted wine;
Give me of the true, —
Whose ample leaves and tendrils curled   15
Among the silver hills of heaven
Draw everlasting dew;
Wine of wine,
Blood of the world,
Form of forms, and mold of statures,   20
That I intoxicated,
And by the draught assimilated,
May float at pleasure through all natures;
The bird-language rightly spell,
And that which roses say so well.   25

Wine that is shed
Like the torrents of the sun
Up the horizon walls,
Or like the Atlantic streams, which run
When the South Sea calls.   30

Water and bread,
Food which needs no transmuting,
Rainbow-flowering, wisdom-fruiting,
Wine which is already man,
Food which teach and reason can.   35

Wine which Music is, —
Music and wine are one, —
That I, drinking this,
Shall hear far Chaos talk with me;
Kings unborn shall walk with me;   40
And the poor grass shall plot and plan
What it will do when it is man.
Quickened so, will I unlock
Every crypt of every rock.

I thank the joyful juice   45
For all I know; —
Winds of remembering
Of the ancient being blow,

And seeming-solid walls of use
Open and flow. 50

Pour, Bacchus! the remembering wine;
Retrieve the loss of me and mine!
Vine for vine be antidote,
And the grape requite the lote!
Haste to cure the old despair, — 55
Reason in Nature's lotus drenched,
The memory of ages quenched;
Give them again to shine;
Let wine repair what this undid;
And where the infection slid, 60
A dazzling memory revive;
Refresh the faded tints,
Recut the aged prints,
And write my old adventures with the pen
Which on the first day drew, 65
Upon the tablets blue,
The dancing Pleiads and eternal men.
1846 1846

MERLIN

I

Thy trivial harp will never please
Or fill my craving ear;
Its chords should ring as blows the breeze,
Free, peremptory, clear.
No jingling serenader's art, 5
Nor tinkle of piano strings,
Can make the wild blood start
In its mystic springs.
The kingly bard
Must smite the chords rudely and hard, 10
As with hammer or with mace;
That they may render back
Artful thunder, which conveys
Secrets of the solar track,
Sparks of the supersolar blaze. 15

Merlin's blows are strokes of fate,
Chiming with the forest tone,
When boughs buffet boughs in the wood;
Chiming with the gasp and moan
Of the ice-imprisoned flood;   20
With the pulse of manly hearts;
With the voice of orators;
With the din of city arts;
With the cannonade of wars;
With the marches of the brave;   25
And prayers of might from martyrs' cave.

Great is the art,
Great be the manners, of the bard.
He shall not his brain encumber
With the coil of rhythm and number;   30
But, leaving rule and pale forethought,
He shall aye climb
For his rhyme.
"Pass in, pass in," the angels say,
"In to the upper doors,   35
Nor count compartments of the floors,
But mount to paradise
By the stairway of surprise."

Blameless master of the games,
King of sport that never shames,   40
He shall daily joy dispense
Hid in song's sweet influence.
Forms more cheerly live and go,
What time the subtle mind
Sings aloud the tune whereto   45
Their pulses beat,
And march their feet,
And their members are combined.

By Sybarites beguiled,
He shall no task decline;   50
Merlin's mighty line
Extremes of nature reconciled, —
Bereaved a tyrant of his will,
And made the lion mild.

Songs can the tempest still, 55
Scattered on the stormy air,
Mold the year to fair increase,
And bring in poetic peace.
He shall not seek to weave,
In weak, unhappy times, 60
Efficacious rhymes;
Wait his returning strength.
Bird that from the nadir's floor
To the zenith's top can soar, —
The soaring orbit of the muse exceeds that journey's length. 65
Nor profane affect to hit
Or compass that, by meddling wit,
Which only the propitious mind
Publishes when 'tis inclined.
There are open hours 70
When the God's will sallies free,
And the dull idiot might see
The flowing fortunes of a thousand years; —
Sudden, at unawares,
Self-moved, fly-to the doors, 75
Nor sword of angels could reveal
What they conceal.

II

The rhyme of the poet
Modulates the king's affairs;
Balance-loving Nature 80
Made all things in pairs.
To every foot its antipode;
Each color with its counter glowed;
To every tone beat answering tones,
Higher or graver; 85
Flavor gladly blends with flavor;
Leaf answers leaf upon the bough;
And match the paired cotyledons.[1]
Hands to hands, and feet to feet,
In one body grooms and brides; 90
Eldest rite, two married sides
In every mortal meet.

[1] Seed leaves in the embryo plant.

Light's far furnace shines,
Smelting balls and bars,
Forging double stars,   95
Glittering twins and trines.
The animals are sick with love,
Lovesick with rhyme;
Each with all propitious Time
Into chorus wove.   100

Like the dancers' ordered band,
Thoughts come also hand in hand;
In equal couples mated,
Or else alternated;
Adding by their mutual gage,   105
One to other, health and age.
Solitary fancies go
Short-lived wandering to and fro,
Most like to bachelors,
Or an ungiven maid,   110
Not ancestors,
With no posterity to make the lie afraid,
Or keep truth undecayed.
Perfect-paired as eagle's wings,
Justice is the rhyme of things;   115
Trade and counting use
The self-same tuneful muse;
And Nemesis,
Who with even matches odd,
Who athwart space redresses   120
The partial wrong,
Fills the just period,
And finishes the song.

Subtle rhymes, with ruin rife,
Murmur in the house of life,   125
Sung by the Sisters as they spin;
In perfect time and measure they
Build and unbuild our echoing clay,
As the two twilights of the day
Fold us music-drunken in.   130
1846   1846

DAYS

Daughters of Time, the hypocritic Days,
Muffled and dumb like barefoot dervishes,
And marching single in an endless file,
Bring diadems and fagots in their hands.
To each they offer gifts after his will,   5
Bread, kingdoms, stars, and sky that holds them all.
I, in my pleachéd garden, watched the pomp,
Forgot my morning wishes, hastily
Took a few herbs and apples, and the Day
Turned and departed silent. I, too late,   10
Under her solemn fillet saw the scorn.
1851   1857

BRAHMA

If the red slayer think he slays,
    Or if the slain think he is slain,
They know not well the subtle ways
    I keep, and pass, and turn again.

Far or forgot to me is near;   5
    Shadow and sunlight are the same;
The vanished gods to me appear;
    And one to me are shame and fame.

They reckon ill who leave me out;
    When me they fly, I am the wings;   10
I am the doubter and the doubt,
    And I the hymn the Brahmin sings.

The strong gods pine for my abode,
    And pine in vain the sacred Seven;
But thou, meek lover of the good!   15
    Find me, and turn thy back on heaven.
1856   1857

MAIA [2]

Illusion works impenetrable,
Weaving webs innumerable,
Her gay pictures never fail,
Crowds each on other, veil on veil,
Charmer who will be believed   5
By man who thirsts to be deceived.

                    1904

TWO RIVERS

Thy summer voice, Musketaquit,[3]
Repeats the music of the rain;
But sweeter rivers pulsing flit
Through thee, as thou through Concord Plain.

Thou in thy narrow banks art pent: 5
The stream I love unbounded goes
Through flood and sea and firmament;
Through light, through life, it forward flows.

I see the inundation sweet,
I hear the spending of the stream   10
Through years, through men, through Nature fleet,
Through love and thought, through power and dream.

Musketaquit, a goblin strong,
Of shard and flint makes jewels gay;
They lose their grief who hear his song,   15
And where he winds is the day of day.

So forth and brighter fares my stream, —
Who drink it shall not thirst again;
No darkness stains its equal gleam,
And ages drop in it like rain.   20

1856   *1858*

2 Illusion.
3 The Concord River.

SEASHORE

I heard or seemed to hear the chiding Sea
Say, Pilgrim, why so late and slow to come?
Am I not always here, thy summer home?
Is not my voice thy music, morn and eve?
My breath thy healthful climate in the heats,   5
My touch thy antidote, my bay thy bath?
Was ever building like my terraces?
Was ever couch magnificent as mine?
Lie on the warm rock-ledges, and there learn
A little hut suffices like a town.   10
I make your sculptured architecture vain,
Vain beside mine. I drive my wedges home,
And carve the coastwise mountain into caves.
Lo! here is Rome and Nineveh and Thebes,
Karnak and Pyramid and Giant's Stairs   15
Half piled or prostrate; and my newest slab
Older than all thy race.

                Behold the Sea,
The opaline, the plentiful and strong,
Yet beautiful as is the rose in June,
Fresh as the trickling rainbow of July;   20
Sea full of food, the nourisher of kinds,
Purger of earth, and medicine of men;
Creating a sweet climate by my breath,
Washing out harms and griefs from memory,
And, in my mathematic ebb and flow,   25
Giving a hint of that which changes not.
Rich are the sea-gods: — who gives gifts but they?
They grope the sea for pearls, but more than pearls:
They pluck Force thence, and give it to the wise.
For every wave is wealth to Daedalus,   30
Wealth to the cunning artist who can work
This matchless strength. Where shall he find, O waves!
A load your Atlas shoulders cannot lift?

  I with my hammer pounding evermore
The rocky coast, smite Andes into dust,   35
Strewing my bed, and, in another age,
Rebuild a continent of better men.

Then I unbar the doors: my paths lead out
The exodus of nations: I disperse
Men to all shores that front the hoary main.   40

  I too have arts and sorceries;
Illusion dwells forever with the wave.
I know what spells are laid. Leave me to deal
With credulous and imaginative man;
For, though he scoop my water in his palm,   45
A few rods off he deems it gems and clouds.
Planting strange fruits and sunshine on the shore,
I make some coast alluring, some lone isle,
To distant men, who must go there, or die.
1856   1867

WALDEINSAMKEIT [4]

I do not count the hours I spend
In wandering by the sea;
The forest is my loyal friend,
Like God it useth me.

In plains that room for shadows make   5
Of skirting hills to lie,
Bound in by streams which give and take
Their colors from the sky;

Or on the mountain-crest sublime,
Or down the oaken glade,   10
O what have I to do with time?
For this the day was made.

Cities of mortals woe-begone
Fantastic care derides,
But in the serious landscape lone   15
Stern benefit abides.

Sheen will tarnish, honey cloy,
And merry is only a mask of sad,
But, sober on a fund of joy,
The woods at heart are glad.   20

[4] Forest solitude.

There the great Planter plants
Of fruitful worlds the grain,
And with a million spells enchants
The souls that walk in pain.

Still on the seeds of all he made   25
The rose of beauty burns;
Through times that wear and forms that fade,
Immortal youth returns.

The black ducks mounting from the lake,
The pigeon in the pines,   30
The bittern's boom, a desert make
Which no false art refines.

Down in yon watery nook,
Where bearded mists divide,
The gray old gods whom Chaos knew,   35
The sires of Nature, hide.

Aloft, in secret veins of air,
Blows the sweet breath of song,
O, few to scale those uplands dare,
Though they to all belong!   40

See thou bring not to field or stone
The fancies found in books;
Leave authors' eyes, and fetch your own,
To brave the landscape's looks.

Oblivion here thy wisdom is,   45
Thy thrift, the sleep of cares;
For a proud idleness like this
Crowns all thy mean affairs.
1857   1858

SONG OF NATURE

Mine are the night and morning,
The pits of air, the gulf of space,
The sportive sun, the gibbous moon,
The innumerable days.

I hide in the solar glory,　　　　　　　　　　5
I am dumb in the pealing song,
I rest on the pitch of the torrent,
In slumber I am strong.

No numbers have counted my tallies,
No tribes my house can fill,　　　　　　　　10
I sit by the shining Fount of Life
And pour the deluge still;

And ever by delicate powers
Gathering along the centuries
From race on race the rarest flowers,　　　15
My wreath shall nothing miss.

And many a thousand summers
My gardens ripened well,
And light from meliorating stars
With firmer glory fell.　　　　　　　　　　20

I wrote the past in characters
Of rock and fire the scroll,
The building in the coral sea,
The planting of the coal.

And thefts from satellites and rings　　　25
And broken stars I drew,
And out of spent and aged things
I formed the world anew;

What time the gods kept carnival,
Tricked out in star and flower,　　　　　　30
And in cramp elf and saurian forms
They swathed their too much power.

Time and Thought were my surveyors,
They laid their courses well,
They boiled the sea, and piled the layers　35
Of granite, marl and shell.

But he, the man-child glorious, —
Where tarries he the while?

The rainbow shines his harbinger,
The sunset gleams his smile. 40

My boreal lights leap upward,
Forthright my planets roll,
And still the man-child is not born,
The summit of the whole.

Must time and tide forever run? 45
Will never my winds go sleep in the west?
Will never my wheels which whirl the sun
And satellites have rest?

Too much of donning and doffing,
Too slow the rainbow fades, 50
I weary of my robe of snow,
My leaves and my cascades;

I tire of globes and races,
Too long the game is played;
What without him is summer's pomp, 55
Or winter's frozen shade?

I travail in pain for him,
My creatures travail and wait;
His couriers come by squadrons,
He comes not to the gate. 30

Twice I have molded an image,
And thrice outstretched my hand,
Made one of day and one of night
And one of the salt sea-sand.

One in a Judaean manger, 65
And one by Avon stream,
One over against the mouths of Nile,
And one in the Academe.

I molded kings and saviors,
And bards o'er kings to rule; — 70
But fell the starry influence short,
The cup was never full.

Yet whirl the glowing wheels once more,
And mix the bowl again;
Seethe, Fate! the ancient elements,   75
Heat, cold, wet, dry, and peace, and pain.

Let war and trade and creeds and song
Blend, ripen race on race,
The sunburnt world a man shall breed
Of all the zones and countless days.   80

No ray is dimmed, no atom worn,
My oldest force is good as new,
And the fresh rose on yonder thorn
Gives back the bending heavens in dew.
1859   1867

TERMINUS [5]

It is time to be old,
To take in sail: —
The god of bounds,
Who sets to seas a shore,
Came to me in his fatal rounds,   5
And said: "No more!
No farther shoot
Thy broad ambitious branches, and thy root.
Fancy departs: no more invent;
Contract thy firmament   10
To compass of a tent.
There's not enough for this and that,
Make thy option which of two;
Economize the failing river,
Not the less revere the Giver,   15
Leave the many and hold the few.
Timely wise accept the terms,
Soften the fall with wary foot;
A little while
Still plan and smile,   20
And, — fault of novel germs, —
Mature the unfallen fruit.

[5] The Roman god of boundaries.

Curse, if thou wilt, thy sires,
Bad husbands of their fires,
Who, when they gave thee breath,   25
Failed to bequeath
The needful sinew stark as once,
The Baresark marrow to thy bones,
But left a legacy of ebbing veins,
Inconstant heat and nerveless reins, —   30
Amid the Muses, left thee deaf and dumb,
Amid the gladiators, halt and numb."

As the bird trims her to the gale,
I trim myself to the storm of time,
I man the rudder, reef the sail,   35
Obey the voice at eve obeyed at prime:
"Lowly faithful, banish fear,
Right onward drive unharmed;
The port, well worth the cruise, is near,
And every wave is charmed."   40

                                        1867

MOTTOES [6]

NATURE

The rounded world is fair to see,
Nine times folded in mystery:
Though baffled seers cannot impart
The secret of its laboring heart,
Throb thine with Nature's throbbing breast,   5
And all is clear from east to west.
Spirit that lurks each form within
Beckons to spirit of its kin;
Self-kindled every atom glows
And hints the future which it owes.   10

                                        1844

---

[6] Other mottoes are to be found as follows: "Nature," p. 21; "Self-Reliance," p. 147; "Circles," p. 168; "The Poet," p. 222; "Politics," p. 241; "Experience," p. 254; and "Fate," p. 330.

NOMINALIST AND REALIST

In countless upward-striving waves
The moon-drawn tide-wave strives;
In thousand far-transplanted grafts
The parent fruit survives;
So, in the new-born millions,   5
The perfect Adam lives.
Not less are summer mornings dear
To every child they wake,
And each with novel life his sphere
Fills for his proper sake.   10

1844

COMPENSATION

The wings of Time are black and white,
Pied with morning and with night.
Mountain tall and ocean deep
Trembling balance duly keep.
In changing moon and tidal wave,   5
Glows the feud of Want and Have.
Gauge of more and less through space,
Electric star or pencil plays.
The lonely Earth amid the balls
That hurry through the eternal halls,   10
A makeweight flying to the void,
Supplemental asteroid,
Or compensatory spark,
Shoots across the neutral Dark.

1847

SPIRITUAL LAWS

The living Heaven thy prayers respect,
House at once and architect,
Quarrying man's rejected hours,
Builds there with eternal towers;
Sole and self-commanded works,   5
Fears not undermining days,
Grows by decays,

And, by the famous might that lurks
In reaction and recoil,
Makes flame to freeze and ice to boil;   10
Forging, through swart arms of Offence,
The silver seat of Innocence.

                                        1847

A R T

Give to barrows, trays and pans
Grace and glimmer of romance;
Bring the moonlight into noon
Hid in gleaming piles of stone;
On the city's pavéd street   5
Plant gardens lined with lilac sweet;
Let spouting fountains cool the air,
Singing in the sun-baked square;
Let statue, picture, park and hall,
Ballad, flag and festival,   10
The past restore, the day adorn
And make tomorrow a new morn.
So shall the drudge in dusty frock
Spy behind the city clock
Retinues of airy kings,   15
Skirts of angels, starry wings,
His fathers shining in bright fables,
His children fed at heavenly tables.
'Tis the privilege of Art
Thus to play its cheerful part,   20
Man on Earth to acclimate
And bend the exile to his fate,
And, molded of one element
With the days and firmament,
Teach him on these as stairs to climb   25
And live on even terms with Time;
Whilst upper life the slender rill
Of human sense doth overfill.

                                        1847

WORSHIP

This is he, who, felled by foes,
Sprung harmless up, refreshed by blows:
He to captivity was sold,
But him no prison-bars would hold:
Though they sealed him in a rock,   5
Mountain chains he can unlock:
Thrown to lions for their meat,
The crouching lion kissed his feet:
Bound to the stake, no flames appalled,
But arched o'er him an honoring vault.   10
This is he men miscall Fate,
Threading dark ways, arriving late,
But ever coming in time to crown
The truth, and hurl wrongdoers down.
He is the oldest, and best known,   15
More near than aught thou call'st thy own,
Yet, greeted in another's eyes,
Disconcerts with glad surprise.
This is Jove, who, deaf to prayers,
Floods with blessings unawares.   20
Draw, if thou canst, the mystic line
Severing rightly his from thine,
Which is human, which divine.

1860

WEALTH

Who shall tell what did befall,
Far away in time, when once,
Over the lifeless ball,
Hung idle stars and suns?
What god the element obeyed?   5
Wings of what wind the lichen bore,
Wafting the puny seeds of power,
Which, lodged in rock, the rock abrade?
And well the primal pioneer
Knew the strong task to it assigned,   10
Patient through Heaven's enormous year
To build in matter home for mind.

From air the creeping centuries drew
The matted thicket low and wide,
This must the leaves of ages strew 15
The granite slab to clothe and hide,
Ere wheat can wave its golden pride.
What smiths, and in what furnace, rolled
(In dizzy aeons dim and mute
The reeling brain can ill compute) 20
Copper and iron, lead and gold?
What oldest star the fame can save
Of races perishing to pave
The planet with a floor of lime?
Dust is their pyramid and mole: 25
Who saw what ferns and palms were pressed
Under the tumbling mountain's breast,
In the safe herbal of the coal?
But when the quarried means were piled,
All is waste and worthless, till 30
Arrives the wise selecting will,
And, out of slime and chaos, Wit
Draws the threads of fair and fit.
Then temples rose, and towns, and marts,
The shop of toil, the hall of arts; 35
Then flew the sail across the seas
To feed the North from tropic trees;
The storm-wind wove, the torrent span,
Where they were bid, the rivers ran;
New slaves fulfilled the poet's dream, 40
Galvanic wire, strong-shouldered steam.
Then docks were built, and crops were stored,
And ingots added to the hoard.
But though light-headed man forget,
Remembering Matter pays her debt: 45
Still, through her motes and masses, draw
Electric thrills and ties of law,
Which bind the strengths of Nature wild
To the conscience of a child.

1860

CONSIDERATIONS BY THE WAY

Hear what British Merlin sung,
Of keenest eye and truest tongue.
Say not, the chiefs who first arrive
Usurp the seats for which all strive;
The forefathers this land who found   5
Failed to plant the vantage-ground;
Ever from one who comes tomorrow
Men wait their good and truth to borrow.
But wilt thou measure all thy road,
See thou lift the lightest load.   10
Who has little, to him who has less, can spare,
And thou, Cyndyllan's son! beware
Ponderous gold and stuffs to bear,
To falter ere thou thy task fulfill, —
Only the light-armed climb the hill.   15
The richest of all lords is Use,
And ruddy Health the loftiest Muse.
Live in the sunshine, swim the sea,
Drink the wild air's salubrity:
Where the star Canope shines in May,   20
Shepherds are thankful and nations gay.
The music that can deepest reach,
And cure all ill, is cordial speech:
Mask thy wisdom with delight,
Toy with the bow, yet hit the white.   25
Of all wit's uses, the main one
Is to live well with who has none.
Cleave to thine acre; the round year
Will fetch all fruits and virtues here:
Fool and foe may harmless roam,   30
Loved and lovers bide at home.
A day for toil, an hour for sport,
But for a friend is life too short.

1860

ILLUSIONS

Flow, flow the waves hated,
Accursed, adored,
The waves of mutation;

No anchorage is.
Sleep is, death is not;   5
Who seem to die live.
House you were born in,
Friends of your spring-time,
Old man and young maid,
Day's toil and its guerdon,   10
They are all vanishing,
Fleeing to fables,
Cannot be moored.
See the stars through them,
Through treacherous marbles.   15
Know the stars yonder,
The stars everlasting,
Are fugitive also,
And emulate, vaulted,
The lambent heat-lightning,   20
And fire-fly's flight.

When thou dost return
On the wave's circulation,
Beholding the shimmer,
The wild dissipation,   25
And, out of endeavor
To change and to flow,
The gas become solid,
And phantoms and nothings
Return to be things,   30
And endless imbroglio
Is law and the world, —
Then first shalt thou know,
That in the wild turmoil,
Horsed on the Proteus,   35
Thou ridest to power,
And to endurance.

1860

QUATRAINS[7]

FATE

Her planted eye today controls,
Is in the morrow most at home,
And sternly calls to being souls
That curse her when they come.

1867

CLIMACTERIC

I am not wiser for my age,
Nor skilful by my grief;
Life loiters at the book's first page, —
Ah! could we turn the leaf.

1867

MEMORY

Night-dreams trace on Memory's wall
Shadows of the thoughts of day,
And thy fortunes, as they fall,
The bias of the will betray.

1867

SACRIFICE

Though love repine, and reason chafe,
There came a voice without reply, —
" 'Tis man's perdition to be safe,
When for the truth he ought to die."

1867

From VOLUNTARIES

So nigh is grandeur to our dust,
So near is God to man,

[7] Note that the second motto to "Self-Reliance" (p. 147) is also a quatrain.
The quatrain "Northman" is in the notes, p. 496.

When Duty whispers low, *Thou must,*
The youth replies, *I can.*

1863

NAHANT

All day the waves assailed the rock,
  I heard no church-bell chime,
The sea-beat scorns the minster clock
  And breaks the glass of Time.

1853   1883

Teach me your mood, O patient stars!
  Who climb each night the ancient sky,
Leaving on space no shade, no scars,
  No trace of age, no fear to die.

1883

Notes

W — *Works* (Centenary Edition)
J — *Journals*
L — *Letters* (Rusk)

Brief references are to books listed under Note on the Text and Further Reading (pp. xxii–xxiii).

NOTE: Materials for studying Emerson's methods of composition and revision may be found by consulting the notes to the following pages: (1) Prose. 24, 148, 158, 215. (2) Poetry. 417, 426, 437, 447, 451, 452, 455.

1803–1832: Discovery

Page 2. *May 7, 1837.* On Emerson's New England heritage, see *Emerson Handbook*, pp. 194–200; also Henry B. Parkes, *The Pragmatic Test* (San Francisco, 1941).

Page 3. *May 6, 1841.* Good general accounts of Mary Moody Emerson are Rosalie Feltenstein, "Mary Moody Emerson: The Gadfly of Concord," *American Quarterly* V (1953) 231–46, and Emerson's own "Mary Moody Emerson" (W X 399–433).

Page 4. *Humanitarians.* Liberals, Unitarians.

Page 5. *[Nov. 25, 1837].* Mostly from "Domestic Life" (1859) but first used in the lecture "Home" (1838). The passage is highly idealized.

Page 7. *Immensum infinitumque.* These words, without the *aliquid,* appear early in Cicero's *De Oratore* (I.6), which Emerson studied in college, where they are used of Cicero's requirement that the accomplished orator must know "everything important." Emerson means that he aspires to meet the most exalted standards of great speaking.

Page 8. *Sept. 27, 1830.* Used in a sermon.

1833–1836: First Fruits

Page 14. *The first philosophy.* In 1835 Emerson put together a statement of "the *first* philosophy, that of mind" (see J III 235–40). A corrected text is printed in Kenneth W. Cameron, *Emerson the Essayist* (Raleigh, N. C., 1945), Vol. I, pp. 191–94.

Page 16. *Jan. 1?, 1834.* Prefixed to one of the MS. Journals.

April 20, 1834. A Sunday. Emerson had just heard two good sermons and was stirred to emulation.

Page 17. *May 3, 1834.* Emerson was thinking out his lecture "Naturalist" (May 7).

June 4, 1836. These points are developed in the lecture "Humanity of Science" (1836). They sum up the Coleridgean view of science that controlled the early lectures on science and also the chapter "Prospects" in *Nature.*

Page 18. *Jan. 13, 1835.* Emerson was preparing his course of lectures on "Biography."

Page 19. *The correspondences.* A term Emerson picked up from the Swedenborgians to denote the emblematic relationship he habitually saw between things and ideas. He develops this point of view at length in the chapter "Language" in *Nature.* On this topic see Matthiessen and the references on pp. 489-90.

Page 20. *Reason and Understanding.* This distinction appears constantly in Emerson's journals and other writings of the early 1830's. It permitted Emerson a "two truth" theory of knowledge — that is, there were empirical truths that were known and dealt with by the logical and practical intelligence, or Understanding; and there were absolute truths, transcending sense experience, which were immediately perceived by intuition, or Reason. The distinction came to him chiefly from Coleridge, who was in turn echoing the Kantian distinction of *Verstand* and *Vernunft.* Kant had been careful not to say that *Vernunft* was a source of absolute knowledge. Coleridge, however, partly following Kant's German successors, Platonized the distinction until it became what Carlyle in his later years sardonically described as "the sublime secret of believing by 'the reason' what 'the understanding' had been obliged to fling out as incredible." Emerson, always the dramatist, pushed the distinction farther in the same direction: his Reason can say, I am God. For a few years it was one of his chief weapons against the common-sense realism and Lockeian empiricism still dominant around him.

Empedocles. Ancient Greek philosopher. Emerson is thinking of the beginning of his Καθαρμοί (Songs of Purification): "An immortal god, and no longer a mortal man, I wander among you," etc.

July 30, 1835. Emerson had had some discussion on the topic with Elizabeth Peabody, at that time Alcott's assistant at the Temple School (see p. 478); the passage is clearly aimed at her. She afterwards ran a kind of "Transcendental bookshop" in Boston.

Aug. 5, 1835. Three days before, Emerson had written of "the depth of obscurity in which the Person of God is hid." Cf. "The Bohemian Hymn" (W IX 359), quite possibly written about this time. This like the next is one of the many passages in Emerson that look ahead to William James — in this case to "The Will to Believe."

NATURE

Pages 21 ff. Leaving aside Plato and the Bible, to which Emerson like most of Western culture is a footnote, the two chief immediate intellectual influences on *Nature* were Samuel Taylor Coleridge, 1772–1834, and Emanuel Swedenborg, 1688–1772. The Coleridge who influenced Emerson was not the author of "The Ancient Mariner" and "Kubla Khan" but the eclectic philosopher of *Biographia Literaria* (1817) and the Anglican homilist of *The Statesman's Manual* (1816), *The Friend* (1818), and *Aids to Reflection* (1825). He conveyed to Emerson some of the key insights of Kant and the post-Kantians mixed with enough Platonism and piety to make them palatable. The chief doctrine Emerson derived from him was the distinction of the Reason and the Understanding. Although from this common point he and Coleridge moved in opposite directions, Coleridge toward a "reconstruction of Christian theology" and he toward Self-Reliance and the God Within, the importance of Coleridge as a catalyst in his thought can hardly be exaggerated. See J. O. McCormick, "Emerson's Theory of Human Greatness," *New England Quarterly* XXVI (1953) 291–314; also *Emerson Handbook*, pp. 223–24.

An Englishman and a contemporary, Coleridge spoke directly to Emerson's condition; Swedenborg was a more remote figure. A distinguished scientist and administrator in the service of the Swedish court for much of his life, at the age of 54 he experienced "the opening of his spiritual sight," whereby he could see the heavens and hells of the spiritual world, converse with spirits and angels, and take down directly at the Lord's dictation the key to the threefold sense of the Scriptures — natural, spiritual, and celestial. Something like forty volumes on these matters came from his indefatigable pen before his death. His influence on Emerson is hard to assess. For one thing, it was in large part indirect, coming through the *New Jerusalem Magazine*, the organ of the American "New Church" or Swedenborgian society, and in particular from one Emerson called his "early oracle," Sampson Reed, whose "Oration on Genius" much impressed him at the end of his senior year at Harvard and whose later *Observations on the Growth of the Mind* (1826) struck him as a revelation. For another, since Swedenborg's commanding intellect was cracked right down the middle, his influence was in part regressive and tended therefore to limit itself. Though Emerson brushed aside his "theological bias," Swedenborg still encouraged one "bred in the old churches" to hope that nature was a Scripture which might somehow be read off into religious truth by "the good." *Nature* was written at about the high point of what Emerson accurately called Swedenborg's "fascination." As he matured intellectually and was weaned of his need of a revelation, he largely outgrew Swedenborg. Yet he continued to feel an "awe and terror" at the man's imposing demonstration of the poet's highest gift, the moral vision that saw natural facts as spiritual emblems (see pp. 237–38). For this reason he never lost his respect for "king Swedenborg." See *Emerson Handbook*, pp. 220–21, and also under Swedenborg in the Index.

In June of 1835 Emerson wrote a friend that he was thinking "of publishing by and by a book of Essays chiefly upon Natural Ethics" in order to help build "the new temple." If he alludes here to *Nature*, he shows that his plan for the book was still vague. That winter he gave a course of lectures on "English Literature," of which the introductory lecture supplied most of the chapter of *Nature* on "Language," the concluding one some paragraphs for "Beauty," and the fifth (on Shakespeare) the second or "poet" section of "Idealism." By March he seems to have been deep in the throes of composition, and by the end of June he could write to his brother, "My little book is nearly done." There he spoke of following it with another essay, "Spirit." In August, however, he had to confess, "The book of Nature still lies on the table. There is, as always, one crack in it not easy to be soldered or welded." Since a good part of the last chapter as we now have it is based on journal entries for the end of June, it seems likely that the projected essay on "Spirit," suggested perhaps by these entries, had since been made the conclusion of *Nature*, and that this expansion of his first purpose had made him feel the need of a bridge chapter, clearly "Idealism," which came hard. He soon solved his problem, however, for the completed book was offered for sale as of September 10, 1836.

Page 21. *Mottoes.* The 1836 motto is actually a condensation of a citation in Ralph Cudworth's *The True Intellectual System of the Universe* (1678), a book Emerson had been reading with enthusiasm, attracted by Cudworth's many quotations from Plato and the Neo-Platonists. See Cameron's chapter on Cudworth in *Emerson the Essayist* and also Vivian C. Hopkins, "Emerson and Cudworth," *American Literature* XXIII (1951) 80–98.

The 1849 motto, like all Emerson's later writings on nature, reflects a sense of "metamorphosis" and evolution in nature which is not present in the book of 1836; cf. "Song of Nature" (p. 455) and the items under Nature in the Index. The best treatment of this development in his thought is in Joseph Warren Beach, *The Concept of Nature in Nineteenth-Century English Poetry* (1936).

Page 22. NOT ME. The terms ME and NOT-ME occur in Thomas Carlyle's *Sartor Resartus*, first published in book form at Boston in 1836 at Emerson's urging and with a preface by him. The terms are Carlyle's version of the German distinction of Self and Not-Self which pervasively conditioned the climate in which *Nature* was written. "How many changes men ring on these two words in and out. It is all our philosophy" (J II 440, 1831).

Emerson called on Carlyle in Scotland in 1833, when the latter was still little known, and began a lifelong friendship somewhat improved by distance, as the two were very different personalities. He saw him again in 1847–48. See the first chapter of *English Traits* and also "Carlyle" (W X 489–98).

Page 24. *In the woods, we return, etc.* This passage is based on an entry in his journal for March 19, 1835:

> As I walked in the woods I felt what I often feel, that nothing can befal me in life, no calamity, no disgrace, (leaving me my eyes) to which Nature will not offer a sweet consolation. Standing on the bare ground with my head bathed by the blithe air, and uplifted into the infinite space, I become happy in my universal relations. The name of the nearest friend sounds then foreign and accidental. I am the heir of uncontained beauty and power. And if then I walk with a companion, he should speak from his Reason to my Reason; that is, both from God. To be brothers, to be acquaintances, master or servant, is then a trifle too insignificant for remembrance. O, keep this humor, (which in your lifetime may not come to you twice,) as the apple of your eye. Set a lamp before it in your memory which shall never be extinguished.

Occult relation. Emerson is thinking of his visit to the Jardin des Plantes in Paris in 1833, of which he wrote at the time:

> Here we are impressed with the inexhaustible riches of nature. The universe is a more amazing puzzle than ever, as you glance along this bewildering series of animated forms, — the hazy butterflies, the carved shells, the birds, beasts, fishes, insects, snakes, and the upheaving principle of life everywhere incipient, in the very rock aping organized forms. Not a form so grotesque, so savage, nor so beautiful but is an expression of some property inherent in man the observer, — an occult relation between the very scorpions and man. I feel the centipede in me, — cayman, carp, eagle, and fox. I am moved by strange sympathies; I say continually, "I will be a naturalist." (J III 163)

Page 25. *"More servants," etc.* Herbert, "Man." See p. 52.

Page 30. *Il più nell' uno.* A phrase picked up from Coleridge.

Page 32. *Every natural fact, etc.* The debt to Swedenborg is obvious here. See, for example, his *Heaven and its Wonders and Hell*, chapter XII.

Page 35. *"The visible," etc.* From a Swedenborgian source.

Page 36. *"Material objects," etc.* From a Swedenborgian source. *"Every scripture," etc.* A doctrine of George Fox, founder of the Society of Friends (Quakers).

Page 40. *Xenophanes.* Sixth-century B.C. Greek philosopher, an early "Idealist." His phrase for God, ἓ καὶ πᾶν, the One and the All (a favorite with Coleridge) constantly recurs in the journals. Cf. "Xenophanes" (W IX 137).

De Staël. Baronne de Staël-Holstein ("Mme. de Staël"), 1766–

1817. Her *De l'Allemagne* (Germany) (1813), early known to Emerson, was influential in spreading a knowledge of the recent literature and philosophy of Germany.

Michael Angelo. Emerson lectured on him in 1835 (W XII 215–44). See F. B. Newman, "Emerson and Buonarroti," *New England Quarterly* XXVI (1952) 524–33.

Page 41. *"The wise man,"* etc. A paraphrase of Emerson's translation of a passage from Goethe (J IV 17).

We are associated, etc. This passage is based on an entry in Emerson's journal some five weeks after the death of his brother Charles (J IV 67–68). Comparison of the two modifies the impression of austerity made by the former alone. Such beliefs were needed to sustain Emerson in the face of repeated sharp personal loss. Cf. J IV 51, 62, and L II 397.

The farewell to Charles appropriately ends the first or lower half of the book.

Page 42. *Idealism.* See p. 487, and also under Idealism in the Index.

Page 44. *The sensual man,* etc. A paraphrase of a favorite quotation from Bacon: "[Poesy] was ever thought to have some participation of divineness, because it doth raise and erect the mind, by submitting the shows of things to the desires of the mind; whereas reason doth buckle and bow the mind unto the nature of things" (*The Advancement of Learning,* Book II; IV, 2).

Page 46. *"The problem,"* etc. Quoted from Coleridge; the source is not Plato but Kant.

Euler. Leonhard Euler, 1707–83, Swiss mathematician and physicist. His remark is quoted by Coleridge.

"These are they," etc. Adapted from Proverbs 8:23–30.

Page 47. *"The things that are seen,"* etc. II Corinthians 4:18.

Viasa. Legendary author of the Hindu Vedas. For an account of Emerson's early knowledge of the Orientals, see the edition by Kenneth W. Cameron of *Indian Superstition* (an early poem), Hanover, N. H., 1954.

Manichean. The Persian Mani in the third century A.D. founded a dualistic religion affirming the universal conflict of Light and Darkness.

Page 50. *"The golden key,"* etc. Milton's *Comus,* ll. 13–14.

Page 51. *Cabinet of natural history.* See note on *Occult relation,* p. 473.

Page 53. *"Poetry comes nearer,"* etc. Not Plato, but a loose version of Aristotle's statement that poetry is something more philosophical and more serious than history (*Poetics,* section 9).

A certain poet. The suggestion has been often made that Emerson is here attempting to render the conversation of his new friend, Bronson Alcott (see pp. 125–31 and notes); certainly the original version of these passages follows immediately in the journals after the record of a visit from Alcott. It seems better to suppose that

Emerson, stimulated perhaps by Alcott, is expressing his own rhap-
sodic vision of redeemed man, a vision the whole book has been building toward, and that he finds he needs "freer speech" than the prose
of a philosophical treatise in order to do so. The matter is carefully
investigated by Cameron (*Emerson the Essayist*, Vol. I, pp. 361–72),
who reprints entire the original MS. journal entries.

Page 54. *The Shakers.* A communistic religious society, an offshoot
of the English Quakers in the later eighteenth century. There was a
Shaker community at Harvard, Mass., which Emerson and Hawthorne
visited in 1842 (cf. pp. 214–15).

1837–1838: Challenge

Page 58. [*Feb. 16, 1837*]. Like others in "Spiritual Laws," this
passage comes from the lecture "Ethics" (1837); there is little or no
journal source.

Page 59. *The soul's mumps, etc.* Emerson is thinking of his own
young days when he plied his aunt with these "threadbare enigmas."

Page 61. *April 29?, 1837.* The "black times" of economic depression are reflected in the tone of the journals. See W. Charvat, "American Romanticism and the Depression of 1837," *Science and Society*
II (1937) 67–82.

Page 62. *May 21, 1837.* Lectures later in 1837 strike a similar
note.

"*I have sinned,*" *etc.* Acts 8:23.

Page 63. *Actual, ideal.* Terms derived from Carlyle.

THE AMERICAN SCHOLAR

Pages 63 ff. The full title in later editions is, "The American
Scholar: An Oration Delivered Before the Phi Beta Kappa Society,
at Cambridge, August 31, 1837." This "theory of the scholar's office,"
as Emerson called it (J IV 259), though prepared at relatively short
notice when another man declined the invitation, was on a topic he
had been meditating for at least two years (see J III 537, 539–40;
IV, 36, 56, 79). A "sermon" to American scholars, it was also an
effort to define his own vocation for himself; see Henry Nash Smith,
"Emerson's Problem of Vocation," *New England Quarterly* XII
(1939) 52–67. A full account of the reception of this address may
be found in Bliss Perry, "Emerson's Most Famous Speech," *The
Praise of Folly and Other Papers* (1923), pp. 81–113.

Page 64. *The old fable.* Such a fable is recounted in Plato's
Symposium and referred to in Plutarch's *Morals* ("Of Brotherly
Love").

Page 71. *Sail for Greece, etc.* Emerson certainly alludes to Washington Irving and Nathaniel Parker Willis here, less certainly to

more recent reputations like Charles Fenno Hoffman or John Lloyd Stephens.

Page 74. *The definition of freedom.* The definition is Kant's.

Page 80. *The Peace party.* The American Peace Society, formed in 1828. On March 12, 1838, Emerson addressed them on "Peace" (W XI 151–76).

Nov. 6?, 1837. Cf. "Heroism" (W II 245–64), a lecture of 1838. Emerson was feeling the threat of poverty if he continued in his free way of life.

Page 81. *Laocoön.* The Athenaeum possessed unusually fine casts of this and other statues.

Page 84. *Nov. 7?, 1837.* Emerson had recently been reading Sir Charles Lyell, *Principles of Geology,* Third Edition (1834).

Oct. 23, 1837. Emerson was preparing his course of lectures on "Human Culture," in which he used many of the above passages. Education was then a much-discussed subject in New England. Cf. under Education in the Index.

Page 86. *April 26, 1838.* The letter to Van Buren is in W XI 89–96; for the circumstances surrounding it, see L II 126–27.

Page 87. *E. H.* Probably Elizabeth Hoar.

Page 89. *Alternation.* A frequent theme at this time when Emerson was much taxed by visitors. Cf. June 13: "Solitude is naught and society is naught. Alternate them and the good of each is seen. . . . Undulation, alternation is the condition of progress, of life."

Caroline Sturgis. Later Tappan. She and her sister Ellen (later Hooper), daughters of a Boston merchant, were "gifted and charming" friends of Margaret Fuller and frequent contributors of poems to *The Dial.* Twenty years old at this time, she is certainly one of the "young persons" Emerson had in mind when he wrote "The Transcendentalist."

Page 90. *The mark of American merit.* The journal specifies Allston, Greenough, Bryant, Everett, Channing, Irving.

June 21, 1838. Not only is this one of the many passages in the journals that treat the theme of "Days," but this and the next selection taken together repeat the same emotional progression as the poem, from joy in the offered gifts to guilt at the lost opportunity.

Page 92. *S. G. Ward.* A Boston banker and lifelong friend of Emerson ("the best man in the city"), he was at this time a young man just back from Europe with a portfolio of art and ideas to match. He contributed several things on art to *The Dial.*

Page 93. *Jones Very.* A tutor of Greek at Harvard, at the time of his visit he had just completed a brief stay at the Charlestown insane asylum. Those who knew him best were uncertain whether he or the society that committed him was the insane party, for his "mania" took the form of a literal acceptance of the doctrine of divine leading such as was taught by the Quakers and also, abstractly, by Emerson. He believed that he had died to this world and was now an organ of the Spirit. Emerson wrote of him in 1838, after this visit, the first of several, "I wish the whole world were as mad as he." His poems, some of which Emerson edited and published (1839), have steadily grown in critical esteem. Cf. *Emerson Handbook*, p. 35.

Page 94. *My angel of Heliodorus.* The "terrible rider" who overthrew the prime minister of Seleucus IV when he came to seize the treasure at the Temple in Jerusalem. See II Maccabees 3 (Apocrypha).

1838: Divinity School Address

Page 98. *Dec. 29, 1834.* Mr. Emerson occupied the northwest second-story chamber of the Manse, Dr. Ripley's home. Hawthorne, when he temporarily occupied the house some ten years later, wrote the *Mosses from an Old Manse* there. — E.W.E.

Page 99. *Every spiritual law, etc.* A typical summary of the doctrine of Compensation which recurs frequently in the early journals and which Emerson finally wrote out in "Compensation." See under Compensation in the Index.

Page 100. *Our aged priest.* Dr. Ezra Ripley.

ADDRESS

Pages 100 ff. The full title is, "An Address Delivered Before the Senior Class in Divinity College, Cambridge, Sunday Evening, July 15, 1838." For the reception of the address, see the references in *Emerson Handbook*, p. 58. Not all who heard or read this address disapproved; among Emerson's vigorous defenders were George Ripley, later to found Brook Farm, and Theodore Parker, the foremost liberal preacher in the Boston area. Through him the address can be said to have inspired the "modernist" interpretation of religion in this country. The controversy over the address is reviewed and excerpts from many of the documents printed in Perry Miller, *The Transcendentalists* (1950), pp. 192–246. Cf. *Freedom and Fate* pp. 39–43.

Page 103. *Evil is merely privative, etc.* The rest of this paragraph is from Emerson's lecture "Ethics" (1837), the tenth in his course on "The Philosophy of History," and has the doctrinaire tone of much of that series. Emerson's enthusiasm for his great discovery of "the infinitude of the private man" — the doctrine both lecture course and address were meant to teach — submerges here the common sense recognition of human duality which later became habitual. That is not to say that the view of evil expressed here is indefensible, nor that he ever repudiated it; it is a version of a classic mystical position which has its own logic — see Bertrand Russell, "Mysticism and Logic," in the book of that title. The baldness of Emerson's formulation of it is to be explained, perhaps, by its pragmatic intention. He is challenging conventional belief with a sweeping counter-statement. When he came to review this challenge in "Uriel" he formulated it more subtly — and more paradoxically.

Page 112. *A devout person.* Reputed to be Lidian.

Page 116. *Oct. 8, 1838.* Dr. Ware had just sent Emerson a copy of his recent sermon on *The Personality of the Deity* with a request for comment.

Page 120. *They call it darkness.* A Swedenborgian echo. Cf. pp. 237–38.

Page 121. *"Saadi."* Cf. p. 489. However Emerson heard of Saadi, a Persian poet, he did not read his *Gulistan* until 1843, when he was pleased to discover that his portrait of the Poet in Oriental dress had corresponded in several particulars to the facts.

1839–1840: Society and Solitude

Page 124. *In ordinary years.* Many years were less than "ordinary." *I call her Asia.* The idea of the Orient had always strong emotional connotations for Emerson: it meant mystery, large faith, feminine passivity, and religious contemplation, thus contrasting with the active, masculine West; it stood for the life of the Soul. See F. I. Carpenter, *Emerson and Asia* (1930).

[Amos Bronson Alcott]

Pages 125 ff. Alcott first came to Emerson's attention as the master of the Temple School in Boston (1834–39), an experiment at what is now known as progressive education which demonstrated Alcott's true greatness as a teacher. The accounts he published of his practice, however, gave his school such notoriety that it had to be abandoned. A group of English reformers meanwhile established an Alcott House School at Ham, Surrey, and in 1842, traveling on funds largely supplied by Emerson, he visited them, soon returning with two of them, full of plans for a new social community. This was established in the summer of 1843 at a farm hopefully named "Fruitlands" but broke up that same winter. Rallying from this bitter disappointment, he tried without much success various means of supporting his family, chief among which were the lecture-discussions he called "Conversations." The Alcotts were kept alive, partly by the efforts of Mrs. Alcott, partly by funds collected for them by Emerson, until at last their daughter Louisa won them financial independence with *Little Women* (1868). By his work as superintendent of the Concord schools (1859 on) and as dean of the Concord School of Philosophy (1879 on) he exerted indirectly a profound influence on American education.

Though Alcott kept voluminous journals which contain much of interest, he was a talker, not a writer. He can be judged fairly only by the impression he made on friends, of whom no one knew him better than Emerson. Their friendship is the subject of Hubert H. Hoeltje, *Sheltering Tree* (1943).

Page 125. *May 19, 1837.* The entry of May 19, 1837 (p. 61) on the insularity of men immediately follows in the journals.

Page 127. *The man for a crisis.* "What a fact, too, that when Higginson went to the Court-House [to rescue the fugitive slave Anthony Burns], having made up his mind that he should not return thence, the only man that followed him into it was Alcott." (J VIII 520, 1855)

Page 129. *Our friends.* Part of the reason for Emerson's sharp tone on Alcott as a reformer was his clash of temperaments with Alcott's arrogant English friend, Charles Lane, who had much to do with accelerating Emerson's developing disaffection with reform and reformers in the early 1840's.

July 8, 1843. Emerson had spent July 4 with the philosophers. What with much time spent in conversation, poor soil and situation, taboos on all animal products, food and service and on all products of slave labor, the subsistence problem at Fruitlands was unpromising, even if Lane had not precipitated a crisis by raising the issue of celibacy.

Page 130. *April, 1844.* After the tragic breaking-down of his Fruitlands endeavor for the ideal life, Mr. Alcott was so grieved that he was in despair and refused food, and was restored to normal life and cheer with difficulty. — E.W.E.

The old paper. The lecture "Tragedy" (1839), published in *The Dial*, April, 1844 (W XII 405–17).

Jan., 1853. In the omitted (and unpublished) portion Emerson discusses the case of Margaret Fuller.

Page 131. *Margaret Fuller.* Given a man's education by her father, Margaret Fuller combined the intellectual force of a man with the passionate nature of a woman in an explosive mixture which impressed, charmed, and sometimes appalled her contemporaries. She was a notable collector of people and early sought out Emerson. Though in the determined assault on his affections that followed she was on the whole defeated, in spite of his own wish to surrender, they remained good friends and constant correspondents, particularly during the period (1840–42) of her editorship of *The Dial*. From 1839 to 1844 she held a remarkable series of educational "Conversations" with the most cultivated women in Boston, from which grew her *Woman in the Nineteenth Century* (1845), a pioneer document of American feminism. After two years on the staff of the New York *Tribune* she went to Europe, where she became an ardent supporter of Mazzini and married one of his followers, the Marquis Angelo Ossoli. Both drowned when the ship bringing them back to the

United States in 1850 was wrecked off Fire Island. Emerson collaborated in writing her memoirs.

Page 132. *A chronicle of sweet romance.* Probably that of Samuel Gray Ward and Anna Barker, whom Emerson had just met and much admired (J V 278–80).

Page 133. *Four persons.* Margaret, Anna Barker, Caroline Sturgis, and Ward.

[*Dec., 1839*]. Continuous in the journals.

Page 136. *Sept. 14, 1839.* Emerson had just attended a convention of teachers addressed by Horace Mann, "a handful of pale men and women in a large church."

Gone up the Merrimack. This trip was the occasion for Thoreau's *A Week on the Concord and Merrimack Rivers* (1849).

Page 139. *Mechanical philosophy.* Cf. Carlyle, "Signs of the Times."

Page 141. *My old essay on Love.* Cf. W II 169–88.

Page 142. [*Nov. 21, 1840*]. A certain estrangement between Emerson and his wife has left its mark on the journals of this and the next few years, as will be clearer when the complete journals are published (cf. J VI 72, 209, 222, 232, 243, 274; also below p. 219). Rusk suggests that one cause was her greater religious conservatism (*Life*, pp. 225–26).

Page 143. *Demoniacal.* The passage from Goethe's *Poetry and Truth* (Autobiography) from which this term derives is printed in the essay "Demonology" (W X 17–18), which is based on a lecture of 1839. With this alleged "monstrous force" in some individuals Emerson associated dreams, hypnotism, "spiritism," omens, luck, magic, and the other wild hints of unknown powers which life brings each man at some moments. Acknowledging their mystery, he firmly subordinated them to the greater wonder of nature's laws and "hidden life" in general; see the whole essay. This use of the term fused with the notion of a "daemonic" region between the human and the divine which Emerson picked up from Plato and the Neo-Platonists and played with from time to time, as in his long poem "Initial, Daemonic and Celestial Love."

A new chapter on Nature. Emerson planned such an essay to follow "Art" in *Essays, First Series* but could not complete it to his satisfaction in time. Presumably "Nature" in *Essays, Second Series,* many pages of which can be traced to the journals of 1840 and 1841, is this essay, though Emerson also lectured on "The Method of Nature" in August, 1841 (W I 191–224). On the persistent dream of deciphering a "secret" from Nature, cf. "The Sphinx," p. 420; see also p. 275.

Page 145. *The new Social Plans.* The founders had reason to suppose Emerson might be interested in Brook Farm, for it, like Thoreau's hut at Walden Pond, aimed at the kind of reform he advocated; as he was soon to phrase it in "Man the Reformer," ". . . there is an infinite worthiness in man, which will appear at the call of worth, and all particular reforms are the removing of some impediment." The aims of this Transcendentalist community, in Ripley's words, were "to insure a more natural union between intellectual and manual labor than now exists; . . . to guarantee the highest mental freedom, by providing all with labor adapted to their tastes and talents, and securing to them the fruits of their industry; . . . and thus to prepare a society of liberal, intelligent, and cultivated persons, whose relations with each other would permit a more wholesome and simple life than can be led amidst the pressure of our competitive institutions." The community lasted relatively long as such experiments went (from 1841 to 1847), though in its later years it became a Fourierist Phalanx and lost Emerson's sympathy. Many years later he wrote an account of it which he added to his "Historic Notes of Life and Letters in New England" (W X 359–69).

SELF-RELIANCE

Pages 147 ff. The topic of this essay had been central to Emerson's thought for over fifteen years. Although he was apparently still "filling the gaps" on Oct. 23, 1840 (see p. 146), all but a few pages are extracts from various lectures and journals of 1832–40. (For details, see below.) Any judgment of its structure should take into account the mosaic method by which it was composed. Emerson himself, with his usual self-disparagement, said he had built no ship in these essays, "only boards and logs tied together." One need not conclude that he considered his essays to have no organization, but simply that he found the construction of them drudgery, since the plan for such an essay as this was made after most of the parts were written. Certainly, if this essay did not attain the organic unity Emerson dreamed of, that has never been any bar to its popularity or force. One reason clearly is that much of the stirring exhortation here was originally directed at himself — certainly the sincerest form of preaching. Its chief fault, as with other essays in the 1841 series, is the unrelieved *forte* that resulted from such a collection of climaxes.

The accompanying table of the original sources of this essay, while neither complete nor definitive, will give some idea of its composition. It is divided into four columns: the page in this book, the first words of each paragraph, the lecture source(s) and date, the journal source(s) and date. Bracketed items are sources for less than half of the paragraph and are followed by a number indicating the approximate number of sentences involved. When they are the same sentences for lecture and journal, the number after the journal item is italicized. Non-bracketed items are sources for most of the paragraph; those italicized are the source of the whole. The rubrics for very short paragraphs are also bracketed.

Table of Sources, "Self-Reliance"

PAGE	PARAGRAPH	LECTURE	JOURNAL
147	I read	["Genius" (1839)] (1)	[J III 550 (1835)] (1)
	There is	["Protest" (1839)] (1)	[J III 14 (1833)] (2)
148	Trust thyself	"Tendencies" (1840)	J IV 471 (1838)
	What pretty	["Education" (1840)] (4)	[J V 54 (1838)] (4)
149	The nonchalance		J V 38 (1838)
	These are		
	Whoso would	["Ethics" (1837)] (2)	[J III 488 (1835)] (3)
			[J IV 419 (1838)] (5)
			[J V 233 (1839)] (9)
150	Virtues are		J V 471 (1840)
151	[What I]	"Ethics" (1837)	[J III 401 (1834)] (1)
	The objection	"Tendencies" (1840)	[J V 234 (1839)] (4)
			[J V 177 (1839)] (9)
			[J IV 290 (1837)] (2)
152	For nonconformity	"Tendencies" (1840)	[J V 41 (1838)] (5)
	[The other]	"Tendencies" (1840)	
	But why		[J IV 484 (1838)] (3)
153	A foolish	"Tendencies" (1840)	
	I suppose	["Present Age" (1837)] (2)	[J IV 76 (1836)] (1)
	There will	"Tendencies" (1840)	[J V 179 (1839)] (4)
			[J II 485 (1832)] (5)
154	I hope	"Politics" (1840)	
155	Let a man	"Human Culture I" (1837)	J IV 329 (1837)
	Our reading		
	The world		
156	The magnetism	["The School" (1838)] (7)	[J V 240 (1839)] (5)
157	The relations	"Duty" (1839)	J V 135 (1838)
	Man is timid	"Religion" (1840)	[J V 230 (1839)] (2)
			[J V 235 (1839)] (5)
	This should	"Duty" (1839)	J V 136 (1838)
158	And now	"Duty" (1839)	[J V 137 (1838)] (5)
			[J IV 416 (1838)] (7)
159	Life only		[J V 477 (1840)] (4)
	This is the		
	[Thus all]		
	But now		[J V 172 (1839)] (2)
			[J V 173 (1839)] (6)
			[J V 188 (1839)] (3)
160	If we cannot		[J V 223 (1839)] (5)
	The populace		[J V 217 (1839)] (6)
161	And truly		J III 285 (1834)
	If any man	["Religion" (1840)] (5)	
	If our young	"Religion" (1840)	J V 207 (1839)
162	[It is easy]		
	1. In what		[J V 220 (1839)] (2)
	Another sort		

Table of Sources, "Self-Reliance" (cont.)

PAGE	PARAGRAPH	LECTURE	JOURNAL
163	As men's	"Duty" (1839)	J IV 487 (1838)
	2. It is for		[J V 95 (1838)] (2)
164	I have no		
	Travelling		J V 210 (1839)
	3. But the		
165	Insist on	["Ethics" (1837)] (2)	[J III 346 (1834)] (2)
	[4. As our]		
	Society never	"Individualism" (1837)	
	The civilized	"Individualism" (1837)	[J III 490 (1835)] (1)
166	There is no	["Individualism" (1837)]	
		(11)	[J III 410 (1834)] (1)
			[J IV 76 (1836)] (4)
	[Society is]	"Individualism" (1837)	J III 291 (1834)
167	And so the		[J V 466 (1840)] (6)
			[J IV 277 (1837)] (1)
	So use all	["Duty" (1839)] (4)	[J V 130 (1838)] (4)

NOTE: Samples of these revisions are included in the notes below.

Page 147. *Ne te quaesiveris extra.* From Persius (*Satire* I.7), whom Emerson studied in college. The context has to do with literary judgments, and the clause has been interpreted in two ways, as meaning either "do not look for yourself outside of yourself" (i.e., "be your own norm") or "do not ask any opinion but your own." In J IV 110 Emerson uses it to mean "do not imitate." All three mottoes date from 1841.

Page 148. *Trust thyself, etc.* The 1840 version of this paragraph (see Table) began with the second sentence and read as follows:

Consent to accept the place the Divine Providence has found for you; the society of your contemporaries; the connexion of events. Live in the new age and be the passive organ of its idea. Great men have always done so and confided themselves to the genius of their age. This is an obscure perception of the great philosophy that the Eternal is stirring at my heart working through my hands and predominates and will predominate in all my being. And we are now men and must accept in the highest mind the same transcendent destiny and not pinched in a corner not cowards fleeing before revolution but pious aspirants to be noble clay plastic in the Almighty effort, we must advance and advance into Chaos and the Dark.

The original journal entry of 1838 begins quite differently, with Napoleon:

If a man is self-exaggerating and does not embrace a great man with his heart and soul, expect no miracles of him. He is a seemer, and the truth is not in him.

Great men again do not brag of their personal attributes, but, like Napoleon, generously belong to the connexion of events. He identified himself with the new age, and owned himself the passive organ of an idea. Great men have always done so, etc. (J IV 471)

Page 149. *A valued adviser.* Probably Mary Moody Emerson.

Page 155. *That popular fable.* Emerson is thinking of the "Induction" to Shakespeare's *The Taming of the Shrew.* The tale was an old one; originating in India, it was included in the Persian *Thousand and One Nights* and was told and dramatized many times in European literature before and after Shakespeare.

Page 158. *And now at last, etc.* This paragraph is a composite of two journal entries. The first is the conclusion of a long entry contrasting intuition with tradition that extends over two days in the journal (Nov. 13–14, 1838) and includes the paragraph immediately preceding this one in the essay (see J V 135–37). From that point on it reads, in obvious allusion to the recent Divinity School *Address* experience:

This palsy of tradition goes so far that when a soul in which the intellectual activity is a balance for the Veneration (whose excess seems to generate this love of the old Word) renounces the superstition out of love for the primary teaching in his heart, the doctors of the church are not glad as they ought to be that a new and original confirmation comes to the truth, but they curse and swear because he scorns their idolatry of the nouns and verbs the vellum and ink in which the same teaching was anciently conveyed. And now at last the highest truth on this subject remains unsaid, probably cannot be said; for, all that we say is the far-off description merely, of the awful truth which in moments of life flashes on us, and bids us go months and years feeding on the remembrance of that light and essaying to tell what we saw. That thought, by what I can nearest approach to say it, is this. When good is near you, when you have life in yourself it is not by any known or appointed way; you shall not discern the footprints of any other; you shall not see the face of man; you shall not hear any name; the way, the thought, the good, shall be wholly strange and new. It shall exclude all other being. There shall be no fear in it. To climb that most holy mountain, you must tread on Fear. You take the way *from* man not *to* man, quit the shore and go out to sea. . . .

The second entry is one of March 24 of the same year:

In the highest moments, we are a vision. There is nothing that can be called gratitude nor properly joy. The soul is raised over passion. It seeth nothing so much as Identity. It is a Perceiving that Truth and Right ARE. Hence it becomes a perfect Peace out of the knowing that all things will go well. Vast spaces of nature the Atlantic Ocean, the South Sea; vast intervals of time years, centuries, are annihilated to it; this which I think and feel underlay that former state of life and circumstances, as it does underlie my present, and will always all circumstance, and what is called life and what is called death.

In the lecture of 1839 he combined the two with a bridge passage as follows: ". . . wholly strange and new. It shall exclude all other being. You take the way from man, not to man. All persons that ever existed are but its perishable ministers. There shall be no fear in it. Fear and hope are alike beneath it. It asks nothing. There is somewhat low even in hope. We are then a vision. . . ." The result became in turn the basis for the present passage.

Page 161. *A sturdy lad, etc.* A passage originally inspired by Thoreau (see J V 207–208).

Page 163. *"To the persevering,"* etc. One of the so-called "Chaldaean oracles" attributed to Zoroaster. Emerson printed a number of them including this one in *The Dial*, April, 1844.

Those foolish Israelites. Adapted from Exodus 20:19.

Page 164. *Traveling is a fool's paradise, etc.* Emerson here revives the tone of the journals he kept during his own year of travel in Europe (cf. J III 62–63, 75–76, and W IX 395–97).

CIRCLES

Pages 168 ff. Nearly all this essay was written in 1840. If one can distinguish between the secure Emerson, safe in the arms of the Over-Soul, and the adventurous Emerson, launched on the seas of life in the bark of self, then this brief and undervalued essay speaks for the second without the first. Its closest analogues in his writings are "Uriel" and an unpublished lecture of 1839 called "The Protest" (see *Freedom and Fate*, pp. 100–103, 126–27). This is the side of Emerson that strongly influenced Nietzsche (see *Emerson Handbook*, pp. 246–49).

Page 168. *Nature centers into balls, etc.* Most of the mottoes in this volume of essays were added to the second edition of 1847. Early drafts of this motto are printed in J VII 212–13 (1846). The "proud ephemerals" are of course man.

St. Augustine described, etc. Apparently in fact the origin of this statement is not known.

One moral we have already deduced. I.e., in "Compensation," in the same volume.

Another dawn, etc. Cf. Milton, *Paradise Lost*, V, 310: "Another morn has risen on mid-noon."

Under every deep, etc. Cf. p. 494.

Page 176. *"Forgive his crimes,"* etc. From Edward Young, *Night Thoughts* (1744).

An endless seeker. The sect of Seekers in the seventeenth century were waiting and seeking for new light from God that would establish the true church. In his early letters Emerson several times spoke of himself as a Seeker.

1841–1843: Lords of Life

Page 180. *Samuel Hoar.* Emerson's neighbor, a lawyer, whose upright character he admired highly.

Page 182. *Mizar and Alcor.* Names of stars. According to Nichol (p. 58), Mizar revolves once around Alcor every 190,000 years.

Page 183. *Berkleian philosophy.* See under Idealism in the Index.

Page 184. *July, 1841.* Emerson's health was poor in the spring of 1841, and in the summer he spent some weeks at the seashore. The lassitude of the time is noticeable in what he wrote.

Page 186. *Sept. 21, 1841.* Cf. pp. 2–4 and notes.

Page 187. *Gothamites.* Ironical: the three wise men of Gotham were famous fools.

Page 189. *Love.* As usual, Emerson means ἀγάπη (charity), not ἔρος (passion); in another mood he might as appropriately have said "moral sentiment." Cf. the conclusion of "Politics" (pp. 251–52).

Page 190. *Champing unleavened bread.* An allusion to dietary reforms like those of Sylvester Graham.

Nourishment of a beard. An allusion to Joseph Palmer, who was later associated with "Fruitlands."

Page 192. *Nov. 12?, 1841.* M. is probably Margaret Fuller.

The Transcendentalist

Pages 192 ff. The full title in the Centenary Edition is: "The Transcendentalist: A Lecture Read at the Masonic Temple, Boston, January, 1842." Actually the date of first delivery was Dec. 23, 1841. It was the fourth in a series of eight lectures on "The Times," a series not planned until nearly November, when Emerson's finances forced him to offer it. Emerson wrote his aunt in June of 1842: "Please observe that in the Transcendental Lecture, I only write biographically, — describing a class of young persons whom I have seen — I hope it is not confession and that, past all hope, I am confounded with my compassionated heroes and heroines." Similarly he wrote his wife in March that the men in New York "fasten me in their thought to 'Transcendentalism,' whereof you know I am wholly guiltless." Though the statement is probably true of what Horace Greeley — or Aunt Mary — considered to be Transcendentalism, one can fairly say that Emerson was well fitted by his own history to interpret this class of young persons. The opening pages of the lecture define, with a dramatic heightening which his disengagement now permits, the essential faith of the author of the concluding chapters of *Nature*. When in the later part of the lecture he turns to the "young persons whom I have seen" his close sympathy is still apparent. Of such youth he had written two years earlier: "The heart of Youth is the regenerator of society; the perpetual hope; the incessant effort of recovery. . . . The world has no interest so deep as to cherish that resistance." The lecture is both "only biographical" and thoroughly personal.

A good modern account of New England Transcendentalism remains to be written. The best available are O. B. Frothingham, *Transcendentalism in New England* (1876); Gray's *Emerson*; H. C. Goddard, *Studies in New England Transcendentalism* (1908); and Perry Miller's anthology, *The Transcendentalists* (1950). Two primary sources are perhaps more use than any of these: Emerson's "Historic Notes of Life and Letters in New England" (W X 323–70); and "Theodore Parker's Experience as a Minister," by Theodore Parker, in John Weiss, *Life and Correspondence of Theodore Parker* (1863).

Page 192. *Idealism.* Cf. the chapter "Idealism" in *Nature* (pp. 42–48) and see under Idealism in the Index. The term denoted first to Emerson the "Ideal Theory" associated with Berkeley and Hume — that is, that all we can know are impressions "in the mind" and not things themselves; second, the assertion of Germans like Fichte and Schelling that the Mind is metaphysically primary, that the external world can be derived dialectically from Self; third, the Platonic assertion that intellectual concepts are more real than changing physical things; and lastly, the pantheistic feeling, associated with the Hindus, that Spirit is the "one and all." That these various strains of Idealism are not consistent with each other is not important to Emerson's purpose, which was never "philosophical" in any but the widest poetic sense. Here he is sketching the working strategy of the transcendentalist in his attack on the self-assurance of the materialist. For a logical exposition of Transcendentalism that demonstrates the superiority of Emerson's dramatic method, see Theodore Parker, "Transcendentalism" (1876), reprinted in G. F. Whicher, ed., *The Transcendentalist Revolt Against Materialism*, Problems in American Civilization (1949).

Page 196. *Jacobi.* Friedrich Heinrich Jacobi (1743–1819), German philosopher. This passage from his "Letter to Fichte" (March, 1799) had been partly quoted by Coleridge in *The Friend*.

Page 197. *It is well known, etc.* Students of Kant will recognize that Kant's precision is not imitated in this summary, which confounds the *transcendental*, or knowledge of "the mode of our knowledge of objects," with the *transcendent*, or "knowledge" that claims to transcend experience. One should add, however, that Emerson's statement compares favorably in this respect with some of his sources; see Carlyle's essay on "Novalis," for example. Though the term

Transcendental was given vogue by Kant, it reached New England very indirectly.

Page 198. *These talkers.* In this passage it is Mr. Alcott that his friend alludes to. — E.W.E.

Page 203. *But to come a little closer, etc.* The next two paragraphs are based on passages (J V 570, VI 77) written before Emerson had conceived of this lecture; the "private experience" they record is certainly his own. The second paragraph in particular is much more personal in the journal version.

Page 204. *Truth, Goodness, and Beauty.* Cf. "The Poet," p. 224.

Page 205. *They complain, etc.* This paragraph was probably written with this address in mind (see J VI 122); the shift in tone is noticeable.

Page 206. *Superior chronometers.* This passage recalls part of the conclusion of the second chapter of *Walden*, as does a passage in the contemporary "Lecture on the Times" (W I 289). Thoreau at this time was living in the Emerson house.

Page 207. *Ellen H[ooper].* The identification is conjectural.
Mary Russell. A friend who had an infant school.

Page 208. *April, 1842.* Cf. Aug. ?, 1851 (p. 325).
Tyburn. Eighteenth-century London gallows.

Page 209. *Charles King Newcomb.* Twenty-two years old, a native of Providence, he was at this time living at Brook Farm. He wrote voluminous unpublished journals (recently edited by J. K. Johnson, *The Journals of Charles King Newcomb*, Brown University, 1946) but published almost nothing. The secret of his brilliance died with his friends.

Page 210. *[March, 1842].* Originally part of an article "Fourier and the Socialists" in *The Dial*, July, 1842, from which the title has been borrowed for this selection. It will do to represent Emerson's now habitual tone on all such schemes.

Page 212. *April 1?, 1842.* On Emerson's considerable interest in dreams and the "night-side" of nature, see p. 480 and Vivian C. Hopkins, *Spires of Form* (1951), pp. 178–83.

Page 213. *Iamblichus.* A fourth-century Neo-Platonist and Neo-Pythagorean. Emerson had been reading his *Life of Pythagoras*, Thomas Taylor, tr. (1818).

Page 215. *The Shaker Village*, Cf. p. 475.
[Nov., 1842]. The journal version (J VI 316) illustrates Emerson's habit of toning down the journals for publication: "The Union is only perfect when all the Uniters are absolutely isolated. Each man being the Universe, if he attempt to join himself to others, he instantly is jostled, crowded, cramped, halved, quartered, or on all sides diminished of his proportion, and, the stricter the union, the less and more pitiful he is," etc. Cf. also J VI 297–98.

Page 217. *Universal of faith.* By 1846 this had become: "As the whole has its law, so each individual has his genius. Obedience to its genius (to speak a little scholastically) is the particular of faith; perception that the tendency of the whole is to the benefit of the individual is the universal of faith." (W XII 87, J VII 186).

Page 218. *Greenough.* See Matthiessen, and C. R. Metzger, *Emerson and Greenough* (1954). Horatio Greenough was an advocate of functionalism in art whose theories attracted and influenced Emerson. They first met in Rome in 1833. His colossal statue of Washington draped in a toga, the product of an earlier period of neoclassicism, proved too heavy for the floor supports of the Rotunda and was finally set to weather outside the Capitol.

Page 219. *Harriet Martineau.* English writer and "philosophic radical." On her visit to the U. S. in 1834 she had met and admired Waldo and Charles Emerson.

June 14, 1842. Cf. p. 480.

Page 221. *Sept., 1843.* Emerson's lecture "The Young American" (1844), as printed in *The Dial*, April, 1844, included a long discussion of the coming of the railroads to New England which used this passage (W I 451–55). Cf. G. F. Cronkhite, "The Transcendental Railroad," *New England Quarterly* XXIV (1951) 306–28.

THE POET

Pages 222 ff. One of the lectures in the series on "The Times" (1841–42) was on "The Poet." Not content with this statement, Emerson immediately began writing a second and almost entirely different piece on the same subject which became the present essay. This was growing steadily in June, 1842; in February, 1844, he spoke of it as completed. Probably the bulk of it was written in 1842, though the last three paragraphs are later. At the same time he was writing much on the same subject in verse: "Saadi" was published in *The Dial* for October, 1842, and a good deal of the never-completed poem "The Poet" was set down around this time (W IX 309–20).

In spite of much literature on the subject, an adequate account of Emerson's theory and practice of poetry remains to be published. A review of the situation is in *Emerson Handbook*, pp. 90–102. In recent years an interesting attempt has been made to treat Emerson as a precursor of modern philosophies of symbolism. These discussions stress the impressive extent to which he saw artistic creation and indeed thought in general to be part of an organic process of interaction between a creature and his environment; "The Poet" certainly supports Cassirer's definition of man as the symbol-making animal. The attempt is analogous to the earlier one of Lindeman and Carpenter to treat Emerson as a precursor of the pragmatism of William James. The modernity of Emerson's psychology, literary and otherwise, still needs a full and clear statement. Stimulating but difficult — in the first case intentionally unsound — are Charles Feidelson, Jr., *Symbolism and American Literature* (1953) and Sherman Paul, *Emerson's*

Angle of Vision (1952). The question of Emerson's pragmatism is reviewed in *Emerson Handbook*, pp. 164–203.

Page 222. *A moody child, etc.* An earlier version of these lines formed part of the poem "The Poet" (W IX 311). On the "musical order" of nature, cf. "Merlin" (p. 449). The second motto is a quotation from "Ode to Beauty," recently published in *The Dial*.

Page 228. *Proclus.* Emerson acquired *The Six Books of Proclus*, Thomas Taylor, tr. (1816) in the summer of 1841. Proclus was a Neo-Platonist, a pupil of Plotinus.

The great ball. The Whigs rolled such balls in the campaign of 1840 to symbolize the gathering majority. The rest of this paragraph is from the first lecture on "The Poet" (1841).

Page 231. *A certain poet.* A Platonic *alter ego.*

Page 235. *A heavenly tree. Timaeus* 90:

> We declare that God has given to each of us, as his daemon, that kind of soul which is housed in the top of our body and which raises us — seeing that we are not an earthly but a heavenly plant — up from earth towards our kindred in the heaven. And herein we speak most truly; for it is by suspending our head and root from that region whence the substance of our soul first came that the Divine Power keeps upright our whole body.

Page 237. *Jacob Behmen,* or Boehme. Seventeenth-century German mystic whose influence reached Emerson from many indirect sources. He anticipated such central ideas of Emerson's as the distinction of Reason and Understanding and the doctrine of Correspondence (see Index). He was the source of a number of "lustres," such as this one.

POLITICS

Pages 241 ff. This essay had a long evolution. Edward Emerson points out that it was based on a lecture "Politics" of 1840; he does not add that the lecture was revised, probably in 1843, nor that much of it was in turn copied from a lecture "Politics" of 1837. The portions of "the lecture" that he prints in his notes to the essay (W III 336–42) all come verbatim from the earlier lecture. The essay is therefore a distillation of nearly a decade of thought on the subject.

One can distinguish four layers: (1) The 1837 layer, devoted chiefly to demonstrating the principle eventually summarized in the essay "History" (W II 3, J IV 118–19): "There is one mind common to all individual men" which is "the only and sovereign agent"; politics, therefore, like history, is controlled by eternal (moral) laws which man can know. The chief remnant of this lecture in the essay is the discussion of persons and property in the early pages. (2) The 1840 layer, stressing the "all-sufficiency of private Character" to remake society. From it comes the opening paragraph of the essay and also the one containing the sentence, "The wise man is the State" (p. 249; cf. J V 360–61) — perhaps the following paragraph also. (3) The later revisions, some borrowed from other lectures, which qualified the confidence of 1840: the "private man's heart" may not influence society but it remains "the consolation of life." (4) The final essay, for which Emerson thoroughly rewrote nearly all the last half of the lecture. The result combines the trust of 1837, the hope of 1840, and the later reservations in a whole delicately balanced between "Experience" and "Idea," criticizing what is and must be in the light of the Promethean promise of human nature that must be also.

Emerson's opinions on public affairs have been the subject of many studies; see *Emerson Handbook*, pp. 186–94. As the essay makes clear, he thought of his transcendental anarchism as beyond all actual parties; in practice he was usually a Whig. "From youthful conservative, to [transcendental] radical, to abolitionist, and back to conservative" — thus Carpenter summarizes his practical political views.

1844–1845: Skepticism

EXPERIENCE

Pages 254 ff. There is no record of this essay's having been given as a lecture, nor does any of it, barring two or three sentences, derive from a lecture. About a quarter of the whole can be traced to the journals, most of it dating from 1842. The experience Emerson is reporting is recent. Two demonstrations of the coherence of this exceptionally well-built essay may be found in W. T. Harris, "Ralph Waldo Emerson," *The Atlantic Monthly* L (1882) 248, and F. I. Carpenter, *R. W. Emerson* (1934), pp. 446–47. A helpful comment on Emerson's way of looking at experience is E. C. Lindeman, "Emerson's Pragmatic Mood," *American Scholar* XVI (1946) 57–64. An extended discussion of this essay is in *Freedom and Fate*, pp. 109–22. See also *Emerson Handbook*, pp. 178–86.

Page 255. *Those that Hermes won, etc.* See Plutarch's *Morals*, "Of Isis and Osiris."

Page 256. *Ate Dea.* Cf. *Iliad* XIX.91.

In the death of my son, etc. See pp. 207–10 and "Threnody," p. 428. Emerson does not mean he has forgotten Waldo; the letter to Caroline Sturgis one week after the event (p. 208) makes the same complaint in the same language. The grief that he cannot grieve is for Emerson a form grief takes, and not the least painful; as he says, he feels cursed.

The Indian, etc. In Robert Southey, *The Curse of Kehama* (1810).

Page 258. *We see young men, etc.* In J VI 371 the reference is to Thoreau. When he spoke of those that "die young," Carpenter suggests, Emerson may have been thinking of Edward and Charles.

That which is its own evidence. Cf. Coleridge: "Reason and religion are their own evidence," "The idea [of God] is its own evidence" (*The Statesman's Manual*).

Page 261. *"There is now no longer,"* etc. Quoted from the *Desatir,* an alleged collection of the writings of the ancient Persian prophets, including Zoroaster. Cf. Carpenter, *Emerson and Asia,* p. 227.

Page 263. *The new molecular philosophy.* Apparently Dalton's Atomic Theory (cf. J VI 207).

Page 267. *The Chinese Mencius.* In June, 1843, Mencius was "wholly new to me, and in its quiet sunshine a dangerous foil to Carlyle's storm lights" (L III 179).

Page 272. *Come out of that.* An echo of a favorite text among Separatist sects, like the Cape Cod "Come-Outers": "Wherefore come out from among them, and be ye separate, saith the Lord" (II Corinthians 6:17).

Page 273. *Law of Adrastia.* Plato, *Phaedrus* 248C.

Page 274. *Your stricture, etc.* Carlyle had written: "I have to object still (what you will call objecting against a Law of Nature) that we find you a Speaker indeed, but as it were a *Soliloquizer* on the eternal mountain-tops only, in vast solitudes where men and their affairs lie all hushed in a very dim remoteness; and only *the man* and the stars and the earth are visible. . . . — By the bye, I ought to say, the sentences are very *brief*; and did not, in my *sheet* reading, always entirely cohere for me. . . . the paragraphs not as a beaten *ingot*, but as a beautiful square *bag of duck-shot* held together by canvas!" (C–E Correspondence II 81–82).

Page 276. *Cyclopean.* The Cyclopes were the legendary builders of certain huge ancient fortifications.

Page 277. *[July, 1844].* The tenth anniversary of the emancipation by Act of Parliament of all slaves in the insular possessions of Great Britain in the West Indies was celebrated in Concord, in the year 1844, by citizens of thirteen Massachusetts towns, and they invited Mr. Emerson to make the Address. — E.W.E. Emerson spoke at other such occasions in the next few years. In the present address Emerson reviewed the history of the emancipation as a sign of the coming victory of the "sentiment of Right" over slavery, though he interpolated a wrathful passage on the failure of Massachusetts to do her part — cf. the condemnation of "New Hampshire" in the "Ode to Channing" (p. 439).

Page 278. *March, 1845* ("A *despair*"). The second paragraph was added later.

Page 279. *[April?, 1845].* The amount of material on Napoleon in the journals is striking testimony to the fascination for Emerson of his polar opposite, the man of action. See the essay in *Representative Men,* and also Perry Miller, "Emersonian Genius and the American Democracy," *New England Quarterly* XXVI (1953) 27–44.

Page 280. *Native American Party.* Later also called "Know Nothings." They held their first national convention in 1845.

Page 282. *Oct 27?, 1845.* Emerson was reading the *Vishnu Purana*, a late Hindu scripture; the same reading produced "Hamatreya" (p. 437) and the passage in "Plato" (W IV 49–51) on the Eastern love of "the Same." A complete copy of the *Bhagavad Gita* had also recently come to hand for the first time. From now on he read extensively in Oriental literature.

Montaigne; or, The Skeptic

Pages 284 ff. This lecture was planned and written in the latter half of 1845, in time for a first reading at Boston on Jan. 1, 1846, as part of that winter's new course on "Representative Men." As Emerson says in the essay, Montaigne in Cotton's translation was an early favorite of his, though not so early as the essay suggests. He valued him from the first for his robust frankness, and also for his vigorous moral sense, — "the wild Gentile stock, I mean, for he has no Grace" (J IV 539, 1835). He was a type of manly force, like Luther, Carlyle, Napoleon, or any Englishman, of the sort in which Emerson always delighted. The stress on his skepticism is a special note of 1845, close in mood to that which controls "Experience." It is hardly necessary to point out that the doubts of "the Skeptic" are more Emerson's than Montaigne's. The Skeptic is a counter-portrait to the Scholar. At the close, of course, Emerson makes his own rejection of skepticism very definite; Grace was indispensable, after all. The last three paragraphs are perhaps his best statement of his peculiar "tragedy of incapacity" and the larger trust with which he learned to meet it — see my "Emerson's Tragic Sense," *American Scholar* XXII (1953) 285–92. The fullest treatment of the subject of this essay is C. L. Young, *Emerson's Montaigne* (1941).

Page 284. *Every fact is related, etc.* This paragraph derives from a passage in the journal for the end of September, 1841 (J VI 60–61). There follows closely in the journal the passage in "The Poet" about the genius that sat near him (225–26); then one about the power of "Idea" to transform the usual solid reality of "Experience." The mood of all three is that of the opening pages of "The Transcendentalist," on which the opening pages of this essay are a commentary.

Page 286. *Cabanis.* P. J. G. Cabanis (1757–1808), French physician and materialist, author of *Relations of the Physical and Moral Nature of Man* (1802), which argues that thought is a secretion of the nervous system.

Page 292. *Old Poz.* Miss Maria Edgeworth's stories for children are so little read in this generation that it may be well to say that Old Poz was a character who bore this nickname because he was positive of his knowledge on all topics. — E.W.E.

Page 293. *Cut these words, etc.* From a journal passage of 1840 (J V 419–20).

Page 296. *San Carlo.* ("St. Charles.") Charles K. Newcomb (p. 488).

Page 301. *"If my bark sink,"* etc. From W. E. Channing, "A Poet's Hope," the last stanza:

> I am not earth-born, though I here delay;
> Hope's child, I summon infiniter powers,
> And laugh to see the mild and sunny day
> Smile on the shrunk and thin autumnal hours.
> I laugh, for Hope hath happy place with me:
> If my bark sinks, 'tis to another sea.

1846–1852: Fate

Page 304. *Nov. 1?, 1845.* On Shakespeare, see R. P. Falk, "Emerson and Shakespeare," *PMLA* LVI (1941) 523–43.

Page 307. *June?, 1846.* These four passages (and another in the MS. journals) are so spaced that it is not clear how many entries they are meant to be. Emerson addressed an Abolitionist gathering on July 4, using some of this material.

Page 308. *Alcott thought,* etc. Alcott had refused to pay his tax four years earlier and now defended Thoreau's gesture against Emerson's charge (Alcott's version) that it was "skulking and mean and in bad taste." Emerson recorded a much more approving comment, however, on the page before this entry (J VII 219).

Page 309. *[July 31, 1846].* The passage is consecutive in the MS.

Page 313. *[March?, 1848].* All after the first sentence is a complete rewriting and expansion of the source in the journals.

Page 315. *Socialism.* Cf. pp. 210–12, 215–16, and 498–99.

Page 318. *July, 1849.* Emerson was reading J. A. Carlyle's translation of the *Inferno.*

Summer, 1867. Emerson was reading T. W. Parsons' translation of the *Inferno.* Cf. *Emerson Handbook,* pp. 218–19.

Page 319. *Sept.?, 1849* *("it seems").* Emerson was reading the first volume of the new Bohn's Library translation. He wrote out his impressions in "Plato: New Readings" for *Representative Men* (1850).

Autumn, 1849. The first two sentences were used in "Montaigne" (p. 299). The passage concludes a MS. journal. It may be compared with the prophecies of the "Orphic poet" in *Nature* (pp. 53–56).

Page 321. *Phalansteries.* The units into which Fourier organized society.

Tartuffe. Moliere's famous hypocrite.

Page 324. *[May?, 1851].* This paragraph was made the conclusion of the essay and the volume (*The Conduct of Life*). For the theme of "Illusions," see under Illusion in the Index.

Page 325. *[Aug.?, 1851].* *Autobiography.* Cf. April, 1842, p. 208. In "Worship" these words are ascribed to a pseudonomous "Benedict" who is, says Edward Emerson, Charles K. Newcomb. In the journal, however, from which the title "Autobiography" is here borrowed, they seem clearly Emerson's own, and Benedict (cf. J VI 166) one of his *alter egos*.

FATE

Pages 330 ff. A course of lectures on "The Conduct of Life" was first given at Pittsburgh in March, 1851, but "Fate" was not one of them. We first hear of this lecture when Emerson gave the course in Boston at the end of the year, "Fate" being read on December 22. A year later he was still tinkering with it (L IV 330); on April 19, 1853, however, he wrote to Carlyle that "I did within a year or eighteen months write a chapter on Fate." We can assume that to all practical purposes the essay was finished in 1852. It reflects the cumulative influence on his mind of his reading in Oriental, particularly Hindu, thought. The unreality of all particulars, total abandonment to an "immense fate," the insignificance of the individual life, and at the same time a continuing belief in the deep identity of the soul with God and a mythology (reincarnation) in which to express it on an adequate scale — these emphases in his later thought all grew up under the influence of "Asia." As the essay also shows, his earlier faith in individual freedom and power has not disappeared but has changed context; Freedom is enclosed between Fate and Necessity. Emerson's Orientalism is treated in F. I. Carpenter, *Emerson and Asia* (1930) and A. E. Christy, *The Orient in American Transcendentalism* (1934); see also *Emerson Handbook*, pp. 210–12. Paul Sakmann has pointed out that the conclusion of the essay resembles the conclusion of Spinoza's *Ethic*.

Page 330. *Delicate omens traced, etc.* A presumably earlier version of this motto has been printed among the "Fragments on the Poet and the Poetic Gift" in *Poems* (W IX 326). The last four lines of the motto were used by Emerson also in his poem "Fate" (W IX 197):

> Deep in the man sits fast his fate
> To mould his fortunes, mean or great:
> Unknown to Cromwell as to me
> Was Cromwell's measure or degree;
> Unknown to him as to his horse,
> If he than his groom be better or worse.
> He works, plots, fights, in rude affairs,
> With squires, lords, kings, his craft compares,
> Till late he learned, through doubt and fear,
> Broad England harbored not his peer:
> Obeying time, the last to own
> The Genius from its cloudy throne.
> For the prevision, etc.

In spite of identical title and conclusion, the two poems are on different aspects of the subject: the motto, the poet's insight; the poem, the hero's power.

By an odd coincidence, etc. In 1850 Emerson himself lectured on this topic, while Alcott gave a "conversation" on it.

Page 333. *Spurzheim, Quetelet.* Johann Gaspar Spurzheim (1776–1832), a phrenologist. Emerson probably heard him in 1832. L. A. J. Quetelet (1796–1874), a Belgian statistician, who wrote on the application of the theory of probability to the moral and political sciences and on the laws of moral statistics.

Page 336. *Oken.* Lorenz Oken (1779–1851), a "transcendental" or *a priori* naturalist of the school of Schelling. The allusion is to his *Die Zeugung* (Generation) (1805).

Page 337. *Knox.* Dr. Robert Knox, of Burke and Hare fame, *The Races of Man*, a fragment (1850). He argued that races, like animal species, were biologically distinct.

To the crab. I.e., the crab apple.

The new science of Statistics. In "Swedenborg" (W IV 109) Emerson speaks of "the terrible tabulation of the French statists" (statisticians). His reason appears in the following, quoted from Quetelet: "The greater the number of individuals, the more does the influence of the individual will disappear" (W VI 342).

Page 340. *"Look not on Nature," etc.* This is one of the "Chaldaean oracles" ascribed to Zoroaster. — E.W.E. It does not appear, however, among the selections Emerson published in *The Dial*, April, 1844.

Page 343. *" 'Tis written," etc.* On this and on the verses on pp. 331 and 348, cf. "Persian Poetry" (W VIII 237–65) and the notes to "Bacchus" (p. 506).

Page 344. *Malignant energy rules.* Mr. Emerson used to tell the story of two bishops who at the worst of the hurricane asked the captain if there was any hope. At his answer, "None but in God," they turned pale, and one said to the other, "And has it come to that!" — E.W.E.

Trim your bark, etc. Cf. the quatrain "Northman": —

> The gale that wrecked you on the sand,
> It helped my rowers to row;
> The storm is my best galley-hand
> And drives me where I go.

Page 348. *"Quisque suos," etc. Manes:* genius, or attendant spirit. The line is spoken by Anchises in Hades, *Aeneid* VI.743. Its precise meaning is uncertain.

Page 350. *Möller.* Identity uncertain; cf. Metzger (see p. 489). The functional ideal of architecture here expressed was the one Emerson welcomed from Greenough.

1853–1860: Crisis

Page 355. [*Spring?*, *1851*]. All but the first and the last two sentences, as well as one sentence from the passage on the Fugitive Slave Law above, were used in "The Fugitive Slave Law" (1851), an address first given in Concord on May 3 and repeated several times the next year as a campaign speech for the Free-Soil candidate for Congress. Emerson spoke again on the Law and Webster in 1854.

Page 356. *Philip Randolph*. A young friend and correspondent of Emerson's in Philadelphia.

Page 358. *Oct.*, *1859* ("*Courage*"). John Brown had visited Concord before his raid to collect money in support of the free state cause in Kansas. Emerson and Thoreau, who of course had no advance knowledge of his plans, were impressed with him and helped him. After his raid and particularly after his speech at his trial, both men spoke out repeatedly in his support.

Oct., *1859* ("*Ideas make*"). The second paragraph is apparently a separate entry in the MS. journal.

Page 361. *If a man has good corn, etc.* These two sentences, which pick up an entry for May, 1840 (J V 392), are the closest thing so far discovered in Emerson's writings to the saying attributed to him: "If a man build a better mouse-trap, the world will beat a path to his door." Probably Emerson improved this passage in a lecture and some hearer built a better saying out of it.

Page 362. *July 21*, *1855*. The story of this letter and its consequences has been told many times; see Rusk's *Life*, pp. 372–74, and *Emerson Handbook*, p. 226. Many of the documents on the Whitman-Emerson relation are collected in *The Shock of Recognition* (1943), ed. Edmund Wilson.

August, 1855. The last six words of the first paragraph are canceled in the MS. It is not clear that the two paragraphs are one entry.

Page 363. *Aug.?*, *1855*. This entry was written four years before the appearance of *The Origin of Species*.

Page 364. [*Spring, 1856*]. Cf. J VI 231–32.

Jan. 9?, *1856*. Illinois was suffering "fierce cold weather" as he wrote.

Works and Days

Pages 365 ff. The portion here omitted amounts to the first ten of twenty-eight pages in the Centenary Edition. There is some indication (L V 53) that Emerson conceived, perhaps wrote, these last eighteen pages first. The lecture was first given at Cincinnati on February 4, 1857; it was published in *Society and Solitude* (1870). Emerson was not as oblivious to the events of the moment as the published version suggests. Edward Emerson prints several sheets from the lecture which applied the general moral to the needs of the hour (W VII 394–95, 399). The criticism of "works" also is colored by the financial panic of 1857.

Page 366. *They come and go, etc.* This germ of the poem "Days" was entered in the journals on May 24, 1847 (J VII 277).

Page 369. HE *lurks, etc.* Cf. p. 303.

Page 370. *I knew a man.* Jones Very (cf. p. 94).

"The gods ever give," etc. Odyssey XVIII.136–37. The passage has been variously interpreted.

Page 371. *The foreign scholar.* This eloquent visitor has not been identified nor is Belleisle on any map. His last two sentences are from J VI 246; one sentence was used in "Experience" (p. 261).

Page 373. *It is a fine fable.* The fable, of course, is Emerson's own.

1861–1882: The War and After

THOREAU

Pages 379 ff. Thoreau died on May 6, 1862, and on May 9 Emerson "read an address of considerable length" at the funeral services. This obituary, with some additions, was printed the next August in *The Atlantic Monthly.* Emerson was first introduced to his fellow-townsman in 1837. He recognized his quality at once, well before anyone else did — Thoreau was then barely twenty — and took the initiative in their long friendship, helping him publish, finding him jobs, and sharing with him many long walks and talks, reflected in the works and journals of both men. In 1841–42 and again while Emerson was absent in England in 1847–48, Thoreau lived in the Emerson house as a kind of handy man. After 1848 they drifted apart. The story is reviewed in *Emerson Handbook,* pp. 27–30; see also the references there. In spite of a certain "alloy of patronage" and an inadequate appreciation of Thoreau's importance as a writer and a social critic, Emerson's portrait is probably the best thing he ever did in that kind and is one of the best likenesses of Thoreau that we have.

Page 381. *One of his friends.* Emerson himself (see J VII 498).

Page 384. *Scott's romance. The Betrothed* (1825).

Page 395. *Feb., 1861* ("*Do the duty*"). The meeting was nearly broken up by a well-dressed mob of "Union-at-any-price" citizens of Boston and the suburban towns. Hearing of the probable danger, Mr. Emerson felt bound to go, and sat upon the platform. The jeers and howls of the mob drowned his attempt at earnest speech. — E.W.E. He did manage to tell a short anecdote.

Page 397. *Nov., 1862.* Clearly intended for a lecture.

Page 399. *The six points of Chartism.* The program of the radical movement of 1838–48 (cf. p. 315): Universal male suffrage; equal electoral districts; no property qualifications for members of Parliament; payment of same; secret ballot; and annual general elections.

Page 402. *April, 1864.* Emerson was preparing to speak at the Saturday Club's celebration of the three hundredth anniversary of Shakespeare's birth. In his *Memoir of Ralph Waldo Emerson* (1887) J. E. Cabot writes: "I remember his getting up at a dinner of the Saturday Club on the Shakespeare anniversary in 1864, to which some guests had been invited, looking about him tranquilly for a minute or two, and then sitting down; serene and unabashed, but unable to say a word upon a subject so familiar to his thoughts from boyhood." Edward Emerson conjectures that he forgot his manuscript, for the speech was written (W XI 447–53).

Page 403. *Franklin Pierce.* Democratic President of the U.S., 1852–56. A college classmate, Hawthorne had written his campaign biography.

Page 404. *May, 1865.* The Bible, nevertheless, was "ploughed into" his mind; echoes of it appear constantly in his writing. Cf. H. R. Zink, "Emerson's Use of the Bible," *Univ. of Nebraska Studies in Language and Literature* (Lincoln, Neb., 1935), No. 14, pp. 61–74.

Page 405. *Westminster Catechisms; Athanasian creeds.* Authoritative statements of faith for, respectively, seventeenth-century Puritans and the Roman and English Catholic churches.

As Parry, etc. Sir William E. Parry attempted to reach the North Pole in 1827 and published an account of the voyage. After his name Emerson left a blank; Franklin is perhaps the name he was looking for; cf. p. 166.

The Abyss. A term used by Boehme (Behmen) to signify the region of nothingness where creation began. Cf. Nov., 1845 (p. 283), and also p. 490.

July 22, 1876. Emma Lazarus was a young New York Jewess whose poems Emerson had criticized and praised; she is now remembered chiefly as the author of the lines on the Statue of Liberty. In spite of this letter, she did make a successful visit in the autumn of 1876.

Poems

All these selections but one come from the Centenary Edition of the *Poems.* Of those problems for the anthologist, the important long "bardic" poems — "Woodnotes," "Monadnoc," "May-Day," "Initial, Daemonic, and Celestial Love," "Threnody" — only the last has been included, as illustrating the characteristics of all and being the most personally felt. When a poem bears two dates, the one on the right is of first publication, that on the left of composition. When this dating is based on information in the Centenary Edition, nothing more is said about it here. The basic dates of publication are 1846 (*Poems*); 1867 (*May-Day*); 1883 (Riverside Edition); and 1904 (Centenary Edition). In addition, a number of poems were first published in *The Dial* (1840–44) and in *The Atlantic Monthly* (1857 on).

Page 412. "*Grace*." The contrast of this poem to Emerson's self-reliance doctrines has often been noticed: see especially G. R. Elliott, "On Emerson's 'Grace' and 'Self-Reliance,' " *New England Quarterly* II (1929) 92–105. The poem expresses a Calvinist-bred mood of self-distrust which he was already endeavoring to throw off (cf. p. 11). The date of composition is that assigned by C. F. Strauch.

"*The Rhodora*." Cf. "Beauty" in *Nature* (p. 26). For critiques more or less severe of this poem, see S. L. Gross, "'Emerson and Poetry," *South Atlantic Quarterly* LIV (1955) 82–94, and Matthiessen, pp. 48–50. For an account of its composition, see Carl F. Strauch, "The Year of Emerson's Poetic Maturity: 1834," *Philological Quarterly* XXXIV (1955) 353–77.

Page 413. "*Each and All*." Though we do not know when this was written, late 1834 seems probable: see Strauch (above), who also gives an account of the intellectual background of this poem and defends its structure, as do Walter Blair and Clarence Faust, "Emerson's Literary Method," *Modern Philology* XLII (1944) 79–95. For a contrary opinion, see Gross (above). The thought is the same as that of the section on "Composition" of the lecture "Naturalist," May 7, 1834 (cf. J III 293, 298). Line 1: *red-cloaked clown*. A reminiscence of Northern Italy (J III 140, 373).

Page 414. "*The Snow-Storm*." Strauch (above) plausibly conjectures that this was written shortly after the great snowstorm of December 29, 1834 (see p. 98). He has some interesting material on the debt of this poem to a discussion of the art of nature and of man in Cudworth (cf. p. 472). See also Matthiessen, pp. 138–40. Whittier used the first part as a motto to "Snowbound," which this poem inspired.

Page 416. "*The Humble-Bee*." A journal entry of May, 1837, the apparent date of composition of this poem, suggests that the shock of the 1837 depression underlies this poem (cf. p. 62): "The humble-bee and the pine-warbler seem to me the proper objects of attention in these disastrous times. . . . I am less inclined to ethics, to history, to aught wise and grave and practick, and feel a new joy in nature." The term "humble-bee" is an alternative to "bumble-bee"; it has nothing to do with humility. Line 3: *Porto Rique*. Emerson's brother Edward spent his last years in Puerto Rico in a vain search for health and died there in 1834.

Page 417. "*The Problem*." Emerson's original title was "The Priest." The germ of the poem is found in a journal entry for August 28, 1838:

> It is very grateful to my feelings to go into a Roman Cathedral, yet I look as my countrymen do at the Roman priesthood. It is very grateful to me to go into an English Church and hear the liturgy read. Yet nothing would induce me to be the English priest. I find an unpleasant

dilemma in this, nearer home. I dislike to be a clergyman and refuse to be one. Yet how rich a music would be to me a holy clergyman in my town. It seems to me he cannot be a man, quite and whole; yet how plain is the need of one, and how high, yes, highest, is the function. Here is division of labor that I like not. A man must sacrifice his manhood for the social good. Something is wrong, I see not what.

There is a reminiscence also of an earlier passage (J IV 31–32) in which he speaks of "the sweetness of that fragrant piety which is almost departed out of the world." For comment see *Emerson Handbook*, pp. 90–91. Line 65: *Chrysostom.* St. John Chrysostom ("Golden Lips"); John of Antioch (307?–407), bishop of Constantinople, whose Homilies earned him his name. Line 68: *Taylor.* Jeremy Taylor (1613–67), author of *Holy Living* and *Holy Dying.* Cf. W IX 406–407.

Page 419. *From "Woodnotes, I."* The passages about the forest seer fit Thoreau so well that the general belief that Mr. Emerson had him in mind may be accepted, but one member of the family recalls his saying that a part of this picture was drawn before he knew Thoreau's gifts and experiences. — E.W.E. Beach (see p. 472) analyzes this poem in detail as "Emerson's great comprehensive nature poem."

Page 420. *"The Sphinx."* In all editions of the poems before 1904 this poem stood first; as Rusk remarks, "many prospective purchasers must have been too dismayed to read further" (*Life*, p. 312). Emerson wrote in 1859:

> I have often been asked the meaning of "The Sphinx." It is this, — The perception of identity unites all things and explains one by another, and the most rare and strange is equally facile as the most common. But if the mind live only in particulars, and see only differences (wanting the power to see the whole — all in each), then the world addresses to this mind a question it cannot answer, and each new fact tears it to pieces, and it is vanquished by the distracting variety. (W IX 412)

The image of Nature as the Sphinx appears in *Nature* (p. 36). The oneness of the riddle and the mind that must read it is mentioned in "History": "This human mind wrote history, and this must read it. The Sphinx must solve her own riddle. If the whole of history is in one man, it is all to be explained from individual experience" (W II 4; cf. J IV 164). The reader who will unite these leads with a careful reading of the poem will not find it so great an enigma. Rusk offers his reading in *Life*, pp. 312–14. Thomas Whitaker, "The Riddle of Emerson's Sphinx," *American Literature* XXVII (1955) 179–95, is an admirable discussion. See also under Fall of Man in the Index. Line 107: *Rue, myrrh and cummin.* Aromatic, presumably healing, plants. Line 119: *Ask on, thou clothed eternity, etc.* An echo of the basic metaphor of Carlyle's *Sartor Resartus*; the chapter "Natural Supernaturalism" is an illuminating commentary on this poem. Line 131: *Who telleth one of my meanings, etc.* The chief riddle of the poem is whether the Sphinx means to imply that the poet has or has not met this condition. This seems to be one of those unresolvable ambiguities which occasionally add to the interest of literature. Whitaker's is the most careful discussion.

Page 424. *"Merops."* Merops, king of Cos, wedded a nymph; when she was taken away, he wished to do away with himself but was granted a place as a soaring eagle among the constellations. The legend is only very generally related to the poem. (Its relevance is made somewhat clearer by an early draft printed in W IX 445–46.) At one time Emerson called this poem "Rhyme."

"The Apology." Natural comparisons to this poem are Words-worth's "Expostulation and Reply" and "The Tables Turned." The accusation of idleness implied here is treated also in "The Tran-scendentalist" (pp. 201–203).

Page 425. *"Suum Cuique."* Omitted in all editions of the poems after 1846; first printed in *The Dial*, Jan., 1841.

"Forerunners." Mr. Emerson said that it came to him as he walked home from Wachusett. — E.W.E. (Wachusett is a hill near Concord.) The first title was "Guides." The thought is similar to that portion of the essay "Nature" (W III 184–94) first published in *The Dial*, Jan., 1844, under the title "Tantalus."

Page 426. *"Uriel."* A recent scholar has summed up the theme of this poem as "the progressive influence of the man of genius." Though the poem thus has a general theme and may be understood in its own terms, the fact is that it is an allegorical treatment of the Divinity School *Address* and its reception; the section of this book on that subject is therefore the best commentary on it. The germ of the poem is probably the journal entry for Oct. 30, 1838 (p. 120). The poem, however, presents the emotion of this entry as recollected in the tranquillity of a later time; irony has replaced apocalyptic prophecy. The title refers to Milton's bright angel of the sun (*Paradise Lost*, III, 648–53):

> one of the seav'n
> Who in God's presence, nearest to his Throne
> Stand ready at command, and are his Eyes
> That run through all the Heav'ns, or down to th' Earth
> Bear his swift errands over moist and dry,
> O're Sea and Land . . .

The allusion underlines the pride of Uriel but also the irony of the poem, for what Emerson's Uriel sees is treason to his Paradise. Line 11: *The young deities, etc.* Three recurrent images in this poem, which ally it to "Circles," emerge early: youth, the sun, and the circle. The young deities discuss bounds; Uriel, on the contrary, sees process and change. Line 15: *low tones that decide.* An apt phrase for Emerson's own platform manner. Line 23: *Evil will bless.* Un-doubtedly this is one of Emerson's statements of the "good of evil" (cf. line 52). (See under Evil in the Index.) As W. T. Harris puts it, "Uriel sees that evil changes on its return into a purifying fire, — a purgatory." Since Uriel is challenging the conventional bounds of good and ill, however, he can be taken also to be urging, like Blake and Nietzsche, a transvaluation of values: "evil" *is* good. A discussion of this passage is in G. F. Whicher, "Unit and Universe . . . ," *Poetry and Civilization* (1955). Line 27: *The stern old war-gods . . . The seraphs.* Initiates can detect Andrews Norton and Henry Ware respectively here. Norton had spoken of "theories which would overturn society and resolve the world into chaos" (W IX 410). Line 35: *A sad self-knowledge.* A knowledge, that is, that he had no place in the conventional Paradise. Line 39: *long gyration, etc.* "Every partial soul must make periods of ascent from and descent into generation, and this forever and ever" (Proclus). Line 41: *by knowledge grown too bright.* Emerson himself (J IV 198) suggests a relation to Shelley's Skylark,

> Like a poet hidden
> In the light of thought,
> Singing hymns unbidden . . .

Line 49: *shrilling from the solar course, etc.* All examples of circular processes in nature, in which Emerson has characteristically mixed together his scientific and his mythological reading. Line 51: *Procession of a soul in matter.* "There are two kinds of souls that descend into the world of matter; the higher order . . . descend for the sake of causing the perfection of the universe. The second class of souls descend because they are condemned to suffer punishment" (Plotinus). Line 52: *the speeding change of water.* In 1834 Emerson had lectured on "Water," stressing its many transformations.

Page 428. *"Threnody."* The first part of this poem was written shortly after Waldo's death in 1842, using phrases from letters written as soon as a week after the event. The second part was probably written in 1843, though Emerson may have worked it over after that time. Blair and Faust (see p. 500) have analyzed the structure of this poem as follows (cf. *Emerson Handbook*, p. 86):

> The first half of the poem describes the feeling of loss and isolation which grief brings: Stanzas 1–2, the separation of the boy from nature; stanzas 3–4, his separation from other men; stanza 5, the resultant feeling of the poet-father that he has lost part of himself. The second half of the poem (beginning: "The deep Heart answered, 'Weepest thou?'") describes the poet's recovery from grief through remembrance of his relation to the whole.

Line 183: *the man of eld.* The description will fit many men; Jacob is perhaps the most likely. Lines 207–208: *Throb thine . . . east to west.* Cf. p. 459.

Page 436. *"Give All to Love."* The view of love dramatized here, the same as that expressed in the essay "Love" and in many other places, is basically Platonic, but also has a strong Puritan flavor; compare the end of "Compensation":

> We cannot let our angels go. We do not see that they only go out that archangels may come in. . . . The death of a dear friend, wife, brother, lover, which seemed nothing but privation, somewhat later assumes the aspect of a guide or genius; for it commonly operates revolutions in our way of life, terminates an epoch of infancy or of youth which was waiting to be closed, breaks up a wonted occupation, or a household, or style of living, and allows the formation of new ones more friendly to the growth of character. (W II 125–26; cf. p. 41 and note.)

Page 437. "*Hamatreya.*" Based on a passage from the *Vishnu Purana* (a late Hindu scripture) which Emerson copied into his journal in the autumn of 1845:

> The words "I and mine" constitute ignorance. . . .
> I will repeat to you, Maitreya, the stanzas that were chanted by Earth. . . : —
> "How great is the folly of princes. . . . 'Thus,' say they, 'will we conquer the ocean-circled earth'; and intent upon their project, behold not death, which is not far off. . . . Foolishness has been the character of every king who has boasted, 'All this earth is mine — everything is mine — it will be in my house forever'; for he is dead. . . . When I hear a king sending word to another by his ambassador, 'This earth is mine; resign your pretensions to it,' — I am at first moved to pity for the infatuated fool."
> These were the verses, Maitreya, which Earth recited and by listening to which ambition fades away like snow before the sun. (J VII 127–29)

Why Emerson wrote "Hamatreya" rather than "Maitreya" has not been explained.

The poem grafts Asia to Concord, the purpose clearly being to produce a shock of recognition at the sudden shift from the local to the cosmic. To do this Emerson recalled the "Historical Discourse" he had given at Concord on the occasion of the town's second centennial in 1835, particularly the opening paragraphs:

> . . . The river, by whose banks most of us were born, every winter, for ages, has spread its crust of ice over the great meadows which, in ages, it had formed. But the little society of men who now, for a few years, fish in this river, plough the fields it washes, mow the grass and reap the corn, shortly shall hurry from its banks as did their forefathers. . . .
> Yet the race survives whilst the individual dies. . . . Here are still around me the lineal descendants of the first settlers of this town. Here is Blood, Flint, Willard, Meriam, Wood, Hosmer, Barrett, Wheeler, Jones, Brown, Buttrick, Brooks, Stow, Hoar, Heywood, Hunt, Miles, — the names of the inhabitants for the first thirty years; and the family

is in many cases represented, when the name is not. If the name of Bulkeley is wanting, the honor you have done me this day, in making me your organ, testifies your persevering kindness to his blood. (W XI 29–30)

(Peter Bulkeley, an ancestor of Emerson's, was a founder of Concord.) With the opening lines, compare "The American Scholar," pp. 77–78.

Page 439. *"Ode Inscribed to W. H. Channing."* William Henry Channing, nephew of the Unitarian leader, William Ellery Channing (not to be confused with another nephew, William Ellery Channing the poet), Unitarian preacher, orator, editor, Transcendentalist, Christian Socialist, was a fervent partisan of all idealistic causes of the day. Emerson saw him and heard him preach in New York in 1843 and described him as "magnanimous, true, apprehensive, heroic," with "purely beautiful" behavior; a "princely person." In 1845 Channing spoke in Concord; some conversation at this time in which Channing urged the anti-slavery cause on Emerson may well have been the occasion for the present poem. If so, Emerson was certainly in no mood to hear activist arguments; see pp. 278–80. Though a Transcendentalist, Channing was opposed to such individualism as Emerson's and Thoreau's, holding that "the true advancement of the individual is dependent upon the advancement of a generation." On reading Emerson's Divinity School *Address* he had written:

> I feel distinctly, my honored friend, in relation to this address, what I feel in relation to all that I have read of your writings, that there is one radical defect, which, like a wound in the bark, wilts and blights the leaf and bloom and fruit of your faith. You deny the Human Race. You stand, or rather seek to stand, a complete Adam. But you cannot do it.

The poem is therefore a reply not merely to an Abolitionist and reformer but to a fundamental criticism of Emerson's whole position. Line 31: *The southern crocodile would grieve.* I.e., no one would grieve, though the South would weep crocodile tears. Line 52: *two laws discrete, etc.* A favorite citation of Irving Babbitt and the "New Humanists" of a generation ago. Other scholars have pointed out that Emerson was as much concerned to show how these two laws were at bottom one. The question relates directly to Emerson's peculiar "dualistic monism" in general and therefore to all the material in this anthology. See particularly under Wealth in the Index. Line 90: *The Cossack eats Poland, etc.* Russia swallowed most of Poland in 1796. Emerson's allusion is probably to the Polish insurrection of 1830–31 and the Decembrist mutiny of some Russian officers in 1830. If so, he ignores the tragic outcome.

Page 442. *"The World-Soul."* The term occurs in Plato and the Neo-Platonists; a disciple of Plotinus, Amelius, taught the unity of souls in the World-Soul.

Page 445. *"Insight."* This poem, not published until after Emerson's death, is undated and is arbitrarily inserted here. The title was added by Edward Emerson. Compare the items under Insight in the Index.

"*Bacchus.*" Mr. Emerson wrote in his own copy of the *Poems* this motto, taken from Plato, to "Bacchus," which sheds light: "The man who is his own master knocks in vain at the doors of poetry." — E.W.E.

Emerson found wine used as a "symbol of intellectual freedom" in the poetry of the Persian Hafiz, whom he read in German translation and translated in 1846 and 1847. The praise of Hafiz which he adapted from his journal of 1847 for his essay on "Persian Poetry" (1865) strikes a note much like the poem (cf. J VII 278–80 and W VIII 247, 420). The debt of this poem to Hafiz has been analyzed in J. D. Yohannan, "The Influence of Persian Poetry on Emerson's Work," *American Literature* XV (March, 1943) 25–41.

Page 447. "*Merlin.*" Emerson refers not so much to the magician of Arthurian legend as to the reputed author of many traditional poems of the Welsh bards. The cult of bardic verse went back at least a century to Gray's "The Bard," being given its chief impetus by the pseudo-bardic effusions of Macpherson's Ossian. To Emerson the name meant a poet who sings with natural inspiration, as an Aeolian harp makes music, whose song is allied to wild and grand forces of nature, and who, above all, has a potency that will change the hearts of men and direct their actions. See N. F. Adkins, "Emerson and the Bardic Tradition," *PMLA* XX (1948) 662–77, and K. W. Cameron, "The Potent Song in Emerson's Merlin Poems," *Philological Quarterly* XXXII (1953) 22–28. That the present poem is not just a dramatic exercise but describes a poetic role Emerson deeply wanted to fill is made clearer in the original draft than in the finished poem:

> I go discontented thro' the world
> Because I cannot strike
> The harp to please my tyrannous ear:
> Gentle touches are not wanted,
> These the yielding gods had granted.
> It shall not tinkle a guitar,
> But strokes of fate, etc.
>
> . . . .
>
> I will not read a pretty tale
> To pretty people in a nice saloon
> Borrowed from their expectation,
> But I will sing aloud and free
> From the heart of the world. (W IX 441)

Line 81: *Made all things in pairs.* The same thought, seen from the other side, introduces the essay "Compensation":

> Polarity, or action and reaction, we meet in every part of nature; in darkness and light; in heat and cold; in the ebb and flow of waters; in

male and female. . . . An inevitable dualism bisects nature, so that each thing is a half, and suggests another thing to make it whole; as, spirit, matter; man, woman; odd, even; subjective, objective; in, out; upper, under; motion, rest; yea, nay. (W II 96–97)

Page 451. *"Days."* In his journal for 1852 Emerson wrote:

I find one state of mind does not remember or conceive of another state. Thus I have written within a twelve-month verses ("Days") which I do not remember the composition or correction of, and could not write the like today, and have only, for proof of their being mine, various external evidences, as the MS. in which I find them, and the circumstance that I have sent copies of them to friends, etc., etc.

The thought was, however, an old one with him — see under "Days" in the Index. For discussions of this poem, which Emerson once said he thought perhaps his best, see *Emerson Handbook*, p. 88.

"Brahma." Unlike "Hamatreya," this does not versify a single source but distills much of Emerson's Hindu reading; the subject is the "doctrine of the absolute unity" that is central both to Hindu thought and Emerson's. Several scholars have assembled the passages that contributed to it — see *Emerson Handbook*, p. 87, and W IX 464–67. A good critical comment is in Mark Van Doren, *Introduction to Poetry* (1951), pp. 90–93. Lines 13–14: *The strong gods . . . the sacred Seven.* W. T. Harris has identified the gods as Indra, god of the sky and wielder of the thunderbolt, Ani, the god of fire, and Yama, the god of death and judgment; and the Seven as the Maharshis or highest saints. Line 16: *turn thy back on heaven.* Cf. "Plato": "That which the soul seeks is resolution into being above form, out of Tartarus and out of heaven, — liberation from nature" (W IV 51). The Hindu doctrine alluded to is that souls which attain to Brahma are freed from returning to life. Cf. "Uriel."

Page 452. *"Maia."* Undated and arbitrarily inserted here. Maya is a Hindu name for Illusion, or the principle of variety.

"Two Rivers." The original prose thought (1856) is printed in W IX 487:

Thy voice is sweet, Musketaquid, and repeats the music of the rain, but sweeter is the silent stream which flows ever through thee, as thou through the land.

Thou art shut in thy banks, but the stream I love flows in thy water, and flows through rocks and through the air and through rays of light as well, and through darkness, and through men and women.

I hear and see the inundation and eternal spending of the stream in winter and in summer, in men and animals, in passion and thought. Happy are they who can hear it. . . .

Cf. J IX 27 for Emerson's revised version of the same passage (with the inadvertent omission of a line). Line 18: *shall not thirst again.* John 4:14.

Page 453. "*Seashore.*" In July, 1856, Mr. Emerson, induced by Dr. Bartol, took his family to spend two weeks at Pigeon Cove, on Cape Ann. The day after our return to Concord, he came into our mother's room, where we were all sitting, with his journal in his hand, and said, "I came in yesterday from walking on the rocks and wrote down what the sea had said to me; and to-day, when I open my book, I find it all reads as blank verse, with scarcely a change." — E.W.E. The journal passage is given in W IX 484–85 (misdated) and in J IX 54–55. Emerson also used an entry of May 23, 1847, from another holiday at Nantasket (J VII 270–71).

Page 454. "*Waldeinsamkeit.*" A brief prose "thought" appears in the journal for early June, 1857 (J IX 97–98). With this poem, cf. "The Apology" (p. 424).

Page 455. "*Song of Nature.*" Completed probably in 1859. Carl F. Strauch, "The Sources of Emerson's 'Song of Nature,' " *Harvard Library Bulletin* IX (1955) 300–34, is a full account of how the poem grew for over fifteen years from a wide variety of reading including Plutarch's *Morals*, Robert Chambers' *Vestiges of Creation* (1845), and the journals of Mary Moody Emerson. The poem makes a convenient comparison with *Nature*. Line 45: *Must time and tide, etc.* The three stanzas which follow echo a passage from Mary Moody Emerson's journal (1834):

> I forget what I meant to say — likely, that Doctor Ripley would not live. But he has to return, and willingly. Ah! as I walked there just now, so sad was wearied nature, that I felt her whisper, "Even these leaves you use to think my better emblems — have lost their charm on me too, and I weary of my pilgrimage, — tired that I must again be clothed in the grandeurs of winter, and anon be bedizened in flowers and cascades. Oh if there be a Power superior to me, (and that there is, my own dread fetters proclaim,) when will he let my lights go out, — my tides cease to an eternal ebb, — my wheels which whirl this ceaseless rotation of suns and satellites stop the great chariot of their maker in mid-career?"

Much of this and other passages is given in "Mary Moody Emerson" (W X 399–433). Line 61: *Twice I have moulded an image, etc.* The best interpretation is that of Charles Malloy, "The Poems of Emerson. Fifth Paper. 'Days,' " *The Coming Age* I (1899) 629–30, who suggested "that the first line, 'Twice I have moulded an image,' indicated the creation of man and woman; the second line, 'And thrice outstretched my hand,' referred to the 'basal or cardinal races'; the third, 'Made one of day and one of night,' referred to the white and black races; and the fourth, 'And one of the salt sea-sand,' indicated the 'middle-race,' presumably the yellow and brown peoples." He is referring to a classification of the races of mankind according to "the march of day from East to West" by a German physiologist, Karl Gustav Carus, which was known to Emerson (see Strauch, pp. 328–29). Line 67: *One over against the mouths of Nile.* Probably Plotinus.

Page 458. *"Terminus."* Though the poem as we have it is certainly about old age, Carl F. Strauch, in "The Date of Emerson's *Terminus,"* *PMLA* LXV (1950) 360–70, has shown that the poem was begun in the 1850's and originally expressed Emerson's distress over the times. Line 28: *Baresark.* I.e., berserk, or savage Viking.

Page 459. *Mottoes.* The mottoes to *Essays, Second Series* were written for the first edition of 1844; most of those to *Essays, First Series* for the second edition of 1847; those to *The Conduct of Life* for the first edition of 1860. In *May-Day and Other Pieces* (1867) Emerson collected a number of them under the heading "Elements"; Edward Emerson added most of the rest in 1904. In a few cases the titles were changed. The selections printed here are under the titles of the original essays. The text of those Emerson himself reprinted is based on *Poems* (W IX), with some corrections from the essays; the text of the rest is the text printed with the respective essays.

"Nature." This was the motto for the essay "Nature" (1844), not the book (1836). It is usually printed with the 1849 motto for the book. Lines 5–6 are also in "Threnody" (p. 433).

Page 460. *"Nominalist and Realist."* Called by Edward Emerson "Promise."

"Compensation." As printed in *Poems,* this looks like the first half of a two-part poem. The *Essays,* however, show it to be a separate motto.

"Spiritual Laws." With the theme, cf. "Uriel" and "Brahma." Variant versions of "the first attempt" are printed in W IX 495–96 and J VII 217. Line 1: *The living heaven thy prayers respect.* Thy prayers are concerned with a Heaven which is *alive,* is the meaning. — E.W.E. The first draft reads, "Heaven is alive." As in "Uriel" and "Brahma," Emerson is distinguishing between "the living Heaven" and the conventional one. Line 12: *The silver seat.* The first draft has "the firm seat," which is closer to the point.

Page 464. *"Considerations by the Way."* Added by Edward Emerson to an entirely different poem, "Merlin's Song." This Merlin is not a potent bard but simply a wise counsellor, a Nestor. Cf. Kenneth W. Cameron, "The Significance of Emerson's Second Merlin Song," *Emerson Society Quarterly,* No. 2 (I Quarter 1956) 2–7. Line 20: *Canope.* I.e., in the south.

Page 466. *Quatrains.* A number of these were printed under this heading in *May-Day;* others are added here. Edward Emerson suggests that Emerson's reading of Persian poetry may have encouraged his taste for this form.

"Climacteric." The "grand climacteric" is the sixty-third birthday.

"Sacrifice." The last two lines are a rendering of a quotation from a seventeenth-century sermon.

"Voluntaries." A long poem in memory of Colonel Robert Gould Shaw, who commanded one of the first colored regiments and was killed at Fort Wagner. These are by far the best-known lines. A "Voluntary" is an organ solo at a service.

Page 467. "*Nahant.*" Cf. J VIII 380, June, 1853.
" '*Teach me your mood.*' " Edward Emerson adds a first stanza
(W IX 340).

Table of Sources

OF SELECTIONS FROM JOURNALS AND LETTERS

Sources are listed in the same order as the selections, under the page
(boldface numbers **2**, **3**, etc.) on which each selection begins. Sources of successive items are separated by a period; of the same item, by a comma. When
selections have been corrected or amplified from the MS., this is so indicated.

2 J IV 229–32. **3** J V 547–48. **4** L IV 178–79. L IV 407–408.
5 J IV 372, W VII 119–21. **6** J I 360–67. **8** L I 170. L I 174–75.
J II 310. **9** J II 409. J II 425. J II 491–92, corr. **10** J II 495–97.
J II 516–17. **11** J II 517. J II 518–19. **13** J III 185–86. **14** J III 196–
97. J III 207–10. **16** J III 233. J III 246. J III 269. J III 277–78.
J III 471–72. **17** J III 557. J III 292–93, 295. J IV 59–60.
18 J III 392–93. J III 440–42. J III 388–90. **19** L I 435. J III 467–
68, ampl. **20** J III 518. J III 537. **21** W II 341–42. **58** J IV 112–13.
J IV 188. W II 131–32. **59** J IV 191–92. **60** J IV 195–97.
61 J IV 238. J IV 215. **62** J IV 247–49. J IV 241–43. **63** J IV 257.
80 J IV 297. J IV 351. J IV 305. **81** J IV 315–16, ampl. J IV 316.
J IV 317–19. **82** J IV 319–20. **83** J IV 331. J IV 343–45.
84 J IV 354–55. J IV 339–40. **85** J IV 401–402. **86** W I 167–69.
J IV 430–31. **87** J IV 440–42. **88** J IV 444. J IV 450–51.
89 J IV 467–68. J IV 478. J IV 480–81. J IV 482. **90** W I 156–57.
J IV 488–89. J IV 489–91. **91** J IV 491–92, ampl. J IV 499.
92 J V 33. J V 76–77, W X 35. **93** J V 98. J V 98–99. **94** J V 104–
106. J V 110. **95** J V 113–14. J V 114–15. J V 132. **98** J III 422–
25. **100** J IV 449. J V 7. **116** J V 30–31. J V 70. L II 166–67.
117 J V 75. J V 77–79, corr. **118** J V 82–83. **119** J V 91–92.
J V 93, 94. **120** J V 108–109. J V 111. J V 123. **121** J V 215–16.
124 C-E Correspondence I 160–61. J V 173–75. **125** J IV 237–38.
126 J V 494. J VI 178. J VI 169–77. **128** J VI 306–10.
129 J VI 420–21. **130** J VI 503–505. J VII 50. J VII 524.
J VIII 362–63, corr. **131** J IX 36. J X 158. J V 292. **132** J V 451–
52. L II 350–51. **133** J V 352. **134** J V 453–54. J V 422–23.
J V 200–201. **135** J V 208. J V 242. W II 361–62. **136** J V 250–52.
137 J V 252–53. J V 253–54. **138** J VI 142. J V 266–68. J V 241–
42. **139** J V 287–89. J V 380–81. J V 334–35. **140** J V 358–59.
141 J V 226–27. J V 476. J V 312–13. J V 411–12. **142** W IV 128–

29. **143** J V 423. J V 420–21. J V 427–28. **144** Letters to a Friend 28–29. J V 468–70. **145** J V 473–74. **146** J V 480. J V 494–95, ampl. J V 506. J V 513–14. **180** J V 508, W I 255–56. **181** J V 395–96. J VI 156. J V 526–27, W I 201–203, W III 180–81. **183** J V 533–34. L II 384–85. **184** E. W. Emerson, Emerson in Concord (1888) 254. Letters to a Friend 35–36. J VI 13–14, W I 205. **185** J VI 18–19. J VI 40. J VI 132. **186** W IV 94. J VI 52–53, 55. **187** J V 236. J VI 74. J VI 76. J VI 58–60. **188** J VI 65, W III 185. W III 234. J VI 80–81. **189** J VI 98. J VI 103. **190** W I 301. J VI 22–23. J VI 101–103, ampl. **191** J VI 99–100. J VI 108–109, W III 191–92. **192** J VI 120–21. J VI 123. **207** J VI 521. J VI 150. J VI 152–53. **208** L III 9–10. J VI 166. J VI 188–90, ampl. **209** J VI 200. J VI 204. J VI 213–14. **210** W X 348–53. **211** J VII 133–34. **212** J VI 180. J VI 178–80. J VI 234–35. **213** J VI 126–28, corr. J VI 240. **214** J VI 258–63. **215** W III 266–67. **216** J VI 301–302. J VI 470–71. **217** J VI 482–83. J VI 317. L III 116. **218** L III 121–22. **219** L III 138. J VI 378–79. J VI 210. **220** J VI 390–91. J VI 397, ampl. J VI 401–402, ampl. **221** J VI 450. J VI 403. L III 178. **274** E-C Correspondence II 84–85. **275** J VI 490–91, ampl. W III 179. J VII 80. **276** J VII 104. J VII 117. J VI 494–95. **277** W XI 143–45. **278** J VII 12, ampl. J VII 12–13. **279** J VII 19. J VII 34. J VII 35, corr. J VII 36. **280** J VII 30. J VII 115–16. J VII 81–82, corr. J VII 82. **281** J VII 83. J VII 91. J VII 112. J VII 75. J VII 96, ampl., W IV 24. **282** J VII 123. J VII 125, corr. J VII 102. **283** J VII 130. J VII 131–32, cf. W IV 46–47. J VII 139–40. **303** J X 189–90, J VII 159–60. **304** J VII 165–66. W IV 206–208. **305** J VII 163. **306** W VIII 115–16. J VII 201–202, cf. W VII 95–96. **307** J VII 205–206. J VII 220–23. **308** J VII 175. **309** J VII 223–24, W XII 48, J VII 162. W X 39. **310** J VII 253–55. J VII 286–87, ampl. J VII 299–300. **311** J VII 326. W X 44–46. **312** J VII 341–42. **313** W VI 241–42, cf. J VII 425, 465. J VII 344–46, W X 489–90. **314** L III 442–43. L IV 33. **315** L IV 54. J VII 427. J VII 428. **316** J VII 430–31, corr. J VII 444–48. **317** J X 188–89, redated. **318** J VII 547. J VIII 33–34. J X 209–10. **319** J VIII 54. J VIII 55. J VIII 64, MS. J "TU." **320** J VIII 79. J VIII 86–87. **321** J VIII 88. J VIII 95. J VIII 112. L IV 209–11. **323** J VIII 122–23, ampl. J VIII 175. J VIII 177. **324** J VIII 219–20, cf. W VI 92–94. J VIII 207, ampl. W VI 325. **325** J VIII 239–40, ampl. **326** J VIII 244. J VIII 292–93. J VIII 296. J VIII 551–52. J VIII 561. **327** J VIII 298–99, ampl. J VIII 300. J VIII 303. **328** J VIII 303–305, ampl. J VIII 311–12. **329** L IV 376–77. **354** J VIII 179. J VIII 202. **355** W XI 187–88, J VIII 236. J VIII 316. J VIII 334–35. **356** J VIII 433–34.

J VIII 531–32. **357** J VIII 544. L V 17–18. **358** W X 256, J IX 213. J IX 246. J IX 249. **359** J VIII 377–78. J VIII 73. 360 J VIII 405–406. J VIII 399–401. **361** J VIII 528–30. **362** J VIII 540–41. R. W. Emerson, Uncollected Writings (1912) 208, corr. J VIII 532–33, ampl. **363** E-C Correspondence II 251. J VIII 557. J VIII 577–78. **364** J IX 24, W XII 303–304. J IX 7–8. 365 J IX 24. **374** J IX 89, corr. J IX 100. J IX 128–29. **375** J IX 182. J IX 183. **376** J IX 181. J IX 188–89. J IX 197–98. J IX 200–201. J IX 216–17. **377** J IX 221. **395** J IX 305. J IX 309. J IX 325–26. 396 J IX 375–76. J IX 556–57. **397** J IX 461–65, corr. **399** J IX 571–73, corr. **400** J X 33. J X 105–106. J X 116. J IX 310–11. 401 J IX 402. J IX 355. J IX 437, ampl. J IX 336–37. **402** J IX 522. J X 28, 31. **403** J X 39–41. **404** J X 47. J X 57. J X 42. J X 96. J X 101–102. **405** J X 166–67. J X 173. J X 171. L VI 296. 406 J VII 137–38, ampl. **407** J IX 472.

Index

Index

OF TITLES, MAJOR NAMES AND SUBJECTS

Titles of essays are in italics; those of poems in quotes. The subject portion of this index undertakes only to list some obvious items under selected general heads, with a few added indications of the area each head is meant to include. Unavoidably some of these areas overlap.